D1481932

DISCARDED

University of Winnipeg, 515 Portage Ave., Winnipeg, MB. R3B 2E9 Canada

SOURCES OF FOUR PLAYS ASCRIBED TO SHAKESPEARE

PR
2875
.S6
1989

SOURCES OF FOUR PLAYS ASCRIBED TO SHAKESPEARE

The Reign of King Edward III
Sir Thomas More
The History of Cardenio
The Two Noble Kinsmen

Edited with an Introduction
By G. Harold Metz

University of Missouri Press
Columbia, 1989

Copyright 1989 by
The Curators of the University of Missouri
University of Missouri Press, Columbia, Missouri 65211
Printed and bound in the United States of America
All rights reserved

Library of Congress Cataloging-in-Publication Data

Sources of four plays ascribed to Shakespeare

Includes index.
1. Shakespeare, William, 1564–1616—Spurious and doubtful works—Sources. 2. English drama—Early modern and Elizabethan, 1500–1600—Sources.
I. Metz, G. Harold (George Harold), 1917–

PR2875.S6 1988 822.3'3 88–4793
ISBN 0-8262-0690-5

∞ This paper meets the minimum requirements of the American National Standard for Permanence of Paper for Printed Library Materials, Z39.48, 1984.

To Mary

PREFACE

The foundation of the Shakespearean dramatic canon was laid by John Heminges and Henry Condell, Shakespeare's fellow players in the King's Men, with the publication of *Mr. William Shakespeare's Comedies, Histories & Tragedies* (the First Folio) in 1623, seven years after his death. The book comprises thirty-six plays, including *Troilus and Cressida*, which was almost excluded (probably because of difficulties over copyright), and *Timon of Athens,* which was originally intended to take the place of *Troilus* when it seemed that play would have to be omitted. Except for this accident of circumstance, we might not have *Timon.* Other plays had been attributed to Shakespeare, incorrectly in most cases, by publishers on the title pages of quarto editions. Seven such plays published from among what is now known as the Shakespeare Apocrypha were printed in the second issue of the Third Folio (1664). The title page reads: "And unto this Impression is added seven Playes, never before Printed in Folio. *viz, Pericles* Prince of *Tyre*. The *London Prodigall*. The History of *Thomas* Ld. *Cromwell*. Sir *John Oldcastle* Lord *Cobham*. The *Puritan Widow*. A *York-shire* Tragedy. The Tragedy of *Locrine*." These plays were also included in the Fourth Folio of 1685. Plays designated "doubtful" and "spurious," including the seven in the second issue of the Third Folio, were sometimes, but not invariably, printed in the editions of Shakespeare published during the eighteenth century. The mere inclusion of such plays did not always indicate a belief in Shakespeare's authorship, and a debate among scholars over authenticity continued. Ultimately a consensus, by no means unanimous, emerged that accepted *Pericles* into the canon and rejected all the others. Thus by the time of Edmond Malone (d. 1812) the settled complement of Shakespeare's plays was thirty-seven—Heminges and Condell's thirty-six plus *Pericles*.

Critics who were not in agreement with this somewhat overly tidy determination constituted the fountainhead of a movement to widen the canon through the first three quarters of the nineteenth century. Numerous attributions were made based on little other than the uncritical impressions on readers of anonymous plays. Ludwig Tieck, one such enthusiast, in a letter of November 1821, credited Shakespeare with a total of fifty-nine plays, including the canon. Richard Simpson compiled in 1875 a list of "Some Plays Attributed to Shakspeare" besides the canonical thirty-seven. This list of thirty plays was not endorsed by Simpson as to authenticity and, in fact, was intended to form the basis of an investigation into authorship. In all, by the dawn of the twentieth century, sixty-six plays in addition to the canon had been assigned to Shakespeare. Almost all these attributions included *Edward III, Sir Thomas More,* or *The Two Noble Kinsmen*, sometimes all three. Simpson, in addition, listed *Double Falshood.*

Meanwhile a countermovement took form, led by Frederick J. Furnivall and Frederick Gard Fleay, colleagues in the New Shakspere Society founded by Furnivall. Employing verse tests and other "scientific" techniques, members of the Society and others successfully attacked the loose assertions of Shakespearean authorship and convincingly demonstrated that many of the early attributions, such as six of the seven additions to the Third Folio, were invalid. In the course of purging the many erroneous ascriptions, however, these investigators decided that there was evidence of fairly extensive interpolation of alien materials into Shakespeare's text. This they took to be the work of contemporaries of Shakespeare, especially but not limited to the "University Wits"—Marlowe, Peele, Nash, Lodge, and Greene—all accomplished playwrights. The process of assigning segments of plays in the Shakespearean canon to other dramatists became known as "disintegration." It reached its peak during the last quarter of the nineteenth century and the first quarter of the twentieth, and its most notable figures were Fleay and J. M. Robertson. A serious and original scholar, Fleay intended to bring to bear the "scientific" methods of the New Shakspere Society to questions of authenticity, but his findings tended to overextend his evidence and he altered his opinions more frequently and more bewilderingly than most scholars. Robertson employed various tests of style and verse to support his impressionistic judgments concerning Shakespearean authorship. He set forth and revised his conclusions in a series of recensions from 1905 to 1930, the net result of which was that he found scarcely any of the plays to be entirely Shakespeare's or entirely free of collaborative contributions, revisions, updatings, or other intrusions. Sir Edmund Chambers brought reason to bear on the welter of unfounded attributions on the one hand and the destructive disintegration of the Shakespearean canon on the other. He disposed of the uncritical ascriptions in his *Elizabethan Stage* (1923) and *William Shakespeare: A Study of Facts and Problems* (1930), and he halted abruptly the disintegration movement in his British Academy annual Shakespeare lecture of 1924 on "The Disintegration of Shakespeare."

The assignment of *Edward III, Sir Thomas More, Cardenio,* and *The Two Noble Kinsmen* to Shakespeare had been set forth earlier from time to time by various individuals. Edward Capell championed the Shakespearean authorship of *Edward III* when he published his text of the play in *Prolusions or Select Pieces of Antient Poetry* in 1760. Simpson propounded a reasoned argument for Shakespeare's hand in *Sir Thomas More* in a brief essay in 1872 and was supported by James Spedding in

1873. Humphrey Moseley registered *The History of Cardenio* for publication in 1653 as "by Mr. Fletcher and Shakespeare," and John Waterson entered "a TragiComedy called the two noble kinsmen by Io: ffletcher & Wm. Shakespeare" in 1634. Not all subsequent critics accepted these attributions. C. F. Tucker Brooke, for example, in his influential *Shakespeare Apocrypha* (1908) examined these four plays, among others, and arrived at the following conclusions: he assigned *Edward III* to Peele; accepted, somewhat hesitantly, the authenticity of the portion of the insurrection scene in Hand D (addition IIc of *Sir Thomas More*); noted that *Cardenio* "has been suggested" to be identical with *Double Falshood* and assigned to Shakespeare, "perhaps fraudulently," by Theobald; and ascribed the non-Fletcherian parts of *The Two Noble Kinsmen* to Massinger.

In *William Shakespeare,* Chambers weighed the divergent claims of the authorship of noncanonical plays in a section entitled "Plays outside the First Folio." He found most such claims lacking in cogency and said "these views now receive little support, and deserve none." Concerning the four plays, he determined that in *Edward III* the Countess episode and the scene (4.4) in which the Black Prince at Crecy refuses to surrender require "serious consideration as Shakespeare's"; that in *Sir Thomas More,* if hand D is Shakespeare's writing, "he was also the author of Addition IIc," and perhaps Addition III; that the external evidence for Shakespeare and Fletcher in *Cardenio* is persuasive (quoting favorably but not endorsing E. H. C. Oliphant's arguments concerning the existence of their work beneath Lewis Theobald's *Double Falshood)*; and that "the non-Fletcherian verse [in *The Two Noble Kinsmen*] agrees with that of Shakespeare, in its latest stage." His balanced, thoughtful evaluation set the plays on a footing that insured serious consideration of them as being at least in part by Shakespeare.

Sir Walter Greg, who was a leading contributor to the decades-long debate concerning Shakespeare's participation in the composition of *Sir Thomas More*, had devoted little attention to the other three plays until he published his study of the First Folio in 1955. Since these plays were not printed in the Folio, his comments were brief but nevertheless incisive. Having earlier made clear his position on *Sir Thomas More,* he limited himself to the observation that most students of the play "now accept the Shakespearean authorship of the three additional pages and possibly a few other lines." He asserted that the Countess episode of *Edward III* is considered by modern critics to be in a hand different from the rest and this "may be Shakespeare's." He noted the early performances of *Cardenio* at court and said that, in spite of some improbabilities in Theobald's account of the origin of *Double Falshood*, "there seems to be no sufficient reason to doubt that he based his version on an early manuscript, perhaps bearing an ascription to Shakespeare." He also observed that *The Two Noble Kinsmen*, along with *Henry VIII*, is "generally held to be the outcome of a collaboration between Shakespeare and John Fletcher about 1613."

Over a period of years beginning in 1953, Kenneth Muir comprehensively reappraised in several essays the potential canonicity of three of the four ascribed plays. He brought together his papers, substantially modified and updated, along with new materials on all four plays in a book entitled *Shakespeare as Collaborator* in 1960. His review of them, specifically of their authorship, constitutes a model of scholarly perspicacity. *Edward III* exhibits "multiple links," primarily of phrasing and imagery, to canonical plays, especially *Henry VI Part 3, Henry V,* and *Measure for Measure.* In regard to *Sir Thomas More* he concluded, "The Shakespearian authorship of part of *Sir Thomas More* is now accepted by all competent critics." As to *Cardenio,* if Theobald "had one or more manuscripts there would be strong reason to believe that *Double Falshood* was a debased version of *Cardenio,* and equally strong reasons for believing that the original authors were Shakespeare and Fletcher." Muir argued that characteristic Shakespearean image clusters in *The Two Noble Kinsmen* establish that he wrote at least three scenes, and this and other tests "make it reasonably certain that Shakespeare wrote" others.

Of course, there have been scholars who have expressed doubts concerning Shakespeare's part in the four plays, although now the predominant opinion of critics who have studied the evidence is that Shakespeare wrote at least part of each of them. The most nearly persuasive counterargument concerns *Cardenio* since there can always be grounds for doubt as long as the play is lost. This lingering ambivalence in the body of scholarly judgment is notably reflected in the decisions concerning the inclusion or exclusion of the four ascribed plays (thus granting or withholding an endorsement) in modern editions of Shakespeare's complete works. George Lyman Kittredge printed *The Two Noble Kinsmen* as the canonical thirty-eighth play in 1936, and Sylvan Barnet included it in the Signet edition of 1972. But Dover Wilson omitted it from his Cambridge *Shakespeare,* as did Alfred Harbage from the Pelican *Works* (1969). David Bevington made the same determination in his complete edition (1980). It was included by G. Blakemore Evans in *The Riverside Shakespeare* (1974) and by Stanley Wells and Gary Taylor in *The Oxford Shakespeare* (1986). Many editors of Shakespeare's complete works have printed a portion of *Sir Thomas More,* frequently only Addition IIc, the last segment of the insurrection sequence, but sometimes also Addition III, most recently by Taylor and by Evans and Wells. C. J. Sisson printed in his *Shakespeare* (1954) a text of the play by Harold Jenkins that inserts all the additions into their proper places. *Edward III* has not been incorporated into any complete *Shakespeare,* although Gary Taylor in *William Shakespeare: A Textual*

Companion to *The Oxford Shakespeare* notes that if the editors "had attempted a thorough reinvestigation of candidates for inclusion in the early dramatic canon, it would have begun with *Edward III*." The text of *Cardenio* being lost, it has of course not been in any editions of Shakespeare's complete works, and no editor seems to have considered reprinting *Double Falshood*.

As reflected in the opinion of the majority of scholars, the cogent evidence for Shakespeare's participation in the composition of these four plays warrants more and deeper study of them. Although there is a significant body of scholarship concerning them, it is nevertheless true that Shakespeareans, perhaps understandably, have tended to neglect them in favor of concentration on the canonical plays. Most studies of the romances have, for example, slighted *The Two Noble Kinsmen*, and very few have taken note of the possibility that the play can be viewed as a significant departure from the path traced in the immediately preceding plays. If this book, which it is hoped will encourage and aid in the study of these four valuable plays, should succeed in its objective, we may anticipate a more thorough exploration of the claims for their admission to the canon.

Scholarly investigation into the sources of Shakespeare's plots began early. Eighteenth-century editors recognized that most of the basic stories around which he wove his poetry were not of his invention. Since almost all these editors had a classical education, they recognized the Plautine substratum upon which he built *The Comedy of Errors*. Their knowledge of Chaucer's *The Knight's Tale* enabled them to identify one of the origins of *A Midsummer Night's Dream*, and familiarity with Plutarch's *Lives* made clear the sources of the Roman plays. Charlotte Ramsey Lennox published in 1753 and 1754 the first extended investigation of Shakespeare's sources in her three-volume *Shakespear Illustrated*, discussing and reprinting all or segments of the sources of twenty-two plays. Richard Farmer, in *An Essay on the Learning of Shakespeare* (1767), corrected previous impressions of Shakespeare's wide-ranging reading of the classics in the originals in search of source materials by showing that much of his knowledge of classical literature was gathered from translations. In the nineteenth century, following the era of the great Shakespearean editors—Johnson, Capell, Steevens, Reed, and Malone—all of whom demonstrated an interest in Shakespeare's sources, the study of the origins of his plots suffered a long-running eclipse that continued well into the current century. "Source-hunting," as it was derisively denominated, was in such disrepute that T. S. Eliot felt constrained to say in his introduction to G. Wilson Knight's *Wheel of Fire*, "The question of 'sources' has its rights."

J. Payne Collier issued in 1843 a two-volume *Shakespeare's Library*, "a collection of romances, novels, poems and histories used by Shakespeare as the foundation of his dramas," which W. Carew Hazlitt expanded to six volumes in 1875, thereby preempting, along with Sir Israel Gollancz's source collection, a New Shakspere Society series of sources and analogues. German scholars Karl Simrock, Albert Cohn, Gregor Sarrazin, and Emil Koeppel were active in origin studies from 1865 until 1904, the year in which H. R. C. Anders published a book-length contribution entitled *Shakespeare's Books.* For the next half-century the investigation of sources was mostly limited to sections of editions of individual plays, to monographs on one aspect of the field, such as the influence of Seneca on Shakespearean tragedy, to portions of works whose principal concern is other than the sources, such as T. W. Baldwin's *William Shakspere's Small Latine and Lesse Greeke,* or to essays on a single topic, of which E. A. J. Honigmann's "Shakespeare's Lost Source Plays" is an example. More significant were two publications by Virgil K. Whitaker in which he called for the revivification of source study, which he said "has been strangely neglected."

In this century the most noteworthy studies of Shakespeare's sources are those of Kenneth Muir, Geoffrey Bullough, and Emrys Jones. By a remarkable stroke of chronological coincidence, Muir and Bullough both first published a book on Shakespeare's sources in 1957. Muir's *Shakespeare's Sources* was limited to the histories and tragedies. It was superseded in 1977 by *The Sources of Shakespeare's Plays*, in which he discussed all thirty-seven canonical plays. Bullough's 1957 book was the first of the eight volumes of his *Narrative and Dramatic Sources of Shakespeare*, which was confined to the received canon and completed in 1975. Jones's *The Origins of Shakespeare* (1970) took a wider view of Shakespeare's dramatic roots and the origin of his plots than a specific source study would have. However, he limited himself to discussing in depth only the early plays up to *King John*, although most of the rest of the canonical thirty-seven—though not all—are touched upon. Neither Muir nor Jones reprinted the sources, but Bullough has done so.

This study attempts in general to emulate for the four ascribed plays Bullough's work on the thirty-seven in the canon. There are some particulars in which it differs from his. The difference in some cases arises from the nature of the specific problem. We have good reason, for example, to believe that we know the primary source of *Cardenio* to be Cervantes' *Don Quixote.* But since the text of that play is lost and Theobald's *Double Falshood* manifestly derives either directly or indirectly (through *Cardenio*) from the same novel, it is under these circumstances virtually impossible to determine if there were any other origin. Thus the only source material reprinted is the appropriate segment of *Don Quixote.* Also, a decision was made generally to omit texts that are merely analogues. The several "lives" of Thomas More include one or perhaps two that may be considered analogues, rather than sources, but all except Roper's are to a greater or lesser extent derivative and it seems unnecessary to reprint them all. Furthermore, possibly one of the minor flaws in Bullough's later work is the proliferation of analogues—thirty-four in his last three volumes. Although they may be of some interest, that interest is peripheral and seems to affect the focus adversely, especially when some are included "whether [Shakespeare] knew them or not" (Bullough, 2:vii). On the other hand, the question of authenticity, which with few exceptions is not a problem to Bullough and therefore receives little attention, is important in regard to all four ascribed plays and has been treated at some length in each case. Biblical and homiletic sources have not been dealt with except occasionally because of their pervasive and diffuse influence. In addition, there are some other, lesser deviations from the plan of Bullough's book. "The aims," in Bullough's words, "have been, not to discover new sources but to make those already known accessible to Shakespeare lovers, and in the introductory essays to indicate (however distantly) the imaginative process informing his dramatic structures" (8:7).

The introductions to the individual plays in this book include sections on publication, date, authorship, sources, and stage history. Because in the case of *Sir Thomas More* a manuscript is extant, there are also discussions of the manuscript itself, the seven hands apparent in it, and the evidence of stage censorship. All four introductions are intended to be comprehensive, but they cannot be exhaustive. The source texts reprinted are those on which there is general scholarly agreement, though not without occasional demur, that they are the ones used in the composition of the plays. Doubtful or possible sources that are controversial have not been reproduced. It is to be regretted that such limitations are necessary, but as Bullough notes, "any attempt to bring together all known parallels must fail by reason of the space required" (1:ix). The source texts are reprinted in the order in which they are first cited in the introduction to each play. There is some minor modernization, such as the substitution of our contemporary letters for the Italian long *s* and the runic thorn.

The selection of the exemplars of the source texts to be reprinted has been guided by the criteria laid down by Bullough. This collection of texts, like his, is intended for the use of the general Shakespearean reader—one who is not a specialist—in the evaluation and understanding of the sources of the four ascribed plays and Shakespeare's participation in them. It is a "working collection" of sources (Bullough 1:x), and as such the touchstone as to which text to reproduce has been its utility to the reader. No text has been reproduced for its own sake or to an extent greater than a comprehension of its use as a source would require. Most are consequently represented by excerpts. Source texts, as well as a few citations in the introductions, originally written in Latin are presented in translation because—to quote Bullough again—"comparatively few readers today can cope with . . . Latin originals" (1:xi).

A brief account of the texts reproduced and the method of their selection may facilitate the use of this book by the student of Shakespearean sources. The principal source of *The Reign of King Edward III* is Froissart's *Chronicle* in the English translation of Lord Berners. The text excerpted is that of William Paton Ker, a distinguished scholar and editor. The portion of Holinshed's *Chronicles* is from the text edited by Sir Henry Ellis, and the Countess of Salisbury novel from Painter's *Palace of Pleasure* is that edited by Joseph Jacobs.

The selection of source texts for *Sir Thomas More* was more complex because the use of the sources by the playwrights is itself rather complicated. Segments extracted from Hall's *Vnion of the Noble and Illustre Famelies of Lancastre & Yorke* were taken from the text prepared by Ellis. The "lives" of More reflected in the play are those of William Rastell, William Roper, Nicholas Harpsfield, Ro: Ba: (possible Sir Robert Bassett), Cresacre More and Thomas Stapleton. The first five existed in various manuscripts at the time the play was composed. The texts selected, except for that of Cresacre More, are those based on the surviving manuscripts and edited for the Early English Text Society by Elsie Vaughan Hitchcock in association with other scholars. Joseph Hunter's edition was used for Cresacre More's *Life*. Stapleton's *Vita* was written and published in Latin at Douai in 1588. It was first translated by Philip E. Hallett and issued in 1928. The text excerpted is that of Monsignor Hallett as edited by E. E. Reynolds and published in 1966. The segment from Foxe's *Actes and Monuments* was reproduced from the fourth edition of 1583. For the two plays—*Lusty Juventus* and *The Disobedient Child*—parts of which formed the basis of the play-within-the-play in *Sir Thomas More*, the type facsimile editions by John S. Farmer for the Early English Drama Society were used.

The History of Cardenio is lost, but from its title it appears that the play was based on the adventures of Cardenio in Cervantes' *Don Quixote*. The text excerpted is the translation of Thomas Shelton edited by James Fitzmaurice-Kelly, an authority on Cervantes.

The prologue of *The Two Noble Kinsmen* says that "Chaucer (of all admir'd) the Story gives." Specifically the source is *The Knight's Tale*, the first of *The Canterbury Tales*. Because printing did not begin in England until three quarters of a century after Chaucer's death, his collection of the stories told by the Canterbury pilgrims was left in the form of manuscripts, many of which are still extant. Since the sixteenth century, the tales and Chaucer's other works have gone through numerous printings. The texts derive ultimately from one or more manuscripts, the editing of which is of varying levels of competency. Highly regarded by Chaucer scholars has been the edition by F. N. Robinson first published in 1933, issued in a second edition in 1957, then reworked by a team of scholars under the general editorship of Larry D. Benson and published in 1987. This edition enables the student of Shakespeare's sources to read *The Knight's Tale* in a reliable text based on documents as close to Chaucer's holograph as it is possible to get. Since *The Two Noble Kinsmen* parallels in its form and arrangement nearly every incident of the Knight's story, the entire tale has been here reproduced. Shakespeare and Fletcher did not, of course, base their play on manuscript sources. Robert Turner, by an admirable stroke of scholarly perception, has demonstrated that they used the second edition of Thomas Speght's *Chaucer*, dated 1602. Speght's versions are known to have had limitations of some consequence—one such slip, in fact, enabled Turner to identify the second edition. Consequently, the best modern edition is here reproduced. The morris dance sequence in *The Two Noble Kinsmen* is patently a theater presentation of the second of two antimasques that form part of Beaumont's *Masque of the Inner Temple and Grayes Inne*, which was danced at court during the celebration of the wedding of James I's daughter in 1613. The text of the masque was printed shortly after the nuptial festivities. From this is reproduced the text of the introduction to the second antimasque, the list of dancers, two stage directions, and a brief account of its favorable reception by the court. The excerpts from Sir Philip Sidney's *Countess of Pembroke's Arcadia* and *Lady of May* are in the texts edited by Albert Feuillerat, which preserve the flavor of the original. The segment of "The Life of Theseus" from Plutarch's *Lives of the Noble Grecians and Romans* is in the translation published under the aegis of John Dryden as issued in the readable text edited by Edmund Fuller in 1959.

All of the texts here reproduced have been selected with a view to their ease of use by the nonspecialist reader. They have been reliably edited—a few are originals—and present exemplars of the sources used by Shakespeare and the other playwrights in composing the four ascribed plays. They will present no special problem to the assumed user and will facilitate the comparison of the sources with the plays that are based on them.

Any student of Shakespeare owes a great deal to the many productive scholars who have earlier explored the same country. I have made a conscious effort to acknowledge such debts in appropriate places, even to the extent that one reader raised a query as to whether the documentation might be excessive. I am more concerned about ideas whose origins have faded from memory and may not have been properly credited. In addition to such general obligations I am specifically and especially indebted for generous help, support, and for such favors as providing materials not yet published, to Giles E. Dawson, Charles R. Forker, Trevor H. Howard-Hill, Harold Jenkins, John Jowett, Arthur F. Kinney, Roslyn L. Knutson, William B. Long, Louis Marder,

Scott McMillin, Giorgio Melchiori, Harrison T. Meserole, S. Schoenbaum, Gary Taylor, Ann Thompson, John W. Velz, and Stanley Wells. It is a pleasure to express my gratitude to each and every one. I also thank Professor Howard-Hill and Cambridge University Press for permission to incorporate in an expanded form elements of my "'voyce and Credyt': The Scholars and *Sir Thomas More*" included in *Shakespeare and Sir Thomas More: Essays on the Play and Its Shakespearian Interest* and the Editorial Board of *Theatre History Studies* and Ron Engle, its editor, for permission similarly to include parts of "*The Two Noble Kinsmen* on the Twentieth Century Stage" and "Stage History of *Cardenio—Double Falshood*" in the stage histories of those plays in this book. In regard to the illustrations I am grateful to Professor Schoenbaum and the Worshipful Company of Stationers for permission to reproduce the *Stationers' Register* entry of *Cardenio*; to the British Library for permission to reproduce the title pages of the 1595 quarto of *Edward III* and of the 1634 quarto of *The Two Noble Kinsmen*; folio 9a of the manuscript of *Sir Thomas More*; and the title page of the first edition (1728) of *Double Falshood*.

I wish also to express my appreciation to the Early English Text Society for permission to reprint passages from its editions of the "lives" of Thomas More by Roper, Harpsfield (including the "Rastell Fragments"), and Ro: Ba:; to Beinecke Library of Yale University for allowing the reprinting of portions of their copies of Foxe's *Actes*, Beaumont's *Masque,* and Sidney's *Lady of May*; to Burns and Oates for permission to reproduce part of the English version of Stapleton's *Vita*; to Houghton Mifflin for permitting the reprinting of the Benson-Robinson text of Chaucer's *Knight's Tale*; to AMS Press for authorizing the use of their reprints of the *Chronicles* and *Don Quixote*; and to Dell Publishing for permission to reproduce a segment of Edmund Fuller's edition of Plutarch's *Lives*. Last but not least, I thank my wife, to whom the book is dedicated, for great patience, unflagging support, and for penetrating questioning of many aspects of this study. The inevitable slips remaining are my responsibility.

Throughout, the abbreviations for the titles of Shakespeare's plays are those employed in the annual annotated *World Shakespeare Bibliography* published as a separate issue of *Shakespeare Quarterly*. To them I have added *Cdo* for *Cardenio* and *DF* for *Double Falshood*. These symbols have been endorsed by Professor Meserole, who serves *Shakespeare Quarterly* as bibliographer. Abbreviations for the titles of scholarly and other journals are also those of the *World Shakespeare Bibliography*.

G. H. M.
9 October 1988

CONTENTS

LIST OF ILLUSTRATIONS

THE REIGN OF KING EDWARD III

THE

RAIGNE OF KING EDVVARD the third:

As it hath bin sundrie times plaied about the Citie of London.

LONDON,
Printed for Cuthbert Burby.
1596.

INTRODUCTION

Publication

"A book Intitled Edward the Third and the blacke prince their warres wth kinge Iohn of Fraunce" was entered by Cuthbert Burby on the *Stationers' Register* on 1 December 1595. The first quarto was issued without authorship attribution dated 1596, under the title *The Raigne of King Edvvard the third* (see figure 1). The second quarto, a reprint of the first with some alterations, followed in 1599, also published by Burby.[1] After the second quarto, the play was not printed again until 1760 when Edward Capell published the first critical edition in *Prolusions*. Capell's text is a conflation of the two quarto texts, freely emended.[2] Subsequent editions of the play were published by Henry Tyrrell, ed., *The Doubtful Plays of Shakespeare* (1851); Ludwig Tieck, ed., *Vier Schauspiele von Shakespeare* (1851); Nicolaus Delius, ed., *Pseudoshakspere'sche Dramen* (1854); and Max Moltke, ed., *Doubtful Plays of William Shakespeare* (1869). All of these are indebted to Capell's edition. J. Payne Collier published *King Edward the Third: A historical play by William Shakespeare* in 1878. In *The Leopold Shakespeare* (1877), Frederick Furnivall reproduced Delius's 1854 text. The first modern edition is that of Karl Warnke and Ludwig Proescholdt, a critical edition based on the text of the first quarto.[3] A. F. Hopkinson published the play in his *Shakespeare's Doubtful Plays* (1891); Thomas Donovan in his *English History Plays* (1896 and 1911); and G. C. Moore Smith in the *Temple Dramatists* series (1897).

The twentieth-century publication history of *Edward III* begins with the edition by Tucker Brooke in his well-known *Shakespeare Apocrypha*, first issued in 1908 and several times reprinted.[4] It was one of James Winny's *Three Elizabethan Plays* and was edited by R. L. Armstrong in E. B.

1. W. W. Greg, ed., *A Bibliography of the English Printed Drama to the Restoration*, 4 vols. (London: The Bibliographical Society, 1939–1959), 1:12, 225–26 (no. 140).

2. Edward Capell, ed., *Prolusions; or, select pieces of Antient Poetry* (London: 1760), pp. i–xi, especially pp. ix–x.

3. Karl Warnke and Ludwig Proescholdt, eds., *Pseudo-Shakesperian Plays*, 5 vols. (Halle: Niemeyer, 1883–1888), vol. 3; *King Edward III*, 1886 (New York: AMS, 1973; rpt., five volumes in one). A useful bibliographical essay on the early literature of the play was published by R. Sachs, "Die Shakespeare zugeschriebenen zweifelhaften Stücke," *SJ* 27 (1892): 183–90.

4. C. F. Tucker Brooke, ed., *The Shakespeare Apocrypha* (Oxford: Clarendon Press, 1908; rpt. 1929, 1947, 1967).

Everitt's *Six Early Plays Related to the Shakespeare Canon.*[5] William A. Armstrong included it in his volume of *Elizabethan History Plays*, and William Kozlenko reprinted Tyrrell's 1851 text in *Disputed Plays of William Shakespeare.*[6] Fred Lapides issued a critical, old-spelling edition based on the first quarto text of *The Raigne of King Edward the Third* in the Garland Renaissance Drama series under the general editorship of Stephen Orgel.[7] The only facsimile reproduction of the first quarto was published by John S. Farmer in 1910, based on British Library copy *C.* 34, *g.* 1.[8] William Poel printed his lightly altered text of the Countess scenes arranged in one act, under the title *Love's Constancy*, in 1906.[9]

Date

The *Stationers' Register* entry of 1 December 1595 provides external evidence concerning the latest possible date of composition. In the preliminaries to his facsimile edition of *Edward III*, Farmer says, "From internal evidence it is clearly shown that the play was written early in 1589," but he does not specify his evidence. The presence in the play of a line that also occurs in Sonnet 94 and an allusion to the story of Lucrece suggests to Sir Edmund Chambers a "date in 1594–1595," while Kenneth Muir, evaluating the same evidence, says, "It is likely to have been written after 1593—because of its allusion to [Shakespeare's] *Lucrece.*"[10] V. Østerberg finds that in thematic, metrical, and stylistic qualities, *Edward III* exhibits characteristics indicating a date of 1592–1594.[11] Thomas Baldwin thinks the casting pattern is that of the Admiral's Men of about 1589.[12] MacDonald Jackson finds that the borrowings from *Edward III* in *The Contention betwixt the two famous Houses of Yorke and Lancaster* and *The True Tragedie of*

5. James Winny, ed., *Three Elizabethan Plays* (London: Chatto & Windus, 1959); R. L. Armstrong, ed., *Edward III. Six Early Plays Related to the Shakespeare Canon*; *Anglistica XIV*, ed. E. B. Everitt (Copenhagen: Rosenkilde and Bagger, 1965).

6. William A. Armstrong, ed., *Elizabethan History Plays* (London: Oxford University Press, 1965); William Kozlenko, *Disputed Plays of William Shakespeare* (New York: Hawthorn, 1974).

7. Fred Lapides, ed., *The Raigne of King Edward the Third* (New York: Garland, 1980).

8. John S. Farmer, ed., *The Reign of King Edward III*, Tudor Facsimile Texts, no. 78 (Edinburgh and London: John S. Farmer, 1910; rpt. New York: AMS, 1970).

9. William Poel, ed., *Love's Constancy*, bound with *Lillies that Fester* (London: Bullen, 1906), pp. 47–74.

10. Farmer, *The Reign of King Edward III*, p. [5]; E. K. Chambers, *William Shakespeare: A Study of Facts and Problems*, 2 vols. (Oxford: Clarendon Press, 1930), 1:517; Kenneth Muir, *Shakespeare as Collaborator* (London: Methuen, 1960), p. 39. Neither Chambers nor Muir offers any evidence in support of the assumed priority in date of the sonnet and *Luc.*

11. V. Østerberg, "The 'Countess Scenes' of *Edward III*," *SJ* 65 (1929): 49.

12. T. W. Baldwin, *On the Literary Genetics of Shakespeare's Plays 1592–1594* (Urbana: University of Illinois Press, 1959), p. 235.

Richard Duke of Yorke, now generally accepted as bad quartos of *2* and *3 Henry VI*, establish a date no "later than 1592." Subsequently he says it was "written in its entirety before 1590."[13] On similar grounds A. S. Cairncross argues that all the Pembroke's Men's plays, including *The Contention* and *The True Tragedie*, existed in 1591, and, if so, then *Edward III* must be of the same era.[14] Robert Smith, emphasizing that *Edward III* is a chronicle play rather than a history play, says that it was written perhaps as early as 1590.[15]

Karl Wentersdorf notes the anachronistic description in the play of the great destructive power of naval artillery at the battle of Sluys, unknown in naval warfare before 1588, more than two centuries later; a reference to a crescent-shaped naval formation at Sluys reminiscent of the Spanish Armada; and an allusion to the English ship "*Nom per illa*" (*The Nonpareil*), which fought against the Spanish fleet in 1588. These, he says, establish a terminus a quo of 1589. The pervasive patriotic spirit of *Edward III* and "the many points of resemblance in diction, imagery and treatment of subject matter to" *1 Henry VI* indicate to Wentersdorf a date "about 1589–1590." Lapides, citing the Armada date and the closing of the playhouses because of plague in 1592, modifies Wentersdorf's conclusion somewhat: "The period 1589–1592 is as specific as we are able to get." G. R. Proudfoot sets a date of 1591–1592 because he determines that the play belonged to Pembroke's Men (who went bankrupt in September 1593); and in consideration of the closing of the theaters for eighteen months because of the plague beginning in June 1592.[16] Gary Taylor, surveying this and other evidence, and placing some emphasis on findings from parallels and studies of style, vocabulary, and metrics, which point away from an early date, concludes that the date of the play is uncertain in the present state of our information. Nevertheless, a date of composition of about 1590–1591 seems to be most in accord with the Armada evidence and a fair assessment of scholarly opinion.[17]

13. MacD. P. Jackson, "*Edward III*, Shakespeare, and Pembroke's Men," *N&Q* 210 (1965): 329–31; "A Note on the Text of *Edward III*," *N&Q* 216 (1971): 453.

14. A. S. Cairncross, "Pembroke's Men and Some Shakesperian Pirates," *SQ* 11 (1960): 335–49.

15. Robert Metcalf Smith, "*Edward III*: A Study of the Authorship of the Drama in the Light of a New Source," *JEGP* 10 (1911): 90–104.

16. Karl P. Wentersdorf, "The Date of *Edward III*," *SQ* 16 (1965): 227–31. Lapides, *The Raigne of King Edward the Third*, p. 37; G. R. Proudfoot, "*The Reign of King Edward the Third* (1596) and Shakespeare," *Proceedings of the British Academy* (London: Oxford University Press, 1986), 71:169–85. Proudfoot's discussion of the date of composition is on pp. 181–82.

17. Gary Taylor, "The Canon and Chronology of Shakespeare's Plays," *William Shakespeare: A Textual Companion*, by Stanley Wells and Gary Taylor with John Jowett and William Montgomery (Oxford: Clarendon Press, 1987), pp. 136–37. Act and scene designations and line numbers cited in the text are those of Lapides's edition. Q1 consists of nineteen scenes, undivided. Capell was the first to divide the play into acts and scenes.

Authorship

The authorship of *Edward III* has been much debated. Many scholars do not accept the hypothesis of Shakespeare's participation in the play, either pointing to the lack of reliable external evidence concerning authorship or simply concluding that the case is not proved. Others argue negatively, citing the unShakespearean structural discontinuity between the two parts of the play (defined as the Countess of Salisbury episode and the later military campaign in France), the pedestrian verse, the static characterization, or what is perceived as the many shortcomings of *Edward III* when compared to Shakespeare's great histories, especially *Henry V*. A few critics see Shakespeare as a reviser of an earlier drama, which was, perhaps, two separate plays.[18] A trend among commentators in the twentieth century has been to accept the hypothesis that Shakespeare wrote part of *Edward III*, either limited to the Countess scenes or to those scenes plus that in which the Black Prince spiritedly refuses to surrender before the battle of Poitiers (4.4). There is no consensus concerning the identity of Shakespeare's posited collaborator, but Peele, Kyd, Marlowe, Lodge, and Greene have been suggested. Finally, some students of the play, including some who have recently studied it most intensively, have concluded that Shakespeare is the sole author of the entire play.[19]

Edward III was first attributed to Shakespeare by Richard Rogers and William Ley in a 1656 play list appended to an edition of Thomas Goff's *Careless Shepherdess*. Scholars have tended to doubt the validity of the ascription because it is late and because the same list also assigns to Shakespeare other plays clearly not his. Two other seventeenth-century catalogues of play titles—those complied by Edward Archer (1656) and Francis Kirkman (1661, expanded 1671)—included *Edward III*, but in neither list is it attributed to Shakespeare or any other playwright.[20] In his edition (1760) of the play, Edward Capell briefly presents a reasoned case for Shake-

Lapides follows the designation in Warnke and Proescholdt's edition and notes differences between them and Capell. Line numbering follows a modified TLN plan. Lapides does not assign line numbers to free-standing stage directions.

18. The unusual use of large type for the opening stage direction of the military sequence in Q1 (sig. E 1v) constitutes a modicum of bibliographical support for the hypothesis that the assumed predecessor play was in two parts. Robert Boies Sharpe, *The Real War of the Theatre: Shakespeare's Fellows in Rivalry with the Admiral's Men, 1594–1603* (New York: The Modern Language Association of America, 1935), p. 39.

19. A comprehensive survey of scholarly opinion on the authorship of *Edward III* to 1957 can be found in Wentersdorf, *The Authorship of Edward III*, Ph.D diss., University of Cincinnati, 1960, pp. 7–60.

20. Sir John Harington and Henry Oxinden each noted an *Edward III* in lists of plays in their collections dated circa 1610 and circa 1663, respectively, but like most of the plays in both lists, it is not attributed. Harington's and Oxinden's lists and the three booksellers' catalogues are reprinted in Greg, *Bibliography*, 3:1306–62. See also Giles E. Dawson, "An Early List of Elizabethan Plays," *Library* 4th ser., 15 (1935): 445–56.

speare's authorship. He acknowledges in his introduction the lack of external evidence but argues, chiefly on stylistic and structural grounds, that the play was written by Shakespeare. This, he says, is conjectural, and he invites others to read the play in his edition and form their own opinions. Many did, but the results have been diverse. Those who until the beginning of the twentieth century arrived at the same conclusion as Capell include Tieck, Ulrici (later recanted), Ortlepp, Tyrrell, Rapp, Moltke, Collier, Tennyson, Teetgen, Phipson, Hopkinson, and Madden. Their reasons, of course, vary, but several note such considerations as the characteristically Shakespearean diction, verse, and ethical content of the play, structural parallels to Shakespeare's acknowledged work, favorable comparisons to the canonical histories, and the expression and content of imagery including the out-of-doors qualities and allusions to field sports. In addition, Collier notes the presence, usually in modified form, in plays of later date such as *Love's Labour's Lost*, *Measure for Measure*, and *Hamlet*, of distinctive thoughts, expressions, and images that first occur in *Edward III*, which he concludes establishes Shakespeare's claim to the authorship of the play.[21]

During the nineteenth century, scholars began to distinguish between the two parts of the play and, as a consequence, a body of thinking developed that denied Shakespeare's authorship of the military episodes, with the possible exception of 4.4, but recognized his hand in the romantic sequence. Those who conclude that the scenes of royal wooing are Shakespearean, perhaps as a revision to, or insertion into, an older text include Fleay, Halliwell-Phillipps, Moore Smith, Brandes, Ward, Schelling, and Moorman. The evidence cited by this varied group of critics, on the basis of which they arrive at a common conclusion concerning the authenticity of the romantic scenes, differs. Fleay notes general style, poetic power, versification, linguistic elements, and characterization.[22] Halliwell-Phillipps cites style and characterization.[23] Moore Smith thinks the treatment of the romantic theme exhibits characteristic Shakespearean power and imagination, while in contrast the military scenes are prolix, clumsy, bathetic, and dull.[24] Ward believes that Shakespeare was refurbishing an older play and that in the course of his work he completely rewrote the body of the first and second acts. For him the Countess of Salisbury belongs with Shakespeare's gallery of heroines.[25] Schelling finds the claims for Shakespearean authorship of the royal courtship of the Countess not

21. Collier, *King Edward the Third: A historical play by William Shakespeare* (1878), pp. vii–xii.

22. F. G. Fleay, *Shakespeare Manual* (London: 1878), pp. 303–6.

23. J. O. Halliwell-Phillipps, *Outlines of the Life of Shakespeare*, 2 vols., 7th ed. (London: 1887), 1:125–27.

24. G. C. Moore Smith, ed., *Edward the Third*, The Temple Dramatists (London: 1897), pp. xiii–xxi.

25. Adolphus William Ward, *A History of English Dramatic Literature to the Death of Queen Anne*, 3 vols., rev. ed. (London: 1899), 2:221–25.

unreasonably advanced.[26] Moorman tells us that superior style, characterization, dramatic effect, versification, and lyricism in the romantic episode set it on a plane above the military scenes, but he rejects the theory that the love scenes are "extraneous matter foisted into the play" or that the disparity in itself furnishes a "reason for assuming double authorship." He thinks the Countess story was an integral part of an earlier *Edward III* that Shakespeare revised, rewriting the love sequence completely but leaving the military episode substantially unchanged.[27]

By a wide margin, critics who until the early part of this century decided that Shakespeare had no hand in *Edward III* outnumbered all others. They include, among others, Knight, Delius, von Friesen, Furnivall, Swinburne, Symonds, Warnke and Praescholdt, Saintsbury, Dowden, Morley, Lee, Liebau, and Rolfe. Almost all cite, occasionally in addition to other reasons, those set forth by Charles Knight, who first elaborated the arguments against Shakespeare's authorship. Knight begins by refuting Ulrici's theory, devised to account for the abrupt transition between the romantic and military sequences, that *Edward III* is actually a two-part play.

> The plan pursued in the *Edward III* is, to say the least, exceedingly inartificial. If the writer of this play had possessed more dramatic skill, he might have made the severance of the action less abrupt. As it is, the link is snapped short. In the first two acts we have the Edward of Romance,—a puling lover, a heartless seducer, a despot, and then a penitent. In the last three acts we have the Edward of history,—the ambitious hero, the stern conqueror, the affectionate husband, the confiding father. . . . Dealing with those incidents which were calculated to call forth the highest poetical efforts, such as the battle of Poitiers and the siege of Calais, the dramatist is strikingly inferior to the fine old chronicler [Froissart]. When Shakspere dealt with heroic subjects, as in his *Henry V*, he kept pretty closely to the original narrative; but he breathed a life into the commonest occurrences. . . . We can easily understand how a new school of writers should, in 1595, have been formed, possessing perhaps, less original genius than some of the earlier founders of the drama, but having an immense advantage over them in the models which the greatest of those founders had produced. Still this consideration does not wholly warrant us in hastily pronouncing the play before us not to be Shakspere's. As in the case of *Arden of Feversham*, we have to look, and we look in vain, for some known writer of the period whose works exhibit a similar combination of excellences.

Concerning the "lilies" line occurring in both the play and Sonnet 94, Knight says, "We are of opinion that the line was original in the sonnet and

26. Felix E. Schelling, *Elizabethan Drama 1558–1642*, 2 vols. (Boston: Houghton-Mifflin, 1908), 1:273.

27. F. W. Moorman, "Plays of Uncertain Authorship Attributed to Shakespeare," *Cambridge History of English Literature*, 15 vols. (Cambridge: Cambridge University Press, 1907–1916), 5:272–76.

transplanted thence into this play. The point is material in considering the date of the sonnet, but it throws no light either upon the date of this play or upon its authorship." He comments favorably on the theatrical effectiveness of the three scenes in which King Edward at Crecy refuses aid to his son (3.5), in which the beleagured Black Prince rejects repeated bids from the French leaders to surrender (4.4), and in which Calais capitulates (5.1), but finds them lacking "in the higher requisites of poetry." The play's great fault, he sums up,

> is tameness; the author does not rise with the elevation of his subject. To judge of its inferiority to the matured power of Shakspere, dealing with a somewhat similar theme, it should be compared with the *Henry V*. The question then should be asked, Will the possible difference of age account for this difference of power? . . . Admitting, which we not, that the best scenes of this play display the same poetical power, though somewhat immature, which is found in Shakspere's historical plays, there is one thing wanting to make the writer [of *Edward III*] a "twin-brother," which is found in *all* those productions. Where is the *comedy* of *Edward III*? The heroic of Shakespeare's histories might be capable of imitation; but the genius which created Faulconbridge, and Cade, and Pistol, and Fluellen (Falstaff is out of the question) could not be approached.[28]

Later critics note these deficiencies, occasionally with some augmentation, frequently in trenchant terms of which some of Frederick Furnivall's and Algernon Swinburne's comments may serve as examples. Furnivall states, "A few wild untrustworthy folk contend that Shakspere wrote the whole play. Against them the internal evidence is clear." He lists differences in style, lack of dramatic unity, want of characterization, "no humour, no wit, no comedy," forced moral tone, and weak versification. He continues, "We come then to those moderate and sensible critics who contend that the King-and-Countess Act alone is Shakspere's. And I willingly grant that the Act is worthy of the young Shakspere," but he concludes by rejecting the idea on the grounds that Shakespeare would not have drawn on an Italian novel for an incident in the life of an English king.

> I submit that it is not my duty to prove the negative; it is the business of the advocates of Shakspere's authorship . . . to prove the affirmative. . . . There were doubtless one-play men in those days, as there have been one-book men since. As at present advised, I refuse to admit the [Countess] episode as Shakspere's.[29]

Swinburne addresses himself to the "brazen-browed and brazen-throated gang of dunces" who subscribe to Capell's

28. Charles Knight, *Studies of Shakespeare* (London: 1849), pp. 279–87. In regard to Knight's concluding point, one wonders how he envisaged the playing of the comic interchange in 2.1 between King Edward and his poet-secretary Lodowick (ll. 394–518).

29. Frederick J. Furnivall, Introduction to *The Leopold Shakspere* (London: 1877), pp. c–ci.

> well nigh still-born theory. . . . The author of *King Edward III* was a devout student and a humble follower of Christopher Marlowe, not yet wholly disengaged by that august and beneficent influence. . . . Whatever in *King Edward III* is mediocre or worse is evidently such as it is through no passionate or slovenly precipitation of handiwork, but through pure incompetence to do better. The blame of the failure, the shame of the shortcoming, cannot be laid to the account of any momentary excess or default in emotion, of passing exhaustion or excitement, of intermittent impulse and reaction; it is an indication of lifelong and irremediable impotence.[30]

Warnke and Proescholdt are as rational in their approach to the problem of authorship as they are sound in their textual criticism. They believe that the story of the military exploits of King Edward and the Black Prince "might well have tempted the pen of a poet like Shakespeare." Furthermore,

> not only the subject itself, but also the manner in which it is treated, reminds the reader of Shakespeare . . . yet though our play is certainly superior to many other contemporary pieces . . . we are nevertheless of opinion that the whole of the play is such as to prevent us from adopting the hypothesis of the authorship.

Unlike the authentic history plays of Shakespeare, *Edward III* "is no more than a versified chronicle." In drawing the picture of Edward III, one of the greatest English kings, Shakespeare would not have had recourse to an anecdote related by an Italian novelist. Structurally, Shakespeare in his plays unites several actions into one, but in none is there so wide a chasm as that between the two parts of *Edward III.* As to the characters, "most suffer from a certain monotony," and some important characters—Warwick, the Prince, and even the Countess—"show real deficiencies such as never occur in Shakespeare." On the whole, Warnke and Proescholdt "are convinced that Shakespeare is not to be regarded as the author of *King Edward III.*" After a review of the arguments of Fleay and Ward for divided authorship they also reject the hypothesis that Shakespeare wrote the Countess episode.[31]

Critics of all persuasions note, but do not always espouse, the possibility that Shakespeare merely retouched an earlier play by another dramatist. The basis for this conception is a recognition that there are some passages in the opening scene and more scattered throughout the later three acts that are reminiscent of Shakespeare, particularly in the imagery; and yet the general impression is that the play does not quite rise to the level of

30. Algernon Charles Swinburne, "Note on the Historical Play of King Edward III," *Gentlemen's Magazine* 247 (1879): 170–81 and 330–49; reprinted in revised form as Appendix 1 in *A Study of Shakespeare* (New York: 1880).

31. Warnke and Proescholdt, *Pseudo-Shakespearian Plays*, pp. xxii–xxxiv.

Shakespeare's acknowledged histories. A few commentators conclude that Shakespeare served merely as an editor, and W. Carew Hazlitt refers to his "editorial hand,"[32] but this is distinctly a minority opinion.

Toward the close of the nineteenth century, Shakespearean scholarship began to search for more objective ways of determining the authorship of disputed plays other than aesthetic judgments. The New Shakspere Society, founded in 1873, with its emphasis on "scientific" methods—which in the event turned out to be mostly statistical expressions of scholarly appraisals—was both a consequence of and a contributing factor to this swelling trend. Some good work was done and the thrust of the society's efforts, and even its errors, helped to point the way toward development of more nearly objective means of settling questions of authorship. However, neither the work of the society nor the more general movement toward objectivity in attribution studies brought a consensus concerning the identity of the playwright who wrote *Edward III.*

The modern era in authorship studies of disputed Shakespearean plays dawned with the publication in 1908 of C. F. Tucker Brooke's edition of *The Shakespeare Apocrypha*, comprising fourteen plays ascribed in whole or in part to Shakespeare on the basis of either significant evidence or persistent tradition. Brooke starts with a list of forty-two "doubtful" plays. From this list, by means of a winnowing process, he selects thirteen plays (including *Edward III*) with which Shakespeare's name had been associated since the seventeenth century and which Brooke regards "as having acquired a real claim to the title" of doubtful Shakespearean plays. To these he adds *Sir Thomas More.*[33] Brooke's edition has been subjected to severe strictures (for example, by Greg),[34] but it remains, three quarters of a century later, the standard for the Shakespeare apocrypha.[35]

Regarding the authorship of *Edward III*, Brooke first asserts that the final three acts are not by Shakespeare. The two passages in act 3 (3.3.1425–27; 3.5.1612–13) referring back to the love intrigue, and the tone and style of the later non-historical scenes they share with the Countess sequence, indicate that the play is the work of a single playwright; but

32. W. Carew Hazlitt, *Shakespear* (London: Quaritch, 1902), pp. 110–11.

33. Brooke, *The Shakespeare Apocrypha*, pp. ix–xi. Brooke apparently did not intend to convey the impression that his list of forty-two titles is substantially complete. There are in fact many more attributions. See Lindley Williams Hubbell, *Note on the Shakespeare Apocrypha*, 4th ed. (Kobe: Ikuta, 1977); and the Introduction to my *Four Plays Ascribed to Shakespeare: An Annotated Bibliography* (New York: Garland, 1982), pp. xiii–xx.

34. W. W. Greg, ed., *The Book of Sir Thomas More*, Malone Society Reprints (Oxford: Oxford University Press, 1911), says, "I have failed to find any principle underlying Mr. Tucker Brooke's procedure: he is not consistent in following the manuscript, neither does he conform either to the ancient or to the modern convention: similar confusion reigns as regards capitals and contractions. His perfunctory and inaccurate introduction does not call for discussion in this place" (p. xxi).

35. G. R. Proudfoot has in preparation a newly edited version of *The Shakespeare Apocrypha* to be published by the Clarendon Press, including *Edward III.*

Shakespeare is incapable of the hollowness and insincerity of the romantic episode and the quibbling mawkishness of Warwick and the Countess, and therefore the play cannot be his. Brooke suggests that the author is George Peele on the basis of similarities between *Edward III* and *David and Bethsabe*, especially in the "basal lack of unity" and the absence of comic relief in both plays. He concedes "that *Edward III* is a finer production than any with which Peele is at present accredited."[36] Subsequently (in 1948) he modified his opinion as to authorship and found good reasons for seeing Shakespeare's hand in the play.[37]

Robert Smith determines that from the complex fusion of materials from two sources (Froissart and Painter) and from the two links in the military scenes, the play was written at one time by one dramatist and that it could not have been Shakespeare because it is not up to his level, is deficient in characterization, and lacks comedy, and because Shakespeare, "as far as is known . . . never consulted Froissart for chronicle history." He specifically challenges "the double authorship theory" and believes it is improbable that any dramatist could have inserted the Countess episode into the play, since there is no evidence of collaboration or revision. He also rejects the suggestions that *Edward III* is the work of Marlowe, Greene, Peele, or Lodge, and he declines to offer any other candidate.[38]

For a period of years after Smith, little was written concerning the authorship of *Edward III* save for a handful of mostly casual comments generally tending to the negative side by John Masefield, Arthur Platt, William A. Neilson and Ashley Thorndike, J. Q. Adams, and S. R. Golding. Golding argues for Robert Wilson as the author on the basis of parallels with *The Cobbler's Prophecy*, *Three Lords and Three Ladies of London*, and, particularly, *A Larum for London*, which he attributes to Wilson on grounds that are less than convincing.[39]

John M. Robertson approaches the authorship problem by reference

36. Brooke, *The Shakespeare Apocrypha*, p. xxiii.

37. Brooke, "The Renaissance," *A Literary History of England*, ed. Albert C. Baugh (New York: Appleton-Century-Crofts, 1948), p. 468.

38. Robert Metcalf Smith, *Froissart and the English Chronicle Play* (New York: Columbia University Press, 1915), pp. 82–85, and "*Edward III*," pp. 103–4. Subsequent studies have shown that Smith, in his assertion that Shakespeare did not use Froissart as a source for his acknowledged plays, is in error. See, for example, J. Dover Wilson, ed., *Richard II*, New Cambridge Shakespeare (Cambridge: Cambridge University Press, 1939), pp. xliv–xlv; E. M. W. Tillyard, *Shakespeare's History Plays* (London: Chatto & Windus, 1948), pp. 252–55; Matthew W. Black, ed., New Variorum *Richard II* (Philadelphia: Lippincott, 1955), pp. 405, 453–62; Geoffrey Bullough, *Narrative and Dramatic Sources of Shakespeare*, 8 vols. (London: Routledge; New York: Columbia University Press, 1957–1975), 3:367–69, 380, 423–31; and Haldeen Braddy, "Shakespeare's Puck and Froissart's Orthon," *SQ* 7 (1956): 276–80.

39. John Masefield, *William Shakespeare* (New York: Holt, 1911), pp. 239–40; Arthur Platt, "*Edward III* and Shakespeare's Sonnets," *MLR* 6 (1911): 511–13; William A. Neilson and Ashley H. Thorndike, *The Facts About Shakespeare* (New York: Macmillan, 1913), pp. 161–62; Joseph Quincy Adams, *A Life of William Shakespeare* (Boston: Houghton-Mifflin, 1923), pp. 163–64; S. R. Golding, "The Authorship of *Edward III*," *N&Q* 154 (1929): 313–15. Golding's attribution to Wilson is effectively countered by E. H. C. Oliphant in "How Not to Play the Game of Parallels," *JEGP* 28 (1929): 1–15.

to comparisons and parallels of thought, diction, verse, and imagery in acknowledged work. He also makes some use of Fleay's verse tests. He does not subscribe to Brooke's assignment of the play to Peele and doubts Shakespeare's participation. Those parts of the play thought to have been written by him are not Shakespearean Marlowesque but Marlowe's authentic hand. Marlowe "planned, opened and largely wrote the play." His principal collaborator was Greene, who "largely rewrote the second act." The style of the Countess sequence is marked by a rapid yet monotonous iambic movement "which is specially characteristic of Greene's later blank verse." Greene also handled parallels to the situation of a virtuous lady besieged by a king in *James IV* and *George-a-Greene*. Peele's hand can be discerned here and there and so can Kyd's, but their contributions are minor.[40]

Ernest A. Gerrard suggests Drayton as the author of *Edward III* on the basis of distinctive verse and stylistic qualities, but his hypothesis drew little notice. H. W. Crundell independently propounded the same attribution in consideration of similarities between the play and Drayton's poem *The Battaile of Agincourt*. This was challenged by Kathleen Tillotson and Bernard H. Newdigate. They dispute Crundell's similarities and point out that there is no evidence that Drayton tried his hand at drama until about 1598.[41]

Østerberg makes most intensively the case for Shakespeare's authorship of the Countess episode. He argues that different hands can be traced in the text because of the palpable difference in dramatic power, art, and style between the "so-called Countess scenes, [which] form a perfect little drama by themselves," and the rest of the play. Close examination of parallels of diction, verse, rhetoric, and imagery between the romantic episode in *Edward III* and *Venus and Adonis*, *The Rape of Lucrece*, *Romeo and Juliet*, and *Love's Labor's Lost* convince Østerberg that the Countess sequence is authentic Shakespeare. Robertson's advocacy of Greene's authorship is not successful except for his suggestion that Greene, with Marlowe and Kyd, might have participated in an assumed early version of *Edward III* written before 1592. This play might have been acquired by Shakespeare's company in 1594, and possibly he refurbished it, inserting his own poem of King and Countess that he may have had in mind as a companion piece to *Lucrece*, which explains in part the many parallels. Shakespeare perhaps touched up the other parts of the play here and there. "The Countess drama [should] be acknowledged as substantially his."[42]

40. J. M. Robertson, *An Introduction to the Study of the Shakespeare Canon* (London: Routledge, 1924), pp. 305–10, 326–38, 352–77, 379–85.

41. Ernest A. Gerrard, *Elizabethan Drama and Dramatists 1583–1603* (Oxford: Oxford University Press, 1928), pp. 266–67; H. W. Crundell, "Drayton and *Edward III*," *N&Q* 176 (1939): 258–60, 356–57; Kathleen Tillotson, "Drayton and *Edward III*," *N&Q* 176 (1939): 318–19; Bernard H. Newdigate, *Michael Drayton and his Circle*, corrected ed. (Oxford: Blackwell, 1961), p. 110.

42. Østerberg, "The 'Countess Scenes' of *Edward III*," pp. 49–91.

In his *William Shakespeare*, Sir Edmund Chambers established the value and cogency of factual external evidence in attribution studies and the dangers of subjective judgments based on frequently slippery and controversial internal evidence. He accepted Shakespeare's part authorship of only two plays where no external evidence of authorship exists, one of which is *Edward III*. He says that modern criticism is right in finding in the play two hands of which only one deserves serious consideration as Shakespeare's. The scenes of the wooing of the Countess by Edward (1.2, from line 263, and 2.1 and 2.2) exhibit a literary quality that is higher than in the bulk of the play. Comparatively free use is made of feminine endings, and there is a constant habit of ringing the changes on individual words in the Shakespearean manner. These qualities are also present in the scene (4.4) in which the Black Prince spurns French urgings to surrender. He cites the reference to *Lucrece* and the links with Sonnets 94 and 146 and concludes that it is quite possible that these scenes may be Shakespeare's. No serious attempt can be made to identify the second hand, but it may be that of Greene or Peele. He does not see any evidence of revision.[43]

Summary comments by John Mackail and E. H. C. Oliphant indicate that their position corresponds to Chambers's. William Wells, however, credits the play to Kyd on the grounds of vocabulary and structural similarities to the *Troublesome Reign of King John*, which he thinks Kyd wrote.[44]

Alfred Hart's statistically based studies of the vocabularies of Shakespeare, Marlowe, Greene, and Peele compared with that of *Edward III* supersede earlier impressionistic judgments of vocabularies and at the same time bring to bear on the authorship question an objective tool, the validity of which any other scholar can test for himself. Hart demonstrates by comparisons of a number of vocabulary features such as the incidence of words having certain prefixes and suffixes and of compound terms and by comparisons of the frequency of neologisms that the vocabulary employed in *Edward III* is very close to Shakespeare's while it is measurably richer than that of Marlowe. Even further removed are Greene and Peele. He shows that the diction of the Countess scenes and that of the remainder of the play exhibit virtually identical qualities, making it unlikely that two playwrights are involved. The only alternative to accepting Shakespeare as the author of the whole of *Edward III* is to "confess our ignorance, and permit the play to remain authorless."[45] Frank O'Connor, citing stylistic features

43. Chambers, *William Shakespeare*, 1:515–18.

44. John W. Mackail, *The Approach to Shakespeare* (Oxford: Oxford University Press, 1930; rpt. Freeport, N.Y.: Books for Libraries, 1970), pp. 107–10; E. H. C. Oliphant, "The Shakespeare Canon," *The Quarterly Review* 259, 513 and 514 (July and October, 1932): 37–40; William Wells, "Thomas Kyd and the Chronicle-History," *N&Q* 178 (1940): 218–24, 238–43.

45. Alfred Hart, "The Vocabulary of *Edward III*," *Shakespeare and the Homilies* (Melbourne: Melbourne University Press, 1934; rpt. New York: Octagon, 1970), pp. 219–41.

of *Richard II*, *King John*, *Julius Caesar*, and *Measure for Measure*, also decides that Shakespeare wrote all of *Edward III*.[46]

E. M. W. Tillyard, in his notable book on *Shakespeare's History Plays* in which he discusses *Edward III* and points out that its unifying theme is the education of princes (King Edward, the Black Prince, the French heir apparent Charles, and King John), is the most respected twentieth-century scholar to deny the participation of Shakespeare in the play. He believes there is a single author who is academic as well as brilliant and whose play is exceedingly thoughtful; but he also maintains that while the style is Shakespearean, as Hart has proved, *Edward III* cannot be Shakespeare's:

> its absence from the First Folio is unthinkable. . . . We may guess that the author was an intellectual, probably young, a university man, in the Southampton circle, intimate with Shakespeare and deeply under his influence, writing in his idiom, . . . a courtier and scholar.[47]

Throughout this period a significant body of critics concluded that the case for Shakespeare's authorship of *Edward III* remained open to doubt, including Thomas Parrott, Sharpe, Hazelton Spencer, Greg, Gerald Bentley, S. Schoenbaum, and Alfred Harbage.[48] M. C. Bradbrook traces the structural similarities between *Henry V* and *Edward III* and compares Edward's wooing of the Countess of Salisbury to Edward IV's wooing of Lady Grey in *3 Henry VI*, finding the latter superior. Parallels between *Edward III* on the one hand and *Henry V* and *Measure for Measure* on the other do not establish common authorship. If Shakespeare had acted in *Edward III* in his early years he may have had it in mind when he wrote the later plays.[49]

Muir adduces evidence for authorship from versification, vocabulary, themes, iterative imagery and image clusters, and structural parallels particularly to *Henry V* and *Measure for Measure*, and, while appropriately expressing caution that such internal evidence must be evaluated with prudent care, he nevertheless concludes that Shakespeare wrote at least the

46. Frank O'Connor, *The Road to Stratford* (London: Methuen, 1948), pp. 24–32 and 44–47.

47. Tillyard, *History Plays*, pp. 111–14 and 121–22.

48. Thomas M. Parrott, *William Shakespeare: A Handbook* (New York: Scribner's, 1934), pp. 181–83; Sharpe, *The Real War of the Theatre*, p. 39; Hazelton Spencer, *The Art and Life of William Shakespeare* (New York: Harcourt, 1940), p. 412, n. 4; W. W. Greg, *The Shakespeare First Folio* (Oxford: Clarendon Press, 1955; rpt. Oxford: Oxford University Press, 1969), p. 99. Gerald Eades Bentley, *Shakespeare: A Biographical Handbook* (New Haven: Yale University Press, 1961), p. 196; S. Schoenbaum, *Internal Evidence and Elizabethan Dramatic Authorship: An Essay in Literary History and Method* (Evanston: Northwestern University Press, 1966), pp. 20, 126–27, 188; Alfred Harbage, ed., "The Canon," *The Complete Pelican Shakespeare* (Baltimore: Penguin, 1969), pp. 18–20.

49. M. C. Bradbrook, *The Living Monument: Shakespeare and the Theatre of his Time* (Cambridge: Cambridge University Press, 1976). See chapter 13, "Shakespeare as Collaborator," pp. 230–32.

scenes of the Countess episode and the scene of the Black Prince's refusal to surrender. While there are occasional passages of poetry in the military part that critics have thought worthy of Shakespeare, the passages are not sustained and sometimes are immediately juxtaposed to other lines that are palpably not authentic. Some of the other evidence is ambiguous, for example the presence of Shakespearean image clusters in the parts of the play not accepted on other grounds as Shakespeare's. There is also the close structural likeness between *Edward III* and *Henry V*, and there are certain images in *Measure for Measure* that echo similar images in *Edward III*. While some of the images in *Measure for Measure* are slightly different, it seems likely that they represent a development from those in *Edward III*. Hundreds of like instances can be found in Shakespeare's undoubted plays. The importance of this is enhanced by the fact that *Henry V* and *Measure for Measure* are almost certainly of a later date than *Edward III*. The evidence taken as a whole suggests that the play was not written by a single author, that it is the result of a Shakespearean collaboration. It appears that the other dramatist was a young poet, capable of writing some fine blank verse "but liable to strange lapses; one whose sense of situation was superior to his power of characterization."[50]

Wentersdorf's doctoral dissertation on the authorship of *Edward III*[51] is the most extensive discussion of this question. Since there is no external evidence other than the not-quite-contemporary and questionable ascription by Rogers and Ley, perforce his treatment is limited to the internal evidence. While various kinds of such evidence are examined, including style, versification, and vocabulary, Wentersdorf's main concern is with imagery. He first examines features such as techniques of characterization, versification, vocabulary, and dramatic structure and finds that the characterization is not unlike Shakespeare's; that verse tests are inconclusive; that applying Hart's vocabulary tests demonstrates that the vocabulary of *Edward III* agrees with Shakespeare's; and that the method of exposition of *Edward III*, its use of mirror-scenes and of dramatic irony, have affinities with the canonical plays. Then he makes a detailed comparison of the images, iterative imagery, and image clusters that occur in *Edward III* and in Shakespeare's acknowledged plays, ranging freely throughout the canon for Shakespearean parallels. Comparisons are also made to selected plays of Kyd, Marlowe, Nashe, Jonson, Chapman, Massinger, and Dekker; and to the non-dramatic work of Bacon and Wyatt. Wentersdorf concludes, "The evidence derived from an analysis of the images strongly favors the hypothesis that the play is the work of one author, and that this author was Shakespeare."[52]

50. Muir, *Collaborator*, pp. 10–55. The passage cited is on p. 53.
51. Wentersdorf, *Authorship of Edward III, passim.*
52. Ibid., p. 489.

Latter day efforts by G. Lambrechts on the grounds of phonetics, syntax, vocabulary, and orthography to establish Kyd as the author of *Edward III*; and by R. G. Howarth to ascribe the work to Greene because of the parallels of structure and theme to *The Scottish Historie of James IV* have not met with scholarly acceptance.[53] As long ago as 1910 Moorman nullified the Greene ascription:

> We have only to compare her [the Countess of Salisbury] with the Ida of Greene's *James IV* to realize the masterly workmanship of the author of *Edward III*. . . . Whereas, in his presentation of the story, Greene wastes every opportunity of bringing the love suit to a dramatic crisis, the author of the countess episode displays the highest art of plot construction.[54]

Similarly, Arthur Freeman disposes of Lambrecht's hypothesis of Kyd's authorship: "Recently G. Lambrechts has troubled an old ghost by crediting Kyd with the 'Shakesperian' *Edward III*, but the very passages he quotes in parallel belie his arguments, and his reasoning along more general lines is nonsensical."[55] Inna Koskenniemi, as a consequence of a study of the themes and images occurring in *Edward III*, and C. H. Hobday, in a review of the "melting sweets" image cluster in the canonical plays, independently decide that the imagery of *Edward III* points to Shakespeare as the author.[56]

In his general study of English history plays, Irving Ribner examines the spectrum of scholarly opinion regarding the authorship of *Edward III*. His summation is a fair representation of the twentieth-century critical judgment:

> Some have been inclined to attribute to Shakespeare only the first two acts, which deal with King Edward's affair with the Countess of Salisbury, and which are far superior to anything else in the play. There has, however, been an equal weight of argument against Shakespeare's hand in any part of the play. All three modern editors [Warnke and Proescholdt, Moore Smith and Brooke], for instance, have concurred in finding nothing Shakespearian in it. . . . Opinion has thus been sharply divided, but modern scholarship has tended more and more to acknowledge Shakespeare's hand in the play. The strongest argument on either side of the issue seems to be that of Kenneth Muir, and I would tend to

53. G. Lambrechts, "*Edward III*, Oeuvre de Thomas Kyd," *Etudes Anglaises* 16 (1963): 160–74; R. G. Howarth, *A Pot of Gillyflowers: Studies and Notes*, mimeograph (Cape Town: R. G. Howarth, 1964).

54. Moorman, "Plays of Uncertain Authorship," *CHEL*, 5:245.

55. Arthur Freeman, *Thomas Kyd: Facts and Problems* (Oxford: Clarendon Press, 1967), p. 180.

56. Inna Koskenniemi, "Themes and Imagery in *Edward III*," *NM* 65 (1964): 446–80; C. H. Hobday, "Why the Sweets Melted: A Study in Shakespeare's Imagery," *SQ* 16 (1965): 3–17.

> agree with him that at least the first two acts and probably a good deal more of the play is the work of William Shakespeare.[57]

Proudfoot expresses a similar view. He notes numerous "points of contact," such as incidents, structural techniques, themes, and images, between *Edward III* and eighteen canonical plays and *Lucrece*. These, he says, are "only illustrative . . . [and adds that] verbal parallels . . . are legion." The casting pattern "corresponds exactly" to that established by Scott McMillin for Pembroke's Men, who acted *Titus Andronicus* and adaptations of Shakespeare's *Taming of the Shrew* and *2* and *3 Henry VI*. That Shakespeare knew *Edward III* well is apparent in his plays "from 1594 onwards," especially *Henry V* and *Measure for Measure*, which "has been fully demonstrated, most impressively by Kenneth Muir." He concludes, "Investigation of the play's language, particularly its exceptionally large vocabulary, and of its imagery, particularly those associative links described as 'image clusters,' is far on the way to demonstrating a kind and degree of connection between the whole play and the early works of Shakespeare that amounts to a strong positive case for his authorship—or that of some person unknown."[58] Lapides examines the internal evidence and concludes that it eliminates every other candidate but Shakespeare.[59]

Most commentators take note of a number of links between *Edward III* and Shakespeare's non-dramatic poetry, particularly the Sonnets. These links may be a general idea or a moral conception (fidelity to an oath), a specific thought (the significance of blushing or pallor), or echoes of a word or two or a whole pentameter line. But the bearing of such parallels between the Sonnets and the play on the question of the authorship of *Edward III*, as distinguished from the problem of sources, has been discussed only casually until recently. Claes Schaar studies the relationship between play and Sonnets and concludes that *Edward III* was originally composed by an unknown playwright who imitated the Sonnets and that "Shakespeare later revised it more or less thoroughly, retaining the imitations." Giorgio Melchiori thinks it improbable that the playwright combined elements from different Sonnets into passages in the play, believing it more likely that Shakespeare, when composing his Sonnets, recalled elements of a play with which he was familiar because he was the author or reviser. Summing up a discussion of authorship, Taylor notes, "The stylistic evidence for Shakespeare's authorship of *Edward III* is greater than that for the additions to *Sir Thomas More* . . . if we [the Oxford editors] had attempted a thorough reinvestigation of candidates for inclusion in the early dramatic canon, it would have begun with *Edward III*."[60]

57. Irving Ribner, *The English History Play in the Age of Shakespeare*, 2d ed., rev. (London: Methuen, 1965; rpt. New York: Octagon, 1979), pp. 142–50.

58. Proudfoot, "*Reign of King Edward the Third*, pp. 180, 181, 182, 184.

59. Lapides, *The Raigne of King Edward the Third*, pp. 3–31.

60. Claes Schaar, *Elizabethan Sonnet Themes and the Dating of Shakespeare's 'Sonnets,'* Lund Studies in English No. 32 (Lund: Ohlsson, 1962), p. 133; Giorgio Melchiori, *Shake-*

The only near-contemporary external evidence concerning the authorship of *Edward III* is the ascription to Shakespeare by Rogers and Ley in their catalog of playbooks printed in *The Careless Shepherdess*. This evidence is suspect because it is dated sixty years after the first quarto and because the play is listed between Marlowe's *Edward II* and Heywood's *Edward IV*, both of which are also attributed to Shakespeare. Elsewhere in the catalog Shakespeare is noted as the author of other plays that almost certainly he did not write. While this is fairly convincing evidence of carelessness, error, or possibly commercial puffery on the part of the publishers in the interest of increased sales, it does not follow that every one of their attributions is wrong. Nevertheless, it must be said that the ascription rests on uneasy foundations.

From the summary above it can be seen that since 1760 there has been extensive presentation of various kinds of internal evidence for authorship. The most controversial has been evidence bearing on the style. While some conservative commentators have rejected on the basis of stylistic investigation any Shakespearean participation at all and critics on the other wing have declared the entire play his, the great majority have concluded that there are some stylistic elements that are reminiscent of Shakespeare. A few conclude that these characteristics are the work of a Shakespearean imitator, but most believe that they are genuine. Verse and imagery studies have been less subject to dispute, and almost all critics point to the presence of Shakespeare, particularly in the Countess scenes. Østerberg's essay mainly on the images of *Edward III* and Wentersdorf's comprehensive analysis of images, iterative imagery, and image clusters based on the work of Caroline Spurgeon lead both scholars to the conclusion that Shakespeare's hand is manifest. Hart's vocabulary studies demonstrate to the satisfaction of most investigators that the play exhibits significant lexical affinities with canonical plays; and also show the absence of such affinities between *Edward III* and the plays of other leading dramatists capable of composing verse comparable to that exhibited in the Countess sequence. Arguments from structure are found on both sides of the question. The palpable similarity of the opening of *Edward III* to that of *Henry V* is taken to support Shakespeare's authorship of the earlier play. In opposition it is urged that the lack of an effective transition from the romantic segment to the military scenes is a disruption so serious that it could not have come from Shakespeare's hand. Others of that opinion find the absence of the play from the 1623 Folio negatively persuasive; but it could have been inadvertently omitted because it was written more than three decades earlier—and for a different acting company—and therefore was not in the memory of Hemings and Condell. Despite Tillyard's persuasive finding

speare's Dramatic Meditations (Oxford: Clarendon Press, 1976), pp. 42–45; Taylor, "Canon and Chronology," p. 137.

that the theme of *Edward III* is the education of princes, some critics continue to assert that the play lacks an organizing conception. The evidence adduced by such leading critics as Chambers, Muir, and Proudfoot makes clear that Shakespeare is the playwright of at least scenes 1.2, 2.1, 2.2, and 4.4, and the convincing arguments set forth by these and other sound scholars concerning Shakespearean structural, lexical, and imagistic elements elsewhere in the play establish the likelihood that his hand is present in scenes other than those four. The hypothesis that he wrote the entire play may be questionable, but it cannot be completely ruled out. If Shakespeare were a budding playwright with his dramatic style as yet not fully formed and with limited understanding of military campaigns, responding in 1589 to a swell of patriotic feeling as a consequence of the victory over the Spanish Armada he might have written with less self-assurance and with his aims less well defined than he did in the romantic sequence. On balance, though, it would appear that the traces of his work in the second half of the play, except for 4.4, which fired his imagination, are not quite sufficient as a basis for the claim that he is the sole author of *Edward III*.

Sources

The earliest recorded comment on the sources of *Edward III* is included in Capell's preface to his *Prolusions* (1760): "The fable of it too is taken from the same books which that author is known to have follow'd in some other plays; to wit, *Holinshed's* Chronicle, and a book of novels call'd the Palace of Pleasure."[61] Holinshed of course devotes a section of his chronicle to the reign of King Edward III (based in part on Froissart) and records much that occurs in the play, but there are several important events in *Edward III* that are not in Holinshed, most notably the Salisbury-Villiers episode. Nevertheless, commentators uncritically repeated Capell's statement for nearly a century, seemingly without investigating other possible sources. Knight struck a new note in 1849 in his *Studies of Shakespeare* by casually but unequivocally calling attention to Froissart's *Chronicles* as a principal source of the play: "The one portion of the drama [the first two acts] pretty closely follows the apochryphal and inconsistent story in 'The Palace of Pleasure.' . . . In the latter portion of the play he [the author] has Froissart before him."[62]

Knight's innovation, although thereafter periodically alluded to, did not immediately attain acceptance, and for another half century Holinshed continued to be viewed as the primary source. Warnke and Proescholdt tell us,

61. Capell, *Prolusions*, pp. ix–x.
62. Knight, *Studies of Shakespeare*, p. 280.

> The greater part of *Edward III* is based on Holinshed's *Chronicle of England*, the [Countess] episode . . . on Holinshed's *Chronicle of Scotland* and on Painter's *Palace of Pleasure*. With the exception of the scenes in which Villiers plays the principal part . . . and which the poet must have derived from some other source, there is no reason to believe that the author of the play consulted any other book.[63]

Moore Smith says, "The main part of the play of *Edward III* deals with the king's wars, and is based upon Holinshed." He notes that the Countess sequence "is not derived like the rest from Holinshed, except in some details about the Countess's conduct during the siege and the sudden departure of the Scots, but from an English translation made through the French from the Italian novelist Bandello, who had himself worked very freely on what he had found in Froissart."[64] Moorman tells us that the sources are Froissart, Holinshed, and Painter.[65]

According to Brooke, "scene 2 of the first act, and the second act of *Edward III* are based in part of Holinshed's *Chronicle of Scotland* and in part on a novel by Bandello, as translated in Painter's *Palace of Pleasure*. The only source of the rest of the drama . . . is Holinshed's *Chronicle of England*; but Knight may be correct in recognizing through the last three acts the influence of Froissart as well. The Villiers-Salisbury episode is not found either in Holinshed or Froissart and is of uncertain derivation."[66]

Robert Smith established Froissart as the primary source of *Edward III* first in his 1911 article and subsequently in a revised and somewhat expanded version in his *Froissart and the English Chronicle Play* (1915). He speculates that when Froissart first visited the English Court in 1361 not long after the death of the Countess of Salisbury he heard the story of her beauty, courage, and virtue, although Smith thinks that he was probably already familiar with it from the version of Jean le Bel. Bandello adapted Froissart's narrative in his novel and added several features that increased its effectiveness by enhancing the dramatic elements, including the addition of a secretary to the King who wrote letters to the Countess, and the solicitation by her mother and father to acquiesce in Edward's illicit proposals. In Bandello, Edward killed the Countess's husband, whereupon she offered to kill herself, inducing the King to offer marriage, which she accepted. This highly colored story was translated by Boisteau and published in his *Histoires Tragiques* (1559), which was in turn translated into English by Painter and included as novel 46 in Tome 1 of his *Palace of Pleasure* (1566). Although the earlier version was available in English in Berners's translation of Froissart (1523–1525) and in Grafton's *Chronicle*

63. Warnke and Proescholdt, *Pseudo-Shakesperian Plays*, p. x.
64. Moore Smith, *Edward the Third*, pp. viii–ix.
65. Moorman, "Plays of Uncertain Authorship," *CHEL*, 5:244.
66. Brooke, *The Shakespeare Apocrypha*, p. xx.

(1568), Smith notes that subsequent English renderings follow that of the Bandello-Boisteau-Painter line of derivation, the most notable of such versions being Drayton's in his *Heroicall Epistles* (1595–1597).

In a scene-by-scene analysis, Smith identifies in the case of each scene the chapter or chapters of Froissart's *Chronicle* from which it was taken. He points out that in regard to certain incidents the source could not have been either Holinshed or Grafton because they appear only in Berners's translation. Most significant of these is the Villiers-Salisbury episode in which the Earl of Salisbury offers to free Villiers without ransom if he will obtain a passport enabling Salisbury to travel through French territory. Until Smith identified the source in Berners's Froissart, it had been overlooked by scholars because in Froissart the incident is related of Sir Gaultier of Manny and an unnamed knight of Normandy. Smith further determines that at least half of the Countess episode is from Froissart and that the borrowings from Painter are mostly concentrated in 2.1. Some incidents occur in the play and in Berners but not in Painter (for example, the Countess's kneeling while welcoming Edward in 1.2). In summary, he points out that Holinshed does not contribute anything which in not more fully set forth in Froissart. He notes also that there are scenes in the play included by Froissart for which Holinshed has no account. Grafton's *Chronicle* parallels Froissart but omits the Sir Gualtier of Manny incident, so it could not have been the source. The play generally follows the sequence of events in Froissart, the playwright's deviations being few. There are also correspondences of detail and phraseology which Smith thinks show that the dramatist worked with the first volume of Berners's book open before him. He concludes that Berners's version of Froissart's *Chronicle* is established as the principal source of *Edward III* with Painter as a secondary source.[67]

Scholarly acceptance of Smith's findings has been general, sometimes expressed implicitly with little comment as in Chambers and Tillyard, or with only passing reference, as by Muir and Wentersdorf.[68] A recent review and discussion in Lapides's 1980 edition concludes:

> Froissart rather than Holinshed is the source of the chronicle material in the play because every incident that is in the play and that is in Holinshed can also be found in greater detail in Froissart. In addition, certain incidents in the play not in Holinshed are to be found in Froissart.

The Countess-Edward love story is based on Painter as well as Froissart. "It follows that Froissart is a more likely source for *Edward III* than Holinshed."[69] Inexplicably, in view of Smith's conclusive study, W. A. Armstrong says that Holinshed and Painter are the sources; and Ribner tells us

67. Robert Smith, *Froissart*, pp. 63–92.

68. Chambers, *William Shakespeare*, 1:518; Tillyard, *History Plays*, pp. 158, 329; Muir, *Collaborator*, p. 10; Wentersdorf, "The Date of *Edward III*," p. 228.

69. Lapides, *The Raigne of King Edward the Third*, p. 42.

that "*Edward III* is drawn chiefly from Holinshed with some suggestions from Froissart," plus the Countess of Salisbury tale from Painter.[70]

R. L. Armstrong looks closely at what is known of the sources in a section of the introduction to his edition. "It used to be assumed," he says, "that as a matter of course *Edward III* was based upon Holinshed's *Chronicle*, but the principal source is in fact Froissart (probably in Lord Berners's translation), which provides some treatment of almost all the material in the play, as Professor R. M. Smith has shown." Froissart furnishes the basic story of Edward's infatuation with the Countess of Salisbury, but in addition several elements are taken from Painter's *Palace of Pleasure*, derived through Boisteau from Bandello's melodramatic account, itself based on Froissart. "With these ascriptions one cannot seriously quarrel. Holinshed has no case against Froissart . . . the clearest evidence of all is provided by the Villiers-Salisbury episode . . . of which Holinshed has no trace." However, it appears to Armstrong that, while Froissart is the chief source, the playwright did look into Holinshed and took some suggestions from him. The taunts by the Countess of Salisbury from her battlements directed at the attacking Scots (229–48) is in neither Froissart nor Painter, but occurs in Holinshed where the Scottish Countess of March does the gibing at the English forces besieging Dunbar Castle. The resort of the English archers to hurling flintstones at the French (2140–43; 2150–53; 2163–65), after having fired all their arrows and driving back a "puisant host of men" (2164) at the Battle of Poitiers, is in Holinshed's account, but not in Froissart's.

Armstrong also finds evidence that the dramatist drew on some source or sources still not identified for other elements of his play. He cites the mention of two French warships, the "*Nom per illa*" and the "*blacke snake of Bullen*," not noted in historical accounts of the Battle of Sluys and "whose names . . . are suspiciously secular;" the Black Prince's device of the pelican feeding her young with her own blood and the motto "*Sic & vos*: 'and so should you,'" which crops up casually at the tag end of 3.5 (1622–26); and the noteworthy reference in 4.4 (1872–77) to "the rough Chatillion," commander of a major French division at Poitiers who has "certain death in pay and service." He also points out two prophesies in the play (1265–70; 1816–26), the originals of which have not been determined.[71] However, these elements in *Edward III* need not require us to

70. W. A. Armstrong, *Elizabethan History Plays*, p. ix; Ribner, *The English History Play*, pp. 143–44.

71. R. L. Armstrong, *Edward III. Six Early Plays*, pp. 195–97, 241 n. 216, 242 nn. 1222 and 1223, 244 nn. 1682 and 1888, 245 n. 1945. Armstrong does not note that Holinshed records the effort of the papal legate to negotiate an agreement between the French and the Black Prince, which may underlie the attempted inducements to surrender in 4.4. The incident is noted more fully in Berners's *Froissart* (Chapter 161, Ker 1:366–69). Proudfoot also concludes that the playwright consulted Holinshed and perhaps even Stow, in "*Reign of King Edward the Third*," pp. 168–69.

posit another source. Wentersdorf elucidates the anachronistic reference to the *Nom per illa*, which he says "was one of Elizabeth I's warships, and that it took a leading part in the fight against the Spanish."[72] Armstrong knows of the Elizabethan *Nonpareil* but does not connect it to the French vessel at Sluys. Lapides, citing Pepys, says that by 1552 the English had a *Bark of Boulogne*, but there is no record that it participated in the Armada battle. The prominence of Chatillion and the description of him as rough and warlike may be simply an instance of the playwright, here as elsewhere, and as Armstrong himself notes, elevating the odds against the English so that their victory, once achieved, would become that much more glorious.[73] Chatillion is perhaps to be identified as the "lorde of Chastellon" mentioned by Froissart as being captured at the battle for Bergerac by Derby's forces and later exchanged under the style of "vycount of Chastellone" with others for the Earl of Oxford (Chapters 103 and 105, Ker 1:238 and 243). In his introduction, Ker more than once refers to Froissart's patron Gui de Blois as Gui de Châtillon (1.xlvii, li, and lxix), the brother of Charles of Blois, who is frequently mentioned in Froissart. Lewis of Blois, their father, was closed in and slain at Crecy (chapter 130, Ker 1:300–301). As to the variant spelling of the name, when one considers that in Froissart and in Berners's translation the names are persistently mangled (see Ker 1:xxxiii: "His Hell of Proper Names"), a slight spelling difference, without even taking into account the predilections of the playwright, is not surprising. Concerning the pelican device, Armstrong points out that it "is among the badges surrounding the prince in at least one portrait of no particular authority, but the device is not generally associated with him, and the source of this passage does not appear." A well-known pelican device was borne by the Pelham family. Historically, Sir William Pelham captured King John at Poitiers. No satisfactory source has yet come to light for the two prophesies, but it is perhaps worth noting that prophecies occur fairly frequently in Shakespeare's early history plays.[74]

Attention has been drawn by one or two scholars to a possible parallel between Edward's attempt at seducing the Countess of Salisbury and a similar plot situation in Greene's *James IV*. Østerberg suggests that Shakespeare "possibly . . . took some hints from Greene's *James IV*," and Howarth thinks that "the theme and treatment are peculiarly Greenian." Al-

72. Wentersdorf, "The Date of *Edward III*," pp. 229–30. See also Lapides, *The Raigne of King Edward the Third*, pp. 34–35; Wm. Laird Clowes, *The Royal Navy*, 5 vols. (Boston and London: 1897), 1:421–22.

73. R. L. Armstrong, *Edward III. Three Early Plays*, n. 1222, p. 242, and p. 197. Lapides, *The Raigne of King Edward the Third*, p. 35.

74. R. L. Armstrong, *Edward III. Three Early Plays*, n. 1682, p. 244; Lapides, *The Raigne of King Edward the Third*, no. 1621, pp. 248–49. W. Gordon Zeefeld, "The Influence of Hall on Shakespeare's Historical Plays," *ELH* 3 (1936): 317–53. For Zeefeld's discussion of prophecies see pp. 347–48.

though he does not state it outright, he hints at influence on *Edward III*.[75] These suggestions have not been well received.

Edward III shares some passages with *Venus and Adonis*, *The Rape of Lucrece*, and certain of Shakespeare's Sonnets. This circumstance has given rise to the hypothesis that these poems are the sources of passages in the play. Scholarly opinion on the question is divided.

In *Edward III* there is an unambiguous allusion to the story of Lucrece, "whose ransackt treasurie hath taskt, The vaine indeuor of so many pens" (990–91). Many critics have taken this to be a reference by the playwright, whether Shakespeare or another, to Shakespeare's poem, but clearly there is nothing in the passage to support the contention. The story was well-known before Shakespeare wrote his *Lucrece*. *Venus and Adonis* and *Edward III* have images and general ideas in common, but verbal parallels are mostly limited to single words and are not exceptional. As evidence of borrowing, none of these common elements is cogent.

A somewhat more extensive series of words and phrases appear to be shared by the play and a few of the Sonnets that scholars generally acknowledge but are at odds to explain. Some think that the passages in the play are echoes of the Sonnets, while others hold that the play has priority and that Shakespeare subsequently incorporated into his Sonnets elements originally in *Edward III*. These may be either borrowings or imitation of the work of an earlier playwright that Shakespeare recalled, perhaps because he acted in the play, or they may be a recasting of his own earlier work. The most notable is the occurrence in the play and in Sonnet 94 (14) of an identical line:

> Lillies that fester, smel far worse than weeds
> (786)

This is spoken by Warwick in his dissembling attempt to persuade his daughter to yield to the King's desires. In the same speech he uses a phrase:

> poyson shows worst in a golden cup,
> (784)

which is reminiscent of a passage in Sonnet 114:

> Mine eye well knows what with his gust is 'greeing,
> And to his palate doth prepare the cup.
> If it be poison'd, 'tis the lesser sin
> That mine eye loves it and doth first begin.
> (11–14)

Earlier, in a dialogue with King Edward, Warwick says,

75. Østerberg, "The 'Countess Scenes' of *Edward III*," p. 90; Howarth, *A Pot of Gillyflowers*, p. 85.

> If nothing but that losse [of my honour] may vantage you,
> I would account that losse my vantage to.
>
> (659–60)

Sonnet 88 has

> The injuries that to myself I do,
> Doing thee vantage, double-vantage me.
>
> (11–12)

When the Countess welcomes King Edward to her castle she says,

> Let not thy presence like the Aprill sunne,
> Flatter our earth, and sodenly be done:
>
> (310–11)

which is close to lines from Sonnet 33

> Full many a glorious morning have I seen
> Flatter the mountain tops with sovereign eye
>
> (1–2)

In the welcoming speech she also uses the word *cost* (322) to mean resplendent as it is similarly used in Sonnet 64 (2), and in Sonnet 91 (10). Edward's poet-secretary, Lodowick, in a soliloquy on the King's infatuation, refers to "scarlet ornaments" (345). The phrase also occurs in Sonnet 142 (6).

Edward, in expressing his admiration for the Countess, says:

> Wisdom is foolishness, but in her tongue,
> Beauty a slander but in her fair face.
>
> (375–76)

Sonnet 127 has

> But now is black beauty's successive heir,
> And beauty slander'd with a bastard shame.
>
> (3–4)

In the same passage the King also says,

> Bid her be free and general as the sun
> Who smiles upon the basest weed that growes
> As lovingly as on the fragrant rose.
>
> (498–500)

The phrases "basest weed" and "fragrant rose" occur in Sonnets 94 (12) and 95 (2).

When the King and the poet are discussing the poem he is to address to the Countess, Edward uses the phrase "when the sunne lifts up his head" (480), which is similar to one in Sonnet 7 (1–2): "when the gracious light lifts up his burning head." It may be significant that in the play passage Edward rhymes *noon* and *sun* (482–3) and Sonnet 7 rhymes *noon* and *son* (13–14).

Some of these links have been noted by critics since Steevens, who called attention to the "lilies" line in 1780, Malone, who pointed out "scarlet ornaments" in 1790, and Lee, who identified the "flatter" image in 1907. In recent studies, other parallels have been identified, particularly by Østerberg, Schaar, and Melchiori, most, but not all, of which have been cited above. The question of influence has been widely discussed. Raymond Alden in 1916[76] found the scholarly community divided over the problem of whether *Edward III* first embodied the passages that subsequently appeared in the Sonnets or whether the playwright borrowed from the sonneteer, with those accepting the priority of the play being in the minority. Editors of the Sonnets, after noting the parallels, have tended to leave the question of influence unanswered.

Østerberg, in his essay on the Countess scenes, calls attention to parallels in *Edward III* to Sonnets 64, 78, 88, 91, 94 ("basest weed"), 98, 99, and 130, in addition to those noticed by earlier scholars. Two of these Østerberg identifies as parallels of ideas. The first is the mutual influence of feminine beauty and the poet's pen, which he finds is intermittent in the discussion between King Edward and Lodowick (400–518) and is also in "Sonnet 78 sqq." The second is in Lodowick's soliloquy on King and Countess (336–59), in which he makes a number of comparisons of the colors white and red (by various terms) in their countenances to those same colors that occur also in Sonnets 98, 99, and 130. One specific term is shared: *coral* is in both the soliloquy (347) and Sonnet 130 (2). Østerberg's judgment is that "not only the tangible identity of wording, but even more the similarity in reasoning connects these texts. . . . Can it be doubted that all the texts hitherto discussed are interlaced like the strands of a cord?" He does not offer an opinion on the problem of priority.[77]

Brooke, in commenting on the "lilies" and "scarlet ornaments" passages, leans toward *Edward III* as the original. In regard to the earlier line he says, "Shakespeare wrote the scene [in the play] in which this line occurs, and is here [in Sonnet 94] purposely quoting it."[78] Hyder Rollins records several of these parallels and has a lengthy note on the "lilies" line, but he does not express a judgment concerning whether the play or the Sonnets came earlier.[79]

T. W. Baldwin believes that Sonnet 54 "adopts a line from *Edward III* which is quoted in Sonnet 94." He does not identify the line, but a later reference to Sonnet 94 and to the "*flower-weed* figure" gives us a hint. "The

76. Raymond Macdonald Alden, *The Sonnets of Shakespeare* (Boston: Riverside, 1916), p. 221.

77. Østerberg, "The 'Countess Scenes' of *Edward III*," pp. 54–56, 73–74.

78. C. F. Tucker Brooke, ed., *Shakespeare's Sonnets* (London: Oxford University Press, 1936), p. 287.

79. Hyder Edward Rollins, ed., New Variorum *Sonnets*, 2 vols. (Philadelphia: Lippincott, 1944), 1:96, 170, 234–35, 290, 364.

conclusion," he says, "is reasonably clear that he [Shakespeare] borrowed from the printed play."[80]

The recent studies of Shakespeare's Sonnets by Schaar and Melchiori have given us two of the most comprehensive discussions thus far of the relationship of *Edward III* to the Sonnets. Schaar analyzes most of the links and finds that in almost every instance the passages are more appropriate to the individual Sonnet and better integrated into the fabric of the poetry than they are in the play. For example,

> Scarlet ornaments has its full force and meaning only in the sonnet. . . . In the play there is no similar motivation for the metaphor as appears clearly from the context. . . . It can hardly be doubted that the phrase was borrowed from the sonnet and tacked onto the description in the play—as an ornament.

Similar reasoning is applied to other parallels. Schaar's conclusion is that the author of *Edward III* had "at his elbow a MS. copy of Shakespeare's sonnets or of some of them, dipping occasionally into the slender volume to appropriate an image or a phrase . . . he was in most cases rather unsuccessful as a borrower. . . . The parallels between *Edward III* and the *Sonnets* are due to the dramatist's imitating Shakespeare."[81]

Melchiori concentrates his attention on the meaning of the passages that the play and Sonnets have in common and on their ethical and moral content, rather than on the phrases themselves. Viewed by these lights he finds, for example, that the "lilies that fester" line in *Edward III* "occurs in the course of a lengthy speech which is nothing else but a repertory of 'sententiae' on the corruption of power, and it fits perfectly into its context." He cites also the appropriateness of the lines from the play linking "basest weeds" and the "fragrant rose," which he says are "conventional expressions, but it seems significant that they should be found identical only in two sonnets [94 (12) and 95 (2)] and nowhere else in Shakespeare's work. It is hardly likely that the author of *Edward III* should have borrowed freely expressions from different Shakespearian sonnets, putting them together in the current conceit on the indiscriminate generosity of the sun. It is much more probable that Shakespeare, writing different sonnets, remembered passages of a play that he knew, and more particularly that he recalled the scenes that he either wrote himself or revised, especially since one of them dealt specifically with the writing of a lyric and the language of love-poetry. What I am suggesting, then, is that Sonnet 94—and a good number of the others—were written *after* and not before *Edward III*." Melchiori further notes that Schaar, while devoting space and care to the analogies between *Edward III* and the Sonnets, "still misses . . . the parallelism

80. T. W. Baldwin, *On the Literary Genetics of Shakespeare's Poems & Sonnets* (Urbana: University of Illinois Press, 1950), pp. 283, 287, 298, 332.

81. Schaar, *Elizabethan Sonnet Themes*, pp. 117–35.

in moral attitude so that he concludes (mistakenly, in my opinion) that the play borrows from the Sonnets."[82] Thus do the two most perceptive recent students of the relationship between *Edward III* and the Sonnets arrive at diametrical conclusions.

If an early date for the composition of the play is accepted, then it follows that the direction of influence is from *Edward III* to the Sonnets; and if the authorship of Shakespeare is accepted for at least the Countess episode—it will be noted that all the links connecting the play and the Sonnets occur in the two earlier of the three Countess scenes—then it also follows that the common ground between the play and the poems represents Shakespeare adapting his own earlier work in writing his Sonnets.

The Reign of King Edward III begins with a recital by the exiled French peer Robert of Artois, newly created Earl of Richmond by King Edward, of the line of descent of French kings from Philip le Beau, whose daughter, Isabel, was Edward's mother. Philip was succeeded on the throne of France by his three sons in order, none of whom had issue. The French magnates thereupon, setting aside Isabel's claim, proclaimed John of Valois[83] their king, but Earl Robert asserts that Edward is "the lyneal watchman of our peace and Iohn of Valoys indirectly climbes" (36–37). The English king is the "true shepheard" (41) of the French commonwealth. Edward, pleased at this, resolves to "approue faire Issabells discent" (48). The Duke of Lorraine arrives as an emissary from King John bidding King Edward to "repaire to France within these forty daies" (62) to do homage for the dukedome of Guyenne, "or else Thy title in that prouince dyes" (65). The English court rejects the demand, Edward defies the French king, and the "gage is throwne" (119). Sir William Montague enters to report that the Scots have broken a truce, have invaded Northumberland, and are besieging the Castle of Roxborough where the Countess of Salisbury is "inclosd" (130). King Edward gives orders to raise troops and to prepare for the campaign in France while he leads the forces at hand to relieve the Countess and to repulse the Scots. This opening scene[84] is, in general, a fairly close rendition of the material in Froissart's *Chronicle* as translated by Lord Berners, chapters (in the order of the events of the play) 25, 5, 24, 26, 28, 32, 33, 35, and 76 [Text I]. The only significant deviation from the source concerns the homage demanded of King Edward by the French king for the Duchy of Guyenne. In Froissart (chapter 24, Ker 1:75–81), Edward first makes a carefully limited homage—he does not put his hands into those of the French king (Ker 1:78)—and only later when he has arranged alliances does he renounce allegiance to the French crown (chapter 35, Ker

82. Melchiori, *Shakespeare's Dramatic Meditations*, pp. 42–48.

83. Historically it was Philip of Valois, John's father, who succeeded upon the death of Philip le Beau's youngest son (*Froissart*, chapter 5, Ker 1:22–23).

84. There is a close resemblance between the incidents in this scene and in their sequence to corresponding scenes in Shakespeare's *Henry V* and the anonymous *Famous Victories of Henry V*. See Muir, *Collaborator*, p. 32.

1:105–6). Sir William Montague's report to the King derives from a later chapter (76, Ker 1:190–93) that leads into the Countess sequence.

The second scene of act 1 and the two scenes of act 2 comprise the Countess of Salisbury episode in which King Edward, smitten with the Countess's grace, beauty, and intelligence, seeks to win her acquiescence in an illicit love affair. Her husband, the Earl of Salisbury, a staunch supporter of the King's claim to the French throne, has fought valiantly in France. Even though the Countess argues indefatigably against the King's suit and in defense of her honor and that of her husband, there are hints in the play that she is not completely beyond temptation. These occur in the two earlier scenes in which her responses to Edward, while ostensibly negative, are couched in language that is less than direct. These and other elements in the episode testify to its composite origin and the ultimate influence of Bandello.

The Countess on her battlements at the opening of 1.2 overhears King David and Earl Douglas as they discuss who shall have her and her jewels when they have taken Roxborough castle. Scottish messengers arrive, warning of King Edward's approach, and the Scots withdraw northward. Upon Edward's arrival with his army, which includes the Countess's father, the Earl of Warwick, the Countess kneels to greet the King and begs him to stay to "honor our roofe" (290). Edward is so bemused by her person that he tries instinctively to pull away to pursue the Scots, but the Countess's invitation is so attractive that he says, "Countesse, albeit my busines vrgeth me, yt shall attend, while I attend on thee" (333–34). The King, who has become uncharacteristically melancholy, instructs his poet-secretary, Lodowick, to write a poem in praise of the Countess, so that she "shall see herselfe the ground of my infirmitie" (392–93). In the only humorous passage in the play, Lodowick pretends not to understand and begins by describing the Countess as "fair and chaste" (476) and "more bould in constancie then Iudith was" (503–4).

The King's criticism of these efforts is not only amusing but also illuminating in that it may provide a clue concerning the process of poetic composition in the time of Shakespeare. The Countess enters to inquire why Edward is discontented, he reveals to her his desire, and she rejects his proposal saying that he is merely trying her faithfulness. She leaves him, and shortly thereafter her father, Warwick, comes to find out why the King is so pensive. Edward tricks Warwick into an oath to relieve his melancholy and then orders him to solicit his daughter. Warwick resolves to abide by the form of his oath, but when he confronts the Countess he announces that he is "an atturnie from the Court of hell" (716). She does not consent. At the beginning of 2.2, there is a diversion when the Earls of Derby and Audley arrive to discuss preparations for the war in France. Prince Edward enters with the same purpose and the King's thoughts veer toward military affairs. However, at this point Lodowick announces that the Countess "with a smiling cheere desires access vnto your Maiestie" (897–98), and he immediately dismisses his son. The Countess hints that Warwick has persuaded her, but she will yield only if he will remove two impediments—his queen and her husband. After a brief demurrer, the King agrees. She shows him two of her wedding knives, gives him one, and then offers to kill her husband with the other by plunging it into her own heart where the earl "my loue . . . lies fast a sleepe within" (970–71). If he would prevent her death she requires that he "stand still [and] sweare to leaue thy most unholie sute and neuer hence forth to solicit me" (976–79). Edward agrees, withdraws his suit, and commends her with the best known lines of the play:

> Arise true English ladie, whom our Ile
> May better boast of then euer Romaine might,
> Of her whose ransackt treasurie hath taskt,
> The vaine endeuor of so many pens:
> (988–91)

The sources of the scenes that comprise the Countess of Salisbury sequence are Froissart's *Chronicle* (Chapter 77, Ker 1:193–95)[85] and Painter's forty-sixth novel in *The Palace of Pleasure* [Text 2]. In a way Froissart is the sole source because, as Gustave Liebau has demonstrated,[86] Bandello developed the alternative version from Froissart's account. Bandello enhanced the story by incorporating a number of strikingly dramatic elements not in Froissart, most of which persisted through the translations and eventually found their way into the play. Robert Smith sums these up:

> He [Bandello] brought into the tale a secretary and letters between Edward and the Countess; he made the father and mother of the lady pander to the King; he killed her husband, and portrayed the Countess about to stab herself, and then begging the King to slay her; and finally made the King propose marriage, and actually marry her.[87]

Bandello's recension, according to Liebau, appeared in the literatures of France, Germany, the Netherlands, and Spain, as well as in English, over a period of four centuries, but there are other traditions, one of which, recorded by Jean le Bel, has Edward raping the Countess during a second visit to the castle after the tournament at London. Antonia Gransden, who has examined this version analytically,[88] shows that, except for a few pe-

85. Froissart continues the story in his account of the feast and jousting that Edward made at London in honor of the Countess (chapter 139, Ker 1:216–18), but the feast and tournament are not in the play.

86. Cited in Robert Smith, *Froissart*, p. 64.

87. Ibid., p. 64.

88. Antonia Gransden, "The alleged rape by Edward III of the countess of Salisbury," *English Historical Review* 87 (1972): 333–44.

ripheral incidents, it has no basis in fact, and she suggests it should be viewed as anti-English French war propaganda, of which there are other examples of the time, intended to show Edward as a brutal aggressor lacking in the finer traits associated with chivalry. Gransden notes that "Froissart explicitly condemned Le Bel's story" in the second redaction of his *Chronicle*, based in part on le Bel's *Vrayes Chroniques*, where he says,

> Jean le Bel relates in his chronicle that the English king raped the countess of Salisbury. Now, I declare that I know England well, where I have lived for long periods mainly at the royal court and also with the great lords of that country. And I have never heard tell of this rape although I have asked people about it who must have known if it had ever happened.[89]

Froissart resided in England from 1361 to 1366, during which time he served at the English court as secretary to Queen Philippa and became the court chronicler. He visited England again for three months in 1395, and at that time he was presented to Richard II by the Duke of York, the king's uncle and one of Edward's and Philippa's famous seven sons.[90] He had ample opportunity while serving as the Queen's secretary to search out the truth of the story of the Countess of Salisbury, and he had perhaps an even better occasion during his visit of 1395, when all the principals had died and were beyond the reach of mere malicious gossip. It appears clear, then, that Froissart, in incorporating into his *Chronicle* le Bel's story of Edward and the Countess, revised it as he did other parts of *Les Vrayes Chroniques*, omitting any mention of rape, perhaps because he concluded that it was false.[91]

The early incidents in the Countess episode follow Berners's translation.[92] The sequence of events in the play is substantially the same as that

89. Quoted by Gransden, "The alleged rape by Edward III," p. 334. See also F. S. Shears, *Froissart Chronicler and Poet* (London: Routledge, 1930), pp. 86–87.

90. Shears, *Froissart Chronicler*, pp. 14–25, 65–69.

91. Kervyn de Lettenhove, editor of Froissart's works, found some errors in le Bel's version and concludes that Froissart was right not to credit le Bel's account. Jules Viard, le Bel's editor, says that le Bel's tale occurs in other French chronicles, but he does not note that those he cites have, in Gransden's words, "a common historiographical archetype" ("The alleged rape by Edward III," pp. 334–35). Gransden also finds an additional reason for questioning le Bel's story in its close affiliation in many particulars to the classical story of the rape of Lucrece (pp. 342–44). For a different interpretation (which does not take into account Gransden's findings), see Michael Packe, *King Edward III* (London: Routledge, 1983), pp. 105–23 and 174–78. Proudfoot, "*Reign of King Edward the Third*," pp. 172–74, inclines toward acceptance of le Bel's account of the rape, calling Froissart's version a "whitewash job."

92. Froissart's *Chronicle* exists in three redactions (of which Berners follows the third) and in many manuscripts that are not all identical (see Shears, *Froissart Chronicler*, pp. 82–87). Ker reprints two incidents in the Introduction to his edition from the second redaction that he says "did not find their way into the vulgate text [the third redaction], and so did not reach Lord Berners," nor, of course, the dramatist who wrote *Edward III*. One of these is an account of a game of chess played by the Countess and Edward during his stay at

in the source, and there is a telling detail in the Countess's kneeling to receive Edward upon his arrival at her castle, an action that is in Froissart (chapter 77, Ker 1:193) and the play (276–82) but is not mentioned by Painter. With the beginning of the second scene of the three in the episode (2.1), the play makes use of Painter's version. It introduces Lodowick, who corresponds to the secretary in *The Palace of Pleasure*. Froissart's *Chronicle* has no such person. Like Painter's secretary, Lodowick carries messages between the King and the Countess. The abortive attempt by Edward and Lodowick at writing amorous verses in the play is analogous to the King's love letter in Painter's novel. Edward's effort to change the Countess's mind by employing her father to persuade her also comes from the novel. The Earl of Warwick is mentioned a number of times by Froissart, including being listed among those at the feast accompanying the jousting in honor of the Countess (chapter 89, Ker 1:217), but he does not connect Warwick with her. Painter identifies the Earl as the Countess's father. The episode in the play concludes, as the *Chronicle* does, with Edward's decision to end his suit for the Countess's love and to return to the wars.

In *The Palace of Pleasure* the King proposes to marry the Countess and make her his Queen. She accepts, the Earl of Salisbury (in Painter's novel) having died in the meantime as a consequence of the rigors of imprisonment. There are a few brief passages in the play reminiscent of words or phrases in either the *Chronicle* or the novel that have been transmuted by the playwright or perhaps merely vaguely remembered in a manner suggestive of Shakespeare; but there is nothing so close that it may be considered a significant borrowing from either Froissart or Painter. The episode in *Edward III* shares with that in *The Palace of Pleasure* fairly frequent references to human color, to blushing, or to paleness, but there are no terms in common. This analysis shows that the two scenes of act 2 are a composite drawn from both sources, with greater reliance on the novel in 2.1, and much less in the other.

The last three acts of the play are in broad outline based on Froissart. The major events of Edward's military campaign in France—the naval battle of Sluys, the land battles of Crecy and Poitiers, and the surrender of Calais—are a fairly faithful rendering of the accounts in the *Chronicle*. Several specific incidents also derive from Froissart. These include the guiding of the English troops under Edward to a safe crossing of the river Somme

---

Roxborough castle in which the King manages to lose his wager, a valuable ruby ring. The Countess tries to persuade Edward to take it back, but he will not accept it. She gives it to one of her damsels with instructions to return it to Edward as he is about to leave the castle, but he again refuses to take it, saying to the damsel, "Let it stay in your keeping" (Ker 1:lxxii–lxxv). This incident occupies in Froissart's second redaction the position that in le Bel's *Chroniques* is occupied by the rape story (Gransden, "The alleged rape by Edward III," p. 334).

by Gobin de Graie (styled by Froissart Gobyn a Grace) and the reward he receives (chapters 126–27, Ker 1:289–93); the objection of the Genoan crossbowmen at going into battle without adequate rest after a long march, their retreat under the English arrows, and their flight through the French host with attendant general disarray (chapter 130, Ker 1:297–98); the refusal by King Edward to send help to the Black Prince beleaguered at the battle of Crecy so that without aid the Prince can clearly demonstrate his valor and win his knighthood (chapter 130, Ker 1:300); the list of the French dead by rank, which in numbers and phrasing is almost identical to that in Froissart (chapter 132, Ker 1:303); the proposal by the Earl of Salisbury that Villiers, whom he holds for ransom, secure a pass so he can travel through French territory to Calais in exchange for Villiers's freedom, the granting of the passport by Prince Charles, and the attempt by the French king to dishonor it (chapter 135, Ker 1:306–8); the grace of King Edward in providing relief to the poor of Calais (chapter 133, Ker 1:305); the capture of King David of Scotland by the squire John Copland at the battle called by Froissart Newcastle-upon-Tyne (also known as the battle of Neville's Cross) and his refusal to yield his prisoner to the Queen, whereupon Edward summons Copland to Calais to explain (chapters 138–39, Ker 1:313–15); the capture of King John at Poitiers (chapter 164, Ker 1:379); the Black Prince's gift to Audley for his bravery in the van at Poitiers and Audley's transferring it to his squires who had fought valiantly at his side (chapters 165 and 167, Ker 1:381–84); the presentation of the six most eminent burgesses of Calais to King Edward, whose purpose is to execute them as an example to the town, although he relents and spares their lives (chapter 146, Ker 1:328–32); and the transporting of the French king as a prisoner to England (chapter 173, Ker 1:392–94).

Most important of these for source studies is the Salisbury-Villiers incident of the safe conduct to Calais. In the play, this action occupies part of three scenes just before the battle of Poitiers. In the first scene (1644–68), the Earl of Salisbury offers to release Villiers without ransom if he will obtain from Charles, Duke of Normandy and heir to King John, a passport enabling Salisbury to travel to Calais. In the second scene (1754–1809), Villiers explains to Charles that he will be quit of his ransom if he obtains the pass, and if not he must return to captivity. Charles counsels Villiers not to return, but Villiers responds that he must honor his oath, whereupon Charles subscribes to the passport. In the third scene (2056–2126), Salisbury is brought a captive to King John, who immediately orders his execution. Salisbury reminds Charles of his safe conduct, and Charles in turn begs his father to honor his signature. The King is reluctant to do so, but Charles insists. The King gives in and in freeing Salisbury tells him to bid King Edward to prepare a grave for "his princely sonne blacke Edward" (2111). This sequence follows closely the events in Froissart (chapter 135, Ker 1:306–8), where the story is told of Sir Gaultier of Manny, a valiant baron of Hainault prominent throughout Edward's French campaign, and an unnamed "knyght of Normandy" (Ker 1:306). The playwright undoubtedly raised the rank of the English adherent to intensify audience interest, and he gave the Norman knight a name that occurs elsewhere in Froissart's *Chronicle*, where it is spelled "Villers" or "Vyllars" (for example, Ker 1:33, 126, 271). Of all the contemporary chronicles, this incident occurs only in Berners's Froissart, establishing it as the prime source of *Edward III*. It is not in Holinshed, with whose *Chronicles* the playwright was familiar, nor in Grafton, who follows Berners, nor in Fabyan or Polydore Vergil, to whom Painter alludes.

There are two incidents pointed out by R. L. Armstrong in his edition that the playwright took from Holinshed. These are the Countess's gibing at the Scots from her battlements (229–42) and the English archers at Poitiers hurling flintstones at the French after they had shot all their arrows (2139–42 and 2163–65) [Text 3].

For four episodes in the play, all dramatically effective, it seems there is no manifest source in Berners's translation, although there are one or two traces of their possible origins. There is nothing in Froissart corresponding to the slanging match between King John and King Edward (1316–1437). Such incidents are, however, common throughout the history plays of the period and frequent in Shakespeare's histories. It is conceivable, although the possibilities may be remote, that they derive from the practice of medieval defiance by which a vassal denied fealty to his feudal overlord. There is nothing in Froissart about the ceremonious arming of the Black Prince before the battle of Crecy by King Edward and the Earls of Derby, Audley, and Richmond, designated Artois in the play (1442–88). In the *Chronicle*, Edward commands every man to be armed (chapter 128, Ker 1:294), but his heir is not mentioned specifically. After the battle, the Prince in *Edward III* is knighted by his father (1600–1605). In Froissart, King Edward descends from his post on the windmill hill, embraces and kisses his son, and commends him for his perseverance and nobility in battle, whereupon the Black Prince "inclyned himselfe to the yerthe, honouryng the kyng his father" (chapter 131, Ker 1:302), as in the play, but he is not knighted nor is any mention made of his accomplishment in defeating in combat and slaying the King of Bohemia. The most noteworthy of these four incidents occurs in scene 4.4 (1904–60) just before the battle of Poitiers when three French heralds successively arrive before the Black Prince, respectively from King John and his sons Charles and Philip, bidding the Prince to withdraw. King John says he will not attack if the Prince and one hundred English men of name will surrender.

Charles sends a swift jennet on which Prince Edward can escape, while Philip's herald, saying that the Prince cannot escape, presents him with a prayer book to prepare himself for his long journey. All three offers are vigorously refused by the Black Prince. The last two can, in their derision, be compared to the French gift of tennis balls to Henry V in Shakespeare's later play, but there is nothing of them in Berners's translation. In regard to King John's offer, however, the *Chronicle* does record the unsuccessful efforts of the Cardinal of "Pyergourt" to bring the two parties into agreement on the very eve of the battle. Both King John and the Black Prince agree to the Cardinal's proposal to make the attempt, but the best offer he can elicit from King John requires that "the prince and a C. of his knyghtes shulde yelde theymselfe into the kynges prison" (chapter 161, Ker 1:367). This is clearly echoed in the play:

> The king of Fraunce my soueraigne Lord and master,
> Greets by me his fo, the Prince of Wals,
> If thou call forth a hundred men of name
> Of Lords, Knights, Esquires and English gentlemen,
> And with thy selfe and those kneele at his feete,
> He straight will fold his bloody collours vp,
> And ransome shall redeeme liues forfeited:
>
> (1905–11)

The playwright's handling of the historical material from his sources is very free and at the same time broadly true to the actual mainstream of events. There are, of course, several significant deviations from recorded history introduced by the dramatist to enhance the effectiveness of his play. Most far-reaching of these, as noted by R. L. Armstrong, is the combination of the reigns of the French kings Philip and John into one, a change that enables the author to oppose a single French monarch, John, to a single English king, Edward. There is a telescoping of time in the case of the main military events. The naval battle of Sluys, which actually occurred in 1340, the two major land battles of Crecy and Poitiers (1346 and 1356), the siege and fall of Calais (1347), and the battle with the Scots at Newcastle alluded to in the play (1346) are brought into close proximity and constitute a drumfire of success achieved by Edward and the Black Prince. Some critics object to this re-ordering of history. R. L. Armstrong says that "the battles of Sluys, Crecy, and Poitiers . . . take place . . . in the course of a week or so,"[93] but the staging in performance is successful, and, in any event, it follows closely the sequence in Froissart's *Chronicle*, where time

93. R. L. Armstrong, *Edward III. Six Early Plays*, p. 197. *Edward III* was written, Proudfoot says, "heavily under the influence of [Marlowe's] *Tamberlaine*" in its heroic figures, in the threats against Calais that echo Tamberlaine's against Damascus, and in its "almost unbroken succession of battles" ("*Reign of King Edward the Third*," pp. 166, 177).

is also in effect telescoped. Theatrical interest is intensified in several incidents, most notably in elevating the rank of the participants in the Salisbury-Villiers sequence, in juxtaposing it to the battle of Poitiers, and in pruning away Froissart's last incident of King John giving Sir Gualtier of Manny (Salisbury) gifts and jewels that he is obliged to return. Events introduced without historical warrant, such as the arming of the Black Prince and the series of calls on him by the heralds, of which there is in Froissart only the barest hint, elevate the theatrical impact of the play. The conclusion of act 5 departs substantially from history to provide a spectacular ending to the play, which Edward sums up succinctly in the final lines:

> God willing then for England wele be shipt,
> Where in a happie houre I trust we shall
> Ariue three kings, two princes, and a queene.
> (2493–95)

In fact, the Scots's King David was detained in custody in England and the Black Prince and his prisoners King John and Prince Philip were in Bordeaux. The playwright's chief deviation from Painter's novel of King and Countess is in his rejection of the ending—their marriage. He further concentrates his structure by having all the action take place at the Earl of Salisbury's castle instead of following his sources for the Countess episode, which place part of the action at London.

In portraying his principal characters, the dramatist adheres fairly closely to Froissart. He enhances them by treating his materials dramatically, rather than factually as in Berners's translation, and by providing for some character development. The King, for example, emerges as a truly regal and chivalric medieval monarch who is not without human weaknesses. While heightened in the play, the King's portrait is consistent with that in the *Chronicle*. The Black Prince is the most thoroughly admirable character in *Edward III*. Hardly more than a lad at the battle of Crecy, he emerges in the course of the play, as indeed he does in history, as a courageous warrior, generous to friend and foe alike, and a veritable exemplar of the ideals of chivalry. In this the character harmonizes with Froissart's view of the Prince. In fact, the only discrepancy is the omission from the play of incidents in the *Chronicle* that further serve to intensify this impression of him. The playwright, for example, makes no use of a notable incident in Froissart of the supper given by the Black Prince to honor his royal prisoner, King John, his son, and his great lords immediately after the battle of Poitiers. The Prince personally served the king "and wolde not syt at the kynges borde for any desyre that the kynge coulde make" because he "sayd he was not suffycient to syt at the table with so great a prince as the kyng was" (chapter 168, Ker 1:384). Also, when they arrived in London the prince escorted his prisoner riding on a "lytell blacke hobbey," while the king rode on a "whyte courser, well aparelled" (chapter 173, Ker 1:393).

The Countess, by the nature of the character, exhibits little development, and this, too, constitutes fidelity to the sources. The play's hints that she is, though effectively, not fully resistant to Edward's blandishments are a reflection of the picture of her in Painter's novel. *The Palace of Pleasure* is also the origin of two important characters in *Edward III*: Lodowick as the king's poet-secretary and the Earl of Warwick as the Countess's father. The Earl is only briefly mentioned here and there in Froissart, and Lodowick not at all. Other important characters, such as King John, Prince Charles, the Earl of Salisbury, and Lord Audley are generally true to Berners's translation with little deviation, as are the minor characters such as Gobin de Graie.

Some students of *Edward III* have argued that the Black Prince is the hero of the play. A reasonably good case can be made out for such a position, but it is evident that the Prince himself believes his father to be the hero. Whenever the two characters are together on the stage, the dramatist makes clear who the leading character is and usually explicitly places the Black Prince in a subordinate posture. But in truth neither King Edward nor his redoubtable son is the protagonist: that role is reserved for England, as it is in Shakespeare's acknowledged history plays. The author employs young Edward to express this theme most clearly in the final scene, although it is frequently and more subtly set forth throughout the whole of the military sequence:

Now father this petition Edward makes,
To thee whose grace hath bin his strongest shield
That as thy pleasure chose me for the man,
To be the instrument to shew thy power,
So thou wilt grant that many princes more
Bred and brought vp within that little Isle,
May still be famous for lyke victories:
(2468–74)

A second important theme is chivalry, exhibited in religious, ethical, and, most notably, interpersonal terms. Almost every scene in *Edward III* makes at least some reference to the knightly code of conduct, and many incidents embody some aspect of the code. The dramatization of the events at Calais affords the playwright a sequence of happenings that felicitously serves this purpose, including King Edward's relief of the poor of the city, the knight-like actions of the six burghers in volunteering to give themselves up to save the general populace, and Edward's yielding to Queen Philippa's plea not to proceed with their execution. These events portray the chivalric

University of Winnipeg, 515 Portage Ave., Winnipeg, MB. R3B 2E9 Canada

ideals of courtesy and care for the weak. In this aspect, R. L. Armstrong compares *Edward III* to *The Troublesome Reign of King John*, also a chronicle play of medieval times: "In contrast with *The Troublesome Reign*, in which from the first speech of the play to the end, motives are sordid and ethics tarnished, *Edward III* is a continuous illustration of [knightly] warrior honor."[94]

The unifying structural element, as Tillyard pointed out in his study of Shakespeare's histories, is the education of princes.[95] King Edward is assisted in learning self-control by the incident with the Countess and is taught magnanimity by Queen Philippa before Calais. The Black Prince is told that he must give up his books and learn to bear the weight of armor, which he does at Crecy. Prince Charles is educated by Villiers about the sacred qualities of oaths, and Charles in turn instructs his father, King John. The linkage in these incidents and the presence in act 3 of two references to the Countess episode (1425–27 and 1612–13) bring the two parts of the play together.

The manner in which the sources of *Edward III* are adapted in structure, character, and theme to dramatic uses exhibits an ingenuity and sophistication only intermittently glimpsed in earlier plays and virtually not at all in those based on chronicle materials, assuming that a date of composition shortly after the Spanish Armada for *Edward III* is accepted. These qualities are remarkably close to those that Geoffrey Bullough describes as Shakespearean in the last volume of his *Narrative and Dramatic Sources of Shakespeare* (8:342–405). While this does not constitute conclusive evidence concerning the identity of the playwright who gave us *Edward III*, at least the use of source materials does not rule out Shakespeare as the author. The handling of source materials may be added to the array of evidence that Proudfoot found "stronger and more various" than can be adduced for other plays of the Shakespeare apocrypha.[96] The case for *Edward III* as an early Shakespearean play of the era of *Titus Andronicus* and *The Comedy of Errors* is as strong as any such case can be when it is based exclusively on internal evidence.

Following is an identification by acts and scenes of the playwright's sources. It is indebted to Robert Smith and Lapides, but is the result of a new study of the play, of Froissart's *Chronicle* in Lord Berners's translation, of Painter's novel 46, and of the two incidents in Holinshed's *Chronicle*. The notation of chapter number alone refers to Berners's Froissart. The sequence of incidents is that of the play.

94. R. L. Armstrong, *Edward III*, p. 197.

95. Tillyard, *History Plays*, pp. 113–14.

96. Proudfoot, "*The Two Noble Kinsmen* and the Apocryphal Plays," *Shakespeare: Select Bibliographical Guides*, ed. Stanley Wells (London: Oxford University Press, 1973), p. 291.

University of Winnipeg, 515 Portage Ave., Winnipeg, MB, R3B 2E9 Canada

Act and scene of *Edward III*	Source
1.1	Chapters 25, 5, 24, 26, 28, 32, 33, 35. Painter, Jacobs, ed., Novel 46, p. 342 (for the identification of the Earl of Warwick as the Countess's father).
1.2, 2.1, 2.2	Chapters 76, 77, 89. Painter, Novel 46 *passim*. Holinshed, Ellis ed., 5:378 (for the gibing at the Scots by the Countess).
3.1	Chapters 123, 50.
3.2	Chapters 122, 123.
3.3	Chapters 126, 127, 128, 129.
3.4 and 3.5	Chapters 130, 131, 132.
4.1	Chapters 68, 135.
4.2	Chapters 133, 138, 139, 146.
4.3	Chapter 135.
4.4	Chapters 159, 161.
4.5	Chapters 130 (for the tempest and flight of crows transferred from Crecy to Poitiers), 135.
4.6 and 4.7	Chapter 162. Holinshed, Ellis ed., 2:665 (for the hurling of the flints by the English archers).
4.8	Chapter 165.
4.9	Chapters 164, 165, 167.
5.1	Chapters 166, 139, 135, 173.

Stage History

The title page of the first quarto, which reads in part, "THE RAIGNE OF KING EDVVARD the third: *As it hath bin sundrie times plaied about the Citie of London*," and the publication of the second quarto point to audience acceptance and continuing presentation of the play, but we have no record of any specific Elizabethan performances. Emil Herz reasons that an "English troupe" performed the play at Danzig (Gdansk) in 1591 or earlier because in that year Philipp Waimer, a Danzig professor, published a dramatized version of Bandello's novel entitled *Elisa*, which he thinks was inspired by *Edward III*. Jerzy Limon notes that Weimer's *Elisa* "is similar to" our play.[97] A protest of 1598 against the unfavorable portrayal of Scots on the London stage is thought by Lapides "possibly" to refer to *Edward III*.[98] Robert Smith believes Heywood's allusion to "King Edward the

97. Emil Herz, *Englische Schauspieler und englisches Schauspiel zur Zeit Shakespeares in Deutschland* (Hamburg und Leipzig, 1903), pp. 5–6; Jerzy Limon, *Gentlemen of a Company: English Players in Central and Eastern Europe, 1590–1660* (Cambridge: Cambridge University Press, 1985), p. 160, n. 1.

98. E. K. Chambers, *The Elizabethan Stage*, 4 vols. (Oxford: Clarendon Press, 1923), 1:323, n. 2; Lapides, *The Raigne of King Edward the Third*, p. 39.

Third" in his *Apology for Actors* (1612) refers to the play and is evidence of continuing performance.[99] Speaight notes six performances of Poel's adaptation of the romantic sequence under the title *The King and Countess* in 1891, 1897, 1911, and 1926; and in the Poel Centenary of 1952.[100]

In spite of the acknowledged superiority of *Edward III* to other early biographical chronicle plays and the excellence of the Countess of Salisbury episode, there is no evidence that the play was produced in its complete form from Jacobean times until recently. The first modern production on record is the presentation in 1986 by the Globe Playhouse of the Shakespeare Society of America in Los Angeles. Joseph Stodder appraised director Dick Dotterer's approach to the problems presented by the play—the structural dichotomy, the time compression of the military segment, and the stylized quality of the battle scenes—as successful on stage. He also found Edward Dloughy as the King, Bill Timoney as the Black Prince, Martita Palmer in the role of the Countess, and Richard German as Warwick, her father, skillful and resourceful performers. The cast, particularly in the Countess sequence, presented sophisticated psychological portraits and made full use of the graceful verse, engaging the interest of the audience in the Countess's moral dilemma. Stodder commended Dotterer for successfully exploiting the comic element in the interplay between Edward and his poet-secretary, Lodowick, in their attempt to write a love poem, a feature frequently overlooked by scholarly readers. The director, Dloughy, and Timoney capably combined their talents to produce credible battle scenes in a series of triumphs, the last of which—the Prince's entry leading the French king captive—brought "the play to a joyous, triumphant conclusion." The company gave twenty-six performances.[101]

The following summer the play was presented originally at the Theatre Clwyd in Mold, North Wales, and later in festival settings at Cambridge and at Taormina, Sicily. The text was cut and adapted with extra dialogue, supplied by Toby Robertson, the director, resulting in a two-hour presentation that had the effect of emphasizing the various messengers' roles, all strongly played by Marc Culwick. "The performance is notable throughout for intelligent, forceful . . . delivery of lines," according to Richard Proudfoot. He also found the scene in which King Edward tries to inspire his secretary to write the love poem "richly comic." Proudfoot complemented Ian McCullough as the King, Annabel Leventon as the Countess, especially in her "resolute but infinitely courteous resistance" to

99. Robert Smith, *Froissart*, pp. 68–69.

100. Robert Speaight, *William Poel and the Elizabethan Revival* (London: Heinemann; and Cambridge: Harvard University Press, 1954), pp. 279–90. Poel published his text in 1906 with the title *Love's Constancy*. See note 9.

101. Joseph H. Stodder, "Three Apocryphal Plays in Los Angeles," *SQ* 38 (1987): 243–48. Another reviewer complimented the acting but found the play text deficient (lacking Shakespearean imagery, poetry, and drama) and both the direction and the production design "static" (*Drama-Logue* [26 July 1986]).

Edward's advances, Colin Hurley as the Black Prince, and several "memorable supporting performances." The ensemble maintained "a strong hold on the attention and imagination of the audience. Shakespeare or not Shakespeare, *Edward III* is revealed at Mold as a gripping play."[102]

There is no external evidence establishing which of the acting companies originally owned the play. Three different troupes have been suggested. On the basis of the structure of the dramatis personae, Baldwin finds that "it is thus evident that *Edward III* was built on the same formula as the plays for the Admiral's men about 1589." Some support for his hypothesis may be found in the fact that the performance at Gdansk in 1591 was given by players who were predominantly former Admiral's Men, to which company some of them subsequently returned.[103] On stylistic grounds and the presence in the play of the "lilies that fester" line, Sharpe decides that it is likely to have been a Chamberlain's play. Roslyn Knutson studies stage conditions in the early to mid-1590s to determine which company owned it. If Shakespeare wrote it, "the odds are excellent that the Chamberlain's men acquired a copy, even if he wrote it before joining the company." If he did not, one of four companies may have come into possession of it when playing resumed in 1594. "In comparison to Derby's, Pembroke's, and Queen's men, the Chamberlain's men were in a better position to acquire the play and perform it '*about the Citie*' [because] their thriving business meant that they had a constant and voracious appetite for new plays."[104] To Jackson, recalled passages from *Edward III* in the memorially reconstructed texts of *2* and *3 Henry VI*, both of which belonged to Pembroke's Men, show that *Edward III* was also theirs. But Taylor evaluates Jackson's evidence as "alleged echoes [which are] weaker than one would desire," and he finds that "the casting pattern would fit the Chamberlain's Men as readily as the pre–1590 Admiral's or what we conjecture about Pembroke's." The absence of external evidence inhibits certainty. One possibility is that Strange's Men (of which Pembroke's was an offshoot), which in 1594 separated from Alleyn and became the Chamberlain's, may have been the original possessors of the play and that *Edward III* may have been passed on to both of the successor companies.[105]

102. Richard Proudfoot, "The Rituals of War," *TLS*, 17 July 1987, p. 770.

103. Baldwin, *On the Literary Genetics of Shakespeare's Poems and Sonnets*, p. 235; Limon, *Gentlemen of a Company*, p. 3.

104. Sharpe, *The Real War of the Theatre*, p. 39; Roslyn Knutson, "The Assignment of Plays to the Repertory of Shakespeare's Company." A brief abstract appears in *ShN* 194 (1987): 25.

105. Jackson, "*Edward III*, Shakespeare and Pembroke's Men," 329–31; Taylor, "Canon and Chronology," p. 137.

1. Source

From *The Chronicle of Froissart*, vol. 1

By Jean Froissart; translated by Sir John Bourchier, Lord Berners, 1523–1525; edited by William Paton Ker, 1901*

Chapter V

Herafter begynneth the occasion wherby the warre moved bitwene the kyngis of Fraunce and Ingland.

Now sheweth the hystory, that this Philyp la Beaw, kyng of Fraunce, had three sonnes, and a feyre doughter named Isabel, maried into Ingland to kyng Edward the second; and these three sonnes, the eldest named Lewes, who was kyng of Navarr in his father's daies, and was called kyng Lewys Hotin; the second had to name Philyp the great, or the long, and the thyrde was called Charles; and all three were kyngis of Fraunce after theyr father's discease by ryght succession eche after other, without havyng any issue male of theyr bodies laufully begoten. So that after the deth of Charlis, last kyng of the three, the twelve piers and all the barons of Fraunce wold nat gyve the realme to Isabell the suster, who was quene of Ingland, bycause they sayd and maynteyned, and yet do, that the realme of Fraunce is so noble that it ought nat to go to a woman; and so consequently to Isabel, nor to the kyng of Inglande her eldest sonne; for they determyned the sonne of the woman to have no ryght nor succession by his mother, syn they declared the mother to have no ryght; so that by these reasons the twelve piers and barons of Fraunce, by theyr comon acord, dyd gyve the realme of Fraunce to the lord Philyp of Valois, nephew somtyme to Philyp la Beawe, kyng of Fraunce, and so put out the quene of Ingland and her sonne, who was as the next heire male, as sonne to the suster of Charles, last kyng of Fraunce. Thus went the realme of Fraunce out of the ryght lynage as it seemed to many folk, wherby great warres hath moved and fallen, and great distructions of people and countries in the realme of Fraunce and other places, as ye may hereafter. This is the very right foundation of this hystory, to recount the great entreprises and great featis of armes that have fortuned and fallen: syth the tyme of the good Charlemaigne, kyng of Fraunce, ther never fell so great adventures.

*Reproduced from *The Chronicle of Froissart* are chapters 5, 24, 25, 26, 28, 32, 33, 35, 50, 68, 76, 77, 89, 122, 123, 126, 127, 128, 129, 130, 131, 132, 133, 135, 138, 139, 146, 159, 161, 162, 164, 165, 166, 167, 168, 173.

Chapter XXIV

Of thomage that kyng Edwarde of Englande, dydde to the kynge of Fraunce, for the duchye of Guyen.

And after that the king had done these two execucyons, he toke newe counselours of the moost noblest and sagest persons of his realme. And so it was about a yere after that Phylip of Valoys was crowned kyng of France, and that all the barones and nobles of the realme had made their homage and fealty to him, except the yong king of England, who had nat done his homage for the duchy of Guyen, nor also he was nat somoned thereto, Than the king of France, by thadvise of all his counsell. sent over into Englande the lorde Ancenis, the lorde Beausalt, and two notable clerkes, maisters of the parlyament of Parys, named maister Peter of Orlyaunce, and maister Peter of Masieres. These iiii. departed fro Paris, and dyd so moch by their journeis that they came to Wysant, and ther they toke see and aryved at Dover, and ther taryed a day to abyde the unshypping of their horses and bagages: and than they rode forth so long that they came to Wynsore, where as the kyng and the yong quene of England lay; and than these foure caused to be knowen to the kynge the occasyon of their commyng. The kyng of Englande, for the honoure of the French kyng his cosyn, caused them to come to his presence, and receyved them honourably: and than they publysshed their message. And the kyng answered them, how that the nobles of his realme, nor his counsell was nat as than about hym, but desyred them to drawe to London, and ther they shulde be answered in such wyse, that of reason they shulde be content. And so they dyned in the kynges chambre, and after departed, and lay the same nyght at Colbroke, and the next day at London. It was nat long after but that the kynge came to his palace of Westmynster, and all his counsell was commaunded to be ther at a certayne day lymited; and whan they were all assembled, than the Frenche embassadours were sent for, and there they declared thoccasyon of their commynge, and delyvered letters fro their maister. Thanne the kynge went a parte with his counsell, to take advyse what was best for hym to do. Thanne was it advysed by his counsell, that they shulde be answered by thordynaunce and style of his predecessours, by the bysshoppe of London. And so the Frenchmen wer called into the counsell chambre: than the bysshop of London sayd, Lordes, that be here assembled for the kyng of Fraunce, the kyngis grace my soveraygne lorde hath harde your wordes, and redde the tenour of your letters; Syrs we say unto you, that we woll counsell the kyng our soveraygne lorde here present, that he go into Fraunce, to se the kynge your maister, his dere cosyn, who ryght amyably hath sent for hym: and as touchyng his faith and homage, he shall do his devour in every thynge that he ought to do of right; and syrs, ye may shewe the kyng your maister, that within short space, the kyng of Englande our maister shall arryve in Fraunce, and do all that reason shall requyre. Than these messangers were feasted, and the kynge rewarded them with many great gyftes and juelles, and they toke their leave and dyd somoche, that at last they came to Parys, wher they found kyng Phylippe, to whome they recounted all their newes; wherof the king was right joyouse, and specially to se the kyng of Englande his cosyn, for he hadde never sene hym before. And whan these tidynges were spredde abrode in the realm of Fraunce, than dukes, erles, and other lordes aparelled them in their best maner; and the kyng of Fraunce wrot his letters to kyng Charles of Behaygne his cosyn, and to the kynge of Navarre, certifyeng theym the day and tyme whan the kyng of England shuld be with hym, desyringe them to be with hym at the same day; and so they came thyder with gret array. Than was it counselled the kynge of Fraunce, that he shulde receyve the kyng of Englande at the cyte of Amyas, and there to make provysion for his commyng. There was chambers, halles, hosteries, and lodgynges made redy, and apparelled, to receyve them all, and their company; and also for the duke of Burgoyne, the duke of Burbon, the duke of Lurren, and syr John of Artoyes. There was purveyaunce for a thousande horse, and for sixe hundred horse that shulde come with the kyng of Englande. The yonge kyng of Englande forgate nat the voyage that he had to do into Fraunce; and so he aparelled for hym and his company, well and sufficiently; and there departed out of Englande in his company, two bysshoppes, besyde the bysshoppe of London, and foure erles, the lorde Henry erle of Derby, his cosyn germayne, sonne to sir Thomas erle of Lancastre, with the wrie necke, the erle of Salisbury, therle of Warwyke, and the erle of Hereforde, and vi. barownes, the lorde Raynolde Cobham, the lorde Thomas Wage marshall of Englande, the lorde Persy, the lorde Manny, and the lorde Mowbray, and mo than xl. other knyghtes; so that the kyng and his company were about a thousand horse; and the kyng was two dayes in passing bytwene Dover and Wysant. Than the kyng and his company rod to Bullayne, and there taryed one day. This was about the myddes of August, the yere of our Lorde God a thousande thre hundred xxix. And anone the tidynges came to kyng Phylip of Fraunce, howe the kynge of Englande was at Bullayne. Than the kynge of Fraunce sent his constable with great plentie of knyghtes to the kynge of Englande, who as thanne was at Monsternell by the see syde, and ther was gret tokens of love and good chere, made on bothe parties. Thanne the kynge of Englande rodde forth withall his rowt, and in his company the constable of Fraunce; and he rodde so long that they came to the cytie of Amyas, wher as kyng Phylippe, and the kynge of Behaygne, the kynge of Mayllorgues, and the kynge of Navarre were redy aparelled to receyve the kynge of Englande, with many other dukes, erles, and great barownes: for there was all the xii. peres of Fraunce, redy to feast and make chere to the kynge of

Englande, and to be there peasably, to bere wytnesse of the kynge of Englandes homage. Ther was the kyng of Englande nobly recyved; and thus these kynges and other princes taryed at Amyas the space of fifteen dayes, and in the meane tyme there were many wordes and ordynaunces devysed; but as farr as I coude knowe, kyng Edwarde of England made his homage to the kynge of Fraunce, all onely by worde, and nat puttyng his handes bytwene the kynge of Fraunce handes, nor none other prince nor prelate lymitted for hym; nor the kynge of Englande wolde nat procede any farther in doyng any more concernyng his homage, but rather he was determyned to returne agayne into Englande; and there was redde openly, the privyleges of auncyent tyme graunted, [in] the which was declared in what maner the kynge shulde do his homage, and howe, and in what wyse he shulde do servyce to the kynge of Fraunce. Than the kynge of Fraunce sayd, Cosyn, we woll nat disceyve you: this that ye have done pleaseth us rightwell, as for this present tyme, tyll such tyme as ye be returned agayne into your realme, and that ye have sene under the seales of your predecessoures, howe, and in what wyse ye shulde do. And so thus the kynge of Englande tooke his leave, and departed fro the kynge of Fraunce ryght amyably, and of all other princes that was there, and retourned agayne into Englande, and laboured so longe that he came to Wyndesor, where his quene receyvedde hym right joyously, and demaunded tidynges of kynge Phylippe her uncle, and of her linage of Fraunce. The kyng shewed her all that he knewe, and of the gret chere and honour that he had there, and sayd, in his mynde, there was no realme coude be compared to the realme of Fraunce. And than within a space after the kyng of Fraunce sent into Englande of his specyall counsell, the byshoppe of Chartres, and the byshoppe of Beauvays, the lorde Loys of Cleremont, the duke of Burbon, therle of Harcourt, and therle of Tankervylle, with dyvers other knyghtes and clerkes, to the counsell of Englande, the which was than holden at London, for the parfourmaunce of the kyng of Englandes homage, as ye have harde before. And also the kyng of England and his counsell, had well oversene the maner and fourme, how his auncyent predecessours had done their homage for the duchy of Acquitayne. There were many as than in Englande that murmured and sayd, how the kyng their lorde was nerer by true succession of herytage to the crowne of Fraunce than Phylippe of Valoys, who was as than kyng of Fraunce. Howbeit the kyng and his counsell wolde nat knowe it nor speke therof, as at that time. Thus was ther great assemble, and moch ado how this homage shulde be parfourmed. These embassadours taryed styll in Englande all that wynter, tyll it was the moneth of May folowyng, or they had aunswere dyffinatyve: howbeit finally, the kynge of Englande, by the advyce of his counsell, and on the syght of his privyleges, where unto they gave great fayth, was determyned to write letters in the maner of patentes, sealed with his great seale, knowlegyng therin the homage that he ought to do to the kyng of Fraunce; the tenour and report of the which letters patentes foloweth:

Edward by the grace of God, kyng of England, lorde of Ireland, and duke of Acquitayne, to them that these present letters shall se or here, send gretyng; we wold it be knowen, that as we made homage at Amyas to the right excellent prince our right dere cosyn, Phylyppe kyng of Fraunce; and there it was requyred by hym, that we shuld knowledge the sayd homage, and to make it to hym expresly, promysinge to bere hym fayth and trouth, the which we did nat as than, bycause we were nat enfourmed of the trouth; we made hym homage by generall wordes, sayeng how we entred into his homage in lyke maner as our predecessours, Dukes of Guyen, in tymes past, had entred into thomage of the kyng of Fraunce for that tyme beyng: and syth that tyme we have ben well enfourmed of the trouth; therfore we knowlege by these presentes, that such homage as we have made in the cyte of Amyas to the kyng of Fraunce in general wordes, was, and ought to be understande this worde, lyege man; and that to hym we owe, to bere faith and trouth, as duke of Acquitayne and pere of Fraunce, erle of Poyters and of Mutterell; and to thentent in tyme commynge that there shulde never be dyscorde. For this cause, we promyse for us and our successours, dukes of Acquitayne, that this homage be made in this manner folowyng; The kyng of Englande, duke of Acquitayne, holdeth his handes bytwene the handes of the kyng of Fraunce; and he that shall addresse these wordes to the kyng of Englande, duke of Acquitayne, shall speke for the kyng of Fraunce in this maner: Ye shall become lyege man to the kynge my lorde here present, as duke of Guyen, and pere of Fraunce; and to hym promyse to bere faythe and trouthe, say, ye: and the kyng of Englande, duke of Guyen, and his successours, sayth, ye. And than the kyng of Fraunce receyveth the kyng of Englande, duke of Guyen, to this sayd homage, as lyege man, with faythe and trouth spoken by mouth, savyng his ryght and all other. And furthermore, whan the sayd kyng entreth in homage to the kyng of Fraunce, for therldome of Poyters, and of Muttrell, he shall putte his handes bytwene the handes of the kyng of Fraunce, for the sayd erledome. And he that shall speke for the kynge of Fraunce, shall addresse his wordes to the kynge and erle, and say thus; Ye shall become liege man to the kyng of Fraunce, my lorde here present, as erle of Poyters, and Muttrell; and to hym promyse to bere fayth and trouth, say, ye, and the kyng, erle of Poyters, sayth, ye. Than the kyng of Fraunce receyveth the kyng and erle to this sayd homage by his fayth, and by his mouth, savyng his ryght and all other. And after this maner it shal be done, and renewed as often as homage shulde be done. And of that we shall delyver, and our succesours, dukes of Guyen, after these sayd homages, made letters patentes, sealed with our great seale, if the kynge of Fraunce requyre it; and beside that, we promyse in good faythe to holde, and to kepe effectuously the peace, and concorde, made bytwene the kynges of Fraunce, and the kynges of Englande, dukes of Guyen, &c.

These letters the lordes of Fraunce brought to the kyng their lorde, and the kyng caused them to be kept in his chauncery.

Chapter XXV

Howe the lorde syr Robert of Artoyse was chased out of the realme of Fraunce.

The man in the world that most ayded kyng Philyppe, to attayne to the Crowne of Fraunce, was syr Robert, erle of Artoyse, who was oone of the most sagest, and greatteste lordes in Fraunce, and of hygh lynage extraughte, fro the blodde royall, and hadde to his wyfe suster jermayn to the sayd kyng Phylyp, and allwayes was his chiefe and speciall compaignyon, and lover in all hys astatis. And the space of iii. yere, all that was done in the realme of Fraunce was done by his advyce, and withoute hym nothyng was done. And after it fortuned, that this kyng Philyppe tooke a mervailouse great displeasure and hatred ageynst this noble man, syr Robert of Artoyse, for a plee that was moved before hym, wherofe the Erle of Artoyse was cause: for he wolde have wonne his entent, by the vertue of a letter that he layd forth, the whiche was nat true, as it was sayde; wherfore the kyng was in suche displeasure, that yf he hadde takyn hym in his ire, surely it hadde coste hym his lyfe, without remedy. So this syr Robert was fayne to voyde the realme of Fraunce, and went to Namure, to the Erle John his Nephewe: than the kyng toke the Erles wyfe, and her two sonnes, who were his owne nephewes, John, and Charles, and dyd put them in prison, and were kept straytly, and the kyng sware that they shulde never come out of prison, as long as they lyved; the kyngis mynde wolde nat be turned by no maner of meanes. Than the kyng in his furye sente hastely to the busshopp Raoul of Liege, and desired hym, at his instaunce, that he wolde defye and make warre agaynst the erle of Namure, without he wolde put out of his countrey syr Roberte erle of Artoyse. And this busshoppe, who greaty loved the kynge of Fraunce, and but lytle loved his neyghbours, dyd as the kyng desired hym. Than the erle of Namure, sore ageynst his wyll, caused the erle of Artoyse to avoyde his lande. Than this erle, syr Robert, went to the duke of Brabant, his cosyn, who right joyously receyved hym, and dyd hym great comforte; and as soone as the kyng of Fraunce knew that, he sent worde to the duke, that if he wold susteyne, maynteyn, or suffre, the erle of Artoyse in his countrey, he shulde have no greatter ennemy than he wold be to hym, and that he wolde make warre ageynst hym, and al his, to the best of his power, with all the realme of Fraunce. Than the duke sent the erle of Artoyse pryvely to Argentuel, to thentent to se what the kyng wolde do forther in the case; and anon the kyng knew it, for he had spyes in every corner. The kyng had great dispyte, that the duke shuld so dele with hym, and within a brief space after, the kyng pourchased, so by reason of his golde and sylver, that the kyng of Behaigne, who was cosin jermayn to the duke of Brabant, and the busshop of Liege, the arche bysshop of Coleyn, the duke of Guerles, the marques of Julyers, the erle of Bare, the lord of Los, the lorde Fawkmount, and divers other lordes, were alied toguyther, al ayenst the duke of Brabant, and defyed hym, and entred with a great oste in to his countrey by Esbayng, and so cam to Hanut, and brent twyse over the countrey where as it pleased them. And the kyng of Fraunce sent with them therle of Ewe, his Constable, with a great oste of men of armes. Than the erle William of Heynaulte, sent his wyfe, suster to the kyng, and his brother, syr John of Heynaulte, lorde Beamont, into Fraunce, to treat for a peace, and sufferaunce of warr, bitwene the kyng and the duke of Brabant. And at last the kyng of France, with moche warke, consented therto, upon condition, that the duke shulde put hymselfe utterly to abyde the ordynaunce of the kyng of Fraunce, and of his counsaile, in every mater that the kyng, and all suche as had defyed hym, had ageynst him; and also within a certayn day lymitted, to avoyde out of his countrey the erle of Artoyse, and to make shorte; al this the duke dyd sore ayenst his wyll.

Chapter XXVI

Howe kyng Edwarde of Ingland toke the towne of Berwyke ageynst the Scottis.

Ye have harde here before recited, of the truce bitwene Inglande and Scotland, for the space of iii. yere; and so the space of oone yere, they kept well the peace, so that in CCC. yere before, there was nat so good peace kept: howbeit, kyng Edward of Ingland was enformed, that the yong kyng David, of Scotland, who had wedded his suster, was seaced of the towne of Berwyke, the whiche ought to apperteyn to the realme of Ingland; for kyng Edward the first, his graunfather, had it in his possession peasably. Also the kyng was enformed, that the realme of Scotlande shulde holde in chiefe of the Crowne of Inglande, and how the yong kyng of Scottis had nat done as than his homage; wherfore the kyng of Ingland sent his ambassad to the kyng of Scottis, desyryng hym to leve his handis of the towne of Berwyke, for it parteyned to his heritage, for kyngis of Inglande, his predecessours, have ben in possession therof: and also they somoned the kyng of Scottis, to come to the kyng of Ingland, to do his homage for the realme of Scotland. Than the kyng of Scottis toke cousaile, howe to answere thys mater: and finally, the kyng answerde the Englisshe ambassadours, and sayd, Syrs, both I and all the nobles of my realme, mervaile greatly of that ye have requyred us to do, for we fynd nat auncientely, that the realme of Scotlande shulde any thyng be bounde, or be subgiet to the realme of Ingland, nother by homage, or any other wayes: nor the kyng of noble memorye, our father, wolde never do homage to the kyngis of Ingland, for any warre that was made unto hym, by any of them; no more in likewyse I am in wyll to do: and also kyng Robert, our father, conquered the towne of Berwyke, by force of armes, agaynst kyng Edwarde, father to the kyng, your maister, that nowe is; and so my father helde it all the dayes of his lyfe as his good heritage; and so in lyke maner we thynke to do, to the best of our power. Howebeit lordes, we require you to be meanes to the kyng your master, whose suster we have maryed, that he wyll suffre us peaseably to enjoye our fraunches and rightis, as his auncetours have done here before; and to lette us enjoye that our father hath wonne, and kept it peaseably all his lyfe dayes; and desyre the kyng your maister, that he wolde nat beleve any evyll counsaile, gyven hym to the contrary: for if ther were any other prince that wolde do us wrong, he shuld aide, succour, and defende us, for the love of his suster, whom we have maryed. Than these ambassadours answerd and said, Syr, we have well understande your answere: we shall shewe it to the kyng our lorde, in lyke maner as ye have said; and so toke theyr leave, and returned into Inglande to the kyng; with the whiche answere the kyng of Ingland was nothyng content. Than he somoned a parliament, to be holden at Westminster, where as all the nobles, and wyse men of the realme were assembled to determine what shuld be best to be done in this mater. And in this meane tyme, syr Robert, erle of Artoys, came into Inglande, dysguysed lyke a marchaunt, and the kyng receyved hym right joyously, and reteyned hym as one of his counsaile, and to hym assigned the erledom of Rychemount. And whan the daye of the parliament aproched, and that all the nobles of the lande were assembled about London, than the kyng caused to be shewed the message, and howe he had wrytten to the kyng of Scottis, and of the answere of the same kyng. Wherfore the kyng desyred all the nobles of his realme, that they wolde gyve hym suche counsaile, as shulde aperteyne to the savyng of his honour and ryght. And whan they were all assembled in counsaile, they thought that the kyng myght no lenger bear by his honour, the injuryes and wronges, that the kyng of Scottis dyd hym dayly; and so they reported their advise to the kyng, exortyng hym to provyde for his force and strength of men of warre, to atteyne therby the towne of Berwike, and to entre into the realme of Scotland, in suche wyse, that he shulde constrayne the kyng of the Scottis, to be joyfull to come and do his homage to hym. And so the nobles and commons of the realme of Ingland, sayd they wold gladly, and willingly, go with hym in that journey: and of theyr good wyls, the kyng thanked them greatly, and desired them to be redy apparailed, at a daye assigned, and to assemble togyther at Newcastell upon Tyne. And than every man went home and prepared for that journey. Than the kyng sent agayn other ambassadours, to the kyng of Scottis, his brother in lawe, sufficiently to sommon hym; and if he wolde nat be other wyse advysed, than the kyng gave them full auctorite to defie hym. And so the day of the assembly of the kyngis oste aproched, at the whiche day, the kynge of Inglande, and all his oste, aryved at New-castell upon Tyne, and there taried iii. dayes, for the residue of his oste, that was comyng after. And on the fourth day, he departed with al his oste toward Scotland, and passed through the landes of the lorde Persy, and of the lorde Nevell, who were two great lordes in Northumberland, and marched on the Scottis. And in lyke wyse so dyd the lorde Rosse, and the lorde Ligy, and the lorde Mombray. Than the kynge and all his oste, drewe toward the cite of Berwyke; for the kyng of Scotland made no other an-swere to these ii. messengers, but as he dyd to the fyrst; wherfore he was openly defied, and somoned. And so the kyng of Ingland and his oste entred into Scotland, for he was counsailed, that he shuld nat tary at siege at Berwike, but to ryde forth, and to burne the countrey, as his graund father dyd: and so he dyd. In whiche journey he wasted and distroyed all the playn countrey of Scotland, and exiled diverse townes that were closed with dykes, and with pales, and toke the strong castell of Edyngburth, and sette therin a garison. And so passed the secund ryver in Scotland, under Douffremlyn, and ran over all the countrey there abowte to Scone, and distroyed the good towne of Douffremlyn, but they dyd no evyll to the abbey, for the kyng of Ingland commaunded that no hurte shuld be done therto. And so the kyng conquered all the countrey to Dondieu, and to Doubreten, a strong castell, standyng on the marches ayenst the wylde Scottis, where as the kyng of Scottis, and the quene his wyfe, were with-drawen unto for suretie; for there were no Scottis that wolde appere afore the Englisshemen, for they were all drawen into the forest of Gedworth, the whiche wer inhabitable, and specially for them, that knew nat the countrey, wherin all the Scottis wer, and all theyr gooddis; and so they set but a lytle by all the remnant. And it was no marvaile, thoughe they were thus dryven: for the kyng their lorde was but xv. yere of age, and the erle of Morrey was but yong, and the nephew of Willyam Duglas, that was slayne in Spayn, was also of the same age: so as at that tyme, the realme of Scotland was dispurveyed of good capiteyns. And whan the kyng of In-gland had ron over all the playne countrey of Scotlande, and taried ther the space of vi. monethes, and sawe that none wold come agaynst hym, than he garnysshed divers castels that he had wonne, and thought by them to make warre to all the other. Than he withdrew fayre and easely toward Berwike; and in his returnyng, he wan the castell of Aluest, parteynyng to the heritage of the erle Duglas: it was a v. leagis fro Edenburge, and therin the kyng set good capitayns, and than rode small journeis, tyll he came to Berwike, the whiche is at the entre of Scotlande, and there the kyng layd rounde about his siege, and sayd, he wolde never depart thens, tyll he had wonne it, or els the kyng of Scottis to come, and to reyse his siege parforce. And within the towne there were good men of warre, set there by the kyng of Scottis: before this cite ther were many assaultis, and sore skrymysshes, nygh every daye, for they of the cite wolde nat yelde them up symply, for alwaies they thought to be rescued; how be it, there was no succour appered. The Scottis, on mornyngis and nyghtis, made many skryes to trouble the oste, but lytle hurte they dyd, for the Englysshe oste was so well kepte, that the Scottis coulde nat entre, but to theyr dammage, and often tymes loste of theyr men. And whan they of Berwike sawe that no comfort, nor ayde, came to them fro any part, and that theyr vitayles began to fayle, and howe they were enclosed both by water and by lande; than they began to fall in a treate with the kyng of Ingland, and desired a truce to endure a moneth; and if within the moneth, kyng David, theyr lorde, or some other for hym, come nat by force to reyse the seige, than they to rendre up the cite, their lyves and gooddis saved, and that the soudiers within, myght safly go into theyr countrey, without any dammage. This treaty was nat lightly graunted; for the kyng of Ingland wolde have had them yelded symply, to have had his pleasure of some of them, bicause they had hold so long ayenst hym: but finally he was content by the counsaile of his lordes. And also syr Robert of Artoys dyd put therto his payne, who had ben all that journeye with the kyng, and had shewed hym alwayes, howe he was next enheriter to the crowne of Fraunce; he wolde gladly that the kyng shuld have made warre into Fraunce, and aleft the warres of Scotland. So his wordes, and others, inclined greatly the kyng to condiscend to the treaty of Berwike; so this truce and treaty was graunted. Than they within the cite sent worde to their kyng, in what case they stode, but for all that, they coulde fynde no remedy to reyse the siege; so the cite was delyvered up at thende of the moneth, and also the castell; and the Marshals of the ost toke possession for the kyng of Ingland, and the burgesses of the cite came and dyd theyr feaute and homage to the kyng, and sware to hold of hym. Than after the kyng entred with great solempnite, and taryed there xii. dayes, and made a capitayn ther, called syr Edward Bailleul: and whan the kyng departed, he lefte with the sayde knyght, certayn yong knyghtis and squiers, to helpe to kepe the landis, that he had conquered of the Scottis, and the fronters therof. Than the kyng and his people returned to London, and every man into theyre owne countres; and the kyng went to Wyndesore, and syr Robert of Artoys with hym, who never ceassed daye nor nyght, in shewyng the kyng what ryght he had to the crowne of Fraunce: and the kyng harkened gladly to his wordis. Thus in this season, the kyng of Ingland wanne the most parte of the realme of

Scotland, who had many expert knyghtis about hym, among other was sir Wylliam Montague, and syr Walter of Manny; they were hardy knyghtis, and dyd many dedis of armes ageynst the Scottis. And the better to have their entre into Scotland, they fortified the bastyde of Rosebourge, and made it a strong castel; and syr Wylliam Montague dyd so well in all his entreprises, that the kyng made hym erle of Salysbury, and maried hym nobly. And also the lorde of Manny was made of the kyngis pryve counsaile, and well advaunsed in the courte.

True it was, that some of the knyghtis of Scotland, dyd ever the anoyaunce they coulde to the Englisshemen, and kept them in the wylde countrey, among marisshes and great forestis, so that no man coulde folowe them. Some season, the Englisshemen folowed them so nere, that all day they skrymysshed toguyther; and in a skrymysshe, this said lorde Wylliam Montague lost one of his yen. In the said forest, the olde kyng Robert, of Scotland, dyd kepe hymselfe, whan kyng Edward the fyrst conquered nygh al Scotland; for he was so often chased, that none durst lodge hym in castell, nor fortresse, for feare of the sayd kyng. And ever whan the kyng was returned into Ingland, than he wolde gather together agayn his people, and conquere townes, castells, and forteresses, juste to Berwike, some by bataile, and some by fayre speche and love: and whan the said kyng Edward hard therof, than wolde he assemble his power, and wyn the realme of Scotlande agayn; thus the chaunce went bitwene these two forsaid kyngis. It was shewed me, howe that this kyng Robert wan, and lost his realme v. tymes. So this contynued tyll the sayd kyng Edwarde died, at Berwike: and whan he sawe that he shulde dye, he called before hym his eldest sonne, who was kyng after hym, and there before all the barones, he caused hym to swere, that as soone as he were deed, that he shulde take his body, and boyle it in a caudron, tyl the flesshe departed clene fro the boones, and than to bury the flesshe, and kepe styll the boons; and that as often as the Scottis shuld rebell ayenst hym, he shulde assemble his people ayenst them, and cary with hym the boones of his father; for he beleved verely, that if they had his boones with them, that the Scottis shulde never attayne any victory ayenst them. The whiche thyng was nat accomplisshed, for whan the kyng was deed, his son caried hym to London, and there he was buryed.

Chapter XXVIII

Howe kyng Edwarde was counselled to make warre agaynst the French kyng.

In this season, whan this croisy was in gret forwardness, for there was no spekyng but therof, syr Robert of Artoies was as than in England, banysshed out of Fraunce, and was ever about kyng Edward; and alwayes he counselled hym to defye the Frenche kyng, who kept his herytages fro hym wrongfully; of the whiche mater the kyng often tymes counselled with them of his secret counsell, for gladly he wolde have had his right, and yf he wyst how. And also he thought, that if he shulde demaunde his ryght, and it refused, what he might do than to amende it. For if he shulde than syt styll, and do nat his devoyre to recover his right, he shulde be more blamed than before: yet he thought it were better to speke nat therof. For he sawe well, that by the puysaunce of his realme, it wolde be harde for hym to subdue the great realme of Fraunce, without helpe of some other gret lordes, outher of the empyre or in other places for his money. The kyng often tymes desyred counsell of his chefe and speciall frendes and counsellours. Fynally, his counsellours answered hym and sayd, Syr, the mater is so weighty, and of so hygh an enterprise, that we dare nat speke therin, nor gyve you any counsell. But syr, this we wolde counsell you to do; sende suffycient messangers, well enfourmed of your intencyon, to therle of Heynaulte, whose doughter ye have maryed, and to syr John of Heynalt, his brother, who hath valyantly served you at all tymes; and desyre them by way of love, that they wolde counsell you in this mater, for they knowe better what parteyneth to suche a mater than we do; and syr, if they agre to your entent, than woll they counsell you what frendes ye may best make. The kyng was content with this answere, and desyred the bysshop of Lyncolne to take on hym this message, and with hym two banerettes, and two doctours: they made them redy, and toke shypping, and aryved at Dunkyrke, and rodde through Flaunders, tyll they came to Valencens, where they founde the erle lyeng in his bedde, sycke of the gout, and with him sir John his brother. They were greatly feasted, and declared the cause of their commyng, and shewed all the reasons and doutes that the kynge their maister had made. Than therle sayd, As helpe me God, yf the kynges mynde might be brought to passe, I wolde be right glad therof: for I had rather the welth of hym that hath maryed my doughter, than of hym that never dyd nothyng for me, though I have maryed his suster. And also he dyd let the maryage of the yonge duke of Brabant, who shuld have maryed one of my doughters. Wherfore, I shall nat fayle to ayde my dere and wel beloved sonne, the kyng of England: I shall gyve hym counsell and ayde to the best of my power, and so shall do John my brother, who hath served hym or this. Howe be it he must have more helpe than ours: for Heynalt is but a small countrey, as to the regard of the realme of Fraunce, and Englande is farr of to ayde us. Than the bysshoppe sayd, Syr, we thanke you in our maisters behalfe, of the comfort that ye gyve us; syr, we desyre you to gyve our maister counsell, what frendes he were best to labour unto to ayde hym. Surely sayd therle, I can nat devyse a more puissant prince to ayde hym, than the duke of Brabant, who is his cosyn germayne; and also the bysshoppe of Liege, the duke of Guerles, who hath his suster to his wyfe; the archbysshop of Colayne, the marques of Jullers, syr Arnolde de Baquehen, and the lorde of Faulquemount; these lordes be thei that may make moost men of warre in short space of any that I know: they arre good men of warre, they may well make x. thousand men of warr, so they have wages therafter; they arre people that wolde gladly wynne advauntage. Yf it were so that the kyng my sonne, your maister, might gette these lordes to be on his part, and so to come into these parties, he might well go over the water of Oysse, and seke out kyng Phylippe to fyght with hym. With this answere, these ambassadours retourned into England to the kyng, and reported all that they had done; wherof the kyng had great joy, and was well comforted. These tidyngis came into Fraunce, and multiplied lytle and lytle, so that kyng Phylippes enterprise of the sayd croysey beganne to asswage and ware cold; and he countermaunded his offycers to sease of makyng of any farther provision, tyll he knewe more what kyng Edward wolde do. Than kyng Edward ordayned x. banerettes, and xl. other knyghtes, and sent them over the see to Valencennes, and the bysshoppe of Lyncolne with theym, to thentent to treat with the lordes of thempyre, suche as therle of Heynalt had named. Whanne they were come to Valencennes, eche of them kept a great estate and part, and spared nothynge, no more than yf the kynge of Englande had bene there in proper persone, wherby they dyd gette great renowme and prayse. They had with them yonge bachelars, who had eche of them one of their eyen closedde with a piece of sylke: it was sayd, how they had made a vowe among the ladyes of their contrey, that they wolde nat se but with one eye, tyll they had done some dedes of armes in Fraunce; how be it they wold nat be knowen therof. And whan thei had ben well feested at Valencennes, than the bysshoppe of Lyncolne, and part of his company, went to the duke of Brabant, who feasted them greatly, and agreed, and promysed to sustayne the kyng of Englande and all his company in his contrey; so that he might go and come, armed and unarmed at his pleasure, and to gyve him the best counsell he coude. And also, yf the kynge of Englande wolde defy the Frenche kyng, that he wolde do the same, and entre into the countrey of Fraunce, with men of warre, so that their wages might be borne, to the nombre of a thousande men of armes. Thus than the lordes retourned agayne to Valencennes, and dyd so moch by messangers, and by promyse of golde and sylver, that the duke of Guerles, who was the kynges brother in lawe, and the marques of Jullers, the archebysshoppe of Colayne, and Waleran his brother, and the lorde of Faulquemount came to Valencennes, to speke with these lordes of Englande, byfore the erle of Haynalt, and the lorde John his brother. And by the meanes of a great somme of florens that eche of them shulde have for themselfe, and for their men, they made promyse to defy the Frenche kyng, and to go with the kyng of England whan it pleased hym, with a certayn men of warre; promysinge also, to gette other lordes to take their part for wages, such as be beyonde the ryver of Ryne, and be able to bringe good nombres of men of warre. Than the lordes of Almayne toke their leave, and retourned into ther owne contreis; and thenglysshmen taryed styll with therle of Heynalt, and sent certayne messangers to the bysshoppe of Lyege, and wolde gladly have hadde hym on their partie; but he wolde never be agaynst the French kyng, for he was become his man, and entred into his feaultie. Kyng Charles of Behaygne, was nat desyred, for they knewe well he was so fermely joyned with the Frenche kyng, by reason of the maryage of John duke of Normandy, who had to wyfe the kyngis doughter, wherby they knewe well he wold do nothyng agaynst the French king.

Chapter XXXII

How kyng Edwarde of England made great alyaunces in the empyre.

After this dysconfeture at Cagaunt, tidynges therof spredde abrode in the countrey. And they of Flaunders sayd, that without reason and agaynst their wylles therle of Flanders had layd there that garyson; and Jaques Dartvell wolde nat it had ben otherwyse, and incontynent he sent messangers to kyng Edwarde, recommendyng hym to his grace with all his hert, counsellyng hym to come thyder, and to passe the see, certyfyenge hym, how the Flemmynges greatly desyred to se hym. Thus the kyng of Englande made great purveyances; and whan the wynter was passed, he toke the see, well accompanyed with dukes, erles, and barownes, and dyvers other knyghtes, and aryved at the towne of Andewarpe, as than pertayning to the duke of Brabant: thyther came people from all partes to se hym, and the great estate that he kept. Than he sent to his cosyn, the duke of Brabant, and to the duke of Guerles, to the marques of Jullers, to the lorde John of Heynalt, and to all such as he trusted to have any conforte of, sayeng, howe he wolde gladly speke with theym; they came all to Andewarp, bytwene Whytsontyde, and the feest of saynte John. And whan the kyng had well feasted them, he desyred to knowe their myndes, whane they wolde begynne that they had promysed: requirynge them to dyspatche the mater brevely, for that intent, he sayd, he was come thyder, and had all his men redy; and howe it shulde be a great damage to hym to defarre the mater long. These lordes had longe counsell among them, and fynally they sayd, Syr, our commynge hyther as nowe, was more to se you, than for any thynge els: we be nat as nowe, purveyed to gyve you a full answere; by your lycence we shall retourne to our people, and come agayne to you at your pleasure, and thane gyve you so playne an answere, that the mater shall nat rest in us. Than they toke day, to come agayn a thre wekes after the feest of saynt John. The kynge shewed them what charges he was at, with so longe abyding, thynkinge whan he came thyther that they had ben full purveyd to have made hym a playne answere, sayng howe that he wolde nat returne into England, tyll he had a full answere. So thus these lordes departed, and the kynge taryed in the abbay of saynt Bernarde, and some of the Englysshe lordes taryed styll at Andewarpe, to kepe the kynge company, and some of the other rode about the countrey in great dyspence. The duke of Brabant went to Lovane, and there taryed a long tyme, and often tymes he sent to the Frenche kyng, desyring hym to have no suspecyons to hym, and nat to byleve any yvell informacion made of hym; for by his wyll, he sayd he wold make none alyance, nor covenant agaynst hym: sayeng also, that the kynge of Englande was his cosyn germayne, wherfore he might nat deny hym to come into his countrey.

The day came that the kyng of Englande loked to have an answere of these lordes: and they excused them, and sayd, howe they were redy and their men, so that the duke of Brabant wold be redy for his part, sayeng, that he was nere than they; and that assone as they might knowe that he were redy, they wolde nat be behynde, but at the begynnyng of the mater, assone as he. Than the kyng dyd so moche, that he spake agayne with the duke, and shewed him the answere of the other lordes, desyring him, by amyte and lynage, that no faut were founde in hym, sayeng, how he parceyved well that he was but cold in the mater, and that without he wer quicker and dyd otherwyse, he douted he shulde lese therby the ayde of all the other lordes of Almayne, through his defaulte. Than the duke sayd, he wolde take counsayle in the mater, and whan he had longe debated the mater, he sayd howe he shulde be as redy as any other, but firste he sayd, he wolde speke agayne with the other lordes; and he dyde sende for them, desyring them to come to hym, wher as they pleased best. Than the day was apoynted about the myddes of August, and this counsell to be at Hale, bycause of the yong erle of Heynalt, who shulde also be ther, and with hym sir John of Heynalt, his uncle. Whane these lordes were all come to this parlyament at Hale, they had longe counsayle togyder; finally, they sayd to the kyng of Englande, Syr, we se no cause why we shulde make defyance to the Frenche kyng, all thynges consydred, without ye can gette thagrement of themperour, and that he wolde commaunde us to do so in his name; the emperour may well thus do, for of long tyme past there was a covenant sworne and sealed, that no kyng of Fraunce ought to take any thyng parteyning to thempyre: and this kynge Philyppe hath taken the castell of Crevecure, in Cambreysis, and the castell of Alues, in Pailleull, and the cytie of Cambray; wherfore themperour hath good cause to defye hym by us: therfore sir, if ye can get his acord, our honour shal be the more; and the kyng sayd, he wolde folowe their counsayle. Than it was ordayned, that the Marques of Jullers shulde go to themperour, and certayne knyghtes, and clerkes of the kynges, and some of the counsell of the duke of Gwerles; but the duke of Brabant wolde sende none fro hym, but he lende the castell of Louayne to the kynge of Englande to lye in. And the Marques and his company founde the emperour at Florebetche, and shewed hym the cause of their commyng. And the lady Margarete of Heynault dydde all her payne to further forthe the matter, whom sir Lewes of Bavyer, than emperour, had wedded. And ther the Marques of Jullers was made an erle, and the duke of Guelders, who byfore was an erle, was than made a duke. And themperour gave commyssion to foure knyghtes, and to two doctours of his counsell, to make kyng Edwarde of Englande, his vycarre generall throughout all the empyre; and therof these sayd lordes hadde instrumentes publyke, confyrmed and sealed suffyciently by the emperour.

Chapter XXXIII

Howe kyng Davyd of Scotlande made alyaunce with kyng Phylyppe of Fraunce.

In this season, the yonge kyng Davyd of Scotlande, who had lost the best part of his lande, and coulde natte recover it out of the holde of thenglysshmen, departed prively with a small company, and the quene his wyfe with hym, and toke shyppyng, and arryved at Bolayne, and so rodde to Pares, to kyng Philyppe, who gretly dyd feast hym; and offred hym of his castels to abyde in, and of his goodes to dyspende, on the condycion that he shulde make no peace with the kynge of Englande, without his counsell and his agrement; for kynge Philyppe knewe well, howe the kynge of Englande apparelled greatly to make hym warre. So thus the kyng ther retayned kyng Davyd, and the quene, a long season, and they had all that they neded, at his coste and charge: for out of Scotlande came but lytell substance to mayntayne withall their estates. And the French king sent certayne messangers into Scotlande, to the lordes ther, such as kept warr agaynst thenglisshmen, offryng them great ayde and confort, so that they wolde take no peace, nor truse, with the kyng of Englande, without it were by his agrement, or by thaccorde of their owne kyng, who had in likewyse promysed and sworne. Than the lordes of Scotlande counselled togyder, and joyously they accorded to his request, and so sealed and sware with the kyng their lorde. Thus this alyance was made bytwene Scotlande and France, the which endured a long season after. And the frenche kyng sent men of warre into Scotland, to kepe warr agaynst thenglysshmen, as syr Arnolde Dandregien, who was after marschall of Fraunce, and the lorde of

Garencieres, and dyverse other knyghtes and squyers. The Frenche kyng thought that the Scottes shuld gyve so moch ado to the realme of England, that thenglysshmen shuld nat come over the see to anoy hym.

Chapter XXXV

Howe kynge Edwarde and all his alyes dyd defye the Frenche kyng.

Thus the wynter passed and somer came, and the feest of saynt John Baptyst aproched: and the lordes of Englande and of Almayne aparelled themselfe to acomplyssh their enterprise; and the Frenche kyng wrought as moch as he coude to the contrary, for he knewe moch of their intentes. Kyng Edwarde made all his provisyon in Englande, and all his men of warr, to be redy to passe the see, incontynent after the feest of saynt John, and so they dyde. Than the kynge went to Vyllenort, and there made his company to be lodged, as many as myght in the towne, and the other without, a long on the ryver syde, in tentes and pavylyons: and ther he taryed fro Maudelyn tyde tyll our lady day in Septembre, abyding wekely for the lordes of thempyre; and specially for the duke of Brabant, on whose commynge all the other abode. And whan the kyng of Englande sawe howe they came nat, he sent great messangers to eche of them, sommonyng them to come, as they had promysed, and to mete with hym at Machlyn, on saynt Gyles day, and than to shewe hym why they had taryed so long. Thus kyng Edwarde lay at Vyllenort, and kepte dayly at his cost and charge, well to the nombre of xvi. hundred men of armes, all come fro thother syde of the see; and x. M. archers, besyde all other provysions; the which was a marveylous great charge, besyde the great rewardes that he had gyven to the lordes, and besyde the great armyes that he had on the see. The Frenche kynge, on his part, had set Genowayes, Normayns, Bretons, Pycardes, and Spanyardes, to be redy on the see, to entre into England, assone as the warr were opened. These lordes of Almayne, at the kyng of Englande somons, came to Machlyn, and with moche besynesse finally they acorded, that the kyng of Englande might well sette forwarde within xv. dayes after; and to thentent that their warr shuld be the more laudable, thei agreed to send their defyances to the French kyng: first, the kyng of England, the duke of Guerles, the marques of Jullers, sir Robert Dartoyse, sir John of Heynalt, the marques of Musse, the marques of Blanquebourc, the lorde of Faulquemont, sir Arnold of Baquehen, the archbysshop of Colayne, sir Galeas, his brother, and al other lordes of thempyre. These defyances were written and sealed by all the lordes, except the duke of Brabant, who sayd he wold do his dede by hymselfe, at tyme convenyent. To bere these defyances into Fraunce, was charged the bysshop of Lyncolne, who bare them to Parys, and dyd his message in suche maner, that he coude nat be reproched nor blamed; and so he had a safe conduct to retourne agayne to his kyng, who was as than at Machlyne.

Chapter L

Of the batell on the see before Sluse in Flaunders bytwene the kyng of England and the Frenchmen.

Nowe let us leave somwhat to speke of therle of Henalt, and of the duke of Normandy, and speke of the kyng of England, who was on the see to the intent to arryve in Flaunders, and so into Heynalt, to make warr agaynst the Frenchmen. This was on mydsomer evyne, in the yer of our lorde M.CCC.xl. all thenglyssh flete was departed out of the ryver of Tames, and toke the way to Sluse. And the same tyme bytwene Blanqueberque and Sluse, on the see, was sir Hewe Kyryell, sir Peter Bahuchet, and Barbnoyr, and mo than sixscore great vessels, besyde other; and they wer of Normayns, bydaulx, Genowes, and Pycardes, about the nombre of xl. M.; ther they wer layd by the French kyng to defend the kyng of Englandes passage. The kyng of England and his came saylyng tyll he came before Sluse; and whan he sawe so great a nombre of shippes that their mastes semed to be lyke a gret wood, he demaunded of the maister of his shyp what peple he thought they were. He answered and sayd, Sir, I thynke they be Normayns layd here by the Frenche kyng, and hath done gret dyspleasur in Englande, brent your towne of Hampton, and taken your great shyppe the Christofer. A quoth the kyng, I have long desyred to fyght with the Frenchmen, and nowe shall I fyght with some of them, by the grace of God and saynt George, for truly they have done me so many dysplesures, that I shall be revenged, and I may. Than the king set all his shyppes in order, the grettest befor, well furnysshed with archers, and ever bytwene two shyppes of archers he had one shypp with men of armes; and than he made another batell to ly alofe with archers, to confort ever them that wer moost wery, yf nede were. And ther were a great nombre of countesses, ladyes, knyghtes wyves, and other damosels, that were goyng to se the quene at Gaunt; these ladyes the kyng caused to be well kept with thre hundred men of armes, and v. C. archers.

Whan the kyng and his marshals had ordered his batayls, he drewe up the seales, and cam with a quarter wynde, to have the vauntage of the sonne: and so at last they tourned a lytell to get the wynde at wyll. And whan the Normayns sawe they recule backe, they had marvell why they dyde so; and some sayd, They thynke themselfe nat mete to medyll with us, wherfore they woll go backe: they sawe well howe the kyng of England was ther personally, by reason of his baners. Than they dyd appareyle their flete in order, for they wer sage and good men of warr on the see, and dyd set the Christofer, the which they had won the yer before, to be formast, with many trumpettes and instrumentes, and so set on their ennemies. Ther began a sore batell on bothe partes; archers and crosbowes began to shote, and men of armes aproched, and fought hande to hande; and the better to come togyder, they had great hokes and grapers of yron, to cast out of one shyppe into another, and so tyed them fast togyder. Ther were many dedes of armes done, takyng, and rescuyng agayne: and at last, the great Christofer was first won by thenglysshmen, and all that were within it taken or slayne. Than ther was great noyse and crye, and thenglysshmen aproched and fortifyed the Christofer with archers, and made hym to passe on byfore to fyght with the Genoweys. This batayle was right fierse and terryble: for the batayls on the see ar more dangerous and fierser, than the batayls by lande; for on the see ther is no reculyng nor fleyng; ther is no remedy but to fight, and to abyde fortune, and every man to shewe his prowes. Of a trouthe, sir Hewe Kyriell, and sir Bahuchet, and Barbe Noyer, were ryght good and expert men of warre. This batayle endured fro the mornyng tyll it was noone, and thenglysshmen endured moche payne, for their ennemies were foure agaynst one, and all good men on the see. Ther the king of England was a noble knight of his owne hande, he was in the flouer of his yongth; in lykewyse so was the erle of Derby, Pembroke, Herforde, Huntyngdon, Northampton and Glocetter, sir Reynolde Cobham, sir Rycharde Stafforde, the lorde Percy, sir Water of Manny, sir Henry of Flaunders, sir John Beauchamp, the lorde Felton, the lorde of Multon, sir Robert Dartoys called erle of Rychmont, and dyverse other lordes and knyghtes, who bare themselfe so valyantly with some socours that they had of Bruges, and of the countrey there about, that they obtayned the vyctorie. So that the Frenchmen, Normayns, and other were dysconfetted, slayne, and drowned: there was nat one that scaped, but all were slayne. Whane this vyctorie was atchyved, the kyng all that nyght abode in his shyppe before Sluse, with great noyse of trumpettes and other instrumentes. Thyder came to se the kynge, dyvers of Flaunders, suche as had herde of the kynges commyng. And than the kyng demaunded of the burgesses of Bruges, howe Jaques Dartvell dyd: they answered, that he was gone to the erle of heynalt, agaynst the duke of Normandy, with lx. M. Flemynges. And on the next day, the which was mydsomer day, the kyng and all his toke lande, and the kyng on fote went a pylgrimage to our lady of Ardenbourge, and there herd masse and dyned, and thane toke his horse and rode to Gaunt, where the quene recyved hym with great joye; and all his caryage came after, lytell and lytell. Than the kyng wrote to therle of Heynault, and to thym within the castell of Thyne, certyfieng them of his arryvall; and whan therle knewe therof, and that he had dysconfyted the army on the see, he dysloged, and gave leve to all the souldyours to depart; and toke with hym to Valencennes, all the great lordes, and ther feasted them honourable, and specially the duke of Brabant, and Jaques Dartvell. And ther Jaques Dartvell, openly in the market place, in the presence of all the lordes, and of all such as wold here hym, declared what right the kyng of Englande had to the crowne of France, and also what puyssaunce the thre countreis were of, Flaunders, Heynault, and Brabant, surely joyned in one alyance. And he dyde so by his great wysdome, and plesaunt wordes, that all people that harde hym, praysed hym moche, and sayd howe he had nobly spoken, and by great experyence. And thus he was greatly praysed, and it was sayd, that he was well worthy to governe the countie of Flaunders. Than the lordes departed, and promysed to mete agayne within viii. dayes at Gaunt, to se the kyng of England: and so they dyd. And the kyng feasted them honorably, and so dyd the quene, who was as than nuly purifyed of a sonne called John, who was after duke of Lancastre, by his wyfe, doughter to duke Henry of Lanncastre. Than ther was a counsell set to be at Vyllenort, and a day lymitted.

Chapter LXVIII

Howe the erle Mountfort dyd homage to the kyng of England for the duchy of Bretayne.

Thus therle Mountfort conquered the countrey, and made hymselfe to be called duke of Bretayne; than he went to a port on the see syde, called Gredo; thane he sent his people abrode to kepe the townes and fortresses that he had won. Than he toke the see, with a certayne with hym, and so arryved in Cornwall, in England, at a port called Chepse; than he enquered where the kynge was, and it was shewed hym howe that he was at Wyndsore. Than he rode thyderwarde, and came to Wyndsore, wher he was receyved with gret joye and feest, bothe of the kyng and of the quene, and of all the lordes. Than he shewed the kynge and his counsayle howe he was in possession of the duchy of Bretayne, fallen to hym by succession, by the deth of his brother, last duke of Breten; but he feared lest that sir Charles of Bloyes, and the Frenche kynge wolde put hym out therof by puyssance, wherfore he sayd, he was come thyder to relyve, and to holde the duchy of the kyng of Englande, by fealtie and homage, for ever, so that he wolde defende hym agaynst the Frenche kynge, and all other that shulde put hym to any trouble for the mater. The kynge of Englande ymagined that his warre agaynste the Frenche kynge shulde be well fortifyed by that meanes, and howe that he coude nat have no more profitable way for hym to entre into France, than by Bretayne, remembring howe the Almayns and Brabances had done lytell or nothyng for hym, but caused hym to spende moche money; wherfore, joyously he condyscended to therle Mountfortes desyre, and there toke homage by the handes of therle, callyng hymselfe duke of Bretaygne. And ther the kyng of Englande, in the presence of suche lordes as were ther, bothe of Bretayne and of Englande, promysed that he wolde ayde, defende, and kepe hym as his liege man, agaynst every man, Frenche kyng and other. This homage and promyses were writen and sealed, and every partie had his part delyverd; besyde that, the kynge and the quene gave to therle and to his company, many great gyftes, in such wyse, that they reputed hym for a noble kyng, and worthy to raygne in gret prosperyte. Than therle toke his leave and departed, and toke agayne the see, and arryved at the forsayd part of Gredo, in base Bretayne, and so came to Nauntes to his wyfe, who sayde howe he had wrought by good and dyscrete counsayle.

Chapter LXXVI

Howe the Scottes besieged a castell of therle of Salysburies.

Than king Davyd was counselled to drawe abacke along by the ryver of Tyne, and to drawe toward Carlyle; and as he went thyderward, he loged that nyght besyde a castel of therle of Salysburies, the whiche was well kept with men a warr; captayne therof was sir Wyllyam Montagu, son to therle of Salysburis suster. The next day the Scottes dysloged to go towarde Carlyle, they had moch caryage with them, of such pyllage as they had won at Dyram. Whan syr Wyllyam Montagu sawe how the Scottes passed by without restyng, than he with xl. with him yssued out a horsbacke, and folowed covertly the hynder trayne of the Scottes, who had horses so charged with baggage, that they might scant go any gret pace. And he overtoke them at thentryng into a wood, and set on them, and ther slewe and hurt of the Scottes mo than CC. and toke mo than sixscore horses charged with pyllage, and so led them toward the castell. The cry and brunt of the flight came to the heryng of syr Wyllyam Duglas, who had the charge of the reregarde, and as than he was past the wood. Whan he sawe the Scottes came fleyng over the dales and mountayns he had great marvell, and than he and all his company ran forth, and rested nat tyll they came to the fote of the castell, and mounted the hyll in hast; but or he came to the bayls, thenglysshumen were entred, and had closed the barryers, and put their pray in saftie. Than the Scottes began to assayle feersly, and they within defended them; ther these two Wyllyams dyd what they might, eche to greve other; this assaut endured so long, that all thoost came thyder, kyng and all. Whan the kyng and his counsell sawe how his men were slayne, lyeng in the felde, and the assylantes sore hurt, without wynning of any thyng, than he commaunded to cease thassaut, and to lodge; than every man began to seke for his logyng, and to gader togyder the deed men, and to dresse theym that were hurt. The next day the kyng of Scottes commaunded that every man shulde be redy to assayle, and they within were redy to defende: there was a sore assaut, and a perylous: ther might a ben sene many noble dedes on both partes. Ther was within present the noble countesse of Salysbury, who was as than reputed for the most sagest and fayrest lady of all England: the castell parteyned to her husbande therle of Salisbury, who was taken prisoner, with the erle of Suffolke, before Lyle in Flanders, as ye have harde before, and was in prison as than in the chatelot of Parys. The kyng of Englande gave the same castel to the sayd erle, whan he maryed first the sayd lady, for the prowes and gode servyce that he had done before, whan he was called but sir Wyllyam Montagu; this noble lady conforted them greatly within, for by the regarde of such a lady, and by her swete conforting, a man ought to be worthe two men at nede. This assaut dured long, and the Scottes lost many of their men, for they adventured themselfe hardely, and caryed wood and tymbre, to have fylled the dykes, to thyntent to bring their engyns to the walles, but they within defended themselfe so valyantly, that the assaylantes were fayne to drawe abacke.

Than the kyng commaunded the ingens to be wel kept that night, and the next day to enforce the assaut; than every man drue to their lodgyng, except those that kept thyngens. Some wept the deth of their frendes, other conforted them that were hurt: they of the castell sawe well, if kynge Davyd contynued his sege, how they shuld have moche ado to defende them and their castell; wherof they toke counsell amonge them, to sende to kyng Edward, who lay at Yorke, as it was shewed them, by suche prisoners as they had taken of the Scottes. Than they loked among them who shulde do the message, but they coude fynde none that wolde leave the castell, and the presence of the fayre lady to do that dede. So ther was among them great stryfe.

Than whan the captayne sir Wyllyam Montagu sawe that, he sayd, Sirs, I se well the trueth and good wyll that ye bere to my lady of this house, so that for the love of her and for you all, I shall put my body in adventur to do this message, for I have suche trust in you, that ye shall right well defende this castell tyll I retourne agayne: and on thother syde, I have suche trust in the king, our soverayne lorde, that I shall shortly bring you suche socours, that shall cause you to be joyfull, and than I trust the kyng shall so rewarde you, that ye shal be content: of these wordes the countesse and all other wer right joyefull. And whan the night came the sayd sir Wyllyam made hym redy, as prively as he might, and it happed so well for hym, that it rayned all night, so that the Scottes kept styll within their lodgynges. Thus at mydnight, sir Wyllyam Montagu passed through thoost, and was nat sene, and so rode forth tyll it was day; than he met ii. Scottes, halfe a leage fro thost, drivyng before them two oxen and a cowe towarde thoost. Syr Wyllyam knewe wel they wer Scottes and set on them, and wounded them bothe, and slewe the catell, to thyntent that they of thost shuld have none ease by them; than he sayd to the two hurt Scottes, Go your wayes, and say to your kyng, that Wyllyam of Montague hath thus passed through his hoost, and is goyng to fetch ayde of the kyng of Englande, and so departed. Than the same mornynge, the kyng of Scottes made a feerse assaut, but nothing coude he wyn, and every day lightly they made assaut: than his counsell sawe how he dyd but lese his men, and that the kyng of England might well come thyder, or the castell were won. Thane they by one acorde counselled their kyng to depart, sayeng, how the abyding ther, was nat for his profet, nor yet for his honour; and sayd, Sir, ye have honourably achyved your enterprise, and have done great dispyte to the Englysshmen, in that ye have ben in this contre a xii. dayes, and taken and distroyed the cytie of Dyrrame; wherfore, sir, all thynges consydred, it were good nowe that ye retourned, and take with you your pyllage that ye have wonne, and another tyme ye may returne agayne whan it pleaseth you. The kyng, who wolde nat do agaynst the opynyons of all his counsell, agreed to them, sore agaynst his mynde: howbeit, the next mornyng he dysloged, and all his host, and toke the way streyght to the great forest of Gedeours, there to tary at their ease, and to knowe what the kyng of Englande wolde do farther, other to goo backe agayne, or els to entre into Scotlande.

Chapter LXXVII

Howe the kyng of Englande was in amours with the countesse of Salisbury.

The same day that the Scottes departed fro the sayd castell, kyng Edward came thyder, with all his host, about noon, and came to the same place wher as the Scottes had loged, and was sore displeased that he founde nat the Scottes ther, for he came thyder in such hast that his horse and men wer sore traveled. Than he commaunded to lodge ther that nyght, and sayd, howe he wolde go se the castell, and the noble lady therin, for he had nat sene her sythe she was maryed before; than every man toke his logyng as he lyst. And assone as the kyng was unarmed, he toke a x. or xii. knyghtes with hym, and went to the castell to salute the countesse of Salisbury, and to se the maner of the assautes of the Scottes, and the defence that was made agaynst them. Assone as the lady knewe of the kynges commyng, she set opyn the gates, and came out so richely be sene, that every man marveyled of her beauty, and coude nat cease to regarde her noblenes with her great beauty, and the gracyous wordes and countenaunce that she made. Whan she came to the kyng, she knelyd downe to the yerth, thankyng hym of his socours, and so ledde hym into the castell, to make hym chere and honour, as she that coude ryght well do it: every man regarded her marvelusly; the king hymselfe coude nat witholde his regardyng of her, for he thought that he never sawe before, so noble, nor so fayre a lady: he was stryken therewith to the hert, with a sparcle of fyne love, that endured longe after; he thought no lady in the worlde so worthy to be beloved as she. Thus they entred into the castell, hande in hande; the lady ledde hym first into the hall, and after into the chambre, nobly aparelled; the kyng regarded so the lady that she was abasshed. At last he went to a wyndo to rest hym and so fell in a gret study: the lady went about to make chere to the lordes and knyghtes that were ther, and commaunded to dresse the hall for dyner. Whan she had al devysed and commaunded, thane she came to the kyng with a mery chere, who was in a gret study, and she sayd Dere syr, why do ye study so? for, your grace nat dyspleased, it aparteyneth nat to you so to do: rather ye shulde make good chere and be joyfull, seyng ye have chased away your enmies, who durst nat abyde you: let other men study for the remynant. Than the kyng sayd, A, dere lady, knowe for trouthe, that syth I entred into the castell, ther is a study come to my mynde, so that I can nat chuse but to muse, nor I can nat tell what shall fall therof; put it out of my herte I can nat. A sir, quoth the lady, ye ought alwayes to make good chere, to confort therwith your peple: God hath ayded you so in your besynes, and hath gyven you so great graces, that ye be the moste douted and honoured prince in all christendome, and if the kyng of Scottes have done you any dyspyte or damage, ye may well amende it whan it shall please you, as ye have done dyverse tymes or this; sir, leave your musyng and come into the hall, if it please you, your dyner is all redy. A, fayre lady, quoth the kyng: other thynges lyeth at my hert that ye knowe nat of: but surely the swete behavyng, the perfyt wysedom, the good grace, noblenes, and exellent beauty that I se in you, hath so sore surprised my hert, that I can nat but love you, and without your love I am but deed. Than the lady sayde, A, ryght noble prince, for Goddes sake mocke nor tempt me nat: I can nat byleve that it is true that ye say, nor that so noble a prince as ye be, wold thynke to dyshonour me and my lorde, my husbande, who is so valyant a knight, and hath done your grace so gode servyce, and as yet lyethe in prison for your quarell; certenly sir, ye shulde in this case have but a small prayse, and nothyng the better therby: I had never as yet such a thought in my hert, nor I trust in God never shall have, for no man lyveng; if I had any suche intencyon, your grace ought nat all onely to blame me, but also to punysshe my body, ye and by true justice to be dismembred. Therwith the lady departed fro the kyng, and went into the hall to hast the dyner; than she returned agayne to the kyng and broght some of his kynghtes with her, and sayd, Sir, yf it please you to come into the hall, your knightes abideth for you to wasshe, ye have ben to long fastyng. than the kyng went into the hall and wassht, and sat down amonge his lordes, and the lady also; the kyng ete but lytell, he sat styll musyng, and as he durst, he cast his eyen upon the lady: of his sadnesse his knyghtes had marvell, for he was nat acustomed so to be; some thought it was bycause the Scottes were scaped fro hym. All that day the kyng taryed ther, and wyst nat what to do: somtyme he ymagined that honour and trouth defended him to set his hert in such a case, to dyshonour such a lady, and so true a knyght as her husband was, who had alwayes well and truely served hym. On thother part, love so constrayned hym, that the power therof surmounted honour and trouth: thus the kyng debated in hymself all that day, and all that night; in the mornyng he arose and dysloged all his hoost, and drewe after the Scottes, to chase them out of his realme. Than he toke leave of the lady, sayeng, My dere lady, to God I commende you tyll I returne agayne, requiryng you to advyse you otherwyse than ye have sayd to me. Noble prince, quoth the lady, God the father glorious be your conduct, and put you out of all vylayne thoughtes; sir, I am, and ever shal be redy to do your grace servyce to your honour and to myne. Therwith the kyng departed all abasshed; and soo folowed the Scottes tyll he came to the cyte of Berwyke, and went and lodged within iiii. leages of the forest of Gedeors, wher as kyng Davyd and all his company were entred, in trust of the great wyldernesse. The kyng of England taryed ther a iii. dayes, to se if the Scottes wold yssue out to fight with hym; in these thre dayes ther were dyvers skirmysshes on bothe parties, and dyvers slayne, taken, and sore hurte amonge the Scottes. Sir Wyllyam Duglas was he that dyd moost trouble to thenglysshemen; he bare azure, a comble sylver, thre starres goules.

Chapter LXXXIX

Of the feest and justynge made at London by the kyng of England for the love of the countesse of Salisbury.

Ye have well harde here before howe the kynge of Englande had great warres in dyvers countreis, and had men of warre in garysons, to his gret cost and charge; as in Picardy, Normandy, Gascoyne, Xaynton, Poyctou, Bretayne, and Scotlande: ye have harde also before how the kyng was stryken in love with the countesse of Salisbury; love quickened hym day and night; her fresshe beautie and godely demeanour was ever in his remembrance, though therle of salisbury was one of the privyest of his counsell, and one of them that had done hym best servyce. So it fell that for the love of this lady, and for the great desyre that the king had to se her, he caused a great feest to be cryed, and a justyng to be holden in the cyti of London in the myddes of August. The which cry was also made in Flaunders, in Heynault, in Brabant, and in Fraunce, gyveng all commers out of every contrey safe conduct to come and go: and had gyven in commaundement through his owne realme that all lordes, knyghtes, squyers, ladyes, and domosels shuld be ther without any excuse, and commaunded expresly the erle of salisbury that the lady his wyfe shulde be ther, and to bring with her all ladyes and damosels of that countrey. Therle graunted the kyng as he that thought none yvell: the gode lady durst nat say nay; howbeit she came sore agaynst her wyll, for she thought well ynough wherfore it was; but she durst nat dyscover the mater to her husband; she thought she wolde deale so, to bringe the kynge fro his opynion. this was a noble feest; there was the erle Wyllyam of Heynalt and sir John of Heynalt his uncle, and a great nombre of lordes and knyghtes of hyghe lynage; there was great daunsynge and justynge the space of xv. dayes; the lorde John, eldyst son to the vycount Beaumonde in England was slayne in the justes. All ladyes and damoselles were fresshely besene accordyng to their degrees, except Alys countesse of Salisbury, for she went as simply as she myght, to the intent that the kyng shulde nat sette his regarde on her, for she was fully determyned to do no maner of thynge that shulde tourne to her dyshonour nor to her husbandes. At this feest was sir Henry with the wrye necke, erle of Lancastre, and sir Henry his sonne, erle of Derby; sir Robert Dartoyes, erle of Rychmount; the erle of Northampton and of Glocetter, the erle of Warwyke, the erle of Salisbury, the erle of Penneforde, the erle of Quenforde, the erle of Suffolke, the baron of Stafforde, and dyvers other lordes and knyghtes of Englande. And or all these nobles departed, the kyng receyved letters fro divers lordes of sundrie countreis, as out of Gascoyne, Bayon, Flaunders, fro Jaques Dartvell, and out of Scotlande fro the lorde Rose and the lorde Persy, and fro sir Edward Baylleull captayne of Berwyke, who sygnifyed the kynge that the Scottes helde but simply the trewse concludedde the yere before, for they newely assembled togyder moch people, for what entent they coude nat tell. Also the captayne in Poyctou, Xanton, Rochell, and Burdeloyes, wrote to the kyng howe the Frenchmen made great preparacions for the warre, for the peace made at Arras was nere expyred, wherfore it was tyme for the kyng to take counsayle and advyse; and so he aunswered the messangers fro poynt to poynt.

Chapter CXXII

Howe the kynge of Englande rode in thre batayls through Normandy.

Whane the kynge of Englande arryved in the Hogue saynt Wast, the kyng yssued out of his shyppe, and the firste fote that he sette on the grounde, he fell so rudely, that the blode brast out of his nose. The knyghtes that were aboute hym toke hym up and sayde, Sir, for Goddessake entre agayne into your shyppe, and come nat a lande this day, for this is but an yvell signe for us. Than the kyng answered quickely and sayd, Wherfore, this is a good token for me, for the land desyreth to have me. Of the whiche answere all his men were right joyfull. So that day and nyght the kyng lodged on the sandes, and in the meane tyme dyscharged the shyppes of their horses and other bagages. There the kyng made two marshals of his hoost, the one the lorde Godfray of Harecourt, and the other therle of Warwyke, and the erle of Arundell constable. And he ordayned that therle of Huntyngdon shulde kepe the flete of shyppes with C. men of armes, and iiii. C. archers: and also he ordayned thre batayls, one to go on his right hande, closyng to the see syde, and the other on his lyfte hande, and the kynge hymselfe in the myddes, and every night to lodge all in one felde. Thus they sette forth as they were ordayned, and they that went by the see toke all the shyppes that they founde in their wayes; and so long they went forthe, what by see and what by lande, that they came to a good port, and to a good towne called Harflewe, the which incontynent was wonne, for they within gave up for feare of dethe. Howebeit, for all that the towne was robbed, and moche golde and sylver there founde, and ryche jewels: there was founde so moche rychesse, that the boyes and vyllayns of the hoost sette nothyng by good furred gownes: they made all the men of the towne to yssue out and to go into the shyppes, bycause they wolde nat suffre them to be behynde them, for feare of rebellyng agayne. After the towne of Harflewe was thus taken and robbed without brennyng, than they spredde abrode in the countrey, and dyd what they lyst, for there was nat to resyst them. At laste they came to a great and a ryche towne called Cherbourgue; the towne they wan and robbed it, and brent parte therof, but into the castell they coude nat come, it was so stronge and well furnysshed with men of warre: thane they passed forthe, and came to Mountbourgue, and toke it and robbed and brent it clene. In this maner they brent many other townes in that countrey, and wan so moche rychesse, that it was marvell to rekyn it. Thanne they came to a great towne well closed, called Quarentyne, where ther was also a strong castell, and many soudyours within to kepe it; thane the lordes came out of their shyppes and feersly made assaut. The burgesses of the towne were in great feare of their lyves, wyves and chyldren: they suffred thenglysshemen to entre into the towne agaynst the wyll of all the soudyours that were ther; they putte all their goodes to thenglysshmens pleasures, they thought that moost advauntage. Whan the soudyours within sawe that, they went into the castell: the Englysshmen went into the towne, and two dayes toguyder they made sore assautes, so that whan they within se no socoure, they yelded up, their lyves and goodes savyed; and so departed. Thenglysshmen had their pleasure of that good towne and castell, and whan they sawe they might nat mentayne to kepe it, they set fyre therin and brent it, and made the burgesses of the towne to entre into their shyppes, as they had done with them of Harflewe, Chyerburgue, and Mountbourge, and of other townes that they had wonne on the see syde; all this was done by the batayle that went by the see syde, and by them on the see togyder. Nowe let us speke of the kinges batayle: whan he had sent his first batayle alonge by the see syde, as ye have harde, wherof one of his marshals therle of Warwyke was captayne, and the lorde Cobham with hym, than he made his other marshall to lede his hoost on his lyft hande, for he knewe the yssues, and entrees of Normandy better than any other dyd ther. The lorde Godfray as marshall rode forthe with fyve hundred men of armes, and rode of fro the kynges batayle as sixe or sevyne leages, in brennynge and exilyng the countrey, the which was plentyfull of every thynge; the granges full of corne, the houses full of all ryches, riche burgesses, cartes and charyottes, horse, swyne, mottons, and other beestes. They toke what them lyst and brought into the kynges hoost, but the soudyours made no count to the kynge nor to none of his offycers of the golde and sylver that they dyd gette, they kept that to themselfe. Thus sir Godfray of Harecourt rode every day of fro the kynges hoost, and for moost parte every nyght resorted to the kynges felde. The kyng toke his way to saynt Lowe, in Constantyne, but or he came ther he lodged by a ryver, abyding for his men that rode along by the see syde; and whan they were come, they sette forthe their caryage, and therle of Warwyke, therle of Suffolke, sir Thomas Hollande and sir Raynolde Cobham, and their company, rode out on the one syde, and wasted and exiled the contrey, as the lorde Harecourt hadde done; and the kynge ever rode bytwene these bataylles, and every nyght they logedde togyder.

Chapter CXXIII

Of the great assemble that the Frenche kynge made to resyst the kyng of Englande.

Thus by thenglysshmen was brent, exyled, robbed, wasted, and pylled, the good plentyfull countrey of Normandy. Thanne the Frenche kyng sent for the lorde John of Heynalt, who came to hym with a great nombre; also the kyng sende for other men of armes, dukes, erles, barownes, knyghtes, and squyers, and assembled togyder the grettest nombre of people that had ben sene in France a hundred yere before. He sent for men into so ferr countreys, that it was longe or they came togyder, wherof the kynge of Englande dyde what hym lyste in the meane season. The French kyng harde well what he dyd, and sware and sayd, howe they shulde never retourne agayne unfought withall, and that suche hurtes and damages as they had done shulde be derely revenged; wherfore he had sent letters to his frendes in thempyre, to suche as wer farthest of, and also to the gentyll kyng of Behayne, and to the lorde Charles his son, who fro thensforthe was called kynge of Almaygne, he was made kynge by the ayde of his father and the Frenche kyng, and had taken on hym the armes of thempyre: the Frenche kyng desyred them to come to hym with all their powers, to thyntent to fyght with the kynge of Englande, who brent and wasted his countrey. These princes and lordes made them redy with great nombre of men of armes, of Almaynes, Behaynoes, and Luxambroses, and so came to the Frenche kyng. Also kyng Philyppe send to the duke of Lorayne, who came to serve hym with CCC. speares: also ther came therle Samynes in Samynoes, therle of Salebruges, the erle of Flaunders, the erle Wyllyam of Namure, every man with a fayre company. Ye have harde here before of the order of thenglysshmen, howe they went in thre batayls, the marshalles on the right hande and on the lyft, the kyng and the prince of Wales his sonne in the myddes. They rode but small journeys, and every day toke their lodgynges bytwene noone and thre of the clocke, and founde the countrey so fruteful, that they neded nat to make no provisyon for their hoost, but all onely for wyne, and yet they founde reasonably sufficyent therof. It was no marveyle though they of the countrey were afrayed, for before that tyme they had never sene men of warre, nor they wyst nat what warre or batayle ment. They fledde away as ferr as they might here spekyng of thenglysshmen, and left their houses well stuffed, and graunges full of corne, they wyst nat howe to save and kepe it. The kynge of Englande and the prince had in their batayle a thre thousand men of armes and sixe thousande archers and a ten thousande men a fote, besyde them that rode with the marshals. Thus as ye have harde, the kyng rode forth, wastynge and brennyng the countrey, without brekyng of his order: he left the cytie of Constance, and went to a great towne called saynt Lowe, a rych towne of drapery, and many riche burgesses. In that towne ther were dwellyng an viii. or nynescore burgesses, crafty men: whanne the kynge came ther, he toke his lodgyng without, for he wolde never lodge in the towne, for feare of fyre, but he sende his men before, and anone the towne was taken and clene robbed: it was harde to thynke the great ryches that there was won, in clothes specially; clothe wolde ther have ben solde good chepe, yf ther had ben any byers. Than the kynge went towarde Cane, the which was a gretter towne, and full of drapery and other marchauntdyse, and riche burgesses, noble ladyes and damosels, and fayre churches, and specially two great and riche abbeys, one of the Trynyte, another of saynt Stephyn; and on the one syde of the towne, one of the fayrest castels of all Normandy, and capitayn therin was Robert of Blargny, with thre hundred Genowayes; and in the towne was therle of Ewe and of Guynes, constable of Fraunce, and therle of Tankervyll, with a good nombre of men of warr. The king of England rode that day in good order, and logedde all his batayls togyder that night, a two leages fro Cane, in a towne with a lytell havyn, called Haustreham, and thyder came also all his navy of shyppes, with therle of Huntyngdone who was governour of them. The constable and other lordes of France that nyght watched well the towne of Cane, and in the mornyng armed them with all them of the towne; than the constable ordayned that none shulde yssue out, but kepe their defences on the walles, gate, bridge, and ryver, and left the subbarbes voyde, bycause they were nat closedde, for they thought they shulde have ynough to do to defende the towne, bycause it was nat closedde but with the ryver; they of the towne sayde howe they wolde yssue out, for they were strong ynough to fyght with the kyng of Englande. Whan the constable sawe their good wyls, he sayd, In the name of God be it, ye shall nat fyght without me. Than they yssued out in good order, and made good face to fyght and to defende theym and to putte their lyves in adventure.

Chapter CXXVI

Howe the French kyng folowed the kyng of Englande into Beauvoysinoys.

Nowe lette us speke of kyng Philyppe, who was at saynt Denyse and his people aboute hym, and dayly encreased. Thane on a day he departed, and rode so longe that he came to Coppygny du Guyse, a thre leages fro Amyense, and there he taryed. The kyng of Englande beyng at Araynes, wyst nat where for to passe the ryver of Some, the which was large and depe, and all briges were broken and the passages well kept. Than at the kynges commaundement his two marshals with M. men of armes and two M. archers, went along the ryver to fynde some passag, and passed by Longpre, and came to the bridge of Atheny, the which was well kept with a gret nombre of knyghtes and squyers and men of the countrey. The Englysshmen alyghted a fote and assayled the Frenchmen from the mornynge tyll it was noone; but the bridge was so well fortifyed and defended, that the Englysshmen departed without wynning of any thynge. Than they went to a great towne called Fountayns on the ryver of Somme, the which was clene robbed and brent, for it was nat closed. Than they went to another towne called Longe in Ponthieu; they coulde nat wynne the bridge, it was so well kept and defended. Than they departed and went to Pyqueny, and founde the towne, the bridge, and the castell so well fortifyed, that it was nat lykely to passe there; the Frenche kyng hadde so well defended the passages, to thentent that the kyng of Englande shulde nat passe the ryver of Somme to fight with hym at his advauntage or els to famysshe hym there. Whane these two marshals had assayed in all places to fynde passage and coude fynde none, they retourned agayne to the king, and shewed howe they coude fynde no passage in no place; the same night the Frenche kynge came to Amyense, with mo than a hundred M. men. The kynge of Englande was right pensyfe, and the next morning harde masse before the sonne rysinge and than dysloged; and every man folowed the marshals baners, and so rode in the countrey of Vimewe, aprochynge to the good towne of Abvyle, and founde a towne therby, wherunto was come moche people of the countrey in trust of a lytell defence that was there; but thenglysshmen anone wanne it, and all they that were within slayne, and many taken of the towne and of the countrey; the kynge toke his lodgynge in a great hospytall that was there. The same day the Frenche kynge departed fro Amyense, and came to Araynes about noone, and thenglysshmen were departed thense in the mornyng. The Frenchmen founde there great provisyon that the Englysshmen had left behynde them, bycause they departed in hast; there they founde flesshe redy on the broches, brede and pastyes in the ovyns, wyne in tonnes and barelles, and the tabuls redy layed. There the Frenche kyng lodged and taryed for his lordes: that nyght the kyng of England was lodged at Osyement. At nyght whane the two marshalles were retourned, (who had that day overrone the countrey to the gates of Abvyl and to saynt Valery, and made a great skirmysshe there,) than the kynge assembled togyder his counsayle and made to be brought before hym certayne prisoners of the countrey of Ponthieu and of Vymeu. The kyng right curtesly demaunded of theym if ther were any among them that knewe any passage byneth Abvyle, that he and his hoost might passe over the ryver of Somme; yf he wolde shewe hym therof, he shulde be quyte of his raunsome, and xx. of his company for his love. Ther was a varlet called Gobyn a Grace, who stept forthe and sayde to the kyng, Sir, I promyse you on the jeopardy of my heed I shall bringe you to suche a place, where as ye and all your hoost shall passe the ryver of Some without paryll. There be certayne places in the passage that ye shall passe xii. men a front two tymes bytwene day and nyght, ye shall nat go in the water to the knees: but whan the fludde cometh, the ryver than waxeth so gret, that no man can passe; but whan the fludde is gon, the whiche is two tymes bytwene day and nyght, than the ryver is so lowe that it may be passed without danger, bothe a horsebacke and a fote. The passage is harde in the botom with whyte stones, so that all your caryage may go surely; therfore the passage is called Blanch Taque; and ye make redy to departe be tymes, ye may be ther by the sonne rysinge. The kynge sayde, If this be trewe that ye say, I quyte thee thy raunsome and all thy company, and moreover shall gyve thee a hundred nobles: than the kynge commaunded every man to be redy at the sounde of the trumpette to departe.

Chapter CXXVII

Of the batayle of Blanchtaque bytwene the kyng of Englande and sir Godmar du Fay.

The kyng of Englande slepte nat moche that nyght, for atte mydnight he arose and sowned his trumpette; than incontynent they made redy caryages and all thynges, and atte the brekynge of the day they departed fro the towne of Oysement, and rode after the guydinge of Gobyn a Grace, so that they came by the sonne rysing to Blanch Taque; but as than the fludde was uppe so that they might nat passe; so the kynge taryed there tyll it was prime, than the ebbe came. The Frenche kyng had his currours in the countrey, who brought hym worde of the demeanoure of the Englysshmen; than he thought to close the kyng of Englande bytwene Abvyle and the ryver of Some, and so to fyght with hym at his pleasure. And whan he was at Amyense he had ordayned a great barowne of Normandy, called sir Godmar du Fay, to go and kepe the passage of Blanche Taque, where the Englysshmen must passe, or els in none other place. He had with hym M. men of armes and sixe thousand a fote, with the Genowayes; soo they went by saynt Reyngnyer in Ponthieu, and fro thens to Crotay, wher as the passage lay; and also he had with hym a great nombre of men of the countrey, and also a great nombre of theym of Mutterell; so that they were a twelfe thousand men one and other. Whan the Englysshe hoost was come thyder, sir Godmar du Fay araunged all his company to defende the passage: the kyng of England lette nat for all that; but whane the fludde was gone, he commaunded his marshals to entre into the water in the name of God and saynt George. Than they were hardy and coragyous entred on bothe parties, and many a man reversed; ther were some of the Frenchmen of Arthoyes and Pycardy, that were as gladde to juste in the water as on the drie lande. The Frenchemen defended so well the passage at the yssuing out of the water, that they had moche to do: the Genowayes dyde them great trouble with their crosbowes; on thother syde the archers of Englande shotte so holly togyder, that the Frenchmen were fayne to gyve place to the Englysshmen. There was a sore batayle, and many a noble feate of armes done on both sydes; finally thenglysshmen passed over and assembled togyder in the felde; the kynge and the prince passed and all the lordes: than the Frenchmen kept none array, but departed he that myght best. Whan sir Godmar sawe that dysconfiture, he fledde and saved hymselfe; some fledde to Abvyle and some to saynt Raygnyer; they that were there a fote coude nat flee, so that ther were slayne a great nombre of them of Abvyle, Muttrell, Arras, and of saynt Raygnier: the chase endured more than a great leag. And as yet all the Englysshmen were nat passed the ryver, and certayne currours of the kyng of Behayne and of sir John of Heynault came on them that were behynd, and toke certayn horses and caryages and slew dyvers or they coude take the passage. The French kyng the same mornynge was departed fro Araynes, trustyng to have founde thenglysshmen bytwene hym and the ryver of Some; but whan he harde howe that sir Godmar du Fay and his company were dysconfyted, he taryed in the felde and demaunded of his marshals what was best to do. They sayd, Sir, ye can nat passe the ryver but at the brige of Abvyll, for the fludde is come in at Blanche taque. Than he retourned and lodged at Abvyle. The kyng of Englande whan he was past the ryver, he thanked God, and so rode forthe in lyke maner as he dyde before. Than he called Gobyn a Grace, and dyd quyte hym his ransome and all his company, and gave hym a hundred nobles and a good horse. And so the kynge rode forthe fayre and easely, and thought to have lodged in a great town called Norell; but whan he knewe that the towne pertayned to the countesse of Dammerle, suster to the lorde Robert of Arthoys, the kyng assured the towne and countrey as moche as pertayned to her, and so went forthe; and his marshalles rode to Crotay on the see syde and brent the towne, and founde in the havyn many shippes and barkes charged with wynes of Poyctou, pertayning to the marchauntes of Xaynton and of Rochell: they brought the best therof to the kynges host. Than one of the marshals rode to the gates of Abvyle, and fro thens to saynt Reygnier, and after to the towne of Rue saynt Esperyte. This was on a Friday, and bothe batayls of the marshals retourned to the kynges hoost about noone, and so lodged all toguyder nere to Cressy in Ponthieu. The kynge of Englande was well enfourmed howe the Frenche kyng folowed after hym to fight. Than he sayd to his company, Lette us take here some plotte of grounde, for we wyll go no farther tylle we have sene our ennemyes; I have good cause here to abyde them, for I am on the ryght herytage of the quene my mother, the which lande was gyven at her maryage; I woll chalenge it of myne adversary Philyppe of Valoys. And bycause that he had nat the eyght part in nombre of men as the Frenche kyng had, therfore he commaunded his marshals to chose a plotte of grounde somwhat for his advauntage; and so they dyde, and thyder the kynge and his hoost went; than he sende his currours to Abvyle, to se if the Frenche kyng drewe that day into the felde or natte. They went forthe and retourned agayne, and sayde howe they coude se none aparence of his commyng; than every man toke their lodgyng for that day, and to be redy in the mornynge, at the sound of the trumpet, in the same place. This Friday the Frenche kynge taryed styll in Abvyle abyding for his company, and sende his two marshals to ryde out to se the dealyng of thenglysshmen; and at nyght they retourned, and sayde howe the Englysshmen were lodged in the feldes. That nyght the Frenche kyng made a supper to all the chefe lordes that were ther with hym; and after supper, thy kyng desyred them to be frendes ech to other: the kyng loked for the erle of Savoy, who shulde come to hym with a thousande speares, for he had receyved wages for a thre monethes of them at Troy in Campaigne.

Chapter CXXVIII

Of the order of the Englysshmen at Cressy, and howe they made thre batayls a fote.

On the Friday, as I sayd before, the kyng of Englande lay in the feldes, for the contrey was plentyfull of wynes and other vytayle, and if nede had ben, they had provisyon folowyng in cartes and other caryages. That night the kyng made a supper to all his chefe lordes of his hoost and made them gode chere: and whan they were all departed to take their rest, than the kynge entred into his oratorie, and kneled downe before the auter, prayeng God devoutly, that if he fought the next day, that he might achyve the journey to his honour; than aboute mydnight he layde hym downe to rest, and in the mornynge he rose betymes and harde masse, and the prince his sonne with hym, and the moste part of his company were confessed and houseled: and after the masse sayde, he commaunded every man to be armed and to drawe to the felde to the same place before apoynted. Than the kyng caused a parke to be made by the wode syde behynde his hoost, and ther was set all cartes and caryages, and within the parke were all their horses, for every man was a fote; and into this parke there was but one entre. Than he ordayned thre batayls; in the first was the yonge prince of Wales, with hym the erle of Warwyke and Canforde, the lorde Godfray of Harecourt, sir Reynolde Cobham, sir Thomas Holande, the lorde Stafforde, the lorde of Manny, the lorde Dalaware, sir John Chandos, sir Bartylmewe de Bomes, sir Robert Nevyll, the lorde Thomas Clyfforde, the lorde Bourchier, the lorde de la Tumyer, and dyvers other knyghtes and squyers that I can nat name; they wer an viii. hundred men of armes and two thousande archers, and a thousande of other with the Walsshmen: every lorde drue to the felde apoynted, under his owne baner and penone. In the second batayle was therle of Northampton, the erle of Arundell, the lorde Rosse, the lorde Lygo, the lorde Wylloughby, the lorde Basset, the lorde of saynt Aubyne, sir Loyes Tueton, the lorde of Myleton, the lorde de la Sell, and dyvers other, about an eight hundred men of armes and twelfe hundred archers. The thirde batayle had the kyng: he had sevyn hundred men of armes and two thousande archers: than the kyng lept on a hobby, with a whyte rodde in his hand, one of his marshals on the one hande and the other on the other hand; he rode fro renke to renke, desyringe every man to take hede that day to his right and honour. He spake it so swetely, and with so good countenance and mery chere, that all suche as were dysconfited toke courage in the seyng and heryng of hym. And whan he had thus visyted all his batayls, it was than nyne of the day; than he caused every man to eate and drinke a lytell, and so they dyde at their leaser. And afterwarde they ordred agayne their bataylles: than every man lay downe on the yerth and by hym his salet and bowe, to be the more fressher whan their ennemyes shulde come.

Chapter CXXIX

Thorder of the Frenchmen at Cressy, and howe they behelde the demeanour of thenglysshmen.

This Saturday the Frenche kynge rose betymes, and harde masse in Abvyle in his lodgyng in the abbey of saynt Peter, and he departed after the sonne rysing. Whan he was out of the towne two leages, aprochyng towarde his ennemyes, some of his lordes sayd to hym, Sir, it were good that ye ordred your batayls, and let all your fotemen passe somwhat on before, that they be nat troubled with the horsemen. Than the kyng sent iiii. knyghtes, the Moyne Bastell, the lorde of Noyers, the lorde of Beaujewe, and the lorde Dambegny to ryde to aviewe thenglysshe hoste, and so they rode so nere that they might well se part of their dealyng. Thenglysshmen sawe them well and knewe well howe they were come thyder to avieu them; they let them alone and made no countenance towarde them, and let them retourne as they came. And whan the Frenche kyng sawe these foure kynghtes retourne agayne, he taryed tyll they came to hym, and sayd, Sirs, what tidynges. These four knyghtes eche of them loked on other, for ther was none wolde speke before his companyon; finally, the kyng sayd to Moyne, who pertayned to the kyng of Behaygne, and had done in his dayes so moch, that he was reputed for one of the valyantest knyghtes of the worlde, Sir, speke you. Than he sayd, Sir, I shall speke, syth it pleaseth you, under the correction of my felawes; sir, we have ryden and sene the behavyng of your ennemyes; knowe ye for trouth they are rested in thre batayls abidyng for you. Sir, I woll counsell you as for my part, savynge your dyspleasure, that you and all your company rest here and lodg for this nyght, for or they that be behynde of your company be come hyther, and or your batayls be set in gode order, it wyll be very late, and your people be wery and out of array, and ye shall fynde your ennemis fresshe and redy to receyve you. Erly in the mornynge ye may order your bataylles at more leaser, and advyse your ennemis at more delyberacyon, and to regarde well what way ye woll assayle theym, for sir, surely they woll abyde you. Than the kynge commaunded that it shuld be so done; than his ii. marshals one rode before, another behynde, sayeng to every baner, Tary and abyde here in the name of God and saynt Denys. They that were formast taryed, but they that were behynde wolde nat tary, but rode forthe, and sayd howe they wolde in no wyse abyde tyll they were as ferr toward as the formast: and whan they before sawe them come on behynde, than they rode forward agayne, so that the kyng nor his marshals coude nat rule them. So they rode without order or good aray, tyll they came in sight of their ennemyes; and assone as the formast sawe them, they reculed them abacke without good aray; wherof they behynde had marvell and were abasshed, and thought that the formast company had ben fightynge; than they might have had leaser and rome to have gone forwarde if they had lyst; some went forthe, and some abode styll. The commons, of whom all the wayes bytwene Abvyle and Cressy were full, whan they sawe that they were nere to their ennemies, they toke their swerdes, and cryed Downe with them, let us sle them all. Ther was no man, though he were present at the journey, that coude ymagen or shewe the trouth of the yvell order that was among the Frenche partie, and yet they were a mervelous great nombre. That I write in this boke I lerned it specially of the Englysshmen, who well behelde their dealyng; and also certayne knyghtes of sir John of Heynaultes, who was alwayes about kyng Philyppe, shewed me as they knewe.

Chapter CXXX

Of the batayle of Cressy bytwene the kyng of England and the Frenche kyng.

Thenglysshmen who were in thre batayls, lyeng on the grounde to rest them, assone as they saw the Frenchmen aproche, they rose upon their fete fayre and easely without any hast, and aranged their batayls: the first, which was the princes batell, the archers there stode in maner of a herse and the men of armes in the botome of the batayle. Therle of Northampton and therle of Arundell with the second batell were on a wyng in good order, redy to confort the princes batayle, if nede were. The lordes and knyghtes of France came nat to the assemble togyder in good order, for some came before and some came after, in such hast and yvell order, that one of them dyd trouble another. Whan the French kyng sawe the Englysshmen, his blode chaunged, and sayde to his marshals, Make the Genowayes go on before, and begynne the batayle in the name of God and saynt Denyse. Ther were of the Genowayes crosbowes, about a fiftene thousand, but they were so wery of goyng a fote that day a six leages armed with their crosbowes, that they sayde to their constables, We be nat well ordred to fyght this day, for we be nat in the case to do any great dede of armes, we have more nede of rest. These wordes came to the erle of Alanson, who sayd, A man is well at ease to be charged with suche a sorte of rascalles, to be faynt and fayle nowe at moost nede. Also the same season there fell a great rayne and a clyps with a terryble thonder, and before the rayne ther came fleyng over bothe batayls a great nombre of crowes, for feare of the tempest commynge. Than anone the eyre beganne to waxe clere, and the sonne to shyne fayre and bright, the which was right in the Frenchmens eyen and on the Englysshmens backes. Whan the Genowayes were assembled toguyder, and beganne to aproche, they made a great leape and crye to abasshe thenglysshmen, but they stode styll and styredde nat for all that. Thane the Genowayes agayne the seconde tyme made another leape and a fell crye, and stepped forwarde a lytell, and thenglysshmen remeved nat one fote. Thirdly, agayne they leapt and cryed, and went forthe tyll they came within shotte: thane they shotte feersly with their crosbowes. Than thenglysshe archers stept forthe one pase, and lette fly their arowes so holly and so thycke, that it semed snowe. Whan the Genowayes felte the arowes persynge through heedes, armes and brestes, many of them cast downe their crosbowes and dyde cutte their strynges, and retourned dysconfited. Whan the Frenche kynge sawe them flye away, he sayd, Slee these rascals, for they shall lette and trouble us without reason. Than ye shulde have sene the men of armes dasshe in amonge them and kylled a great nombre of them; and ever styll the Englysshmen shot where as they sawe thyckest preace; the sharpe arowes ranne into the men of armes and into their horses, and many fell, horse and men, amonge the Genowayes, and whan they were downe, they coude nat relyve agayne, the preace was so thycke that one overthrewe another. And also amonge the Englysshemen there were certayne rascalles that went a fote with great knyves, and they went in among the men of armes, and slewe and murdredde many as they lay on the grounde, bothe erles, barownes, knyghtes, and squyers, wherof the kyng of Englande was after dyspleased, for he had rather they had bene taken prisoners. The valyant kyng of Behaygne, called Charles of Luzenbourge, sonne to the noble emperour Henry of Luzenbourge, for all that he was nyghe blynde, whan he understode the order of the batayle, he sayde to them about hym, where is the lorde Charles my son. His men sayde, Sir, we can nat tell, we thynke he be fightynge. Than he sayde, Sirs, ye ar my men, my companyons, and frendes in this journey, I requyre you bring me so farre forwarde, that I may stryke one stroke with my swerde. They sayde they wolde do his commaundement, and to the intent that they shulde nat lese hym in the prease, they tyed all their raynes of their bridelles eche to other, and sette the kynge before to acomplysshe his desyre, and so thei went on their ennemyes. The lorde Charles of Behaygne his sonne, who wrote hymselfe kyng of Almaygne, and bare the armes, he came in good order to the batayle; but whane he sawe that the matter wente awrie on their partie, he departed, I can nat tell you whiche waye. The kynge his father was so farre forewarde, that he strake a stroke with his swerde, ye and mo than foure, and fought valyantly and so dyde his company; and they adventured themselfe so forwarde, that they were ther all slayne, and the next day they were founde in the place about the kyng, and all their horses tyed eche to other. The erle of Alansone came to the batayle right ordynatly and fought with thenglysshmen; and the erle of Flaunders also on his parte; these two lordes with their companyes coosted the Englysshe archers and came to the princes batayle, and there fought valyantly longe. The Frenche kynge wolde fayne have come thyder whanne he sawe their baners, but there was a great hedge of archers before hym. The same day the Frenche kynge hadde gyven a great blacke courser to sir Johan of Heynault, and he made the lorde Johan of Fussels to ride on hym, and to bere his banerre. The same horse tooke the bridell in the tethe, and brought hym through all the currours of thenglysshmen, and as he wolde have retourned agayne, he fell in a great dyke and was sore hurt, and had ben ther deed, and his page had nat ben, who folowed hym through all the batayls and sawe wher his maister lay in the dyke, and had none other lette but for his horse, for thenglysshmen wolde nat yssue out of their batayle, for takyng of any prisoner; thane the page alyghted and relyved his maister; than he went nat backe agayn the same way that they came, there was tc many in his way. This batayle bytwene Broy and Cressy this Saturday was ryght cruell and fell, and many a feat of armes done that came nat to my knowledge. In the night dyverse knyghtes and squyers lost their maisters, and somtyme came on thenglysshmen, who receyved theym in suche wyse, that they were ever nighe slayne, for there was none taken to mercy nor to raunsome, for so the Englysshmen were determyned. In the mornyng the day of the batayle certayne Frenchemen and Almaygnes perforce opyned the archers of the princes batayle, and came and fought with the men of armes hande to hande. Than the seconde batayle of thenglysshmen came to socour the princes batayle, the whiche was tyme, for they had as than moche ado; and they with the prince sent a messanger to the kynge, who was on a lytell wyndmyll hyll. Than the knyght sayd to the kyng, Sir, therle of Warwyke, and therle of Canfort, sir Reynolde Cobham and other, suche as be about the prince your sonne, ar feersly fought with all and are sore handled, wherfore they desyre you that you and your batayle wolle come and ayde them; for if the Frenchmen encrease, as they dout they woll, your sonne and they shall have moche ado. Than the kynge sayde, Is my sonne deed or hurt, or on the yerthe felled? No sir, quoth the knyght, but he is hardely matched, wherfore he hathe nede of your ayde. Well, sayde the kyng, retourne to hym, and to them that sent you hyther, and say to them that they sende no more to me for any adventure that falleth, as long as my sonne is alyve; and also say to them that they suffre hym this day to wynne his spurres; for if God be pleased, I woll this journey be his and the honoure therof, and to them that be aboute hym. Than the knyght retourned agayn to them, and shewed the kynges wordes, the which gretly encouraged them, and repoyned in that they had sende to the kynge as they dyd. Sir Godfray of harecourt wolde gladly that the erle of Harecourt his brother myght have bene saved; for he hard say by them that sawe his baner, howe that he was ther in the felde on the Frenche partie, but sir Godfray coude nat come to hym betymes, for he was slayne or he coude come at hym, and so was also the erle of Almare, his nephue. In another place, the erle of Alenson, and therle of Flaunders, fought valyantly, every lorde under his owne baner; but finally, they coude nat resyst agaynst the puyssaunce of the Englysshemen, and so ther they were also slayne, and dyvers other knyghtes and squyers. Also therle Lewes of Bloyes, nephue to the Frenche kyng, and the duke of Lorayne fought under their baners, but at last they were closed in among a company of Englysshmen and Walsshemen, and there were slayne, for all their prowes. Also there was slayne the erle of Ausser, therle of saynt Poule and many other. In the evenynge the Frenche kynge, who had lefte about hym no mo than a threscore persons, one and other, wherof sir John of Heynalt was one, who had remounted ones the kynge, for his horse was slayne with an arowe; than he sayde to the kynge, Sir, departe hense, for it is tyme; lese nat yourselfe wylfully; if ye have losse at this tyme, ye shall recover it agayne another season. And soo he toke the kynges horse by the bridell, and ledde hym away in a maner perforce. Than the kyng rode tyll he came to the castell of Broy. The gate was closed, bycause it was by that tyme darke; than the kynge called the captayne, who came to the walles, and sayd, Who is that calleth there this tyme of nyght. Than the kynge sayde, Opyn your gate quickely, for this is the fortune of Fraunce. The captayne knewe than it was the kyng, and opyned the gate, and let downe the bridge; than the kyng entred, and he had with hym but fyve barownes, sir Johan of Heynault, sir Charles of Momorency, the lorde of Beaujewe, the lorde Dabegny, and the lorde of Mountfort. The kynge wolde nat tary there, but dranke and departed thense about mydnyght, and so rode by suche guydes as knewe the countrey, tyll he came in the mornynge to Amyense, and there he rested. This Saturday, the Englysshemen never departed fro their batayls for chasynge of any man, but kept styll their felde, and ever defended themselfe agaynst all such as came to assayle them. This batayle ended aboute evynsonge tyme.

Chapter CXXXI

Howe the next day after the batell the Englyssh-men disconfyted dyverse Frenchemen.

On this Saturday, whan the nyght was come and that thenglysshmen hard no more noyse of the Frenchemen, than they reputed themselfe to have the vyctorie, and the Frenchmen to be dysconfited, slayne and fledde away. Than they made great fyers and lyghted up torchesse and candelles, bycause it was very darke; than the kyng avayled downe fro the lytell hyll where as he stode; and of all that day tyll than, his helme came never of on his heed. Than he went with all his batayle to his sonne the prince and enbrased hym in his armes and kyst hym, and sayde, Fayre sonne, God gyve you good perseverance; ye ar my good son, thus ye have aquyted you nobly; ye ar worthy to kepe a realme; the prince inclyned himselfe to the yerthe, honouryng the kyng his father. This night they thanked God for their good adventure and made no boost therof, for the kynge wolde that no manne shulde be proude or make boost, but every man humbly to thanke God. On the Sonday in the mornyng there was suche a myst, that a man myght nat se the bredethe of an acre of lande fro hym. Than there departed fro the hoost, by the commaundement of the kyng and marshalles fyve hundred speares and two thousand archers, to se if they might se any Frenchemen gathered agayne togyder in any place. The same mornyng out of Abvyle and saynt Reyngnyer in Ponthieu, the commons of Rone, and of Beaujoys, yssued out of their townes, natte knowyng of the dysconfiture the day before. They met with thenglysshmen, wenyng they had bene Frenchmen; and whan thenglysshmen sawe them, they sette on them fresshly, and there was a sore batayle, but at last the Frenchemen fledde and kept none array. Their were slayne in the wayes and in hedges and busshes, mo thane sevyn thousande, and if the day had ben clere, there had never a one scaped. Anone after, another company of Frenchmen were mette by the Englysshmen, the archebysshoppe of Rone, and the great priour of Fraunce, who also knewe nothynge of the dysconfiture the day before, for they harde that the Frenche kynge shulde a fought the same Sonday, and they were goynge thyderwarde. Whane they mette with the Englysshmen, there was a great batayle, for they were a great nombre, but they coude nat endure agaynst the Englysshmen, for they were nyghe all slayne, fewe scaped, the two lordes were slayne. This mornyng thenglysshmen mette with dyverse Frenchmen, that had loste their way on the Saturday and had layen all nyght in the feldes, and wyst nat where the kyng was nor the captayns. They were all slayne, as many as were met with; and it was shewed me, that of the commons and men a fote of the cyties and good townes of France, ther was slayne foure tymes as many as were slayne the Saturday in the great batayle.

Chapter CXXXII

How the next day after the batayle of Cressey they that were deed were nombred by thenglysshmen.

The same Sonday, as the kyng of Englande came fro masse, suche as had ben sente forthe retourned and shewed the kyng what they had sene and done, and sayde, Sir, we thinke surely ther is now no more aparence of any of our ennemyes. Than the kyng sende to serche howe many were slayne, and what they were. Sir Reynolde Cobham, and sir Richard Stafforde with thre haraldes went to serche the felde and contrey; they visyted all them that were slayne and rode all day in the feldes, and retourned agayne to the hoost as the kyng was goynge to supper: they made just report of that they had sene, and sayde howe ther were xi. great princes deed, fourscore baners, xii. C. knyghtes, and mo than xxx. thousande other. Thenglysshmen kept styll their felde all that nyght; on the Monday in the mornyng the kyng prepared to depart. The kyng caused the deed bodyes of the great lordes to be taken up, and conveyed to Mutterell, and there buryed in holy grounde, and made a crye in the countrey to graunt truse for thre dayes, to thyntent that they of the countrey might serche the felde of Cressy to bury the deed bodyes. Than the kynge went forthe and came before the towne of Muttrell, by the see, and his marshals ranne towarde Hedyn and brent Vambam, and Seram, but they dyd nothyng to the castel, it was so strong and so well kept; they lodged that night on the ryver of Hedyn, towardes Blangy. The next day they rode towarde Bolayne and came to the towne of Wysame, there the kyng and the prince lodged, and taryed there a day to refresshe his men; and on the Wednysday the kyng came before the stronge towne of Calys.

Chapter CXXXIII

Howe the kyng of Englande layd siege to Calys, and howe all the poore people were put out of the towne.

In the towne of Calys ther was captayne a knyght of Burgone, called sir John de Vien, and with hym was sir Andrewe Dandrehen, sir John de Sury, sir Bardon de Belborne, sir Godfray de Lament, sir Pepyn de Urmue, and dyvers other knyghtes and squyers. Whan the kyng of England was come before Calys, he layd his siege and ordayned bastides bytwene the towne and the ryver; he made carpenters to make houses and lodgynges of great tymbre, and set the houses lyke stretes and coverd them with rede and brome, so that it was lyke a lytell towne; and there was every thynge to sell, and a markette place to be kept every Tuesday and Saturday for flesshe and fyssh, mercery ware, houses for cloth, for bredde, wyne, and all other thynges necessarie, such as came out of England or out of Flanders; ther they might bye what they lyst. Thenglysshmen ran often tymes into the countrey of Guynes, and into Trivynois, and to the gates of saynt Omers, and somtyme to Boleyn: they brought into their hoost great prayes. The kyng wolde nat assayle the towne of Calys, for he thought it but a lost labour; he spared his peple and his artillery, and sayd, howe he wolde famysshe them in the towne with long siege, without the French kyng come and reyse his siege perforce. Whan the capten of Calys sawe the manner and thorder of thenglysshmen, than he constrayned all poore and meane peple to yssue out of the towne: and on a Wednysday ther yssued out of men, women, and chyldren, mo than xvii. C. and as they passed through the hoost they were demaunded why they departed, and they answered and sayde, bycause they had nothyng to lyve on. Than the kyng dyd them that grace, that he suffred them to passe through his host without danger, and gave them mete and drinke to dyner, and every person ii.d. sterlyng in almes, for the which dyvers many of them prayed for the kynges prosperyte.

Chapter CXXXV

Howe sir Gaultier of Manny rode through all Fraunce by save conduct to Calys.

It was nat long after, but that sir Gaultier of Manny fell in communycation with a knyght of Normandy, who was his prisoner, and demaunded of hym what money he wolde pay for his raunsome. The knyght answered and sayde he wolde gladly pay thre M. crownes. Well, quoth the lorde Gaultyer, I knowe well ye be kynne to the duke of Normandy and wel beloved with hym, that I am sure, and if I wolde sore oppresse you, I am sure ye wolde gladly pay x. thousand crownes, but I shall deale otherwyse with you. I woll trust you on your faythe and promyse; ye shall go to the duke your lorde, and by your meanes gette a save conduct for me and xx. other of my company to ryde through Fraunce to Calys, payeng curtesly for all our expenses. And if ye can get this of the duke or of the kyng, I shall clerely quyte you your ransome with moche thanke, for I greatly desyre to se the kynge my maister, nor I wyll lye but one nyght in a place, tyll I come there; and if ye can nat do this, retourne agayn hyder within a moneth, and yelde yourself styll as my prisoner. The knyght was content and so went to Parys to the duke his lorde, and he obtayned this pasport for sir Gaultier of Manny, and xx. horse with hym all onely: this knyght retourned to Aguyllon, and brought it to sir Gaultier, and ther he quyted the knyght Norman of his raunsome. Than anone after, sir Gaultier toke his way and xx. horse with hym, and so rode through Auvergne and whan he taryed in any place, he shewed his letter and so was lette passe but whan he came to Orleaunce, for all his letter he was arested and brought to Parys, and there put in prison in the Chatelet. Whan the duke of Normandy knewe therof, he went to the kynge his father and shewed him howe sir Gaultier of Manny had his save conduct, wherfore he requyred the kynge as moche as he might to delyver hym, or els it shulde be sayde howe he had betrayed hym. The kyng answered and sayd howe he shulde be put to dethe, for he reputed hym for his great ennemy. Than sayd the duke, Sir, if ye do so, surely I shall never bere armour agaynst the kynge of Englande, nor all suche as I may let. And at his departyng, he sayd, that he wolde never entre agayn into the kynges host: thus the mater stode a certayne tyme. There was a knyght of Heynalt, called sir Mansart de Sue; he purchased all that he myght to helpe sir Water of Manny, and went often in and out to the duke of Normandy. Finally, the kyng was so counselled, that he was delyverd out of prison and all his costes payed: and the kynge sende for hym to his lodgyng of Nesle in Parys, and there he dyned with the kynge, and the kynge presented hym great gyftes and jewels, to the value of a thousand floreyns. Sir Gaultier of Manny receyved them on a condycion, that whan he cam to Cales, that if the kyng of Englande his maister were pleased that he shulde take them, than he was content to kepe them, or els to sende them agayne to the Frenche kyng, who sayd he spake lyke a noble man. Thane he toke his leave and departed, and rode so long by his journeys that he came into Heynalt, and taryed at Valencennes thre dayes, and so fro thens he went to Cales, and was welcome to the kynge. But whan the kyng harde that sir Gaultier of Manny had receyved gyftes of the Frenche kynge, he sayde to hym, Sir Gaultier, ye have hytherto truely served us, and shall do, as we trust: sende agayn to kyng Philyppe the gyftes that he gave you, ye have no cause to kepe theym: we thanke God we have ynough for us and for you: we be in good purpose to do moche good for you, acordyng to the good servyce that ye have done. Thanne sir Gaultier toke all those jewels and delyverd them to a cosyn of his called Mansac, and sayd, Ryde into Fraunce to the kynge there and recommend me unto hym, and say howe I thanke hym M. tymes for the gyft that he gave me, but shewe hym howe it is nat the pleasure of the kyng my maister that I shulde kepe them, therfore I sende them agayne to hym. This knyght rode to Parys and shewed all this to the kyng, who wolde nat receyve agayne the jewelles, but dyde gyve them to the same knyght sir Mansac, who thanked the kyng, and was nat in wyll to say nay.

Chapter CXXXVIII

Of the batayle of Newcastell upon Tyne bytwene the quene of England and the kyng of Scottes.

The quene of England, who desyred to defende her contrey, came to Newcastell upon Tyne and there taryed for her men, who came dayly fro all partes. Whan the Scottes knewe that the Englysshemen assembled at Newcastell, they drue thyderwarde and their currours came rennynge before the towne; and at their retournynge they brent certayne small hamelettes there about, so that the smoke therof came into the towne of Newcastell: some of the Englysshmen wolde a yssued out to have fought with them that made the fyers, but the captayns wolde nat suffre theym to yssue out. The next day the kyng of Scottes, with a xl. thousande men, one and other, came and lodged within thre lytell Englysshe myle of Newcastell in the lande of the lorde Nevyll, and the kyng sent to them within the towne, that if they wolde yssue out into the felde, he wolde fyght with theym gladly. The lordes and prelates of England sayd they were content to adventure their lyves with the ryght and herytage of the kynge of Englande their maister; than they all yssued out of the towne, and were in nombre a twelfe hundred men of armes, thre thousand archers, and sevyne thousande of other, with the Walsshmen. Than the Scottes came and lodged agaynst theym nere togyder: than every man was sette in order of batayle: than the quene came among her men and there was ordayned four batayls, one to ayde another. The firste had in governaunce the bysshoppe of Dyrham and the lorde Percy: the seconde the archbysshoppe of Yorke and the lorde nevyll: the thyrde the bysshoppe of Lyncolne, and the lorde Mombray: the fourth the lorde Edwarde de Baylleule, captayne of Berwyke, the archbysshoppe of Canterbury and the lorde Rose: every batayle had lyke nombre, after their quantyte. The quene went fro batayle to batayle desyring them to do their devoyre to defende the honoure of her lorde the kyng of Englande, and in the name of God every man to be of good hert and courage, promysyng them that to her power she wolde remembre theym as well or better as thoughe her lorde the kyng were ther personally. Than the quene departed fro them, recommendyng them to God and to saynt George. Than anone after, the bataylles of the Scottes began to set forwarde, and in lykewyse so dyd thenglysshmen. Than the archers began to shote on bothe parties, but the shot of the Scottes endured but a short space, but the archers of Englande shot so feersly, so that whan the batayls aproched, there was a harde batell. They began at nyne and endured tyll noone: the Scottes had great axes sharpe and harde, and gave with them many great strokes; howbeit finally thenglysshmen obtayned the place and vyctorie, but they lost many of their men. There were slayne of the Scottes, therle of Sys, therle of Ostre, the erle Patrys, therle of Surlant, therle Dastredare, therle of Mare, therle John Duglas, and the lorde Alysaunder Ramsey, who bare the kynges baner, and dyvers other knyghtes and squyers. And there the kynge was taken, who fought valiantly, and was sore hurt; a squyer of Northumberland toke hym, called John Coplande, and assone as he had taken the kynge, he went with hym out of the felde, with viii. of his servauntes with hym, and soo rode all that day, tyll he was a fyftene leages fro the place of the batayle, and at nyght he came to a castell called Orgulus; and than he sayde he wolde nat delyver the kyng of Scottes to no man nor woman lyveyng, but all onely to the kynge of Englande, his lorde. The same day there was also taken in the felde the erle Morette, the erle of Marche, the lorde Wyllyam Duglas, the lorde Robert Vesy, the bysshoppe of Dadudame, the bysshoppe of saynt Andrewes, and dyvers other knyghtes and barownes. And ther were slayne of one and other a xv. thousande, and the other saved themself as well as they might: this batell was besyde Newcastell, the yere of our lorde M.CCC.xlvi. the Saturday next after saynt Mychaell.

Chapter CXXXIX

How John Copland had the kyng of Scottes prisoner, and what profet he gatte therby.

Whan the quene of Englande, beyng at Newcastell understode howe the journey was for her and her men, she than rode to the place where the batayle hade ben: thane it was shewed her howe the kynge of Scottes was taken by a squyer called John Coplande, and he hadde caryed away the kyng no man knewe whyder. Than the quene wrote to the squyer commaundyng hym to bring his prisoner the kyng of Scottes, and howe he had nat well done to depart with hym without leave. All that day thenglysshmen taryed styll in the same place and the quene with them, and the next day they retourned to Newcastell. Whan the quenes letter was brought to Johan Coplande, he answered and sayd, that as for the kyng of Scottes his prisoner, he wolde nat delyver hym to no man nor woman lyveng, but all onely to the kynge of Englande his soverayne lorde; as for the kynge of Scottes, he sayd he shuld be savely kept, so that he wolde gyve acompte for hym. Thanne the quene sende letters to the kyng to Calays, wherby the kyng was enfourmed of the state of his realme. Than the kyng sende incontynent to Johan Coplande, that he shulde come over the see to hym to the siege before Calays. Than the same Johan dyd putte his prisoner in save kepynge in a stronge castell, and so rode through England tyll he came to Dover, and there toke the see and arryved before Calays. Whan the kyng of Englande sawe the squyer, he toke hym by the hande and sayde, A welcome my squyer, that by your valyantnesse hath taken myne adversary, the kyng of Scottes. The squyer kneled downe and sayde, Sir, yf God by his grace have suffred me to take the king of Scottes by true conquest of armes, sir, I thynke no man ought to have any envy thereat, for as well God may sende by his grace suche a fortune to fall to a poore squyer, as to a great lorde; and sir, I requyre your grace be nat myscontent with me, though I dyde nat delyver the kynge of Scottes at the commaundement of the quene. Sir, I holde of you, as myne othe is to you, and nat to her but in all good maner. The kyng sayd, Johan, the good servyce that ye have done and your valyantnesse is so moche worthe, that hit must countervayle your trespasse and be taken for your excuse, and shame have they that bere you any yvell wyll therfore. Ye shall retourne agayne home to your house, and thane my pleasure is that ye delyver your prisoner to the quene my wyfe, and in a rewarde I assigne you nere to your house, where as ye thynke best yourselfe, fyve hundred pounde sterlyng of yerely rent to you and to your heyres for ever, and here I make you squyer for my body. Thane the thyrde day he departed and retourned agayne into Englande, and whan he came home to his owne house, he assembled toguyder his frendes and kynne, and so they toke the kyng of Scottes, and rode with hym to the cytie of Yorke, and there fro the kyng his lorde he presented the kyng of Scottes to the quene, and excused hym so largely, that the quene and her counsell were content. Than the quene made good provisyon for the cytie of Yorke, the castell of Rosbourg, the cyte of Dyrham, the towne of Newcastell upon Tyne, and in all other garysons on the marchesse of Scotlande, and left in those marchesse the lorde Percy and the lorde Nevyll, as governoure there. Thanne the quene departed fro Yorke towardes London. Than she sette the kynge of Scottes in the strong towre of London, and therle Morette and all other prisoners, and sette good kepyng over them. Than she went to Dover and there tooke the see, and had so good wynde, that in a shorte space she arryved before Calays, thre dayes before the feest of Al Sayntes, for whose commyng the kyng made a great feest and dyner, to all the lordes and ladyes that were ther. The quene brought many ladyes and damoselles with her, as well to acompany her as to se their husbandes, fathers, bretherne and other frendes that lay at siege there before Calays and had done a longe space.

Chapter CXLVI

Howe the towne of Calys was gyven up to the kyng of England.

After that the Frenche kyng was thus departed fro Sangate, they within Calays sawe well howe their socoure fayled them, for the whiche they were in great sorowe. Than they desyred so moche their captayne sir John of Vyen, that he went to the walles of the towne and made a sygne to speke with some person of the hoost. Whan the kyng harde therof, he sende thyder sir Gaultier of Manny and sir Basset: than sir John of Vyen sayd to them, Sirs, ye be right valyant knyghtes in dedes of armes, and ye knowe well howe the kynge my maister hath sende me and other to this towne, and commaunded us to kepe it to his behofe, in suche wyse that we take no blame nor to hym no dammage; and we have done all that lyeth in oure power. Nowe our socours hath fayled us, and we be so sore strayned that we have nat to lyve withall, but that we muste all dye or els enrage for famyn, without the noble and gentyll kyng of yours woll take mercy on us: the which to do we requyre you to desyre hym, to have pyte on us and to let us go and depart as we be, and lette hym take the towne and castell and all the goodes that be therin, the whiche is great habundaunce. Than sir Gaultyer of Manny sayde, Sir, we knowe somwhat of the entencyon of the kynge our maister, for he hath shewed it unto us; surely knowe for trouth it is nat his mynde that ye nor they within the towne shulde departe so, for it is his wyll that ye all shulde put your selfes into his pure wyll, to ransome all suche as pleaseth hym and to putte to dethe suche as he lyste: for they of Calays hath done hym suche contraryes and dispyghtes, and hathe caused hym to dyspende soo moche good, and loste many of his menne, that he is sore greved agaynst them. Than the captayne sayde, Sir, this is to harde a mater to us; we ar here within, a small sorte of knyghtes and squyers, who hath trewely served the kynge our maister as well as ye serve yours in lyke case, and we have endured moche payne and unease; but we shall yet endure asmoche payne as ever knyghtes dyd rather thanne to consent that the worst ladde in the towne shulde have any more yvell than the grettest of us all: therfore, sir, we pray you that of your humylite, yet that ye woll go and speke to the kynge of Englande and desyre hym to have pytie of us, for we truste in hym somoche gentylnesse, that by the grace of God his purpose shall chaung. Sir Gaultier of Manny and sir Basset retourned to the kynge and declared to hym all that hadde ben sayde. The kynge sayde he wolde none otherwyse but that they shulde yelde theym up symply to his pleasure. Than sir Gaultyer sayde, Sir, savyng you dyspleasure in this, ye may be in the wronge, for ye shall gyve by this an yvell ensample: if ye sende any of us your servauntes into any fortresse, we woll nat be very gladde to go if ye putte any of theym in the towne to dethe after they be yelded, for in lykewise they woll deale with us if the case fell lyke: the whiche wordes dyverse other lordes that were there present sustayned and maynteyned. Than the kynge sayde, Sirs, I woll nat be alone agaynst you all; therfore, sir Gaultyer of Manny, ye shall goo and say to the capytayne that all the grace that he shall finde nowe in me is that they lette sixe of the chiefe burgesses of the towne come out bare heeded, bare foted and bare legged, and in their shertes, with haulters about their neckes, with the kayes of the towne and castell in their handes and lette theym sixe yelde themselfe purely to my wyll, and the resydewe I wyll take to mercy. Than sir Gaultyer retourned and founde sir John of Vyen styll on the wall, abydinge for an answere: thanne sir Gaultier shewed hym all the grace that he coulde gette of the kynge. Well, quoth sir Johan, sir, I requyre you tary here a certayne space tyll I go into the towne and shewe this to the commons of the towne, who sent me hyder. Than sir John went unto the market place and sowned the common bell. Than incontynent men and women assembled there; than the captayne made reporte of all that he had done, and sayde, Sirs, it wyll be none otherwyse; therfore nowe take advyse and make a shorte aunswere. Thanne all the people beganne to wepe and to make such sorowe, that there was nat so hard a hert if they had sene them but that wolde have had great pytie of theym; the captayne hym selfe wepte pyteously. At last the moost riche burgesse of all the towne, called Ewstace of saynt Peters, rose up and sayde openly, Sirs, great and small, great myschiefe it shulde be to suffre to dye suche people as be in this towne, other by famyn or otherwyse, whan there is a meane to save theym: I thynke he or they shulde have great merytte of our Lorde God that myght kepe theym fro suche myschief: as for my parte, I have so good truste in our Lorde God, that if I dye in the quarell to save the residewe, that God wolde pardone me; wherfore, to save them, I wyll be the first to putte my lyfe in jeopardy. Whan he had thus sayde, every man worshypped hym, and dyvers kneled downe at his fete with sore wepyng and sore sighes. Than another honest burgesse rose and sayde, I wyll kepe company with my gossyppe Ewstace; he was called John Dayre. Than rose up Jaques of Wyssant, who was riche in goodes and herytage; he sayd also that he wolde holde company with his two cosyns; in likwyse so dyd Peter of Wyssant his brother: and thane rose two other; they sayde they wolde do the same. Thanne they went and aparelled them as the kynge desyred. Than the captayne went with them to the gate: ther was great lamentacyon made of men, women, and chyldren at their departyng: than the gate was opyned and he yssued out with the vi. burgesses and closed the gate agayne, so that they were bytwene the gate and the barriers. Than he sayd to sir Gaultier of Manny, Sir, I delyver here to you as captayne of Calays, by the hole consent of all the peple of the towne, these six burgesses; and I swere to you truely that they be and were to day moost honourable, riche, and most notable burgesses of all the towne of Calys; wherfore, gentyll knyght, I requyre you pray the kyng to have mercy on theym, that they dye nat. Quoth sir Gaultier, I can nat say what the kyng wyll do, but I shall do for them the best I can. Thane the barryers were opyned, the sixe burgesses went towardes the kyng, and the captayne entred agayne into the towne. Whan sir Gaultier presented these burgesses to the kyng, they kneled downe and helde up their handes and sayd, Gentyll kyng, beholde here we sixe, who were burgesses of Calays and great marchantes: we have brought to you the kayes of the towne and of the castell and we submyt oure selfe clerely into your wyll and pleasure, to save the resydue of the people of Calys, who have suffred great payne. Sir, we beseche your grace to have mercy and pytie on us through your hygh nobles: than all the erles and barownes, and other that were there, wept for pytie. The kyng loked felly on theym, for greatly he hated the people of Calys, for the gret damages and dyspleasures they had done hym on the see before. Than he commaunded their heedes to be stryken of. Than every man requyred the kyng for mercy, but he wolde here no man in that behalfe. Than sir Gaultier of Manny sayd, A noble kyng, for Goddessake, refrayne your courage; ye have the name of soverayne nobles, therfore nowe do nat a thyng that shulde blemysshe your renome, nor to gyve cause to some to speke of you villany; every man woll say it is a great cruelty to put to deth suche honest persons, who by their owne wylles putte themselfe into your grace to save their company. Than the kyng wryed away fro hym, and commaunded to sende for the hangman, and sayd, They of Calys had caused many of my men to be slayne, wherfore these shall dye in likewyse. Than the quene beynge great with chylde, kneled downe and sore wepyng, sayd, A gentyll sir, syth I passed the see in great parell, I have desyred nothyng of you; therfore nowe I humbly requyre you, in the honour of the Son of the Virgyn Mary and for the love of me that ye woll take mercy of these sixe burgesses. The kyng behelde the quene and stode styll in a study a space, and than sayd, A dame, I wold ye had ben as nowe in some other place, ye make suche request to me that I can nat deny you; wherfore I gyve them to you, to do your pleasure with theym. Than the quene caused them to be brought into her chambre, and made the halters to be taken fro their neckes, and caused them to be newe clothed, and gave them their dyner at their leser; and than she gave ech of them sixe nobles and made them to be brought out of thoost in savegard and set at their lyberte.

Chapter CLIX

Of the great hoost that the Frenche kyng brought to the Batayle of Poycters.

After the takyng of the castell of Remorentyne and of them that were therin, the prince than and his company rode as they dyde before, distroyeng the countre aprochyng to Anjowe and to Tourayne. The Frenche kyng, who was at Charters, departed and came to Bloyes and ther taryed two dayes, and than to Amboyse and the next day to Loches; and than he herde howe that the prince was at Towrayne and how that he was retournyng by Poyctou: ever the Englysshmen were costed by certayne expert knyghtes of France, who alway made report to the kyng what the Englysshmen dyd. Than the kynge came to the Haye in Towrayne, and his men had passed the ryver of Loyre, some at the bridge of Orleance and some at Mehun, at Saulmure, at Bloyes, and at Towrs and wher as they might; they were in nombre a xx. thousande men of armes besyde other; ther were a xxvi. dukes and erles and mo than sixscore baners, and the foure sonnes of the kyng, who were but yonge, the duke Charles of Normandy, the lorde Loyes, that was fro thensforthe duke of Anjewe, and the lorde Johan duke of Berry, and the lorde Philyppe, who was after duke of Burgoyne. The same season pope Innocent the sixt send the lorde Bertrand, cardynall of Pyergourt and the lorde Nycholas, cardynall of the Egle, into France, to treat for a peace bytwene the Frenche kyng and all his enemyes; first bytwene hym and the kyng of Naverr, who was in prison: and these cardynalles often tymes spake to the kyng for his delyverance duryng the sege at Bretuell, but they coude do nothyng in that behalfe. Than the cardynall of Pyergourt went to Tours, ther he herde howe the Frenche kynge hasted sore to fynde the Englysshmen; than he rode to Poycters, for he herde howe bothe the hoostes drewe thyderward. The Frenche kyng herde howe the prince hasted greatly to retourne, and the kyng feared that he shulde scape hym and so departed fro Hay in Tourayne, and all his company, and rode to Chauvygny, wher he taryed that Thursday in the towne and without along by the ryver of Creuse; and the next day the kyng passed the ryver at the bridge there, wenyng that the Englysshemen had ben before hym, but they were nat. Howe be it they pursued after and passed the bridge that day mo than threscore thousand horses, and dyvers other passed at Chastelerault, and ever as they passed they tooke theyr where the Frenchmen were, but they supposed that they were nat farre of, for they coude nat fynde no more forage, wherby they had gret faut in the hoost of vitayle, and some of them repented that they had distroyed so moch as they had done before whan they were in Berry, Anjowe and Torayne, and in that they had made no better provision. The same Friday thre great lordes of France, the lorde of Craon, the lorde Raoull of Coucy and therle of Joigny, taryed all day in the towne of Chauvygny, and part of their companyes; the Saturday they passed the bridge and folowed the kyng, who was than a thre leages before, and tooke the waye amonge busshes without a wode syde to go to Poicters. The same Saturdaye the prince and his company dysloged fro a lytell vyllage therby, and sent before hym certayne currours to se if they myght fynde any adventure and to here where the Frenchmen were; they were in nombre a threscore men of armes well horsed, and with them was the lorde Eustace Dambreticourt, and the lorde John of Guystelles: and by adventure the Englysshmen and Frenchemen mette togyder by forsayde wode syde. The Frenchmen knewe anone howe they were their ennemyes; than in hast they dyd on their helmyttes and displayed their baners and came a great pase towardes thenglysshmen; they were in nombre a two hundred men of armes. Whan the Englysshmen sawe them, and that they were so great a nombre, than they determined to fly and let the Frenchmen chase them, for they knewe well the prince with his hoost was nat farre behynde; than they tourned their horses and toke the corner of the wood, and the Frenchmen after theym cryenge their cryes and made great noyse. And as they chased, they came on the princes batayle or they were ware therof themselfe: the prince taryed ther to have worde agayne fro them that he send forthe: the lorde Raoll of Coucy with his baner went so farre forward that he was under the princes baner; ther was a sore batayle and the knyght fought valiantly. Howe be it he was there takenne; and the erle of Wynguy, the vycount of Bruce, the lorde of Chavygny and all the other takene or slayne, but a fewe that scaped. And by the prisoners the prince knewe howe the French kynge folowed hym in suche wyse that he coude nat eschue the batayle; than he assembled togyder all his men and commaunded that no man shulde go before the marshals baners. Thus the prince rode that Saturday fro the mornyng tyll it was agaynst night, so that he came within two lytell leages of Poicters: than the captall de Buz, sir Aymenon of Punyers, the lorde Bartylmewe of Brunes and the lorde Eustace Dambretycourt, all these the prince sende forthe to se yf they myght knowe what the Frenchmen dyd. These knyghtes departed with two hundred men of armes well horsed; they rodde so farre that they sawe the great batayle of the kynges; they sawe all the feldes covered with men of armes. These Englysshmen coud nat forbere, but sette on the tayle of Frenche hoost and cast downe many to the yerth and toke dyvers prisoners, so that the hooste beganne to styre, and tidynges therof came to the Frenche kyng as he was entryng into the cytie of Poycters. Than he retourned agayne and made all his hoost do the same, so that Saturday it was very late or he was lodged in the felde. Thenglissh currours retourned agayne to the prince and shewed hym all that they sawe and knewe, and said howe the Frenche hoost was a great numbre of people. Well, sayde the prince, in the name of God lette us now study howe we shall fyght with them at our advauntage. That night the Englysshmen lodged in a strong place among hedges, vynes and busshes, and their hoost well watched, and so was the Frenche hoost.

Chapter CLXI

Howe the cardynall of Pyergourt treated to make agrement bytwene the Frenche kyng and the prince before the batell of Poycters.

Whan the Frenche kynges batayls was ordered and every lorde under his banner among their owne men, than it was commaunded that every man shulde cutte their speres to a fyve fote long and every man to put of their spurres. Thus as they were redy to aproche, the cardinall of Piergort came in great hast to the king; he came the same mornynge from Poycters; he kneled downe to the kyng and helde up his handes and desyred hym for Goddessake a lytell to absteyne settynge forwarde tyll he had spoken with hym; than he sayde, Sir, ye have here all the floure of your realme agaynst a handfull of Englysshmen, as to regarde your company: and sir, if ye may have them acorded to you without batayle, it shal be more profitable and honourable to have theym by that maner rather than to adventure so noble chivalry as ye have here present: sir, I requyre you in the name of God and humylyte, that I may ryde to the prince, and shewe hym what danger ye have hym in. The kynge sayd, It pleaseth me well, but retourne agayne shortely. The cardynall departed and dilygently he rode to the prince, who was among his men afote: than the cardynall alighted and came to the prince, who receyved hym curtesly. Than the cardynall, after his salutacyon made, he sayde, Certaynly, fayre son, if you and your counsayle advyse justely the puyssaunce of the Frenche kynge, ye woll suffre me to treat to make a peace bytwene you and I may. The prince, who was yong and lusty, said Sir, the honour of me and of my people saved, I wolde gladly fall to any reasonable way. Than the cardynall sayd, Sir, ye say well, and I shall acorde you and I can; for it shulde be great pytie yf so many noble men and other as be here on bothe parties shulde come togyder by batayle. Than the cardynall rode agayne to the kyng (and sayd) Sir, ye nede nat to make any great haste to fyght with your ennemyes, for they canne nat flye fro you though they wolde, they be in suche a ground; wherfore, sir, I requyre you forbere for this day tyll to morowe the son rysinge. The kynge was lothe to agree therto, for some of his counsayle wolde nat conset to it; but finally the cardynall shewed such reasons, that the kyng acorded that respyte: and in the same place there was pyght up a pavilyon of reed sylke fresshe and rych, and gave leave for that day every man to drawe to their lodgynges, except the constables and marshalles batayls. That Sonday all the day the cardynall traveyled in ridynge fro the one hoost to the other gladly to agree them; but the Frenche kynge wolde nat agree without he myght have foure of the princypallest of the Englysshmen at his pleasure, and the prince and all the other to yelde themselfe simply; howe be it ther were many great offers made. The prince offred to rendre into the kynges handes all that ever he had wonne in that voyage, townes and castels, and to quyte all prisoners that he or any of his men had taken in that season, and also to swere nat to be armed agaynst the Frenche kyng in sevyn yere after; but the kyng and his counsayle wolde none therof: the uttermast that he wolde do was, that the prince and a C. of his knyghtes shulde yelde theymselfe into the kynges prison, otherwyse he wolde nat; the whiche the prince wolde in no wyse agre unto. In the meane season that the cardynall rode thus bytwene the hoostes in trust to do some good, certayne knyghtes of France and of Englande bothe rode forthe the same Sonday, bycause it was truse for that day, to cost the hoostes and to beholde the dealyng of their enemyes. So it fortuned that the lorde John Chandos rode the same day coostyng the French host, and in like maner the lorde of Cleremont, one of the Frenche marshalles, had ryden forthe and aviewed the state of the Englysshe hoost; and as these two knyghtes retourned towardes their hoostes they mette togyder; eche of theym bare one maner of devyce, a blewe lady enbraudred in a sone beame above on their apayrell. Than the lorde Cleremont sayd, Chandos, howe long have ye taken on you to bere my devyce? Nay, ye bere myne, sayd Chandos, for it is as well myne as yours. I deny that, sayd Cleremont, but and it were nat for the truse this day bytwene us, I shulde make it good on you incontynent that ye have no right to bere my devyce. A sir, sayd Chandos, ye shall fynde me to morowe redy to defend you and to prove by feate of armes that it is as well myne as yours. Than Cleremont sayd, Chandos, these be well the wordes of you Englysshmen, for ye can devyce nothyng of newe, but all that ye se is good and fayre. So they departed without any more doyng, and eche of them returned to their hoost. The cardynall of Pyergort coude in no wyse that Sonday make any agrement bytwene the parties, and whan it was nere nyght he returned to Poicters. That night the Frenchmen toke their ease: they had provision ynough, and the Englysshmen had great defaut; they coude get no forage, nor they coude nat depart thense without danger of their ennemyes. That Sonday thenglysshmen made great dykes and hedges about their archers to be the more stronger; and on the Monday in the mornynge the prince and his company were redy apayrelled as they were before, and about the sonne rysing in lyke maner were the Frenchmen. The same morning be tymes the cardynall came agayne to the Frenche hoost and thought by his preachyng to pacify the parties; but than the Frenchmen sayd to hym, Retourne whyder ye woll; bring hyder no mo wordes of treaty nor peace; and ye love yourselfe depart shortely. Whan the cardynall sawe that he traveyled in vayne, he toke leave of the kyng and than he went to the prince and sayd, Sir, do what ye canne, their is no remedy but to abyde the batayle, for I can fynde none acorde in the Frenche kyng. Than the prince sayd, The same is our entent and all our people; God helpe the right. So the cardynall retourned to Poycters. In his company there were certayne knyghtes and squyers, men of armes, who were more favourable to the Frenche kyng than to the prince; and whan they sawe that the parties shulde fight, they stale fro their maisters and went to the Frenche hoost, and they made their captayne the catelayne of Ampostre, who was as than ther with the cardynall, who knewe nothynge therof tyll he was come to Poycters. The certentie of the order of the Englysshmen was shewed to the Frenche kyng, except they had ordayned thre hundred men a horsebacke, and as many archers a horsebacke, to coost under covert of the mountayne and to strike into the batayle of the duke of Normandy, who was under the mountayne afote. This ordynaunce they had made of newe, that the Frenchmen knewe nat of; the prince was with his batayle downe amonge the vynes, and had closed in the wekyst parte with their caryages. Nowe wyll I name some of the princypall lordes and knyghtes that were ther with the prince: the erle of Warwyke, therle of Suffolke, the erle of Salisbury, therle of Stafford, the lorde John Chandos, the lorde Richarde Stafford, the lorde Reynold Cobham, the lorde Spencer, the lorde James Audeley, the lorde Peter his brother, the lorde Bercley, the lord Basset, the lord Waren, the lorde Dalawar, the lorde Maulyne, the lorde Wylly, the lorde Bartylmewe de Brunes, the lord of Felton, the lorde Rychard of Pembruge, the lorde Stephyne of Constracyon, the lorde

Braffeton, and other Englysshmen: and of Gascon, there was the lorde of Prunes, the lorde of Buger, the captall of Buz, the lorde Johan of Chamont, the lorde Delaspare, the lorde of Rosen, the lorde of Conseu, the lorde of Montferant, the lorde of Landuras, the lorde Soulech of Lestrade, and other that I can nat name: and of Heynowers, the lorde Eustace Dambretycourt, the lorde John of Guystels, and two other strangers, the lorde Danyell Phasell, and the lorde Denyce of Moerbertre. All the princes company past nat an viii. M. men one and other, and the Frenchmen were a lx. M. fightyng men, wherof ther were mo than thre thousande knightes.

Chapter CLXII

Of the batell of Poycters bytwene the prince of Wales and the Frenche kyng.

Whanne the prince sawe that he shuld have batell and that the cardynall was gone without any peace or trewse makynge, and sawe that the Frenche kyng dyd sette but lytell store by him, he said than to his men, Now sirs, though we be but a small company as in regarde to the puyssance of our ennemyes, let us nat be abasshed therfore: for the vyctorie lyeth nat in the multitude of people, but wher as God wyll sende it. Yf it fortune that the journey be ours, we shal be the moost honoured people of all the worlde; and if we dye in our right quarell, I have the kyng my father and bretherne, and also ye have good frendes and kynsmen; these shall revenge us: therfor sirs, for Goddessake, I requyre you do your devoyers this day; for if God be pleased and saynt George, this day ye shall se me a good knyght. These wordes and suche other that the prince spake conforted all his people. The lorde sir John Chandos that day never went fro the prince, nor also the lorde James Audeley of a great season: but whane he sawe that they shulde nedes fight, he sayd to the prince, Sir, I have served alwayes truely my lorde your father and you also, and shall do as long as I lyve; I say this bicause I made ones a vowe that the first batayle that other the kynge your father or any of his chyldren shulde be at, howe that I wolde be one of the first setters on, or els to dye in the payne; therfore I requyre your grace, as in rewarde for any servyce that ever I dyde to the king your father or to you, that you woll gyve me lycence to depart fro you and to sette my selfe there as I may acomplysshe my vowe. The prince acorded to his desyre and sayde, Sir James, God gyve you this day that grace to be the best knyght of all other: and so toke hym by the hande. Than the knyght departed fro the prince, and went to the formast front of all the batayles, all onely acompanyed with foure squyers, who promysed nat to fayle hym. This lorde James was a right sage and a valyant knyght, and by hym was moche of the hoost ordayned and governed the day before. Thus sir James was in the front of the batayle redy to fight with the batayle of the marshalles of Fraunce. In lykewyse the lorde Eustace Dambreticourt dyd his payne to be one of the formast to sette on; whan sir James Audeley began to sette forwarde to his ennemyes, it fortuned to sir Eustace Dambretycourt as ye shall here after. Ye have herde before howe the Almayns in the French host were apoynted to be styll a horsebacke. Sir Eustace beyng a horsebacke layed his spear in the rest and ran into the Frenche batayle; and than a knyght of Almaygne, called the lorde Loyes of Coucoubras, who bare a shelde sylver, fyve rosses goules; and sir Eustace bare ermyns, two hamedes of goules. Whan this Almaygne sawe the lorde Eustace come fro his company, he rode agaynst hym and they mette so rudely, that bothe knightes fell to the yerth. The Almayne was hurt in the shoulder, therfore he rose nat so quickely as dyde sir Eustace, who whan he was up and had taken his breth, he came to the other knyght as he lay on the grounde: but thane fyve other knyghtes of Almayne came on hym all at ones and bare hym to the yerth; and so perforce there he was taken prisoner and brought to the erle of Nosco, who as than toke no hede of hym; and I can nat say whyther they sware him prisoner or no, but they tyed hym to a chare and there lette hym stande. Than the batayle began on all partes, and the batayls of the marshals of Fraunce aproched, and they set forthe that were apoynted to breke the ray of the archers. They entred a horsebacke into the way where the great hedges were on bothe sydes sette full of archers; assone as the men of armes entred, the archers began to shote on bothe sydes and dyd slee and hurt horses and knyghtes, so that the horses whan they felt the sharpe arowes they wolde in no wyse go forward, but drewe abacke and flang and toke on so feersly, that many of them fell on their maisters, so that for preace they coude nat ryse agayne; in so moche that the marshals batayle coude never come at the prince: certayne knyghtes and squyers that were well horsed passed through tharchers and thought to aproche to the prince, but they coude nat. The lorde James Audeley, with his four squyers was in the front of that batell and there dyd marvels in armes; and by great prowes he came and fought with sir Arnolde Dandrehen under his owne baner, and ther they fought longe togyder, and sir Arnolde was there sore handled. The batayle of the marshals began to dysorder by reason of the shot of the archers with the ayde of the men of armes, who came in among them and slewe of them and dyd what they lyst; and ther was the lorde Arnold Dandrehen taken prisoner by other men than by sir James Audeley or by his four squiers, for that day he never toke prisoner, but alwayes fought and went on his enemyes. Also on the French partie, the lorde Johan Cleremont fought under his owne baner as long as he coude endure, but ther he was beten downe and coude nat be relyved nor ransomed, but was slayne without mercy; some sayde it was bicause of the wordes that he had the day before to sir John Chandos. So within a short space the marshals batayls were disconfyted, for they fell one upon another and coude nat go forth; and the Frenchmen that were behynde and coude nat get forwarde reculed backe and came on the batayle of the duke of Normandy, the which was great and thicke and were afote: but anon they began to opyn behynde: for whan they knewe that the marshals batayle was dysconfited, they toke their horses and departed, he that might best. Also they sawe a rowt of Englysshmen commynge downe a lytell mountayne a horsebacke, and many archers with them, who brake in on the syde of the dukes batayle. Trewe to say, the archers dyd their company that day great advauntage, for they shotte so thicke that the Frenchmen wyst nat on what syde to take hede; and lytell and lytell the Englysshmen wanne grounde on theym. And whan the men of armes of Englande sawe that the marshals batayle was dysconfited and that the dukes batayle begane to dysorder and opyn, they lept than on their horses, the whiche they had redy by them; than they assembled togyder and cryed Saynt George, Gyen: and the lorde Chandos sayd to the prince, Sir, take your horse and ryde forth, this journey is yours: God is this day in your handes: gette us to the French kynges batayle, for ther lyeth all the sore of the mater; I thynke verily by his valyantnesse he woll not flye: I trust we shall have hym by the grace of God and saynt George, so he be well fought withall; and sir, I herde you say that this day I shulde se you a good knyght. The prince sayde, Lette us go forthe, ye shall nat se me this day retourne backe, and sayd, Avaunce baner, in the name of God and of saynt George. The knyght that bare it dyde his commaundement: there was than a sore batayle and a perylous, and many a man overthrowen, and he that was ones downe coud nat be relyved agayne without great socoure and ayde. As the prince rode and entred in amonge his ennemyes, he sawe on his ryght hande, in a lytell busshe lyeng deed the lorde Robert of Duras and his baner by hym, and a ten or twelfe of his men about hym. Than the prince sayd to two of his squyers and to thre archers, Sirs, take the body of this knyght on a targe and bere hym to Poycters, and present him fro me to the cardynall of Pyergourt, and say howe I salute hym by that token; and this was done. The prince was enformed that the cardynalles men were on the felde agaynst hym, the which was nat pertayning to the right order of armes, for men of the churche that cometh and goeth for treaty of peace ought nat by reason to ber harnes nor to fyght for neyther of the parties: they ought to be indyfferent: and bycuse these men had done so, the prince was dyspleased with the cardynall, and therfore he sende unto hym his nephue the lorde Robert of Duras deed. And the cathelayn of Ampostre was takenne, and the prince wolde have had his heed stryken of, bycause he was pertaynynge to the cardynall, but than the lorde Chandos sayd, Sir, suffre for a season; entende to a gretter mater, and paradventure the cardynall wyll make suche excuse that ye shal be content. Than the prince and his company dressed them on the batayle of the duke of Athenes, constable of France: there was many a manne slayne and cast to the yerth. As the Frenchmen fought in companyes, they cryed Mountjoy saynt Denyce, and the Englysshmen Saynt George, Gyen. Anone the prince with his company met with the batayle of Almaygnes, wherof the erle of Salesbruce, the erle Nosco, and therle Neydo were capitayns, but in a short space they were put to flyght: the archers shotte so holly togyder that none durst come in their dangers; they slewe many a man that coulde nat come to no raunsome; these thre erles was ther slayne, and dyvers other knyghtes and squyers of their company: and ther was the lorde Dambretycourt rescued by his owne men and sette on horsebacke, and after he dyde that day many feates of armes and toke gode prisoners. Whan the duke of Normandyes batayle sawe the prince aproche, they thought to save themselfe, and so the duke and the kynges chyldren, the erle of Poycters, and the erle of Tourayne, who were ryght yong, byleved their governours and so departed fro the felde, and with them mo than eyght hundred speares, that strake no stroke that day. Howbeit the lorde Guysshard Dangle, and the lorde John of Sayntre, who were with the erle of Poicters, wolde nat flye, but entred into the thyckest prease of the batayle. The kynges thre sonnes toke the way to Chamigny; and the lorde John of Landas, and the lorde Thybault of Woodney, who were sette to awayt on the duke of Normandy, whan they had brought the duke a long leage fro the batayle, than they tooke leave of the duke and desyred the lorde of saynt Venant, that he shulde nat leave the duke, but to bring hym in savegarde, wherby he shulde wyn more thanke of the kynge than to abyde styll in the felde; than they met also the duke of Orleaunce and a great company with hym, who were also departed fro the felde, yet they hadde rather a dyed, than to have had any reproche. Than the kynges batayle came on the Englysshmen; there was a sore fyght and many a great stroke gyven and receyved. The kyng and his yongest sonne mette with the batayle of thenglysshe marshalles, therle of Warwyke and therle of Suffolke, and with theym the Gascons, the captall of Buz, the lorde of Pomyers, the lorde Amery of Charre, the lorde of Mucydent, the lorde of Languran, and the lorde de la Strade. To the Frenche partie there came tyme ynough, the lorde Johan of Landas, and the lorde of Woodney; they alyghted afote and wente into the kynges batayle; and a lytell besyde fought the duke of Athenes, constable of France, and a lytell above hym the duke of Burbone, and many good knyghtes of Burbonoyse, and of Picardy with hym; and a lytell on the one syde ther were the Poytevyns, the lorde de Pons, the lorde of Partney, the lorde of Dampmare, the lorde of Montaboton the lorde of Suggeres, the lorde Johan Sayntre, the lorde Guyssharde Dangle, the lorde Argenton, the lorde of Lymyers, the lorde of Mountandre, and dyverse other, also the Vycount of Rochevart, and the erle of Daunoy: and of Burgone, the lorde James of Beauyeu, the lorde de la Castell Vilayn, and other: in another parte, there was the erle of Vantadowre, and of Mounpenser, the lorde James of Burbone, the lorde Johan Darthoyes, and also the lorde James his brother, the lorde Arnolde of Cervolle, called the Arche preest, armed for the yonge erle of Alansonne: and of Auvergne, there was the lorde of Marcuell, the lorde de la Towre, the lorde of Chalenton, the lorde of Montague, the lorde of Rochfort, the lorde de la Chayre, the lorde Dachone; and of Lymosyn, there was the lorde Delmall, the lorde of Norwell, the lorde of Pers Buffier: and of Pycardie, there was the lorde Wyllyam of Nerle, the lorde Arnolde of Renewall, the lorde Geffray of saynt Dygier, the lorde of Chamy, the lorde of Heley, the lorde of Mounsaunt, the lorde of Hangyes and dyvers other: and also in the kynges batayle ther was therle Duglas of Scotland, who fought a season right valyantly, but whan he sawe the dysconfyture, he departed and saved hymselfe, for in no wyse he wolde be takenne of the Englysshmen, he had rather ben there slayne. On the Englysshe parte the lorde James Awdeley with the ayde of his foure squyers fought alwayes in the chyefe of the batayle: he was soore hurte in the body and in the vysage; as longe as his breth served hym he fought; at laste at the ende of the batayle his foure squyers tooke and brought hym oute of the felde, and layed hym under a hedge syde for to refresshe hym, and they unarmed hym, and bounde up his woundes as well as they coulde. On the Frenche partie kynge Johan was that day a full right good knyght; if the fourth part of his menne hadde done their devoyers as well as he dydde, the journey hadde ben his by all lykelyhode. Howebeit they were all slayne and takenne that were there, excepte a fewe that saved themselfe that were with the kynge. There was slayne the duke peter of Burbon, the lorde Guyssharde of Beaujeu, the lorde of Landas, and the duke of Athenes, constable of Fraunce, the bysshoppe of Chalons in Champayne, the lorde Wyllyam of Neell, the lorde Eustace of Rybamont, the lorde de la Towre, the lorde Wyllyam of Montagu, sir Guyuenton of Chambley, sir Baudrin de la house, and many other, as they fought by companyes: and ther were taken prisoners the lorde of Wodney, the lorde of Pompador, and the archpreest, sore hurte, the erle of Vandos, the erle of Mons, the erle of Genvyll, the erle of Vandone, sir Loyes of Melwall, the lorde Pyers Buffyer, and the lorde of Senerache; ther were at that brunt slayne and taken mo than two hundred knyghtes.

Chapter CLXIIII

Howe kyng John was taken prisoner at the batayle of Poycters.

Often tymes the adventures of amours and of war are more fortunate and marvelous than any man canne thynke or wysshe; truly this batayle, the which was nere to Poycters in the feldes of Beaumont and Malpertuis, was right great and peryllous, and many dedes of armes there was done the which all came nat to knowlege. The fyghters on bothe parties endured moche payne; kyng John with his owne handes dyd that day marvels in armes; he had an axe in his handes wherwith he defended hymselfe and fought in the brekynge of the prease. Nere to the kyng there was taken the erle of Tankervyll, sir Jaques of Burbon, erle of Ponthieu, and the lorde Johan of Arthoyes, erle of Ewe; and a lytell above that under the baner of the captall of Buz was taken sir Charles of Arthoys and dyvers other knyghtes and squyers. The chase endured to the gates of Poiters: ther were many slayne and beaten downe, horse and man, for they of Poyters closed their gates and wolde suffre none to entre; wherfore in the strete before the gate was horrible murdre, men hurt and beaten downe. The Frenchemen yelded themselfe as farre of as they might know an Englysshman; ther were dyvers Englysshe archers that had iiii. v. or vi. prisoners: the lorde of Pons, a gret baron of Poitou, was ther slayne, and many other knyghtes and squyers: and ther was taken therle of Rochuart, the lorde of Dannauement, the lorde of Pertney; and of Xaynton, the lorde of Montendre, and the lorde John of Sayntre, but he was so sore hurt that he had never helth after; he was reputed for one of the best knightes in France. And ther was left for deed among other deed men, the lorde Rychard Dangle, who fought that day by the kyng right valyantly, and so dyd the lorde of Charny, on whom was great prease, bycause he bare the soverayne baner of the kynges: his owne baner was also in the felde, the which was of goules, thre schochyns sylver. So many Englysshmen and Gascons came to that part, that perforce they opyned the kynges batell, so that the Frenchmen were so mengled amonge their ennemyes that somtyme there was fyve men upon one gentylman. Ther was taken the lord of Pompadour, and the lorde Bartylmewe de Brunes, and ther was slayne sir Geffray of Charny with the kynges baner in his handes; also the lorde Reynold Cobham slewe therle of Dammartyn: than ther was a great prease to take the kynge, and such as knewe hym cryed Sir, yelde you, or els ye ar deed. Ther was a knyght of saynt Omers, retayned in wages with the kyng of England, called sir Denyce Morbecke, who had served the Englysshmen v. yere before, bycause in his youth he had forfayted the realme of France, for a murdre that he dyd at saynt Omers. It happenyd so well for hym, that he was next to the kynge whan they were about to take hym; he stepte forthe into the prease, and by strength of his body and armes, he came to the Frenche kyng, and sayd in gode Frenche, Sir, yelde you. The kyng behelde the knyght and sayde, To whom shall I yelde me; where is my cosyn the prince of Wales, yf I myght se hym, I wolde speke with hym. Denyce answered and sayd, Sir, he is nat here, but yelde you to me and I shall bringe you to hym. Who be you, quoth the kynge. Sir, quoth he, I am Denyce of Morbecke, a knyght of Arthoys, but I serve the kyng of Englande bycause I am banysshed the realme of Fraunce and I have forfaytedde all that I had there. Than the kynge gave hym his ryght gauntlet, sayeng, I yelde me to you. There was a great prease about the kynge, for every man enforsed hym to say, I have taken him, so that the kyng coude nat go forwarde with his yonge sonne the lorde Philyppe with hym bycause of the prease. The prince of Wales, who was coragious and cruell as a lyon, toke that day great pleasure to fight and to chase his ennemyes. The lorde John Chandos, who was with hym, of all that day never left hym nor never toke hede of takynge of any prisoner: than at the ende of the batayle, he sayde to the prince Sir, it were good that you rested her and sette your baner a high in this busshe, that your people may drawe hyther, for they be sore spredde abrode, nor I can se no mo baners nor penons of the Frenche partie: wherfore sir, rest and refresshe you, for ye be sore chafed. Than the princes baner was sette uppe a hygh on a busshe, and trumpettes and clarions began to sowne. Than the prince dyd of his basenet, and the knyghtes for his body and they of his chambre were redy aboute hym, and a reed pavilyon pyght uppe, and than drinke was brought forthe to the prince and for suche lordes as were aboute hym, the whiche styll encreased as they came fro the chase: ther they taryed and their prisoners with theym. And whan the two marshalles were come to the prince, he demaunded of them if they knewe any tidynges of the Frenche kyng. They answered and sayde, Sir, we here none of certenty, but we thinke verily he is other deed or taken, for he is nat gone out of the batels. Than the prince sayd to therle of Warwyke and to sir Reynolde Cobham, Sirs, I requyre you goo forthe and se what ye can knowe, that at your retourne ye may shewe me the trouth. These two lordes toke their horses and departed fro the prince, and rode up a lytell hyll to loke about them; than they parcyved a flocke of men of armes commynge togyder right werely; there was the Frenche kyng afote in great parell, for Englysshmen and Gascoyns were his maisters, they had taken hym fro sir Denyce Morbecke perforce; and suche as were moost of force sayd, I have taken hym, Nay, quoth another, I have taken hym: so they strave which shulde have him. Than the French kyng, to eschue that peryll, sayd, Sirs, stryve nat, lede me courtesly, and my sonne, to my cosyn the prince, and stryve nat for my takynge, for I am so great a lorde to make you all riche. The kynges wordes somwhat apeased them; howebeit ever as they went they made ryot and brauled for the takyng of the king. Whan the two foresayd lordes sawe and herde that noyse and stryfe among them, they came to them and sayd, Sirs, what is the mater that ye stryve for. Sirs, sayd one of them, it is for the Frenche kyng, who is here taken prisoner, and there be mo than x. knyghtes and squyers that chalengeth the takynge of hym and of his sonne. Thane the two lordes entred into the prease and caused every man to drawe abacke, and commaunded them in the princes name on peyne of their heedes to make no more noise nor to aproche the kyng no nerer, without they were commaunded: thane every man gave rowme to the lordes, and they alyghted and dyd their reverence to the kyng, and so brought hym and his son in peace and rest to the prince of Wales.

Chapter CLXV

Of the gyft that the prince gave to the lorde Audeley after the batell of Poycters.

Assone as therle of Warwyke and the lorde Cobham were departed fro the prince, as ye have herde before, than the prince demaunded of the knyghtes that were about hym for the lorde Audeley, yf any knewe any thyng of hym. Some knyghtes that were ther answerd and sayd, Sir, he is sore hurt and lyeth in a lytter her besyde. By my faith, sayde the prince, of his hurtes I am right sorie: go and knowe yf he may be brought hyder, or els I woll go and se hym there as he is. Thane two knyghtes came to the lorde Awdeley, and sayde, Sir, the prince desyreth greatly to se you, outher ye must go to hym or els he woll come to you. A sir, sayde the knyght, thanke the prince, whan he thynketh on so poore a knyght as I am. Than he called eyght of his servantes and caused theym to bere hym in his lytter to the place wereas the prince was: than the prince tooke hym in his armes, and kyst hym, and made hym great chere, and sayd, Sir James, I ought gretly to honour you, for by your valyaunce ye have this day achyved the grace and renome of us all, and ye ar reputed for the moost valyant of all other. A sir, sayde the knyght, ye say as it pleaseth you: I wolde it were so, and if I have this day any thynge avaunced myselfe to serve you and to acomplysshe the vowe that I made, it ought nat to be reputed to me any prowes. Sir James, sayde the prince, I and all ours take you in this journey for the best doar in armes; and to thyntent to furnysshe you the better to pursue the warres, I retayne you for ever to be my knight, with fyve hundred markes of yerely revenewes, the which I shall assigne you on myne herytage in Englande. Sir, sayde the knyght, God graunt me to deserve the great goodnesse that ye shewe me; and so he toke his leave of the prince, for he was right feble, and so his servauntes brought hym to his lodgyng. And assone as he was gone, the erle of Warwyke and the lorde Combham retourned to the prince and presented to hym the Frenche kyng: the prince made lowly reverence to the kynge and caused wyne and spyces to be brought forthe, and hymselfe served the kynge in signe of great love.

Chapter CLXVI

Howe the Englysshmen wan gretly at the batayle of Poycters.

Thus this batayle was dysconfyted, as ye have herd, the which was in the feldes of Malpertuesse, a two leages fro Poyters, the xxii. day of Septembre the yere of our Lorde M.CCC.lvii. It began in the mornyng and endyd at noon, but as than all the Englysshmen wer nat retourned fro the chase, therfore the princes baner stode on a busshe to drawe all his men togyder, but it was ny night or all came fro the chase. And as it was reported, there was slayne all the floure of Fraunce, and there was taken with the kyng and the lorde Philyppe his sonne a sevyntene erles, besyde barones, knyghtes and squyers, and slayne a fyve or sixe thousande of one and other. Whan every man was come fro the chase, they had twyse as many prisoners as they were in nombre in all; than it was counsayled among them bycause of the great charge and dout to kepe so many, that they shulde put many of them to raunsome incontynent in the felde, and so they dyd; and the prisoners founde the Englysshemen and Gascoyns right courtesse; ther were many that day putte to raunsome and lette go, all onely on their promyse of faythe and trauth to retourne agayne bytwene that and Christmas to Burdeux with their raunsomes. Than that nyght they lay in the felde besyde where as the batayle had been; some unarmed theym, but nat all, and unarmed all their prisoners, and every man made good chere to his prisoner: for that day who soever toke any prisoner, he was clere his, and myght quyte or raunsome hym at his pleasure. All suche as were there with the prince were all made ryche with honour and goodes, as well by ransomyng of prisoners as by wynnynge of golde, sylver, plate, jewelles, that was there founde; there was no man that dyd set any thyng by riche harnesse, wherof there was great plentie, for the Frenchmen came thyder richely besene, wenynge to have had the journey for them.

Chapter CLXVII

Howe the lorde James Audley gave to his foure squyers the v. C. markes of revenewes that the prince had gyven hym.

Whan sir James Awdeley was brought to his logynge, than he send for sir Peter Audeley his brother and for the lorde Bartylmewe of Brunes, the lorde Stephane of Gousenton, the lorde of Wylly, and the lorde Raffe Ferres: all these were of his lynage; and than he called before them his four squiers, that had served hym that day well and trewly. Than he sayd to the sayd lordes, Sirs, it hath pleased my lorde the prince to gyve me fyve hundred markes of revenewes by yere in herytage, for the whiche I have done hym but small servyce with my body; sirs, beholde here these four squyers, who hath alwayes served me truely, and specially this day; that honour that I have is by their valyantnesse. Wherfore I woll rewarde them: I gyve and resigne into their handes the gyft that my lorde the prince hath gyven me of fyve hundred markes of yerely revenewes, to them and to their heyres for ever, in lyke maner as it was gyven me; I clerely disheryte me therof and inheryte them without any rebell of condycion. The lordes and other that were ther, every man beheld other and sayde among themselfe, It commeth of a great noblenes to gyve this gyft. They answered hym with one voyce, Sir, be it as Godde wyll, we shall bere wytnesse in this behalfe wher soever we be come. Thane they departed fro hym, and some of them went to the prince, who the same nyght wolde make a supper to the Frenche kynge and to the other prisoners, for they had than ynough to do withall of that the Frenchemen brought with them, for the Englysshmen wanted vitayle before, for some in thre dayes hadde no bredde before.

Chapter CLXVIII

Howe the prince made a supper to the French kyng the same day of the batayle.

The same day of the batayle at night the prince made a supper in his lodgynge to the Frenche kyng and to the moost parte of the great lordes that were prisoners. The prince made the kynge and his son, the lorde James of Burbone, the lorde John Darthoys, the erle of Tankervyll, therle of Stampes, therle Dampmartyne, the erle of Gravyll, and the lorde of Pertenay to syt all at one borde, and other lordes, knyghtes and squiers at other tables; and alwayes the prince served before the king as humbly as he coude, and wolde nat syt at the kynges borde for any desyre that the kynge coulde make: but he sayd he was nat suffycient to syt at the table with so great a prince as the kyng was. But than he sayd to the kyng, Sir, for Goddessake make non yvell nor hevy chere, though God this day dyde nat consent to folowe your wyll: for sir, surely the kynge my father shall bere you as moche honour and amyte as he may do, and shall acorde with you so reasonably that ye shall ever be frendes toguyder after; and sir, methynke ye ought to rejoyse, though the journey be nat as ye wolde have had it, for this day ye have wonne the hygh renome of prowes and have past this day in valyantnesse all other of your partie: sir, I say natte this to mocke you, for all that be on our partie that sawe every mannes dedes, ar playnly acorded by true sentence to gyve you the price and chapelette.

Therwith the Frenchemen began to murmure and sayde among themselfe howe the prince had spoken nobly, and that by all estimacion he shulde prove a noble man, if God sende hym lyfe, and to perceyver in suche good fortune.

Chapter CLXXIII

Howe the prince conveyed the Frenche kyng fro Burdeux into Englande.

After the deth of this knight, sir Godfray of Harcourt, the Frenchmen retourned to Constances with their prisoners and pyllage, and anone after they went into France to the duke of Normandy, who as than was called regent of France, and to the thre estates, who receyved them right honourable. So fro thensforth saynt Savyour le Vycont was Englysshe and all the landes pertayning to sir Godfray of Harcourt, for he had solde it to the kyng of England after his dyscease and disheryted the lorde Loys of Harcort his nephue, bycause he wolde nat take his part. Assone as the kyng of Englande herde tidynges of the dethe of the lorde Godfray of Harcort, he was sorie therof; than he sent incontynent men of armes, knyghtes, squyers and archers, mo than CCC. by see to go and take possessyon for hym of saynt Savyour le Vycont, the which was worth xxx. M. frankes by yere, and made captayne of those landes the lorde Johan Lyle. The thre estates all that season studyed on the ordinance of the realme of France, and it was all governed by them. The same wynter the prince of Wales and suche of Englande as were with hym at Burdeux ordayned for shyppes, to convey the Frenche kyng and his sonne and all the other prisoners into Englande; and whan the tyme of his departure aproched, than he commaunded the lorde Dalbert, the lorde of Musydent, the lorde de Laspare, the lorde of Punyers, and the lorde of Rosen to kepe the contre there, tyll his retourne agayne. Than he toke the see, and certayne lordes of Gascoyne with hym; the Frenche kyng was in a vessell by hymself, to be the more at his ease, acompanyed with two hundred men of armes and two thousand archers: for it was shewed the prince that the tre estates by whom the realme of France was governed had layed in Normandy and Crotoy two great armyes, to the entent to mete with hym and to gette the Frenche kynge out of his handes, if they might; but ther were no suche that apered, and yet thei were on the see xi. dayes, and on the xii. day they aryved at Sandwych. Than they yssued out of their shyppe and lay there all that night, and taryed there two dayes to refresshe them; and on the thirde day they rode to Canterbury. Whan the kynge of Englande knewe of their commynge, he commaunded them of London to prepare theym and their cyte to recyve suche a man as the Frenche kyng was. Than they of London arrayed themselfe by companyes and the chiefe maisters clothyng dyfferent fro the other; at saynt Thomas of Caunterbury the Frenche kyng and the prince made their offerynges and there taryed a day, and than rode to Rochester and taryed there that day, and the nexte day to Dartforde and the fourth day to London, wher they were honourably receyved, and so they were in every good towne as they passed. The Frenche kynge rode through London on a whyte courser, well aparelled, and the prince on a lytell blacke hobbey by hym: thus he conveyed along the cyte tyll he came to the Savoy, the which house pertayned to the herytage of the duke of Lancastre; there the French kyng kept his house a long season, and thyder came to se hym the kyng and the quene often tymes and made hym gret feest and chere. Anone after by the commaundement of pope Innocent the sixt there came into Englande the lorde Taylleran, cardynall of Pyergort, and the lorde Nycholas, cardynall of Dargell; they treated for a peace bytwene the two kynges but they coude bring nothyng to effect, but at last by good meanes they procured a truse bytwene the two kynges and all their assysters, to endure tyll the feest of saynt Johan the Baptyst in the yere of our Lorde God M.CCC.lix. and out of this truse was excepted the lorde Philyppe of Naverr and his alyes, the countesse of Mountfort and the duchy of Bretayne. Anone after, the French kyng was removed fro the Savoy to the castell of Wyndsore, and all his householde, and went a huntyng and a haukyng ther about at his pleasur, and the lorde Philypp his son with hym: and all the other prisoners abode styll at London, and went to se the kyng at their pleasure, and were receyved all onely on their faythes.

2. Source

From *The Palace of Pleasure* (1575 edition): *The Countesse of Salesburie*

By William Painter; edited by Joseph Jacobs, 1890

The Forty-sixth Nouell

A King of England loued the daughter of one of his noble men, which was Countesse of Salesburie, who after great sute to atchieue that he could not winne, for the entire loue he bare her, and her greate constancie, hee made her his queene and wife.

This historie ensuinge, describing the perfect figure of womanhode, the naturall qualitie of loue incensinge the hartes indifferently of all nature's children, the liuely image of a good condicioned Prince, the zealous loue of parentes and the glorious reward that chastitie conduceth to her imbracers, I deeme worthie to be annexed to the former Nouell, wherein as you haue hearde, bee contayned the straunge aduentures of a fayre and innocente Duchesse: whose life tried like gould in the fornace, glittereth at this daye like a bright starry planet, shining in the firmament with moste splendent brightnesse aboue all the rest, to the eternal prayse of feminine kinde. And as a noble man of Spaine, by heate of Loue's rage, pursued the louinge trace of a king of England's sister: euen so a renowmed and most victorious Prince (as the Auctour of theim both affirmeth) thorow the furie of that passion, which (as Apuleus sayth) in the firste heate is but small, but aboundinge by increase, doth set all men on fier, maketh earnest sute by discourse of wordes to a Lady herselfe, a Countesse, and Earle's doughter, a beautifull and faire wighte, a creature incomparable, the wife of a noble man his own subiect: who seing her constante forte to be impregnable, after pleasaunte sute and milde requeste, attempteth by vndermining to inuade, and when with siege prolixe, hee perceiueth no ingenious deuise can atchieue that long and painfull worke, he threateth mighte and maine, dire and cruell assaultes, to winne and gette the same: and laste of all surrendred into his hands, and the prisoner cryinge for mercie, he mercifully is contented to mitigate his conceyued rigour, and pitifully to release the Lady, whom for her womanlye stoutnesse and coragious constancie hee imbraceth and entertayneth for his owne. This greate and worthy king, by the first viewe of a delicate Ladie, thorowe the sappe of loue soaked into his noble harte, was transported into manye passions, and rapte with infinite pangues, which afterwards bredde him great disquietnes. This worthie Prince (I say) who before that time like an Alexander, was able to conquere and gain whole kingdomes, and made all Fraunce to quake for feare, at whose approch the gates of euery Citie did flie open, and fame of him prouoked ech Frenchman's knee to bowe, whose helmet was made of manhods trampe, and mace well steeled with stoute attemptes, was by the weakest staye of dame Nature's frame, a woman (shaped with no visage sterne or vglie loke) affrighted and appalled: whose harte was armed with no lethal sworde or deadly launce, but with a curat of honour and weapon of womanhode, and for all his glorious conquests, she durst by singuler combat to giue refusall to his face: which singuler perseueration in defence of her chastitie inexpugnable, esclarisheth to the whole flocke of womankinde the brighte beames of wisedome, vertue and honestie. No prayers, intreatie, suplication, teares, sobbes, sighes, or other like humaine actions, poured forth of a Princesse hart, could withdrawe her from the boundes of honestie. No promise, present, practise, deuise, sute, freinde, parent, letter or counsellour, could make her to stray oute of the limites of vertue. No threate, menace, rigour, feare, punishmente, exile, terror or other crueltie, could diuert her from the siege of constancie. In her youthly time till her mariage day, shee delighted in virginitie: from her mariage day during her widow state, she reioysed in chastity: the one she conserued like a hardie Cloelia, the other she kept like a constant Panthea. This notable hisstorie therfore I haue purposed to make common, aswel for encouragement of Ladies to imbrace constancie, as to imbolden them in the refusal of dishonest sutes, for which if they do not acquire semblable honour, as this Lady did, yet they shall not be frustrate of the due reward incidente to honour, which is fame and immortall prayse. Gentlemen may learne by the successe of this discourse, what tormentes be in Loue, what trauailes in pursute, what passions like ague fittes, what disconueniences, what loste labour, what plaints, what griefes: what vnnatural attemptes be forced. Many other notorious examples be contayned in the same, to the greate comforte and pleasure as I trust, of the wel aduised reader: and although the auctour of the same, perchaunce hath not rightly touched the proper names of the aucthours of this tragedie, by perfecte appellations: as Edward the third for his eldest sonne Edward the Prince of Wales (who as I read in Fabian) maried the Countesse of Salesburie, which before was Countesse of Kent, and wife vnto sir Thomas Holland: and whose name, (as Polidore sayth) was Iane, daughter to Edmond Earle of Kent, of whom the same Prince Edward begat Edward that died in his childish yeres, and Richard that afterwards was king of England the second of that name, and for that she was kin to him, was deuorced: whose sayde father maried Philip, daughter to the earle of Henault, and had by her vii. sonnes: and Aelips for the name of the sayde Countesse, beinge none suche amonges our vulgare termes, but Frosard remembreth her name to be Alice, which in deede is common amonges vs: and the Castell of Salesburie, where there is none by that name, vppon the frontiers of Scotlande, albeit the same Frosard doth make mention of a castell of the Earle of Salesburie's giuen vnto him by Edward the third when he was sir William Montague and maried the saide Lady Alice for his seruice and prowesse against the Scottes: and Rosamburghe for Roxboroughe: and that the said Edwarde when hee saw that hee could not by loue and other perswasions attaine the Countesse but by force, maried the same Countesse, which is altogether vntrue, for that Polydore and other aucthors do remember but one wife that hee had, which was the sayde vertuous Queene Philip, with other like defaults: yet the grace of the historie for all those errours is not diminished. Wherof I thoughte good to giue this aduertisement: and waying with my selfe that by the publishing hereof no dishonour can dedounde to the illustre race of our noble kinges and Princes, ne yet to the blemishinge of the fame of that noble kinge, eternized for his victories and vertues in the auncient Annales, Chronicles and Monuments, forren and domesticall, (because all nature's children be thrall and subiecte to the infirmities of their first parentes,) I do with submission humblie referre the same to the iudgement and correction of them, to whom it shall appartaine: which beinge considered, the Nouell doth begin in this forme and order.

There was a kinge of Englande named Edwarde, which had to his first wyfe the doughter of the Counte of Henault of whom hee had children, the eldest whereof was called also Edward, the renowmed Prince of Wales, who besides Poictiers subdued the French men, toke Iohn the French king prisoner, and sent him into England. This Edwarde father of the Prince of Wales, was not onely a capitall eunemie of the Frenchmen, but also had continual warres with the Scottes his neighbours, and seing himself so disquieted on euery side, ordayned for his Lieutenant vpon the frontiers of Scotland, one of his Captaynes, named William, Lord Montague: to whom because he had fortified Roxborough, and addressed many enterprises against the enemies, he gaue the Earledome of Sarisburie, and maried him honourablie with one of the fairest Ladies of England. Certaine dayes after, kinge Edward sent him into Flaunders, in the companie of the Earle of Suffolke, where fortune was so contrarie, as they were both taken prisoners, by the Frenchmen, and sente to the Louure at Paris. The Scottes hearing tell of their discomfiture, and how the marches were destitute of a gouernour, they speedely sente thether an armie, with intente to take the Countesse Prisoner, to rase her Castle, and to make bootie of the riches that was there. But the Earle of Sarisburie before his departure, had giuen so good order, that their successe was not such as they hoped: for they wer so liuely repelled by them that wer within, as not able to endure their furie, in steede of making their approches, they were constrayned to go further of. And hauinge intelligence by certaine spies, that the king of England was departed from London, with a great armie, to come to succour the Countesse, preceyuing that a farre of, they were able to do litle good, they were faine shortly to retire home again to their shame. King Edward departed from London, trauayling by great iourneyes with his armye towardes Sarisburie, was aduertized, that the Scottes were discamped, and fled againe into Scotland. Albeit they had so spoyled the castle in manye places, as the markes gaue sufficiente witnesse, what their intente and meaning was. And althoughe the kinge had thoughte to retourne backe againe vppon their retire, yet being aduertised of the great battrie, and of the hotte assault they had giuen to the Castell, he went foorth to visit the place. The Countesse whose name was Aelips, vnderstanding of the kinge's comming, causing all things to bee in so good readinesse, as the shortnesse of the time could serue, furnished her selfe so well as shee could with a certaine nomber of Gentlewomen and Souldiours that remained, to issue forth to meete the king, who besides her natural beautie, for the which she was recommended aboue all the Ladies of her prouince, was enriched with the furniture of vertue and curtesie, which made her so incomparable, that at one instante, she rauished the hartes of all the Princes and Lordes that did behold her, in such wise, as there was no talke in all the armie but of her graces and vertue, and specially of her excellent and surpassing beauty. The kinge hauing made reuerence vnto her, after hee had well viewed all her gestures and countenaunces, thoughte that hee had neuer seen a more goodlier creature. Then rapte with an incredible admiration he said vnto her: "Madame Countesse, I do beleeue, that if in this attire and furniture wherein you now be, accompanied with so rare and excellente beautie, ye had beene placed vppon one of the rampiers of your Castell, you had made more breaches with the lokes and beames of your sparkling eyes, in the hartes of your ennemyes, than they had beene able to haue done in your castel, with their thundring ordinaunce." The Countesse somewhat shamefast and abashed, to heare herselfe so greatly praysed of a Prince so greate, began to blushe and taint with roseall colour, the whitenesse of her alablaster face. Then lifting vp her bashfull eyes, somewhat towards the king, she said vnto him: "My soueraigne Lord, your grace may speake your pleasure, but I am well assured, that if you had seen the nomber of the shotte, which by the space of xii. houres were bestowed so thicke as hayle, vpon euery part of the fort, you might haue iudged what good wil the Scots did beare vnto mee and my people. And for my selfe I am assured, that if I had made proufe of that which you saye, and submitted myselfe to their mercie, my bodye nowe had been dissolued into duste." The king astonned with so sage and wise aunswere, chaunging his minde, went towarde the castell: where after interteignement and accustomed welcome, he began by litle and litle, to feele himselfe attached wyth a newe fier. Which the more he laboured to resist, the more it inflamed: and feelinge this new mutacion in himselfe, there came into his mind, an infinite nomber of matters, balancing betwene hope and feare, somtimes determining to yeld vnto his passions, and somtimes thinking clerely to cut them of, for feare least by committinge himselfe to his affections, the vrgent affayres of the warres, wherewith hee was inuolued, should haue ill successe. But in the ende vanquished wyth Loue, hee purposed to proue the hart of the Countesse, and the better to attayne the same he toke her by the hande, and prayed her to shewe him the commodities of the fortresse. Which shee did so well, and with so good grace intertaigne them all the whyle wyth infinite talke of diuers matters, that the litle grifts of loue which were scarcely planted, began to growe so farre as the rootes remayned fast grounded in the depthe of his harte. And the kyng not able any longer to endure such a charge in his minde, pressed with griefe, deuised by what meanes he might enioye her, which was the cause of his disquiet. But the Countesse seing him so pensife, without any apparaunt occasion, sayde vnto him: "Sir, I doe not a litle maruell to see you reduced into these alterations: for (me thincke) your grace is maruelously chaunged within these two or thre houres, that your highnes vouchsaued to enter into this castel for my succour and reliefe in so good time, as al the dayes of my life, both I and mine be greatly bound vnto you, as to him which is not onely content liberally to haue bestowed vpon vs the goods which we possesse, but also by his generositie, doth conserue and defend vs from the incursions of the enemie. Wherein your grace doth deserue double prayse, for a deede so charitable: but I cannot tell nor yet deuise, what should bee the cause that your highnesse is so pensife and sorowful, sith without great losse on your parte, your enemies vnderstandinge of your stoute approche, be retired, which ought, as I suppose, to driue awaye the Melancholie from your Stomacke, and to revoke your former ioy, for so much as victorie acquired withoute effusion of bloud, is alwayes most noble and acceptable before God." The king hearing this angel's voyce, so amiably pronouncing these words, thinking that of her owne accord shee came to make him mery, determined to let her vnderstand his griefe, vpon so conueniente occasion offred. Then with a trembling voice he said vnto her: "Ah Madame, how farre be my thoughtes farre different from those which you do thincke me to haue: I feele my hart so opprest with care, as it is impossible to tell you what it is, howbeit the same hath not beene of long continuance, being attached therewithall, since my comminge hether, which troubleth me so sore, as I cannot tell whereupon well to determine." The Countesse seing the king thus moued, not knowing the cause whye, was vncertaine what aunswere to make. Which the king perceyuing, said vnto her, fetching a deepe sighe from the bottome of his stomacke: "And what say you Madame thereunto, can you giue mee no remedie?" The Countesse, which neuer thoughte that any such discurtesie could take place in the kinge's hart, taking things in good part, said vnto him: "Syr, I know not what remedie to giue you, if first you do not discouer vnto me the griefe. But if it trouble you, that the Scottishe kinge hath spoyled your countrie, the losse is not soe greate, as therewith a Prince so mightie as you be, neede to be offended: sithens by the grace of God, the vengeaunce lieth in your handes, and you may in time chasten him, as at other times you haue done." Whereunto the kinge seinge her simplicitie, aunsweared: "Madame, the beginninge of my griefe ryseth not of that, but my wounde resteth in the inwarde parte of my harte, which pricketh mee so soore, as if I desire from henceforth to prolonge my life, I muste open the same vnto you, reseruing the cause thereof so secrete, as none but you and I must be partakers. I must now then confesse vnto you, that in comminge to your Castell, and castinge downe my head to behold your celestiall face, and the rest of the graces, wherewith the heauens haue prodigally endued you, I haue felt (vnhappie man as I am) such a sodaine alteration, in al the most sensible partes of my body, as knowing my forces diminished, I cannot tel to whom to make complaint of my libertie lost (which of long time I haue so happily preserued) but onely to you, that like a faithfull keeper and onely treasurer of my hart, you may by some shining beame of pitie bring againe to his former mirth and ioye, that which you desire in me: and by the contrarie, you may procure to me a life more painefull and greeuous than a thousand deathes together." When he had ended these woordes, hee helde his peace, to let her speake, attendinge none other thing by her aunswere, but the last decree either of death or life. But the Countesse with a grauitie conformable to her honestie and honour, without other mouing, said vnto him: "If any other besides your grace had been so forgetful of himself to enter in these termes, or to vse such talke vnto me, I knowe what should be mine aunswere, and so it might be, that he shoulde haue occasion not to be well contented, but knowing this your attempt to proceede rather from the pleasantnes of your hart, that for other affection, I wil beleue from henceforth, and perswade my selfe, that a Prince so renowmed and gentle as you be doth not thincke, and much lesse meane, to attempt any thing against mine honour, which is a thousand times dearer vnto mee than life. And I am perswaded, that you do not so litle esteeme my father and my husband, who is for your seruice prisoner in the hands of the Frenchmen, our mortal enemies, as in their absence to procure vnto them such defamation and slaunder. And by making this request your grace doth swarue from the bounds of honestie very farre, and you do greate iniury to your fame, if men should know what termes you do vse vnto me. In like maner, I purpose not to violate the faith, which I haue giuen to my husband, but I intend to keepe the same vnspotted, so long as my soule shalbe caried in the Chariot of this mortall body. And if I should so far forget my self, as willingly to commit a thing so dishonest, your grace oughte for the loyal seruice of my father and husband toward you, sharpely to rebuke me, and to punish me according to my desert. For this cause (most dradde soueraigne Lord) you which are accustomed to vanquishe and subdue other, bee nowe a conquerour ouer your selfe, and throughly bridle that concupiscence (if there be any) vnder the raynes of reason, that being quenched and ouercome, they may no more reuiue in you, and hauing liuely resisted the first assaultes, the victorie is but easie, which shalbe a thousande times more glorious and gaineful for you, than if you had conquered a kingdome." The Countesse had scarce made an ende of her tale, but one came to tell them that the Tables were couered for dinner: the king well fedde with Loue, dined for that time very soberly, and not able to eate but vppon amorous dishes, did caste his lokes inconstantly here and there, and still his eyes threw the last loke vppon that part of the table where the Countesse sate, meaninge thereby to extinguish the boiling flames, which incessantly did burne him, howbeit by thinking to coole them, he further plonged himselfe therein. And wandering thus in diuers cogitacions, the wise aunsweare that the Countesse made, like a vaunt currour, was continually in his remembraunce, and was well assured of her inuincible chastitie. By reason whereof, seing that so hard an enterprise required a longer abode, and that a hart so chast, could not so quickly be remoued from purpose, carefull on the other side to giue order to the waightie affayres of his realme, disquieted also on euery side, through the turmoile of warres, determined to depart the next day in the morning, reseruing till another time more conuenient the pursute of his loue. Hauing taken order for his departure, in the morning he wente to seeke the Countesse, and taking his leaue of her, praied her to thinke better of the talke made vnto her the daye before, but aboue al, he besought her to haue pitie vpon him. Wherunto the Countesse aunswered, that not onely shee praied God incessantly to giue him victory ouer his outward enemies, but also grace to tame the carnal passion, which did so torment him. Certaine dayes after that king Edward was arriued at London, which was the place of his ordinarie abode, the Countesse of Sarisburie was aduertised, that the Earle her husband, being out of pryson, consumed with griefe and sicknes, died by the way homewards. And because they had no children, the Earledome retourned to the kinge, which first gaue the same vnto him. And after she had lamented the death of her husband the space of many dayes, shee returned to her father's house, which was Earle of Warwike. And for so much as he was one of the king's priuie Counsel, and the most part of the affayres of the Realme passed by his aduise and counsell, he continued at London, that hee might be more neare vnto the kinge's person. The king aduertised of the comming of the Countesse, thoughte that fortune had opened a way to bring his enterprise to desired effect, specially for that the death of her husband, and the witnesse of his earnest good will, woulde make her more tractable. The kinge seing all thing (as he thought) to succede after his desire, began to renue his first affections, seeking by all meanes to practice the good will of the Countesse, who then was of the age of xxvi. yeares. Afterwards he ordeyned many triumphes at the Tilt and Torney, Maskes, Momeries, Feastes, Banquettes, and other like pastimes, whereat ladies accustomably doe assemble, who made much of theym all, and secretely talked wyth them. Notwithstanding he could not so well disguise and counterfaite his passions, but that he still shewed himselfe to beare beste good will to the Countesse. Thus the kinge could not vse such discretion in loue, but that from his secret fier, some euident flames did issue oute: but the Countesse which was a wise and curteous Ladye, did easely perceiue, how the king by chaunging the place, had not altered his affection, and that hee still prosecuted his talke begon at Sarisburie. She despising all his amorous countenaunces, continued her firme and chaste minde: and if it chaunced that sometimes the king made more of her than discretion required, sodainly might haue been discried a certaine palenesse in her face, which declared the litle pleasure that she toke in his toyes, with certaine rigour appearinge, that yelded to the king an assured testimonie that he laboured in vaine. Neuerthelesse, she, to cut of all meanes of the kinges pursute, kept still her father's house, shewinge herselfe in no place where the king mighte see her. The king offended, seing himselfe depriued and banished her presence, whom he esteemed as the comfort of his life, made his secretarie priuie to the whole matter, whose fidelity he had wel proued in matters daungerous, with mind to pursue her by other way, if it chaunced that she persisted in her wonted rigor and refusal. Howbeit before he proceded any further, sithe he could not secretely talke with her, he purposed to send her a letter, the tenor whereof insueth:

"MADAME, if you please by good aduise to consider the beginning of my Loue, the continuance of the same, and then the last issue wherunto it tendeth, I am assured that laying your hand on your hart, you wil accuse your selfe, not only of your curst and froward stomacke hitherto appearing, but also of that newe ingratitude, which you shewe vnto me at this houre, whoe not contented to bathe and plondge mee into the missehappe of my paines paste, but by a newe onset, to abandon your selfe from my presence, as from the sighte of your mortall eunemie: wherein I finde that heauen and all his influences, doe crie out for myne ouerthrowe, whereunto I doe agree, since my life taking no vigor and increase, being onely sustained by the fauour of your diuine graces, can not be maintained one onely minute of a daye, without the liberall helpe of your sweetenesse and vertue: beseching you, that if the hartie prayers of any mortal tormented man, may euer haue force and power to moue you to pitie, it may please you miraculously to deliuer from henceforth this my poore miserable afflicted mynde, either from death or martyrdome:

He that is more yours than his ownne,
Edward, the desolate king of England."

The letter written with his own hande, and sealed with his seale, he commaunded the Secretarie to go to the Countesse, at her father's house, and secretly to deliuer the same. The Countesse hauing red and perused it, sayd to the Secretarie: "My frende, you shall tell the kyng, that I doe besech him most humbly, to sende me no more letters or messages touching the matters whereof he hath written: for I am in such wyse resolued in the aunswere, which I made him in my castle, as I wyll persiste immutable, to the ende of my life." The Secretaire retorninge the aunswere of the Countesse, the king rapte with an impacient and extreme choler, desired eftsones to giue another attempt: and consuming by litle and litle in his amorous fier, began to sort out of the limits of reason. And almoste out of his wittes, demaunded of his Secretarie: "Do you thinke it expedient that I make request to her father, whose counsell I want in other thinges?" To whome the Secretarie boldly aunswered, that he thought it vnreasonable to seeke ayde at a father's handes to corrupt the doughter: faithfully telling to the king, the reproche and infamie that would followe thereof, as well for the olde seruice, that her father hadde done to his auncestours, as for his great prowesse in armes for which he was so greatly commended. But loue, the mortall enemie of all good counsell, so blinded the eyes of the kyng, that without anye further deliberation, he commaunded the Secretarie to go seke the father, to demande his counsell for matters of importance: whiche the Earle vnderstanding, obeyed incontinently, where the king alone in a chamber lying vpon a bed, after hee had commaunded him to shut the dore and to sit downe by him, sayde these wordes: "My lorde, I haue caused you to come hither for a certaine occasion, whiche toucheth me so nighe, as the losse or preseruation of my life. For neuer through any assaut of fortune (the sharpenesse wherof I haue often felt) haue I bene vanquished with so great disquiet, as nowe. For I am so vexed with my passions, as being ouercome by them, I haue none other refuge, but to a most unhappie death that euer man can suffer, if presently I bee not holpen. Knowe ye therefore, that I deeme him onely to be happy that by Reason can rule his wyttes, not suffering hym selfe to be caried into vayne desires: in whiche pointe wee do differ from beastes, who being lead onely by naturall order, doe indifferently runne headlong, whether their appetite doth guide them: but we with the measure of Reason, ought to moderate our doinges with suche prouidence, as without straying we may choose the right way of equitie and iustice: and if at any time, the weake fleshe doth faint and giue ouer, we haue none to blame but our selues: who deceiued by the fading shadow and false apparaunce of things, fal into the ditche by our selues prepared. And that which I do alleage, is proued, not without manifest reason, wherof I nowe doe fele experience, hauing let slip the raynes of the bridle to farre ouer my disordinate affections, beyng drawen from the right hande, and traiterously deceiued. And neuerthelesse I can not tell howe to retire to take the right waye, or howe to retourne my back from that which doth me hurt. Wherefore nowe (vnfortunate and miserable that I am) I acknowledge my selfe to be like vnto him, that followeth his game in the thicket of a woode, rushing through thicke and thynne at all aduentures, not knowing howe to finde the waye he entred in, but rather the more he desireth to follow the trace, the more in the ende he is wrapped in the bushes. So it is my Lorde, that I can not and may not for all my foresayd allegations, so colour my fault, or purge myne error, but that I must confesse and acknowledge it to be in me: but I speake to this ende, that seeking a farre of the originall of my griefe, you would helpe me to complayne, and thereby to take pitie vpon me. For to tell you the truthe, I am so intricated in the labarinthe of my vnbrideled will, as the more I doe aspire to the better (alas) the worsse I am. Haue not I good cause to complaine my Lorde, that after so manye famous victories achieued by Sea and Lande, wherewith I haue renowmed the memorie of my name in all places, am now bound and daunted with an appetite so outragious, as I can not helpe my selfe, whereby myne owne life, or rather death, is consumed in suche anguishe and mortall paine, as I am become the very mansion of all mischiefs, and onely receptacle of all miseries? What sufficient excuse for my fault may I henceforth alleage, that in the end will not display it to be both vnprofitable and voyde of reason? But what shall be the buckeler of my shame, if not my youthly age, which pricketh me forewarde to loue like a sharpe nedle, the force whereof I haue so ofte repelled, as nowe being vanquished, I haue no place for rest, but in thy mercy, who in my father's dayes diddest liberally spende thy bloud, in manye notable enterprises in his seruice, whiche afterwardes thou haste so well continued, that in many daungerous affaires, I haue diuers times proued the fidelitie of thy counsell, whereby I haue brought to passe thinges of great importaunce, and therein hitherto neuer founde thee slacke and vnfaythfull. Whiche when I remember doe prouoke me to be bolde to declare vnto you mine entent, whiche by youre onely worde you may procure, the fruite whereof being gotten, you shall winne the heart of a king, to be vsed as you liste for euer. And the more the thing shal seeme harde, difficult or painefull, the greater shall your merite be, and the more firmely shall he be bounde, whiche doth receive it. Consider then my Lorde, howe profitable it is, to haue a king at your commaundement. You haue also foure sonnes, whom you cannot honourably aduaunce with out my fauour: swearing unto you by my regall Scepter, that if you comfort me in these my troubles, I will endue the three yongest with so large possessions, as they shall haue no cause to be offended with their eldest brother. Remember likewyse, what rewardes I haue bestowed vpon them that serue me. And If you haue knowen how liberall I haue bene towardes other, thinke then I praye you, how bountifully you bynde me towardes you, vpon whome my life and deathe dependeth." The king ending his sorowfull complainte, stopped by sobbes and sighes, helde his peace. And the Earle who tenderly loued his Prince, hearing this pitifull discourse, (the faithfull witnesse of his inward passion) and not able to coniecture the occasion, was maruellously troubled in him selfe, and without longer aduise, ouercome with pitie, he made a liberall and very sodayne offer to the king of his life, his children, and of all that he was able to doe. "Commaunde, my soueraigne Lorde (quod he with weaping teares) what it shall please you to haue me doe, if it be, euen to bestowe my life for your sake. For by the faithe and fealtie that I do owe to God and to your grace, I sweare, that many dayes and yeares paste, I haue bound my selfe inuiolably, and all mine abilitie without exception, so long as this tongue is able to sturre, and breathe shall remaine within this bodye, faithfully and truely to serue your maiestie, not onely for that dutie bindeth me, but if it were for your sake, to transgresse and exceede the bondes of mine honour." But the good olde Earle, whiche neuer thought that a request so vniust and dishonest would haue proceeded out of the mouth of a king, with franke and open harte made that liberall offer. The king then hauing sounded the depth of the Earle's affection, chaunging colour, his eyes fixed on the grounde, sayde vnto him: "Your doughter the Countesse of Sarisburie, (my Lorde) is the onely medicine of my trauayles, whome I doe loue better than mine owne life, and doe feele my selfe so inflamed with her heauenly beautie, as without her grace and fauour I am not able hereafter to liue: for this consideration, sith you desire to doe me seruice, and to preserue my life, I praye you to deale with her, that she with compassion may looke vpon me. Crauing this request at your handes, not without extreme shame, considering as well your honorable state, as your auncient merites imploied vpon me and my progenitours: but according to your modestie and accustomed goodnesse, impute the faulte vpon amorous loue, which in such wise hath alienated my libertie, and confounded my heart, that now ranging out of the boundes of honour and reason, I feele my selfe tormented and vexed in mynde. Whereby I am prouoked to make this request, and not able to expel the mortall poyson out of my hart, which hath diminished my force, intoxicated my sense, and hath depriued my minde from all good counsell, as I can not tell what to doe but to seeke to you for helpe, hauing no kinde of rest but when I see her, when I speake of her, or thinke vppon her. And I am at this present reduced into so pitiful plight as being not able to wynne her by intreaties, offers, presentes, sutes, ambassages and letters, my onely and last refuge and assured port of all my miseries, resteth in you, either by death to ende my life, or by force to obtayne my desire." The Earle hearing the vnciuile and beastly demaunde of his soueraigne Lorde, blushing for shame, and throughly astonned, filled also with a certaine honest and vertuous disdayne, was not able to dissolue his tongue to render a worthy aunswere to the afflicted Prince. Finally, like one awaked from his dead sleepe, he said vnto him: "Sir, my wittes fayle, my vertue reuolteth, my tongue is mute, at the wordes that proceede from you, whereby I fele my selfe brought into two strange and perillous pointes, as passing either by one or other, I must nedes fall into very great daunger. But to resolue vpon that which is most expedient, hauing geuen vnto you my faithe in pledge, to succour and helpe you euen to the abandoning of honor and life, I will not be contrarie to my woordes. And touching my daughter, for whom you make request, I will reueale vnto her the effecte of your demaunde: yet of one thing I must tell you, sir, power I haue to entreate her, but none at all to force her. Inough it is that she vnderstnd of me, what hart and affection you beare vnto her. But I doe maruell, yea and complaine of you, pardon me (most drad soueraigne) and suffer me without offence to discharge my grief before your presence, rather than to your shame and mine eternal infamie, it should be manifested and published abrode by other. I say, that I maruell, sir, what occasion moued you to commit such reproch in my stock and bloud, and by an act so shamefull and lasciuious, to dishonour the same: whiche neuer disdained to serue both you and yours to the vttermost of their powers. Alas, vnhappy father that I am, is this the guerdon and recompence that I and my children shall expect for our trusty and faithfull seruice? O sir, for God's sake, if you liste not to be liberall of your owne, seke not to dishonour vs, and to inflict vpon our race such notable infamie. But who can loke for worse at the handes of his mortall and cruell enemie? It is you, euen you it is (most noble Prince) that doth rauishe my daughter's honor, dispoyle me of my contentation, ye take from my children hardinesse to shewe their faces, and from all our whole house, the auncient fame and glorie. It is you that doth obscure the clearenesse of my bloud, with an attempt so dishonest and detestable, as the memorie therof shall neuer be forgotten. It is you that doth constraine me to be the infamous minister of the totall destruction of my progenie, and to be a shamelesse Pandarus of my daughter's honor. Doe you thinke to helpe and succour me, when others shall attempt to obiect vnto my face this slaunder and reproche? but if your selfe doe hurt me, where shall I hereafter seke reliefe and succour. If the hande which ought to helpe me, be the very same that doth giue me the wounde, where shall the hope bee of my recouerie? For this cause, may it please your maiestie, whether iustlie I do make my complainte, and whether you geue me cause to aduance my cries vp into the heauens, your selfe shall be the iudge: for, if like a iudge in deede you doe geue ouer your disordinate affection, I then appeale to the iudgement of your inuincible minde, of late accomplished with all curtesie and gentlenesse. On the other side, I doe lament your fortune, when I thinke vpon the reasons which you haue alleaged, and the greater cause I haue to plaine, because I haue knowen you from your youth, and haue alwayes deemed you at libertie and free from such passions, not thral or subiect to the flames of loue, but rather geuen to exercise of armes. And nowe seing you to become a prisoner of an affection vnworthy your estate, I can not tell what to thinke, the noueltie of this sodain chaunce semeth to be so straunge. Remember sir, that for a litle suspicion of adulterie, you caused Roger Mortimer to be put to death. And (being skarce able to tell it without teares) you caused your owne mother miserablie to die in pryson: and God knoweth howe simple your accusations were, and vpon howe light ground your suspicion was conceived. Do not you knowe howe wounderfully you be molested with warres, and that your enemies, trauell day and night to circumuent you, both by Sea and Lande? Is it nowe tyme then to geue your selfe to delightes, and to captiuate your mynde in the pleasures of Ladies? Where is the auncient generositie and nobilitie of your bloud? Wher is magnanimitie and valour, wherewith you haue astonned your eunemies, shewed your selfe amiable to your frends, and wonderfull to your subiects? Touching the last point, wherin you threaten, that if my doughter doe not agree to your desire, you will forcibly enioye her, I can neuer confesse that to be the fact of a valiaunt and true king, but of a vile, cowardly, cruell and libidinous Tyraunt. I trust it be not the pleasure of God, that nowe at the age you be of, you wil begin to force Gentlewomen that be your humble subiects, which if you do, this iland shall lose the name of a Realme, and hereafter shalbe deemed none other, but a sanctuarie of theues and murderers. If then, (to conclude this my sorowefull and heauie complaint) you may, or can by your flatteries, promisses and presents, allure my doughter to your vnbrideled appetites, I shall haue occasion to bewayle her dishonestie, and to deeme her, as an incontinent daughter, degenerated from the vertues of her progenitors. But touching your owne persone, I haue nothing to saye, but that herein you doe followe the common sort of men, that be sutors to Ladies, willing to please their fansies. There resteth onely nowe for me to aunswere the fauour, whiche in time to come you promise to me and my children: I couet not after any thing reprochfull to me or them, or to any of our posteritie, that may make us ashamed, knowing in what contempt and reputation they be, which being borne of base parentage, be arriued to goods and honour, by gratifying and obeying Princes and kinges in their dishonest lustes and appetites. Remember sir, that within these fewe dayes, being in campe against the Scottes, you vpbrayded a certaine man (which shalbe namelesse) for being a minister of your father's loue, who from the state of a barber, was aduaunced to the degree of an Earle, and how you sayd, that if in time to come he amended not his manners, you would sende him to the shop againe. And for my part, I am of opinion, that honest pouertie hath euer bene the auncient and greatest inheritaunce amonges the noble Romaines, which if it be condemned by the ignoraunt multitude, and if we therefore should geue place, making greater accompt and estimation of richesse and treasures, then of vertue: I doe say for mine own part, that by the grace of God, I am abundantly prouided, for the maintenance of me and mine, not like an ambicious man or couetous, but as one satisfied with the good wil of fortune. I do most humbly then besech you (sir) for conclusion, to take in good parte, that which my dutie and honour do constraine me to speake. And so by your grace's leaue, I will departe towarde my daughter, to let her vnderstande from point to point your maiestie's pleasure." And without tarying for other replie of the kyng, he went his way discoursing diuers thinges in his minde, vpon that which had passed betwene the king and him. The reasons which the Earle had made, so pearced the affections of the passionate Prince, as vncertaine what to saye, he condemned himselfe, knowing verie well, that the Earle not only vpon right and iust cause, had pronounced these wordes: but also that he had done the office of a faithfull seruaunt and trustie counseller, in such sort, as feling his conscience touched at the quicke, he could not excuse himself from committing a dishonest charge to a father so commendable and vertuous in the behalfe of his daughter. Thus he determined to chaunge his opinion. Afterwardes when he had throwen forth many sighes, hee spake these wordes to himselfe. "O miserable man, cut of this amorous practise, howe arte thou defrauded of right sense to cast thy mynd vpon her, whom thou oughtest to vse with such reuerence as thou wouldest doe thine own proper sister, for the seruice which thou and thy progenitors haue receiued of the good Earle her father? Open the eyes of thine vnderstanding and knowe thy selfe, geue place to reason, and reforme thy vnshamefull and disordinate appetites.

Resist with al thy power this wanton will which doth enuiron thee. Suffer not this tyraunt loue to bewitch or deceiue thee." Sodainly after he had spoken those wordes, the beautie of the Countesse representing it self before his eyes, made him to alter his minde again, and to reiect that which he before allowed, saying thus: "I feele in minde the cause of mine offence, and thereby doe acknowledge the wrong, but what shall I doe? sithe I am not able any longer to withstande beautie, that cruell murderer, whiche doth force and maister me so much? Let fortune then and loue doe what they list, the faire Countesse shalbe myne, whatsoeuer come of it. Is it a notable vice in a king to loue his subiecte's daughter? Am I the first vpon whome such inconueniene hath come?" This talke ended, he deluded himself, and thinking vpon the contrary, he accused himself again, and then from this he altered again to the other. And being in this perplexitie, he passed daye and night, with such anguish and dolor, as euery man doubted his health: and floting thus betwene hope and dispaire, he resolued in thend to attend the father's answere. The Earle then being gone out of the king's chambre, aggrauated with sorowfull thoughtes, full of rage and discontent, thought good to delay the matter till the next day, before he spake to his daughter: and then calling her vnto him, and causing her to sit against him, he reasoned the matter in such wise. "I am assured, deare daughter, that you will no lesse maruell than be astonned to heare what I shal say vnto you, and so much the more, when you doe see, how farre my tale shall exceade the order of Reason. But for so much as of twoo euils the least is to be chosen, I doubt not, but like a sage and wise woman, which I haue alwayes knowen you to be, you will stay vpon that whiche I haue determined. Touching my self, sith it hath pleased God to geue me knowledge of good and il, hitherto I haue still preferred honour before life, bicause (after mine opinion) it is a lesse matter to die innocently, than to liue in dishonour and shame of the worlde. But you know what libertie he hath, which is vnder the power of another, being sometime constrayned to make faire weather of thinges not onely cleane contrarie to his myndc, but also (which is worse) against his owne conscience, being oftentymes forced according to the qualitie of the tyme, and pleasure of the state, to chaunge his maners, and to put on newe affections. Whereof I haue thought good to put you in remembraunce, because it toucheth the matter, whiche I purpose to tell you. Thus it is (deare daughter) that yesterday after dynner, the kyng sent for mee, and being come before him, with a very instant and pitiful prayer, he required me (his eyes full of teares) to doe a thing for hym that touched his life. I whiche (besides that I am his subiect and seruaunt) haue alwayes borne a particuler affection to his father and him, without deliberation what the matter should be, betrothed to him my faith to obey his request, if it coste me the price of mine honour and life. He assuring himselfe of my liberall promise, after many wordes ioyned with an infinite number of sighes, discouering vnto me the secrete of his harte, told me, that the torment which he indured, proceded no where els but of the feruent loue that he bare vnto you. But, O immortall God, what man of any discretion would haue thought that a king could be so impudent and vnshamefast, as to committe to a father a charge so dishonest towardes his own daughter?" The Earle hauing recited in order the historie past betwene hym and the kyng, sayde thus vnto her: "Consider you, swete daughter, myne vnaduised and simple promisse, and the vnbrideled mynde of an amorous kyng, to whome I made aunswere, that intreate you thereunto I was able, but force you I coulde not. For this cause (deare daughter) I doe praye you at this instant to obeye the kynge's pleasure, and thereby to make a present by your father of your honest chastitie, so dearely estemed and regarded by you, specially, that the thing may so secretly be done as the fault be not bruted in the eares of other. Neuerthelesse, the choyse resteth in you, and the key of your honour is in your own hands, and that which I haue sayde vnto you, is but to kepe promise with the king." The Countesse all the while that her father thus talked, chaunged her colour with a comly shamefastnesse, inflamed with a vertuous disdaine, that he whiche had behold her then, would haue thought her rather some celestial goddesse than a humaine creature: and after long silence, with an humble grauitie she began thus to make her aunswere: "Your wordes haue so confounded me, and brought me into suche admiration (my Lorde and right honourable father) that if all the partes of my bodie were conuerted into tongues, they could not bee sufficient worthely to expresse the least part of my sorrowe and disquietnesse: and truely very iustly may I complayne of you, for the litle estimation you haue of me, which am deriued of your owne fleshe: and for the ransome of the fraile and transitorie life which you haue geuen me vpon earth, you wyll for recompence nowe defraude me of myne honour: whereby I do perceiue that not onely al nature's lawes be cancelled and mortified in you, but which is worse, you doe exceede therin the cruelties of beastes, who for all their brutishenesse be not so vnnatural to do wrong to their owne yong, or to offer their fruite to the mercie of an other, as you haue done yours to the pleasure of a Kyng: for notwithstandynge the straight charge and aucthoritie whiche you haue ouer mee, to commaunde me being your right humble and very obedient daughter, yet you ought to thinke and remember, that you haue neuer seene in mee any acte, mocion, signe, or woorde, to incite you to moue sutch dishonest talk. And although the king many times, with infinite number of prayers, presentes, messages and other such allurementes of persuasion hath displayed and vttered all the art of his mynde to seduce and corrupt me, yet he was neuer able to receiue other aunswere of me, but that honor was a thousand times derer vnto me then life, which still I meant to kepe secret from your knowledge euen as I haue done from other of mine aliaunce, for feare least you should be induced to commit some trespas, or conspire against our king, forseing the straunge accidentes whiche haue chaunced for like matters, to the ruine of many cities and prouinces. But, good God, my doubt is nothing to purpose, sithe that your selfe is the shamelesse post of an act so dishonest: and to conclude in fewe wordes, daily I had good hope, that the king seing me at a point still to conserue my chastitie inuiolable he would give ouer to pursue me any longer, and would haue suffered me hereafter to liue in quiet with mine equals, but if so be he doe continue obstinate in his olde folly, I am determined rather to die, than to doe the thing that shall hurt me and pleasure him: and for feare that he take from me by force that which of mine owne accord I will not graunt, following your counsell, of twoo euilles I will chose the least, thinking it more honourable to destroy and kill my selfe with mine own handes, then to suffer such blot or shame to obscure the glorie of my name, being desirous to committe nothing in secrete, that sometime hereafter being published, may make me ashamed and chaunge colour. And wher you say that you haue sworne and gaged your faith to the king, for the assuraunce of your promise, it was very ill done, before you did consider, what power fathers haue ouer their children, whiche is so well defined by the lawe of God, as they be not bound to their parentes in that which is against his deuine commaundementes: much lesse may they bynde vs to things incestuous and dishonest, which specially and straightly be inioyned vs not to perfourme, if we therunto be required: and it had bene farre more decent, and excusable before God, if when you made that foolyshe promise to the kyng you had promised him, rather to strangle mee with youre owne handes, than to consent to let me fall into a faulte so abhominable: and to thend I may tell you the last determination, and conclusion of that whiche I am determined by good aduise and immutable counsell: thus it is. You shall tell the king, that I had rather lose my life after the moste cruell and shameful maner that may be deuised, then to consent to a thing so dishonest, hauing long time fixed this saying in mind, '*That honest death doth honor and beautifie the forepassed life.*'" The father hearing the wise aunswere of his daughter, gaue her his blessing, in his hart praysing her godly minde, beseching God to helpe her and to kepe her vnder his protection, and to confirme her in that holy and vertuous determination. Then feling him greatly comforted, he repaired to the king, to whom he said: "Pleaseth your grace, to thintent I might obserue my promise, I sweare by the faith that I doe owe vnto God and you, that I haue done what I can with my daughter, disclosing vnto her your whole minde and pleasure, and exhorting her to satisfy your request, but for a resolute aunswere she saith, that rather she is contented to suffer most cruel death than to commit a thing so contrarie to her honour. You know (sir) what I sayd vnto you still, that I might entreate her, but force her I could not: hauing then obeied your commaundement, and accomplished my promise, it may please you to geue me leaue to go home to one of my Castels, from henceforth to recline my selfe to quietnesse, and to ease my decrepite and feeble age." Which the king willingly graunted. The same daye hee departed from the Courte with his sonnes and went home to his Countrie, leauing at London his wife and daughter and the reste of his housholde, thinking therby to discharge himself of those thinges with out the kinge's displeasure. The king on the other side was no soner aduertised of the Earle's departure, and that he had left his daughter behinde him at London, but he knew the father's minde and purpose, and fell in suche dispaire of his loue, as he was like to haue runne out of his wittes for sorrowe. The nightes and dayes were all one to him, for hee could take no rest, he gaue ouer vse of armes and administration of iustice, hunting and hauking, wherin before that time he had great delight: and all his study was many times to passe and repasse before the gate of the Countesse, to proue if he might attaine to haue some sight of her: and thinges were brought to so pitifull state, that within fewe dayes the citizens and other gentlemen began to perceiue the raging loue of their Prince, euery of them with common voice blaming the crueltie of the Countesse that was vnmarried, who the more she proued the king inflamed with her loue, the more squeymish she was of her beautie. The peres and noble men seing their king reduced to such extremitie, moued with pitie and compassion, began secretly to pratise for him, some with threatninges, some with flatteries and persuasions: some went to the mother, declaring vnto her the eternall rest and quiet prepared for her and all her friendes, if she would persuade her daughter to encline to the kinge's mind, and contrariwyse the daunger iminent ouer her head. But all these deuises were in vayne, for the Countesse moued no more then a harde rocke beaten with diuerse tempestes: and at length seing that euery man spake diuersly, as their affections ledde them, shee was so troubled and pensife in harte, as fearing to bee taken, and that the kyng vanquished with his strong passion, by succession of tyme would vse his force, and violentlye oppresse her, founde meanes to get a great sharpe knife, whiche she caried about her secretly vnder her gowne, of purpose, that if she sawe perill to be defloured, shee might kill her selfe. The Courtiers offended with the martyrdome of their master, and desyrous to gratifie and seeke meanes to doe hym pleasure, conspyred all against the Earle's familie, lettyng the kynge to vnderstande that it were most expedient, for that thinges were out of hope, to cause Aelips to be brought to his Palace, that there he might vse her by force. Wherunto the king (being dronke in his own passion) did willingly agree: notwithstanding, before hee passed any further, for that hee faithfully loued the Countesse, he determined to aduertise her mother of that whiche he intended to doe, and commaunded his Secretarie to go seke her with diligence, and without concealing any thing from her knowledge, to instructe her of the whole. The Secretarie finding the mother of the countesse, said vnto her: "Madame, the king hath willed me to say vnto you that he hath done what he can, and more then his estate requireth, to win the grace and loue of your daughter, but for that she hath despised his long sute, disdained his presence, and abhorred his griefes and complaintes, knowing not what to do any more, his last refuge is in force, doing you to vnderstande hereof, to the intent that you and shee may consider what is to be done in this behalf: for he hath determined whether you will or no, to fetch her out openly by force, to the great dishonour, slaunder and infamie of al your kinne. And where in time past, he hath loued and fauoured the Earle your husband, he meaneth shortly to make him vnderstand what is the effect of the iust indignation of such a Prince as he is." The good Lady hearing this sodaine and cruell message, was astonned in such wise, as she thought how she sawe her daughter already trained by the heares of her head, her garmentes haled and torne in pieces, with rufull and lamentable voyce crying out to him for mercy: for this cause with blubbering teares, trembling for feare, she fell down at the Secretarie's feete, and straightlye imbracing his knees, sayde vnto hym: "Maister Secretarie, my deare louing friend: beseche the king in my name to remember the payne and seruice done by our auncestours. Intreate him not to dishonoure my house in the absence of the Earle my husbande: and if you be not able by your perswasion to mollifie his hard hart, desire him for a while to take pacience, vntill I haue aduertised my daughter of his will and pleasure, whom I hope to perswade, that shee shall satisfie the kinge's request." When she had made this aunswere, the Secretary declared the same to the kinge, who madde with anger and passioned with loue, was content, and neuerthelesse commaunded his gentlemen to be in readinesse to seeke the Countesse. In the meane time the mother of faire Aelips went to her daughter's chamber, and after she had commaunded all her maids, which accompanied her, to withdraw themselues out of the chamber, shee began in few woordes to recite vnto her the message done vnto her by the Secretary: finally with sobbinge sighes she said vnto her: "The dayes haue been (deare daughter) that I haue seene thee to keepe thy state amonges the chiefeste of all the Ladies of this Realme: and I haue counted my self most happie that euer I did beare the in my wombe, and haue thoughte, by meanes of thy beautie and vertue, one day to see thee become the ioye and comfort of all thy frendes: but now my cogitacions be turned cleane contrary, through thine vnluckie fate: nowe I thincke thee to be borne not onely for the vniuersall ruine of all oure familie, but also (which greeueth me most) to be an occasion and instrument of my death, and desolation of all thy frendes: but if thou wilt somewhat moderate thy rygor all this heauines shortly may be tourned to ioye: for our king and soueraign Lorde is not onely in loue with thee, but for the ardent affection and amitie that he beareth thee, is out of his wittes, and now doth conspire against vs, as though we were traytors and murderers of our Prince: in whose handes (as thou knowest) doth rest the life, honor and goods both of thy selfe and of vs all: and what glory and triumphe shall be reported of thee to our posterity, when they shal know how by thy obstinate crueltie, thou haste procured the death of thine old father, the death of thy hooreheaded mother, and the destruction of thy valiaunt and coragious brethren, and dispoyled the rest of thy bloud of their possessions and abilitie? But what sorrowe and griefe will it be, to see them wander in the world like vagabounds banished from their liuings, and remaine in continuall pouertie, without place and refuge of their miserie? who in steede of blessing or praysinge the houre of thy birth, will cursse the in their minds a thousand times, as the cause of all their ouerthrow and ill fortune. Thinke and consider vpon the same (deare daughter) for in thee alone resteth the conseruacion of our liues, and hope of all our frendes." This lamentable discourse ended, the afflicted Countesse not able anye longer to resiste that pangue, began to waxe so faint as wyth her armes a crosse she fell downe halfe deade vpon her doughter: who seinge her without mouinge and without any apparaunce of life, and all the partes of her bodye to waxe cold, she quicklye layde her downe, and then with helpe and other thinges apt for sowninges, shee made her come to herselfe againe, and thinking wholy to recouer her, she earnestly promised to do what she would haue her, saying vnto her: "Do awaye your teares (Madame) moderate your tormentes, reuoke your former ioye, and be of good cheere, for I am disposed to obey you. God defende that I should be the cause of the paine which I see you to suffer: nowe am I ready to goe with you to the kinge, where if it shall please you, wee two withoute other company will do our owne errande and attempt the beginning of our enterprise." The mother full of ioye, lifting vp her hands to the heauens, tenderly embraced her daughter, and manye times did kisse her, and after shee had commaunded her Coche to be made readye, she wente forth with her doughter, accompanied onelye with two Gentlewomen to the kinge's Palace. Being come thither, they sente worde to the Secretary, that brought her the message, who conducted them to the kinge's chamber, and presenting them before him, sayde: "Syr, beholde the companye which you haue so long time desired: who are come to do your grace humble reuerence." The king greatly astonied, went forth to meete them, and with iouful countinaunce saide: "Welcome, Lady Countesse, and your long desired company. But what good fortune hath broughte you hither nowe?" The Countesse hauing made her obeysance, yet all frighted with feare, aunswered him: "Beholde here my Lorde your fayre Aelips so long time wished for, who taking repentaunce for her former cruelty and rigor, is come to render herselfe at your commaundement." Then the king beholding the yong Countesse tremblinge for feare, like a leafe shaken with the winde (with her eyes fixed on the grounde) approching neer her, toke her by the hande, and kissing her, sayd: "Welcome, my life and soule." But she no more moued than a fierce lion enuironed with cruell beastes, stood still and helde her peace, her harte so constrayned for sorrow and despite, as she was not able to aunsweare a word. The kinge who thoughte that such passion proceeded of shame, commaunded the Gentlewomen, that were in her company, to departe the chamber, sauing the mother which broughte her to the entrie of his chamber, who withdrawing herselfe backe, left her to the mercy of loue and the kinge. So sone as the king was entred the chamber he shutte the doore after him. Which Aelips perceiuinge beganne to feele a furious combate betweene her honour and life, fearing to be defloured, and seing her abandoned of al humaine succour, falling downe prostrate at his feete, she sayd vnto him: "Gracious and redoubted Prince, sithe my heauy fortune hath broughte mee hither, like an innocente Lambe to the sacrifice, and that my parents amazed through your furie, are become rauishers of me against my will, and contrary to the duety of their honor, haue deliuered me into your handes, I humbly beseech your maiestie, if there remaine in your noble personage any sparke of vertue and Princely affection, before you passe any further to satisfy your desire, to let me proue and vnderstande by effecte, if your loue be such, as oftentimes by letters and mouth you haue declared vnto me. The requeste which I will make vnto you shall be but easie, and yet shall satisfie mee more than all the contentacion of the world. Otherwise (sir) doe not thinke that so longe as my life doth continue, I am able to do that which can contente your desire. And if my sute shall seeme reasonable, and grounded vppon equitie, before I doe open and declare the same more at large, assure the performaunce thereof vnto me by oth." The king hearing her prayer to be so reasonable, wherunto rather then to refuse it, he swore by his Scepter, taking God to witnesse and all the heauenly powers for confirmacion of that which he pretended to promise: saide vnto her: "Madame, the onely maistresse and keper of my louing harte, sith of your grace and curtesie you haue vouchsafed to come vnto my Palace, to make request of my onely fauoure and good will, which now I irreuocably do consent and graunt, swearing vnto you by that honourable sacramente of Baptism, whereby I was incorporated to the Church of God, and for the loue that I beare you (for greater assuraunce I cannot giue) I will not refuse any thing, that is in my power and abilitie, to the intent you may not be in doubt whether I do loue you, and intend hereafter to imploy my selfe to serue and pleasure you: for otherwyse I should falsify my faith, and more feruently I cannot bind my selfe if I shoulde sweare by all the othes of the worlde." The fayre Countesse sitting still vpon her knees, although the king many times prayed her to rise vp, reuerently toke the king by the hand, saying: "And I do kisse this royal hand for loyall testimonie of the fauour which your grace doth shew me." Then plucking out a sharpe knife, which was hidden under her kirtle, all bathed and washed in teares, reclining her pitifull eyes towardes the king, that was appalled with that sight, she said vnto him: "Sir, the gift that I require, and wherfore your faith is bound, is this. I most humblie desire you, that rather then to dispoile me of mine honour, with the sworde girded by your side, you do vouchsafe to ende my life, or to suffer me presently, with this sharpe pointed knife in my hand to thrust it to my hart, that mine innocent bloud, doing the funerall honour, may beare witnesse before God of my vndefiled chastity, as being vtterly resolued honourablie to die. And that rather then to lose mine honoure, I may murther my selfe before you wyth this blade and knife in present hand." The king burning with amorous heate, beholding this pitifull spectacle, and consideringe the inuincible constancie and chastitie of the Countesse, vanquished by remorse of conscience, ioyned with like pitie, taking her by the hand, said: "Rise vp Lady, and liue from henceforth assured: for I will not ne yet pretende all the dayes of my life, to commit any thing in you against your will." And plucking the knife out of her hand, exclaimed: "This knife hereafter shall bee the pursiuant before God and men of this thine inexpugnable chastitie, the force whereof wanton loue was not able to endure, rather yelding place to vertue, which being not alienated from me, hath made me at one instant victorious ouer my selfe, which by and by I will make you to vnderstande to your greate contentacion and greater maruel. For assuraunce wherof I desire none other thing of you, but a chaste kisse." Which receyued, hee opened the doore and caused the Countesse to come in with the Secretarie and the gentlewomen, and same time hee called also the Courtiers and Piers of the Realme, which were then in the base Court of the Palace, among whom was the Archbishop of Yorke, a man of great reputacion and singuler learning, to whom with the knife in his hand he recited particulerly the discourse of his loue: and after he toke the Countesse by the hande, and sayde vnto her: "Madame, the houre is come that for recompence of your honest chastity and vertue, I wil and consent to take you to wife, if you thincke good." The Countesse hearinge those wordes began to recoloure her bleake and pale face with a vermilion teinte and roseal rudde, and accomplished with incredible delight and ioye, falling downe at his feete, said vnto him "My Lord, for asmuch as I neuer loked to be aduaunced to so honourable state as fortune nowe doth offer, for merite of a benefit so high and great which you present vnto me, vouchsauing to abase your selfe to the espousal of so poore a Lady, your maiesties pleasure being such, behold me ready at your commaundement." The king taking her vp from kneeling on the ground, commaunded the Bishop to pronounce with highe voice the vsual words of Matrimonie. Then drawing a riche Diamond from his finger hee gaue it to the Countesse, and kissing her, saide: "Madame, you be Queene of England, and presently I doe giue you thirty thousande angells by the yeare for your reuenew. And the Duchie of Lancaster being by confiscation fallen into my hands, I guie also vnto you, to bestowe vppon your selfe and your frends." Al which inrolled according to the maner of the countrie, the king (accomplishing the mariage) rewarded the Countesse for the rigorous interestes of his so long loue, with suche hap and content as they may iudge which haue made assay of like pleasure, and recouered the fruite of so long pursute. And the more magnificently to solemnize the mariage, the kinge assembled all the Nobilitie of Englande, and somoned them to be at London the first day of July then folowinge, to beautifie and assist the Nupcialles and coronation of the Queene. Then he sente for the father and brethren of the Queene, whom he embraced one after an other, honouring the Earle as his father, and his sonnes as his brethren, wherof the Earle wonderfully reioysed, seinge the conceyued hope of his daughter's honour sorted to so happie effecte, as well to the perpetual fame of him and his, as to the euerlasting aduauncement of his house. At the appointed day the Queene was broughte from her father's house apparelled with Royall vestures, euen to the Palace, and conducted with an infinite nomber of Lords and Ladies to the Church, where when seruice was done, the kinge was maried (againe) openly, and the same celebrated, shee was conueyed vp into a publike place, and proclamed Queene of England, to the exceedinge gratulacion and ioye incredible of all the subiectes.

3. Source

From *The Chronicles of England, Scotland and Ireland* (1587 edition), vols. 2 and 5

By Raphael Holinshed; edited by Sir Henry Ellis, 1807–1808

England vol. 2

The cardinal of Piergort the popes legat, as then lieng in the citie of Poictiers, came that morning to the king, and required him to absteine from battell, till he might vnderstand whether the prince would condescend vnto such conditions of peace as he himselfe should think reasonable, which if it might be brought to passe, the same should be more honorable for him, than to adventure so manie noble men as were there with him at that present in hazard of battell. The king was contented that the cardinall should go to the prince, and see what he could doo with him. The cardinall rode to the prince, and talked with him till he was contented to come to a treatie. The cardinall returned to the French king, and required of him that a truce might be granted till the next daies sun-rising: which truce obteined, he spent that daie in riding to and fro betwixt them.

The prince offered to render into the kings hands all that he had woone in that voiage, as well townes as castels, and also to release all the prisoners, which he or any of his men had taken in that iournie: and further he was contented to haue beene sworne not to beare armour against the French king within the terme of seuen yeares next following. But the French king would not agree therevnto: the vttermost that he would agree vnto, was this, that the prince and an hundred of his knights should yeeld themselues as prisoners vnto him, otherwise he would not haue the matter taken vp. But it was the French kings hap after (notwithstanding his hautines) to be taken captiue, as Okland noteth, saieng,

——— seruilia sub iuga missus
Disceret vt domino regi parêre Britanno.

But the prince in no wise cold be brought to any such vnreasonable conditions, and so the cardinall could not make them fre'ends, although he trauelled earnestlie betwixt them all that daie. When it drew towards night, he returned toward Poictiers.

The Englishmen were not idle, whilest the cardinall was thus in hand to bring the parties to some good agreement, but cast great ditches, and made hedges, and other fortifications about the place where their archers stood, and on the next morning, being mondaie, the prince and his people prepared themselues to receiue battell, as they had doone before, hauing passed the day before and that night in great defect of necessarie things, for they could not stir abroad to fetch forrage or other prouisions without danger to be surprised of their enimies. The cardinall came againe earlie in the morning vnto the French king, and found the French armie readie in order of battell by that time the sunne was vp, and though he eftsoones fell in hand to exhort the king to an agreement, yet it would not be. So he went to the prince, and declared to him how he could doo no good in the matter, and therefore he must abide the hazard of battell for ought that he could see: wherewith the prince was content, and so the cardinall returned vnto Poictiers.

Here is to be remembred, that when (as Thomas Walsingham writeth) this cardinall of Piergort was sent from the pope to trauell betwixt the parties for a peace to be had, and that the pope exhorted him verie earnestlie to shew his vttermost diligence and indeuour therein: at his setting foorth to go on that message, the said cardinall (as was said) made this answer: Most blessed father (said he) either we will persuade them to peace and quietnesse, either else shall the verie flintstones crie out of it. But this he spake not of himselfe, as it was supposed, but being a prelate in that time, he prophesied what should follow; for when the English archers had bestowed all their arrowes vpon their enimies, they tooke vp pebles from the place where they stood, being full of those kind of stones, and approching to their enimies, they threw the same with such violence on them, that lighting against their helmets, armor, and targets, they made a great ringing noise, so that the cardinals prophesie was fulfilled, that he would either persuade a peace, or else the stones should crie out thereof.

Scotland vol. 5

About the same time sir William Montacute earle of Salisburie, togither with the earle of Arundell came into Scotland with a great power of men, and besieged the castell of Dunbar, lieng at the same for the space of 22 weeks. [At which battell also was king Edward, the earle of Glocester, the lords Persie and Neuill, being in the yeare 1337, as saith *Scala chron.*] Within the said castell was the countesse hir selfe, surnamed blacke Agnes of Dunbar, who shewed such manlie defense, that no gaine was to be got anie waies forth at hir hands, so that in the end they were constreined to raise their siege, and to depart without speed of their purpose. It is said, that this countesse vsed manie pleasant words in iesting and tawnting at the enimies dooings, thereby the more to incourage hir souldiers.

One day it chanced that the Englishmen had deuised an engine called a sow, vnder the pentise or couert wherof they might approch safelie to the wals: she beholding this engine, merilie said, that vnlesse the Englishmen kept their sow the better, she would make hir to cast hir pigs: and so after destroied it.

SIR THOMAS MORE

9

all marry god forbid that
moo nay certainly you ar
for to the king god hath his offyc lent
of dread of Iustyce, power and Comaund
hath bid him rule, and willd you to obay
and to add ampler maiestie to this
he ~~god~~ hath not ~~le~~ only lent the king his figure
his throne ~~his~~ sword, but gyven him his owne name
calls him a god on earth, what do you then
rysing gainst him that god himsealf enstalls
but ryse gainst god, what do you to your sowles
in doing this o desperat ~~ar~~ as you are.
wash your foule mynds with teares and those same hands
that you lyke rebells lyft against the peace
lift vp for peace, and your vnreuerent knees
~~that~~ make them your feet to kneele to be forgyven
~~is safer warrs, then ever you can make~~
~~whose discipline is ryot; why euen your warrs hurly~~
~~cannot proceed but by obedienc~~ what rebell captaine
as mutynes ar incident, by his name
can still the rout who will obay a traytor
or howe can well that proclamation sounde
when ther is no adicion but a rebell
to quallyfy a rebell, youle put downe straingers
kill them cutt their throts possesse their howses
and leade the matie of lawe in liom
to slipp him lyke a hound; ~~sayeng~~ say nowe the king
as he is clement, yf thoffendor moorne
shoold so much com to short of your great trespas
as but to banysh you, whether woold you go.
what Country by the nature of your error
shoold gyve you harber go you to ffraunc or flanders
to any Iarman province, ~~to~~ spane or portigall
nay any where ~~why you~~ that not adheres to Ingland
why you must needs be straingers, woold you be pleasd
to find a nation of such barbarous temper
that breaking out in hiddious violence
woold not afoord you, an abode on earth
whett their detested knyves against your throtes
spurne you lyke dogges, and lyke as yf that god
owed not nor made not you, nor that the elaments
wer not all appropriat to ~~ther~~ your Comforts.
but charterd vnto them, what woold you thinck
to be thus vsd, this is the straingers case
and this your mountanish inhumanyty

all fayth a saies trewe letts vs do as we may be doon by

~~all~~ Linco weele be ruld by you master moor yf youle stand our
freind to procure our pdon

moor Submit you to theise noble gentlemen
entreate their mediation to the kinge
geve vp your sealf to forme obay the maiestrate
and thers no doubt, but mercy may be found yf you so seek

INTRODUCTION

Sir Thomas More survives in the form of a manuscript entitled *The Booke of Sir Thomas Moore* (see figure 2). The earliest recorded evidence of the existence of the manuscript is dated 1727. John Murray, a book collector and possibly a book dealer, lent the manuscript to Thomas Hearne, a well-known Oxford antiquary who in a journal noted this remark on the following 15 January:

> On the 12th of Oct. last M^r^. Murray lent me a thin folio Paper MS. done or sowed up in a Vellum Cover; on wch it is intitled, *The Booke of Sir Thomas Moore*. This I have read over. It is wrote in the nature of a Play or Interlude, soon after his death I believe. Tho' it appears from thence plainly, what a great, wise, good, and charitable man Sir Thomas was, yet there is no particular of History in it, but what we know already. It is the original, being in many places strangely scored & in others so altered that 'tis hard to make some things out.[1]

The description of its condition and the precision of the transcription of its title leave no doubt that the manuscript Hearne "read over" is the one that survives as Ms. Harley 7386 in the British Library. Hearne and Murray were both known to Edward Harley, second Earl of Oxford, who perhaps procured the manuscript from Murray and added it to his collection, which came to rest in the library of the British Museum (now the British Library) in 1753. Nothing is known of its earlier provenance.

Publication

Sir Thomas More was first published in 1844 by the Reverend Alexander Dyce for the Shakespeare Society. His text is a good one and preserves some readings that have since disappeared because of the deterioration of the manuscript. A. F. Hopkinson issued a modern-spelling version in 1902 based on Dyce's text, and it was reprinted in 1915. C. F. Tucker Brooke included in his *Shakespeare Apocrypha* (1908) a critical edition based on a fresh transcription. Dyce's and Brooke's editions (and of course the derivative edition by Hopkinson) have been censured for presenting a version intermingling readings from the original and from the additions, which results in a mixed text that fails to represent either the original or the re-

1. Thomas Hearne, *Remarks and Collections*, ed. H. E. Salter for the Oxford Historical Society (Oxford: Clarendon Press, 1914), 9:392–93.

vised play. F. G. Fleay says of Dyce's edition that the result is "neither the original version nor the altered, but a farrago of the two."[2]

The first edition prepared in accord with modern editorial standards is that published by Sir Walter W. Greg as one of the Malone Society Reprints (1911). This *Book of Sir Thomas More* is a type facsimile presenting everything in the manuscript that remains, carefully keeping separate the original text and the additions, and rigorously conforming to the canons of modern bibliographical scholarship. An especially lucid introduction illuminates the many potentially confusing features of the manuscript. Greg's Malone Society version remains, three quarters of a century after it was first published, the standard for the play. A reissue of 1961 with a useful supplement to the introduction by Harold Jenkins remains in print.

Canon John Shirley published a modern-spelling version of Greg's edition in 1938. Herbert Farjeon included in his Nonesuch *Shakespeare* (1953) a transcription of Greg's edition with some readings from Dyce's edition. The text is a conflation of the original with the additions inserted in what Farjeon considers to be appropriate places. Harold Jenkins published in C. J. Sisson's *Complete Works* (1954) a modern-spelling text representing the revised version of the play. It incorporates all the additions and takes fully into account—though not always adopting—all the deletions and corrections. In his introduction, Jenkins notes that since the play "was not brought to finality," it is impossible to arrive at a true final version. However, beginning with a fresh reexamination of the manuscript and aiming, with balanced scholarly judgment, at a smoothly flowing play, he has produced a text that is probably as close to the playwrights' final intention as is possible. It is the only one of its kind.[3]

Excerpts from *Sir Thomas More* are frequently reprinted, usually limited to Addition IIc (the last portion of the riot scene), but sometimes also including Addition III (More's soliloquy on greatness), the passages generally thought to be Shakespeare's. The most important of these are those of Sir Edward Maunde Thompson, Greg, and R. C. Bald. Thompson published his transcription of Addition IIc in his *Shakespeare's Handwriting*; and Greg printed his in the symposium on *Sir Thomas More*, brought together under the leadership of Alfred W. Pollard. While these two, and that in Greg's earlier edition of the play, "differ in a number of details" (as Greg says in *Shakespeare's Hand*, p. 228), they are essentially very similar, as is Bald's independent transcription. Greg also contributed to the Pollard

2. Frederick Gard Fleay, *A Biographical Chronicle of the English Stage*, 2 vols. (London, 1891; rpt. New York: Franklin, 1969), 2:312.

3. Harold Jenkins, ed., *Sir Thomas More*. *Works*, ed. C. J. Sisson (London: Odhams 1954), pp. 1235–66. Vittorio Gabrieli and Giorgio Melchiori, who issued a modern spelling text with apparatus in Italian (Bari: Adriatica, 1981), have in preparation an edition in the Revels plays series.

symposium a "consecutive and more or less readable text of [all] the insurrection scenes" in the original spelling.[4]

Photographic renderings of the posited Shakespearean portions of the play have been about as numerous as transcripts. John Farmer published a photographic facsimile of the complete manuscript in the Tudor Facsimile Texts series. It is of the first importance not only because it is the only facsimile of the entire manuscript but also because it preserves readings that have since disappeared or become illegible. In the original 1911 issue and the 1961 reprint of Greg's edition, portions of six folios are reproduced, exhibiting the hands in the manuscript. Thompson reproduced folios 8^a, 8^b, and 9^a in *Shakespeare's Handwriting* that are distinctly superior to most other photographic facsimiles of these pages. There are good quality photographic reproductions of pages of the manuscript in whole or in part in *Shakespeare's Hand* (plates 3 and 4), in Greg's *Dramatic Documents*, "Prompt Books" (plates 2A and 2B), in Bald's *Shakespeare Survey* essay (plates 13–15), in P. J. Croft's *Autograph Poetry*, and in the Riverside *Shakespeare* (pp. 1698–1700). Samuel Schoenbaum, in his *William Shakespeare: Records and Images* (items 52, 53, and 54), reproduces not only folios 8^a, 8^b, and 9^a but also the single word *all* on 9^b, probably a speech prefix, first noted by Peter Blayney.[5] There are numerous other photographic facsimiles of individual pages and portions of pages extracted from what are alluded to as "the three pages," especially in paleographic studies of the different hands.

The Manuscript

The *Booke of Sir Thomas Moore* consists of an original version of the play and a series of emendations and expansions. These take the form of additions, of which there are six of varying extent, and of alterations in the

4. Edward Maunde Thompson, *Shakespeare's Handwriting* (Oxford: Clarendon Press, 1916); W. W. Greg, "The Handwritings of the Manuscript," *Shakespeare's Hand in the Play of Sir Thomas More*, ed. Alfred W. Pollard (Cambridge: Cambridge University Press, 1923; rpt. 1967); R. C. Bald, "*The Booke of Sir Thomas More* and its Problems," *ShS* 2 (1949): 44–61. Additions IIc and III are reprinted in the collected *Works*, eds. John Munro, G. Blakemore Evans, and Stanley Wells and Gary Taylor; John Munro, ed., *London Shakespeare*, 6 vols. (London: Eyre and Spottiswood; New York: Simon & Schuster, 1957), 4:1255–78; G. Blakemore Evans, ed., *Riverside Shakespeare* (Boston: Houghton Mifflin, 1974), pp. 1683–97. Stanley Wells and Gary Taylor, eds., *Oxford Shakespeare* (Oxford: Clarendon Press, 1986), pp. 889–92.

5. John S. Farmer, ed., *The Book of Sir Thomas Moore*, Tudor Facsimile Texts, no. 65 (Edinburgh and London: by the editor, 1910; rpt. New York: AMS, 1970); W. W. Greg, *Dramatic Documents from the Elizabethan Playhouses*, 2 vols. (Oxford: Clarendon Press, 1931); P. J. Croft, *Autograph Poetry in the English Language* (London: Cassell, 1973), vol. 1, no. 23; Evans, *Riverside Shakespeare*, pp. 1698–1700; S. Schoenbaum, *William Shakespeare: Records and Images* (New York: Oxford University Press, 1981); Peter W. M. Blayney, "*The Booke of Sir Thomas Moore* re-examined," *SP* 69 (1972): 167–91.

original text, both *currente calamo* and as editorial changes. There are two lacunae in the original version representing leaves removed because the original text was, or was intended to be, superseded. In one instance (after folio 11), it is fairly certain that only one leaf was extracted; in the other instance (after folio 5), it may have been one or two leaves. As a consequence of the many changes, the omissions, the insertion of additions, the employment of links that are not always complete or clear, and the extensive emendations in the original version, the text gives the appearance of being in a confused state, leading some scholars to conclude that the play as we have it may be unfinished. In total, the manuscript comprises twenty-two leaves. The first two are the original vellum wrapper extracted from a medieval devotional book, and the remaining twenty leaves contain the text.

The Hands

There are seven hands in the manuscript. The original fair copy throughout is in a single hand (Hand S)[6] that has been identified as that of Anthony Munday, who was the author of part, but probably not all, of that version. A second hand that appears throughout (Hand C), writing some fairly long stretches of dialogue and also making numerous less extensive but nevertheless important changes in the text, in the stage directions and in the speech prefixes, is that of a playhouse scribe. The hand of Edmund Tilney occurs here and there in the original version of the play noting passages for deletion or change, because he found them unacceptable, and writing an unequivocal instruction at the head of the manuscript (folio 3^{a}):

> <Leaue out> ye insur <rection> wholy & ye Cause ther off & <b>egin w^{t} s^{r} Tho: Moore att ye mayors sessions w^{t} a reportt afterwards off his good servic' don being' Shriue off Londõ vppõ a mutiny Agaynst ye Lũbards only by A shortt reportt & nott otherwise att your own perilles E Tyllney. (p. 1)[7]

Greg's observation that Tilney's hand does not appear in the additions has general scholarly support. Besides Hand C, there are in the six additions

6. The letters designating the hands are those assigned by Greg in his edition. S stands for scribe. Letters A through E identify five hands in the order in which they first appear in the additions to the original play. The seventh hand is that of Edmund Tilney, Master of the Revels and official censor of the drama.

7. Giorgio Melchiori reports that he and Peter Croft determined that one phrase reads, "w^{t} ye Cause ther off," instead of "& ye Cause," as Greg has it. Giorgio Melchiori, "*The Booke of Sir Thomas Moore*: A Chronology of Revision," *SQ* 37 (1986): 291–308; see n. 27, p. 299. Page numbers in the Introduction and notes, unless otherwise indicated, refer to W. W. Greg, ed. *The Book of Sir Thomas More* (Oxford: Oxford University Press, for the Malone Society, 1911).

four hands assigned, as Jenkins says, following Pollard (p. xxxiv), "with varying degrees of confidence," as Henry Chettle (Hand A), Thomas Heywood (Hand B), William Shakespeare (Hand D), and Thomas Dekker (Hand E). The identification of Chettle and Dekker with Hands A and E on paleographic grounds is regarded as reasonably certain. Critics are divided on whether Hand B is Heywood's, and the identification of D as Shakespeare's hand is more widely disputed. Finally there are a few intrusions of no great significance in another hand, but this is generally acknowledged as modern and may be disregarded.

Except for Tilney's, none of the hands is identified in the manuscript itself.[8] The various assignments are made on the basis of paleographic, literary, and theatrical evidence that is subject to differences of opinion, and not all scholars accept the evidence. Since there is significant disagreement in regard to Hands B and D, they will be discussed after Hands S, A, C, and E.

The hand in which the original fair copy is written was designated by Greg in his edition as S for Scribe, because he considered him to be merely a copyist and not an original playwright. This determination was supported by the fact that the hand is a good, reasonably clear English secretary, exhibiting few idiosyncracies, and further that in at least two instances S apparently made copyist's errors. One year after Greg's edition of the play was published, Farmer issued in his Tudor Texts series a collatype facsimile of *John a Kent and John a Cumber*, a play signed at the end by "Anthony Mundy." A paleographic comparison of the handwriting in *John a Kent* with that of *Sir Thomas More* by Greg and independently by Thompson established S as Munday's hand,[9] and, in this, scholarly opinion attains a consensus. Since Munday at any possible date for *Sir Thomas More* was already a successful playwright, the idea that he was merely a copyist was untenable.

Primarily as an aid to the authentication of literary manuscripts, Greg published in 1925 the first volume of his *English Literary Autographs*.

8. Scholarly discussion of the identification of the hands, and of the broader question of authorship, is extensive, multifarious, and scattered. Useful summary accounts may be found in R. W. Chambers, *Man's Unconquerable Mind* (London: Cape, 1939; rpt. New York: Haskell, 1967), pp. 227–48; Bald, "*Booke*"; Jenkins's supplement to the Introduction to Greg ed., *The Booke of Sir Thomas More*, 1961 issue, xxxiii–xlv; Kenneth Muir, *Shakespeare as Collaborator* (London: Methuen, 1960), pp. 4–6; and S. Schoenbaum, *Internal Evidence and Elizabethan Dramatic Authorship* (Evanston: Northwestern University Press, 1966), pp. 104–7, 124. For a list of materials published to 1930, see E. K. Chambers, *William Shakespeare: A Study of Facts and Problems*, 2 vols. (Oxford: Clarendon Press, 1930), 1:499–500; for those published after 1930, see my annotated bibliography on the four ascribed plays, one of which is *Sir Thomas More* (New York: Garland, 1982), pp. 69–117.

9. W. W. Greg, "Autograph Plays by Anthony Munday," *MLR* 8 (1913): 89–90; *Shakespeare's Hand*, p. 48; E. M. Thompson, "Autograph MSS. of Anthony Munday," *Transactions of the Bibliographical Society*, no. 14, October 1915 to March 1917 (1919), pp. 325–53.

Among them Samuel Tannenbaum recognized Hand A as that of Henry Chettle.[10] He supports his contention with a detailed analysis and comparison of writing habits and letter forms, especially of the characteristic formation of certain letters, combinations of letters, and the use of the digraph *ct*. He also pointed out an unusual form of the minuscule *i* that occurs only in Hand A and Chettle's writing in Henslowe's *Diary*. This identification is confirmed by Greg, McKerrow, Sisson, Jenkins, and recently by Anthony Petti, and has been generally accepted.[11]

Greg's evidence for identifying the writer of Hand C as a playhouse functionary includes the presence of the hand in many parts of the manuscript performing such functions as making "tidying up" changes, revising stage directions, adding warning notes, fitting the additions into their places, attempting to clear up at least one textual tangle (in Hand D), and transcribing one draft passage originally written in Hand B—both versions surviving. He appears to have been a bookkeeper. Greg's judgment was confirmed when he discovered the same hand in two theatrical plots, in the second part of *The Seven Deadly Sins* at Dulwich College and in a fragment of another plot, which is likely to be *2 Fortune's Tennis*, in the British Library.[12] The owner of Hand C has not thus far been successfully associated with a name. Tannenbaum made an effort to identify C as Thomas Kyd on the basis of comparisons with the handwriting in surviving documents generally acknowledged to be in Kyd's hand. The similarities are not as convincing as those in the instance of, for example, Henry Chettle. Tannenbaum candidly lists the weaknesses in his case, which are of considerable significance, but he attempts to explain them away as variations of common occurrence and subsequently ignores them. Greg, in his review of Tannenbaum's book cited above, substantially demolishes the case for Kyd, and it has been generally rejected.[13]

As with Hand A, Hand E is identified by comparison with a series of entries recording financial transactions in Henslowe's *Diary* either partly or entirely in the hand of Thomas Dekker. Greg was almost certain of the

10. Samuel A. Tannenbaum, "*The Booke of Sir Thomas Moore*" (*A Bibliotic Study*) (New York: Tenny, 1927), pp. 53–55; W. W. Greg, ed., *English Literary Autographs 1550–1650* (Oxford: Oxford University Press, 1925; rpt. Oxford, 1932, and Nendeln: Kraus, 1968), Part 1: Dramatists.

11. W. W. Greg, review of Tannenbaum's *Booke*, *Library* 9, 2 (1928): 202–11; McKerrow, review of Tannenbaum's *Booke*, *RES* 4 (1928): 237–41; C. J. Sisson, review of Tannenbaum's *Booke*, *MLR* 23 (1928): 231–34; Harold Jenkins, *The Life and Work of Henry Chettle* (London: Sidgwick & Jackson, 1934), p. 63; Anthony G. Petti, *English literary hands from Chaucer to Dryden* (Cambridge: Harvard University Press, 1977), p. 95.

12. W. W. Greg, *Dramatic Documents*, "Reproductions and Transcripts," pls. 2 and 4, and "Commentary," pp. 105–22, 130–37.

13. Tannenbaum, *Booke*, pp. 35–50. Bald ("*Booke*," p. 60 n. 10) tentatively hints at Goodale, whose name appears in the manuscript (p. 89), and Acheson nominates Peele. Arthur Acheson, *Shakespeare, Chapman and Sir Thomas More* (London: Quaritch, 1931; rpt. New York: AMS, 1970), pp. 265–73. Neither of the latter suggestions, like that by Tannenbaum, has received any support.

assignment at the time of his edition (pp. ix–x), but he was inhibited by the hesitation of Sir George Warner, keeper of manuscripts at the British Library. By the time of his contribution to *Shakespeare's Hand* Greg's conjecture had hardened into a certainty and in this he is supported by Thompson (pp. 83–84). The identification has been widely accepted.

In the same book, Greg neutrally discussed the writing of the hand he had designated B and in a footnote (p. 44) he put forth a suggestion:

> Hand B should be compared with that of *The Captives*, &c., MS. Egerton 1994 (fols. 52–95) at the British Museum, which is presumably Thomas Heywood's. There is a considerable resemblance both in the writing and the spelling, but there are also differences which make it impossible to venture on an identification.

Subsequently he added the thought that "the probable difference of twenty to thirty years in date would of course allow considerable latitude for change."[14] Tannenbaum picked up the thread and elaborates an argument in favor of B being Heywood, employing a technique known as "bibliotics."[15] He begins by accepting without discussion that two plays, *The Captives* and *The Escapes of Jupiter* (the latter composed of elements from Heywood's *Golden Age* and *Silver Age*), bound together in British Library MS. Edgerton 1994, are written in the same hand; and that it has been proved by Alexander C. Judson, and independently by Greg, that it is Heywood.[16] "With this mass of manuscript material," says Tannenbaum, available "as a standard of comparison," it should be possible to determine conclusively whether or not Heywood wrote the parts of *Sir Thomas More* on folios 7[a] and 16, especially when due allowance is made for those "changes in a person's chirography as inevitably develop as one grows older." Heywood's writing is notoriously difficult. Tannenbaum calls his penmanship "atrocious." Petti says it is "abominable," and on the occasion of the first printing of *The Captives* (1885), A. H. Bullen described it as "detestable."

14. Greg, *Literary Autographs*, Pl. 22, Thomas Heywood.

15. "Bibliotics" is defined by Tannenbaum as "the science which studies the characteristics of a document for the purpose of determining its genuineness or spuriousness and of establishing the identity of the person who wrote it" (*Booke*, p. 9). He cites forensic authorities. In his review of Tannenbaum's book, Greg pointed out, with some justice, that "the problems that come before the courts, almost always involve questions either of forgery or of abnormal circumstances, illness, disguise, or the like. It very seldom happens that any question arises as to whether two perfectly normal documents were written by one hand or not. But this is an habitual problem of palaeography." It should be noted that forensic methods, like bibliotics (scarcely a science), have sometimes resulted in indecisiveness, such as that exhibited in R. A. Huber's study (discussed later), or in stupendous failure, as in the erroneous handwriting identifications in the notorious Howard Hughes-Clifford Irving and Mark Hofmann cases.

16. Alexander C. Judson, ed., *The Captives* (New Haven: Yale University Press, 1921), pp. 9–13; W. W. Greg, "*The Escapes of Jupiter*. An Autograph Play of Thomas Heywood's," in "Anglica," *Palaestra* 148, band 2 (1925): 211–43; rpt. W. W. Greg, *Collected Papers*, ed. J. C. Maxwell (Oxford: Clarendon Press, 1966), pp. 156–83.

Even Heywood himself called it "difficult."[17] From this it might be thought that a comparison of Hand B with Heywood's writing would be relatively simple, since the control material is so distinctive, but it has not proved so. Tannenbaum describes in some depth the many similarities between the two hands: both are small and almost illegible, the slant of the letters is the same, the form of the letters exhibit only a slight resemblance to the correct forms, the linkage between letters, or the lack of it, is virtually identical, the writing is cramped and angular, the distinctive formation of several minuscules is the same. Tannenbaum then proceeds to list eighteen ways in which the two hands differ. He explains the contradiction by citing the passage of time between B's addition to *Sir Thomas More* and the other two plays, and then, relying on common spellings that he acknowledges are not dependable as a guide to identification, he accepts B as Heywood. Greg says in his *Library* review article that as a consequence of Tannenbaum's argument he studied the evidence afresh and, while not denying the possibility that B may be Heywood, concluded that he is, if anything, more skeptical. Since that review, scholars have been divided on the question. Joining Greg in his skepticism are McKerrow, E. K. Chambers, Law, Bald, Nosworthy, Ribner, and Petti. Those who accept B as Heywood, sometimes with reservations, include Sisson, Clark, Douglas Collins, Deutschberger, Munro, Partridge, Blayney, Schoenbaum, and Chillington. Jenkins sums up:

> Heywood's writing . . . is like B in more than its badness: they are bad in the same way, with some similar aberrant forms and similar joins and breaks between letters. The resemblance was first pointed out by Greg . . . [who] repeatedly urged caution, stressing the differences between the hands as well as their similarities. . . . Yet in view of the long time interval, it seems reasonable to give the greater weight to similarities; and there is some support from peculiarities of spelling, though here again differences have been pointed out. . . . I cannot regard the identification as improbable; but the matter is undecided.[18]

17. Tannenbaum, *Booke*, pp. 56–57, 64; Petti, *English literary hands*, p. 111. Bullen is cited in Judson's edition of *The Captives*, p. 13. Heywood's published comment is reprinted in the Malone Society edition of *The Captives*, ed. Arthur Brown (Oxford: Oxford University Press, 1953), p. viii.

18. For Greg's and McKerrow's reviews, see note 11 above; Chambers, *William Shakespeare*, 1:503–4; Robert Adger Law, "Is Heywood's Hand in *Sir Thomas More*?" *TSE* 11 (1931): 24–31; Bald, "*Booke*," p. 46; J. M. Nosworthy, "Hand B in *Sir Thomas More*," *Library*, series 5, 11 (1956): 47–50; Irving Ribner, *The English History Play in the Age of Shakespeare*, 2d ed., rev. (London: Methuen, 1965; rpt. New York: Octagon, 1979), pp. 210–11; Petti, *English literary hands*, p. 111. Sisson (in the review cited in note 11 above), says, "It is reasonably certain to my mind," p. 233; Arthur Melville Clark, *Thomas Heywood Playwright and Miscellanist* (Oxford: Blackwell, 1931), pp. viii, 9–10; D. C. Collins, "On the Date of *Sir Thomas More*," *RES* 10 (1934): 401; Paul Deutschberger, "Shakespeare and *Sir Thomas Moore*," *SAB* 15 (1943): 75; Munro, *London Shakespeare*, 4:1255; A. C. Partridge, *Orthography in Shakespeare and Elizabethan Drama: A Study of Colloquial Contractions, Elision,*

Richard Simpson in his seminal 1871 article on this play[19] first suggested that Addition IIc was in Shakespeare's own handwriting, the hand subsequently lettered D. He found this hand to be one of four in the manuscript. James Spedding confirmed Simpson's suggestion of Hand D as Shakespeare's in a response the following year,[20] one of six hands he distinguishes. Brooke accepts D as Shakespeare and concludes there are five hands in the manuscript, but he also records Frederick Furnivall's opinion that there are clearly six and perhaps seven.[21] In his edition, Greg at first adopts a neutral stance on Hand D, merely saying, "It is this hand which has been thought to be Shakespeare's" (p. ix). After describing how D works as seen in the manuscript, he notes that "the passage is undoubtedly autograph" (p. xiii). Later he says that "D may be the hand of Shakespeare himself."[22]

The first comprehensive paleographic analysis of Hand D was undertaken by Thompson and published in his *Shakespeare's Handwriting* (1916). He begins with a professional examination of Shakespeare's penmanship as exhibited in the only authenticated exemplars, the six surviving signatures, three in the will with the words "By me," and three in other legal documents. He then examines in general and in particular the calligraphy of Addition IIc. In the course of this investigation, Thompson finds that there is substantial correspondence between unusual letter formations in the handwriting of the signatures and that of the addition. These similarities are the "spurred" *a*, the four forms of *k*, the minuscules *p*, *e*, *m*, *w*, *r*, and the Italian long *s*; the majuscules *W* and *S*, the *ha* ligature, the upstrokes attached to some letters, and the needle eye loop. Thompson concludes that Hand D is Shakespeare's:

> We venture to submit that, despite the scanty examples of Shakespeare's hitherto acknowledged handwriting, the cumulative evidence in favour of the identity of the writing of the signatures with that of the addition of the play of *Sir Thomas More*, which has been elicited by the scrutiny of the documents, is far more conclusive than might have been anticipated. We commend it to the careful consideration of the impartial reader.[23]

Prosody and Punctuation (London: Arnold; and Lincoln: Nebraska University Press, 1964), pp. 44–50, 63; Blayney, "*The Booke of Sir Thomas Moore* re-examined," p. 167; Schoenbaum, *William Shakespeare: A Documentary Life* (New York: Oxford University Press in association with The Scolar Press, 1975), p. 157; Carol A. Chillington, "Playwrights at Work: Henslowe's, Not Shakespeare's, *Book of Sir Thomas More*," *ELR* 10, 3 (1980): 439–79; Jenkins, in Greg, *Sir Thomas More*, pp. xxxv–xxxvi.

19. Richard Simpson, "Are There Any Extant MSS. in Shakespeare's Handwriting?" *N&Q* 183 (1871): 1–3.

20. James Spedding, "Shakespeare's Handwriting," *N&Q* 184 (1872): 227–28.

21. C. F. Tucker Brooke, ed. *The Shakespeare Apocrypha* (Oxford: Clarendon Press, 1908; rpt. 1929, 1947, 1967), pp. xlvi n. 6, xlviii–xlvix.

22. Greg, *Shakespeare's Hand*, p. 47.

23. Thompson, *Shakespeare's Handwriting*, p. 63.

Later, Thompson proposed "to analyse and compare still more closely the individual letters of these writings and record the results of such further study" in a manner intended specifically to be useful to Shakespearean scholars. The result of this renewed analysis was a confirmation of the identity of Hand D, supported this time by a more extensive showing of both the general resemblance between the hand in the play and that in the signatures, and of the presence in both of certain letter forms (particularly *a*, *k*, and *p*) exhibiting a "peculiarity" which may be regarded as personal, thus affording a more certain identification. Furthermore, Hand D and Shakespeare use only one letter in the Italian style, a medial long *s*, the hands otherwise using exclusively the English secretary alphabet. Finally, in both writings there occur examples of a rare ornamental upstroke attached to some letters with a needle eye loop at the bottom.[24]

The weakness in this otherwise persuasive exposition of paleographic scholarship is the shortage of authentic Shakespearean handwriting for comparison with Addition IIc. Given the fact that Thompson had only the six signatures and the words "By me" with which to work, he has made out a fairly convincing case. However, those critics who come to examine that case with skepticism find it possible to attack the fundamental deficiency in the indispensable control.

Early objections to equating Hand D with Shakespeare on paleographic grounds came from Sir George Greenwood and Sir Sidney Lee. Lee finds the proofs "incomplete," because the control is "too scant to offer positive marks of identification." He prudently adds, "In the absence of trustworthy external testimony, doubt attaches to any purely palaeographical deduction."[25] Greenwood mounts a detailed contradiction to Thompson's hypothesis and challenges, to some effect at least, a few of his key tenets. However, Greenwood's admitted limited paleographic knowledge coupled with his *parti pris* approach, which prevents him from recognizing anything useful in Thompson's findings, tends to invalidate his counterargument, especially since he offers no positive suggestions of his own.[26]

Much more worthy opposition to the recognition of D as Shakespeare's hand is provided by Levin L. Schücking and Tannenbaum, who have provided a service to scholarship by testing the validity of the conjectural conclusions of others. Both critics are to a limited degree successful in illuminating the weaknesses in the paleographic findings and in shaking the arguments for identification. Schücking's scholarship and Tannenbaum's acute insights—and, not least, their pertinacious opposition—

24. Thompson, *Shakespeare's Hand*, pp. 57–112.

25. Sir Sidney Lee, *A Life of William Shakespeare*, 14th ed. (London: Macmillan, 1931; rpt. New York: Dover, 1968), "Additional Notes and Passages," p. 735.

26. Sir George Greenwood, *The Shakspere Signatures and "Sir Thomas More"* (London: Palmer, 1924). Greenwood weakens his case by a Robertsonian attack on the canon and by comment, apparently meant to be derogatory, on Thompson's advanced age.

established a tradition of skepticism that has endured and is still alive. While their arguments in general are not entirely convincing, the one great weakness in their position is the lack of an alternate candidate. To the hypothetical question, "If it isn't Shakespeare, who is it?" they offer no reasoned response. Tannenbaum's approach is mainly, though not exclusively, paleographic. In his successive reviews of the handwriting of D, he closely tracks the analyses of Greg and Thompson, frequently agreeing with their descriptions of the graphic qualities of the hand, but as frequently disagreeing with their interpretation.[27] In his first effort, "Autographs," he reviews exhaustively the handwriting of the Shakespeare signatures, discussing the differing circumstances in which they were written, the effect of such circumstances on the writing, and describing the hand in minute detail. He surveys Thompson's findings, paying particular attention to the form and use of letters, symbols, and some of the incidental pen-strokes, all of which Thompson concluded were sufficiently unusual and could therefore serve as grounds for the identification of Hand D with the signatures. Tannenbaum then takes up each of Thompson's assertions and in twenty-five numbered paragraphs denies the validity of all except possibly the evidence of the *ha* ligature and one of the forms of the letter *k*. A few of Tannenbaum's pointed observations strike home, notably his perceptive explication of the authorial alteration of the word *warre* to *warrs* (p. 77), which Thompson mistakenly thought constituted the use of the Italian long *s*; but Tannenbaum is manifestly wrong—though equally as confident—in other cases such as his denial of the exceptional quality of the spurred *a*. While he succeeds in challenging a few of Thompson's propositions, he does not accomplish his chief purpose—to demolish the heart of the paleographer's case—and he certainly does not adduce cogent facts to support his conclusion that "the weight of the evidence is overwhelming against the theory that in folios 8 and 9 of *The Booke of Sir Thomas Moore* we have a Shakspere holograph."[28] While continuing to deny that D is Shakespeare's hand, Tannenbaum acknowledges that the differences in handwriting he emphasizes "are not of a nature to prove that he [Shakespeare] could not possibly have been the author and writer of the revision in the insurrection scene." He notes that we lack adequate specimens of the handwriting of no fewer than eleven other Elizabethan playwrights, but he does not suggest that any of them is D.[29]

27. Tannenbaum's most important contributions, in addition to his *Booke*, are "Shakespeare's Unquestioned Autographs and the Addition to *Sir Thomas Moore*," *SP* 22 (1925): 133–60, rpt. in *Problems in Shakspere's Penmanship* (New York: Modern Language Association, 1927), pp. 179–211; *Shakspere and "Sir Thomas Moore"* (New York: Tenny; and London: Laurie, 1929); and *An Object Lesson in Shaksperian Research* (New York: Tenny, 1931).

28. Tannenbaum, *Problems*, p. 211. Incidental to his general discussion, Tannenbaum, a respected physician, conclusively disposes of the speculation that Shakespeare's signatures exhibit symptoms of writer's cramp.

29. Tannenbaum, *Booke*, p. 70.

Greg summarized the state of the paleographic study of Hand D to the end of 1927 in an essay in the *Times Literary Supplement*. He acknowledged that the strictures of some commentators, including Tannenbaum, had demonstrated that there were some weaknesses in Thompson's paleographic case. For example, Thompson had originally identified three instances in Addition IIc of the Italian long *s*, but subsequently he abandoned one and Greg agreed with Tannenbaum that the *s* in *warrs* is not an italic form of the letter. Thus, Greg says, Thompson occasionally claimed a little more than he had actually proved in this and in a few other instances. However, Thompson's case rests in the first instance on the general resemblances between the hands and on the judgment of a talented paleographer with decades of experience in reading documents in the secretary hand, and only partly on specific points of identity. The lack of really adequate material on both sides of the equation, but especially the few samples of Shakespeare's writing, Greg says, makes complete proof impossible; but when considered together with the other independent lines of argument the case appears sound. As to the identification, Greg advances the following propositions:

> 1. The paleographical case for the hands of S[hakespeare] and D being the same is stronger than any that can be made out for their being different.
> 2. The hand of S is more nearly paralleled in D than in any other dramatic document known to us.
> 3. Setting S aside, it can be shown that D was not written by any dramatist of whose hand we have adequate knowledge.

Greg continues,

> If these propositions can be established, I think that together they incline the balance of probability in favour of identification. More than this I would not claim. I feel tempted, however, to add one more proposition of a somewhat challenging nature, namely:
>
> 4. On purely paleographical grounds there is less reason to suppose that all six signatures were written by the same hand than there is, granting this identity, to suppose that the hand of the signatures also wrote the addition to *More*.[30]

Sir Edmund Chambers in his cautious and lucid way reviewed the status of the Hand D identification in 1930 by first assessing the surviving

30. Greg, "Shakespeare's Hand Once More," *TLS*, 24 November 1927, p. 871; rpt. in Greg, *Collected Papers*, ed. Maxwell, pp. 192–200. Taylor notes that recent paleographic studies of Hand D by P. J. Croft, R. E. Alton, and Giles E. Dawson have endorsed the conclusion that D is Shakespeare. "The Canon and Chronology of Shakespeare's Plays," *William Shakespeare: A Textual Companion*, eds. Stanley Wells and Gary Taylor with John Jowett and William Montgomery (Oxford: Clarendon Press, 1987), p. 124.

authentic Shakespearean material, which he finds, as a basis for comparison, "slight." The two hands are normal for the period, but Thompson has found distinctive "minor peculiarities" which Chambers accepts as significant. Chambers cites the forms of *k*, *p*, *s*, the spurred *a*, the dotted capital *W*, and the looped *per* symbol to which Thompson had called attention. Tannenbaum's objections are noted, but Chambers concludes that although the paleographic case "does not approach complete proof," he is inclined to accept it.[31] Other notable students of the play, among them Robert Boies Sharpe, Hazleton Spencer, M. M. Reese, Albert Feuillerat, and I. A. Shapiro, attack the paucity of paleographic data on which a judgment could be made or the interpretation of such evidence. They are joined by Deutschberger, who restates and summarily rejects all the arguments in favor of identifying D as Shakespeare.[32]

In a book devoted to an examination of the methods employed by scholars in authorship studies and in which he tirelessly exposes the numerous errors of attribution based on internal evidence, Schoenbaum finds one shining exception to the muddle of misattribution: the Pollard symposium on *Sir Thomas More*. Schücking and Tannenbaum sturdily took issue with the findings, but "in neither instance was the opposition damaging. . . . The work . . . serves as a stunning vindication of the role of internal evidence in attribution study." On the basis of this he concludes, "Shakespeare's hand is now universally recognized to be present in *Sir Thomas More*."[33]

A comparison of the spellings in *Sir Thomas More* with those in *Much Ado About Nothing*, *2 Henry IV*, *Midsummer Night's Dream*, and *Merchant of Venice* leads Ralph H. Lane to conclude that they are different and therefore that Shakespeare is disqualified as the penman who wrote Hand D. R. A. Huber, a staff sergeant associated with the Royal Canadian Mounted Police crime detection laboratory, as a result of an admittedly limited study (restricted to photographic reproductions), concludes that Shakespeare is only one of a group of writers who could have written Hand D. In comment on Huber's paper, C. J. Sisson, in the same volume, cites two items of evidence of prime importance in the identification of Hand D as that of Shakespeare: the spurred *a* and the spelling *scilens*. In forty years of reading

31. Chambers, *William Shakespeare*, 1:507–9.

32. Robert Boies Sharpe, *The Real War of the Theatres: Shakespeare's Fellows in Rivalry with the Admiral's Men, 1594–1603* (New York: The Modern Language Association of America, 1935), p. 91; Hazelton Spencer, *The Art and Life of William Shakespeare* (New York: Harcourt, 1940), pp. 413–14; M. M. Reese, *Shakespeare: His World & His Work*, 2d ed., rev. (London: St. Martin's, 1980), pp. 193–98; Albert Feuillerat, *The Composition of Shakespeare's Plays: Authorship, Chronology* (New Haven: Yale University Press, 1953), pp. 48–49 n.; I. A. Shapiro, "Shakespeare and Mundy," *ShS* 14 (1961): 25–33; Deutschberger, "Shakespeare and *Sir Thomas Moore*," 156–67.

33. Schoenbaum, *Internal Evidence*, pp. xix, 104–7.

an estimated half a million sheets of contemporary manuscripts, Sisson did not find these forms duplicated.[34]

Michael Hays attacks the identification, in the first instance, for employing the Shakespearean signatures as a control because they are insufficient. He cites comments by Thompson and Greg on this difficulty and by Hilary Jenkinson on the further possibility that the will may have been signed, as other such documents were, on behalf of a terminally ill testator, by a scribe in the presence of several witnesses. If this is the case, then we are left with only three signatures, two of which are poor, and the external evidence to prove Hand D is reduced almost to the vanishing point. Hays also impugns the interpretation of some of the evidence, particularly in regard to the key letter formations, but his position is weakened by the fact that he was unable to examine MS. Harley 7368 at first hand and is forced to rely on Farmer's facsimile. He also criticizes paleographic inquiries as not being scientific. In a companion article he reports on an investigation of the watermarks and chain-lines in the paper of the manuscript, examined at his request by Professor William Ingram. On the basis primarily of qualities of the chain-lines, Hays develops a hypothesis that folios 7 and 16 were once conjugate, which, he says, raises the possibility that Hands C and D may be the same. Since this theory rests on an interpretation by Hays of physical evidence developed by another scholar, it is, at least, somewhat doubtful.[35]

Paul Ramsey, relying in part on Huber but independently expressing reservations, doubts that D is Shakespeare's hand. In his judgment, the paleographic evidence does not establish a positive identification and is actually "slightly negative." Jane Cox of the Public Record Office raises a similar doubt about the authenticity of four of the six Shakespearean signatures generally accepted as genuine. "It is obvious at a glance," she says, "that these signatures, with the exception of the last two [those on the second and third sheets of the will], are not the signatures of the same man. Almost every letter is formed in a different way in each. . . . Which of the signatures . . . is the genuine article is anybody's guess." This is a finding reminiscent of Greg's fourth "challenging" proposition of 1927. Cox notes

34. Ralph H. Lane, "Shakespearean Spelling," *ShN* 8, 4 (September 1958): 28; R. A. Huber, "On Looking over Shakespeare's 'Secretarie,'" *Stratford Papers on Shakespeare 1960*, ed. B. A. W. Jackson (Toronto: Gage, 1961), pp. 53–70, which is preceded by an editor's note (pp. 52–53) and followed by a postscript by C. J. Sisson (pp. 70–77). Huber's technique is described by Jackson as "modern police methods of handwriting identification," and as such it is forensic in orientation. Therefore, it is akin to the "bibliotic" procedures employed by Tannenbaum and has the same limitations.

35. Michael L. Hays, "Shakespeare's Hand in *Sir Thomas More*. Some Aspects of the Palaeographic Argument," *ShakS* 8 (1975): 241–53; "Watermarks in the Manuscript of *Sir Thomas More* and a Possible Collation," *SQ* 26, 1 (1975): 66–69; Hilary Jenkinson, "Elizabethan Handwritings: A Preliminary Sketch," *Library* 4, 3 (1922): 1–34. See also Melchiori, "A Chronology," p. 292, n. 5.

Jenkinson's suggestion that the signatures may have been appended to the will and to the other documents by law clerks and also cites the known practice in the Canterbury Prerogative Court. In fifty-five wills proved in the court in the same month as Shakespeare's, she says, "There are numerous examples of 'forgeries' of witnesses' signatures; the attorney's clerk simply wrote the names on the document." She finds no positive evidence that Shakespeare did not sign his will but concludes that the will signatures have no better claim to authenticity than those on the other documents. Charles Hamilton, a disputed documents expert, determined by a study of Shakespeare's signatures, of Hand D, and of Schoenbaum's facsimile of Shakespeare's will that the entire will is in Shakespeare's hand. Hamilton also identifies other documents as having been written by Shakespeare, such as that of the Welcombe enclosure and the three applications for a coat of arms. He describes the credentials of professional handwriting experts like himself and says they must be able to expose a forgery at a glance. However, his authentication of the notorious Mormon forgeries perpetrated by Mark W. Hofmann, which he publicly acknowledged to be in error, casts serious doubt on his Shakespearean discoveries.[36]

The case for identifying the writer of Hand D as Shakespeare's, even if it falls short of being absolutely conclusive, is nevertheless on balance so strong as to leave little room for doubt. The paleographic evidence, appraised independently of other evidence, is as sound as it is possible for it to be, given the high degree of variability in handwriting of the Elizabethan era. Important signatures certifying financial and legal documents written within a single week will vary even today, and the signatures of some penmen may vary materially. Writing samples exhibit even greater differences if separated by years, as Hand D's and Shakespeare's were. Under these circumstances, minutely examining the form of individual letters is of less cogency than the overall impression of identity arrived at upon a general inspection of the style of two samples by a skilled paleographer who has spent years examining a great number of documents. This is why scholars have accepted the verdict of such students of paleography as Thompson, Greg, Sisson, Jenkins, Blayney, Evans, Croft, Alton, and others rather than the opinions of Greenwood and of Tannenbaum and his followers, whose credentials in paleography have been less impressive and who have generally concentrated on the specific characteristics of handwriting. The tendency to employ evidence developed by the forensic type of handwriting analyses has not proved helpful to the negative cause. In

36. Paul Ramsey, "Shakespeare and *Sir Thomas More* Revisited: or, A Mounty on the Trail," *PBSA* 70 (1976): 333–46; *Shakespeare in the Public Records*, text and selection of documents by David Thomas, section on the will and signatures by Jane Cox (London: HM Stationery Office, 1985), pp. 33–34; Charles Hamilton, *In Search of Shakespeare* (New York: Harcourt, 1985); *New York Times*, 11 February 1987, p. A20.

regard to the identification of hands other than D—and B, on which there is still some dispute—there has been agreement between the factions in regard to S (Munday), A (Chettle), first recognized by Tannenbaum and promptly accepted by Greg, and E (Dekker), but it is worthy of note that the two sides emphasize different aspects of the evidence in arriving at their judgments.

Authorship

The question of the authorship of *Sir Thomas More* is distinct from that of the identity of the penmen. Scholars are generally agreed that the passages in Hands A, B, D, and E were composed by the playwrights in whose hands they are written. Munday, indisputably the penman of Hand S, wrote out the fair copy of the original, and it is acknowledged by almost all students of the play that he is at least part author. Some critics have concluded that the entire early form of the play is his work, but there are two bits of evidence which many commentators believe indicate that Munday was copying from a draft that included some passages composed by at least one other playwright. Hand C has been identified as the writing of a playhouse functionary because of the kinds of alterations he makes in the contributions of the dramatists and because his hand has been found in two playhouse plots. It is most probable that he was a bookkeeper, but his name is not known. After Munday's, C's writing is the most extensive in the manuscript. Since he inserts, corrects, and augments stage directions and speech prefixes, copies cleanly into Addition V (2–7, p. 89) a passage manifestly revised *currente calamo* in Addition VI (68–73, p. 93), and does other "housekeeping" tasks, it is evident that he is not a playwright (pp. xvii–xviii). This prompts a question concerning the identity of the author or authors of the passages in Hand C. Those who have examined the problems of Munday's possible collaborator or collaborators in the original play and of the authors of the passages in Hand C have generally sought candidates among the other dramatists—A, B, D, and E. This seems reasonable in view of the fact that there were four playwrights more or less simultaneously revising the original play composed by at least one other author who is not present in the additions. Only one writer outside this group of dramatists has been suggested.

Greg, in his discussion of Hand S when he still considered the writer to be a scribe and before he had identified the handwriting as Munday's, adduced two pieces of evidence pointing to the conclusion that the original play was of mixed authorship. The first is the presence in the manuscript of two different versions of the play's ending (†1956–64 and †1965–85, pp. 64–5). The first version is "marked for omission and crossed out" (p. 64 n. 1956). The second is clearly an authorial improvement. Greg explains (p. xvi) that "the duplicate endings . . . show that the draft was either written by the author himself, or under his immediate supervision, but the latter is perhaps as likely as the former." His second evidence is the word "*fashis*" (†1847, p. 61), a meaningless misreading of *fashiõ* (*fashion*), which Greg points out is "quite an easy mistake, for the two resemble one another closely in some [secretary] hands, but it is a mistake of which it is almost impossible to suppose that an author would be guilty in copying his own work."[37] His conclusion is that "the original text of the play is not autograph," a determination he subsequently modified after his recognition of Hand S as Munday's. E. H. C. Oliphant addresses himself to the questions of whether Munday had associates in writing the original and, if so, who they could have been, conducting his examination on literary grounds. He determined that "three different styles were discernible in the original version of the play." The first style is "somewhat old-fashioned," the second is "much jerkier and less regular," and the third is "much finer and more impressive verse than either of the others." He assigns these sections of the original draft to, respectively, Munday, Heywood, and Chettle, with a minor reservation about Heywood. He also thinks that Dekker participated, because he would not have taken part in the revision if he had not been one of the original authors, but his contribution does not seem to be evident in the fair copy and probably was deleted while it was still in draft form.[38]

Jenkins finds nothing improbable in the suggestion that Chettle may have collaborated with Munday on the original text, "since Chettle was a close friend of Munday at least from 1592 . . . but the case is by no means clear, and the opposite view has also been expressed." Greg is one of those who had reservations that the original text was a collaboration, but by 1923 he had become receptive to the idea.[39] Bald inclines toward acceptance of

37. Efforts by a few scholars to explain away the error have not proved persuasive. MacDonald Jackson, while acknowledging the mistake, seeks to excuse it: "It seems to me no less difficult to imagine a copyist of Munday's intelligence misreading a manuscript so absurdly, than to imagine that the author himself made such a mistake." Yet Munday did misread his original and it is inherently more likely that he did so while copying someone else's work rather than his own. Richard Beebe offers examples of penslips in *John a Kent and John a Cumber* and in *Sir Thomas More* in an effort to prove that *fashis* "is not necessarily a copyist's error," but he fails to prove his point. Shapiro does not discuss the *fashis* question but asserts that *Sir Thomas More* "was conceived, as well as written, wholly by Anthony Mundy." He promises us his evidence in a future "study of the *Sir Thomas More* problem" that has not appeared. Jackson, "Anthony Mundy and *Sir Thomas More*," *N&Q* 208 (1963): 96; Richard Beebe, "*Fashis* in *The Booke of Sir Thomas More*," *N&Q* 216 (1971): 452–53; Shapiro, "Shakespeare and Mundy," pp. 25–33. For a counterargument by Jackson, see "Anthony Munday and the Play of Thomas More," *Moreana* 22, 85 (1985): 83–84. Jackson states my position incorrectly in his opening sentence.

38. E. H. C. Oliphant, "*Sir Thomas More*," *JEGP* 18 (1919): 226–35. The first style he discovered in lines 1-†877 (pp. 1–30); the second in two places, lines †878-†1157 (pp. 30–39) and †1603-†1987 (pp. 53–65); the third in lines †1158-†1602 (pp. 39–53).

39. Harold Jenkins, *The Life and Work of Henry Chettle* (London: Sidgwick & Jackson, 1934), pp. 59–71. In his Supplement to the Introduction to Greg's *Sir Thomas More* edition, Jenkins maintains his position (pp. xxxviii–xxxix); Greg, *Shakespeare's Hand*, pp. 47–48.

Oliphant's hypothesis: "It would seem, then, that Munday, Chettle, and B (Heywood?) first collaborated on the play; Dekker may also have done so, or may have come in later as a reviser."[40] Nosworthy, finding that "there is ample evidence, both bibliographical and stylistic, that he [Munday] was not the sole author," searches for indications of possible collaborators in Henslowe's *Diary*. In entries ranging in date from 1597 to 1602, he finds Munday and Chettle working together, sometimes with other dramatists, on five plays; and Munday and Dekker, again with others, on four. He eliminates, as collaborators, Hand B, who is "unidentified," Hand C, because he is a "professional scribe," and Hand D, "since Shakespeare's *locus standi* has yet to be ascertained," and concludes that Munday's associates in the original draft of *More* were Chettle and Dekker. A. C. Partridge analyzes the use of contractions and the spelling, grammar, punctuation, and vocabulary of each of the playwrights, then tests Oliphant's proposition in the light of his investigations. This process, he finds, tends to support Oliphant: "The above analyses, if they prove anything at all, serve to confirm the triple authorship of *Sir Thomas More* by Munday, Heywood (?) and Chettle, on the lines indicated by Oliphant, and largely accepted by Greg." Blayney finds an additional nine instances in which Munday seems to have erred in transcribing from his copy, some parts of which he thinks "may have been altered in rough, and that Munday has misunderstood deletion marks."[41]

John Jowett investigates the possibility of Chettle's presence in the original version of the play. He reviews the evidence earlier adduced for collaboration, including Greg's two items, and decides that the duplicate endings show "Munday making a fundamental revision [of the contribution of another playwright] which he added after transcribing his copy." In regard to the nonsense word *fashis*, he adopts Jackson's view and concludes that "*fashis* is not therefore good evidence for copy in another hand." Jowett then "presents a reading more likely to arise from misinterpretation of copy," the error *Lord* for *Lordship*, which he explains as "an inadequate representation of a copy abbreviation 'L' or 'Lo.'" Munday corrected his error by inserting *ship* above the line (*757, p. 26). Jowett states, "The interlineation indicates that Munday did not write this part of the text." He sets forth an array of Chettle's lexical, metrical, and grammatical preferences, which he deduces from *Hoffman* along with other tests devised by Partridge, Blayney, and Warren Austin—a total of ten in all—and compares them with similar indices of phenomena noted in Munday's *John a Kent and John a Cumber*. Jowett says it may be difficult to establish "the exact extent of Chettle's contribution, [but that] he did contribute

40. Bald, "*Booke*," p. 47.

41. J. M. Nosworthy, "Shakespeare and *Sir Thomas More*," *RES* n.s. 6 (1955): 12–25; Partridge, *Orthography*, pp. 43–66, 169–71; Blayney, "*The Booke of Sir Thomas Moore* re-examined," pp. 172–73.

to the original text must now be difficult to dispute." A cautious estimate of Chettle's role "would assign to him six or perhaps seven scenes [1, 6, 7, 8, 10, 13, and possibly 2] . . . over one-third of the original text."[42]

Giorgio Melchiori, in his and Gabrieli's edition of the play and in three essays, contends that Munday is the sole author of the play and rejects, sometimes implicitly, sometimes overtly, evidence presented for mixed authorship. However, in his contribution to the symposium on *Sir Thomas More* edited by Howard-Hill, he modifies his view of Munday's role somewhat. Of the word *fashis* he says, "At least at that point he was copying a word written by somebody else." He maintains his position that the second ending is Munday revising. "He might not have been the sole author, but the transcriber of a text written in collaboration with others." His conclusion on the general authorship question leads him "to describe *The Book of Sir Thomas More* as a play by Anthony Munday, revised by Henry Chettle, Thomas Dekker, probably William Shakespeare, and possibly Thomas Heywood and/or others."[43]

Chettle is the author of the seventy-one lines of Addition I (More in melancholy) in his hand (A), which does not appear elsewhere in the manuscript. He may, in addition, have made the contribution to the original that Oliphant first noted and that Partridge, Blayney, and Jowett have ably confirmed. Heywood (if Hand B is his) writes in his own hand the first portion of the three-part Addition II and all of Addition VI, except for the opening stage direction. He may be the author of the two segments of the original assigned to him by Oliphant. Addition IIa (1–64, pp. 69–71) shows the insurrection approaching a climax. In Addition IIb (66–122, pp. 71–2; l. 65 is doubtful) the Lord Mayor and members of the Privy Council discuss corrective measures, and More proposes to appease "with a calm breath this flux of discontent" (107, p. 72). IIb is written in Hand C. Addition IIc comprises the famous lines in Hand D (123–270, pp. 73–8) in which More persuades the rioters to lay by their weapons and sue for clemency. Hand B is clearly the reviser as well as the penman of Addition IIa since he can be seen making insertions and changes while writing. The revision is a relatively unimaginative reworking of original lines 412–52 (pp. 14–16) undertaken apparently for the purpose of creating, along with other

42. Partridge, *Orthography*, pp. 43–66; Blayney, "*The Booke of Sir Thomas Moore* re-examined," pp. 182–88; Warren B. Austin, *A Computer Aided Technique for Stylistic Discrimination: The Authorship of Greene's Groatsworth of Wit* (Washington: U.S. Office of Education, 1969); John Jowett, "Henry Chettle and the Original Text of *Sir Thomas More*," *Shakespeare and Sir Thomas More: Essays on the Play and its Shakespearian Interest*, ed. Trevor H. Howard-Hill (Cambridge: Cambridge University Press), forthcoming.

43. Gabrieli and Melchiori, *The Book of Sir Thomas More*, pp. 37–48, 319–20; Giorgio Melchiori, "The Contextualization of Source Material: The Play within the Play in *Sir Thomas More*," *Le Forme del Teatro* 3 (1984): 59–94; "Hand D in *Sir Thomas More*: An Essay in Misinterpretation," *ShS* 38 (1985): 101–14; "*The Booke of Sir Thomas Moore*: A Chronology of Revision," *SQ* 37 (1986): 291–308; "*The Book of Sir Thomas More*," *Shakespeare and Sir Thomas More*, ed. Howard-Hill, forthcoming.

changes in the margins of the original manuscript (for example, *638–41 and *647–58, pp. 22–23), the part of the Clown, as Melchiori points out in his "*Book of Sir Thomas More.*" Almost all the forty-one lines of the early text are carried over to Addition IIa by Heywood with but a few incidental alterations. Addition IIb is continuous both physically and in dramatic action to both IIa and IIc. Although they are distinct, Greg sees the "three different scribes working however in conjunction" (p. 69n.). If Addition IIb, in the hand of the playhouse reviser, could be taken to have authorial affinity to one of the other two parts of Addition II, then it is at least a possibility that in Addition IIb, Hand C is copying the work of Hand B. (It is apparent that Addition IIb is not the work of Hand D.) There are a few minor locutions in Addition IIb that seem consistent with Heywood's original lines in Addition IIa and in Addition VI. Their presence would lend some support to such an assignment, and there seems to be no stylistic disparity to prohibit it.

Addition VI (pp. 91–93), all composed by Hand B, is an original continuation of the players' scene intended to show More's shrewdness and generosity. Its literary qualities point to Heywood. In sum, then, Heywood appears to be part author as well as the penman of Addition IIa and sole author of Addition VI. He may also have been the author of Addition IIb. Hand E was determined early by Greg to be Dekker. Only thirty-one lines of Addition IV are in Dekker's hand. These are at the end of the second segment of the More-Faulkner scene (212–42, pp. 87–88). The preceding lines, 1 to 211, of Addition IV are in Hand C. But Dekker inserted three words ("I am *ipse*") in line 193 (identified by Tannenbaum but not previously noted by Greg), manifestly showing the author emending his own text although it is written by Hand C. Most scholars now accept Dekker as the author of all 242 lines of Addition IV.

Simpson first names Shakespeare as part author of *Sir Thomas More* in 1871, assigning to him the insurrection scene, More's soliloquy, and the Faulkner sequence. Spedding's response a year later endorsed Simpson's determination that Shakespeare composed the third part of the insurrection scene (Addition IIc), but he doubted Shakespeare's authorship of the other two passages primarily because he distinguished Hand C from Hand D, which Simpson had not done. Hopkinson reverts in part to Simpson's position, concluding that Shakespeare is the author of the insurrection scene, of More's soliloquy, and of the Faulkner-Erasmus sequence, but not the author of the part of Addition IV that is in Dekker's hand.[44] Citing opinions of paleographers, Brooke assigns to Shakespeare the scenes of the Lord Mayor's conference on the riot, More's pacification of the insurrectionists

44. Simpson, "Are There Any Extant MSS. in Shakespeare's Handwriting?" and Spedding, "Shakespeare's Handwriting," (see ns. 19 and 20). A. F. Hopkinson, ed., *Sir Thomas More* (London: Sims, 1902; rpt. 1915), p. xxviii.

and his soliloquy, the Faulkner-Erasmus sequence, and the brief segment in which the Lord Mayor's visit to Chelsea is announced.[45]

In the Malone Society reprint, Greg imposed some order on the early scholarly speculations in regard to authorship. With bibliographical precision he limited the participation of Hand D to folios 8ª, 8ᵇ, and 9ª, setting aside the suggested alternate assignments, including Addition III, which had earlier been put forth largely as a consequence of a failure to discriminate Hand C from Hand D. Greg adds that Hand D's lines, which have "undoubted literary merit," are possibly in Shakespeare's hand, but he cannot "regard them with the admiration they have aroused in some critics" (p. xiii). A dozen years later in *Shakespeare's Hand* (p. 47), Greg says, "D may perhaps be the hand of Shakespeare himself." Dover Wilson in his essay in the Pollard collection compares letter formations and spellings exhibited in Addition IIc of the manuscript with misprints and related bibliographic evidence in fifteen good Shakespearean quarto texts, demonstrating that the forms in *Sir Thomas More* could have led to misprints such as are present in the quartos. He sets forth an impressive array of bibliographic detail to show what took place, but his most notable contribution is finding two rare spellings in the manuscript and in Shakespearean quartos that occur infrequently elsewhere—*straing* for *strange* and *scilens* for *silence*. The latter spelling is of prime importance since bibliographers have found it eighteen times in the quarto of *2 Henry IV*, where it is a character's name, and in only two other plays.[46] In the same collection, R. W. Chambers discusses the expression of ideas—particularly political ideas—in the three pages of Addition IIc and in the canon. There is a remarkable concurrence in conceptions of social structure, the evils of civil unrest, and the sympathetic portrayal of the common people between the insurrection scene and a number of Shakespearean plays—*2 Henry VI* (the Cade scenes), *Julius Caesar*, *Troilus and Cressida*, and *Coriolanus* especially (this type of concurrence can also be found in less explicit or less comprehensive form in other plays—for example, *Richard II*, *Hamlet*, and *The Winter's Tale*). Chambers emphasizes that while the ideas, which in themselves are indicative of the authorship of the 147 lines, are important, they are less so than the linkages of underlying thought they reveal. Though sometimes clothed in completely different expressions, the same ideas and even the specific sequences of thought are identifiable in canonical plays. Chambers supports his contention that Addition IIc contains characteristic Shakespearean ideas with striking examples.

John Velz reexamines and extends the conclusions to Chambers's ca-

45. Brooke, *The Shakespeare Apocrypha*, pp. xlviii–xlix.

46. The spelling occurs once in both the apocryphal *The Puritan* and John Mason's *The Turk*. F. P. Wilson, *Shakespeare and the New Bibliography*, rev. ed. Helen Gardner (Oxford: Clarendon Press, 1970), p. 111, n. 1*.

nonical approach to the authorship question. His essay is "intended to be indicative rather than definitive," but the extension of Chambers is more significant than Velz's statement of objectives would indicate. He adduces new evidence that supports and strengthens Chambers's thesis. In the second part of his paper, he demonstrates that there are links between *Sir Thomas More* and several canonical plays: *Midsummer Night's Dream*, *Love's Labor's Lost*, *Hamlet*, *Richard III*, and especially—and substantially—*Henry VIII*. Velz's evidence also shows from the content of the links that Shakespeare had a fairly intimate knowledge of the original text of *Sir Thomas More* and apparently was not, as some commentators have conjectured, ignorant of the parts of the play composed by the other playwrights.[47]

The significance of the collection of studies in *Shakespeare's Hand*, including the essays by Greg and by Thompson and Pollard's preface, lies in its synergism. The confluence of the disparate findings of literary, paleographic, bibliographic, imagistic, and what has sometimes been called "psychological" disciplines, all of which individually tend to support the Shakespearean authorship of Addition IIc and which collectively present a reinforcing argument, established the symposium that Pollard brought together as a peak in the history of the scholarship of the play equal to that of Greg's Malone Society edition. Schoenbaum summarizes, "The varieties of evidence presented in the Pollard collection . . . converge upon a single destination; all roads lead to Shakespeare."[48] Greg's 1927 propositions, quoted above, which are generally confined to the paleographic question of the identity of the penman of Hand D, nevertheless indirectly bear on the question of authorship. It is notable that he does not restate his earlier reservations about Shakespeare's authorship of Addition IIc. By the time he arrived at his ultimate statement of the canon in 1955, Greg, in a note, said, "In the present discussion it will be assumed that the three pages are in Shakespeare's autograph," and that "most English students now accept the Shakesperian authorship of the three additional pages."[49]

Tannenbaum and Schücking strongly opposed Shakespeare's authorship of Addition IIc, just as they rejected the identification of Hand D as his. Tannenbaum's attack in a stream of books and articles seeks to deny the Shakespearean authorship of the 147 lines. He argues tenaciously, but

47. Chambers reworked his essay three or four times as a lecture and for publication and printed his definitive version in *Man's Unconquerable Mind* (London: Cape, 1939; rpt. New York: Haskell, 1967), pp. 204–49. John W. Velz, "*Sir Thomas More* and the Shakespeare Canon," *Shakespeare and Sir Thomas More*, ed. Howard-Hill, forthcoming.

48. Schoenbaum, *Internal Evidence*, p. 106. Schoenbaum repeats this view in *Shakespeare's Lives* (Oxford: Clarendon Press; New York: Oxford University Press, 1970), p. 696; in *Documentary Life*, p. 158; and in *Records and Images*, pp. 111–12.

49. W. W. Greg, *The Shakespeare First Folio* (Oxford: Clarendon Press, 1955; rpt. 1969), p. 99. He also says, "The masterly statement of the case by R. W. Chambers in his essay on 'Shakespeare and the Play of More' in *Man's Unconquerable Mind* . . . comes as near to formal proof as its nature allows, and is likely to be held conclusive by anyone capable of judging evidence."

the combination of his insistence that whatever he presents as evidence should be accepted without question, his immoderate style of debate, the waywardness of some aspects of his rationale inextricably mingled with sound scholarship, and his unwillingness to credit the most palpably valid elements of his opponents' case—plus his inability to nominate any other dramatist as Hand D—induces a reluctance on the part of more balanced scholars to accept his argument against the Shakespearean authorship of Addition IIc. In contrast to this, witness the universal assent, even from those he regards as opponents, to his perceptive recognition of Hand A as Chettle's.[50] Schücking's case against Shakespeare's participation in *Sir Thomas More*, stated and restated in his three articles, is grounded on literary considerations. He does not find a trace in Addition IIc of Shakespeare's habitually clear conception of his play or of his insight into human motives, and the appeal to the mob's reason in the play compares poorly to, for example, Anthony's rabble-rousing oration in *Julius Caesar*. The implied threat in More's speech is clearly not Shakespearean. Taking a hint from Pollard, and quoting a passage from his Introduction to *Shakespeare's Hand*, Schücking decides that assigning Addition IIc to Heywood rather than to Shakespeare is nearer to the mark.[51] He thinks that the sentimentality in More's crucial speech is typically Heywood, and he supports this conjecture with verbal parallels between *Sir Thomas More* and some of Heywood's plays. The fact that the hand in which Addition IIc is written is not Heywood's "should not cause us to abandon the idea of his possible authorship . . . the final judgment must needs be that Shakespeare's authorship of the '147 lines' is more than doubtful."[52] Tannenbaum and Schücking were worthy disputants who incisively tested the hypothesis that Shakespeare is the author of Addition IIc. However, observers who adopted a neutral posture toward the debate concluded that, in Schoenbaum's words, "in neither instance was the opposition damaging."[53]

50. Tannenbaum admits that his evidence, while casting doubt on Shakespeare's authorship of the 147 lines, does not conclusively disprove it. See *Booke*, p. 70.

51. Levin L. Schücking, "Das Datum des Pseudo-Shakespeareschen *Sir Thomas Moore*," *Englische Studien* 46 (1912–1913): 228–51; "Shakespeare and *Sir Thomas More*," *RES* 1 (1925): 40–59; "Über Einige Probleme der Neueren und Neuesten Shakespeare-Forschung," *GRM* 33 (1951–1952): 208–28. In support of his assignment of Addition IIc to Heywood, Schücking quotes Pollard in "Shakespeare and *Sir Thomas More*," p. 57. Pollard says, "If these three pages were not Shakespeare's work the dramatist to whom on the ground of style and temper I would most readily assign them (despite a difficulty about the date) would be Thomas Heywood. But Heywood is definitely ruled out by his handwriting, that is to say, that if Sir Edward [Maunde Thompson] was right, even to this limited extent, Shakespeare survives a test which excludes Heywood, and not only Heywood but all the other dramatists of whose handwriting specimens are known to exist" (*Shakespeare's Hand*, p. 14). Schücking omits without warning Pollard's parenthesis and ends his quote at "Thomas Heywood," thus substantially changing Pollard's meaning.

52. R. W. Chambers, *Man's Unconquerable Mind*, pp. 230–39, effectively negates Schücking's championship of Heywood as the author of Addition IIc.

53. Schoenbaum, *Internal Evidence*, p. 107.

R. W. Chambers touched on the imagery in the three pages of the *Sir Thomas More* text, but since his primary interest lay elsewhere it was Caroline Spurgeon who first systematically analyzed it. She had been studying the canonical plays for a number of years, identifying and cataloguing the images to define characteristic Shakespearean patterns. She undertook to add to the previous examinations of Addition IIc "a detailed study and comparison of the imagery in this fragment with that in the known work of Shakespeare." Twelve images are identified, and examples from acknowledged plays are compared to those in the three pages. Spurgeon points out that recurring Shakespearean images do not involve repetition: "certain ideas or pictures [are] to be found again and again in varied form and with different applications." Of the twelve images in the 147 lines, all of which are paralleled in Shakespeare's known plays, seven express a particular application that recurs many times in Shakespeare and three others have identifiable peculiarities. All fall into image categories established by study of the canon. In conclusion Spurgeon asks, "Is it too much to claim that the cumulative evidence they offer forms one more link in the gradually strengthening chain of proof which is leading some of us to believe that the fragment was written by Shakespeare?"[54] Karl Wentersdorf adds an image from More's speech on insurrection to those previously described: the unnatural savagery of pagans. He finds this image at two places in the Addition, especially in the phrase "momtanish inhumanyty" (263, p. 78)—the inhuman cruelty of the infidel Mohammedans (the Turks)—and in ten plays of the canon, three of which specifically mention Turks.[55]

Addition III is the twenty-one line soliloquy by the Lord Chancellor on his rise to power, on his relationship to his father, whom he now outranks, and on the risks of eminence in government under Henry VIII. The Addition is written in Hand C, but it must have been composed by one of the playwrights. Simpson, Hopkinson, and Brooke considered it Shakespeare's, but Spedding and Greg did not, since they made a paleographic distinction between Hands C and D. Sir Edmund Chambers and Bald, who seem to have been studying Addition III from a literary viewpoint at about the same time, arrived at conclusions that are remarkably similar. Chambers asks,

> If Shakespeare wrote Addition II(c), is it not possible that he also wrote Addition III, although it is in C's hand? . . . My attention was first called to the passage by the parallel in the first line to *Oth.* i.3.322. . . . But the whole is at least as good as anything in Addition II(c). The vocabulary is

54. Caroline F. E. Spurgeon, "Imagery in the *Sir Thomas More* Fragment," *RES* 6 (1930): 257–70.

55. Karl P. Wentersdorf, "Linkages of Thought and Imagery in Shakespeare and *More*," *MLQ* 34 (1973): 384–505. In regard to the variant *momtanish* (= *mahometanish*), see Wentersdorf's note on "A Crux in the Putative Shakespearian Addition to *Sir Thomas More*," *ELN* 10 (1972): 8–10.

> consistent with Shakespeare's. The coupling of words, especially of the English "smooth" with the Latin "dexter" is like him. Even the pun [on More's name] in the fourteenth line is characteristic.

He supports his point on the agreement in vocabulary with thirteen examples from ten accepted plays. Bald says that the internal evidence of verbal parallels, echoes, and a few identical phrases from eight canonical plays is sufficient to establish Shakespeare's authorship. All have the genuine Shakespearean ring.[56] H. W. Crundell drew attention to two characteristically Shakespearean ideas that are intertwined in Addition III: the "law of children"—More's relations with his father—and "corruption of the blood," a criminal law conception regarding such crimes as treason. He cites *Julius Caesar*, 3.1.36–42, and the "treason of Goneril," apparently in *King Lear*, 2.4.152–68.

In a response, R. W. Chambers endorses Crundell's twin points and accepts the assignment of Addition III to Shakespeare, adding that any such finding "might be regarded as subsidiary evidence that Shakespeare had a hand in the play as a whole" and that his claim as "the author of the '147 lines' . . . would therefore be strengthened."[57] Nosworthy critically examines the evidence presented to support Shakespeare's authorship of the soliloquy, especially the lexical parallels and the thought content, in the light of accepted work of Shakespeare and decides that

> Addition III . . . is demonstrably Shakespearian in tone, style, thought, and dramatic function. It bears no clear resemblance to the style of any other dramatist of the period and, on grounds of quality, seems beyond the scope of most. Its relationship to the canonical works turns out to be closely parallel, on all counts, with that established for the three pages of Addition II.[58]

Munro cites in his edition an unpublished letter of 11 February 1882 from S. A. Abbott to Furnivall in which Abbott finds likenesses between Shakespeare's work and Addition III. Munro disagrees. "These 21 lines," he says, "from their style, have been thought possibly or probably Shakespeare's in origin," but a comparison to a similar passage in *Thomas Lord Cromwell* inclines him to think that they are "the work of an author concerned with *Cromwell*, and that this excludes Shakespeare."[59]

Bald examined the state of scholarship of *Sir Thomas More* twenty-six years after the publication of *Shakespeare's Hand*. He finds that while not

56. E. K. Chambers, *William Shakespeare*, 1:514–15; R. C. Bald, "Addition III of *Sir Thomas More*," *RES* 7 (1931): 67–69. See also H. W. Crundell, "Shakespeare and *Sir Thomas More*," *London Mercury* 25 (1931–1932): 288–89.

57. H. W. Crundell, "Shakespeare and the Play of More," *TLS*, 20 May 1939, pp. 297–98. R. W. Chambers, "Shakespeare and More," *TLS*, 3 June 1939, p. 327.

58. Nosworthy, "Shakespeare and *Sir Thomas More*," pp. 17–24.

59. Munro, *London Shakespeare*, pp. 1255, 1256, and 1260.

all the arguments for Shakespeare's presence in the play have withstood the scrutiny of adverse critics, the essential case remains intact, and the studies of scholars subsequent to the symposium of 1923—he cites Spurgeon's essay and the conclusive form of R. W. Chambers's paper on the thought exhibited in the play—have strengthened the case. The only playwrights other than Shakespeare who might have written Addition IIc are Marlowe, Chapman, and Jonson, but their distinctive voices are not that of the Addition. The play was intended for the Admiral's Men, but because Henslowe was buying few plays in 1600, since he was building the Fortune and the players were in the country, Munday and his associates offered it to the Chamberlain's Men. When revisions became necessary, Shakespeare participated.[60] Muir reviews the literary evidence and concludes that, even if we had no manuscript, the images, style, sequences of thought, characterization, and the sympathetic portrayal of the mob—fickle, simple-minded, dangerous, but in the end submissive—would lead to Shakespeare. The comparable scenes in *Henry VI*, *Julius Caesar*, and *Coriolanus* "seem to have been written by the same hand." The whole rhythm and movement of the speech "is palpably Shakespearian and phrase after phrase reminds us of the master. The Shakespearian authorship of this scene is now generally accepted and one other speech [Addition III] . . . appears to have the genuine Shakespearian ring."[61]

On the fiftieth anniversary of Greg's landmark edition, Jenkins surveyed the authorship debate. In spite of the attacks by Schücking on the literary arguments and by Tannenbaum on the paleographic arguments, the case stands. Jenkins endorses Greg's 1927 reappraisal. He finds particularly sound R. W. Chambers's evidence from sequences of thought in Addition IIc and in the Shakespeare canon and says they "might themselves be conclusive. Attributions have certainly been accepted on much less." When the other evidence, notably the spelling arguments, is taken into account, "the combination of resemblances outstrips any credible coincidence." The twenty-one lines of Addition III "are much in Shakespeare's manner." Nosworthy's analysis of vocabulary and ideas in the Addition "makes . . . a very formidable case." Although Jenkins does not cite it, when Crundell's linkage of "corruption of the blood" and the "law of children" is taken into account, Nosworthy's case is even stronger. He accepts the assignment of both additions to Shakespeare.[62] Ramsey extends his agnosticism concerning Shakespeare as penman D to his possible authorship of Addition IIc. He denies the identification on the basis of metrical, rhythmical, and literary evidences, which are stronger for Heywood than for Shakespeare, who is "probably not" the author. William Matchett cites parallels of words and ideas between *The Merchant of Venice* and Addition

60. Bald, "*Booke*," pp. 59–60.
61. Muir, *Collaborator*, pp. 5–9.
62. Jenkins in Greg, *Sir Thomas More*, pp. xxxvii–xxxviii.

IIc, which he considers to be associational links between the two plays and which constitute "yet another of the many arguments confirming that Shakespeare was its author."[63]

G. Blakemore Evans brings into focus current scholarly thinking on the authorship of both Additions IIc and III in his introduction to the reprint of the two additions. Both "are now generally accepted as the work of Shakespeare. . . . The evidence advanced to connect Shakespeare with the two passages commonly attributed to him is significantly of various kinds." He lists the painstaking handwriting analyses, "the surprisingly large number of uncommon spelling links" to Shakespearean quarto and folio texts, R. W. Chambers's "expression of ideas," and metrical and vocabulary studies. "The real strength of the case for Shakespeare's authorship of these two passages rests, then, not on any single piece or kind of evidence but on the quite remarkable manner in which several independent lines of approach support and reinforce one another in pointing to a single conclusion—the 'hand' of Shakespeare."[64] Carol Chillington offers a novel theory of the authorship of *Sir Thomas More* inspired by a comment by Pollard that if a date as late as 1599 is assigned he would regard it "as an obstacle to Shakespeare's authorship of the three pages so great as to be almost fatal" (*Shakespeare's Hand*, p. 31). Following Collins and Bald, Chillington determines that the cause of Tilney's sensitivity to the insurrection sequence is the Essex rebellion of 1601. This means that Shakespeare is eliminated from the collaboration, since he "would hardly have been willing to redeem a failing play like *Sir Thomas More* for a rival company." Recalling Greg's conclusion that if Hand D is not Shakespeare, then "D was not written by any dramatist of whose hand we have adequate knowledge," she puts forth as her candidate for identification with D a playwright of whose writing no specimen survives: "the young John Webster." She justifies this by an analysis of the imagery, dramatic style, and technique in Webster's known plays and a comparison to similar features in *Sir Thomas More*. Schücking found these qualities reminiscent of Heywood, which, Chillington explains, could be a young playwright imitating an established craftsman who directed the collaboration of Henslowe dramatists. She posits a "sharing out of the scenes," assigning to Webster folios 8^a, 8^b, 9^a, 10^a, and describes in detail "the process by which *Sir Thomas More* was written and revised," including the discovery "that Hand D—Webster" wrote part of the original play. She also thinks "it is quite

63. Ramsey, "Shakespeare and *Sir Thomas More* Revisited," pp. 345–46. In his essay in the Howard-Hill symposium, Ramsey reiterates his stand, saying that his "conclusion will still be agnostic, though more negative" than in 1976. "The literary evidence is strongly, though not quite conclusively, against Shakespeare." William H. Matchett, "Shylock, Iago, and *Sir Thomas More*: with Some Further Discussion of Shakespeare's Imagination," *PMLA* 92 (1977): 217–30. J. H. P. Pafford draws attention to "another grain to add to the evidence" in the Shakespearean use of the word *dung* in Addition IIc (134–35, p. 73). See Pafford's "The Play of *Sir Thomas More*," *N&Q* 226 (1981): 145.

64. Evans, *Riverside Shakespeare*, pp. 1683–85.

possible" that an entry in Henslowe's *Diary* of a payment to Heywood and Chettle, not Webster, for a play whose title is not included in the entry "refers to *Sir Thomas More*." At Queen Elizabeth's death the "syndicate dispersed"—Heywood, for example, may have become active in seeking royal patronage for Worcester's Men, who subsequently became Queen Anne's—and the play was abandoned. Dismissing the evidence for identification adduced in *Shakespeare's Hand*, Chillington says, "The attribution of Shakespeare has had little but venerability to justify it."[65]

In reflecting on the years of debate regarding the authorship of the 147 lines, Dover Wilson summed up the situation in 1956 in his typically thought-provoking manner: "We shall probably never be able to prove that Shakespeare wrote the Three Pages in *Sir Thomas More*. But a case, which in Greg's words rests on 'the convergence of a number of independent lines of argument . . . and not on any one alone,' can never be *dis*proved and is bound to win acceptance from an ever-widening circle of scholars."[66] His appraisal has proved to be prophetic.

Date

Two dates of composition must be established for *Sir Thomas More*: the date of the original and the date of the revision. Most critics who have made a study of the question have concluded that the alterations and additions were made shortly after the original, not more than a year or so later.[67] The original date of composition has been sharply debated. Almost

65. Chillington, "Playwrights at Work," *passim*. Some scholars accept Chillington's hypothesis as worthy of serious consideration. See George Walton Williams, "The Year's Contribution to Shakespearian Study 3 Textual Studies," *ShS* 35 (1982): 190–91; and Andrew Gurr, "Paying for Plays," *TLS*, 15 February 1985, p. 174; but Charles Forker and Gary Taylor demonstrate the weakness of her conjecture in essays in the Howard-Hill collection. Taylor further notes that "if the [recently discovered] Melbourne manuscript . . . is indeed in Webster's hand, then Webster is certainly not Hand D, [and that the cumulative] internal evidence has persuaded us, as it has most scholars, that Hand D is Shakespeare" (*Textual Companion*, p. 125, and illustration 2, pp. 8–9). Thomas Merriam has put forth a suggestion that "about 90% of the play was composed by Shakespeare" based on a study employing his own modification of a system of statistically based stylometric analysis developed by Andrew Q. Morton and his colleagues at the University of Edinburgh. It has been received by *Sir Thomas More* scholars with reactions ranging from caution to disbelief (Thomas Merriam, "The Authorship of Sir Thomas More," *ALLCB* 10 [1982]: 1–7). For the Edinburgh system of stylometry, see Andrew Q. Morton, *Literary Detection* (Epping: Bowker, 1978). Merriam advises me (in a private letter of 21 April 1988) that he did not intend "to ascribe authorship for all the *More* additions to W. S."

66. J. Dover Wilson, "The New Way with Shakespeare's Texts; an Introduction for Lay Readers, III: In Sight of Shakespeare's Manuscripts," *ShS* 9 (1956): 69–80. Greg's comment is quoted from his 1927 review of the paleographic case, *Collected Papers*, p. 200.

67. For example, D. C. Collins, "On the Date of Sir Thomas More," *RES* 10 (1934): 401–11; I. A. Shapiro, "The Significance of a Date," *ShS* 8 (1955): 102; Wentersdorf, "The Date of the Additions in *Sir Thomas More*," *SJW* (1965): 305–25; Blayney, "*The Booke of Sir Thomas Moore* re-examined," p. 190, among others.

every year from 1586, suggested by Simpson, to 1605, proposed by Schücking, has been put forth. While there is no consensus, an examination of the numerous dates suggested by scholars reveals that there tend to be three clusters: 1586–1594; 1595–1599; and 1600–1605. For these groupings, which tend to merge into each other, a variety of reasons have been set forth. An early date has generally been grounded on two propositions: acceptance of Hand D as Shakespeare and the fact that Hand C, whose early associations may have been with either Strange's or the Admiral's Men but who later was possibly associated with the Admiral's, could only conceivably be found working together when the two troupes were playing in a kind of amalgamation, the precise nature of which is not known. The topical character of the scenes of Ill May Day, which historically took place in 1517, suggest to some that the play was composed at the time of or soon after similar mutinous incidents in 1586, 1593, and 1595, although in fact there was restiveness among the ranks of artificers during almost any of the years in which the play could have been written.

Paleographic evidence of date comes from Munday holographs. In addition to the original fair copy of *Sir Thomas More*, we have also his play *John a Kent and John a Cumber* and his dedication of a translation of an Italian devotional work entitled *The Heaven of the Mynde*. The latter is dated 1602 in Munday's own hand. *John a Kent* is signed by Munday and has a subscribed date (in Hand C, as William Long has demonstrated)[68] that had been read as 1596 (or occasionally 1595) but that Shapiro has shown (see discussion below) is actually 1590. Greg, writing before Shapiro, concluded that Munday's hand in *Sir Thomas More* has forms related to both of the other texts, which places it between *John a Kent* and *Heaven of the Mynde*. On the basis of this evidence, Greg suggests a date of composition of 1598–1600. Shortly thereafter, Thompson reviewed the same evidence and pointed out that the date of 1596 for *John a Kent* was only a downward limit, that it may have been written as early as 1590, that Munday's writing in *Sir Thomas More* "lies much closer chronologically" to *John a Kent*, and that an appropriate date for the collaborative play would be 1592–1593. In the 1923 symposium, Greg conditionally accepts Thompson's suggestion for the date of original composition, saying, "Should *John a Kent* prove to be before 1596, as it well may, a correspondingly earlier date must be assigned to *More*" (p. 51). In a later list of manuscript plays, he notes, as to date, merely "c. 1593?"[69]

In *William Shakespeare*, Sir Edmund Chambers is ambivalent about the

68. William B. Long, "The Occasion of *The Booke of Sir Thomas Moore*," forthcoming in the Howard-Hill symposium.

69. Greg, "Autograph Plays," pp. 89–90; Thompson, "Autograph Manuscripts," pp. 327–34; W. W. Greg, *The Editorial Problem in Shakespeare: A Survey of the Foundations of the Text*, 3d ed. (Oxford: Clarendon Press, 1954), p. 23, n. 1. Pollard thinks that the insurrection sequence is a topical comment on the apprentice riots of the mid 1590s, and he assigns a date of 1593–1595, *Shakespeare's Hand*, pp. 22–31.

alternatives of an early or late date of composition. He lists a number of verse features such as double endings and extra mid-line syllables and notes that their incidence "for what it is worth, does not suggest the earliest Shakespeare." After a review of "the clues to date," he says, "If Shakespeare wrote the Addition, these facts would perhaps fit best with a date in 1592–3," but that date "would be rather early" for Dekker's and Heywood's participation. He thinks Schücking's date is ruled out by the paleographical evidence and concludes, "The date, or dates, must remain undetermined."[70]

The date appended to *John a Kent and John a Cumber* was closely examined in facsimile by Shapiro, who provisionally determined that it read 1590 rather than 1595 or 1596. This was verified by staff members at the Huntington Library after a close examination of the manuscript, and Shapiro prints a convincing photograph of the date. On the basis of Thompson's opinion that Munday's writing in *Sir Thomas More* is close to the date of *John a Kent* and a reference to that play in a Martinist tract of September 1589, Shapiro concludes that Munday's original version "would have to be dated not later than 1591 and . . . possibly earlier," and that the revision may have occurred "about 1593, when Lord Strange's men, who then included Shakespeare [and the writer of Hand C], were temporarily associated with the Admiral's company."[71] Jenkins also emphasizes the contemporaneous presence of Shakespeare and Hand C and decides that the additions would have to have been written before the reconstitution of the companies in 1594. "The dates which best fit the evidence seem to be *c.* 1590–3 for the original composition and *c.* 1594–5 for the revision." On the same grounds, Wentersdorf settles on dates of 1592, when "the original play must have been written for Edward Alleyn and the Strange's men," and the late spring of 1594, when "the manuscript of *More* was hastily revised by Shakespeare and the dramatists working for Henslowe."

Blayney studies the style and vocabulary of four of Chettle's pamphlets in view of Tannenbaum's unchallenged identification of his hand in Addition I and because of the suspicion that Chettle may be present in the original. He searches for echoes of thoughts, expressions, and words from *Sir Thomas More*, and, in *Kind-Harts Dreame*, he finds echoes "strongly reminiscent of Shakespeare's part of the play . . . under circumstances suggesting association." This evidence, he says, affords an opportunity to date Addition IIc with rather unusual precision, "a fairly certain date for the Shakespeare addition of October/November 1592." The composition of

70. Chambers, *William Shakespeare*, 1:509, n. 2; 513. In regard to Dekker's and Heywood's participation, he cites their birthdates, which would set their ages at approximately twenty in 1592–1593. His view that the date is early for them is, of course, personal. To me it seems possible that young men of twenty could have been the authors of the passages in their hands.

71. Shapiro, "Date," p. 102.

the original began in the "early months" of 1592, and it was submitted in June to Tilney, who returned it in August with notes of his objections to "prison-breaking, street brawls, and general trouble with prentices." By November, "the necessary revision is made by Chettle, Shakespeare, Heywood and C, [and] the MS is re-submitted," only to have Tilney object in his well-known note "to the 'Ill May Day' episode as a whole." Although further revisions are planned, the continuing unrest in London over aliens caused the effort to be abandoned. Some of the details of Blayney's case do not by their nature lend themselves to conclusive proof. Proudfoot notes that Blayney saw some things in the manuscript "which escaped even the keen eye of Greg," but that he "is least convincing on the subject of the likely chronology of the revisions, where he attaches undue weight to the existence of certain verbal similarities between various parts of the play, including Hand D's addition, and Chettle's *Kind Heart's Dream*." Taylor re-examines Blayney's case in general and especially in regard to the dating of the additions. He finds that most of Blayney's identification of "key words" and of verbal parallels do not convince him of any link between the play and the pamphlet.[72]

Evans finds two main points favoring an early date for both sections of the play. The first is the paleographic evidence from Munday's handwriting supported by Shapiro's reading of the date in *John a Kent*. The other is the association of Hands C and D in the same manuscript. The most likely time, he says, "for an association [of Hand C] with D would have been prior to, or very shortly after, the official formation of the Lord Chamberlain's Men (Shakespeare's company) in 1594." Most critics prefer "a date between 1590 and 1593 for the original play and of 1594 or 1595 for the revisions." Long, who "attempts to fix both date and company," considers C's participation in *Sir Thomas More* "vital" to the determination of the date because in addition to being bookkeeper of that play he also performed the same function for *John a Kent* and wrote the plot of *2 Seven Deadly Sins*, both of which can be dated circa 1590. This evidence and the presence of Goodale's name in *Sir Thomas More* firmly place it, along with *John a Kent*, "with Lord Strange's Men at the Curtain, 1590–1593. It would seem most likely that *More* was planned as a performance by Strange's Men for the theatrical season of 1592–1593." Melchiori, in an essay "aimed essentially at establishing the order of composition and insertion of the various additions and revisions," says that he has evidence in the form of topi-

72. Jenkins, Greg, *Sir Thomas More*, p. xliii; Wentersdorf, "Date of Additions," p. 325; Blayney, "*The Booke of Sir Thomas Moore* re-examined," pp. 188–90; Proudfoot, "The Year's Contribution to Shakespearian Study 3. Textual Studies," *ShS* 26 (1973): 183; Gary Taylor, "The Date and Auspices of the Additions to *Sir Thomas More*," in the forthcoming Howard-Hill collection. In a note (n. 32), Taylor reports that Blayney told him that he (Blayney) "had come to share Proudfoot's reservations about the second half of the article," that is, the dating of the additions immediately after the original.

cal allusions and echoes that would date the additions "not later than 1593–94," which will be published in his and Gabrieli's edition of *Sir Thomas More* in the Revels Plays series.[73]

In 1912, Schücking suggested a late date of composition (1605) primarily by reference to the dates of other plays, especially *Thomas Lord Cromwell*, with which he thinks *Sir Thomas More* has affinities, but his proposal received little notice or support. Oliphant, on the basis of a comparison with the known dates of Munday's other dramatic writings, says "'More' should date not earlier than 1598–9." G. B. Harrison applied an internal stop test to forty-one lines of Addition IIc and compared his counts to the frequency of the same type of metrical phenomena in the canonical plays which R. W. Chambers cited in his contribution to *Shakespeare's Hand*. The incidence of internal stops in the forty-one lines of the addition is comparable to that of *Julius Caesar* and *Troilus and Cressida*, and consequently "it seems difficult, then, on internal evidence to place the More speech before *Julius Caesar*; indeed, if the rhythmical tests, which are usually applied to date Shakespeare's plays, count for anything, it is later. It is still more difficult to believe that Shakespeare could have written it between 1595 and 1597." Immediately thereafter, Pollard applied the same test, using Harrison's method, to two speeches in act 4 of *The Merchant of Venice*, comprising together thirty-seven lines, and found a slightly higher incidence of internal stops in *The Merchant of Venice* than Harrison found in *Sir Thomas More* This fact leads Pollard to conclude, "I cannot myself see any difficulty in Shakespeare having written this speech of More about the same date as the *Merchant*," that is, 1594–1595.[74]

73. Evans, *Riverside Shakespeare*, p. 1684; Long, "The Occasion of *The Booke of Sir Thomas Moore*," in the Howard-Hill symposium; Melchiori, "A Chronology," pp. 306–8.

74. Schücking, "Datum," pp. 250–51; Oliphant, "*Sir Thomas More*," pp. 232–33; G. B. Harrison, "The Date of *Sir Thomas More*," *RES* 1, 3 (1925): 337–39; Alfred W. Pollard, "Verse Tests and the Date of *Sir Thomas More*," *RES* 1, 4 (1925): 441–43. Harrison's note, which has proved to be influential on the thinking of a number of scholars who came after him, employs techniques that are subject to question. Because he elected to compare what he counts as forty-one lines of Addition IIc (220–63, pp. 77–78) to texts of the Globe edition, he found it "first desirable to bring the More speech into line with the familiar [Globe] text by modernising the spelling and punctuation. . . . It is especially desirable to gain this new perspective because the author of the three pages had such rudimentary theories of spelling and punctuation." He reprints the passage in modern spelling with his own punctuation for comparison to four plays in the Globe edition. There is no way of knowing whether the Globe editors would have pointed the passage in *Sir Thomas More* as Harrison has, since they did not include it in their edition. The passage he chose includes the notable crux at 235–37, which D corrected *currente calamo*, probably twice, and which C deleted, substituting a half-line of his own. Harrison omits the three genuine lines by D, two of which are hypermetrical, and retains C's spurious half-line. The result manifestly deviates in substance from the passage in Greg's transcription of Addition IIc. By Harrison's count, as he has punctuated the passage, it has ten internal stops in forty-one lines, a proportion, he says, of one in four. Greg's transcription of the same passage shows only one period and one semi-colon that are internal stops, plus numerous commas, most of which are not stops. By a different method of editorial punctuation, three of Harrison's internal stops are unneces-

Douglas Collins notes that "no serious study has been made of the emotional disturbances arising from the conditions of the time" that would account for the severity of Tilney's strictures. He calls attention to astrologically alarming events, the political conditions that led to the Essex rebellion, and economic and sociological troubles such as the throng of loose and masterless men about the city. He decides that, in view of these circumstances that certainly would have worried Tilney, "a date about 1601 has much to commend it." Collins cites in support Harrison's internal stop test and comments by Sir Edmund Chambers. In consultation with Harrison he decides on this chronology: Dekker, Heywood, and Munday wrote the play for the Admiral's Men in 1601. The Admiral's prompter began preparation of the script for production, but it was offered to the Chamberlain's Men when the company decided not to proceed with it and returned it to the authors. Shakespeare touched up one scene, and the play was submitted to Tilney, who required such drastic alterations that it was never acted.[75] Bald finds it hard to ignore Harrison's evidence and decides that "his general contention for a date *c.* 1600 rather than *c.* 1595 on metrical grounds is well founded." He also cites Collins's argument that the best explanation for Tilney's refusal to permit the insurrection scenes to be played lies in the Essex rebellion. In late 1600, the Fortune was being built and the Admiral's Men were on tour, so it would be natural for Henslowe's dramatists to offer their new play to the Chamberlain's company. "According to this hypothesis . . ." Bald says, "*Sir Thomas More* was begun in the latter part of 1600."[76]

Nosworthy studies the vocabulary characteristics of Addition IIc, finding that there are a few unique words and, more useful, a number of uncommon words that occur in canonical plays. He finds twenty-six words in plays ranging from *2 Henry VI* to *The Tempest.* Although "such usages

---

sary, yielding by this scheme of punctuation a frequency of 1 in 5.9 lines. If the three deleted lines were retained, redistributed as four regular lines, which appears possible, and C's half-line deleted, the count of internal stops to lines would then be 7 in 45 lines, or 1 in 6.4, statistically a significant difference when compared to Harrison's ratio of 1 in (actually) 4.1. This is admittedly not much more than an exercise, but it shows that there is a serious weakness in Harrison's method.

Equally as pertinent is the fact that Harrison proposes to limit the application of the internal stop test to four canonical plays to which, he says, R. W. Chambers has reference: *R2*, *JC*, *Tro.*, and *Cor.* He give us his results for the first three plays, but we hear nothing more about *Cor.* Pollard, in his response, accepts Harrison's statistics without demur but effectively counters his contention that internal stops are more frequent in late as compared to early plays by showing that *MV* has a higher incidence of internal stops (1 in 3.4 lines) than *Tro.* (1 in 4.8 lines), Harrison's prime example. It is perhaps worthy of note that of the scholars who in the ensuing discussion refer to Harrison's paper or cite his evidence as support for a late date (Collins, Bald, Ribner, Spikes, Lake, and Chillington), none discusses or even mentions Pollard's corrective paper.

75. Collins, "On the Date of Sir Thomas More," pp. 402–4, 410–11.

76. Bald, "*Booke*," pp. 51–54.

cannot be cited as absolute proof of anything . . . it may legitimately be claimed that the vocabulary of the three pages is entirely characteristic of Shakespeare's verbal habits for, roughly, the period 1598–1602." He adds that *Henry V* is "on a purely mathematical basis . . . the most relevant play," which would suggest a date of 1599, but because of R. W. Chambers's showing of the affinity between *Sir Thomas More* and *Troilus and Cressida*, even though the latter "is but slenderly represented in the lexical tabulation," he settles on a date of 1601–1602.[77] Partridge prefaces a study of the play with a "statement of what is already known, accepted or conjectured" about it. Probably it was "written between 1593 and 1598, though some critics have argued for a date as late as 1600." He analyzes the contractions, grammatical forms, spelling, and punctuation of Addition IIc and finds relationships to the canonical middle plays. In his "Conclusions," he tells us that "the original play was probably written between 1593 and 1597, and the revisions, at any rate Dekker's and Shakespeare's, between 1598 and 1601. In either case the later dates are to be preferred." Matchett determines a later date as a result of the relationship he has defined between *Sir Thomas More* and *The Merchant of Venice*. He makes a fairly convincing case that the two plays share significant imagery and lexical preferences, but his case for the priority of *The Merchant of Venice* is weak. However, on the basis of an assumption that the canonical play is the earlier, he tells us that he is "naturally prepared to argue that the *More* fragment must have been written after the writing of *The Merchant of Venice*, which is to say at the 1600 end of the usual dating spectrum."[78] Jackson presents indices of selected colloquial forms in all the plays of the canon based on earlier counts by Frederick Waller and shows that their use by Shakespeare increases steadily, with only a few aberrations, from the earliest to the latest plays. There is a notable shift to more frequent use of such forms around 1600, *Twelfth Night*, for example, showing a three-fold increase compared to *As You Like It*. The frequency of these colloquial forms "unequivocally associates Hand D of *Sir Thomas More* with the post-1600 Shakespeare plays, . . . everything points to composition no earlier than 1600." Jackson thinks that Shakespeare's addition is most unlikely to have been written before 1600 and that "he might well have written it several years later." He offers no opinion regarding the date of composition of the original version.[79]

77. Nosworthy, "Shakespeare and *Sir Thomas More*," pp. 14–17. What Nosworthy means by the expression "purely mathematical basis" as applied to *H5* is unclear. In his lexical tabulation, it occurs four times, as contrasted to three for the "slenderly represented" *Tro.*, to eight for *Ham.* and seven for *2H4*. Nosworthy is silent about four occurrences in *2H6*, the same as for *H5*. Some further explanation would have been in order.

78. Partridge, *Orthography*, pp. 43, 57–64; Matchett, "Shylock, Iago, and *Sir Thomas More*," p. 221.

79. MacD. P. Jackson, "Linguistic Evidence for the Date of Shakespeare's Addition of *Sir Thomas More*," *N&Q* 223 (1978): 154–56. For an additional comment and correction,

Thus we have two primary schools of scholarly thinking in regard to the date of composition of the two elements of *The Booke of Sir Thomas Moore*. Those who favor an early date for the original and a date for the revisions of a year or two thereafter are in the mainstream of criticism, in company with some of the most eminent students of the play. The alternative line of thought, possibly shaped by the spectacular failure of the Essex rebellion,[80] sets the original date of composition at about the turn of the century, and, again, with the additions composed soon after. There is a third conception, not so much separate from the other two but rather in the nature of a synthesis, latterly represented by the thinking of D. J. Lake, Taylor and McMillin, that posits an early date for the original version and a post-1600 date for the additions. Pollard hinted at it in *Shakespeare's Hand* when he noted "the further possibility . . . that the play was drafted at one of the early dates and rewritten with additions at one of the later ones" (p. 21). Sir Edmund Chambers thinks "it is possible that *Sir Thomas More* was laid aside when Tilney sent it back, and taken up later by new writers, with different literary notions from Munday's, in the hope that the political cloud had blown by and that Tilney might now be persuaded to allow the main original structure to stand." He does not say how much time he assumes between the two efforts, but it appears he was thinking of at least a few years.

Lake has little doubt "that the original play . . . belongs to the early 1590s." He then examines the Shakespeare and Dekker additions, finding the Shakespearean style "unmistakably mature" based on indices of frequency of feminine endings, alexandrines, and half lines in the range found in *The Merry Wives of Windsor*, *Hamlet*, *Measure for Measure*, *Macbeth*, and *Antony and Cleopatra*. Dekker's use of colloquialisms in *Sir Thomas More* as compared to his plays written after 1600 seems to show that his addition was written shortly before *Satiromastix* and *2 Honest Whore*, both dated 1605–1607 by Fredson Bowers. Neither Shakespeare's nor Dekker's addi-

---

see also Jackson, "Hand D of *Sir Thomas More*," *N&Q* 226 (1981): 146. For the work on which Jackson bases his case, see Frederick O. Waller, "The Use of Linguistic Criteria in Determining the Copy and Dates for Shakespeare's Plays," *Pacific Coast Studies in Shakespeare*, eds. Waldo F. McNeir and Thelma N. Greenfield (Eugene: University of Oregon Press, 1966), 1–19. Jackson acknowledges the limitations of his data: "Obviously the absolute figures are too small to allow of any confident inference" ("Linguistic Evidence," p. 156). In Jackson's table of colloquial forms there is one play that is manifestly anomalous. "*The Taming of the Shrew*," as he points out, "is the only early play which exhibits in its orthography anything like the degree of colloquialism evident in the later plays." It is quite possible that Addition IIc, which Jackson finds to be highly colloquial also, may be just such another statistical aberration and therefore closer in time to *Shr.* than to the middle plays.

80. Jenkins (in Greg, *Sir Thomas More*, p. xli) says, "The idea that it [*Sir Thomas More*] reflects the Essex rebellion . . . seems to originate in the fascination Essex exerts over the minds of modern scholars. The hypothesis might follow if a suitable date for *More* could first be established; it cannot help to establish one."

tions, according to Lake, were written "earlier than 1600. They may well be several years later than that."[81]

Taylor presents a solution that involves an early date for the original and a late date for the revisions, a suggestion that faces the twin challenges of the paleographic evidence and the association of Hands C and D. According to his conception, the play was composed probably by Munday and Chettle, and the fair copy was prepared by Munday sometime between autumn 1592 and May 1595, the later limit set by the riot in that year followed by the executions. These events rule out any participation by Munday, a government undercover agent, after that date. It was submitted to Tilney, whose criticisms "effectively disembowelled" the play, so it was laid aside. The several different vocabulary and metrical studies of the additions by Jackson, Lake, Nosworthy, and R. W. Chambers—substantiated by a test of "colloquialisms in verse" of Taylor's own devising—point "unequivocally to the first few years after 1600" when the play was again taken up. This is supported by the presence of profanity in each addition, which indicates a date before the 1606 *Acte to Restraine Abuses of Players*; Faulkner's reference to the scouring of Moorditch, which occurred in 1603; and parallels to Addition IIc in Chettle's *Hoffman*, dated 1603–1604. Revisions were begun circa 1603–1604 to update and to improve the play, but the alterations may also have been intended to forestall the possibility that Tilney would recognize it as one that he had censored a decade before; if he did recognize it, the players could plausibly "claim that the play had been considerably revised." It is even possible that it may have been submitted not to Tilney but to Sir George Buc, who had become acting Master of the Revels on 23 June 1603. Taylor conjectures that the event that initiated the reworking of the play was its acquisition by the Chamberlain's-King's Men (possibly by purchase from Henslowe), which explains Shakespeare's participation in Addition II, and the presence of Goodale's name and of Hand C, who, according to Taylor's theory, had never left the Chamberlain's. This hypothesis takes into account the paleographical constraints, provides for the absence of Tilney and Munday from the additions in the manuscript, and offers a solution to the presence of Shakespeare and Hand C in the same manuscript. It reconciles the paleographic evidence for an early date for Munday's transcript with the stylistic evidence for a later date for the additions.

On the basis of testimony from paleographical, authorial, and textual

81. Chambers, *William Shakespeare*, 1:511–12; D. J. Lake, "The Date of the *Sir Thomas More* Additions by Dekker and Shakespeare," *N&Q* 222 (1977): 114–16. Lake recognizes that his statistics are based on a small sample: "It may be objected that the shortness of the *More* text—eighty lines, only nine speeches—renders these comparisons a little suspect" (p. 115). For a conjectural reconstruction of events based on an assumed early date for both the original and the revision, see Metz, "The Master of the Revels and *The Booke of Sir Thomas Moore*," *SQ* 33 (1982): 493–95.

studies, and new evidence adduced chiefly from dramatic and theatrical sources, McMillin develops answers to the questions of dating the play and identifying the acting company or companies for which it was written. He postulates an original date of composition before the separation of the Admiral's and the Chamberlain's combination in June 1594. The play was intended for Lord Strange's Men, the earlier name for the Chamberlain's troupe (the name changed because of their patron's change of title), and for Edward Alleyn, who was playing with them. McMillin determines this by finding that Strange's Men had the number of talented players to pro-produce a play with twenty-two speaking parts and a principal role of more than eight hundred lines; and that *Sir Thomas More* matched their "repertory and the general character of the company." Since the theaters were closed because of plague for most of the two years preceding the division of the companies in 1594, he selects a "speculative [date sometime] between the summer of 1592 and the summer of 1593." After Tilney's censure, it was set aside because with the theaters closed there was no immediate need for it. The original play was written by Munday, Chettle, and Hand D, who was perhaps Shakespeare. Hand D must have been a participant because he does not appear to know what the other playwrights are attempting to do in the course of the revisions, probably because he composed his part before the revisions were written, and because the beginning of Addition IIc on folio 8[a] in his hand seems to be in medias res. McMillin also points out, "No direct evidence places Hand D's pages at the same time as the other revisions and none places the other revisions at the same time as the original." In general, plays were not revised soon after having been first written. This usually occurred upon revival when changes in the company or in theatrical style might necessitate changes in the text. McMillin finds that "the primary motive that can be detected in most of the additions . . . [is] the . . . easing [of] the casting demands of an unusually large play." Since *Sir Thomas More* is not mentioned in Henslowe, it must have been revived "after March 1603, when the *Diary* ceases to be a systematic account." It may have been in the possession of Henslowe or Alleyn since 1594. Four of the six playhouse hands discernible in the manuscript "are known to have been associated with the Admiral's men after 1600." They were working primarily on revivals for Alleyn, who had come out of retirement, and on new plays on Tudor history. *Sir Thomas More*, of course, is both. The date of the revision is "sometime after March 1603; . . . On the assumption that the Admiral's men revised the play after Elizabeth's death" on 23 March, it is understandable that the revising playwrights show no sign of heeding Tilney's stern admonition of a decade earlier regarding the Ill May Day sequence. The presence of Goodale's name is anomalous, but there is no record of him after 1599 and it is possible that he "joined the Admiral's men after 1603 . . . in time for the *More* revision."

In sum, the play was originally written for Alleyn and Strange's Men in 1592–1593. It was revised and cut down ten years later for the Admiral's Men when they were reviving Alleyn's big roles. "The evidence for these assertions comes from the theatrical characteristics implied by the manuscript . . . let Munday, Chettle, and Shakespeare be the collaborators of the original . . . let Dekker, Heywood, and perhaps Chettle be the revisers . . . let Hand C be present on both occasions."[82]

McMillin's and Taylor's scenarios agree on many points. There are some secondary differences, but the primary difference is the dating of Hand D's pages. Taylor places them late, at the same time as the other revisions (c. 1603); McMillin sees them as having been written contemporaneously with Munday's contribution (c. 1593). Perhaps further studies will harmonize these differences, but at this time Collins's comment of a half-century ago remains valid: "In spite of all this spade work, no satisfactory conjectural date has been forthcoming. There are a number of difficulties which have to be considered, and no date proposed so far has eliminated all of them";[83] though it must be said that Taylor's and McMillin's suggestions come very close to doing so.

Sources

Considering the volume of the scholarly literature on *Sir Thomas More*, there has been relatively little written about the play's sources. Much of what has been written is notably casual. In the first edition of the play (1844), Dyce reprints two items under the heading "Illustrations of the Earlier Scenes of the Play." These comprise a portion of Edward Hall's *Union of the two Noble and Illustre Famelies of Lancastre and Yorke*, in which the chronicler tells of the events of Ill May Day 1517; and a ballad entitled "The Story of Ill May Day in the time of King Henry VIII., and why it was so called, and how Queen Catherine begged the lives of Two Thousand London Apprentices." Dyce does not comment on either "illustration," but it is clear that the ballad is an analogue rather than a source of the Ill May Day scenes. In his commentary notes, Dyce reprints other "illustrations." There are six passages of illustrations from Roper's *Life*, three from Hall (one paraphrased), and three from Cresacre More's *Life*. Dyce also notes that the play performed by the Lord Cardinal's Players in *Sir Thomas More*, entitled *The Marriage of Wit and Wisdom*, is actually "a por-

82. Taylor, "The Date and Auspices of the Additions to *Sir Thomas More*," forthcoming in the Howard-Hill collection. See also Taylor's "Canon and Chronology," pp. 124–25, 139, 461–62; Scott McMillin, *The Elizabethan Theatre and The Book of Sir Thomas More* (Ithaca: Cornell University Press, 1987), *passim*. Passages cited are on pp. 53–54, 72–73, 75, 76, 90, 93–94, and 156.

83. Collins, "On the Date of Sir Thomas More," pp. 401–2.

tion of *Lusty Juventus* . . . with alterations and a few additions,—the additions perhaps being borrowed from some other ancient drama" that he does not name. In his notes, Dyce reprints fifty-one lines from *Lusty Juventus*.[84]

In a brief paragraph and following a cautionary word on sources, Hopkinson says that for the earlier scenes the author "no doubt went to Hall's *Chronicle*. . . . For later scenes he may have gone to Hall, Stowe or Holinshed." He thinks it probable that the playwright had access to a manuscript of Roper's *Life*, and he notes that "stories and traditions of More were current at the time" and that John Foxe's *Actes and Monuments* was probably laid under contribution for the account of More's execution.[85] Brooke concludes, "The main source of the drama is doubtless Hall's *Chronicle* . . . however, the story of More's life and death was such common property in the reign of Elizabeth that it is unsafe perhaps to fix upon any one authority." He announces that he has found in Foxe an account of the fight in Pannier Alley and the source of the long-haired Faulkner episode. He adds, "The stock account of More's execution . . . will be found in the same work."[86]

Greg's Malone Society edition concerns itself almost exclusively with the manuscript and the text, and in his preface he does not discuss sources except for one brief paragraph on *The Marriage of Wit and Wisdom*, which he says (p. xix) is "a somewhat altered version of a scene from *Lusty Juventus* to which is prefixed a prologue of which the first eight lines are taken from that to the *Disobedient Child*." The only source mentioned by Pollard is Foxe, although a curious negative comment in a discussion of date may indicate his ideas of other sources: "There is no mention of anti-alien riots [of 1586] in Holinshed or Stowe."[87] The subject of sources does not come up in Sir Edmund Chambers's *William Shakespeare*. Comments on the sources of *Sir Thomas More* in the decade following *Shakespeare's Hand* (until 1933) are generally brief and mostly limited to an affirmation of Dyce's "illustrations," especially Hall and Roper.

In the first significant source study, published in 1933, Marie Schütt analyzed all the scenes in the play and determined sources in most instances.[88] She categorized the possible sources as Protestant, therefore unsympathetic to More; as Catholic, in which he is the saint and martyr; and as originating in the oral tradition, in which he is a man of spirit, wit, and

84. Alexander Dyce, ed., *Sir Thomas More* (London: for the Shakespeare Society, 1844). The excerpt from Hall's *Union* and the ballad are printed on pp. vii–xxiii. The other "illustrations" are included in notes on pages 13, 48–49, 61–63, 67, 72, 88, 89, 93, 97, 98, 99–100, and 100–101.

85. Hopkinson, *Sir Thomas More*, 1915 issue, pp. xxxiv–xxxv.

86. Brooke, *The Shakespeare Apocrypha*, p. liv.

87. *Shakespeare's Hand*, pp. 2, 25.

88. Marie Schütt, "Die Quellen des 'Book of Sir Thomas More,'" *Englische Studien* 68 (1933): 209–26.

humor. The five biographies of More of the sixteenth and early seventeenth centuries, by Roper, Harpsfield, Stapleton, Ro: Ba:, and Cresacre More, are listed and briefly described. It is clear that Schütt considers the *Lives* collectively as the major, though not the only, source. The insurrection sequence and the council scene are derived from Hall, and the long-haired ruffian incident is derived from Foxe. Hall also supplies some minor elements in the concluding Tower and execution scenes. The major portion of the play comes from one of the biographies supplemented from the oral tradition, with which the playwrights were no doubt familiar—Brooke's "common property." The four incidents for which Schütt does not suggest sources are the play-within-a-play, except, of course, More's participation that derives from Roper, the presentation of the Articles to the Council for signature, Fisher at the Tower, and the scene of More's serving men. In the case of each of these four, a source can be suggested where Schütt does not do so. Her conclusion, in which she says that the principal origins of the play are Hall's *Chronicle* and Ro: Ba:'s biography, is subject to exception as to Ro: Ba because in almost every instance in which she cites his biography as the source, he is merely copying or adapting from an earlier *Life*, usually Harpsfield's or Stapleton's; and, of course, through them from Roper's. Only one general criticism has been made regarding the integrity of her essay. Greg, in a note in his study of the Shakespeare First Folio, says: "A careful inquiry into sources by Marie Schütt . . . produces some curious results."[89] Unfortunately, he does not tell us to what he refers. Perhaps it is her designation of Ro: Ba:'s *Life* as a principal source, virtually without argument, even though the work is late and acknowledged by Ro: Ba: himself to be largely derivative. Furthermore, the play rarely exhibits linguistic sharing with his text.

Most other scholars who have commented on the sources of *Sir Thomas More* since Schütt have accepted Hall's *Union* as the main source. They also cite Foxe and *Lusty Juventus* but are less certain of the playwright's use of the biographies. Occasionally, other less likely possibilities are noted, such as in Erasmus's letter to Ulrich von Hutten. Sources of minor elements in the play, including the urinal jest (†1751–55, p. 58), which first appeared in print in Sir John Harington's *The Metamorphosis of Ajax* (1596), are even more rarely noticed. R. W. Chambers states, "Hall's *Chronicle* provided the most important source of fact . . . [but] beyond this it is difficult to say how far the play draws upon recollections of what Roper or Stapleton had written, and how far it is dependent upon London tradition."[90] Jenkins emphasizes "the lively tradition of anecdote" as a source, second only to Hall, which was directly followed and was a main

89. Greg, *First Folio*, p. 99.

90. R. W. Chambers, *Thomas More* (London: Cape, 1935; rpt. Ann Arbor: University of Michigan Press, 1958), pp. 45–46.

source for the first part of the play. He continues, "Any direct relation between the biographies and the play is most unlikely."[91] He believes that "for episodes of More's personal life (as distinct from public events) the play draws on traditional popular legends."[92]

A minority of students of the play favor Roper's *Life* as the primary source. Following a discussion of the diversity of the play Ribner says,

> For all of their material the authors seem to have gone mainly to Roper's life of More, although some use must also have been made of John Foxe's *Acts and Monuments*, from whence came the anecdote of the long-haired servant, which Foxe attributes to Thomas Cromwell, but which our authors decided to give to More.[93]

In a study devoted mainly to an assessment of the structure, themes, and organization, Judith Doolin Spikes points out that "many, perhaps most, of the virtues of the play are those of its principal source, William Roper's *Life of Sir Thomas More*." The playwrights had also read Foxe and Hall, but "the correspondences between the play and Roper's *Life* are so numerous and so close that its status as the principal source cannot be doubted, even though use of it may well have been made at second or third hand," presumably as incorporated into subsequent *Lives*. Spikes also raises a question concerning the manner in which it came into the playwrights' hands.[94] Michael Anderegg, one of the most knowledgeable Morean biographical scholars, favorably summarizes Spikes's position and says that Schütt's "evidence strongly suggests that the authors of *Sir Thomas More* were quite familiar with William Roper's *Life of More* (either directly or through Nicholas Harpsfield's *Life*) and perhaps with Thomas Stapleton's *Tres Thomae* (1588)." He also undertakes, in response to Spikes's question, to "suggest a possible way that a manuscript of Roper's (or Harpsfield's) biography could have come to the attention of at least one of the playwrights involved in the composition of *Sir Thomas More*." He recalls that a copy of Harpsfield's *Life* was found in the study of Thomas More, the chancellor's grandson, when he was arrested by Richard Topcliffe at Cambridge on 13 April 1582, according to a note written in the manuscript itself, at present in the Emmanuel College Library. Topcliffe, well known as a recusant hunter, was a superior of Munday, whom he employed "to guard and take bonds of recusants." Anderegg conjectures that under circumstances similar to those in which the Harpsfield *Life* was found, Munday may have come upon a manuscript copy of Roper's and "might have

91. Jenkins, *Sir Thomas More*, p. 1235.
92. Personal letter of 21 March 1984.
93. Ribner, *English History Play*, pp. 212–13.
94. Judith Doolin Spikes, "*The Book of Sir Thomas More*: Structure and Meaning," *Moreana* 43–44 (1974): 25–39.

seen in it the germ of a play." He believes that "the early lives of More are very much in the background of *Sir Thomas More*."[95]

Among those who have studied the problem of the play's sources, it has become habitual to assume that the playwrights borrowed Foxe's anecdote of the long-haired ruffian and substituted More for Cromwell as the protagonist in the play's version of the story. Pollard says that it is "rather unhappily transferred to More" and almost all later commentators have followed Pollard's lead. Another explanation appears possible. That the playwrights were acquainted with the Morean anecdotal tradition is generally accepted. Perhaps they knew a form of the story with More rather than Cromwell as the principal. One of the collaborators may have read Foxe's version in *Actes and Monuments* and decided to use it in the play, with More restored as the hero in accord with the version transmitted orally. This explanation is admittedly speculative but no more so than Pollard's assertion, for which he has no superior warrant. I believe it is even possible that Foxe knew the oral tradition of the anecdote with More as the central figure and adapted it to his purposes in his eulogistic presentation of Thomas Cromwell, whom he greatly admired, calling him "a continual nourisher of peace."[96] In an essay by Frank Wilson on Shakespeare's reading, he traces the image of humanity preying on itself that occurs in Addition IIc (209–10, p. 76) to a book by John Poynet (1556), who in turn cites Theodoretus, a Church father.[97]

The written sources that may have provided the materials for a dramatic biography of More (as distinguished from oral tradition) are the chronicles, the various *Lives*, brief notices in the nature of memoirs or eulogies incorporated into letters or non-biographical books, and some other minor literary writings. The earliest influential chronicle, that of Polydore Vergil, is not a source of *Sir Thomas More*. He has an account of Ill May Day 1517, including the causes of the insurrection and the aftermath of executions and pardons, but More's involvement is not chronicled. Polydore mentions More only twice, both times very briefly. He notes that he was the speaker of the House of Commons and tells of his conflict with Henry and his execution in few words.[98]

95. Michael A. Anderegg, "*The Book of Sir Thomas More* and its Sources," *Moreana* 14, 53 (1977): 57–62. For a different interpretation of some of Anderegg's evidence, see Metz, "The Play of *Sir Thomas More*: the Problem of the Primary Source," *Moreana* 21, 82 (1984): 41–48.

96. Pollard, *Shakespeare's Hand*, p. 2. Why the transfer should be unhappy is not clear. The handling of the story in the play is anything but unhappy. It is dramatically effective, and in the latter part of the scene in Addition IV, where Dekker is rewriting and extending the incident, it is quite lively, possibly theatrically the play's best, other than Addition IIc. Metz, "Thomas More, Thomas Cromwell and Jack Faulkner," *N&Q* 230 (1985): 28–30.

97. F. P. Wilson, "Shakespeare's Reading," *ShS* 3 (1950): 14–21.

98. Polydori Vergilii Vrbinatis, *Angliae Historiae*, 1555 Facsimile rpt. (Menston: Scolar, 1972), pp. 650–52, 676, 689. For an excerpt comprehending the reigns of Henry VII

Edward Hall's account of Henry's reign is of particular value because he lived through the events that are dramatized in *Sir Thomas More*. His Protestant and Tudor leanings make him less objective when writing of More than he might otherwise have been, but, except for an occasional lapse, the *Union* is a reasonably fair recital of the historical events on which the play is based. It is clear that he is not sympathetic to More and seems to lack the capability of understanding him in all his complexities. The chronicles of Grafton, Stow, and Holinshed are, for the events of the play, dependent in large part on Hall.[99]

Five *Lives* of More have been considered potential sources on which the playwrights may have drawn. The authors are William Roper, an attorney and More's son-in-law; Nicholas Harpsfield, archdeacon of Canterbury and a friend of Roper's; Thomas Stapleton, a literary and ecclesiastical scholar and religious controversialist; Ro: Ba:, who is perhaps Sir Robert Bassett, Margaret Roper's grandson and therefore More's great-grandson; and Cresacre More, the chancellor's great-grandson in the direct line. Except for Roper's text, which "for all the More *Lives* . . . ranks as the *biographia princeps*," as Elsie Vaughan Hitchcock says, each of these biographies is dependent to some degree on the preceding *Life* or *Lives*, a relationship that is specifically acknowledged by Harpsfield, Ro: Ba:, and Cresacre More. Stapleton appears to have made use of Roper and of Harpsfield.[100] Each, however, adds some new material that was probably, and, in the case of Stapleton, was certainly, received orally from surviving family members. Cresacre More's *Life* is least valuable, since the last of the family who knew the Chancellor intimately that Cresacre might have consulted was William Roper himself, who died in 1578 when Cresacre was only six years old. (John Harris, sometime secretary to the Chancellor lived until circa 1588, but he had been continuously in exile from 1565.) It is also the least likely of the biographies to have been a source of *Sir Thomas More* because it was composed after 1615 and apparently was not completed until 1625. The book would therefore have been unavailable to the playwrights

---

and Henry VIII and an English translation see Denys Hay, ed., *Anglica Historica of Polydore Vergil A.D. 1485–1537*, Camden Series, vol. 74 (London: Royal Historical Society, 1950), pp. 243–47, 307, 333–35.

99. For a discussion of the limitations of the various chronicles and in particular the relationships of Grafton, Stow, and Holinshed to Hall, see Charles Lethbridge Kingsford, *English Historical Literature in the Fifteenth Century* (Oxford: Clarendon Press, 1913), pp. 103–7, 140–49, 253–74.

100. William Roper, *The Lyfe of Sir Thomas Moore, knighte*, ed. Elsie Vaughan Hitchcock, EETS O.S. 197 (Oxford: Oxford University Press, 1935) (composed c. 1556–1557, first printed 1626), p. xlxii. Stapleton lists his sources in the preface to his *Vita*, but he does not mention Roper. In his introduction to Msgr. Hallett's English translation of Stapleton's *Vita* (p. xii), E. E. Reynolds says that Stapleton "had a manuscript copy of William Roper's *Life* by him, and perhaps one of Harpsfield's *Life*." His determination is based on allusions in the text.

in any form until at least 1616 and probably not until 1625. It seems reasonable to eliminate it from consideration as a source of the play.[101]

In addition to these *Lives*, there are a series of shorter sketches that may have been sources, a few so brief as to amount to no more than passing allusions in books or pamphlets on another subject. Among them are Erasmus's "portrait" of More in his letter to Ulrich von Hutten; sketches in Richard Pace's *De Fructu qui ex Doctrina Percipitur* and Reginald Pole's *Pro Ecclesiasticae unitatis defensione*; allusions in the "Rastell Fragments"; "Richard Hall's" *Life of Fisher*; and Sir John Harington's *A New Discourse of a Stale Subject, called The Metamorphosis of Ajax*. Of these works listed, it appears that the one most likely to have been used by the authors of the play is Erasmus's letter. Harington's *Metamorphosis* may also have supplied anecdotes. There are other potential sources that are neither chronicles nor biographies. The most important of these are John Foxe's *Actes and Monuments*, the early plays *Lusty Juventus* (c. 1565) and *The Disobedient Child* (c. 1569), and the *Paris News Letter*.

The oral tradition, which preserved and transmitted much information on More, by its very nature was generally not recorded. Some elements of this tradition, however—usually in the form of anecdotes, apothegms, sententious sayings, or jests—found their way into print, some in the possible sources already named above and also in More's *English Works*, in his Latin *Epigrams*, in collections such as Camden's *Remains*, and in sixteenth-century joke books. A few have survived in manuscript form.[102] There is rather more material thus recorded than might have been anticipated.[103]

101. For a useful account of the early biographies and their interrelationships, see Michael A. Anderegg, "The Tradition of Early More Biography," *Essential Articles for the Study of Thomas More*, eds. R. S. Sylvester and G. P. Marc'hadour (Hamden, Connecticut: Archon, 1977), pp. 3–25.

102. For example, marginal notes by Gabriel Harvey in a book dated 1567 and a diary entry by John Manningham dated 25 June 1602. See Samuel A. Tannenbaum, "Some Unpublished Harvey Marginalia," *MLR* 25 (1930): 327–31; and Robert Parker Sorlien, "Thomas More Anecdotes in an Elizabethan Diary," *Moreana* 34 (1972): 81–82.

103. Listed here in order of date of composition are the potential sources of *Sir Thomas More* to which reference is made in the discussion that follows: Desiderius Erasmus, 1517 letter to Ulrich von Hutten, *The Epistles of Erasmus*, ed. Francis Morgan Nichols, 3 vols. (London: Longmans, 1917–1718; rpt. New York: Russell, 1962), 3:387–401 (first printed 1519); anonymous, *Discours sur le procez et exécution de Thomas Morus, Chancellier d'Angleterre* [*The Paris News Letter*], n.d. (between 6 and 22 July 1535), trans. *Expositio fidelis de morte D. Thomae Mori & quorundam aliorum insignium virorum in Anglia*, rpt. in Harpsfield, *Life*, eds. Hitchcock and Chambers, pp. 253–66 (Latin translation dated 23 July 1535, first printed 1535); Edward Hall, *The Union of the Two Noble and Illustre Famelies of Lancastre and Yorke* (London: 1548, 1550; 2d ed. 1560), rpt. under the title *Hall's Chronicle*, ed. Sir Henry Ellis (London: 1809; rpt. New York: AMS, 1965) (composed c. 1534–1542); William Rastell, *Sir Thomas Moores lyfe*, which is lost but partially preserved in *Certen brief notes apperteyning to Bushope Fisher collected out of Sir Thomas Moores lyfe writt by Master Justice Restall* ["The Rastell Fragments"], rpt. in Harpsfield, *Life*, eds. Hitchcock and Chambers, pp. 219–52 (composed

All but two of the potential sources of the play—the exceptions being Harington's *Metamorphosis* (1596) and Ro: Ba:'s *Life* (1599)—were available to the playwrights of the collaboration at any date from 1588 onward. Already in print by that year were the sketch by Erasmus (1519), the *Paris News Letter* and its Latin recension *Expositio fidelis* (both 1535), Hall's *Union* (1548), Foxe's *Actes and Monuments* (1563, augmented fourth edition, 1583) and Stapleton's *Vita Thomae Mori* (1588). There is some clear evidence that the biographies written by Rastell (c. 1548–1553), Roper (c. 1556–1557), and Harpsfield (c. 1557) circulated in manuscript throughout the last half of the sixteenth century and into the seventeenth. Rastell's lost *Sir Thomas Moores lyfe* was probably completed circa 1553 and is mentioned by Sanders in 1585. The extant excerpts from it in MS. Arundel 152 are dated circa 1576. Hitchcock says of Roper's *Life* (p. xxv) that it "had circulated in manuscript for many years before it was printed." She demonstrates (p. xxi) that between Roper's original and the surviving thirteen manuscripts, most dated "late sixteenth century" (pp. xi–xiii), there existed eleven earlier manuscripts "now lost." Similarly, Hitchcock shows that in addition to the eight manuscripts of Harpsfield's *Life* we now have (also dated "late sixteenth century"), there had been seven lost manuscripts (p. xxiv). Furthermore, in the case of Harpsfield, we have an item of conclusive evidence that it circulated in manuscript: the well-known note in the Emmanuel College manuscript that was found by Richard Topcliff among the papers in "Mr. Thomas Moares Studdye" on 13 April 1582 (pp. xiii, 294–96).

---

in Belgium c. 1548–1553, cited by Nicholas Sanders in *De origine Schismatis*, 1585, fol. 15, and first printed in 1891); William Roper, *The Lyfe of Sir Thomas Moore, knighte*, ed. Elsie Vaughan Hitchcock, EETS O.S. 197 (Oxford: Oxford University Press, 1935) (composed c. 1556–1557, first printed 1626); Nicholas Harpsfield, *The life and death of Sr Thomas Moore, sometymes Lord high Chancellor of England*, eds. Elsie Vaughan Hitchcock and R. W. Chambers, EETS O.S. 186 (Oxford: Oxford University Press, 1932) (composed c. 1557, first printed 1932); John Foxe, *Actes and Monuments of matters most speciall and memorable* (augmented 4th ed. October 1583) (composed c. 1561–1562), first issued in an incomplete Latin version under the title *Commentarii rerum in ecclasia gestarum* (1554) and first printed in English under the title *Actes and monuments of these latter and perillous dayes* (1563); Thomas Stapleton, *Vita et Illvstre Martyrium Thomae Mori, Angliae Quondam Svpremi Cancellarii*, published as Part 3 of *Tres Thomae* (Douai: 1588) (composed c. 1586–1587), trans. Philip E. Hallett and published under the title *The Life and Illustrious Martyrdom of Sir Thomas More* (London: Burns & Oates, 1928), rpt. ed. E. E. Reynolds (London: Burns & Oates; New York: Fordham University Press, 1966); John Harington, *A New Discovrse of a Stale Svbiect, Called the Metamorphosis of AIAX*, ed. Elizabeth Story Donno (London: Routledge; and New York: Columbia University Press, 1962) (composed c. 1595–1596, first printed 1596); Ro: Ba:, *The Lyfe of Syr Thomas More, Sometymes Lord Chancellor of England*, eds. Elsie Vaughan Hitchcock and P. E. Hallett, with additional notes and appendices by A. W. Reed, EETS O.S. 222 (London: Oxford University Press, 1950) (composed c. 1599, first printed 1810); Cresacre More, *The Life of Sir Thomas More*, ed. Joseph Hunter (London: 1828) (composed after 1615, first printed Douai, 1626).

The source of the opening dramatic movement of *Sir Thomas More*, the Ill May Day riot of 1517, is Hall's *Union* [Text 1].[104] The events of scenes 1, 3, 4, the abbreviated and partially cancelled scenes 5, 5a, and 6—both the revised part of the scene in Addition II and the extant portion in the original text—and scene 7, are all in Hall (pp. 1–5 to l. 103; p. 11 l. 316 to p. 25 l. *734). This set of scenes comprises the representation of the causes of the discontent of the London crafts; their frustration at the lack of a means of seeking redress; the bill of grievances and strangers' insolences; the Council's discussion of the problem and the report they receive of an imminent mutiny; the plans of the mob to attack the strangers and burn their houses; the aroused prentices playing at bucklers (*cudgels* in *Sir Thomas More*) and the wounding of Sir John Munday; breaking open the Counters and Newgate and releasing the prisoners; the Council discussion with the Lord Mayor and the suggestion that Sheriff More may be able to restore order; his speech to the rebellious Londoners and their agreement to submit and sue for clemency if More will make their peace with the King; the execution of Lincoln, the reprieve for the rest of the insurrectionists on More's plea; and the King's pardon for all the rioters. Not only are all of these in Hall but the sequence of events in his *Union* is also followed with virtually no deviation by the playwrights. The hinge of the play's action immediately prior to the uprising (79–91, p. 4) is Lincoln's bill of particulars that was taken over from Hall verbatim except for some eight minor changes, half of which are the omission of the words *to* and *poor* and the definite article. The others are an alteration in word order, a change in the form of a verb, the omission of the expression "so highly," and a revision of Hall's "set to" to "see to," all of which adds up to a slight theatrical improvement but no significant revision in Hall's text.

A comparison of the names in the insurrection scenes in *Sir Thomas More*, other than those of prominent persons such as More himself and the Earls of Surrey and Shrewsbury, shows that Hall supplied Lincoln, Betts, de Barde, Caveler, Mewtas (Hall has Mutuas), Williamson, Sherwin, Sir Thomas Palmer, Sir Roger Cholmley (Hall has Sir Richard), Sir John Munday (though Anthony Munday certainly knew of him), and Dr. Beale. One name from Hall, Nicholas Downes, strayed to scene 13, but the context in which it occurs there shows its Ill May Day connection (†1560–62, p. 51). There are many lesser but still important details borrowed from Hall, such as the story of Williamson and his stockdoves, that of de Barde and Sherwin's wife, and the allusion to the mayor's wife. These specific correspondences are of prime significance for the establishment of Hall's *Union* as the source of the Ill May Day scenes, but they also demonstrate

104. More himself tells us something of Ill May Day in his *Apologye*, but he makes no reference to his own part in quelling the riot. *The Apologye of Syr Thomas More Knyght*, ed. Arthur Irving Taft, EETS O.S. 180 (London: Oxford Univeristy Press, 1930), pp. 177–78.

the mutuality of interest exhibited by the playwrights on the one side and by Hall as seen in his book on the other. He is an admirer of the Tudor regime, an unswerving adherent of Henry VIII's—he finds few things to criticize in Henry's most controversial actions and these are minor—and a confirmed supporter of London's causes. These views are also those of the play's collaborators. They may be perhaps a trifle less uncritical of Henry and the Tudor monarchy than Hall is, but as Londoners—either born or by choice—they also favor the city. We need not seek to determine in this connection whether the dramatists were influenced by Hall or whether their predilections biased them to find his book congenial. The important consideration is that they all knew of More's popularity with Londoners and his reputation as "a specyall lover and ffrende in the Busynesses and Causes of this Citie."[105] The collaborators' sentiments can be seen when Shrewsbury returns from making his report to Henry on the pacification of the riot. He brings the King's "loouing thankes" (*525, p. 18) and a knighthood for More, to which the Lord Mayor responds

> His maiestie hath honord much the cittie
> in this his princely choise.
> (*545–46, p. 19)

In a later scene, the Lord Mayor says to More in regard to his service to the city during the insurrection:

> My Lord, you set a glosse on Londons fame
> and make it happie euer by your name.
> Needs must we say, when we remember *Moore*
> Twas he that droue rebellion from our doore.
> with graue discretions milde and gentle breath,
> sheelding a many subiects liues from death.
> And with your vertues our endeuours crownde.
> (†967–72, p. 33)

Hall, who tends to be critical of More, nevertheless admires his steadfast advocacy of London. To practicing playwrights, all of this meant that More was an eminently appropriate subject for a dramatic biography to be presented before the people of London.[106]

105. Harpsfield, *Life*, ed. Hitchcock and Chambers, p. 314.

106. Why Munday, who spied on the English College at Rome and was a recusant hunter, should have chosen (if the choice was his) More the controversialist on behalf of the old faith as the subject of a biographical drama, or agreed to collaborate in writing it, is a puzzle. Possibly it was because he shared with More an enthusiasm for the business and causes of London. Perhaps, as a professional playwright, he viewed the story of More's life as a good plot for a play, disregarding other considerations; or, as Long ("The Occasion of *The Booke of Sir Thomas Moore*") has suggested, perhaps he was carrying out an assignment from a responsible official of Elizabeth's government, possibly transmitted to him by Richard Topcliffe, to show on the stage as vividly as only the theater can do, the evils of riotous resistance to the royal will as a warning and a corrective to the endemic London unrest.

In the discussion above, Holinshed's *Chronicle* is occasionally referred to as a possible source, usually in conjunction with Roper's *Life*, Foxe's *Actes*, or Hall's *Union*. Vittorio Gabrieli, in an essay devoted in part to the sources of *Sir Thomas More*, offers the hypothesis that the immediate source of the Ill May Day sequence is Holinshed. While acknowledging the priority of Hall, as Holinshed at seven places in his account also does, Gabrieli presents a fairly extensive array of evidence in support of his proposition. Most persuasive are his points that the spelling and punctuation of Lincoln's bill of complaints in the play closely follows that in Holinshed even though it is quite different from Hall's, and that the play reproduces Holinshed's "fatherlesse children" where Hall has "poore fatherles chyldren." In addition, he notes that the dramatists adopt names from Holinshed, but not those in Hall omitted by Holinshed, and follow Holinshed's spellings of the names *Standish* and *Downes* and of the word *kennel*, which are differently spelled in Hall; that the wording in *Sir Thomas More* of More's speech to the rioters is closer to Holinshed and that Hall lacks the phrase "almost persuaded the people to depart"; that the name of the Picard *Mewtas* is spelled thus in the play and Holinshed, but *Mutuas* in Hall; that his house is called "Greene gate" by Holinshed, which is the way the play has it; and that Holinshed's comment on the king's mercy—not in Hall—is echoed in a speech by Surrey (*716–32, p. 24). Gabrieli's findings about Lincoln's bill and the spellings of *Standish*, *Downes*, *kennel*, and *Mewtas* are obviously correct. His conjecture about the source of Surrey's speech, while less compelling, may also be valid. As to the names in the play, it is true that there are two names in Hall not in Holinshed or in the play, but there are also four names in Holinshed not in Hall or in the play, so it would appear that not much can be made of the absence from the play of names that occur in the chronicles. Gabrieli also says that of the historical sources "only Holinshed mentions Sherwin's name"; in fact, Sherwin is named by Hall in a sentence that is copied verbatim by Holinshed except for the spelling, the omission of one word (*day*), and the substitution of the word *seuenth* for the numeral *vii*. Regarding the phrase in Holinshed that "sir Thomas More and others . . . had almost persuaded the people to depart," it is true that it is not in Hall. However, in the same place in Hall's account of the order of events, he says, "Syr Thomas Moore and other . . . had almost brought them to a staye." This may well be the model for Holinshed's altered phrase; but, more important, the action in the play is closer to Hall than to Holinshed in that the people stay their riot but do not depart. Hall also has the phrase "persuading the rebellious persons to cease." Gabrieli's discussion of the expression "Greene gate" in Holinshed ("greene gate" in the play [419, p. 15]) fails to point out that Hall also mentions "Grenegate."

Some of the evidence that Gabrieli has marshaled is cogent, but some is doubtful, at least to one reader. It may be, however, that the playwrights' working source for the Ill May Day scenes was initially Holinshed, especially in view of Gabrieli's reminder that Hall's *Union* was not as readily available at the time of composition as Holinshed's *Chronicle*; but, though it may have been rare, copies were to be had, as the list in the *Short Title Catalogue* of nearly forty, still extant, demonstrates. Perhaps it may be conjectured that Munday, certainly at least part author of the original *Sir Thomas More*, noting in the copy of Holinshed, from which he may have been working, its repeated acknowledgment of Hall as its source, sought out a copy of the *Union* and made use of it, which thus became a dual source, both directly and indirectly through Holinshed. In a later scene-by-scene identification of the sources, Gabrieli modifies some of the points made in his article and makes Hall's contribution somewhat clearer, but he does not alter his central contention—that the dramatic presentation of the May Day rising is based on Holinshed's *Chronicle*. Giorgio Melchiori tells us that the Ill May Day sequence is "an extremely able rehandling of historical events and incidents of early 1517 as reported by a specific source: pages 840–4 of the 1587 edition . . . of the third volume of Holinshed's *Chronicles*. The fact that most of the material of the chronicles is derived from Edward Hall's history is irrelevant: a study of the surviving scenes of the play's original version shows that the author was following Holinshed closely even in matters of spelling and punctuation, as well as wording."[107]

The second scene of *Sir Thomas More*, the Lifter-Suresby episode, is the earliest of several in the play that might have been derived either from one of the narrative biographies of More or from oral tradition. That such a tradition flourished throughout the sixteenth century and at least into the early decades of the seventeenth century is authenticated in a number of ways, but it can easily be traced as it repeatedly surfaces in the biographies until that of Cresacre More. In his *Life*, Cresacre More incorporates several items drawn from popular tales of More that had been recorded by his predecessors and adds a few more that had not previously been committed to print, indicating that this lively anecdotal vein continued to flourish at least as late as 1615.[108] Clearly the stories transmitted orally were available to the collaborators, who no doubt enjoyed a merry tale as much as anybody, since they made repeated use of them. The Lifter-Suresby scene is anecdotal. Of the possible sources, it occurs in Stapleton's *Vita Thomae*

107. Vittorio Gabrieli, "*Sir Thomas More*: Sources, Characters, Ideas," *Moreana* 23, 90 (1986): 17–43; Melchiori, "Hand D," p. 110 and n. 15; "The Sources of *More* by Scenes" in the Howard-Hill symposium.

108. Michael A. Anderegg, "The Anecdotal Tradition of Thomas More: A Note," *Moreana* 35 (1972): 55–56; Gabrieli, "Sources, Characters, Ideas," pp. 28–29, suggests that the ultimate source of the Lifter-Suresby incident is to be found in More's *Four Last Things*, but the anecdote there related by More lacks the most important aspects of the scene in the play.

Mori [Text 2] and in Ro: Ba:'s *Life* [Text 3]. It does not appear in Roper, Harpsfield, or any of the early memoirs. Stapleton's version is of course narrative rather than dramatic and relatively brief compared to that in the play. There are some small differences between his account and scene 2. The *Vita*, for example, has More on the bench, and he initiates the collection. The action takes place over two days. However, the principal elements of the scene are to be found in Stapleton. His and the play's versions do not appear to share any common lexical ground, although it is guesswork as to how a sixteenth-century dramatist would render Stapleton's Latin. Ro: Ba:'s account follows Stapleton's, with only a few minor changes. On balance it seems reasonable to conclude that Stapleton is the source, perhaps acting in effect as proxy for the anecdotal tradition.[109]

More's soliloquy on his elevation to high office and its accompanying perils (Addition III, p. 79), which may have been a brief independent scene or may have been meant to serve as the initial portion of scene 8, has not been traced to any clearly identifiable source. Schütt suggests without explanation a passage in Ro: Ba:'s *Life* on More's integrity, perhaps because the words *honors*, *offices*, and *wealth* occur in Ro: Ba: and are used in the same order in Addition III. While this has some evidential value, it is limited to a less important element of the speech concerned mainly with the exhilarating sense of power that comes with high position, its potential effect on More's relationships with others, particularly his father, and the grave danger of a misstep, perhaps leading to his undoing. Another possible source is a combination of More's reluctance to accept the appointment as Lord Chancellor, his habit of seeking his father's blessing openly in the Court of the King's Bench, his deference to his father when they were at readings in Lincoln's Inn, and his recognition of the precariousness of his position as a royal retainer, to which he alludes in his comment to Roper that Henry would sacrifice him promptly if it would win a castle in France. Roper refers obliquely to More's reluctance to accept the Chancellorship [Text 4], but Harpsfield [Text 5] is unequivocal concerning this matter.[110] If these elements constitute the origin of Addition III, there is a presumption in favor of Harpsfield.

The manuscript *Booke of Sir Thomas Moore* provides some evidence that the combined Erasmus-Faulkner scene (8) may have been originally two scenes. One of Dekker's contributions in writing the replacement for

109. Stapleton, *Vita*, ed. Reynolds, who says (p. 125, n. 5) of the episode: "Perhaps to be regarded as one of the folk-tales about More." Gabrieli, "Sources, Characters, Ideas," p. 30, dismisses Ro: Ba: as a possible source: "there is no evidence at all that they [the dramatists] knew the biography compiled by Ro: Ba:." His judgment is based on Ro: Ba:'s own admission that his *Life* is derived from Harpsfield and Stapleton.

110. For a different view of More's reluctance, see J. A. Guy, *The Public Career of Sir Thomas More* (New Haven: Yale University Press, 1980), pp. 6–11. Guy's assessment is illuminating but emphasizes perhaps a little too heavily More's pragmatism in his approach to royal service. Men's motives are seldom so unmixed as Guy portrays them.

the original scene or scenes was apparently the merging of the Faulkner incident and the original Erasmus episode. This amalgamation is dramatically effective, adding variety and contrast to what is otherwise possibly the most pedestrian segment of the play. Hand C, acting as a scribe here, as elsewhere, copied Dekker's draft. The playwright, in reviewing C's fair copy, seems to have decided to add the distinctly livelier new ending. This conjecture is based on the style and manner of the two parts and on the insertion in Dekker's hand of the phrase "I am *ipse*" appended to line 193, which demonstrates that Dekker emended C's copy.

The source of the Faulkner incident is manifestly Foxe's *Actes and Monuments* [Text 6]. The enlarged fourth edition of his book appeared in 1583 and is almost certainly the one used by Dekker. Foxe tells the story of the long-haired ruffian with Thomas Lord Cromwell as the principal, not More.[111] The passage in Foxe's account begins with a report of a fray arranged by the combatants to take place in Paternoster Row. This is incorporated in the form of a summary report, but otherwise unchanged, into *Sir Thomas More*, even including the point that although the exits from Paternoster Row were closed with carts to inhibit the authorities from breaking up the fray, Pannier's Alley was open. Similarly, Foxe's report of the unrelated questioning of the long-haired ruffian by Cromwell is adapted to the play by Dekker, who elaborates the conversation between Cromwell and the ruffian somewhat, allowing the opportunity for the play's protagonist, More, not Cromwell, and Faulkner to exchange witticisms. The playwright also changes the prison to Newgate from the Marshalsea. The combination of the incident of the Paternoster Row fray with that of the long-haired ruffian is the work of Dekker. The two happen to be juxtaposed in Foxe but are not otherwise associated except insofar as Cromwell is the principal in both. The long hair of the retainer, the commitment to prison, the haircut, the commendation of the ruffian by the principal (Cromwell or More) on his improved appearance, and, most important, the main outline and the sequence of incidents are the same in both versions.

The other part of scene 8, the first meeting of More and Erasmus, is one of the best known in the Morean traditional vein. The widely disseminated exchange in Latin between the two at the moment of mutual recognition is noted in a jotting in Addition IV (p. 85), but no use of it is made in the dialogue. Harpsfield tells the story, which he says he had from More's friend, Antonio Bonvisi, of a debate at table between More and a learned foreign theologian, whom he does not name, in which More distinguished himself. Ro: Ba: follows Harpsfield closely, copying several phrases verbatim. Cresacre More, whose account is essentially the same as Harpsfield's, adds some details, such as the specific identification of Eras-

111. Metz, "Thomas More, Thomas Cromwell and Jack Faulkner."

mus, that the meeting was arranged without either More or Erasmus knowing the other, and the concluding recognition and exchange. Of these elements in Cresacre More, only the identification of Erasmus is in *Sir Thomas More*. T. E. Bridgett recounts two versions of the meeting from traditional sources.[112] That the oral tradition preserved more than one variant of the incident can be safely assumed. The specific source of this part of scene 8 is Harpsfield or possibly the oral tradition, of which Harpsfield would then be an exemplar. The disguising element in the scene—Randall wearing More's clothes in an unsuccessful effort to assume the Lord Chancellor's identity—is unlikely to have been traditional. Disguisings, and specifically one character in a play appearing in another's clothes, is a theatrical device of which Tudor and Stuart dramatists were particularly fond. No specific source need be sought.

More's impromptu participation in the play-within-a-play (scene 9) has its origin in a passage in Roper in which he relates that More as a lad (apparently about twelve or thirteen years of age) would step in among the players presenting a play at Christmastime in Cardinal Morton's house and extemporaneously make a part for himself. Roper is followed by Harpsfield, Ro: Ba:, and Cresacre More, but they add nothing to the account. Roper, or course, could not possibly have been a witness to such an incident and he must therefore have received the information from family sources, possibly from Sir John More. Erasmus, in his memoir addressed to von Hutten, mentions More's acting, though not extemporaneously, noting, "When quite a youth, he wrote '*comoediolas*' and acted them."[113] The players, "ffoure men and a boy," are "My Lord Cardinalles" (†907, †932, pp. 31–2), which also comes from Roper (he mentions Cardinal Morton just before and immediately after the story of More's impromptu playing). When More asks the actors in the play what they have to offer, they mention seven plays, from which he selects *The Marriage of Wit and Wisdom*. When presented, this play turns out to be not the extant play of that name but part of *Lusty Juventus* preceded by a twelve line prologue of which the first eight lines are borrowed verbatim (except for spelling) from the prologue to *The Disobedient Child* [Text 7]. Only the opening song and some three dozen other lines are taken from different parts of *Lusty Juventus* [Text 8], some altered, and the whole pieced out with links to preserve continuity. More briefly plays the part of Good Counsel, substituting for a player who had gone to a wigmaker's to obtain a false beard. He speaks

112. T. E. Bridgett, *Life and Writings of Sir Thomas More* (London: Burns & Oates, 1891; rpt. 1924), p. 38 n.

113. *Epistles of Erasmus*, ed. Nichols, 3:391. The Latin *comoediolas*, translated by Nichols as *farces*, may also be rendered *comic playlets*. In a letter to John Holt dated November 1501, More, then twenty-three years old, refers to his "comediam . . . de Salemone" in *The Correspondence of Sir Thomas More*, ed. Elizabeth Frances Rogers (Princeton: Princeton University Press, 1947), p. 3.

only ten lines, none from *Lusty Juventus*. Two of his lines (†1025–26, p. 35) allude to the thinness of his beard, which Schütt traces to Erasmus's physical description of More in his letter to von Hutten.[114] The performance of *Wit and Wisdom* is interrupted by the return of the actor, whereupon More suggests that his guests taste of the banquet:

> And then they shall begin the play againe,
> which through the fellowes absence, and by me,
> in sted of helping, hath bin hindered.
> Prepare against we come: Lights there I say,
> thus fooles oft times doo help to marre the play.
> (†1142–46, p.38)

This may possibly be an echo of a sentiment expressed by the Chancellor himself in his *History of King Richard III*, where he warns against interference by lesser men in the affairs of princes:

> In a stage play all the people know right wel, that he that playeth the sowdayne [sultan] is percase a sowter [cobbler]. Yet if one should can so lyttle good, to shewe out of seasonne what acquaintance he hath with him, and calls him by his owne name whyle he standeth in his magestie, one of his tormentors might hap to breake his head, and worthy for marring of the play. And so they said that these matters bee Kynges games, as it were stage playes, and for the more part plaied vpon scafoldes. In which pore men be but y[e] lokers on. And thei y[t] wise be, wil medle no farther. For they that sometyme step vp and playe w[t] them, when they cannot play their partes, they disorder the play & do themself no good.[115]

The comparison of the stage to the world of royal affairs, or to the great world itself, is, of course, very old. Richard Sylvester cites a passage from Lucian's *Menippus* and also notes that it is "a favorite metaphor of More's." He points out that it can be found in *The Four Last Things*, in *Utopia*, and elsewhere in More's writing.[116] The occurrence in *Sir Thomas More* of the expressions "weele not haue our play marde," "the play . . . hath bin hindered," and "fooles oft times doo . . . marre the play" (†1115–16, †1142–44, †1146, pp. 37–8) perhaps evidence something more than a mere resemblance to the passage in More's biography.

The concluding action of *Sir Thomas More* begins with scene 10. The setting is a meeting of the Council, but their deliberations on the alliance with the Emperor in opposition to the French are interrupted when Sir Thomas Palmer enters with "Articles" sent by the king to the members of

114. Schütt, "Die Quellen des 'Book of Sir Thomas More,'" p. 215. Her suggestion lacks cogency, especially since the thinness of More's beard could have been part of the oral tradition, but if she is right perhaps the playwrights did know Erasmus's letter.

115. *The History of King Richard III*, in *The Complete Works of St. Thomas More*, ed. Richard S. Sylvester (New Haven: Yale University Press, 1963), 2:81.

116. Ibid., pp. lxi, ci, 258.

the Council to be read and signed. The Articles are not described here or at any other point in the play. Surrey, Shrewsbury, and other Council members sign. The Bishop of Rochester refuses and is immediately summoned to present himself before the king. More resigns his office as Lord Chancellor and says he needs time to think. Palmer responds that the king orders him to Chelsea under house arrest. He goes home to find Lady More, his daughters, and his son-in-law, Roper, apprehensively waiting for him (scene 11). He reports what has happened and insists that all should be merry and not weep at his fall.

The source of the early part of scene 10 is Hall's *Union*. Hall tells in this work of Henry's financial support of the Emperor and specifically mentions that in acknowledgment the Emperor wore a cross of St. George with a rose. This is echoed in the play by Shrewsbury:

> the Emperour is a man of royall faith.
> His looue vnto our Sovereigne, brings him downe,
> from his emperiall seate, to march in pay
> vnder our English fflagge, and weare the crosse
> like some high order on his manly breast.
> (†1206–10, p. 40)

The heart of this and the next scene (10 and 11), however, is the series of events leading up to More's resignation, the resignation itself, and the consequences. Roper records the king's importunate efforts to gain More's consent to his divorce, the drift of which of course More foresaw. After he had been Lord Chancellor for a while (historically, two and a half years), he petitioned his friend, the Duke of Norfolk, to move Henry to relieve him of the chancellorship. Norfolk at length secured More's release, after which More gave up the great seal and the perquisites of office and retired to Chelsea. He told his family what had occurred and explained that they must live modestly and thus be able to continue together. Harpsfield, Stapleton, and Ro: Ba: follow Roper, who was a participant in these events. More's house arrest is a reflection of Roper's account of his detention in the custody of the Abbot of Westminster. Hall briefly tells of More's resignation and says that he "was with the kynges fauor discharged." Roper's *Life* may also be the source of More's jesting with his family in scene 11 over his loss of title. The "my Lord is gone" jest is told by Roper, and, while the play does not re-tell the tale, there is a possible echo in this brief exchange:

> *Lady* [More]. will your Lordship in?
> *Moore*. Lordship? no wife, that's gon,
> (†1347–48, p. 45)

Between Roper's and Hall's accounts, Roper's circumstantial details, intermixed with some anecdotal elements, indicate that his version is the chief source of scenes 10 and 11.

The scene of Bishop Fisher's commitment to the Tower (scene 12) is brief and few details are distinctive. All of the potential sources allude to Rochester's imprisonment, but there is one version—that in the "Rastell Fragments"—that is closer than the others to the short scene in *Sir Thomas More*. In the "Fragments," as in the play, the bishop thanks his escort, speaks lightly of his imprisonment, and expresses his happiness to accept death in Christ's cause. There are two near-correspondences in language. Rastell has Rochester say, "I thank you Masters all," and *Sir Thomas More* reads, "Honorable Lords, I can but thank ye." In both works he is addressing the members of his escort who have conveyed him to the Tower. Rastell mentions Fisher's amiable countenance, and in the play Shrewsbury speaks of his happy private thoughts. These may be no more than mere commonplaces, although the spirit of both accounts is the same: the Bishop of Rochester cheerfully confronts his destiny [Text 9].

Of the concluding five scenes (13 through 17) of *Sir Thomas More*, the substance of four is to be found in greater or less detail in all of the possible sources. Scene 15 is the exception. It is a domestic incident lacking the dramatic intensity of the other four, and theatrically it does not advance the action. There are a number of such static scenes in Shakespearean canonical plays, their purpose being to present significant matters of thought, rather than action, that have a bearing on the theme or the underlying message of the play, or to set or reflect a mood. Hereward T. Price, who has written on such "mirror scenes," describes them as symbolic rather than dramatic and employed to express an informing idea. He has identified mirror scenes in twenty of Shakespeare's plays. It is characteristic of them to be episodic and detachable as scene 15 is.[117] The informing idea appears to be to remind the audience of the exceptional personal (as distinguished from public) qualities of the man about to be beheaded. It has two elements, the purpose of the first being to show in what great respect More's servants—and by extension the common people of London—hold him; the second is to exhibit his generosity. Theatrically the scene is employed to lower the dramatic tension (as the porter's scene does in *Macbeth*) that has been building up and that, after scene 15, intensifies again. There is nothing sufficiently specific in any one of the potential sources to show that it serves as the origin of this scene. Roper, followed by Harpsfield and Stapleton, refers to More's care for his servants, and Erasmus and Stapleton briefly tell of More's charity, but the accounts provide only a bare hint of the Morean quality circumstantially set forth in the play. Perhaps here again—especially in view of the scene's focus on mundane concerns—we may have an element drawn from oral tradition.

More's arrest, his commitment to the Tower, his preparations for his

117. Hereward T. Price, "Mirror Scenes in Shakespeare," in *Joseph Quincy Adams Memorial Studies*, eds. James G. McManaway, Giles E. Dawson, and Edwin E. Willoughby (Washington: Folger Shakespeare Library, 1948), pp. 101–13.

death, and his execution are presented in scenes 13, 14, 16, and 17. Hall, Foxe (citing Hall as his source), Roper, Harpsfield, Stapleton, Ro: Ba:, and Cresacre More all relate the story of the decline, fall, and death of the Lord Chancellor. Hall and Foxe express little sympathy for the dissenter, while Roper and his followers tend to venerate the martyr. Neither of these attitudes is reflected unchanged in *Sir Thomas More*, which rather treats the events with an air of uncomplicated realism much like that characteristic of More himself. Neither he nor his beloved Londoners, including the playwrights, seem to have viewed his sacrifice as an exercise in exceptional heroism; instead, they viewed it as just one more of those many things in life that one does because one must. That it was, in the event, heroic they have no doubt, but it was heroic only in the significance of the sacrifice, different in magnitude, not in kind.

All the sources relate the story of More's commitment to prison in the Tower. Hall's account is brief, that of the *Lives* more extended. Scene 13 begins with a family discussion of More's resignation of the chancellorship, in the course of which he is openly chided by his wife, who says, "We are exilde the Courte" (†1443, p. 48), and more gently by Roper and Catesbie. The Earls of Surrey and Shrewsbury arrive, accompanied by Downes, bearing a message from the king insisting that More sign the Articles and reminding him that Rochester for his refusal has been imprisoned in the Tower. Lady More begs him to sign, but he refuses and is arrested for high treason by Downes. He takes leave of his family and goes off to prison escorted by the two noblemen. Scene 14 immediately following depicts his arrival at the Tower, where he is turned over to the lieutenant and his gentleman porter. The earls wish him well and leave him. More finds some virtue at being imprisoned because now the poor suitor, the fatherless orphan, and the distressed widow shall not disturb his sleep, and God is as strong here (in his place of confinement) as abroad (†1670–74, p. 55). More's own account of the event included in his letters to his daughter Margaret written from the Tower is cited by Roper, who summarizes More's arrest briefly beginning with the attempt by the royal commissioners at Lambeth Palace to persuade More to sign the oath. There is nothing in Roper about his reception into prison. Harpsfield follows Roper, making somewhat more use of More's letters to his daughter in paraphrase. Stapleton quotes the principal letter fully as does Ro: Ba:, who includes a few sentences omitted by Stapleton.

In *Sir Thomas More*, the playwrights have two of More's friends from his Council days, Surrey and Shrewsbury, convey him to prison. As regards the specific persons mentioned, this is, strictly speaking, unhistorical. However, More was attended on three different occasions by sympathetic escorts. He was moved from Lambeth to the Tower, according to Roper, in the custody of Richard Cromwell, the nephew of Sir Thomas

Cromwell, who was, at this point, still not unfriendly toward More. Later, after his trial, More was returned to the Tower by Sir William Kingston, who was, Roper says, his very dear friend. And the court official chosen to notify More of his impending execution was Sir Thomas Pope, who, again according to Roper, was More's singular friend. None of these details are included in Hall's *Union*.

In these scenes (13 and 14) there is an increasingly frequent use of traditional elements, including two intentionally misleading comments by More seemingly indicating that he is prepared to submit to the royal demands. When Surrey and Shrewsbury urge More in friendly fashion to sign the Articles, he responds, "Ile now satisfye the Kings good pleasure." His daughters and the earls express their relief at this, but More quickly adds, "I will subscribe to go vnto the Tower" (†1575, †1580, p. 52). Later, in scene 16, More's family visits him in his cell, and they again attempt to persuade him to yield to the king's will. To this appeal More gives a riddling answer, saying he had deceived himself and to correct it would be no disparagement. Lady More is led by this statement to think he will conform and offers to certify so to the king. More quickly explains that he merely meant that he had planned to have his beard trimmed, but had realized this would be labor lost since it would be cut off tomorrow along with his head. Among the crowd awaiting More's arrival at the Tower in the play is the poor woman whose evidence More as Chancellor had in his possession. She asks him about her writings, and he responds that she will have to apply to the king, who has relieved him. Shortly thereafter the Gentleman Porter reminds More that by custom his uppermost garment is forfeit, so More gives him his cap, but the porter tells More what he knows very well, that it should be the uppermost on his back. Hall recites both the anecdotes of More's cap and the poor woman's evidence. Roper tells only the story of the cap. Harpsfield has both, and his editors cite Hall as his source for the story of the poor woman's papers. Stapleton tells both anecdotes, and it is evident that he knows Hall's *Chronicle* because he cites it earlier on another matter in his *Life*. Ro: Ba: omits the anecdote of More's cap.

Scene 16 presents More hearing the news that his day of execution is to be the following day, a fact that he discusses calmly with the lieutenant of the Tower. This friendly conversation between the lieutenant and More is in Roper, but the content of the conversation is completely different. The visit of More's family to him in the Tower is also recounted by Roper, but More's misleading responses to their attempts to persuade him are not in his *Life*. As in *Sir Thomas More*, his answer to their importunities is lively, even witty, but in Roper it is more dignified and thoughtful. The source of More's misleading reply in scene 16 is almost certainly Stapleton's *Vita*. There the story is told of a royal courtier, who, in response to his repeated exhortations to conform, receives from More the comment that he has changed his opinion. Like Lady More, the courtier offers to tell the king, but unlike her he actually does so. Henry sends him back to require More to put it in writing, and when he does More reveals that he had changed his opinion only about shaving his beard.[118]

Harpsfield, following Roper, has the dialogue with the lieutenant and the visit of More's family. Stapleton briefly alludes to a conversation between More and his jailer, but he describes him as wicked or avaricious rather than as friendly, and he also notes Dame Alice's visit to the Tower. Ro: Ba:'s account is the same as Stapleton's. Hall has nothing on the substance of this scene.

In the exchange between More and the lieutenant, there are again anecdotal elements. After having been informed that the warrant for his execution has arrived, More says that he had had a sore fit of the stone at night but that the king has sent him a rare receipt to cure it. He calls for his urinal and examines the water, giving his opinion that "the man were likely to liue long enough . . . so pleasde the King" (†1754–55, p. 58). He and the lieutenant discuss More's wealth, and he explains that he has little because

Moore with moste parte of my coyne,
I haue purchased as straunge comodities
as euer you heard tell of in your life.
Lieu. Commodities my Lord?
might I (with out offence) enquire of them?
Moore Croutches (Mr Lieutenant) and bare cloakes.
ffor halting Soldiours, and poore needie
Schollers.
(†1779–85, pp. 58–59)

He says that this is due to his being partly a poet.

That parte of Poett that was giuen me
made me a very vnthrift.
ffor this is the disease attends vs all,
Poets were neuer thriftie, neuer shall.
(†1790–93, p. 59)

More's relief of the poor is recorded by all his biographers except Roper. Erasmus, in his sketch written for von Hutten, first mentions it. Harpsfield repeats the passage from Erasmus, somewhat altered. Stapleton is the first to tell of the house in Chelsea that More provided at his own expense in which the destitute were cared for (which is not in the play), and Ro: Ba: adopts Stapleton. The beard joke, without More's misleading reply, and the urinal jest occur together in Harington's *Metamorphosis*, which first prints the latter story. Only Ro: Ba: of the biographers associ-

118. Stapleton, *Vita*, ed. Reynolds, pp. 161–63. More's use of the expression "my lord" has led some to speculate that the courtier may have been Cromwell.

ates the urinal and the beard stories, which indicates that he had probably read Harington's book.[119] Schütt speculates that both writers may have independently derived the tales from oral tradition, which is, of course, entirely possible. There is some lexical community between the jests in the sources and in the play, but More's charitable actions are rendered more economically by the dramatists than by the biographers, and the diction is different. It is noteworthy that the playwrights did not see fit to make use of the animated, colloquial—and first-hand—account of the visit of More's family to him in the Tower as it is in Roper's *Life*, with its lively revelation of the personality of Dame Alice.

The execution scene (17) is brief and concludes on an epitaphic note. The lieutenant ushers More onto the scene, where they take leave of each other, More thanking the lieutenant for his wife's hospitality and saying she made a "very wanton" of him. He greets the two sheriffs who will convey him to the scaffold, recognizing one as having attended his lectures on St. Augustine's *De Civitate Dei* at St. Laurence Jewry and the other as of counsel with him on a cause. As he ascends the stair, Surrey and Shrewsbury arrive to bid him farewell and to tell him that he should publish his offense to the king. He gives his purse to the executioner and tells him that unless he does the beheading handsomely More will not deal with him hereafter, and that he should take heed not to cut off his beard. More forsakes all mirth and places his head on the block. Surrey concludes:

> A very learned woorthie Gentleman
> Seales errour with his blood.[120]
> (†1983–84, p. 65)

The quips and jests in this final scene, all of which have a colloquial ring, may be from the oral tradition. More says his memory is so bad he shall forget his head, and that he is on a headless errand. He asks for help going up the scaffold, "As for my comming downe, let me alone" (†1917–18, p. 63).

Both Hall and Roper recount the essential elements of this scene. Hall omits the customary gift of money to the executioner and once again dem-

119. Gabrieli, in "Sources, Characters, Ideas," says "the two apophthegms were obviously part of current oral tradition, so that there is no proof of the dependence of either text on the other." He also notes, "The extraordinary verbal similarities between Harington and the play text may be due, in Giorgio Melchiori's opinion, to the fact that Sir John Harington, at the time of writing his book, was a brilliant young courtier and wit and a frequenter of the theatres . . . so that it is not inconceivable that the players may have shown him, hoping to get his support, the manuscript 'book' of *STM* which had fallen foul of the censor" (p. 29).

120. Error, in a sense, may be the subject of the play. Long, "The Occasion of *The Booke of Sir Thomas Moore*," makes the intriguing observation that "the theme of *Sir Thomas More* is neither the anti-alien riot . . . nor the career and death of More himself, but the unfortunate consequences of disobedience to the rule of the sovereign." Lincoln and More made the fatal error of challenging the regal authority.

onstrates his inability to comprehend More, saying, in regard to the second beard jest, "thus with a mocke he ended his life." The sole source of More's reference to himself as a "wanton" is Roper's *Life*, where it occurs as part of a conversation in the Tower in which More explains to Margaret that he is content, even happy, with his lot, that "God maketh me a wanton, and setteth me on His lap and dandleth me." Although the other biographers all follow Roper, even reproducing parts of his account word for word, none has this comment. Harpsfield, Stapleton, and Ro: Ba: tell of the *De Civitate Dei* lectures, the jest of help up the scaffold, forgiveness and the present of money to the hangman, and the witty comment concerning a clean beheading. In Hall's *Chronicle*, the account of the execution includes anecdotes that in the play occur earlier, such as More's giving his cap as his "uppermost garment" to the Gentleman Porter and the incident of the poor woman's evidence. The chronicler credits More with great wit but adds that it was mingled with taunting and mocking. R. W. Chambers points out[121] that the playwrights applied a corrective to Hall's unsympathetic view when they have More say, in apology after his response to the poor woman's plea for the return of her evidence:

> I cannot help thee, thou must beare with me.

to which she responds:

> Ah gentle hart, my soule for thee is sad,
> farewell the best friend that the poore ere had.
> (†1646–48, p. 54)

Another element of this concluding scene is More's series of comments about his physical decline. He speaks of his failing memory (†1888–89, p. 62), says he is old and has a bad voice (†1933, p. 64), and that his eyes are weaker (†1968, p. 65). Harpsfield in four places mentions More's debility, but the specific difficulties alluded to in the play are not in his *Life*. *The Paris New Letter* and Roper briefly refer to his failing health, and of course it could have been part of the oral tradition.[122]

It is evident from this analysis that the two primary sources of *Sir Thomas More* are Hall's *Union of the Two Noble and Illustre Famelies of Lancastre & Yorke* and Roper's *Life of Syr Thomas Moore, knighte*. From Hall the play derives all the events of the Ill May Day episode, comprised of six scenes and more than five hundred lines, equivalent to almost one-fourth of the whole and clearly important for reasons other than mere extent. The play's London tone may be considered to have been derived at least in part

121. Chambers, *Thomas More*, pp. 45–47.

122. Harpsfield, *Life*, ed. Hitchcock and Chambers, pp. 59, 142, 175, 184; Roper, *Life*, ed. Hitchcock, p. 51. The editors give the source of Harpsfield's last allusion as *The Paris News Letter*. Harpsfield also mentions that More was "greeued in the reynes by reason of grauell and stone," which may have been the origin of the urinal jest.

from Hall, as well as from the oral tradition. The portrait of More is, in this aspect, historically authentic, and we are reminded of this by the opening words of his epitaph that he himself wrote: "Thomas Morvs vrbe Londinensi."[123] The orally transmitted tales are essentially, although not exclusively, a London tradition, in which Hall and the playwrights shared. The dramatists also borrowed from Hall significant elements other than the Ill May Day sequence, the most important of which is the council meeting that opens scene 10.

An equally important portion of the play is drawn from Roper's biography. His *Life* is the source of some incidents in the early scenes, and more extensive and explicit borrowings run from scene 9 through to the final scene (17). Some details come from other sources, but most of the events of each of the scenes making up the latter half of the play can be found in Roper's *Life*.[124]

The third principal source is less precisely definable, although it is frequently cited in the foregoing discussion. It is also materially less significant as a source in comparison with Hall and Roper. The unwritten story of the life and career of More manifestly contributed to the play. Some of the many tales told of him found their way into the sources, while others did not. An example of one that did is the Lifter-Suresby cutpurse incident (scene 2), which is related in Stapleton's *Vita Thomae Mori*. Perhaps one of the playwrights developed the scene from Stapleton, but it is possible that his *Life* and the play stand in the same relationship to the story, that they are parallel renderings of an anecdote in the oral tradition. The apologetic tone of More's response to the poor woman whose legal writings had been in his possession when he was Lord Chancellor and her reply attest to the existence of a continuing tradition variant from Hall's version. Also, the

123. Harpsfield, *Life*, eds. Hitchcock and Chambers, p. 279. More's monument, exhibiting his epitaph, survives in his parish church, Chelsea Old Church, in London, in spite of a 1941 bombing.

124. Gabrieli, in "Sources, Characters, Ideas," p. 19, says, "When we consider the main biographical sources of *Sir Thomas More*, especially in scene x–xvii, we are faced with the indisputable fact that . . . the authors of the play resorted directly to Harpsfield's *Life*, and not to Roper's memoir . . . its 'finger prints' can be easily detected in most of the second half of *Sir Thomas More*." Gabrieli does not provide detailed information on the "finger prints," but subsequently he discusses "five anecdotes connected with More's death" that are incorporated into *Sir Thomas More*. Of these, he says in reference to one, the incident of the gentleman porter and More's upper garment, "the play relied mainly on Harpsfield" (p. 22); but the paragraph in Harpsfield (eds. Hitchcock and Chambers, p. 170) is taken over from Roper with only changes in spelling and the alteration of one word—the substitution of *saide* for *quoth* (ed. Hitchcock, p. 75). There is nothing in either version to show that it could not have been adopted by the playwrights from Roper's *Life*. Perhaps Gabrieli thinks of Harpsfield as the prime biographical source of *Sir Thomas More* because he records incidents that Roper does not. By my count there are some five incidents or allusions in Harpsfield that are reflected in the play (Text 5) that Roper does not supply. These show that the playwrights made use of Harpsfield, but they do not seem to be of sufficient significance to support Gabrieli's rejection of Roper.

anecdote of the first meeting of More and Erasmus almost certainly existed in the London tradition at the date of composition of the play, although it was not printed, with Erasmus identified, until 1626 when Cresacre More's *Life* was published. (Harpsfield's theologian is anonymous.) It is the type of story that may have been retailed by word of mouth or may have been in one of the early sixteenth-century jestbooks now lost.

Sources that might be termed secondary only because limited use was made of them in the play include Foxe's *Actes and Monuments*, for the story of the long-haired ruffian; *Lusty Juventus* and *The Disobedient Child*; Stapleton and possibly also Erasmus, for More's relief of the poor; and probably Harpsfield, for More's soliloquy on the perils of greatness. All of these are significant for the importance of their content if not for the extensiveness of their use.

In transforming their materials from the chronicle, biographical, and oral sources into drama, the playwrights follow rather faithfully the broad outline of the original from which they were working. They felt free to adapt their sources to suit theatrical needs, sometimes condensing as in the instance of More's relief of the poor, which in the play is reduced to eight lines, or expanding as in the case of Stapleton's story of the cutpurse incident, which is acted out in the play rather than narrated and occupies more than two hundred lines. Here and there the collaborators altered the historical timing. For example, they telescope the interval between More's resignation and the presentation of oaths to be signed so that in the play they occur in immediate sequence. Historically there was about a year between the two events. Sometimes important details are altered apparently to intensify the dramatic qualities incipient in the source or perhaps to make use of a form of the story available in the oral legends.

The most significant of such changes is the deviation from the source in Addition IIc. In Hall's recital of the events of Ill May Day 1517, which has all the immediacy and vivid detail of an eye witness account and is, in any event, surely authentic, More fails to quell the riot; in the play, because of his eloquence and the respect in which he is held by the common people of London, he is able to persuade the rioters to desist and to sue to the king for clemency. The riot sequence as a whole in *Sir Thomas More* barely deviates from Hall, but in this instance it happily alters the historical account or, perhaps, chooses a different version, without which the play would have lacked its most dramatically effective moment. Another instance is the adjustment of historical events in the careers of Fisher and More so that the sequence of More's downfall and execution is adumbrated in the corresponding, though, in the play, slightly earlier, phase of Fisher's public career. On the occasion of the presentation of the Articles for signature at the Council meeting, Rochester immediately refuses to sign and is promptly summoned to appear before the king; in the meantime, the Lord Chancellor bargains for time and hopes to avoid being forced to a decision. Soon thereafter, Fisher is sent to the Tower, while More's fate is as yet, at that point, not determined. He is taken into custody in the next ensuing scene and is reminded that Fisher has been committed for a like obstinacy. More subsequently arrives at the Tower in a scene closely parallel to Fisher's, even to the point that each scene is concluded by the protagonist welcoming his imprisonment. Later, immediately after More is informed that the warrant for his execution has been received at the Tower, he asks for news of Rochester and is told that he was put to death yesterday morning. More shortly shares that fate. In these and in other instances, the version as presented in the play is enhanced from what is sometimes a pedestrian narrative to the level of veritable drama. Such skillfully orchestrated structural adaptations of the sources, associated with other alterations designed to elevate the dramatic and theatrical qualities, amount to an admirable play in conception if not always in execution. If this is so, it seems to point to the hand or hands of one or both of the two most accomplished dramatists in the collaboration—Shakespeare and Munday. While certainly Shakespeare was capable even early in his career (if we assume an early date for the play) of developing the plan for *Sir Thomas More*, Munday, "our best plotter" according to Francis Meres, may equally as well have devised it.[125] Or we may even—if it does not strain the bounds of credibility—postulate a cooperative effort between the rising Shakespeare and the experienced playwright. In any event it seems a fair assessment to say that the plan of the play exhibits the work of a professional dramatist of which either Shakespeare or Munday could be proud.

Censorship and *Sir Thomas More*

The manuscript *Booke of Sir Thomas Moore* is one of only a small number of play manuscripts surviving from the Elizabethan era that shows the censor actually at work on a script. The censorship responsibility was assigned to the Master of the Revels, who was under the general direction of the Lord Chamberlain of the royal household. The surviving records do not clearly establish that the review and "reformation" of plays prior to performance was a duty of the Master of the Revels when Edmund Tilney was appointed the first regular incumbent in that office in 1579. However, in a special commission issued 24 December 1581 that arose out of a rivalry between the London corporation and the Privy Council for control of the

125. Chambers reprints some of Meres's comments, including the one about Munday, in *William Shakespeare*, 2:195.

stage, including plays, actors, playwrights, and playing places, the responsibility was clearly assigned to the Master of the Revels.[126]

Tilney's explicit charge at the head of folio 3ª of *The Booke of Sir Thomas Moore* leaves no doubt either of his authority to censor plays submitted to him or of the kind of play content that concerned the government. The two most important subjects considered inappropriate for playhouse entertainment were political topics, including criticism of court personages, and matters of religion. Tilney could not in conscience encourage the sympathetic treatment of sedition on stage and consequently ordered the spectacle of civil disorder to be reduced to a neutral report. As to controversial religious topics, the dramatists of *Sir Thomas More* successfully avoid them completely.

The precise relationship between the censor and the manuscript *Booke of Sir Thomas Moore* poses another scholarly puzzle. Greg identified Tilney's hand at several places in the play in addition to the note on folio 3ª. He made marks of disapproval, comments, "MEND Yis" opposite line 320 (p. 12), and "ALL ALTR" at line †1256 (p. 42), but Greg says (p. xiv) that his hand does not seem to occur in any of the revisions. The *Booke* has been examined at first hand by a number of students of the play, and all concur in this determination although it is recognized that some of the marks in the additions are not sufficiently distinctive to be identifiable. Before Greg's Malone Society reprint, some scholars believed that the additions had been written in response to Tilney's strictures (for example, Simpson, Ward, and Brooke),[127] but Greg's explanation has proved so cogent that no later critic accepts the earlier hypothesis. He sums up his discussion with the assertion that no "notice whatever [has] been taken of the censor's orders" (p. xiv).

A variety of solutions has been proposed to the problem of determining in what form the play was submitted to Tilney for his review, what the process was, and, if possible, what the date was. Before Greg's edition, scholars decided, without much analysis, that the authors submitted to Tilney the original fair copy in Munday's hand. Greg's determination led him to conclude that "every indication in the manuscript points to its having been submitted for license in its present form" (p. xiv), that is, the

126. E. K. Chambers, *The Elizabethan Stage*, 4 vols. (Oxford: Clarendon Press, 1923; rpt., 1945), Appendix D, 4:286. For the development of stage censorship, see 1:269–307, 317–28, concisely summarized by Chambers in his *William Shakespeare* 1:98–105. Greg discusses censorship in the course of describing extant promptbooks in *Dramatic Documents*, "Commentary," pp. 189–369. Anne Lancashire sets forth the evidence for and the effects of censorship in her edition of the manuscript play, *The Second Maiden's Tragedy* (Manchester: Manchester University Press; Baltimore: Johns Hopkins University Press, 1978), pp. 8–15, 275–85.

127. Simpson, "Are There Any Extant MSS. in Shakespeare's Handwriting?" p. 1; Adolphus William Ward, *A History of English Dramatic Literature*, rev. ed., 3 vols. (London: Macmillan, 1899), 1:214; Brooke, *The Shakespeare Apocrypha*, pp. xlix–l.

original text plus the revisions and additions as the manuscript now stands. Sir Edmund Chambers objects. Greg's argument, he says, "obliges us to suppose that the play was sent to Tilney in a most untidy and in places almost unintelligible condition; in a variety of hands; with long passages only marked for deletion by marginal lines; with Addition I fitted into the wrong scene; with Addition VI so fitted in as to break the continuity of sc. ix, and still containing a draft of part of Addition V." He thinks the script "was laid aside when Tilney sent it back, and taken up later by new writers" who composed the additions. Some critics who have written since Chambers have accepted Greg's view that the additions do not respond to Tilney's strictures but have elected to follow one or another version of Chambers's conjecture as to the sequence of events. The weakness in this theory is that it does not offer a satisfactory explanation for Tilney's absence from the additions. Sir Edmund's reason for rejecting Greg's hypothesis is that it is unreasonable to assume that Tilney would review an untidy script. But the censor may have accepted it even though the manuscript was not easy to read. Wentersdorf points out that we know next to nothing about Tilney's relationship with the players and that he might have raised no objection to reviewing a messy manuscript, especially if, as Wentersdorf speculates, the company proffered an additional fee. Greg notes that those who argue that Tilney accepted the *Booke* for allowance in its chaotic state can point to the late play *The Launching of the Mary*, which was reviewed and allowed by Sir Henry Herbert in a state of "extreme untidiness."[128]

While most scholars settle for either Greg's or Chambers's theory, a few have attempted to devise an explanation for all aspects of the case. Bald analyzed the conflicting suggestions of Greg and Chambers and noted that in Addition IIb the aliens are "Lombards" rather than French, Dutch, or strangers. This may mean that the playwrights had learned that Tilney did not object to the foreigners being Lombards, perhaps because Lombardy had virtually become enemy (that is, Spanish) territory. This leads Bald to "surmise that the play was submitted to Tilney not once, but twice: the first time he made only a few minor deletions in the early scenes, but altered the references to the aliens' nationality, and confined his attention mainly to the scenes on the missing leaves . . . [and he] insisted on seeing that his instructions had been observed in the revisions. . . . When the play was re-submitted, Tilney proved, perhaps owing to recent political developments, even more rigorous than he had been on the first occasion, and the actors, in spite of the fact that they had gone so far as to cast the play, decided that it was useless to attempt any further revision." Bald acknowledges that his solution is "almost all pure conjecture," but he thinks it

128. Chambers, *William Shakespeare*, 1:511–12; Wentersdorf, "Date of the Additions," pp. 311–13; Greg, *Dramatic Documents*, "Commentary" p. 200.

"more satisfactory" than Chambers's. Dover Wilson describes the problem and tells us that the play as it stands is in the process of being drastically overhauled. "In some way . . . the instructions of the censor must be related to the disorderly condition of the 'booke.'" This he calls "the chief puzzle of the manuscript," but he, uncharacteristically, has no solution to offer. In his review of the scholarship to 1961, Jenkins says "Tilney's censorship of the play—or rather the relation between his censorship and the revisions—remains an enigma." He does not subscribe to Greg's conjecture and cannot believe that the additions followed shortly after the original text because "Munday's hand is absent from them." Furthermore, the additions "bear no mark recognizable as Tilney's and there is no reason to think he read them. It seems clear to me that the confusions of the present manuscript are due to alterations begun and not perfected." Bald's hypothesis "involves supposing that the play was submitted to the censor (on the second occasion) unfinished and chaotic, and it leaves the other additions entirely out of account. I therefore incline to the alternative, tentatively suggested by Sir Edmund Chambers, that what Tilney read was the original version of the play."[129]

Blayney finds "two distinct biasses in the censorship, first against prentice riots and prison breaking, second against anti-alien trouble." He suggests the following sequence of events: the play is drafted and Munday prepares a fair copy, which is submitted to Tilney; he censors the references to prison breaking, street brawls, and prentice troubles and returns the manuscript; revisions are made and the play resubmitted; Tilney now objects "to the 'Ill May Day' episode as a whole" and returns the manuscript; revisions are planned but an outbreak of plague closes the theaters and the play is abandoned. Blayney's solution involves two submissions for allowances and two stages of revisions, the second of which was planned but not carried out. Chillington believes that sometime in 1601–1602 Tilney saw the original draft of the play, which he returned with the admonition on folio 3[a]. His hand is not in the additions "because he had not seen them." The playwrights did not take Tilney's orders literally and began a revision that would make some concession to his requirements, but they did not think it necessary to abandon completely the presentation of Ill May Day. To obtain a license, they relied on their ability to negotiate with Tilney via "back-alley communications with the Revels Office" to gain his acceptance of a partial recasting of the script. But Elizabeth's death and an onset of plague closed the playhouses and caused the collaborators to abandon the play.[130] Another explanation conjectures that Tilney's review of the *Booke*

129. Bald, "*Booke*," pp. 50–51 and n. 11; J. Dover Wilson, "A New Way with Shakespeare's Texts," p. 72; Jenkins in Greg, *Sir Thomas More*, pp. xxxix–xl.

130. Blayney, "*The Booke of Sir Thomas Moore* re-examined," pp. 190–91; Chillington, "Playwrights at Work," pp. 469–76. The passages quoted are in n. 21, p. 471.

and the changes attributable to literary and theatrical considerations took place at the same time, that the company interested in the play arranged for revisions, working from the foul papers, after the fair copy had been sent to the Master of the Revels but before it was returned to them. This hypothesis obviates the necessity to explain why Tilney would accept a confused copy for review and accounts for his absence from the additions—he never saw them.[131] All these explanations are, of course, speculative since there is no external evidence and the only thing approaching "hard" internal evidence is the absence of Tilney's hand from the revisions.

Stage History

Scholars are not agreed as to whether or not *Sir Thomas More* was performed either at the time the first version was composed or after the play had been revised. Tilney's comment at the top of folio 3[a] is considered by Greg to be "a very conditional [acting] license" (p. x). That is, if the major requirement to "leave out the insurrection wholly and the cause thereof" were complied with and a few other changes marked in the text were made, then the play could be produced. There is, however, no evidence that the collaborators came to grips with Tilney's admonition. While we may conjecture that the revision of the original text embodied in Addition II is less inflammatory than the earlier version, which is lost, it does not conform to Tilney's order to omit the insurrection and may be taken to indicate that the collaborators did not intend to try to do so. Some students of the play think that from the point of view of preparation for performance, the text is deficient. Greg says, "It is evident throughout that the manuscript has not been finally revised for presentation . . . [and it] was consequently laid aside and the play never came on the boards" (p. xv). Chambers notes that the insertions of new pages are not perfected, that there are "ragged edges" left by the deletions, and that a few missing entries, exits, and speech prefixes need to be supplied.[132] Of course, even if we accept the theory that the manuscript as it is could not have been used as a promptbook, that does not prove that a promptbook was not prepared from it. McMillin studies the manuscript as a playhouse document. He has

131. Metz, "The Master of the Revels and *The Booke of Sir Thomas Moore*," *SQ* 33 (1982): 493–95. Concerning my suggestion, Professor Jenkins, in a private letter of 23 January 1984, comments, "Except that it avoids . . . other implausibilities, would one have thought it plausible that revision and censorship would be going on simultaneously? One would have expected the authors to do necessary revision before sending the play in or not to embark on revision until they got it back. But the facts about this play are so odd and so seemingly contradictory that hardly anything can be ruled out." For a different view, see Taylor, "Date and Auspices," n. 57, in the Howard-Hill symposium.

132. Chambers, *William Shakespeare*, 1:512.

shown that, although the play may not be completely satisfactory from a literary point of view, it has, except for some relatively minor difficulties, been made reasonably coherent as a theatrical text. Possibly it could not itself serve to regulate a performance, but a promptbook could have been prepared from it with little difficulty. In this connection it should be noted that the manuscript is designated as "The Booke" and that it was enclosed in vellum, which indicates that someone in the theater thought of it as a promptbook. McMillin also believes that the principal purpose of some of the revisions is to facilitate casting and points out that Addition VI (p. 93) includes, in a section of dialogue between Luggins and the Vice, two speech prefixes at lines sixty-one and sixty-six that read "clo" (clown) instead of Vice, as would have been expected. This shows that the playwright knew that the actor who would play the part of the clown would double as the Vice in *The Marriage of Wit and Wisdom*. Thus, "the revisers attended to the specific casting of the play as they worked."[133]

There are some other bits of evidence that the play may have been acted. Goodale's name in the "Booke" is clear evidence that the play could have been cast. In his notes to the transcription of the Ill May Day scenes, Greg points out that in two separate entry directions in the additions (in Hand C), no entry is provided for Sherwin, although he was in the original text, and that two of his lines have been reassigned to other speakers. Greg concludes, "This attempt to get rid of a minor but still important character can only be due to difficulties of casting and corroborates the evidence afforded by the occurrence of Goodale's name . . . that the parts were actually assigned."[134] Baldwin notes that it is possible the actors' parts were prepared in conformance with the censor's instructions, and he is convinced that the play was produced.[135] W. J. Lawrence interprets the Goodale note and a preceding cross within a circle as a prompt warning and finds four others in the manuscript. "Either these are prompters warnings or they are meaningless," he says. "The inference is that the whole play as we have it, *plus* the lacunae, formed a prompt copy," and that the play was therefore acted. He observes that Henslowe's *Diary* shows that a number of plays were revised, but always by a single playwright, and the many hands in the manuscript might therefore indicate successive revisions that would only have been undertaken if performances were possible.[136] Greg's response is to question the validity of Lawrence's designating two of the marginal notations as prompt warnings, but he adds, "It certainly seems

133. Scott McMillin, "*The Book of Sir Thomas More*: A Theatrical View," *MP* 68 (1970): 10–24. See also his *The Elizabethan Theatre and The Book of Sir Thomas More*, pp. 97–112.

134. *Shakespeare's Hand*, pp. 202, 208, 209.

135. Thomas Whitford Baldwin, *The Organization and Personnel of the Shakespearean Company* (Princeton: Princeton University Press, 1927; rpt. New York: Russel, 1961), pp. 131–34.

136. W. J. Lawrence, "Was *Sir Thomas More* Ever Acted?" *TLS* 1 July 1920, p. 421.

probable that the preparations for performance had reached a fairly advanced stage." However, "the work of incorporating the alterations was never completed and this is an even more formidable objection to supposing that the play was actually performed."[137] Muriel St. Clare Byrne, who addresses herself primarily to another aspect of Lawrence's discussion, the date of composition, briefly comments on his prompt copy hypothesis: "His contention that this play was acted—contrary as it is to the opinion hitherto more generally held—is certainly a satisfying one."[138] In the summation of his case, Lawrence adds two stage directions that mention properties in support of his theory that the manuscript is a promptbook, but he modifies his contention regarding prompt warnings to state, "One sheet has an unmistakable prompt warning and . . . on a few others there are possible warnings."[139]

There is also some evidence that reflections of one or two incidents in the play can be seen in other contemporary plays. C. R. Baskervill has identified a number of parallels between *Sir Thomas More* and Jonson's *Bartholomew Fair* in the cutpurse episodes in both plays. These are the censure of the cutpurse's victim, the plan to teach the censurer a lesson, the victimizing of the censorious person, the way in which the loss is revealed, and the drawing of the moral to correct the censurer. Baskervill cites in addition a passage from Jonson's play that he says alludes to *Sir Thomas More.*

> Nay, once from the seat
> Of judgment so great
> A judge there did lose a fair pouch of velvet.

He notes that there are in both plays a play-within-a-play (a puppet show in *Bartholomew Fair*), and in each case a list of shows by title, and an initial delay in starting the entertainment accompanied by joking about the performance. He finds close similarities, both general and specific, between pairs of characters from the two plays—for example, Suresbie and Overdo, both justices, and Faulkner and Waspe, both ruffians—and he also cites a number of correspondences in language and detail between the two plays. He sums up, "It is only in this play of *Sir Thomas More* . . . that I have found a main motive and situation of *Bartholomew Fair* combined with many of its details." He believes that Jonson knew *Sir Thomas More*, and if this is the case it could only have been in performance.[140] S. R. Golding quotes some lines from *The Death of Robert, Earl of Huntingdon* that link

137. W. W. Greg, "Was *Sir Thomas More* Ever Acted?" *TLS*, 8 July 1920, p. 440. There is a further exchange on 15 July 1920, p. 456, and 29 July 1920, p. 488.

138. Muriel St. Clare Byrne, "The Date of *Sir Thomas More*. Some Further Points," *TLS*, 12 August 1920, pp. 520–21. Lawrence replies 2 September 1920, p. 568.

139. W. J. Lawrence, *Pre-Restoration Stage Studies* (Cambridge: Harvard University Press, 1927; rpt. New York: Blom, 1967), pp. 387–92.

140. C. R. Baskervill, "Some Parallels to *Bartholomew Fair*," *MP* 6 (1909): 1–19; *Ben Jonson: Bartholomew Fair*, ed. Eugene M. Waith (New Haven: Yale University Press, 1963), 3.5.94–96.

Lady Vanity and long-haired ruffians. This could refer to *Sir Thomas More.* "The reference," he adds,

> seems to imply that "More" had recently been performed on the stage, since an allusion of this kind would have been unintelligible to the audience, if the play had only existed in manuscript or if the production of "More" had ante-dated that of "The Death" by several years. If, therefore, my interpretation of the passage quoted is correct, there are adequate reasons for the belief that "Sir Thomas More" was acted towards the close of 1597.[141]

Jenkins finds that "it is generally assumed that the play can never have reached performance . . . but the evidence is not conclusive. . . . To make a coherent fair copy of the play might not be an easy task; but it would surely not be beyond an experienced playhouse book-keeper. . . . The manuscript that survives is in the nature of an author's fair copy hacked about and supplemented by the foul papers of a revision, but because it would not itself do for a promptbook, it does not follow that one was not made" (pp. xliii–xliv). Greg concludes his discussion, saying, "The only deduction the evidence warrants is that the play was cast which is . . . by no means the same thing" as production (pp. xv–xvi). There is, however, sufficient show of evidence to constitute a challenge to Greg's position, and neither he nor any other critic has successfully disposed of the various arguments for Elizabethan performance of the play. The question is not conclusively settled.

There is no external evidence indicating to which acting company the play belonged. The presence in the manuscript of the name Goodale, a Lord Strange's player (Addition V, p. 89), indicates that the play may have been written for that company or at least was at sometime in their possession. Alternatively, perhaps it was originally the joint property of Strange's and the Admiral's Men, when the two troupes were acting together in the early 1590s. The playwrights who have been identified as participants in the collaboration, except Shakespeare, wrote other plays for the Admiral's Men. The playhouse functionary (Hand C) associated with Strange's Men circa 1590 was later connected with the Admiral's Men, but his affiliation at the time *Sir Thomas More* was written is unknown. Sharpe offers the opinion that it may have belonged to either the Admiral's or Pembroke's Men based on the general tone and social sympathies. If the playhouse scribe was a Henslowe employee rather than an Admiral's, as some think possible, then *Sir Thomas More* may have been a Worcester's play.[142]

141. S. R. Golding, "Further Notes on Robert Wilson and *Sir Thomas More,*" *N&Q* 155 (1928): 237–40. There is also some lexical connection between *Sir Thomas More* and Chettle's *Hoffman*, but we need not assume performance to explain it.

142. Sharpe, *The Real War of the Theatres*, p. 91. Taylor decides that the play belonged to the Chamberlain's Men ("Date and Auspices" in the forthcoming Howard-Hill symposium); McMillin to the Admiral's Men (*Elizabethan Theatre*, pp. 91–95).

There is no record of any production of *Sir Thomas More* until the twentieth century. The earliest are non-professional. Three performances were given by students at Birkbeck College, London, in 1922, and there was a presentation at Crosby Hall. A dramatic reading of the play was presented at the Ambassador's Theatre, London, in 1935, with Lewis Casson in the title role. Three performances by the students of the King's School were presented in the chapter house at Canterbury in 1938, directed by Canon John Shirley, who subsequently published his text. The Ill May Day scenes were broadcast by the BBC in 1948.[143]

The first professional stage production came in June 1954 in an arena setting at the Theatre Centre in London. There were eight performances, the first four in Elizabethan dress, the second four in modern costumes, produced by Brian Way with Michael Beint in the title role. *The Times* reviewer found the performance "overproduced," noting that More "bids life a cheerful farewell so many times that his last speech at the blade is an anti-climax." The players "are continuously spirited and play some of the better constructed scenes with good effect. Mr. Michael Beint speaks the hero's part with alert expressiveness."[144]

Richard Flatter presented a play at the Badischen Staatstheater, Karlsruhe, in 1960 entitled *Heinrich VIII und Sir Thomas More* composed of the Shakespearean elements of *Henry VIII* plus scenes from *Sir Thomas More*, principally the sequence of his conflict with the king, his imprisonment, and his execution. The result was, according to Karl Brinkmann, merely a sketch that lacked dramatic force and unity and amounted to no more than an artificial compilation by four writers: Shakespeare, Fletcher, and Munday, and Flatter, who assembled and translated it. Neither the superior staging of Richard Skraup nor the acting of a fine cast was able to transform the synthetic script into drama. It was only "a rather loose sequence of historical pageants."[145]

The most noteworthy presentation in the stage history of the play was that of the Nottingham Playhouse in 1964, featuring an admired performance by Ian McKellen in the title role. *The Times* was critical of the lack of focus in the mob scenes but praised the efforts of the producer (Frank Dunlop, who found the play Brechtian) to make clear the grounds of the conflict between Henry and More and Fisher, including having the Duke of Norfolk read "a passage from the actual edict." The principal was well supported by a young cast, and McKellen gave a beautifully modulated

143. Jenkins, *Sir Thomas More*, p. 1236; Arthur Melville Clark, *Thomas Heywood, Playwright, and Miscellanist* (Oxford: Blackwell, 1931), p. 10, n. 2; Marie-Claude Rousseau, "Les représentations de *Sir Thomas More*," *Moreana* 18, 71–72 (1981): 164–65.

144. Mary C. Hyde, compiler, "Current Theater Notes," *SQ* 6 (1955): 67–88. "Shakespeare Productions in the United Kingdom: 1954," *ShS* 9 (1956): 120; *The Times*, 23 June 1954, p. 11.

145. Karl Brinkmann, "Bühnenbericht 1960," *SJ* 97 (1961): 215; Karl Brinkmann and Wolfgang Clemen, "International Notes Germany," *ShS* 15 (1962): 134.

performance. He kept "the jocularity within the bounds of character [and he] jests his way to the scaffold, but unblatantly." There were thirteen performances.[146] The first production outside of England was mounted at the Mayfair Theatre, Dunedin, New Zealand, using a text edited by Alistair Fox and directed by Jane Oakshott, both of Otago University. There were five performances. Reactions of reviewers were mixed, mainly because of an unwieldy ad hoc cast of fifty-five, which included professors, lecturers, and a local magistrate, who was hanged on stage. Ern Joyce was praised for his portrayal of the Chancellor.[147] The Poor Players, a group of Bristol Old Vic Theatre School and Bristol University drama students, in 1981 acted the play seven times, three at the Vandyck, Bristol, and four at London's Young Vic. Although Tony Howard was critical of a number of aspects of the production, he found other points admirable and concluded his review by saying, "This was an illuminating revival." The amateur Richmond Shakespeare Society produced the play at the Mary Wallace Theatre, Twickenham, in 1982, in conjunction with Bolt's *A Man for All Seasons*.[148] BBC Radio presented a two-hour version of *Sir Thomas More* based on Jenkins's text on 25 December 1983.[149]

The North American premier took place in Los Angeles at the Shakespeare Society of America's Globe Playhouse as part of the cultural program associated with the twenty-third Olympiad in 1984. It was presented in repertory with *Antony and Cleopatra*. The *Los Angeles Times* reviewer found it "a mildly interesting testimonial but not much of a drama." The pacification of the riot, "depict[ing] More coping with a crisis . . . [was] the best part." There were twelve performances.[150]

146. J. L Styan, "Dwarfed by Shakespeare. In Search of an Elizabethan Heritage," *Plays and Players* (July 1964): 8–12; *The Times*, 11 June 1964, p. 17.

147. Robert H. Leek, "A Year of Shakespeare in Kiwiland," *SQ* 30 (1979): 272–77; Mary O'Neill, "First Thomas More prize," *Moreana* 22, 85 (April 1985): 109–10.

148. Tony Howard, "Census of Renaissance Drama Productions, 1981," *RORD* 25 (1982): 115–30; "Census of Renaissance Drama Productions, 1982–83," *RORD* 26 (1983): 79.

149. Rousseau, "*Sir Thomas More*: Du Texte à la Scène," *Moreana* 21, 83–84 (December 1984): 133–35.

150. *Los Angeles Times*, 14 August 1984.

1. Source

From the *Vnion of the Two Noble and Illustre Famelies of Lancastre & Yorke* (1548 edition)

By Edward Hall

Kyng Henry the VIII

While these thynges were thus in commonynge and imagenyng. Themperour Maximilian and all his seruauntes whiche were reteyned with the kyng of England in wages by the day, euery person accordynge to his degree, and Themperour as the kynges soldioure ware a Crosse of sayncte George with a Rose, and so he and all his trayne came to the kynges campe the. xiii. day of August beyng Frydaye, and there was receyued with greate magnyficence and brought to a tente of cloth of golde all ready and apparelled accordynge to his estate, for all the tente within was styled with clothe of golde and blewe veluet, and all the blewe veluet was embrowdered with. H. K. of fyne golde, and hys cupboorde was rychely furnyshed and officers appoyncted to geue on hym attendaunce: and there he taried tyll Sonday, and from thence he went agayne to Ayre for his pleasure.

In this ceason, the Genowayes, Frenchemen and other straungiers sayde and boasted them selfes to be in suche fauour with the kyng and hys counsayll, that they set naughte by the rulers of the citie: and the multitude of straungers was so great about London, that the poore Englishe artificers coulde skace get any lyuynge. And most of all the straungers were so proude, that they disdained, mocked and oppressed the Englishemen, whiche was the beginning of the grudge. For amonge all other thynges, there was a Carpenter in London called Willyamson, whiche bought two stockdoues in Chepe. and as he was about to paye for them, a Frencheman tooke them oute of hys hande, and said they were not meate for a carpenter: well sayde the Englishman I haue bought them and now payd for them, and therefore I will haue them, naye sayde the Frencheman I will haue them for my lorde the Ambassador, and so for better or worse, the Frencheman called the Englisheman knaue, and went awaye with the stockdoues. The straungiers came to the Frenche Ambassadour, & surmysed a cōplaynt agaynste the poore carpenter, and the Ambassadour came to my lorde Mayre, and said so muche, that the carpenter was sent to prison: and yet not contented with this, so complayned to the kynges counsail, that the kynges commaundement was layde on hym. And when syr Ihon Baker knyght and other worshipfull persones sued to the Ambassadour for hym, he aūswered, by the body of God that the English knaue shoulde lose his lyfe, for he sayde no Englisheman shoulde deny that the Frenchemen required, and other aunswer had they none.

Also a Frencheman that had slayne a man, should abiure the realme & had a crosse in his hande, & then sodeinly came a great sorte of Frēchmen about him, & one of them said to the Constable that led him, syr is this crosse the price to kyll an Englishman. The Cōstable was somwhat astonyed and aunswered not. Then said another Frencheman, on that pryce we would be banyshed all by the masse, this saiyng was noted to be spoken spitefully. Howebeit, the Frenchemen were not alonely oppressors of the Englishemen for a Lombarde called Fraunces de bard, entised a mannes wyfe in Lombarde strete to come to his chābre with her husbandes plate, whiche thynge she dyd. After when her husbande knewe it, he demaunded hys wyfe, but aunswer was made he shoulde not haue her, then he demaunded his plate, and in lyke maner aunswer was made that he shoulde neither haue plate nor wyfe. And whē he had sewed an accion against the straunger in the Guylde hall, the straunger so faced the Englisheman, that he faynted in his sute. And then the Lombarde arrested the poore man for his wyfes boorde, while he kept her frō her husbād in his chāber. This mocke was much noted, and for these and many other oppressions done by them, there encreased suche a malice in the English mennes hartes, that at the laste it brast oute. For amongest other that sore grudged at these matters, there was a broker in London called Ihon Lyncoln, whiche wrote a bill before Easter, desyring doctor Standyche at hys sermon at sainct Marye Spyttell the Mondaye in Easter weke, too moue the Mayre and Aldermen, to take parte with the comminaltie agaynst the straungiers: The doctor aunswered that it became not hym too moue anye suche thynge in a sermon. From hym he departed, and came to a Chanon in sayncte Mary spittell, a doctor in Deuinitie, called doctor Bele, and lamentably declared to hym, how miserably the common artificers lyued, and skase coulde get any woorke to fynde them, their wyfes and chyldren, for there were such a nūber of artificers straungers, that tooke awaye all the lyuynge in maner. And also howe the Englishe merchauntes coulde haue no vtteraunce, for the merchaunt straungers brynge in all Sylkes, clothe of Golde, Wyne, Oyle, Iron and suche other merchaundise, that no man almoost byeth of an Englisheman. And also outwarde, they carye so muche Englishe Wolle, Tynne, and Leade, that Englishmen that auenture outwarde can haue no lyuyng: Whiche thynges sayd Lyncoln hathe bene shewed to the counsayll, & cannot be heard. And farther sayde he, the straungiers compasse the cytye rounde aboute, in Southwarke, in Westminster, Temple barre, Holborne, Sayncte Martynes, Sayncte Ihons strete, Algate, Towre hyll, and sayncte Katherynes, and forstall the market, so that no good thynge for them commeth to the market: whiche is the cause that Englishemen want and sterue, and they lyue haboundantly in great pleasure. Wherefore sayde Lyncolne master doctor, syth you were borne in Lōdon, & se the oppression of the straūgers, & the great misery of your awne natyue countray, exhorte all the cytiezens to ioyne in one against these straungers, raueners and destroyers of your countrey. Master doctor hearynge this, sayde he muche lamented the case if it were as Lyncoln hadde declared, yes sayde Lyncolne, that it is and muche more, for the Dutchemē bryng ouer Iron, Tymber, lether and Weynskot ready wrought, as Nayles, Lockes, Baskettes, Cupbordes, Stooles, Tables, Chestes, gyrdels, with poyntes, sadelles & painted clothes so that if it were wrought here, Englishmen might haue some worke & lyuynge by it. And besyde this, they growe into such a multitude that it is to be looked vpon, for I sawe on a Sondaye this Lent. vi. C. straūgiers shotyng at y[e] Popyngaye with Crosbowes, and they kepe such assemblyes and fraternities together, & make such a gathering to their cōmon boxe, that euery botcher will holde plee with the citye of Lōdō: wel sayd the doctor, I will do for a reformacion of this matter asmuche as a priest may do, & so receaued Lincolnes byl & studyed for his purpose. Then Lyncoln very ioyous of hys enterprice went from man to man, saiyng that shortly they shoulde heare newes, and daily excited younge people and artificers to beare malice to the straungiers. When Ester came and doctor Bele shoulde preache the Twesdaye in Easter weke, he came into the pulpit, and there declared that to him was brought a pitifull bill, and red it in this wyse. To all you the worshipful lordes and masters of this citie, that will take cōpassion ouer the poore people your neighbours, and also of the great importable hurtes, losses and hynderaunces, whereof procedeth the extreme pouertie too all the kynges subiectes that inhabite within this citie and suburbes of thesame, for so it is that the alyens and straūgiers eate the bread from the poore fatherles chyldren, and take the liuynge from all the artificers, and the entercourse from all merchauntes, wherby pouertie is so nuche encreased that euery man bewaileth the misery of other, for craftes mē be brought to beggery and merchauntes to nedynes: wherefore the premisses considred, the redresse must be of the commons, knyt and vnyte to one parte, and as the hurt and dammage greueth all men, so muste all men set to their willyng power for remedy, and not to suffre thesayd alyens so highly in their wealth, and the naturall borne men of his region too come to confusion. Of this letter was more, but the doctor red nǫ farther, and then he began *Caelum caeli domino, terram autem dedit filijs hominum*, and vpon thys text he intreated, that this lande was geuen too Englishemen, and as byrdes woulde defende their nest, so oughte Englishemen to cheryshe and defende them selfes, and to hurt and greue aliens for the common weale. And vpon this text *pugna pro patria*, he brought in, howe by Goddes lawe it was lawfull to fight for their coūtrey, and euer he subtellye moued the people to rebell against the straūgiers, and breake the kynges peace, nothynge regardynge the league betwene princes and the kynges honoure. Of this Sermon many a light person tooke courage, and openly spake against straungiers. And as the deuell woulde, the Sundaye after at Grenewiche in y[e] kynges gallery was Fraunces de bard, whiche as you harde kept an Englishe mans wife and his goodes, and yet he could haue no remedy, & with him were Domyngo, Anthony Caueler, and many mo straũgiers, and ther they talkynge with syr Thomas Palmer knyght, Iested and laughed howe that Fraunces kepte the Englishemans wyfe, saiynge y[t] if they had the Mayres wife of London, they would kepe her: syr Thomas sayd, Sirs you haue to muche fauour in England. There were diuerse Englishe merchauntes by, and harde them laugh, and were not content, in somuche as one William bolt a Mercer sayd, wel you whoreson Lombardes, you reioyse and laugh, by the masse we will one daye haue a daye at you, come when it will, and that saiynge the other merchauntes affirmed. This tale was reported aboute London, and the younge and euell disposed people sayde, they woulde be reuenged on the merchaunt straungiers, aswell as on the artificers straungiers.

The IX. Yere

VPon this rumour the. xxviii. daye of Aprill, diuerse yoũge men of the citie assauted the Alyens as they passed by the stretes, and some were strikẽ, & some buffeted, & some throwen in the canel. Wherfore the Mayre sent diuerse persõs to ward, as Stephyn Studley skynner, and Bettes and Stephenson & diuerse other, some to one coũter, & some to another, and some to Newgate. Then sodenly was a cõmen secret rumour, & no mã could tell how it began, that on May daye next, the citie would rebell & slaye all Aliens, in somuche as diuerse straungers fled oute of the citie. This brute ranne so farre that it came to the kynges coũsayll, insomuch as the Cardinall beyng lord Chaũcelour, sent for Ihon Rest Mayre of the citie, and other of the counsaill of the citie, & demaũded of the Mayre in what case the citie stode, to whome he aunswered that it was wel & in good quyet: Nay sayd the Cardinal, it is informed vs that your yoũg and ryotous people will ryse & distresse the straungiers, heare ye of no such thing? No surely sayd the Mayre, & I trust so to gouerne thẽ that the kynges peace shalbe obserued, & that I dare vndertake if I & my brethren the Aldermen may be suffered. Wel sayd y[e] Cardinal, go home & wisely forsee this matter, for & if any suche thing be, you may shortly preuent it. The Mayre came from the Cardinals at. iiii. of the clocke at after none on May euen, & demaũded of the officers what they harde, diuerse of thẽ aunswered that the voyce of the people was so, & has ben so. ii. or. iii. dayes before. This heryng the Mayre sent for al his brethrẽ to the Guylde hall in great hast, & almost. vii. of the clocke or the assemble was set. Then was declared to thẽ by Master brooke y[e] recorder how that the kynges coũsail had reported to thē y[t] the cōminaltie that night would ryse, & distresse all the Aliēs & straungers y[t] inhabited in the citie of Lōdon: the Aldermē aūswered they harde say so, but they mistrusted not the matter, but yet they sayde that it was well done to forsee it. Then sayd the recorder it were best that a substācial watche were set of honest persons, housholders, which might withstand the euell doers. An Alderman sayde, that it was euell to rayse men in harneys, for if suche a thinge were entended, they coulde not tell who woulde take their parte. Another Alderman sayd, that it were best to kepe the younge men asonder, and euery man to shut in hys dores, and kepe hys seruauntes within. Then with these opinions was the Recorder sent to y[e] Cardinal before. viii. of the clocke, and then he with suche as were of the kynges counsaill at hys place, commaūded that in no wyse watche should be kept, but that euery man shoulde repayre to his awne house, and there to kepe hym and hys seruauntes tyl. vii. of the clocke of the mornynge: with whiche commaundement, the sayde Rycharde brooke sergeaunt at the law and recorder, and syr Thomas Moore, late vndershrife of Lōdon, & then of the kynges of coūsaill, came to the Guylde hall halfe houre and before. ix. of the clocke, and there shewed the commaundemēt of the kynges counsayl. Then in all hast, euery Alderman sent to his warde that no man should styrre after. ix. of the clocke out of his house, but to kepe his doores shut, and hys seruauntes within tyll, vii. of the clocke in the mornynge. After this commaundement, syr Ihon Monday Alderman came from hys warde, and founde two young men in chepe plaiynge at Buckelers, and a great company of young men lokynge on thē for the commaundement was then skace knowen, for then it was but. ix. of the clocke. Master Mondy seyng that, bade them leaue, and the one younge man asked hym why? and then he sayd thou shalt know, & toke hym by the arme to haue had him to the counter. Then all the yoūg mē resisted the Alderman & toke him from master Mondy, and cryed prentyses and clubbes. Then out at euery doore came clubbes and weapōs and the Alderman fled, and was in great daungier. Then more people arose out of euery quarter, and oute came seruynge men, and water men and Courtiers, and by a. xi. of the clocke there were in Chepe. vi. or. vii. hundreth. And oute of Paules churcheyarde came. iii. hundreth, which wist not of the other, and so out of all places they gathered, and brake vp the counters, and tooke out the prisoners, that the Mayre had thether committed for hurtynge of the straungers, and came to Newgate and tooke out Studley and Petyt, committed thether for that cause. The Mayre and Shrifes were there present, and made Proclamaciō in the kynges name, but nothynge was obeyed. Thus they ranne a plump thorow sainct Nycholas Shābles, & at saynct Martyns gate, there met with them syr Thomas Moore and other, desyrynge theym to go to their lodgynges: And as they were intreatyng, and had almost brought them to a staye: The people of saynct Martynes threwe oute stones and battes, and hurte dyuerse honest persones, that were persuadynge the ryotous people to ceasse, and they bade them holde their handes, but still they threwe oute bryckes and hoate water. Then a sergeaunt of Armes called Nycholas dounes, whiche was there with master Moore, entreatynge them, beynge sore hurte, in a furye cryed doune with them. Then all the misruled persones ranne to the dores and wyndowes of saynct Martyn, and spoyled all that they founde, and caste it into the strete, and lefte fewe houses vnspoyled. And after that they ranne hedlynge into Cornehill by Leaden hal to the house of one Mutuas a Frencheman or Pycarde borne, whiche was a greate bearer of Frenchemen, where they pyckpursses, or howe euell disposicion soeuer they were of, and within hys gate, called Grenegate, dwelled dyuerse Frenchmen that kalendred Worsted, contrary to the kynges lawes: & all they were so borne out by thesame Mutuas, y[t] no mā durst medle w[t] them, wherfore he was sore hated, & if the people had found him in their fury, they would haue striken of his head: but whē they foūd hym not, the water men, & certayne young priestes that were there fell to riflynge: some ranne to Blāchechapelton, & brake the straungers houses, & threwe shooes and bootes into the strete: This from x. or. xi. of the clocke, continued these ryotous people durynge whiche tyme a knight called syr Thomas parr, in great hast went to the Cardinall & told him of thys ryot, which incōtinent strengthened his house with men & ordinaunce. And after, this knight roade to the king to Richemōd, & made y[e] report much more then it was: Wherfore the king hastely sent to Lōdō, & was truly aduertised of the matter, & how that the ryot was ceassed, & many of the doers apprehēded. But while this ruffling cōtinued, syr Richard Cholmeley knight, Lieutenaūt of the Towre, no great frende to the citie, in a frantyke furye losed certayn peces of ordinaunce, & shot into y[e] citie, whiche did litle harme, howbeit his good wil apered. About. iii. of the clocke, these ryotous persons seuered and went to their places of resorte, & by the waye they were taken by the Mayre and the heddes of the citie, and some sent to the Towre, and some to Newgate, and some to the Counters, to the number of. iii. C. some fled, and specially the watermen and priestes, & seruyng men, but the poore prentises were taken. About fyue of the clocke, the erles of Shrewesbury and Surrey, whiche had harde of this ryot, came to London with suche strength as they had, so dyd the Innes of court, and diuerse noble men: but or they came all the ryot was ceased, and many taken as you haue heard.

Then were the prisoners examined, & the sermon of docter Bele called to remembraunce, and he taken and sent to the Towre, & so was Ihon Lyncoln: but with this ryot the Cardinall was sore displeased. Then y[e]. iiii. day of May was an Oyer & determiner at Londō before y[e] Mayre, the duke of Norffolke, the erle of Surrey and other. The citie thought that the duke bare them grudge for a lewde priest of his, which the yere before was slayn in Chepe, in so much the duke then in his fury sayd, I pray God I may once haue the citizẽs in my daungier: & the duke also thought that they bare him no good wil, wherfore he came into the citie with. xiii. C. men in harneys to kepe the Oyer & determiner. And vpõ examinaciõ it could neuer be proued of any metyng, gathering, talking or conuenticle at any daye or tyme before y^t^ day, but that the chaũce so happened w^t^out any matter prepensed of any creature sauing Lyncoln & neuer an honest person in maner was taken but onely he. Then Proclamacions were made that no womẽ shoulde come together to bable & talke, but all men should kepe their wyues in their houses. All the stretes y^t^ were notable stode full of harnessed men, which spake many opprobrious wordes to the citezens, which greued them sore: & if they woulde haue bene reuenged, the other had had the worsse, for the citizẽs were. ii. C. to one: but lyke true subiectes they suffred paciently.

When the lordes wer set, the prisoners were brought in thorough ye stretes tyed in ropes, some men, some laddes, some chyldren of. xiii. yere. There was a great mourning of fathers & frendes for their chyldren & knysfolke. Emong the prisoners many were not of the citie, some were priestes, and some husbandmen & laborers, the whole some of the prisoners were. ii. C. lxxviii. persons. The cause of the treason was, because the kyng had amitie with all Christen princes, that they had brokẽ the truce & league cõtrary to the statute of kyng Hẽry the. v. Of this treasõ diuerse were endited, & so for y^t^ tyme, the lordes departed. And the next day the duke came agayn, & the erle of Surrey with. ii. M. armed men, which kept the stretes. Whẽ the Mayre, the duke, & ye erle of Shrewesbury & Surrey were set, the prisoners were arreigned, and. xiii. founde giltye of high treason, & adiudged to be hanged, drawen & quartered, & for execucion wherof, were set vp xi. payre of galowes in diuerse places where the offences were done, as at Algate, at Blãche-chapeltõ, Gracious strete, Leadẽ hal, & before euery coũter one, & at Newgate, at s. Martens, at Aldrisgate, at Bishopsgate. This sight sore greued the people to se galowes set in the kynges chãber. Then were ye prysoners y^t^ were iudged, brought to the places of execuciõ, & executed in most rygorous maner, for the lord Edmõd Haward sonne to the duke of Northfolke, & knight Mershal shewed no mercy, but extreme cruelty to the poore yõgelinges in their execuciõ, & likewise the dukes seruaũtes spake many opprobrious wordes, some bad hãge, some bad drawe, some bad set the citie on fyer, but all was suffred.

On Thursday the. vii. day of May was Lyncoln, Shyrwyn, & two brethrẽ called Bets, and diuerse other adiudged to dye. Then Lyncoln said, my lordes, I meant wel, for & you knew the mischief that is ensued in this realme by straugers, you would remedy it, & many tymes I haue cõplayned, & then I was called a busy felow: now our lord haue mercy on me. Then all thesayd persons were layd on the hardels, & drawen to the standarde in Chepe, & first was Ihon Lyncoln executed, & as the other had the rope about their neckes, there came a commaūdemēt frō the kyng to respite execucion. Then the people cryed, God saue y[e] king. Then was the Oyer and determiner deferred tyll another daye, and the prisoners sent agayne to warde, and the harnessed men departed oute of London, and all thynges quyet.

The. xi. daye of Maye the kynge came to his maner of Grenewiche, where the recorder of London & diuerse Aldermen came to speke with his grace, and al ware gounes of black coloure. And when they perceaued the king comming out of his priuie chambre into his chābre of presence, they kneled doune, & y[e] recorder sayd: Our most natural, beninge and souereigne lorde, we knowe well that your grace is displeased with vs of your citie of Lōdon for the great ryot late done: we assertein your grace that none of vs, nor no honest person were condisendynge to that enormitie, and yet we, oure wyfes and chyldrē euery houre lament that your fauour shoulde be taken from vs, and forasmuche as light & ydle persones were the doers of thesame, we moost hūbly besche your grace to haue mercy of vs for our negligence, & compassion of the offendours for their offence and trespasse.

Truly sayd the kyng, you haue highly displeased and offended vs, & ye oughte to wayle and be sory for thesame, and where ye saye that you the substanciall persons were not concentyng to thesame, it appereth to the contrary, for you neuer moued to let theim nor sturred once to fight with theim, whiche you saye were so small a numbre of light persones, wherefore we must thynke, and you cannot deny, but you dyd wyncke at the matter, but at this tyme we will graunt to you neither our fauour nor good will, nor to thoffenders mercy, but resort to the Cardinall our lord Chaūcelour, & he shall make you an answer, & declare our pleasure, and with this answer y[e] lōdoners departed & make relaciō to y[e] Maior.

Thursdaye the. xxii. day of May the kynge came into Westmynster hall, for whome at the vpper ende was set a clothe of estate, & the place hanged with Arras, with him was the Cardinal, the dukes of Northfolke & Suffolke, y[e] erles of Shrewsbury, of Essex & Wilshyre, of Surrey, with many lordes & other of the kinges coūsail. The Mayre & Aldermē, & al the chief of the citie were there in their best liuery (according as the Cardinal had thē apoynted) by. ix. of the clock. Then the kynge cōmaunded y[t] all the prisoners should be brought foorth. Then came in the poore yoūglinges & olde false knaues boūde in ropes all along, one after another in their shertes, & euery one a halter about his neck, to the nūber of. iiii. C. mē &. xi. womē. And whē all were come before y[e] kinges presence, the Cardinal sore laied to the Mayre & cōminaltie their negligēce, & to the prisoners he declared y[t] they had deserued death for their offence: Then al the prisoners together cryed mercy gracious lord, mercy. Then the lordes altogether besought his grace of mercy, at whose request the kyng pardoned thē al. And then the Cardinal gaue vnto thē a good exhortacion to the great gladnes of the herers. And whē the generall pardō was pronoūced, all ye prisoners shouted atonce, & altogether cast vp their halters into ye hall roffe, so y^t^ the kyng might perceaue they were none of the discretest sorte. Here is to be noted y^t^ diuerse offenders which were not takē, hering y^t^ the king was inclined to mercy, came wel appareled to Westmynster, & sodeynly stryped thē into their shertes w^t^ halters, & came in emōg the prisoners willingly, to be partakers of the kynges pardon, by the whiche doyng, it was well knowen that one Ihō Gelson yoman of the Croune, was the first that began to spoyle, and exhorted other to dooe thesame, and because he fled and was not taken, he came in the rope with the other prisoners, and so had his pardon. This compaignie was after called the blacke Wagon. Then were all the galowes within the citee taken doune and many a good praier saied for the kyng, and the citezens toke more hede to their seruauntes.

The twenty and three day of October, the kyng came to his Manor of Grenewiche, and there muche consulted with his counsaill, for a mete manne to bee his Chauncellour, so that in no wise he were no manne of the Spiritualtie, and so after long debate, the Kyng resoluted himself vpon sir Thomas More knight, Chauncellour of the Duchie of Lancastre, a manne well learned in the toungues, and also in the Common Lawe, whose witte was fyne, and full of imaginacions, by reason wherof, he was to muche geuen to mockyng, whiche was to his grauitie a greate blemishe. And then on the Sondaie, the twentie and foure daie of thesame monethe, the kyng made hym his Chauncellour, and deliuered him the great Seale, which Lorde Chauncellour, the next morow after, was ledde into the Chauncery, by the two dukes of Norffolk and Suffolk, and there sworne, and then the Mace was borne before hym.

After whiche prorogacion, sir Thomas More Chaunceller of Englāde, after long sutes made to the kyng to be discharged of that office, the. xvi. daie of Maie he deliuered to the kyng, at Westminster, the greate Seale of Englande, and was with the kynges fauor discharged, whiche Seale the kyng kept til Whitsontide folowyng, and on the Mondaie in Whitson weke, he dubbed Thomas Awdeley, Speker of the parliament knight, and made hym lorde keper of the great Seale, and so was he called.

The xxx. day of Marche the Parliament was proroged, and there euery lorde and burges and all other, were sworne to the act of succession, and subscribed their handes to a Parchement fixed to thesame othe. This Parliament was proroged till the third day of Nouember next. After this, commissions were sent ouer all England to take the othe of all men and women to the act of succession, at whiche fewe repyned, except doctor Ihon Fysher, sir Thomas Moore knight late lorde Chaūcelor, and doctor Nicholas Wylson parson of saint Thomas Apostles in London: wherfore these thre persones, after long exhortacion to them made by the bishop of Cauntorbury at Lambeth, and expresse denyal of them to be sworne, they were sent to the Tower where they remayned and were often tymes mocioned to be sworne: but the Bishoppe and sir Thomas More sayd that thei had in their writynges written the princes dowager Quene, and therfore they might not go against that, and the doctor sayd that he in preachying called her quene, whiche he would not withsay, howbeit at length he was very wel contented, and dissembled the matter and so escaped: But the other twayne stode against all the realme in their opinion.

And the xix. day of Iune was thre Monkes of the Charterhouse hanged, drawen, and quartred at Tyborne and their quarters set vp about Lōdon for deniyng the kyng to be supreme head of the Churche. Their names were Exmewe, Myddlemore, and Nudigate. These men when they wer arreigned at Westminster, behaued them selfes very stifly & stubbornly, for hearyng their inditement red how trayterously they had spoken against the kynges Maiestie his croune and dignitie, they neither blushed nor bashed at it, but very folishly & hipocritically knowleged their treason whiche maliciously they auouched, hauyng no lernyng for their defēce, but rather beyng asked dyuers questions, they vsed a malicious silence, thinkyng as by their examinacions afterward in the Tower of London it did appeare, for so they sayd, y^t they thought those men which was ye lorde Crūmwel & other that there satte vpon them in iudgement to be heretiques and not of the Churche of God, and therfore not worthy to be either aunswered or spoken vnto. And therfore as they deserued, they receiued as you haue heard before.

Also the xxii. day of thesame moneth Ihon Fysher bishop of Rochester was beheaded, and his head set vpon London bridge. This bishop was of very many menne lamented, for he was reported to be a man of great learnyng, and a man of very good life, but therin wonderfully deceiued, for he maintained the Pope to be supreme head of ye Church, and very maliciously refused the kynges tytle of supreme head. It was sayd that the Pope, for that he helde so manfully with him and stoode so stifly in his cause, did elect him a Cardinal, and sent the Cardinalles hat as farre as Caleys, but the head it should haue stande on, was as high as Lōdon bridge or euer the hat could come to Bishop Fysher, & then it was to late and therfore he neither ware it nor enioyed his office. This man as I sayd was accoumpted learned, yea, and that very notably learned, and yet haue you heard howe he was deceiued with Elizabeth Barton that called herself the holy mayd of Kent, and no doubt so was he in the defence of that vsurped authoritie, the more pitie: wonderfull it is that a man beyng lerned should be so blind in the scriptures of God that proueth the supreme aucthoritie of princes so manyfestly. Also the vi. day of Iulye was sir Thomas More beheaded for the like treason before rehersed, which as you haue heard was for the deniyng of the kynges Maiesties supremitie. This manne was also coumpted learned, & as you haue heard before he was lorde Chauncelor of England, and in that tyme a great persecutor of suche as detested the supremacy of the bishop of Rome, whiche he himselfe so highly fauored that he stoode to it till he was brought to the Skaffolde on the Tower hill where on a blocke his head was striken from his shoulders and had no more harme. I cannot tell whether I should call him a foolishe wyseman, or a wyse foolishman, for vndoubtedly he beside his learnyng, had a great witte, but it was so mińgled with tauntyng and mockyng, that it semed to them that best knew him, that he thought nothing to be wel spoken except he had ministered some mocke in the communcacion insomuche as at is commyng to the Tower, one of the officers demaũded his vpper garment for his fee, meanyng his goune, and he answered, he should haue it, and tooke him his cappe, saiyng it was the vppermoste garment that he had. Lykewise, euen goyng to his death at the Tower gate, a poore woman called vnto him and besought him to declare that he had certain euidences of hers in the tyme that he was in office (which after he was apprehēded she could not come by) and that he would intreate she might haue them agayn, or els she was vndone. He answered, good woman haue pacience a litle while, for the kyng is so good vnto me that euen within this halfe houre he will discharge me of all busynesses, and helpe thee himselfe. Also when he went vp the stayer on the Skaffolde, he desired one of the Shiriffes officers to geue him his hand to helpe him vp, and sayd, when I come doune againe, let me shift for my selfe aswell as I can. Also the hāgman kneled doune to him askyng him for forgiuenes of his death (as the maner is) to whom he sayd I forgeue thee, but I promise thee that thou shalt neuer haue honestie of the strykyng of my head, my necke is so short. Also euen when he shuld lay doune his head on the blocke, he hauyng a great gray beard, striked out his beard and sayd to the hangmā, I pray you let me lay my beard ouer the blocke least ye should cut it, thus wt a mocke he ended his life.

2. Source

From *Vita et Illustre Martyrium Thomae Mori, Angliae Quondam Svpremi Cancellarii*

By Thomas Stapleton; translated by Philip E. Hallett, 1928; edited and annotated by E. E. Reynolds, 1966

To his charity towards his neighbour, his constant generous almsgiving bears witness. He used personally to go into dark courts and visit the families of the poor, helping them not with small gifts but with two, three, or four pieces of gold, as their need required. Afterwards, when his dignity as Chancellor forbade him to act thus, he used to send some of his household who would dispense his gifts faithfully to needy families, and especially to the sick and the aged. This task was often laid upon Margaret Giggs, the wife of John Clement, whom More had brought up with his own daughters. The chief festivals of the year were his favourite times for sending such gifts. Very often he invited his poorer neighbours to his table, receiving them graciously and familiarly. The rich were rarely invited, the nobility hardly ever. Moreover, in his parish, Chelsea, he hired a house in which he placed many who were infirm, poor, or old, providing for them at his own expense. In her father's absence, Margaret Roper took charge of these. One poor widow, named Paula, who had spent all her money in litigation, he took into his own family and supported. Whenever he undertook the causes of widows and orphans, his services were always given gratuitously.

But to pass on, he was engaged in many important embassies. Often did he go to France to draw up treaties or to claim property. He accompanied Henry to France when that King and Francis I of France visited each other at Ardres. It was there that More had the pleasure of meeting his friend Budé, as is mentioned in the extract from his letter to Budé, which we have given above. Twice he went on missions to Flanders with great state, in company with Cuthbert Tunstal. But though others might be dazzled by the splendour of these embassies, they were quite out of harmony with More's modest and humble disposition. We quote from another letter to Erasmus: "You would hardly believe how unwilling I am to be involved in all these negotiations of princes: nothing could be more distasteful to me than this legation." And in another letter to the same: "The work of an ambassador has never had much attraction for me." And again in an unprinted letter to Tunstal: "What possible gain is it to me to be employed in embassies, for although my Prince is generously inclined towards me, yet far from seeking advancement at Court I turn away from it with loathing."

The incident which I shall now relate was not only a proof of his cleverness, but also very amusing. It took place in open court; for, as we shall see, not only in the law-courts, but even in prison and on the scaffold, More's humour would burst out.

One day, when More was on the bench of magistrates, some pickpockets were brought before them. Those whose purses had been stolen were complaining of the losses they had sustained, when one of the magistrates, a very dignified old gentleman, with some asperity began to lecture them for not guarding their purses more carefully, and for providing, by their negligence and thoughtlessness, an opportunity for rogues of this kind to exercise their trade. Thus did he inveigh against those for whom he should have given judgment. A speech of this nature was little to More's taste, and accordingly, as the case was adjourned, he had one of the thieves brought from the prison privately to him that night, and arranged with him that at the next session he should steal the purse of the magistrate who had thus inveighed against the innocent, as he sat in court. The thief was quite willing, and More promised him his favour for this one occasion. When, then, More and the other magistrates were again assembled in court, the thief was one of the first to be called upon to answer the charge made against him. He replied that he could clear himself if he were allowed to whisper some secret information to one of the magistrates. Being asked to choose whichever one he wished, he fixed upon that particular old gentleman. Coming close to him to whisper his story into his ear, he skilfully cut off the well-filled purse which was hanging at his side. When he had finished what he had to say, he returned to his place and gave a sign to More that he had succeeded. A little while after More suggested that help should be given to some poor fellow who was in danger of death and permitted a public collection to be made on his behalf. It began with him and his magistrates. The old gentleman, wishing to give an alms, then discovered that he had lost his purse: with shame and annoyance he averred that he certainly had had it when he took his place on the bench. More then suggested that he should not be too severe on others who suffered a like misfortune and bade the thief restore the purse. All who were present enjoyed the joke and appreciated the wisdom that was intertwined with More's humour. To incidents of this nature More was referring, I imagine, when in his Epitaph he wrote: "He was neither odious to the nobility, nor unpleasant to the people." For by his kindness and cheerfulness he made himself pleasing to all, and of all did he gain the goodwill. Although there was never any bitterness or malice in his humour, yet often with the greatest cleverness he turned the laugh against pretentious vanity.

The following instance shows his prudence and modesty no less than his ready wit. After he had resigned the Chancellorship, whilst as yet no one knew what had occurred, he came from London to his home and went at once to the church, where Vespers were being sung. Out of respect for his rank, his wife had a private closed pew. At the end of the office he went to the place and said to his wife, as usually one of his servants would say, "If you please, Madam, my Lord Chancellor is gone." Seeing him making the announcement in person, she thought he was joking. "No doubt it pleases you, Master More," she said, "to joke in this fashion." He replied: "I speak seriously and it is as I say: my Lord Chancellor is gone and is no longer here." In great astonishment she rose at once, and when she had learned the whole truth of the matter, womanlike she was in great distress at her husband's loss of position. By this humorous way of making the announcement, More wished both to soften the blow for his wife and to show what little account he made of his high honour.

At his imprisonment, on his entry into the Tower, when according to custom he was asked by the porter for his upper garment he handed him his cap. ("This certainly," he said, "rests in the highest place.") What the porter really demanded, with the warrant of custom, was his cloak.

When he was in the Tower, he was entertained at the table of the Lieutenant, according to his rank and position, as is the custom. (The Lieutenant, as is nearly always the case in the Tower, was a Knight.) Once the Lieutenant was politely apologising for the fare set before him. More answered, "If any one of us" (the others present were his fellow-captives) "is not satisfied with his fare, then I think you should turn him out of house and let him go and be hanged."

When later on the rigour of his confinement was increased and all his books and papers were taken away, he kept the blinds of his windows drawn down day and night. His gaoler asked why he acted thus. He answered: "Now that the goods and the implements are taken away, the shop must be closed."

When he was going up on to the scaffold where he was to die, he stretched out his hand for help: "I pray you," he said, "see me safe up: as for my coming down I will not trouble anyone."

When the executioner according to custom asked his pardon, "I am sorry," he replied, "that my neck is so short, for you will find it difficult to cut off my head creditably."

Many other witty sayings of a similar kind are related, but there is no need to recount them all here, nor is there reliable authority for all of them. His rivals and the heretics took offence at what they called his foolish levity in laughing and joking at so solemn a time. Edward Hall, the chronicler, for example, calls More therefore a foolish sage or a wise fool.

At the time, however, the King bade More, in treating the question, to say nothing and do nothing but what his conscience dictated, and place before his eyes God in the first place, and only in the second place the King. It may be that the King up to this time was really indifferent in the matter, although, taking into account the fall of Wolsey and other matters soon to be mentioned, we do not consider this probable. Or it may be that knowing More's utter sincerity he thought there was no other way of dealing with him.

More, anxious, as in duty bound, to obey the King and to make a thorough examination of the whole case, begged him to deign to name some others who might help him in his investigations. For this purpose the King appointed Cranmer, afterwards Archbishop of Canterbury, Lee, afterwards Archbishop of York, Richard Fox, and Nicholas [de Burgo], an Italian, all of whom were doctors of theology or canon law. More now discussed the matter thoroughly with these learned doctors: he read through and through all that he could find upon the matter, by whomsoever written, and studied the question as deeply as he could. He allowed no prejudice to influence him, but looked at the matter impartially and conformed himself to the judgment of the others as far as reason allowed, as the doctors we have mentioned afterwards testified to the King. But after all his study his opinion remained the same. Again he opened his mind to the King, protesting that he would far more willingly have followed the royal desire in the matter than receive any honours or revenues whatsoever from him, either those he had already received or those he might hope to receive in the future. The King, whether sincerely or not, received More's reply and protestation with the greatest kindness. For the future, however, those only did he admit to treat of the affair of his marriage, those only did he employ whose consciences he saw could without any scruple approve of the divorce. But More and the many others whose consciences forbade approval he made use of in other affairs of State, for up to this time he forced the conscience of no man and made no trouble or difficulty with anyone in this matter.

After this More acted so loyally in the matter of the divorce that although he read gladly all the books that were published on the King's part, yet he would never so much as look at any published against the divorce, although many men at home in English and abroad in Latin had written against it. A certain book, written by the Bishop of Bath against the divorce at the time when the Papal Legates were holding their Court, More afterwards found amongst his papers; but he delivered it up to the flames.

The details I have here transcribed are taken from a letter which after his resignation of the Chancellorship More wrote to Thomas Cromwell, then of the King's Council. My purpose has been to show what may have been the first cause of the King's annoyance with More, although at this time it was in no way apparent; to show how loyally, wisely, and sincerely More behaved so that he might offend neither against the King nor against his own conscience; and finally to show how anxious the King was to draw More over to his side.

For the whole time during which More was Chancellor the affair of the divorce remained undecided. As the King, however, continued to follow his desire or rather his lust, and wished at all costs to satisfy it, More who foresaw only too well the troubles that afterwards occurred, by earnest and repeated prayers, obtained from the King permission to resign the dignity and the burden of the Chancellorship, after he had borne that great charge with the highest integrity for a period of two and a half years. It was on October 26, 1529, that he was appointed, and on May 15, 1532, he resigned.

But the following anecdote is especially amusing, and yet a remarkable witness to his utter tranquillity and peace of heart in prospect of imminent death. Many men of high position used to visit him in prison, either of their own accord, or sent by the King. The latter is more probable, for access to the prisoners in the Tower of London is usually not so easy. Amongst these visitors was one whose attempts to move More were vehement rather than prudent. His warnings, his pleadings were incessantly repeated. He begged More to change his opinion, and not to be obstinate, and yet in all that he said there was no word of the divorce or the oath. More, either out of fun, or to rid himself of the man's importunity or to rebuke his want of courtesy, at length answered him with apparent seriousness. "Indeed, my lord, I will tell you how the matter stands. After giving everything most careful consideration, I have changed my opinion and I intend to act quite differently from the manner I had proposed." The good man, hearing this, waited for nothing further, but showed himself delighted at More's words and begged him to remain firm in the new course he had chosen. In all haste he went to the King and announced to him that More had changed his opinion. The King readily believed what it gave him such pleasure to hear, but wishing for complete certainty, "Return," he said, "to More, and say that I am delighted to hear that he has conformed his opinion to mine. I ask one thing only, that he should put into writing the change of his mind and intention, so that as many as have been scandalised by his obstinacy may now be edified by his retractation." The foolish man returned to More in prison and acquainted him with the King's words and good pleasure. On hearing him, More professed the greatest astonishment. "Have you, then, been to the King?" he said. "Have you reported to the King's Majesty the words we here privately interchanged?" "Why should I not report," said the other, "what I knew would be so pleasing to the King's Majesty?" "But at least," said More, "you should have understood my words better before you carried them to any one else, most of all to the King." "But I understood what you said quite clearly," replied the other, "that after most careful consideration you had changed your opinion." "Indeed," said More, "you have done a ridiculous thing. I have indeed changed my opinion, and told you so in familiar conversation, and I would have finished what I had to say if you had waited to hear it; but as regards the grave matter of the oath that was offered to me I have not changed my opinion. On that subject you did not speak to me, nor did I refer to it." "In what other way, then," asked the other, "have you changed your opinion?" "I will tell you clearly," answered More. "You know that during all the time I have been at Court, I have always been clean-shaven like the other members of the King's Council, and as is the custom amongst lawyers. But while I have been in prison my beard has grown long, as you see, and for some time now I had determined to shave it before going to execution so that I should not appear strange to those who know me. But now I have entirely changed my mind, and I intend to allow my beard to suffer the same fate as my head." The other was filled with confusion, as the King had ordered him to return to inform him of the matter. "So," said the King, "does this man still mock us with his jests."

Thus, then, was More tempted and gravely tempted again and again in prison, but nevertheless he was always merry and cheerful. Almost every day he sang psalms to himself, showing thus the deep and perpetual peace of his soul, according to the words of St. James: "Is any one cheerful in mind? Let him sing." In short, he said to his daughter Margaret, on his faith, that never had he received a greater benefit from the King than his imprisonment in the Tower, on account of the incredibly great spiritual progress that, as he hoped, he was there making.

After receiving sentence of death and being led back to the Tower on July 1, 1535, Thomas More prepared himself for approaching death. He was in no way cast down or anxious in mind: he was not only quite resigned, as we have seen, but even cheerful and merry, according to his wont. Of this we shall soon have proof. But not for a moment did he put aside the fear of the Lord. "Blessed is the man that is always fearful." During those last days, within the narrow limits of his prison, he would walk up and down clad in a linen sheet, like a corpse about to be buried, and severely discipline himself. Mark the holiness of the man who had, though innocent, suffered for so long such heavy punishment, but was as unrelenting towards himself as if he had ever lived in pampered luxury and had committed the grossest crimes. Woe to us who live delicately, who are puffed up with pride, green with envy, mean, avaricious, gross, impure, but yet are unwilling to bear any hardship for Christ's sake or for our own good. But "the kingdom of heaven suffereth violence, and the violent bear it away." Thomas More had learnt this lesson thoroughly, and to the last day of his life he willed to be harsh and to do violence to himself. He knew that in the race the strong runner, as he approaches his goal, increases his efforts and his speed.

When the day had arrived which was to bring to More death, or rather life, he was led out of his prison. His beard was long and disordered, his face was pale and thin from the rigour of his confinement. He held in his hand a red cross and raised his eyes to heaven. His robe was of the very poorest and coarsest. He had decided to make his journey in a better garment and to put on the gown of camlet, which Bonvisi had given him in prison, both to please his friend and to be able to give it to the executioner. But through the avarice or wickedness of his gaoler, he, so great and renowned, he who had held such high office, went out clad in his servant's gown made of the basest material that we call frieze. But this was for Thomas More a fitting nuptial garment: by it he was made like to Christ, who willed to be poor: clothed in it he hastened to drink the Chalice of Christ and to celebrate the Nuptial Feast of the Lamb.

Margaret Giggs, the wife of John Clement, once showed me a life-like image, made with great skill, of More going out to the place of execution, and in accordance with that image I have described here his appearance and demeanour. She was present at More's death and assisted the other Margaret, Roper's wife, to bury him.

As he was passing on his way, a certain woman offered him wine, but he refused it, saying, "Christ in his passion was given not wine, but vinegar, to drink."

Another woman shouted at him and demanded to know what he had done with certain documents which she had entrusted to him while he was Chancellor. "Good woman," he replied, "as for your documents, have patience, I beseech you, for the space of one short hour. For then from the care of your documents and from every other burden, the King's Majesty in his goodness will give me complete relief."

He was again interrupted by another woman, who perhaps felt she had a grievance or perhaps was suborned by others, and now cried out that he had done her a grave injury while he was Chancellor. "I remember your case quite well," he gravely replied, "and if I had to pass sentence again, it would be just the same as before."

When he arrived at the place of execution and was about to mount the scaffold, he stretched out his hand for assistance, saying, "I pray you see me safe up, and for my coming down let me shift for myself." On the scaffold he wished to speak to the people, but was forbidden to do so by the Sheriff. He contented himself, therefore, with saying: "I call you to witness, brothers, that I die the faithful servant of God and the King, and in the faith of the Catholic Church." Such were his words; and in truth no one in the kingdom could be matched with him for fidelity to the King: God he served with the greatest zeal and holiness of life.

3. Possible Source

From *The Lyfe of Syr Thomas More, Sometymes Lord Chancellor of England*

By Ro: Ba:; edited by Elsie Vaughan Hitchcock and Philip E. Hallett, 1950

Sir Thomas More spent most of his life in worldly honors and highe Offices, where much wealth might be had. Yet, *inuentus est sine macula, nec post aurum abijt*, "he was found without spote, nor coueting after gold." The office of Chancellourshipp being the greatest office in this Realme of

England, and in dignitie next to the king, he was very vnwillinge to take it vpon him; and he had vtterly refused it, had it not bene vnmeete and vnseemlie obstinately to gainsay and contradict the kinges pleasure, who, of entire affection and loue, made choice of him, as thinking him the meetest man of all others for that place.

Sir Thomas [was] so well knowne to the learned abroade that his opinion was thought sufficient to decide any controuersie. It happined once that a very excellent learned man, a stranger, satt at the table at a great mans howse in this Realme with Sir Thomas More, whom this stranger had neuer before seene. There was great reasoning betweene the stranger and some others of deepe points of learning. At length Sir Thomas set in foot, & demeaned him selfe so cunninglie that the stranger, who was a religious man, was astonished to heare so profound reasons at a laymans handes. Wherevpon he enquired of those that satt next him what his name was: which when he vnderstoode, said, as Queen Saba said to Solomon: *Verus est sermo quem audiui in terra mea super sapientia huius; non credebam narrantibus mihi, donec veni et vide*; "True is the fame I haue hard in my Countrie of this mans wisdome. I did not beleeve them that told it; but now I am come my selfe, and I find it to be true, yea, and more I finde then was reported."

At an other tyme, Sir Thomas sitting as Iudge, some litle petie fellowes were brought before him for picking and cutting of purses. (Cutpurse art was not then so frequent, nor yet so heynous, as now.) Y[ey] that were endomaged made meanes for theire losses, and one of [the] Iujstices, a graue and an old man, all to ratled the poore men, affirming that they were in greate fault that had no better care of theire money, for theire negligence and carelesnes made theeues, by giuings them so faire occasions that y[ey] could hardly but doe as they did. Sir Thomas, seeing the importunitie of the old man, sought occasion to depart for that present, referring the hearing of these matters till the next morninge.

In the meane tyme he caused the theefe to be sent for to his chamber; and there, after he had throughlie chidden him, said vnto him, "I haue good hope thou wilt do better hereafter, and see it proue so. For this tyme I will stand your friend, but you must shew me a tricke of your cunning. You heard yesterday how the old gentleman chid them that lost there purses. If thou canst take his purse from him, & let me know when it is done, I will warrant thee for this tyme thou shalt take no harme."

The poore knaue promised his diligence, and being the next day the first man that was called to his aunswere, made a request to the Bench that it would please them to giue him leaue to speake, for he doubted not but to satisfie them at the full. But the matter he was to vtter was secret; therefore he desired he might tell it to some one first in secret. Y[t] was granted him; and when it was asked him whome he would haue, "Sir, if it might be you," said the theefe, pointing to the old angrie gentleman, "to you I would tell it." Then he and the old man went apart. The old mans purse was made fast to his girdle, which the theefe spying, gaue it the loosing. And after he had told a friuolous tale to him, he retourned and gaue notice of the purse to Sir Thomas. Sir Thomas, taking occasion by giuing an almes to a prisoner whose discharge was staied for lacke of money to defrey the keepers fees, request[ed] the gentlem[e]n on the bench to help the poore man. He himselfe gaue first. When it came to the old Iustice, he put his hand to his pouche, and found it to be taken away: as angrie as ashamed, affirming verie seriouslie that he had his purse when he came to the hall, and he merueiled what was become of [it]. "It is well," said Sir Thomas, "you will now leaue to chide my neighbours, who had as litle care but not so good hap as you, for you shall haue your purse againe;" so told who had it.

He would neuer strike anie of his seruantes, nor giue them any wordes of contumelie or reproche. If he had any occasion to chide, then it was in such mild sort that his verie chiding made him more to be loued. They would be glad to haue giuen occasion in some light matter (yet feared to giue occasion) that they might enioy his sweet and louing chiding.

4. Source

From *The Lyfe of Sir Thomas Moore, knighte*

By William Roper; edited by Elsie Vaughan Hitchcock, 1935

This S*ir* Thomas Moore, after he had bine brought vpp in the Latyne tongue at St. Anthonies in London, was by his fathers p*ro*curem*en*t receaved into the house of the right reu*er*end, wise, *and* learned prelate Cardinall Mourton; where, thoughe he was younge of yeares, yeat wold he at Christmas tyde sodenly sometimes steppe in among the players, *and* neuer studyeng for the matter, make a p*ar*te of his owne there presently among them, w*hi*ch made the lookers on more sporte then all the plaiers beside. In whose witt *and* towardnes the Cardinall muche delightynge, wold often say of him vnto the nobles that divers tymes dined w*i*th him: "This child here wayting at the table, whosoeu*er* shall liue to see it, will proue a mervailous man."

Wherupon for his [better] furtheraunce in learninge, he placed him at Oxford; where when he was both in the greake *and* latine tongue sufficiently instructed, He was then for the study of the lawe of the Realme put to an Inne of Chauncery called Newe Inne, where for his tyme he very well p*ro*spered; And from thence was admitted to Lincolnes Inne, with very small allowans, contynewinge there his study vntill he was made *and* accompted a worthy vtter barrister.

After this, to his greate commendacion, he redde for a good space a publike lecture of St. Augustine, *de civitate dei*, in the Churche of St. Lawrens in the old Jury; whereunto there resorted Doctor Grosin, an excellent [cunninge] man, *and* all the cheif learned of the City of London.

Then was he made reader of Fvrnivals Inne, so remayninge by the space of three yeares and more.

After [this] he was made one of the vndershirifs of London, by w*hi*ch office *and* his learninge together (as I haue herd him say) he gayned without greif not so litle as foure hundreth pound*es* [by the] yeare; Sithe there was at that tyme in none of the princes court*es* of the lawes of this realme, any matter of importans in controu*er*sie wherein he was not with the one p*ar*te of Councell. Of whom, for his learninge, wisdome, knowledge, *and* experiens, men had such estimacion that, before he [came] to the seruice of king Henrye the eight, at the suite *and* instaunce of the Englishe merchaunt*es*, he was by the kings consent made twise Embassador in certaine greate causes betweene them *and* [the] merchaunt*es* of the Stilliarde: Whose wise *and* discreete dealinge therin, to his highe comendacion, coming to the kings vnderstanding, p*ro*voked his highnes to cause Cardinall Wolsey (then Lord Chauncelor) to p*ro*cure him to his seruice. And albeit the Cardinall, according to the kinges request, earnestly travailed w*i*th him therefore, amonge many other his p*er*swasions alleaging vnto him howe deare his service must needes be vnto his ma*ies*tie, w*hi*ch could not, [with] his honor, w*i*th les then he should yearly leese thereby, seeme to recompence him; yeat he, loth to chainge his estate, made such meanes to the kinge, by the Cardinall, to the contrary, that his grace, for that tyme, was well satisfied.

And for the pleasure he took in his company, would his grace sodenly sometimes come home to his house att Chelsey, to be merry with him; whither on a tyme, vnloked for, he came to dinner [to him]; *and* after dinner, in a faire garden of his, walked with him by the space of an houre, holdinge his arme aboute his necke. As soone as his grace was gone, I reioycing thereat, told S*ir* Thom*as* Moore howe happy he was, whom the king had so familiarly entertayned, as I neuer had seene him to doe to any [other] excepte Cardinall Wolsey, whom I sawe [his grace] once walke with, arme in arme. "I thancke our lord, sonne," quoth he, "I find his grace my very good lord indeed, *and* I beleeave he dothe as singulerly favour me as any subiect w*i*thin [this] realme. Howbeit, sonne Roper, I may tell thee I haue no cawse to be prowd thereof, for if my head [could] winne him a castle in Fraunce (for than was there warre betweene vs) it should not faile to goe."

[More,] betweene the Dukes of Norffolke *and* Suffolk, being brought throwghe Westminster Hall to his place in the Chancery, The Duke of Norffolke, in Audiens of all the people there assembled, shewed that he was from the kinge himself straightly charged, by speciall comission, there openly, in presens of them all, to make declaration howe much all England was beholdinge to S*ir* Thom*as* Moore for his good service, *and* howe w*or*thy he was to haue the highest roome in the realme, and howe dearly his grace loved *and* trusted him, for w*hi*ch, said the duke, he had greate cause to reioyce. Wherunto S*ir* Thom*as* Moore, among many other his hvmble *and* wise sayengs not nowe in my memory, awneswered, That althoughe he had good cause to take comforte of his highnes singuler Favour towards him, that he had, farre aboue his desert*es*, so highly comended him, to whom [therfore] he acknowledged himself most deeply bounded; yeat, neu*er*theles, he must for his owne p*ar*te needes confes, that in all things by his grace alleaged he had done no more then was his duty; And further disabled himself as vnmeete for that roome, wherein, considering howe wise *and* honourable a prelate had lately before taken so greate a fall, he had, he said, thereof no cause to reioice. And as they had [before], on the kings behalf, charged him vprightly to minister indifferent iustice to the people, w*i*thout corruption or affection, So did he likewise charge them againe, that if they sawe him, at any time, in any thinge, digresse from any p*ar*te of his duty in th*a*t honorable office, euen as they wold discharge theyr owne duty *and* fidelitye to god *and* the kinge, so should they not faile [to disclose it] to his grace, who otherwise might haue iust occasion to lay his fault wholy to their Charge.

Whensoeuer he passed throughe westminster hall to his place in the Chauncery by the courte of the kinges Benche, if his father, one of the Judges there[of], had bine sate ere he came, he wold goe into the same courte, *and* there reuerently kneeling downe in the sight of them all, duly aske his fathers blessinge. And if it fortuned that his father *and* he, at readings in Lincolnes Inne, mett together, as they sometime did, notwithstanding his highe office, he wold offer in argument the prehemynens to his father, thoughe he, for his office sake, wold refuse to take it. And for the better declaration of his naturall affection towards his father, he not only, while he lay [on] his death bedd, [accordinge to his dutie], ofte times with comfortable wordes most kindly came to visite him, But also at his dep*a*rture out of the world, with teares taking him about the necke, most lovingly kissed *and* imbraced him, co*m*mending him into the mercifull hand*es* of almighty god, *and* so dep*a*rted from him.

Nowe shortly vppon his entry into the highe office of the Chauncelorshipp, the king [yeat] eftssoones agayne moved him to waighe and consider his greate matter; who, falling downe vppon his knees, hvmbly besought his highnes to stand his gratious sou*er*aigne, as [he] euer since his entry into his gra[ces] service had founde him; sayeng there was nothing in the world had bine so greiuous vnto his harte as to remember [that] he was not able, as he willingly wold, with the losse of one of his limbes, for that matter any thing to finde wherby he could, [with his consciens, safely] serve his graces contentac*ion*; As he that alwaies bare in mynde the most godly word*es* th*a*t his highnes spake vnto him at his first coming into his noble service, the most vertuous lesson that euer prince taught his servant, willing him first to looke vnto god, *and* after god to him; as, in good faith, he said, he did, or els might his grace well accompt him his most vnworthy servaunt. To this the kinge awneswered, that if he could not [therein] with his consciens serue him, he was content taccept his service otherwise; And vsing the aduice of other [of] his learned councell, whose consciences could well inough agre therewith, wold neu*er*theles contynewe his gratious favour tow*a*rds him, *and* neuer with that matter molest his consciens after.

But S*ir* Thom*as* Moore, in processe of time, seing the king fully [determined to p*ro*ceede [forthe] in the mariage of Queene Anne, and when he, w*i*th the Bishopps *and* nobles of the higher house of the parliament, were, for the furtheraunce of that mariage, comaunded by the kinge to goe downe to the comon house, to shewe vnto them both what the vniu*er*sities, aswell of other p*ar*tes beyond the seas as [of] Oxford *and* Cambridge, had done in that behalf, *and* their seales also testifyenge the same—All w*hi*ch matters, at the kings request, not shewing of what minde himself was therein, he opened to the lower house of the parliament—Neu*er*theles, doubtinge least further attempt*es* after should followe, *which*, contrary to his consciens, by reson of his office, he was likely to be putt vnto, He made sute vnto the Duke of Norfolk, his singuler deere freind, to be a meane to the kinge that he might, with his grac*es* favour, be discharged of that chargeable roome of [the] Chauncelo*ur*shippe, wherein, for certaine infirmities of his bodye, he pretended himself vnable any longer to serve.

When the Duke, beinge therunto often sollicited, by importunate sute had at length of the king obtayned for S*ir* Thom*as* Moore a cleere discharge of his office, Then, at a tyme convenient, by his highnes apointm*ent*, re-payred he to his grace, to yealde vpp vnto him the greate seale. Which, as his grace, w*i*th thancks and prayse for his worthy service in that office, courteously at his hand*es* receaved, so pleased it his highnes [further] to say vnto him, that for the service that he before had done hym, in anye sute w*hi*ch he should after haue vnto him, that either should concerne his honor (for that word it liked his highnes to vse vnto him) or that should app*er*taine vnto his p*ro*fitt, he should find his highnes good and gratious Lord vnto him.

After he had thus geuen ouer the Chauncelo*ur*shipp, and placed all his gentlemen *and* yeomen w*i*th Byshoppes *and* noble men, *and* his eight watermen w*i*th the Lord Awdley, that in the same office succeded him, to whom also he gaue his greate barge, Then, calling vs all that were his children, vnto him, *and* asking our advise howe we mighte nowe, in this decay of his abilyty (by the surrender of his office so impaired that he could not, as he was wont, and gladly wold, beare out the whole charges of them all himself) from [t]hencforth be able to liue *and* contynewe together, as he wished we should.

After this, as the duke of Norfolke *and* S*ir* Thom*as* Moore chaunced to falle in familiar talke together, the duke said vnto him: "By the masse, m*aster* Moore, it is p*er*illous stryvinge withe princes. And therfore I wold wishe you somewhat to inclyne to the kings pleasure; For by god body, master Moore, *Indignatio principis mors est.*"

"Is that all, my Lord?" quothe he. "Then in good faith is there no mo*re* differens betweene yo*ur* grace *and* me, but that I shall dye today, *and* yow tomorowe."

So fell it oute, within a moneth or thereaboutes after the makinge of the statute for the oathe of the supremacye *and* matrimonye, that all the preistes of London and Westminster, *and* no temporall men but he, were sente for to appeare att Lambethe before the Byshoppe of Cant*er*bury, the lord Chauncelo*ur*, *and* Secretory Cromwell, Comissioners appointed there to tender the oathe vnto them.

Then S*ir* Thom*as* Moore, as his accostomed manner was alwaies, ere he entered into any matter of importaunce, as when he was firste chosen of the kings privy Councell, when he was sent Embassado*ur*, appointed speaker of the p*ar*liamente, made Lord Chauncelo*ur*, or when he tooke any like waighty matter vppon him, To goe to church *and* be confessed, to heare masse and be howsled, So did he likewise in the mornynge earlye the self same day that he was summoned to appeare before the Lord*es* at Lambeth. And whereas he evermore vsed before, at his dep*ar*ture from his wife *and* children, whom he tenderly loved, to haue them bring him to his boate, *and* there to kisse them all, and bidd them farewell, Then wold he Suffer none of them forthe of the gate to followe him, but pulled the wickatt after him, *and* shutt them all from him; *and* w*i*th an heauy harte, as by his countenaunce it appeared, w*i*th me and our foure servant*es* there tooke he his boate towards Lambithe. Wherein sitting still sadly a while, at the last he [sodainely] rounded me in the yeare, *and* said: "Sonne Roper, I thancke our Lord the feild is wonne." What he ment thereby I then wist not, yeat loth to seeme ignorant, I awneswered: "S*ir*, I am thereof very glad." But as I coniectured afterward*es*, it was for [that] the loue he had to god wrought in him so effectually that it conquered all his carnall affections vtterlye.

[Nowe] At his cominge to Lambithe, howe wisely he behaved himself before the Comissioners, at the ministration of the oathe vnto him, may be found in certaine letters of his, sent to my wife, remayning in a greate booke of his workes. Where, by the space of foure daies, he was betaken to the custody of the Abbott of Westminster, during w*hi*ch tyme the king consulted with his councell what order were meete to be taken with him. And albeit in the beginninge they were resolued that with an othe not to be acknowen whether he had to the supremacye bine sworne, or what he thoughte thereof, he should be dischardged, yeat did Queene Anne, by her impo*ur*tunate clamo*ur*, so sore exasperate the kinge againste him, that contrary to his former resolucion, he caused the said othe of the Supremacye to be ministred vnto him. Who, albeit he made a discreete qualified awnswer, neu*er*theles was forthw*i*th comitted to the tower.

Who[m], as he was going thitherward, wearing, as he comonly did, a chayne of gould about his necke, S*ir* Richard Cromewell, that had the charge of his conveyans thither, advised him to send home his chayne to his wife, or to some of his children. "Nay, S*ir*," quoth he, "that I will not; for if I were taken in the feild by my enemies, I wold they shold somewhat fare the better by me."

At whose landing m*aster* Leiuetenant [at] the tower gate was ready to receaue him, wheare the Porter demaunded of him his vpper garment. "M*aster* Porter," quoth he, "here it is;" *and* tooke of his cappe, and deliu*er*id it [him], saying, "I am very sory it is no better for you." "No, S*ir*," quoth the Porter, "I must have yo*ur* gowne."

And so was he by m*aster* Leiuetenaunte convayed to his lodginge, where he called vnto him one John A wood, his owne servaunte, there apointed to attend vppon him [who coulde neither write nor rede]; and sware him before the Leiuetenaunte that if he should heare or see him, att any tyme, speake or write any manner of things against the king, the Councell, or the State of the realme, he shoulde open it to the Leiuetenaunte, that [the Leiuetenaunte] mighte incontinent reveale it to the Councell.

Nowe when [he] had remayned in the Tower a litle more then a monethe, my wife, longinge to see her father, by her ernest suite at length got leaue to goe to him. At whose cominge, after the seuen psalmes *and* letany said (w*hi*ch, whensoeu*er* she came to him, ere he fell in talke of any worldly matters, he vsed accustomably to say with her) Amonge other communicacion he said vnto her: "I beleeve, Megge, that they that have putt me heare, weene they haue done me a high displeasure. But I assure [thee], on my faithe, my owne good daughter, if it had not byne for my wife *and* you that be my children, whom I accompte the cheife p*ar*te of my charge, I wold not haue fayled longe ere this to haue closed my self in as straighte a roome, and straighter too. But since I am come hither without myne owne deserte, I trust that god of his goodnes will discharge me of my care, *and* w*i*th his graciouse helpe supply my lack amonge you. I find no cause, I thanck god, Megge, to reckon my self in wors case heare then in my owne house. For me thinckethe god makethe me a wanton, *and* settethe me on his lappe and dandlethe me." Thus by his gratious demeano*ur* in tribulac*i*on appeared it that all the trowble[s] that euer chaunced [vnto] him, by his patient sufferaunce thereof, were to him no paynefull punishment*es*, but of his paciens profitable exercises.

And att another tyme, when he had first questioned with my wife a while of the order of his wife, children, *and* state of his howse in his absens, he asked her how queene Anne did. "In faith, father," quoth she, "never better." "Never better! Megge," quothe he. "Alas! Megge, alas! it pitieth me to remember in[to] what misery, poore soule, she shall shortly come."

After this, m*aster* Lieutenant, cominge into his chamber to visite him, rehearced the benefittes and freindshipp that he had many waies receaved at his hand*es*, *and* howe much bounden he was therefore freindly to intertayne him, *and* make him good cheare; w*hi*ch, since the case standing as it did, he could not do w*i*thout the kinges indignation, he trusted, he said, he wold accepte his good will, *and* suche poore cheare as he had. "Maister Lievetenaunt," quothe he againe, "I veryly beleeve, as you may, so you are my good freind indeede, and wold, as you say, with your best cheere intertaine me, for the w*hi*ch I most hartely thancke you; and assure yo*ur* self, m*aster* Leivetenant, I doe not myslike my cheare; But whensoeu*er* I soe doe, then thruste me out of yo*ur* doores."

Whereas the oath confirminge the supremacye *and* matrimonie was by the first statute in fewe wordes comprised, The Lord Chauncelor *and* Master Secretary did of their owne heads adde more words vnto it, to make it appeare vnto the kinges cares more pleasaunt *and* plausible. And that oath, so amplified, caused they to be ministred to S*ir* Thomas Moore, *and* to all other throughout the Realme. W*hi*ch S*ir* Thomas Moore p*er*ceyuinge, said vnto my wife: "I may tell thee, Megg, they that haue committed me hither, for refusinge of [this] oath not agreable w*i*th the statute, are not by theyr owne lawe able to iustifye my imprisonem*ent*. And surely, daughter, it is greate pitye that any Christian prince should by a flexible Councell ready to followe his affections, and by a weake Cleargie lackinge grace constantly to stand to their learninge, w*i*th Flatterye be so shamefully abused." But at length the Lord Chauncelo*ur* *and* m*aster* Secretorye, espieng their [owne] ou*er*sight in that behalf, were fayne afterward*es* to find the meanes that another statute shold be made for the confirmacion of the oath so amplified w*i*th their additions.

When S*ir* Thomas Moore had continued a good while in the Tower, my Lady, his wife, obtayned lycens to see him; who, at her first cominge, like a simple ignorant woman, *and* somewhat worldly too, with this manner of salutacion bluntlye saluted him:

"What the good yere, m*aster* Moore," quoth she, "I mervaile that you, that have bine alwaies hitherto taken for so wise a man, will nowe so play the foole to lye heare in this close, filthy prison, and be content thus to be shut vpp amongst mise *and* rattes, when you might be abroade at yo*ur* libertye, *and* w*i*th the favo*ur* and good will both of the kinge *and* his Councell, If yow wold but doe as all the Byshops *and* best learned of this realme [haue] done. And seinge you have at Chelsey a right faire house, yo*ur* library, yo*ur* bookes, yo*ur* gallery, your garden, yo*ur* orchard, *and* all other necessaries so handsome aboute you, where you might in the company of me your wife, [your] children, *and* howshold be meerye, I muse what a gods name you meane heare still thus fondly to tarye."

After he had a while quietly heard her, with a chearefull countenaunce he said vnto her:

"I pray thee, good m*istris* Alice, tell me one thinge."

"What is that?" quoth shee.

"Is not this house," quoth he, "as nighe heauen as my owne?"

To whom shee, after hir accustomed homely fashion, not liking such talke, awneswered, "Tylle valle, Tylle valle!"

"Howe say you, m*istris* Alice," quoth he, "is itt not so?"

"Bone deus, bone deus, [man], will this geare neuer be lefte?" quoth shee.

"Well then, m*istris* Ales, if it be so," [quoth he], "it is very well. For I see no greate cause why I should much Ioye [either] of my gay house or [of] any thinge belonginge therunto; when, if I should but seuen yeares lye buried vnder the ground, and then arise *and* come [t]hither againe, I should not faile to find some therein that wold bid me get [me] out of doores, and tell me it were none of mine. What cause haue I then to like such an house as wold so soone forgett his m*aster*?"

So her p*er*swasions moved him but a litle.

Not longe after came there to him the Lord Chauncelo*ur*, the dukes of Norfolke *and* Suffolk, with m*aster* Secretory *and* certaine other of the privy Counsaile, at two seu*er*all times, by all pollicies possible p*ro*curinge him, eyther precisely to confesse the sup*re*macy, or precisely to denye it; wherunto, as appeareth by his examination[s] in the said great book, they could neuer bringe him.

Shortlye herevppon, m*aster* Riche, afterward*es* Lord Riche, then newlye made the kings Solicitor, S*ir* Ri*chard* Sowthwell, and one m*aster* Palmer, servaunt to the Secretory, were sent to S*ir* Thom*as* Moore into the tower, to fetche away his bookes from him. And while S*ir* Ri*chard* Southwell and m*aster* Palmer were busye in the trussing vppe of his bookes, m*aster* Rich, pretending freindly talke w*i*th him, amonge other things, of a sett cours, as it seemed, saide thus vnto him:

"Forasmuch as it is well knowen, master Moore, that you are a man bothe wise *and* well learned aswell in the lawes of the realme as otherwise, I pray you therefore, S*ir*, lett me be so bold as of good will to putte vnto you this case. Admitt there were, S*ir*," quoth he, "an acte of p*ar*liam*ent* that all the Realme should take me for kinge. Wold not you, m*aster* Moore, take me for kinge?"

"Yes, sir," quoth S*ir* Thomas Moore, "that wold I."

"I put case further," quoth m*aster* Riche, "that there were an acte of p*ar*liament that all the Realme should take me for Pope. Wold not you then, m*aster* Moore, take me for Pope?"

"For awneswer, [Sir]," quoth S*ir* Thomas Moore, "to yo*ur* firste case: the p*ar*liam*ent* may well, m*aster* Riche, medle w*i*th the state of temporall princes. But to make awneswer to yo*ur* other case, I will put you this case: Suppose the p*ar*liam*ent* wold make a lawe that god shold not be god. Wold you then, m*aster* Riche, say that god were not god?"

"No S*ir*," quoth he, "that wold I not, sith no p*ar*liam*ent* maye make any such lawe."

"No more," said S*ir* Thomas Moore, as m*aster* Riche reported of him, "could the p*ar*liam*ent* make the kinge Supreame head of the churche." Vppon whose onlye reporte was Sir Thomas Moore indicted of treason vppon the statute [whereby] it was made treason to denye the kinge to be supreame head of the churche.

After whiche ended, the Comissioners yeat further curteouslye offred him, if he had any thinge els to alleage for his defence, to graunt him favorable audience. Who awneswered: "More haue I not to say, my Lord*es*, but that like as the blessed Apostles St Pawle, as we read in thact*es* of the Apostles, was present, *and* consented to the death of St Stephen, and kepte their clothes th*a*t stoned him to deathe, and yeat be they [nowe] both twayne holy Sainctes in heaven, and shall continue there frendes for euer, So I verily [truste], *and* shall therefore right hartelye pray, that thoughe yo*ur* lordshippes haue nowe [here] in earthe bine Judges to my condemnacion, we may yeat hereafter in heaven meerily all meete together, to our eu*er*lasting saluac*ion*."

Thus much towching S*ir* Thomas Moores arrainem*ent*, being not thereat present my self, haue I by the credyble reporte, [partely] of the right worshipp*fu*ll S*ir* Anthony Seintleger, knight, *and* p*ar*tely of Ri*chard* Heywood *and* John Webbe, gentlemen, withe others of good creditt, at the hearing thereof present themselves, as farre as my poore witt *and* memory wold serue me, here truly rehersed vnto you.

Nowe, after this arraignem*ent*, dep*ar*ted he from the barre to the Tower againe, ledde by S*ir* William Kingston, a talle, stronge, *and* comely knighte, Constable of the Tower, *and* his very deare freind. Who, when he had brought him from westminster to the old Swanne towards the Tower, there w*i*th an heavy harte, the teares runinge downe by his cheekes, bade him farewell. S*ir* Thom*a*s Moore, seinge him so sorowefull, comforted him w*i*th as good words as he could, sayenge: "Good m*aster* Kingston, trouble not yo*ur* self, but be of good cheare; for I will pray for you, *and* my good Lady, yo*ur* wife, that we may meete in heuen together, where we shalbe meery for ever *and* ever.

Soone after, S*ir* will*iam* Kingston, talking w*i*th me of S*ir* Thomas Moore, said: "In good faith, m*aster* Roper, I was ashamed of my self, that, at my dep*ar*ting from yo*ur* father, I found my harte so feeble, *and* his so stronge, that he was fayne to comforte me, wh*i*ch should rather have comforted him."

And so vppon the next morowe, beinge Tuesdaye, St Thomas even, *and* the vtas of Saincte Peeter, in the yeare of our lord, one thowsand five hundreth thirtye *and* five (according as he in his letter [the daye] before had wished) earlye in the morninge came to him S*ir* Thomas Pope, his singuler freind, on message from the kinge *and* his Councell, That he should before nyne of the clock the same morning suffer death; and that therefore furthw*i*th he should prepare him self therunto:

"M*aster* Pope," quoth he, "for yo*ur* good tydings I most hartelye thancke you. I haue bine alwaies much bounden to the Kings highnes for the benefit*es and* honoures that he hath still from tyme to tyme most bountyfully heaped vppon me; and yeat more bound am I to his grace for puttinge me into this place, where I haue had convenient time *and* space to haue remembraunce of my end. And so helpe me, god, most of all, m*aster* Pope, am I bound to his highnes that it pleaseath him so shortly to ridde me out of the miseries of this wretched woorld. And therefore will I not faile ernestly to pray for his grace, bothe heare *and* also in another world."

"The kings pleasure is further," quoth m*aster* Pope, "that at yo*ur* execution you shall not vse many words."

"M*aster* Pope," quothe he, "you do well to geeue me warninge of his graces pleasure, for otherwise I had purposed at that tyme somewhat to have spoken, but of no matter wherew*i*th his grace, or any other, should haue had cause to be offended. Neu*er*theles, whatsoeuer I intended, I am ready obediently to conforme my self to his graces commandem*ent*es. And I beseeke you, good m*aster* Pope, to be a meene vnto his highnes that my daughter Margaret may be at my buriall."

"The kinge is content already," quoth m*aster* Pope, "that yo*ur* wife, children *and* other [your] freinds shall haue libertie to be present thereat."

"O howe much beholden then," said S*ir* Thomas Moore, "am I to his grace, that vnto my poore buriall vouchsafeth to haue so graciouse consideracion."

Wherewithall m*aster* Pope, takinge his leaue of hym, could not refrayne from wepinge. Which S*ir* Thomas Moore p*er*ceiuinge, comforted him in this wise: "Quiet yo*ur* self, good m*aster* Pope, *and* be not discomforted; For I trust that we shall, once in heaven, see eche other full merily, where we shalbe sure to live *and* loue together, in ioyful blisse eternally."

Vppon whose dep*ar*ture, S*ir* Thom*as* Moore, as one that had bine invited to [some] solempne feaste, chaunged himself into his best apparell; w*hi*ch m*aster* Leiuetenaunt espienge, advised him to put it of, sayenge that he that should haue it was but a Javill.

"What, m*aster* Leiuetenaunt," quoth he, "shall I accompte him a Javill that shall doe me this day so singuler a benefitt: Nay, I assure you, were it clothe of gold, I wolde accompt it well bestowed on him, as St Ciprian did, who gaue his executioner thirtie peeces of gould." And albeit at length, throughe m*aster* Leiuetenaunt*es* importunate p*er*suasion, he altered his apparell, yeat after thexample of that holy martir St Ciprian, did he, of that litle money that was lefte him, send one Angell of gold to his executioner.

And so was he by m*aster* Leiuetenaunte brought out of the Tower, *and* from thence led to[wardes] the place of execution. Where, goinge vppe the scaffold, w*hi*ch was so weake that it was ready to fall, he saide merily to m*aster* Leiuetenaunte; "I pray you, m*aster* Leiue-tenaunte, see me salf vppe, *and* for my cominge downe let me shifte for my self."

Then desired he all the people thereaboute to pray for him, *and* to beare witnes w*i*th him that he should [nowe there] suffer death in *and* for the faith of the holy chatholik churche. Whiche done, he kneled downe, and after his prayers said, turned to thexecutioner, *and* w*i*th a cheerefull countenaunce spake [thus] to him: "Plucke vpp thy spirites, man, *and* be not afrayde to do thine office; my necke is very shorte; take heede therefore thow strike not awrye, for savinge of thine honestye."

So passed Sir Thomas Moore out of this world to god, vppon the very same daye in w*hi*ch himself had most desired.

5. Source

From *The life and death of S[r] Thomas Moore, knight, sometymes Lord high Chancellor of England*

By Nicholas Harpsfield; edited by Elsie Vaughan Hitchcock and R. W. Chambers, 1932

In the saide Citie, at S[t] Antonies schoole, he learned the principles of the latine tongue, in the knowledge whereof when he had in short space farre surmounted his coequalls, his father, seeing the towardlynes and actiuitie of his sonne, and being carefull for his farther good and vertuous education, procured and obteyned that he shoulde be brought vp in the house of the right reuerende, the wise and learned prelate, Cardinall Morton; who, being a man of quicke witt and deepe iudgement, soone espied the childes excellent dispositio*n* and nature; who, among many other tokens of his quicke and pregnant witt, being very yonge, would yet notwithstanding vpon the [soden] stepp in among the Christmas players, and forthwith, without any other forethinking or premeditation, playe a part with them himselfe, so fitly, so plausibly and so pleasantly, that the Auditours tooke muche admiration, and more comfort and pleasure thereof then of all the players besydes; and especially the Cardinall, vpon whose table he wayted. And often would he tell to the nobles sitting at the table with him: "Whosoeuer liueth to see it, shall see this childe come to an excellent and meruailous proufe." To whose very likely, then, and probable foreiudgement, thende and issue of this mans life hath plainly, openly and truely aunswered. And so farre as we may, as it were for a wonderfull but yet for a true surplusage, adde to his coniecturall foreiudgement our sure, constant, stable and grounded iudgement, that he was and is the oddest and the notablest man of all Inglande, And that he atchieued such an excellent state of woorthines, fame and glory as neuer did (especially laye man) in Inglande before, and muche doubt is there whether anye man shall hereafter. Which my saying I trust I shall iustifie hereafter. In the meane season, good Reader, if thou thinke I passe and exceede iust measure, and wouldest I should shew by and by what motions I haue that leade me to this censure, I praye thee spare me a litle while, and geue the more vigilant and attentiue eare to the due and deepe consideration of that I shall truely and faythfully sett forth touching this man. And then I hope I shall, if thou be any thing indifferent, satisfie my promise and thy expectation also.

This Cardinall then that had raysed both to himself and others such an expectation to this childe, being nowe more and more carefull to haue him well trayned vp, that his goodly budd might be a faire flower, and at length bring forth such fruit as he and the others expected and looked for, thought it best he should be sent to the Vniuersite of Oxforde, and so he was; where, for the short time of his abode (being not fully two yeres) and for his age, he wonderfully profited in the knowledge of the latin and greeke tonges; where, if he had setled and fixed himselfe, and hadd runne his full race in the study of the liberall sciences and diuinitie, I trowe he would haue beene the singuler and the onely spectacle of this our time for learning. But his father minded that he should treade after his steppes, and settle his whole minde and studie vpon the lawes of the Realme. And so being plucked from the vniuersities of studies and learning*es*, he was sett to the studies of the lawes onely of this Realme. Which studie he co*m*menced first at Newe Inne, one of the Innes of Chauncerie. And when he had welfauouredly profited therein, he was admitted to Lincolnes Inne, and there, with small allowance, so farre forth pursued his studie that he was made, as he was well woorthy, an vtter barrester. Nowe is the lawe of the Realme, and the studie thereof, such as would require a whole man, wholly and entierly thereto addicted, and a whole and entier mans life, to growe to any excellencie therein. Neyther were vtter barresters commonlye made then but after many yeres studie. But this mans speedie and yet substantiall profiting was such that he enioyed some prerogatiue of time; and yet in this notwithstanding did he cutt off from the studie of the lawe muche time, which he employed to his former studies that he vsed in Oxforde; and especially to the reading of S[t] Augustine *de Ciuitate Dei*, which though it be a booke very harde for a well learned man to vnderstande, and cannot be profoundly and exactly vnderstanded, [and] especially cannot be with co*m*mendation openly read, of any man that is not well and substantially furnished as well with diuinite as prophane knowledge; yet did M*aster* More, being so yonge, being so distracted also and occupied in the studie of the co*m*mon lawes, openly reade in the Churche of S[t] Laurence in London the bokes of the saide S[t] Augustine *de Ciuitate Dei*, to his no small co*m*mendation, and to the great admiration of all his audience. . . . Neuer the more discontinuing his studie of the lawe at Lincolnes Inne, but applying still the same vntill he was called to the bench, and had read there twise, which is as often as ordinarily and Judge of the lawe doth reade.

Before which time he had placed himselfe and his wife in Bucklersbury in London, where he had by her three daughters and one sonne (called John More, to whom Erasmus did dedicate Aristotles workes, printed by Bebelius; and three daughters, Margarete, maried to M*aster* Will*ia*m Roper; Cicelie, maried to M*aster* Giles Heron; and Elizabeth, wife to M*aster* Will*ia*m Dancie): which children from their youth he brought vp in vertue, and knowledge both in the latin and the greeke tonges, whom he would often exhort to take vertue and learning for their meate, and playe for their [sauce].

As he was borne in London, so was he as well of others as of the saide Citie derely beloued, and inioyed there the first office that he had, being made vnder sheriffe of the [saide] Citie. The saide office, as it is woorshipfull, so is it not verye combersome: for the Judge sitteth vpon Thursday onely, once in the weeke, before noone; no man dispatched in the same office more causes then he did; No man euer vsed himselfe more sincerely and vprightly to the suters, to whom often times he forgaue his owne fee and dutie. In the saide Court it is the order, before they co*m*mence their matter, that the Plaintiffe put downe three grotes, and the defendant as muche; more it is not lawfull to require of them; by the which office, and his learned counsaile that he gaue his client*es*, he gayned without grudge, griefe or touche of his owne conscience, and without the grudge, griefe of iniurie of any other man, aboue fowre hundred poundes yerely.

Neither was there any matter in controuersie of weight and importance in any of the Princes courtes of the lawes of the Realme that he was not retayned for counsaile of the one or the other partie; yea, he grewe shortly in suche woorthy credite for his witt, learning, wisdome and experience, that before he came to the seruice of king Henry the eight, he was at the sute and instance of the englishe merchauntes, and by the kinges consent, for great important matters betweene the said merchautes and the merchaunt*es* of the Stilliarde (albeit co*m*monly suche ambassades are co*m*mitted to Ciuilians) sent twise Ambassadour ouer the Seas. He of his owne selfe and of nature neither desired nor well lyked to be intricated with Princes affaires, and of all other offices he had little minde and fancie to be any ambassadour, And least to this ambassade; for that he lyked not to haue his abode (as he had) and, as it were, to be shutt vp in a Towne nere to the Sea, where neither the grounde nor the ayre was good and wholsome.

Moreouer the king was in hande w*i*th Cardinall Woolsey, then Lorde Chauncell*our*, to winne him and to procure him to his graces seruice. The Cardinall did not forslowe the matter, but incontinentlye trauelled, and that very earnestly, with him, with many persuasions, which he did amonge other inforce with this, that his seruice must needes be deere to his Maiestie, which could not with his hono*ur* with lesse then he should leese thereby seeme to recompence him. Yet he, being very lothe to shifte and chaunge his state and condition, wrought so with the Cardinall that by the Cardinall the king was satisfied for the time, and accepted M*aster* Mores excuse. I say for the time. For this mans woorthy estimation and fame so grewe on euery day more then other, that a while after the king could by no maner of intreatie be induced any longer to forbeare his seruice, and that vpon this occasion.

There chaunced a great shipp of his that then was Pope to arriue at Southampton, the which the king claymed as a forfeyture. Wherevpon the popes ambassadour, then resident in the Realme, vpon sute obteyned of the king that he might retaine for his master some Counsailers learned in the lawes of the Realme, and that in his owne presence (him selfe being a singuler Ciuilian) the matter might in some publike place be openly heard, debated and discoursed. Among all the lawyers, no one could be founde so apte and meete as M*aster* More, As one that was able to report to the Ambassadour all the reasons and argumentes on both sides proposed and alleaged. Vpon this the Counsailers of either partie, in the presence of the Lorde Chauncell*our* and other the Judges in the Starre chamber, had audience accordingly. At what time M*aster* More was not onely a bare reporter to the Ambassadour, but argued himselfe also so learnedly and so substantially that he recouered and wonne to the pope the saide forfaiture, and to himselfe high co*m*mendation and renowne.

Being then vpon this occasion retained in the kinges seruice, the king gaue him a notable and woorthye lesson and charge, that in all his doinges and affaires touching the king, he should first respect and regarde God, and afterwarde the king his master. Which lesson and instruction neuer was there, I trowe, any Princes seruaunt that more willingly heard, or more faithfully and effectually executed and accomplished, as ye shall here-after better vnderstande.

At his first entraunce, being [then] no better rowme voyde, he was made master of the requestes, and within a moneth he was made knight and one of the kinges priuie Councell. After the death of M*aster* Weston, he was made vnder Treasourer of Theschequer; and then afterwarde, vpon the death of Sir Richarde Wingefelde, Chauncello*ur* of the Douchie of Lancaster; and at length aduaunced to be Lorde Chancello*ur* of Inglande. The which offices, as he obteyned by the kinges goodnes, by his meere voluntary and free disposition, without any sute or solicitation of his owne behalfe, so did he vse him selfe therein with all good dexteritie, wisedome and equitie, sinceritie and incorruption, and in this race of the kinges seruice he ranne painfully, wisely and honorably, twentie yeres and aboue.

Neyther was there any one man that the king vsed more familierly, [nor] with whom he more debated, not onely for publike affaires, but in matters of learning, withall taking a great comfort besides in his merie and pleasantly conceyted witt. And tooke such pleasure in his company that he woulde sometime, upon the sodaine, come to his house at Chelsey to be merye with him. Whither on a time, vnlooked for, he came to diner to him; and after diner, in a faire garden of his, walked with him by the space of an howre, holding his arme about his necke. Of all the which fauour he made no more accompt then a deepe wise man should doo, And as the nature and disposition of the king (which he deepely and throughlye perceaued) did require, and as in deede he afterwarde in himselfe most of all men experienced. Wherefore euen at this time, when flattering fortune seemed most pleasantly to smile vppon him, and all thinges seemed as faire and beautifull as the lustry of a bright diamonde, he well thought as well vpon the disposition and inclination of the saide Prince as vpon the fraile, instable and brickle state of suche as seeme to be in high fauo*ur* of their Princes.

Wherefore, when that after the kinges departure his sonne in lawe, M*aster* Will*iam* Roper, reioycingly came to him, saying these wordes: "S*ir*, howe happy are you whom the king hath so familierly interteyned, as I neuer haue seene him to doo anye other except Cardinall Wolsey, whom I sawe his grace walke with-all arme in arme;" S*ir* Thomas More aunswered in this sort; "I thanke our Lorde, sonne, I finde his grace my verye good Lorde in deede; And I beleeue he doth as singulerly fauour me as he doth any subiect within this Realme. Howbeit, sonne Roper, I may tell thee I haue no cause to be proude thereof; For if my head could winne him a castle in Fraunce" (for then was there warre betweene Fraunce and vs) "it should not faile to serue his turne."

And doubtlesse, if S*ir* Thomas More had beene of so high, immoderate aspiring minde as was the Cardinall, he might haue perchaunce geuen him a fall longe ere he tooke his fall, and haue shifted him from the saddle of the Lorde Chauncellourshipp, and might haue sitt therein before he did; whose fall and ruine he neither procured nor desired, as the world well knoweth, and much lesse his great office, wherevnto he woorthily succeeded. Yea, the Cardinall himselfe, when he sawe he should needes forgoe the same, though he neuer bare him, as I haue saide, true hartie affection, yet did he confesse that S*ir* Thomas More was the aptest and fittest man in the Realme for the same: whose great excellent witt and learning, whose singuler qualities, graces and giftes, whose profounde pollitike head in the ciuill affaires, as well inwardly as outwardly, the saide Cardinall by longe time [certainly], and, as I might say, feelingly knewe.

But nowe lett vs returne to S*ir* Thomas More, newly made Lorde Chauncell*our*, which office, I suppose verilye he was of himselfe very vnwilling to take vpon him, and would haue earnestly refused the same, but that he thought it vnmeete and vnseemely to gainsay and contrary the will and pleasure of the king, that so highly and entierly fauored and loued him, and also an euill part to withdrawe and denye his seruice to the whole Realme, that with gladfull and meruailous good mind towarde him wisshed and desired that he of all men might enioye the saide office; who betweene the dukes of Norfolke and Suffolke being brought through Westminster hall to his place in the Chauncerie, the duke of Norffolke, in open audience of all the people there assembled, shewed that he was from the king himselfe straightly charged by speciall Commission, there openly in presence of them all, to make declaration howe much all Inglande was beholding vnto S*ir* Thomas More for his good seruice, and howe woorthy he was to haue the highest roome in the Realme, and howe derely his grace loued and trusted him, for which (saide the duke) he had great cause to reioyce. Wherevnto S*ir* Thomas More, among many other his humble and wise sayinges not nowe in my memorie, aunswered that although he had good cause to take comfort of his highnes singuler fauour towardes him, that he had, farre aboue his desertes, so highly co*m*mended him, to whom therefore he acknowledged himselfe most deepely bounden; Yet neuerthelesse he must for his owne part needes confesse that in all thinges by his grace alleaged he had done no more than was his dutie, and further disallowed himselfe as vnmeete for that roome, Wherein, considering howe wise and honorable a Prelate had lately before taken so great a fall, he had, he saide, [therof] no cause to reioyce. And as they had before, on the kinges behalfe, charged him vprightly to minister indifferent Justice to the people, without corruption or affection; so did he likewise charge them againe, that if they sawe him, at any time, in any thing, digresse from any part of his dutie in that honorable office, euen as they would discharge their owne dutie and fidelitie to God and the king, so should they not faile to disclose it to his grace, who otherwise might haue iust occasion to laye his fault whollye to their charge.

Whensoeuer he passed through Westminster hall to his place in the Chauncerie by the Court of the kinges benche, if his Father (one of the judges thereof) had bene sett ere he came, he would goe into the same court, and there reuerently kneeling downe in the sight of them all, dulye aske his fathers blessing. And if it fortuned that his father and he at readinges [in] Lincolnes Inn mett together, as they sometime did, [notwithstanding his high office] he would offer in argument the preheminence to his father, though he, for his office sake, would refuse to take it. And for better declaration of his naturall affection towarde his father, he not only while he laye on his death bedd, according to his dutie, often times with comfortable wordes most kindly came to visite him, but also at his departure out of this world, with teares taking him about the necke, most louingly kissed and embraced him, commending him into the mercifull handes of almightie God, and so departed from him.

All the while he was Lorde Chauncell*our*, yea, and before also, there was nothing in the world that more pleased or comforted him then when he had done some good to other men; of whom some he relieued with his money, some by his authoritie, some by his good worde and commendac*i*on, some with his good counsaile. Neither was there euer any man (woorthy to be relieued) that sought reliefe and helpe at his hande, that went not from him merie and cheerfull. For he was (as a man may say) the publique patrone of all the poore; And thought that he did procure to himselfe a great benefite and treasure as often as he could by his counsaile deliuer and ridd any man in any perplexitie and difficile cause, as often as he could pacifie and reconcile any that were at variance and debate.

Nowe a litle to speake againe of the kinges great affaires then in hande. The king, shortlye vpon his entrie into the office of the Chauncellourshipp, moued eftsones S*ir* Thomas More to weigh and consider his great matter; who, falling downe vpon his knees, humbly besought his highnes to stande his gratious Soueraine, as he euer since [his] entrie first into his graces seruice had founde him, saying there was nothing in the worlde had beene so grieuous vnto his heart as to remember that he was not able, as he willingly would with the losse of one of his limmes, for that matter any thing to finde whereby he could with his conscience safely serue his graces contentation; as he that alway bare in minde the most godly wordes that his highnes spake vnto him at his first co*m*ming into his noble seruice, the most vertuous lesson that euer Prince taught his seruaunt, willing him first to looke vnto God, and after God vnto him, as, in good fayth, he saide he did, or els might his grace well accompt him his most vnwoorthy seruaunt. To this the king aunswered, that if he could not therin with his conscience serue him, he was content to accept his seruice otherwise; and vsing the aduise of other of his learned Councell, whose consciences could well ynough agree therewith, would neuerthelesse continue his gratious fauoure towarde him, and neuer with that matter molest his conscience after.

But S*ir* Thomas More, in processe of time, seing the king fully determined to proceede forth in the mariage of Queene Anne, when he with Bisshopps and nobles of the higher house of the Parliament were, for the furtherance of that mariage, co*m*maunded by the king to goe downe to the common house, to shewe vnto them both what the vniuersities, as well of other partes beyonde the Seas as of Oxforde and Cambridge, had done in that behalfe, and their Seales also testifying the same—All which matters, at the kinges request, not shewing of what minde himselfe was therein, he opened to the lower house of the Parliament—Neuertheless, doubting least further attemptes should after folowe, which, contrary to his conscience, by reason of his office, he was likely to be put vnto, he made sute to the duke of Norffolke, his singuler deere frend, to be a meane to the king that he might, with his graces fauo*ur*, be discharged of that chargeable roome of the Chauncello*ur*shipp, wherein, for certaine infirmities of his bodie, he pretended himselfe vnable any longer to serue.

At the commencement of which Parliament, S*ir* Thomas More, standing at the right hande of the king, behinde the barre, made an eloquent oration. The effect thereof was that the office of a Shepherd did most liuely resemble the office and gouernment of a king, whose riches if [ye] respect, he is but a riche man; if his hono*ur*, he is but honorable; and so forth; but the office of a Shepherde, as he well and wittilye declared, acco*m*modating the prosequution thereof to his purpose and the summoning of the present Parliament, comprised in a maner all or the chiefe and principall function of a king.

Nowe, whereas I declared that S*ir* Thomas More, vpon consideration and deepe foresight of thinges hanging vpon the Realme and imminent, was desirous to be exonerated and discharged of that office, pretending infirmities, Truth it is that this was no bare and naked pretence, but that it was so with him in very deede; for he was troubled with a disease in his brest, which continuing with him many monethes, after he consulted with the phisitians, who made him aunswere that longe diseases were daungerous; adding further that his disease could not shortly be holpen, but by a litle and litle, with continuance of longe time, by rest, good diet and phisicke, and yet could not they appoint any certaine time when he should recouer, or be quite ridd and cured. This thing S*ir* Thomas More well weighing with himselfe, and that eyther he must forgoe the office, or forslowe some part of his requisite and dutifull diligence, seing him selfe not able to welde and dispatche the manifolde and weightie affaires of that office, and that with longe continuance in the office he was like to be bereaued of the office and his life withall, determined with himselfe rather to forgoe the one then both.

So it is true also that he was most fauourably and honorably dimissed, after longe sute, from the saide office. At the which time the king saide to him that in any sute that he should afterwarde haue to his grace, that eyther should concerne the saide S*ir* Thomas Mores hono*ur* (for that worde it liked his highnes to vse to him) or that should apperteyne to his profite, he should finde his highnes a good and gratious Lorde to him.

But because we are in hande with the bookes and learning of the saide S*ir* Thomas More, I will nowe tell you this one thing onely, that I haue heard him report that he would at table and otherwhere wonderfull deepely and clarkely talke with learned men, as well englishe as of other countries; and that he once knewe when a very excellent learned man (as he was taken), a straunger, being in this Realme, chaunced to be at the table with S*ir* Thomas More, whom he knewe not. At which table there was great reasoning between the saide straunger and others of many great pointes of learning. At length S*ir* Thomas More sett in a foote, and coped with the saide straunger, and demained himselfe so cunningly and so learnedlye that the saide straunger, which was a religious man, was muche astonied and abashed to heare such profounde reasons at a laye mans hande. And therevpon inquired of suche as were neerest at hande to him what his name was: which when he once vnderstoode, he had no great pleasure afterwarde to encounter any more with him.

He enioyed the health of his body full well; and though he were not very stronge of body, yet was he able to goe throughe with any labour and paine meete and conuenient for him for to dispatche his busines and affaires. He was very litle infested and incombred with sickenes, sauing a litle before he gaue ouer the office of the Lorde Chaun:cello*ur*, and especially afterwarde, when he was shutt vp in the towre.

So fell it out within a moneth or thereaboutes after the making of the Statute for the othe of the Supremacie and matrimonie, that all the Priestes of London and Westminster, and no moe temporall men but he, were sent for to appere at Lambeth before the Bisshopp of Caunterbury, the Lord Chauncello*ur*, and Secretary Cromwell, Commissioners appointed there to tender the othe vnto them.

Then S*ir* Thomas More, as his accustomed maner was (as we haue declared) when he had any matter of weight in hande, went to Churche and was confessed, and heard Masse and was houseled, in the morning early the selfe same day that he was summoned to appere before the Lordes at Lambeth. And whereas he euermore vsed before, at his departure from his wife and children, whom he tenderly loued, to haue them bring him to his boate, and there to kisse them all and bidd them farewell, then would he suffer none of them forth of the gate to folowe him, but pulled the wickett after him, and shett them all from him. And with an heauy heart, as by his countenaunce it appered, with M*aster* Will*ia*m Roper and their fowre seruauntes tooke he his boate there towarde Lambeth. Wherein sitting still sadly a while, at the last he sodenlye rounded M*aster* Will*ia*m Roper in the eare, and saide: "Sonne Roper, I thanke our Lorde the field is wonne." What he meant thereby M*aster* Will*ia*m Roper then wist not; yet lothe to seeme ignorant, he aunswered: "S*ir*, I am thereof very gladd." But, as he coniectured afterwarde, it was for that the loue [he had to] God wrought in him so effectually that it conquered all his carnall affections vtterly from his wife and children, whom he moste deerely loued.

The saide Co*m*missioners required him to take the othe lately appointed by the Parliament for the Succession; to who*m* S*ir* Thomas More aunswered that his purpose was not to put any fault eyther in the acte [or] any man that made it, or in the othe or any man that sware it, nor to condemne the conscience of any other man. "But as for my selfe," saide he, "my conscience so moueth me in the matter, that though I would not denye to sweare to the Succession, yet vnto [that] othe that there was offered me I cannot sweare without the hazarding of my soule to perpetuall damnation." And farther saide that if they doubted whether he did refuse the othe onely for the grudge of his conscience, or for any other phantasie, he was ready therein to satisfie them by his othe. Which, if they trusted not, what should they be the better to geue him [any] othe? And if they trusted that he would therein sweare true, then trusted he that of their goodnes they would not moue him to sweare the othe that they offred him, perceaving that for to sweare it was against his conscience.

Vpon this they shewed him a Roll, wherin were the names of the Lordes and the Commons which at the determination and ending of the saide Parliament had sworne to the saide Succession, and subscrybed their names. Which when they sawe that notwithstanding S*ir* Thomas More still refuse[d] it, they co*m*maunded him to goe downe to the garden.

In the meane while were there called in doct*our* Wilson and all the Clergie of the Citie of London, which all receaued the othe saving the said doct*our* Wilson. Wherevpon he was co*m*mitted to the towre; and so was also the good Bisshopp of Rochester, John Fisher, that was called in before them that day, and refused the foresaide othe.

When they were gone, then was S*ir* Thomas More called vp againe, and there was declared vnto him what a number had sworne euen since he went aside, gladly, without any sticking. And laide to him obstinacie, that he would neyther take the othe, nor yet tell the cause whye he refused to sweare: which, he saide, he would doo, sauing he feared that he should exasperate thereby the kinges displeasure the more against him. And yet at length, when they pressed him, he was content to open and disclose the saide causes in wryting vpon the kinges gratious licence, or vpon his co*m*maundement. But it was aunswered that if the king would geue licence, it would not serue against the Statue. Whervpon S*ir* Thomas More by and bye inferred, that seing he could not declare the causes without perill, then to leaue them vndeclared was no obstinacie in him.

And whereas he saide that he did not condemne the conscience of other men, the Archbisshopp of Caunterbury, taking holde thereon, saide that it seemed by that the matter wherevpon he stoode was not very sure and certaine; And therefore he should therein obey his soueraine Lorde and king, to whom he was certaine he was bounde to obey. S*ir* Thomas More aunswered that he thought that was one of the causes in which he was bounde not to obey his Prince. And if that reason may conclude, then haue we a way to auoide all perplexities; for in whatsoeuer matters the doctours stande in great doubt, the kinges co*m*maundement, geuen vpon whether side he list, soyleth all the doubtes.

When they could gett none other aunswere of him, he was co*m*mitted to the custodie of the abbott of Westminster by the space of fowre dayes; during which time the king consulted with his counsaile what order were meete to be taken with him. And albeit in the beginning they were resolued that with an othe, not to be acknowen whether he had to the Supremacie beene sworne, or what he thought thereof, he should be discharged, yet did Queene Anne by her importunate clamo*ur* so sore exasperate the king against him that, contrary to his former resolution, he caused the saide othe of the Supremacie to be ministred vnto him; who albeit he made a discrete qualified answere, neuerthelesse was forthwith co*m*mitted to the towre.

Whom, as he was going thitherwarde, wearing (as he co*m*monly did) a cheine of golde about his necke, S*ir* [Richard] Cromwell, that had the charge of his conueyance thither, aduised to sende home, his chyne to his wife or to some of his children. "No, S*ir*," quoth he, "that I will not; for if I were taken in the fielde by mine enemies, I would they should somewhat fare the better by me."

At whose landing M*aster* Lieftenant at the towre gate was ready to receaue him, where the Porter demaunded of him his vpper garment. "M*aster* Porter," saide he, "here it is," and tooke off his cappe, and deliuered it to him, saying: "I am very sory it is no better for you." "Noe, S*ir*," quoth the Porter, "I must haue your gowne."

The which Lieftenant, on a certaine time comming to his chamber to visite him, rehearsed the benefites and frendshipp that he had many wayes receaued at his handes, and howe muche bounden he was therefore frendly to interteyne him and make him good cheere. Which, since the case standing as it did he could not doo without the kinges indignation, he trusted, he saide, he would accept his good will and such poor cheere as he had. "M*aster* Lieftenant," quoth he againe, "I verily beleeue, as you may, you are my good frende in deede, and would, as you say, with your best cheere interteyne me, for which I most heartily thanke you. And assure your selfe, M*aster* Lieftenant, I doo not mislyke my cheere, but whensoeuer I so doo, then you maye thrust me out of your dores."

And as besyde his olde disease of his brest, he was now greeued in the reynes by reason of grauell and stone, and with the crampe that diuers nightes gryped his legges, so dayly more and more there grewe toward him many other great causes of griefe and sorowes; which all he did moderate and temper with patient and spirituall consolation and comfort to heauenwarde.

"Concerning nowe the matters you charge and challenge me withall, the articles are so prolixe and longe that I feare, what for my longe imprisonment, what for my longe lingring disease, what for my present weaknes and debilitie, that neyther my witt, nor my memorie, nor yet my voice, will serue to make so full, so effectuall and sufficient aunswere as the weight and importance of these matters doth craue."

When he had thus spoken, susteyning his weake and feeble body with a staffe he had in his hande, commaundement was geuen to bring him a chaire; wherein being set, he commenced his answere muche after this sort and fasshion.

After which ended, the Commissioners yet further courteouslye offred him, if he had any thing els to alleage for his defence, to graunt him fauorable audience. Who aunswered; "More haue I not to say, my Lordes, but that like as the blessed Apostle S[t] Paule, as we reade in the Actes of the Apostles, was present and consented to the death of S[t] Steuen, and kept their clothes that stoned him to death, and yet be they nowe both twaine holy Saintes in heauen, and shall continue there frendes together for euer, so I verily trust, and shall therefore right heartily praye, that though your Lordshipps haue nowe here in earth beene Judges to my condemnation, we may yet hereafter in heauen merily all meete together, to our euerlasting saluation. And thus I desire Almightie God to preserue and defende the kinges Maiestie, and to send him good counsaile."

Thus muche nowe concerning his arraignement. After the which he departed from the barre to the towre againe, ledd by S*ir* Will*ia*m Kingeston, a tall, stronge and comely knight, Constable of the Towre, and his very deere frende. Who, when he had brought him from Westminster to the Olde Swanne towarde the towre, there with an heauy hart, the teares running downe by his cheekes, bad him farewell. S*ir* Thomas More, seing him so sory, comforted him with as good wordes as he could, saying: "Good M*aster* Kingeston, trouble not you selfe, but be of good cheere, for I will praye for you and my good Lady your wife, that we may meete in heauen together, where we shall be merie for euer."

Soone after this S*ir* William Kingeston, talking with M*aster* Will*ia*m Roper of S*ir* Thomas More, saide: "In good fayth, M*aster* Roper, I was ashamed of my selfe that at my depart[ing] from your father, I founde my heart so feeble and his so stronge, that he was faine to comfort me, [which] should rather haue comforted him."

And so vpon the next morowe, being Tuesday, S[t] Thomas Even, and the Vtas of S[t] Peter, in the yere of our Lorde 1535 (according as he in his letter the day before had wisshed), early in the morning came to him S*ir* Thomas Pope, his singuler frende, on message from the king and his Counsaile, that he should before nyne of the clocke the same morning suffer death, and that therefore, forthwith he should prepare himselfe thereto.

"M*aster* Pope," quoth he, "for your good tydinges I most heartily thanke you. I haue beene alwayes muche bounden to the kinges highnes for the benefites and honours that he hath still from time to time moste bountifully heaped vpon me; and yet more bounden am I to his grace for putting me vnto this place, where I haue had conuenient time and space to haue remembraunce of mine ende. And so helpe me God, most of all, M*aster* Pope, am I bounden to his highnes that it [pleaseth] him so shortly to ridd me out of the miseries of this wretched world, and therefore will I not fayle earnestlye to praye for his grace, both here, and also in another world."

"The kinges pleasure is further," quoth M*aster* Pope, "that at your execution you shall not vse many wordes."

"M*aster* Pope," quoth he, "you doo well to geue me warning of his graces pleasure, for otherwise I had purposed at that time somewhat to haue spoken, but of no matter wherewith his grace, or any other, should haue had cause to be offended. Neuerthelesse, whatsoeuer I intended, I am ready obedientlye to conforme my selfe to his graces co*m*maundement. And I beseeche you, good M*aster* Pope, to be a meane vnto his highnes that my daughter Margarete may be at my buriall."

"The king is content already," quoth M*aster* Pope, "that your wife, children and other your frendes shall haue libertie to be present thereat."

"Oh, howe muche beholden then," saide S*ir* Thomas More, "am I to his grace, that vnto my poore buriall vouchsafeth to haue such gratious consideration."

Wherewithall M*aster* Pope, taking his leaue of him, could not refraine from weeping. Which S*ir* Thomas More perceaving, comforted him in this wise: "Quiet your selfe, good M*aster* Pope, and be not discomforted; for I trust that we shall, once in heauen, see eche other full merilye, where we shall be sure to liue and loue together, in ioyful blisse eternallye."

Vpon whose departure, S*ir* Thomas More, as one that had beene inuited to some solemne feast, chaunged himselfe into his best apparell. Which M*aster* Lieftenant espying, aduised him to put it off, saying that he that should haue it was but a iavell. "What, M*aster* Lieftenant," quoth he, "should I accompt him a iavell that shall doo me this day so singuler a benefite? Nay, I assure you, were it cloth of golde, I would accompt it well bestowed on him as S[t] Ciprian did, who gaue to his executioner thirtie peeces of golde." And albeit at length, through M*aster* Lieftenant*es* importune persuasion, he altered his apparell, yet after the example of that holy Martyr Saint Ciprian, did he, of that litle money that was lefte him, sende one angell of golde to his executioner; and so was he by M*aster* Lieftenant brought out of the towre, and from thence led towarde the place of execution.

When he was thus passing to his death, a certaine woman called to him at the towre gate, beseeching him to notifie and declare that he had certaine euidences of hers that were deliuered to him when he was in office, saying that after he was once apprehended, she [could] not come by them; And that he would intreate that she might recouer her saide euidences againe, the losse of which [would] import her vtter vndoing. "Good woman," sayth he, "content thy selfe, and take patience a litle while, for the king is so good and gratious to me, that euen within this halfe howre he will disburden me of all worldly busines, and helpe thee himselfe."

When he was going vp to the scaffolde, which was so weake that it was redy to fall, he saide merily to M*aster* Lieftenant: "I praye you, M*aster* Lieftenant, see me safe vp, and for my co*m*ming downe lett me shifte for my selfe."

The*n* desired he all the people thereabout to praye for him, and to beare witnes with him that he should nowe [there] suffer death in and for the fayth of the holy Catholike Churche. Which done, he kneeled downe, and after his prayers sayde, turned to the executioner, and with a cheerefull countenance spake thus vnto him: "Plucke vp thy spirites, man, and be not afraide to doo thine office; my necke is very short; take heede therfore thou stryke not awrye, for saving of thine honestie."

So passed S*ir* Thomas More out of this world to God, vpon the verye same day in which himselfe had moste desired.

6. Source

From *Actes and Monuments of matters most speciall and memorable* (1583 edition)
By John Foxe

Not the presence of him onely but also the hearing of the coming of Cromwell brake many fraies and much euill rule: as well appeareth by a certain notorious fray or riot appointed to be fought by a company of ruffins in the streete of London called Paternoster rowe, where carts were set on both sides of purpose prepared to enclose them, that none might break in to part them. It happened that as this desperate skirmish should begin, the Lord Cromwell comming the same time from the Court through Paules churchyard, and entering into chepe, had intelligence of the great fray toward, and because of the carts he could not come at them, but was forced to go about the little conduit, and so came upon them through Pannier Alley.

Thus as the conflict began to waxe hote, and the people were standing by in great expectation to see them fight, sodenly at the noice of the Lord Cromwels commyng, the campe broke vp and the Ruffins to go, neither could the cartes kepe in those so couragious campers, but well was he that first could be gone. And so ceased this tumultuous outrage, without any other parting, only through the authoritie of the Lord Cromwels name.

One example more of the like affinitie commeth here in mynd, which ought not to be omitted, concerning a certain serving man of the like ruffenly order who thinking to disceuer himselfe from the common usage of all other men in strange newfanglenes of fashions by himself (as many there be whom nothing doth please, which is dailie seene and receiued) used to go with his haire hangyng about his eares downe vnto his shoulders, after a strange monstrous maner, counterfeiting belyke the wyld Irish men, or els Crinitas Ioppas, which Virgil speaketh of, as one wearie of his owne English fashion: or els as one ashamed to be seene lyke a man, would rather go lyke a woman or lyke to one of the Gorgon sisters, but most of all lyke to himself, that is, lyke to a Ruffin, that could not tell how to go.

As this Ruffin ruffling thus with his locks was walking in the streetes, as chance was, who should meet him but the Lord Cromwell, who beholding the deforme and unseemly maner of his disguised goyng, full of much vanitie and hurtful example, called the man to question with him whose servant he was, which being declared, then was demanded, whether his maister or any of his felowes used so to go with such haire about their shoulders, as he did, or no? Which when he denied and was not able to yeld any reason for refuge of that his monstrous disguising, at lẽgth he fell to this excuse that he had made a vow. To this the Lord Cromwell answered agayne that for so much as he had made himself a votarie, he would not force him to breake his vowe, but untill his vow should be expired, he should lye the meane tyme in prison, and so sente him immediately to the Marshalsey: where he endured, till at length this intonsus Cato beyng perswaded by hys maister to cut his haire, by sute and petition of frends, hee was brought agayne to the Lord Cromwell with his hed polled according to the accustomed sort of his other fellowes, and so was dismissed.

7. Source

From *The Disobedient Child* (c. 1560)

By Thomas Ingelend; edited by John S. Farmer, 1905

The Prologue

The Prologue Speaker. Now, forasmuch as in these latter days,
Throughout the whole world in every land,
Vice doth encrease, and virtue decays,
Iniquity having the upper hand;
We therefore intend, good gentle audience,
A pretty short interlude to play at this present:
Desiring your leave and quiet silence
To show the same, as is meet and expedient.

8. Source

From *Lusty Juventus* (1550)

By R[ichard] Wever; edited by John S. Farmer, 1905

[*Here entereth Lusty Juventus, or Youth, singing as followeth*:

In a herber green, asleep where as I lay,
The birds sang sweet in the middes of the day
I dreamed fast of mirth and play:
  In youth is pleasure, in youth is pleasure.
Methought I walked still to and fro,

And from her company I could not go;
But when I waked, it was not so:
  In youth is pleasure, in youth is pleasure.
Therefore my heart is surely pight,
Of her alone to have a sight,
Which is my joy and heart's delight:
  In youth is pleasure, in youth is pleasure.
    Finis.

★ ★ ★

Hyp. The ground is the better on the which she doth go;
For she will make better cheer with that little, which she can get,
Than many a one can with a great banket of meat.
Juv. To be in her company my heart is set;
Therefore, I pray you, let us be gone.
F'ship. She will come for us herself anon;
For I told her before, where we would stand,
And then, she said she would beck us with her hand.
Juv. Now, by the mass, I perceive that she is a gallant;
What, will she take pains to come for us hither?
Hyp. Yea, I warrant you; therefore you must be familiar with her:
When she cometh in place,
You must her embrace
Somewhat handsomely;
Lest she think it danger,
Because you are a stranger,
To come in your company.
Juv. Yea, by God's foot, that I will be busy.

★ ★ ★

Hyp. What, Unknown Honesty? a word!
[*Draws A. L. aside.*
You shall not go yet, by God I swear;
Here is none but your friends, you need not to fray,
Although this strange young gentleman be here.
Juv. I trust, in me she will think no danger;
For I love well the company of fair women.
Ab. Liv. Who, you? nay, ye are such a holy man,
That to touch one ye dare not be bold;
I think, you would not kiss a young woman,
If one would give you twenty pound in gold.
Juv. Yes, by the mass, that I would;
I could find in my heart to kiss you in your smock.
Ab. Liv. My back is broad enough to bear away that mock;

For one hath told me many a time,
That you have said you would use no such wanton's company as mine.

* * *

Hyp. She did nothing else but prove,
Whether a little thing would you move
To be angry and fret;
What, and if one had said so?
Let such trifling matters go,
And be good to men's flesh for all that.
Juv. To kiss her since she came I had clean forgot:

9. Source

From *Certen brief notes apperteyning to Bushope Fisher* ("The Rastell Fragments")

By William Rastell; in Harpsfield's *Life*; edited by Elsie Vaughan Hitchcock and R. W. Chambers, 1932

Vpon this [point, and onelie by this wyttnesse of the] king*es* owne messeng*er* sent to the byshopp, w[ere the 12 men charged to find the holy lerned] byshopp gyltie of Treas[on. But before the enquest of 12 men went from the Barr to agree vpon ther verdict, there was layd to the byshopes charge, by some of his judges, high pride and great presumption, that he and a few other did dissent and vary in this matter of the kinges supremacie] from the whole nomber of the byshop*es*, lord*es*, lerned men *and* co*m*mons, gathered together [in the parlia]ment, with dyu*er*se other thing*es*. Vnto all whiche he aunswered in effect as the holy fathers [Cart]husians *and* Docto*ur* Reynold*es* had done; wherein he shewed hymeself excellentlie *and* p*r*ofowndlie [le]rned, of great co*n*stancie *and* of a m*ar*velouse godlie corage; And declared the whole matter [so] lernedlie, *and* therew*i*th so godlie, th*a*t it made many of them ther present, *and* some of his Judg*es* also, [so] inwardlie to lament, that ther eyes brast owt w*i*th teares to see such a great famouse clarke [and] vertuouse byshopp to be co*n*demned to so crewell death by such impyouse lawes *and* by such an vnlawfull *and* detestable wyttnesse, co*n*trarie to all humayne honestye *and* fidelitie *and* the word *and* p*r*omyse of the king hymeself.

But pytie, m*er*cye, equytie, nor Justice had ther no place. For the xij men gaue ther verdite th*a*t he was gyltie of the treason, whiche they did by the p*er*swasion *and* threatt*es* of some [o]f his Judg*es* *and* of the kyng*es* lerned consell; neu*er*thelesse the mostp*ar*te of the xij me*n*n did this [so]re agaynst ther owne co*n*scyence; And yet durst do no nother for feare of losse of ther owne [l]yves, w*i*th whiche they were sore manased in case they shulde haue discharged this innocent godlie byshope of Treason.

Then Imediatlie vpon this verdite that same Thursdaye, [t]he xvij day of June, was lyke Judgem*ent* of treason gyven agaynst hyme as was agaynst the holy Carthusyans, of drawing, hanging, cutting downe alyue, throwing to the ground, his bowell*es* to be taken out of his belly, *and* be burnt, he being alyve, *and* his head to be cutt of, *and* his body to be deuyded in fowre part*es*, *and* his head *and* qu*arteres* to be putt where the king shuld appoynt.

But this crewell Judgm*ent* thus gyven was not all executed on hyme. For the king p*er*doned hyme all other crewelties saving heading. And so was he onely beheaded, as you shall redde in the next chapiter. And the cause why he was but onely beheaded, was (as me*n* saye) thought not for any pitie or co*m*passion that this crewell king had on this innocent vertuouse byshop, but for th*a*t the king thought that, if he shuld be drawen on [a] hurdell throwe London to the place of execution, as the Carthusyans were, it were lykelie that he, being aged, sycke *and* very weeke, shuld dye by the waye; W*hi*che the king in no wise wold, but that the byshopp shuld suffer death by open *and* publicke execution, to the Terro*ur* of all other byshopp*es* *and* lerned devynes th*a*t shuld grudge *and* repyne at his supremacie.

Of the man*er* of the martirdom of this blissed byshoppe.

When this crewell Judgem*ent* was thus gyven agaynst hyme at Westmy*n*ster Hall, he was, parte on horsebacke *and* p*a*rte by Foot, Frome thence co*n*veyed agayne to the Tower of London, w*i*th a great nombre of officers *and* me*n*n bearing halberd*es* and wepons abowt hyme *and* before hyme *and* behynd hyme, w*i*th the axe of the Tower borne all the way before hyme, the edge toward*es* hyme, as the fashyon is in England whe*n*n any co*n*dempned of treason is brought frome Judgm*ent*.

And when he came to the Tower gate, he turned hyme unto thos that thus had brought hyme fro the Towre to Westm*inster*, *and* frome thence to the Towre agayne, *and* sayed unto the*m*: "I thanke you, Maisters all, for the paynes ye haue taken with me this day in goyng *and* comyng frome hens to Westm*inster* and hyther agayne." And this spake he w*i*th so lustie a corage *and* so amyable a countenaunce, *and* his color so well come to hyme as though he had come from a great *and* honorable fest. And his gesture *and* his behavyo*ur* shewed such a certayne inward gladnes in his hart, that any [mann] myght easelie see that he ioyouslie longed *and* looked for the blisse *and* Joyes of heaven, and [that he] inwardlie reioyced th*a*t he was so nere unto his death for Christ*es* cause.

THE HISTORY OF CARDENIO

The History of Cardenio, by Mr. Fletcher. & Shakespeare.

Hannah Birch Jr. 643.d. 841.d.32

Double Falſhood;

OR,

The DISTREST LOVERS.

A

P L A Y,

As it is Acted at the

THEATRE-ROYAL

IN

D R U R Y-L A N E.

Written Originally by *W. SHAKESPEARE*;
And now Reviſed and Adapted to the Stage
By Mr. THEOBALD, the Author of *Shakeſpeare Reſtor'd.*

——— *Quod optanti Divûm promittere nemo*
Auderet, volvenda Dies, en! attulit ultrò. Virg.

LONDON:
Printed by J. WATTS, at the Printing-Office in *Wild-Court* near *Lincolns-Inn Fields.*

M DCC XXVIII.

INTRODUCTION

The History of Cardenio was entered on the *Stationers' Register* by Humphrey Moseley on 9 September 1653. The play is stated on the register to have been written "by Mr. Fletcher. & Shakespeare." (See figure 3). It was performed at least twice at court, once during the 1612–1613 Christmas festivities and again on 13 June 1613. Lewis Theobald, the noted Shakespearean editor, who was also a less noted writer and adapter of plays, produced *Double Falshood*, or *The Distrest Lovers*, first acted on 13 December 1727 at the Drury Lane Theatre, which he said was his revision of a play by Shakespeare "built upon a Novel in *Don Quixot*." *The History of Cardenio* is lost, while *Double Falshood* survives. As a consequence of the loss of the text of the earlier play, the relationship between the two plays remains an unsolved puzzle.

Publication

If Moseley published *Cardenio* following the *Stationers' Register* entry,[1] no copy is extant. Eduard Castle conjectures that the play may have been printed but that the issue perished in the Great Fire of 1666. The writer of the lives of the dramatists in Lardner's *Cyclopaedia* says, of the dual authorship of *The Two Noble Kinsmen* and *Cardenio*, "For this assertion, there is no other evidence than the fact that when these dramas were printed (1634 and 1653), they were ascribed to both writers." Dyce's impression is that he "speak[s] of it [*Cardenio*] as if he had read it." There is no other record of such a print.[2]

Theobald published the text of his play in 1728 with the title page as shown in figure 4.[3] A "second edition," so designated on its title page, was

1. W. W. Greg, ed., *A Bibliography of the English Printed Drama to the Restoration*, 4 vols. (London: The Bibliographical Society, 1939–1959), 1:60–61; 2:981. S. Schoenbaum, *William Shakespeare: Records and Images* (New York: Oxford University Press in association with Scolar Press, 1975), p. 230. The spelling *Cardenio* is sanctioned by Shelton's translation and by the *Stationers' Register* entry, in which it is clear and eminently readable (Schoenbaum provides a photographic facsimile). Here and there in the literature, the spelling *Cardennio* occurs (for example, E. K. Chambers, *William Shakespeare: A Study of Facts and Problems*, 2 vols. [Oxford: Clarendon Press, 1930], 1:539), apparently influenced by the spellings in the Chamber accounts ("*Cardenno*" and "*Cardenna*").

2. Eduard Castle, "Theobald's *Double Falsehood* and *The History of Cardenio* by Fletcher and Shakespeare," *Ärchiv für das Studium der Neueren Sprachen und Literaturen* 169 (1936): 182–99; Dionysius Lardner, ed., *The Cabinet Cyclopaedia* (London: 1837), 2:249; Alexander Dyce, ed., *The Works of Beaumont & Fletcher* (London: 1843), 1:xliii, n. k.

3. The title page of the British Library copy has been collated with the Folger Shakespeare Library copy and with the editor's copy. There are no variants.

issued also dated 1728. This is in fact a reprint of the first edition except for the altered title page and a revised preface.[4] Later reprints were published at Dublin in 1728, and at London in 1740, 1767, and 1770.[5] C. F. Tucker Brooke briefly mentions *Cardenio* and *Double Falshood* in his *Shakespeare Apocrypha* but does not reprint the latter play. The only scholarly edition of *Double Falshood* is a modified diplomatic reprint of the first edition published by Walter Graham in 1920. The Cornmarket Press issued in 1970 a photographic facsimile of the Birmingham Shakespeare Library's copy of the first edition, with an introduction by Kenneth Muir, in its second series of adaptations of Shakespeare's plays. In an appendix, Theobald's revised preface to the second edition is reproduced from the same library's copy of that edition.[6]

Date

The History of Cardenio was probably written during the summer of 1612. As will be more fully discussed below, the tale of Cardenio and Luscinda derives from Don Quixote's Sierra Moreno adventure in Cervantes's masterpiece as translated into English by Thomas Shelton. The version by Shelton was entered on the *Stationers' Register* on 19 January 1611/1612 and subsequently published in 1612. In his dedication, which is not dated, Shelton says that he completed the work in forty days "some five or sixe yeares agoe." His translation is based on the Spanish edition published at Brussels in 1607. Thus, the English *Don Quixote* was available in print in 1612 and perhaps in manuscript form as many as three or four years earlier.[7] If Mose-

4. For the "second edition," the setting of type from the title page of the first edition was used except that the legend "*The* SECOND EDITION" is inserted between rules after the motto and before the imprint. According to contemporary notices in the press, the first edition, though dated 1728, was published late in December 1727; and the second edition was published in the middle of March 1728 (Thomas R. Lounsbury, *The Text of Shakespeare* [New York: Scribner's, 1906], p. 299; reprinted under the title *The First Editors of Shakespeare* [*Pope and Theobald*] [London: Nutt, 1906]; John Freehafer, "*Cardenio*, by Shakespeare and Fletcher," *PMLA* 84 [1969]: 501–13). Freehafer discusses the dates on pp. 508–9.

5. William Jaggard, *Shakespeare Bibliography* (Stratford-on-Avon: Shakespeare Press, 1911), pp. 303–4; H. L. Ford, *Shakespeare 1700–1740: A Collation of the Editions and Separate Plays* (Oxford: Oxford University Press, 1935), p. 141. Ford is in error in saying that the second edition is a reissue of the first except for the title page.

6. C. F. Tucker Brooke, ed., *The Shakespeare Apocrypha* (Oxford: Clarendon Press, 1908; rpt. 1967); Walter Graham, ed., *Double Falsehood*, Western Reserve Studies, vol. 1, no. 6 (Cleveland: Western Reserve University, 1920); Kenneth Muir, ed., *Double Falshood: Lewis Theobald 1728*, the second series of adaptations of Shakespeare's plays, gen. ed. H. Neville Davies (London: Cornmarket, 1970). Richard Proudfoot plans to include an edition of *Double Falshood*, ed. Brean S. Hammond, in his new *Shakespeare Apocrypha*, currently in preparation.

7. James Fitzmaurice-Kelly, ed., *The History of Don Quixote of the Mancha Translated from the Spanish of Miguel de Cervantes by Thomas Shelton* (London, 1896; rpt. New York: AMS, 1967), p. 3. References are to this edition. Fitzmaurice-Kelly gives convincing bib-

ley's authorship attribution to Fletcher and Shakespeare is accepted, then *Cardenio* is probably the first of three possible collaborations between the two poets, the other two being *Henry VIII* (*All is True*) and *The Two Noble Kinsmen*, most likely in that order. *All is True*, according to a letter of 4 July 1613 from Henry Bluett in London to his uncle, Richard Weeks, concerning the burning of the Globe to the ground "on Tuesday last" [29 June 1613], "had been acted not passing 2 or 3 times before" the disastrous fire. It was therefore a new play.[8] The approximate date of composition of *The Two Noble Kinsmen*, summer 1613, is known because it incorporates an adaptation of an antimasque first performed at Whitehall on 20 February 1613. A date in the autumn of 1612 for *Cardenio* places it before the other two plays.

Authorship

The authorship question is twofold. Scholars must first determine who wrote *Cardenio*; and, independently of that determination, it must be decided whether *Double Falshood* was composed in its entirety by Theobald, or whether it was based on the earlier play attributed to Fletcher and Shakespeare. Since the text of *Cardenio* is lost, a solution to the problem of its authorship is dependent on the slimmest evidence of any of the doubtful plays reasonably associated with Shakespeare's name.[9] Moseley's *Stationers' Register* entry of *Cardenio* crediting the play to Fletcher and Shakespeare is clear and explicit external evidence and, in the absence of any countervailing testimony, would have to be accepted, at least presumptively, as determinative of the authorship of the play. But doubts about the reliability of

liographical and lexical reasons for the identification of the edition Shelton used (pp. xxx–xxxii). In this determination, he appears to have been preceded by H. E. Watts, *Miguel de Cervantes, his Life and Works*, rev. ed. (London: Black, 1895); and supported by Edwin B. Knowles, "The First and Second Editions of Shelton's *Don Quixote* Part I: A Collation and Dating," *Hispanic Review* 9 (1941): 254 and n. 5. Andrew Gurr, in the introduction to his edition of *The Knight of the Burning Pestle* (Edinburgh: Oliver and Boyd, 1968), which he dates 1607, says, "Shelton's manuscript was in circulation for some years before it appeared in print" (p. 3). He cites as evidence the allusion to *Don Quixote* in the epistle to *The Knight* (p. 17) and similar references by Wilkins, Middleton, and Jonson between 1607 and 1609.

8. Maija Jansson Cole, "A New Account of the Burning of the Globe," *SQ* 32 (1981): 352; E. K. Chambers, *Elizabethan Stage*, 4 vols. (Oxford: Clarendon Press, 1923), 2:419–23, prints other accounts.

9. The only play credibly assigned to Shakespeare about which we know less is *Love's Labor's Won*, of which we have only the title included in a list of Shakespeare's plays by Francis Meres, *Palladis Tamia: Wits Treasury* (London: 1598); facsimile reprint edited by Don Cameron Allen (New York: Scholars' Facsimiles and Reprints, 1938). A series of excerpts, including the segment on the twelve plays, is printed by Chambers, *William Shakespeare*, 2:193–95. See also T. W. Baldwin, *Shakespeare's Love's Labor's Won* (Carbondale, Ill.: Southern Illinois University Press, 1957); and Metz, "*Wonne* is 'lost, quite lost,'" *MLS* 16 (1986): 3–12.

Moseley have been repeatedly raised. In some of his *Stationers' Register* entries, he listed what purport to be the main title and an alternate title of a single play when each is actually a title for two different plays. It has been supposed that his purpose was to secure the copyright to two plays for a single six pence entrance fee.[10] Also, he seems to have erroneously—or perhaps fraudulently—attributed at least one other play to Shakespeare—*The Merry Devil of Edmonton*—which certainly is not his. However, the eighteenth-century doubts concerning Theobald's assertion that *Double Falshood* is based on a Shakespearean original arose as a consequence of natural skepticism and as a reaction to his deteriorating reputation rather than as a question about Moseley's ascription, which almost all scholars, until recently, believed was not likely to have been known to either Theobald or his critics in 1728.[11]

Among his contemporaries, Theobald's good name had suffered because of incidents that had occurred earlier. One was the controversy that arose about a play Theobald claimed to have written entitled *The Perfidious Brother*. A city watchmaker named Henry Meystayer brought him a draft script with the request that he adapt it for the stage. Theobald judged it to be so poor that he found it necessary to rewrite it completely and had it produced as a work of his own. Meystayer promptly claimed it as his, and Theobald lamely explained that since it had been completely recast and had cost him four months' work he was entitled to take credit for it.[12] Also controversial was the publication of his frontal attack on Pope's edition of Shakespeare in his *Shakespeare Restored, or a Specimen of the many errors as well Committed as Unamended by Mr. Pope in his late edition of this poet* (1726). Theobald's book, largely devoted to *Hamlet* but touching in an appendix on almost all the plays, was greatly resented by Pope and his numerous faction. The animosity thus engendered created a situation assuring that any future work by Theobald would be scrutinized for every conceivable flaw, no matter how minute. It was in this unfavorable climate that *Double Falshood* was first produced in the following year (1727). Theobald invited critical debate in a series of notices in the press. Whatever other effect Theobald may have sought by the notices, they did draw attention to the play, which proved to be exceptionally popular.

10. For a discussion of Moseley's entry of 9 September 1653, which includes such double titles, see W. W. Greg, "The Bakings of Betsy," *Library* 2 (1911): 225–59; reprinted in *Collected Papers*, ed. J. C. Maxwell (Oxford: Clarendon Press, 1966), pp. 48–74. Greg suggests an alternative explanation of the double entries that does not impugn Moseley's honesty (*Collected Papers*, pp. 70–74).

11. Freehafer, "*Cardenio*, by Shakespeare and Fletcher," pp. 510–11, thinks that Theobald knew of the *Stationers' Register* entry. Harriet Frazier, *A Babble of Ancestral Voices* (The Hague: Mouton, 1974), p. 150, concludes that he was aware of both Moseley's entry and of the records of court performances.

12. J. Churton Collins, "Lewis Theobald," *DNB* 19: 599. See also Lounsbury, *Text of Shakespeare*, pp. 139, 142–45; and Richard Foster Jones, *Lewis Theobald* (New York: Columbia University Press, 1919), pp. 21–22.

The debate on Theobald's claim that the source play was Shakespeare's was lively, with many of the critical community, especially Pope's adherents, extremely skeptical; but Theobald's claim did not lack supporters. One, signing himself "Dramaticus," is an enthusiast of the theater. He writes, "By the unanimous Applause, with which this Play was receiv'd by considerable Audiences, for *ten* nights, the true Friends of the *Drama* had the satisfaction of seeing that *Author* [Shakespeare] restor'd to his rightful Possession of the stage." Regarding authorship, he is a believer, citing "several strong testimonies, besides the Judgment of the Gentlemen [Gildon, possibly, and Theobald], who rescu'd it from Oblivion, and prepared it for the stage, and whose Veneration for the Genius of that Author, appears, from what he [Theobald] has published in justice to him [Shakespeare], to be too sincere, to permit him [Theobald] to impose a spurious piece on the World in his [Shakespeare's] Name."[13] He does not, unfortunately, detail the "several strong testimonies."

A voice on the other side of the question is that of "a young Gentleman of *Cambridge*:"

See T———leaves the Lawyer's gainful train,
To wrack with poetry his tortur'd brain:
Fir'd, or not fir'd, to write resolves with rage,
And constant pores o'er SHAKESPEAR'S sacred page
———Then starting cries, I something will be thought:
I'll write—then—boldly swear 'twas SHAKESPEAR wrote.
Strange! he in Poetry no forgery fears,
That knows so well in Law he'd lose his ears.[14]

Though disclaiming to do so, Theobald responded to his critics in the prolegomena to his printed version, but unfortunately his remarks are general and, in some particulars, regrettably vague.[15] In his dedication to George Dodington, he notes the pleasure he feels

13. In a letter addressed "To the Author of the British Gazetteer," *The Weekly Journal: or the British Gazetteer*, 10 February 1728, p. 142. "Dramaticus" has been identified as Sir William Yonge. See Freehafer, "*Cardenio*, by Shakespeare and Fletcher," p. 509.

14. "The Modern Poets," *The Gentlemen's Magazine* 1, 11 (November 1731): 493. George Winchester Stone, Jr., identifies the author of "The Modern Poets" as Pope ("Shakespeare in the Periodicals 1700–1743," Part 2, *SQ* 3 [1952]: 321).

15. A notable example of Theobald's lack of precision is in the passage concerning the number of manuscript copies of his source play that he has. In discussing in his Preface the contentions of his opponents that it is "incredible that such a Curiosity [as a Shakespearean play] should be stifled and lost to the World for above a Century," he says, "One of the Manuscript Copies which I have, is of above Sixty Years Standing, in the Handwriting of Mr. Downes, the famous Old Prompter. . . . There is a Tradition (which I have from the Noble Person, who supply'd me with One of my Copies) that it was given by our Author, as a Present of Value, to a Natural Daughter of his. . . . Two other Copies I have, (One of which I was glad to purchase at a very good Rate,) which may not, perhaps, be quite so old as the Former; but One of Them is much more perfect, and has fewer Flaws and Interruptions in the Sense." At first reading it might appear that the manuscript in Downes's hand is different from the one presented to him by the Noble Person, and the later phrase—"Two

> from the Universal Applause which crowns this *Orphan* Play, than this Other which I take in presuming to shelter it under Your Name. I bear so dear an Affection to the Writings and Memory of SHAKESPEARE, that, as it is my good Fortune to retrieve this Remnant of his Pen from Obscurity, so it is my greatest Ambition that this Piece should be received into the Protection of such a Patron.

Dodington, he says, is a person of "*fine Discernment*" and

> a distinguish'd *Friend* of the *Muses*. . . . And from hence it is I flatter Myself, that if You shall think fit to pronounce this Piece genuine, it will silence the Censures of those *Unbelievers*, who think it impossible a Manuscript of *Shakespeare* could so long have lain dormant; and who are blindly paying Me a greater Compliment than either They design, or I can merit, while they cannot but confess Themselves *pleased*, yet would fain insinuate that they are *imposed upon*. I should esteem it some Sort of *Virtue*, were I able to commit so *agreeable a Cheat*.

He concludes with the wish that Dodington "would look with a Tender Eye on this *dear Relick*." In the editor's preface in the first edition, he tells us that the success of the play has almost made a preface unnecessary and therefore that it is in his intention "rather to wipe out a flying Objection ro [*sic*] two, than to labour at proving it the Production of *Shakespeare*."

The first objection he takes up is the allegation that a play of Shakespeare's could not have lain unnoticed for more than a century. His not very persuasive response, apparently offered in an attempt to establish a provenance, is that he has some old manuscripts, "one in the handwriting of Mr. *Downes*, the famous Old Prompter." The second objection is that since the play is based on *Don Quixote*, "Chronology is against" Shakespeare being the author, but Theobald disposes of this by reference to the date of publication of Shelton's English version. (He actually cites 1611, possibly in reliance on the *Stationers' Register* entry, which is dated "19 no Januarij 1611," that is, 1612, the year of publication.) The third objection of his opponents is the contention "that tho' the Play may have some Resemblances of *Shakespeare* yet the *Colouring, Diction*, and *Characters*, come nearer to the Style and Manner of FLETCHER." His response to this is that it "is far from deserving any Answer; I submit it to the Determination of better Judgments."

other Copies"—would seem to raise the total to four. However, the ensuing expression—"not . . . quite so old as the Former"—seems to mean that the first two copies mentioned are one and the same, making the total three. On the other hand, the word *former* need not be construed as singular—its sense could be *former ones*. It is little wonder that scholars are divided over whether Theobald says he has three or four manuscripts. Most think he meant three, but Chambers epitomizes the confusion when he alludes to "the three (or was it four?) manuscripts which Theobald claimed to possess" (*William Shakespeare*, 1 : 542). Muir, in his introduction to the Cornmarket Press facsimile, states flatly that Theobald claims that "he possessed four manuscripts of the play."

In the revised and expanded preface to the "second edition," Theobald subjoins an additional nineteen lines to the above comments, telling us that he

> had once design'd a *Dissertation* to prove this Play to be of *Shakespeare's* Writing, from some of its remarkable peculiarities in the *Language*, and Nature of the *Thoughts*: but as I could not be sure but that the Play might be attack'd I found it advisable . . . to reserve *that* Part to my *Defense*. That Danger, I think is now over, so I must look out for a better Occasion.

He has been honored with solicitations to restore Shakespeare's text in its entirety, and though "*private Property*" may prevent his producing an edition of Shakespeare, he plans to issue "his *whole* WORKS corrected. . . . This may furnish an Occasion for speaking more at large concerning the present *Play*: For which Reason I shall now drop it for another Subject." There are two other changes in the preface. He alters the passage on the publication of *Don Quixote* to cite the date of the original Spanish edition rather than that of Shelton's translation: "But it happens, that the *First* Part of *Don Quixot*, which contains the Novel upon which the Tale of this Play seems to be built, was publish'd in the Year 1605, and our *Shakespeare* did not dye till *April* 1616; an Interval of no less than Eleven Years, and more than sufficient for All that we want granted." He also revises the comment on his admiration for Shakespeare so that it reads: "tho' my Partiality for *Shakespeare* makes me wish that Every Thing which is good, or pleasing, in that other great Poet [Fletcher], had been owing to *his* Pen."

The significance of two of these three changes has been debated. Virtually no one has commented on the altered passage in regard to the date of publication of *Don Quixote*. A few critics have detected in the second alteration (the change of the expression from "Every Thing which is good, or pleasing, in our Tongue" to "Every Thing which is good, or pleasing, in that other great Poet") an inclination on the part of Theobald to retreat from his absolute rejection of Fletcher's presence in the source play. This idea was rather casually tossed off originally by Richard Foster Jones without supporting argument in his biography of Theobald.[16] In regard to the third change, some have attached significance to the fact that Theobald never published his defense of the attribution of the original play to Shakespeare, concluding that he failed to do so because it would not have been successful. There is, however, very little in either of these last two revisions by Theobald to support such relatively large conclusions. The change to allude directly to Fletcher, whom Theobald admired, may have been motivated by no more than a desire to focus more specifically on his point.

16. Jones, *Lewis Theobald*, p. 103. Jones's brief comment is that the substitution "leads me to believe Theobald saw signs of Fletcher in the play." For a review article on Jones's biography, see Edward B. Koster, *ES* 4 (1922): 20–31; 49–60.

As to his defensive dissertation, his promise to publish it is distinctly tentative and dependent on the emergence of an appropriate occasion. The difficulties he experienced in publishing his edition of Shakespeare and his concurrent time-consuming cataloging work for Lord Orrery must have left him little leisure to devote to an essay on a question he may have thought was receding into the past. One other element of evidence that may bear on the third question is the royal patent granted to him on 5 December 1727, which exhibits a license "for the sole Printing and Publishing [of *Double Falshood*] . . . for the Term of Fourteen Years." The complete text of the patent is published opposite the title page of both the first and second editions. The drawer of the patent, granted "By His Majesty's Command," appears to accept a Shakespearean play, as the source play, but this may have been based solely on Theobald's representation. He sold his patent to his publisher, John Watts, for one hundred guineas on 31 July 1728 when it still had more than thirteen years to run.[17]

Shortly after the publication of the text of *Double Falshood*, Theobald was pilloried by Pope, successively in his *Treatise on the Bathos* and in the first edition of the *Dunciad* (both 1728). "Pope's satire," Collins says, "is chiefly directed against Theobald's pedantry, dulness, poverty, and ingratitude,"[18] and some of his comments refer specifically to *Double Falshood*. Most notable of Pope's remarks (in the *Dunciad*) is an extended note on the *Double Falshood* line

> None but Itself can be its Parallel

which Pope alters to read:

> None but Thy self can be thy parallel.

He comments, "A marvellous line of *Theobald*; unless the Play call'd the *Double Falshood* be (as he would have it believed) *Shakespear's*. But whether this line be his or not, he proves *Shakespear* to have written as bad [by parallels from *Hamlet* and *The Winter's Tale*] . . . no man doubts but herein he is able to imitate *Shakespear*."[19] He appends an elaborate note on *Double*

17. Eu. Hood, "Fly Leaves.—No. XVII. Literary Contracts continued," *Gentlemen's Magazine* 94, 1 (March 1824): 223. The note reads in part: "Lewis Theobald, for one hundred guineas, on 31st of July, 1728, sold to Watts 'the copy of a play, intituled Double Falshood, or the Distrest Lovers, written originally by W. Shakspeare, and now revised and adapted to the stage by the said Lewis Theobald.' " The quoted language parallels that of the patent and the title page and leaves open the possibility that the word "copy," if it is not merely short for "copyright," may refer to one of Theobald's manuscripts. Hood has been identified as Joseph Haslewood (Freehafer, "*Cardenio*, by Shakespeare and Fletcher," p. 504, n. 27).

18. *DNB* 19: 600.

19. *The Dunciad*, The Twickenham Edition, vol. 5, ed. James Sutherland (London: Methuen; and New Haven: Yale University Press, 1943), pp. 180–82. The original *Double Falshood* line occurs at 3.1.18. A later comment by Pope on *Double Falshood* is significant. In a letter to Aaron Hill of 9 June 1738 he says, "I never supposed [the play] to be his [Theobald's]: He gave it as *Shakespear's*, and I take it to be of that Age" (*The Correspondence of Alexander Pope*, ed. George Sherburn, 5 vols. [Oxford: Clarendon Press, 1956], 4:102).

Falshood parodying Theobald's style of note-writing in *Shakespeare Restored*. In a restrained though unequivocal voice, Theobald refuted the general accusations in periodicals and in his edition of Shakespeare, and specifically in regard to *Double Falshood* in a note on a passage in *1H6*:

> I have produced these Authorities, in Reply to a Criticism of Mr. *Pope's* because, in the Gaiety of his *Wit* and *good Humour*, he was pleas'd to be very smart upon me, as he thought, for a Line, in a *posthumous* Play of our Author's which I brought upon the Stage.
> Double Falshood:
>
> > *Nought, but* itself, *can be its* Parallel.
> > It is spoken of an Action so enormous, that the Poet meant, it had no Equal upon Record. I have Shewn from Examples, that such a License in Expression was practis'd in our *English* Writers: I'll subjoin a few instances of the same Liberty, taken by the best *Roman* Classics.

He lists seven passages from Plautus, Ovid, Seneca, and Terence.[20]

In spite of Theobald's efforts, however, the debate regarding the authenticity of the Shakespearean original continued. Richard Farmer, in his *Essay on the Learning of Shakespeare*, decides that such a play could not have been the work of Shakespeare partly on the basis of the fact that in *Double Falshood* the word *aspect* is accented on the first syllable, "which I am confident, in *any* sense of it, was never the case in the time of Shakespeare . . . the *Double Falshood* is superior to Theobald . . . and from every mark of Style and Manner, I make no doubt of ascribing it to Shirley." Farmer arrived at this conclusion based on a statement by "Mr. Langbaine [who] informs us that he [Shirley] left some plays in MS. . . . Perhaps the mistake arose from an *abbreviation* of the name."[21]

David Erskine Baker notes, "Theobald endeavored to persuade the world (but with little success) [that the play] was written by Shakespeare."[22] Citing similar lines in *Double Falshood* and Massinger's *Duke of Milan*, Malone concludes that if the line were not "an interpolation of Theobald's [it] would serve to confirm Massinger's title to this play, he

20. *Works*, ed. Theobald, 7 vols. (London: 1733), 4:188.

21. Richard Farmer, *An Essay on the Learning of Shakespeare* (1767); reprinted in *Eighteenth Century Essays on Shakespeare*, edited by D. Nichol Smith (Glasgow, 1903). Smith's collection was reprinted (New York: Russell, 1962), pp. 179–81; Gerard Langbaine, *An Account of the English Dramatick Poets* (Oxford, 1691; rpt. New York: Burt Franklin, n.d.), p. 475. In his discussion of the accent on *aspect*, Farmer appears not to have taken into account the effects of Theobald's adaptation. See Weber, *The Works of Beaumont and Fletcher*, 1:xxiv; and Gamaliel Bradford, Jr., "*The History of Cardenio* by Mr. Fletcher and Shakespeare," *MLN* 25 (1910): 51–56.

22. David Erskine Baker, *Biographia Dramatica; or, A Companion to the Playhouse* (London: 1764; continued to 1782 by Isaac Reed, and to 1811 by Stephen Jones, 3 vols., London: 1812), 2:173.

having very frequently imitated Shakespeare."[23] Henry Weber rejects the proposed authorship of *Cardenio* by Shirley or Massinger, since they were not writing for the stage circa 1613 and thinks that "the testimony of the Stationers' Books does not appear questionable with regard to Fletcher . . . [that] Shakspeare . . . is more doubtful; but, if we admit that he assisted Fletcher in The Two Noble Kinsmen, the matter will not be altogether improbable."[24] Dyce notes that Farmer ascribes the play to Shirley and adds that "internal evidence corroborates his conjecture," but he does not detail the internal evidence.[25] J. O. Halliwell-Phillips leans against Theobald's ascription because the history of the manuscripts "is not satisfactory."[26]

Fleay, in his *Biographical Chronicle of the English Drama*, cites the *Stationers' Register* entry as to authorship; but he equates *The History of Cardenio* with Shirley's *Love's Pilgrimage* chiefly because the latter has a character named Cardenas, which he thinks is equivalent to Cardenio.[27] Churton Collins, after briefly reviewing the opinions of earlier critics on the origin of *Double Falshood*, concludes, "To the present writer it seems all but certain that it was founded on some old play, the plot being borrowed from the story of Cardenio in 'Don Quixote,' but that it is for the most part from Theobald's own pen." Earlier he had raised a doubt about Theobald's responsibility for the memorable "parallel" line.[28] Sir Sidney Lee thinks the evidence for a Shakespearean cooperation with Fletcher in *Cardenio* "too slender to admit of a conclusion. . . . The title of the play leaves no doubt that it was a dramatic version of the adventures of the lovelorn Cardenio which are related in the first part of *Don Quixote* . . . [but] there is no evidence of Shakespeare's acquaintance with Cervantes' great work." He makes brief mention of *Double Falshood* but finds "nothing in the play . . . to suggest Shakespeare's hand."[29] William Jaggard finds *Double Falshood* to be the earliest fraud that was "seriously accepted as Shakespeare's work . . . no small compliment to Theobald," who deceived

23. Edmond Malone, *Supplement to the Edition of Shakespeare's Plays Published in 1778 by Samuel Johnson and George Steevens*, 2 vols. (London: 1780), 2:718–19.

24. Henry Weber, ed., *Works of Beaumont and Fletcher*, 14 vols. (Edinburgh: 1812), 1:xxiii–xxiv.

25. In "Some Account of Shirley and his Writings" prefaced to Dyce's and William Gifford's edition of *The Dramatic Works and Poems of James Shirley*, 6 vols. (London: 1833; rpt. New York: Russell, 1966), 1:lix–lxi. Dyce reiterates the ascription to Shirley in his edition of *The Works of Beaumont and Fletcher*, 11 vols. (London: 1843–1846), 1:xlii–xliv.

26. J. O. Halliwell-Phillips, *Outlines of the Life of Shakespeare*, 7th ed, 2 vols. (London: 1887), 2:413–14.

27. Fleay, *Biographical Chronicle*, 2 vols. (London: 1891; rpt. New York: Franklin, 1969), 1:194.

28. Collins, *DNB* 19: 600, and "The Porson of Shakspearian Criticism," in *Essays and Studies* (London: 1895), p. 313.

29. Sir Sidney Lee, *A Life of William Shakespeare*, 14th ed. (London: Macmillan, 1931; rpt. New York: Dover, 1968), pp. 437–39.

Farmer and Malone, but Reed "discovered Theobald's handiwork, and denounced him."[30]

A new voice was heard on the question of the authorship of *Cardenio* in 1909 (preliminarily) and 1910 (more comprehensively), that of Gamaliel Bradford.[31] He denies the validity of the attribution of *Double Falshood* to Shirley and to Massinger and says, surprisingly, that the great body of critical authority has dismissed the supposition that the piece was the composition of Theobald himself. He points out that betrayal of friendship forms the subject of *The Two Noble Kinsmen* as well as *Double Falshood*, that the madness of Julio is the counterpart of that of the Jailer's Daughter, and that Fletcher was fond of going to Cervantes for plots.[32] The characterization is the type familiar in dramatic romances, including those of Fletcher and Shakespeare. The question of style is of paramount importance. The early part of *Double Falshood*, from the beginning through 3.2, is Theobald's minutely altered version of the source play, everything flattened to the level of eighteenth-century commonplace. Yet beneath "this obscuring haze" the reader can "distinguish another touch, firm, vivid, masculine, high-wrought, imaginative, all the more marked for standing out so strongly against the emptiness that surrounds it." Bradford cannot be positive about the identity of the writer.

Another hand appears beginning at 3.3. Under Theobald's revision Bradford finds the style of Fletcher. He supports his case with examples of lexical, structural, and metrical features characteristic of Fletcher's plays. In the latter part of the play he finds an intermingling of the two styles.

> We have, then, in *Double Falshood* a play on a subject supposed to have been treated by Shakespeare and Fletcher [in *Cardenio*] containing in one portion many Elizabethan touches quite different from Fletcher, in another distinct portion many more touches so Fletcherian that it is difficult to believe them not Fletcher's.

Perhaps Theobald wrote the play in imitation of Fletcher, and possibly in imitation of Shakespeare, but this seems improbable since it is unlikely that he knew of the *Cardenio* records; and if he did, why did he fail to cite them in support of his authorship contention? He concludes that his evidence does not prove Shakespeare's association with either *Cardenio* or *Double Falshood*, but he believes that in the latter we have "the remains of a play which was almost indisputably Fletcher's" and which has "at least some claim to be classed among Fletcher's collaborations" with Shakespeare. At

30. William Jaggard, *Shakespearean frauds* (Stratford-on-Avon: Shakespeare Press, 1911; rpt. Folcroft, Pa.: Folcroft Library Editions, 1972), pp. 1–2.

31. Bradford, "*The History of Cardenio* by Mr. Fletcher and Shakespeare." He first enunciated his view in "*The History of Cardenio*," *Nation* 88 (1909): 328.

32. Bradford cites Orie Latham Hatcher, *John Fletcher: A Study in Dramatic Method* (Chicago: University of Chicago Press, 1905; rpt. New York: Haskell, 1973), pp. 47–53.

a later date, in writing to Graham, Bradford says that he "cannot resist the conviction that they [passages in the first two acts and a half] are Shakespeare" because they exhibit "that peculiar elaboration and intricacy of style, of the invention and distortion of words, which is at once the charm and the danger of Shakespeare's later manner."[33]

In 1911, Rudolph Schevill, as a corollary to a *Double Falshood* source study to be discussed below, concluded that Theobald had drawn on an analogue of the Cardenio story published in 1729 that is clearly of contemporary origin and therefore that he had no Elizabethan manuscripts and must himself be the author of the play.[34] Robert Forsythe dismisses the charges of forgery against Theobald since "there is no reason to believe that Theobald did not have the MSS. which he claimed to possess." No reasonable attempt can be made to determine the original authorship of the play because of the "unmistakeable signs of Theobald's hand throughout." Citing Collins's judgment as "most just," and in view of Theobald's facility as a writer of blank verse, Forsythe concludes, "A considerable part [of the play] is Theobald's."[35]

Graham accepted and supported Bradford's view of the authorship question in a 1916 article, the substance of which he later incorporated into the introduction to his edition of *Double Falshood*.[36] Graham's support consists primarily of a series of verse tests, such as measures of feminine endings, run-on lines, and weak and light endings. Using these tests he compares *Double Falshood* to Theobald's *Persian Princess*, *Electra*, and *Orestes*; the two segments of *Double Falshood* against each other; and separately against the Shakespeare and Fletcher segments of *Henry VIII* and *The Two Noble Kinsmen*.[37] His conclusions are that *Double Falshood* shows an appreciable variance from Theobald's dramatic compositions both earlier and later; that there is a real stylistic difference between the two parts of *Double Falshood* as Bradford distinguished them; and that the metrical tests support Moseley's assignment of *Cardenio* "correctly to Fletcher, at least, if not to Shakespere." Though Graham acknowledges the limitations of metrical

33. Bradford, "*The History of Cardenio* by Mr. Fletcher and Shakespeare," pp. 55–56; Graham, *Double Falsehood*, p. 19.

34. Rudolph Schevill, "Theobald's *Double Falsehood?*" *MP* 9 (1911): 269–85.

35. Robert Stanley Forsythe, *The Relations of Shirley's Plays to the Elizabethan Drama* (New York: Columbia University Press, 1914; rpt. New York: Blom, 1965), pp. 431–33.

36. Walter Graham, "The *Cardenio-Double Falsehood* Problem," *MP* 14 (1916): 269–80; and *Double Falsehood*, pp. 8–24. There are typographical errors of some consequence in the *MP* article that Graham corrected in a subsequent note. See "Note on the *Cardenio-Double Falsehood* Problem," *MP* 15 (1917): 568.

37. Graham, "The *Cardenio-Double Falsehood* Problem," p. 277 n., uses the division of *Henry VIII* between Shakespeare and Fletcher as determined by Ashley H. Thorndike, *The Influence of Beaumont and Fletcher on Shakspere* (Worcester, Mass.: Wood, 1901; rpt. New York: AMS, 1966), pp. 40–41; and the division of *The Two Noble Kinsmen* by William A. Neilson and Ashley H. Thorndike, *The Facts about Shakespeare* (New York: Macmillan, 1913), p. 160.

studies of an adapted text, he nevertheless concludes, "From these investigations . . . the following facts seem to be established: (1) The immediate source of *Double Falshood* was Shelton's *Don Quixote.* (2) The style of the play as a whole, and the second part in particular, differs appreciably from Theobald's acknowledged work. (3) There are unmistakable evidences of two styles. (4) These distinct styles show a general similarity to those in *Two Noble Kinsmen* and *Henry VIII*, which are now recognized as belonging to Shakspere and Fletcher."[38]

E. H. C. Oliphant three years later (1919) undertook, at Bradford's suggestion, a fresh assessment of the authorship question.[39] After a brief discussion of the sparse external evidence, he turns to an examination of Theobald's claims. Three charges have been adduced against Theobald: the unlikelihood of his having three manuscripts; the question concerning their disappearance; and the omission of the play from his edition of Shakespeare. As to the first, Oliphant thinks it only natural that Theobald would have sought out all available copies to support and protect his claim for a royal patent. The disappearance of the manuscripts is not unusual; other old play manuscripts have disappeared. The absence of the play from his edition of Shakespeare can be explained as a precaution to protect his patent.[40] He concludes that there is no sound reason for doubting Theobald's honesty. Next he examines Moseley's *Cardenio* attribution. Oliphant acknowledges Moseley's peccadilloes and that the authorship ascription is late, but he says there are reasons for accepting the *Stationers' Register* entry as genuine. First, Moseley is not known to have deliberately misassigned any play; second, there are the records of the performances of 1612–1613 by the King's Men, the acting company for which both Shakespeare and Fletcher wrote their plays; third, the production of *Cardenio* synchronizes with the production of the supposed collaborative plays, *Henry VIII* and *The Two Noble Kinsmen*; and, fourth, these facts fit in with Theobald's contentions. Moseley did not include *Cardenio* in the 1647 Beaumont and Fletcher folio because he did not have it until 1653, and the 1679 folio added only previously published plays. Similarly, the first two Shakespeare folios were too early, and the second issue of the third folio (1664) added only

38. Graham, "*Cardenio-Double Falsehood*," pp. 270–74; 279; 280.

39. E. H. C. Oliphant, "*Double Falsehood*: Shakespeare, Fletcher and Theobald," *N&Q* 164 (1919): 30–32, 60–62, 86–88. Included in revised and expanded form in *The Plays of Beaumont and Fletcher* (New Haven: Yale University Press; London: Oxford University Press, 1927; rpt. New York: Phaeton, 1970), pp. 284–90.

40. Oliphant does not mention that Theobald sold his patent in 1728 to Watts, five years before his edition of Shakespeare (1733). This circumstance supports Oliphant's contention, since Theobald would be doubly obligated to protect Watts's title. Freehafer, "*Cardenio*, by Shakespeare and Fletcher," pp. 211–13, discusses the significance of the patent itself. See also Giles E. Dawson, "The Copyright of Shakespeare's Dramatic Works," in *Studies in Honor of A. H. R. Fairchild*, edited by Charles T. Prouty (Columbia: University of Missouri Studies, 1946), pp. 9–35, especially pp. 26–28.

previously published plays attributed to Shakespeare. Theobald's rejection of the suggestion that *Double Falshood* is reminiscent of Fletcher shows his sincerity, because if he had known of Moseley's attribution he would certainly have welcomed such a suggestion. His rejection amounts to the denial of an argument favorable to his cause. Oliphant finds the ascriptions to Shirley and Massinger unacceptable, but he is reminded in some places of Beaumont, though not so strongly as to suppose him to be involved. If *Double Falshood* is to be considered a forgery by Theobald, it must be assumed that, though he knew nothing of the collaboration of Shakespeare and Fletcher on *Cardenio*, halfway through his play he abruptly changed style and wrote a remarkable imitation of Fletcher. Acceptance of such a theory is too much for Oliphant, who prefers to believe that *Double Falshood* was "genuinely based on an Elizabethan drama . . . the early author of the latter portion . . . must on internal evidence be set down as Fletcher . . . [and] if so much be granted, we are faced with the possibility that Fletcher's collaborator . . . was Shakespeare."[41]

In his 1920 edition of *Double Falshood*, Graham reexamines the authorship debate, weighing all the arguments raised to prove that Theobald composed the play, most of which he disposes of by reference to Bradford's and Oliphant's studies. "Most modern scholars who have investigated the matter see no real reason for attributing the authorship of the piece to Theobald, altho on his own testimony it is known that he made revisions and additions." This conclusion, however, does not prove that it is Shakespeare's and Fletcher's. In his summation entitled "The Problem as it Stands Today," he finds that

> the presence of Fletcher's hand in the play seems clearly evident, and there may also be sufficient proof to warrant our attributing parts of the drama to him. . . . The external evidence confirms this view, and on the whole, may be said to establish a sound case for Fletcher. Since this external evidence makes Shakespeare Fletcher's collaborator, it renders probable the supposition that the other original writer, whose work is still perceptible in the lines, is our great master-dramatist. Yet in spite of the evidence, internal and external, which has been accumulated, no scholar is yet ready to declare unreservedly his belief in Shakespeare's participation. . . . The whole matter may forever remain what it is at the present time—one of the most fascinating and baffling of literary problems.[42]

Sir Edmund Chambers ponders the contradictory behavior of Theobald particularly in not publishing the unadapted Elizabethan text; the disappearance of the manuscripts; the external evidence, such as it is; and the opinions of scholars. He sums up, "On the whole, with the *Cardenio* rec-

41. Oliphant, "*Double Falsehood*," p. 87.
42. Graham, *Double Falsehood*, pp. 11, 23–24.

ord and Moseley's statement to go upon, it seems to me less likely that Theobald was responsible for a fabrication, than that he had an old play of some sort . . . [but] it does not follow that Shakespeare had anything to do with the play. I cannot share Oliphant's confidence in Moseley on this point. The play itself, as it stands [*Double Falshood*], is a very poor one. And while I can see traces that may well be Fletcher's, I cannot find a single passage which compels a belief in Shakespeare."[43]

Alfred Harbage, in an important essay designed to establish the relationship between Elizabethan manuscript plays and Restoration adaptations, which he thinks were more numerous than previously suspected, sets out to trace the provenance of the significant body of earlier dramatic manuscripts, known to have been in the possession of Richard Marriott, Francis Kirkman, and, most important, Humphrey Moseley, about the time of the Restoration. One of Moseley's manuscripts was *The History of Cardenio*, listed in the 1653 *Stationers' Register* entry as by Fletcher and Shakespeare. Harbage thinks "the ascription of authorship is fairly credible in view of the collaboration of Fletcher and Shakespeare in 1613." He sees no reason to doubt that Theobald got hold of the Moseley manuscript, or copies of it, and even his account of how he obtained the manuscript may have a reasonable explanation. The "natural daughter" of the tradition relayed by the noble person from whom Theobald received one of his copies is "otherwise unknown, but possibly Mary Davenant is indicated. . . . In the early eighteenth century Sir William Davenant [Mary's husband] was rumoured to have been Shakespeare's illegitimate son: Theobald may have been guilty only of misconstruing and elaborating common gossip." Mary, "as the widow of Sir William Davenant, active about the theatre long after her husband's death . . . is not at all unlikely to have possessed such a relic."[44]

John Cadwalader reprints a Theobald letter in support of the belief that he actually had a manuscript of Shakespeare's day. The letter, dated 10 December 1727, three days before the play's premier, is addressed to the Countess of Oxford enclosing "twelve box tickets" for Theobald's benefit and asking her to "disperse them." A postscript reads, "If your Honour has any mind to read the play in manuscript, upon the earliest intimation of your pleasure you shall command it."[45] In regard to this offer, Harbage

43. Chambers, *William Shakespeare*, 1:542.

44. Alfred Harbage, "Elizabethan-Restoration Palimpsest," *MLR* 35 (1940): 287–319. Reprinted in *Shakespeare Without Words and Other Essays* (Cambridge: Harvard University Press, 1972), pp. 170–218. Harbage makes much of the practice of Restoration adapters of rewriting Elizabethan plays without acknowledging their source plays, but he does not cite Theobald's acknowledgment of his source as an evidence of his honesty.

45. John Cadwalader, "Theobald's Alleged Shakespeare Manuscript," *MLN* 55 (1940): 108–9. Cited from the catalog of manuscripts of the Duke of Portland by the Historical Manuscripts Commission (vol. 29, part 6, p. 20).

comments, "It is well worth noting that Theobald was willing to exhibit the old manuscript upon which *Double Falsehood* was based."[46] Cadwalader and Harbage rely on a phrase in the opening sentence of the letter ("I have the good fortune to introduce an original play of Shakespeare to the town") to identify the "manuscript" of the postscript with *Cardenio*, but some critics think Theobald refers to the manuscript of his adaptation.

Baldwin Maxwell believes there is every reason to question the ascription of *Cardenio* to Fletcher and Shakespeare by the "ambitious publisher Humphrey Moseley" because of his insincere or misinformed assignment of other doubtful plays to Shakespeare. The only evidence for collaboration is the fact that both playwrights wrote plays for the same company.[47] Leonard Schwartzstein compares passages in *Double Falshood* with similar lines in Shakespeare and decides that they are verbal and situational echoes suggesting "deliberate imitation of Shakespeare on the part of someone" not named. Marco Mincoff thinks that "there is very good reason indeed to suppose that Theobald was working from a genuine original by the pair."[48]

Sir Walter Greg briefly summarizes his findings in regard to *Cardenio*: "Moseley's attributions though most likely derived from the manuscripts, do not always carry weight. However, Cervantes's tale, with altered names, supplies the plot of a play called *Double Falsehood*. . . . Revised and Adapted to the Stage by Mr. Theobald. . . . In spite of some improbabilities in Lewis Theobald's account, there seems no sufficient reason to doubt that he based his version on an early manuscript, perhaps bearing an ascription to Shakespeare, or to believe that he was perpetrating 'so agreeable a Cheat' as that of which, even at the time, he was accused. His indignant repudiation of the suggestion that the original might have been by Fletcher precludes our supposing that he had somehow acquired Moseley's manuscript or even knew of his entrance."[49]

Kenneth Muir finds Theobald's account of his "three or four" Shakespearean manuscripts vague and not above suspicion. It is especially strange that he did not include the play in his edition of Shakespeare unless it be assumed that he changed his mind about the authorship.

> But, when all allowances have been made, it is remarkable, to say the least, that, if the play was Theobald's own, he should have chosen for his plot one which the author of *Cardenio* used, for there is no reason to

46. Harbage, "Palimpsest," p. 297.

47. Baldwin Maxwell, *Studies in Beaumont, Fletcher and Massinger* (Chapel Hill: University of North Carolina Press, 1939; rpt. New York: Octagon, 1974), pp. 56–57.

48. Leonard Schwartzstein, "The Text of *The Double Falsehood*," *N&Q* 199 (1954): 471–72; M. Mincoff, "The Authorship of *The Two Noble Kinsmen*," *Englische Studien* 33 (1952): 97–115. The passage cited is on p. 99.

49. W. W. Greg, *The Shakespeare First Folio* (Oxford: Clarendon Press, 1955), pp. 98–99.

> believe that he knew of the Court performances—he denied that the play had ever been acted—and if he had known of Moseley's entry he would have used it to support the play's authenticity, rather than have denied that Fletcher had had a hand in it.

Fletcher has been generally recognized, especially in the last two acts, which are less adulterated by Theobald. In the non-Fletcherian part of *Double Falshood*, there are wholesale echoes of Shakespeare, some manifest (from *Hamlet*, *Troilus and Cressida*, and *Romeo and Juliet*), others that seem to be clever reflections of Shakespeare's style in his last period. While it is clearly impossible to come to any definite conclusions about the play,

> it seems more likely that Theobald was working on an old manuscript than that he knew of Moseley's entry of *Cardenio* and that he composed scenes in two different styles while asserting Shakespeare's sole authorship. He probably believed at first that the play was by Shakespeare, but was afterwards sufficiently shaken in his view not to include the play in his edition of Shakespeare. If, indeed, he had one or more manuscripts, there would be strong reason to believe that *Double Falshood* was a debased version of *Cardenio*, and equally strong reasons for believing that the original authors were Shakespeare and Fletcher.

Critics have endeavored to escape this conclusion and have suggested other Jacobean playwrights, but "there is no need to argue the case against any of these dramatists, since there is no evidence, either internal or external, that any of them had a hand in *Cardenio*." Muir's conclusion, hedged with reservations, is that the lost *Cardenio* was the play that Theobald adapted.[50]

Clifford Leech's reading of *Double Falshood* leads him to believe that

50. Kenneth Muir, "Cardenio," *Etudes Anglaises* 11 (1958): 202–9. Reprinted with modifications as chapter 8 of Muir's *Shakespeare as Collaborator* (London: Methuen, 1960), pp. 148–60. Quotations in the text are from the book. In subsequent papers, Muir analyzes Theobald's adaptation of *Richard II* for the light it might shed on the *Cardenio–Double Falshood* problem, but he draws no conclusions ("Three Shakespearean Adaptations," *Proceedings of the Leeds Philosophical and Literary Society* 8 [1959]: 233–40); and calls attention to the presence in Shakespeare's romances and "strangely . . . in Theobald's *Double Falsehood*" of internal rhyme, perfect or imperfect, in the same or in successive lines ("A Trick of Style and Some Implications," *ShakS* 6 [1970]: 305–10). In his introduction to the Cornmarket Press facsimile, Muir adds, "There are signs that Henriquez's long speech on p. 14 [of *Double Falshood*] was originally in verse, as it contains ten lines of verse, printed as prose. Theobald's revising hand may be at work here. The stratagem of the hearse on p. 46, which is not in *Don Quixote*, is not properly developed, and there seems to be little point in reintroducing the hearse on p. 55. Perhaps the purpose has been blurred in Theobald's adaptation." Curt A. Zimansky, in a review of Muir's *Etudes Anglaises* paper, adds to the evidence on Theobald's manuscripts by calling attention to Gildon's comments in *The Post-Man Robb'd of his Mail* (1719) about a play by Shakespeare and Beaumont and Fletcher (see below, n. 56); but he also asserts that Theobald "made no reference to [*Double Falshood*] when editing Shakespeare," which is not a fact. In addition, he accepts Jones's conjecture that Theobald did not believe the play to be Shakespeare's and arrives at a novel conclusion: "Theobald was telling a partial truth, but thought he was lying" (*PQ* 38 [1959]: 358–59).

Cardenio is "a play to which Shakespeare made some contribution while the total effect was closer to that characteristic of Fletcher's work." Scholars who have examined *Double Falshood* "have come to a position of near-unanimity in deciding that the first half of the play contains passages with 'something of a Shakespearean turn' . . . [in] Bradford's expression. . . . If it is correct that the beginning was at least partially Shakespeare's, the ending Fletcher's, there may be a special interest in the fact that" *Double Falshood* may have been linked with *All's Well That Ends Well*, *The Winter's Tale*, *Cymbeline*, and *Philaster*. Leech correctly doubts that this throws light on authorship, but, for what it is worth, it is reminiscent of Fletcher's practice in other undoubted plays of his. "The conclusion does indeed seem irresistible that Theobald made some use of a Jacobean original and that this was either identical with or derivative from the play performed at court and the play entered by Moseley. In addition, Moseley's evidence along with the suggestions of Shakespeare's style in the first half of the play point—though not conclusively—to a collaboration between Shakespeare and Fletcher."[51]

Under the rubric "Shakespearean Frauds and Forgeries," Louis Marder, the chronicler of Shakespeare's reputation, discusses *Double Falshood.* No copy of *Cardenio* had ever been found, so Theobald apparently took steps to supply one. Even though he claimed to have four manuscript copies, he did not include the play in his edition of Shakespeare nor did he publish it in its original form or show it to anyone. It is not mentioned in the catalog issued at the sale of his library after his death. Thus, even the external circumstances point to a fraud.[52]

In his book on *The Two Noble Kinsmen*, Paul Bertram devotes a chapter to "*Cardenio* and Theobald."[53] Because his thesis is that Shakespeare is the sole author of *The Two Noble Kinsmen* and because the posited collaboration of Shakespeare and Fletcher in the composition of both *Cardenio* and *Henry VIII* is often cited as supporting evidence for a similar collaboration on *The Two Noble Kinsmen*, he brings a large measure of skepticism to an assessment of the *Cardenio-Double Falshood* authorship question. He examines the studies by Bradford, Oliphant, and Graham, the summary opinions offered by Chambers and Greg, and Muir's analysis. He quotes from Jones's biography of Theobald in which doubt is cast on Theobald's bona fides because of his manifest inconsistencies, then elaborates, under the heading of "An Explanation" (pp. 186–89), a comprehensive discussion of Theobald's behavior in connection with *Double Falshood*. The substance of

51. Clifford Leech, *The John Fletcher Plays* (Cambridge: Harvard University Press, 1962), pp. 150–53.

52. Louis Marder, *His Exits and His Entrances: The Story of Shakespeare's Reputation* (London: Murray; and Philadelphia: Lippincott, 1964), pp. 213–15.

53. Paul Bertram, *Shakespeare and The Two Noble Kinsmen* (New Brunswick: Rutgers University Press, 1965), chapter 4, pp. 180–96.

his explanation is that Theobald knew full well that at least part of *Cardenio* was written by Fletcher, that Shakespeare did not write any part of it, and that Theobald dishonestly repudiated Fletcher's participation because it would have weakened his attribution to Shakespeare. His motive was financial. If his original manuscript "had been costly, he wished to recoup his original losses [*sic*]." His behavior is described as "venal," and Bertram speculates that he may have "perhaps liquidated his manuscripts." He says, in summation,

> The lingering belief in Shakespeare's co-authorship . . . is based primarily upon four assumptions: (1) That Shakespeare and Fletcher collaborated on *Henry VIII* and *The Two Noble Kinsmen* near the time *Cardenio* was first acted . . . (2) That Theobald's *Double Falsehood* was based on *Cardenio* . . . (3) That the absence of dialogue in *Double Falsehood* that can seriously be claimed for Shakespeare is due to a sweeping revision of *Cardenio* by Theobald . . . (4) That Theobald's denial of Fletcher's connection with *Double Falshood* tends to validate the 1653 Moseley attribution of *Cardenio* to Shakespeare and Fletcher.

He rejects three of these, but of the second he says, "This assumption is very probably correct." His conclusion is that "Theobald's behavior is easily intelligible on the hypothesis of Jones and others that his repudiation of Fletcher was insincere, and the most reasonable position with respect to the authorship of *Cardenio* is that, whoever wrote the play, Shakespeare had nothing to do with it."[54]

John Freehafer, in a closely reasoned essay, sets forth suggested solutions to almost all the puzzles associated with the authorship of *Cardenio-Double Falshood*.[55] Theobald's account of the manuscript in Downes's hand he finds "altogether plausible" (p. 502). Betterton was associated with Downes for many years, and Theobald's statement about Betterton must be true for several reasons: he had been active in the theater virtually until his death in 1710; actors who had known him were still alive in 1727; and his protégé, Barton Booth, actually played the part of Julio during the last few performances of the first run of *Double Falshood*. The assertion that the play was considered for production immediately after the Restoration is persuasive since Betterton successfully portrayed, in *Hamlet* and in Fletcher's *Mad Lover*, parts similar to Cardenio, and furthermore Shakespeare's and Fletcher's other two collaborations had been produced (in 1663 and 1664). Theobald's statement, applied by implication to the manuscript

54. Ibid., pp. 195–96. Bertram's challenge to the scholarly advocates of a partial Shakespearean authorship of *Cardenio* is a useful testing of the validity of that judgment. At the minimum, it makes clear the dimensions of the problem. However, the thrust of his counterargument is vitiated to some degree by his thesis, that Shakespeare is the sole author of *The Two Noble Kinsmen*, which seems to predispose him against Shakespearean collaboration in any play.

55. Freehafer, "*Cardenio*, by Shakespeare and Fletcher," *passim*.

in Downes's hand, that it had "Flaws and Interruptions in the Sense," suggests that it was cut and perhaps altered for performance. Freehafer decides that the Downes manuscript is the one that the "Noble Person . . . supply'd" to Theobald, and the tradition of the natural daughter refers, as Harbage suggested, to Lady Mary Davenant, who succeeded her husband as manager of the Duke's Company and was in turn succeeded in that capacity by Betterton. Charles Gildon, Freehafer believes, was referring to *Cardenio* in his complaint about actor-managers because he explicitly cites a play written by Beaumont and Fletcher and by "the immortal Shakespeare" a few years before he died. Gildon also says that there is infallible proof that the copy is genuine, but he does not say what the proof is. Presumably it was Gildon himself, although he alludes to "a Friend," who offered the play for production and suffered rejection due to the ignorant management of the players.[56] He was well known to Charles Boyle, Lord Orrery (to whom he dedicated a book), who was also Theobald's patron. Freehafer identifies Charles's son, the fifth Earl, as the "Noble Person" of Theobald's preface. The provenance of the Downes manuscript would thus be as follows (p. 504): at Moseley's death (January 1661), *Cardenio*, among other plays, came into the possession of Davenant, who was seeking pre-Restoration plays for his newly reconstituted acting company; he had Downes prepare a fair copy of a previously cut and probably altered acting version based on Moseley's manuscript; Davenant left it, along with other manuscripts, to his widow, from whom it passed through the hands of Betterton to Gildon, who bought it along with other manuscripts at Betterton's death; and it passed from Gildon to Boyle, who presented it to Theobald. Of the other manuscripts, we know less except that one, as Theobald says in his preface, "has fewer Flaws and Interruptions in the Sense," which indicates that it is Moseley's uncut manuscript, or a copy of it. The fact that *Cardenio* was never published does not prove to Freehafer that the play was not the work of Shakespeare and Fletcher. Theobald's omission of it from his edition of Shakespeare is explained by the fact that under the copyright laws and the customs of the time, it was not his to print since he had sold the rights to Watts. Perhaps Theobald could have

56. Charles Gildon, *The Post-Man Robb'd of his Mail: or, the Packet Broke Open* (London: 1719; rpt. New York: Garland, 1972), Letter 13, pp. 264–68. The pertinent passage in the letter reads, "By this Means [that is, selecting plays for production by a throw of the dice] a valuable Jewel, Lately brought to them by a Friend of mine, might have had a Chance of obliging the Town with a noble Diversion. I mean, a Play written by *Beaumont and Fletcher*, and the immortal *Shakespear*, in the Maturity of his Judgment, a few Years before he dy'd. A Piece so excellent, that a Gentleman, who is allow'd a Master of the Stage, tells me, that after reading it seven times, it pleas'd and transported him, and that it is far beyond any of the Collegue Poets [Beaumont and Fletcher], and inferior to few of the other Poets [Shakespeare] which are in Print. There is infallible Proof that the Copy is genuine; yet this Rarity, this noble Piece of Antiquity, cannot make its way to the Stage, because a Person that is concern'd in it, is a Person, who of all Persons Mr. C_____ [Colley Cibber] does not approve."

secured Watts's consent, but he was probably inhibited from seeking it because he, in company with other contemporary scholars, had accepted the canon as determined by the Shakespeare First Folio. Furthermore, in keeping with the practice of the time, once he had published his adapted text, the original "incorrect" version was superseded. The internal evidence for authorship, Freehafer says, is incomplete. *Double Falshood* probably represents a heavily cut and rearranged *Cardenio*. The result is little more than half as long as most of the First Folio plays and most of the cuts, combinations of scenes, rearrangements, and some resulting aborted motifs occur in the first half, the Shakespearean part, in which the taste of the age would have called for drastic alteration. Fletcher's part required less. Theobald made similar "sweeping changes" (p. 505) when he adapted *Richard II*, because Theobald believed Shakespeare knew little of the true rules of art.[57] Theobald made the changes because of a tradition of substantial revision of Shakespeare, a need to cater to the current taste, and a desire for success and thus for financial gain. Freehafer points out that it has been well known that Theobald had earlier imitated Shakespeare, and some have thought this proof that he did so in *Double Falshood*. Parallels to canonical plays have been cited in support of this contention, but Freehafer says that the passages cited, which are certainly reminiscent of Shakespeare, are mingled with elements from Shelton's story of Cardenio and Luscinda and this would tend to show that they are the work of Shakespeare rather than Theobald. Evidence for Fletcher's participation—feminine endings, alliteration, repetition, Fletcherian turns of action, Fletcherian characters, especially the two old fathers who are not significant in *Don Quixote*—is strong enough to have won general scholarly acceptance. There is some external evidence of the collaboration. The three commentators who "examined the manuscripts of *Cardenio*" (p. 508) and who left evidence—Moseley, Gildon, and Theobald—speak of Shakespeare and Fletcher, or of Shakespeare and Beaumont and Fletcher, in discussing the playwrights. Moseley's entry is particularly significant because he was the publisher of Fletcher, not of Shakespeare. The punctuation of the entry, especially the period after Fletcher's name, seems to indicate that Shakespeare's name was added as an afterthought.[58] Freehafer carefully weighs what little evidence there is tending to establish Theobald's knowledge of Fletcher's presence in *Cardenio* and concludes that it is likely that Theobald knew of Moseley's *Stationers' Register* entry. He learned about it, however, after he had already

57. "Our *Shakespeare*, with all his easy Nature about him, for want of the Knowledge of the true Rules of Art, falls frequently into this vicious Manner [the ostentatious Affectation of abstruse Learning]" (*Works*, ed. Theobald, 1:xlvi–xlvii).

58. Too much should not be read into the punctuation of the *Stationers' Register* entry. The pointing of the titles of other plays in the same entry could support a contention that the variable use of commas and periods by the stationers' clerk is random (Greg, *Bibliography*, 1:60–61; Schoenbaum, *Records and Images*, p. 230).

announced, on the representation of the "Noble Person" who gave him the Downes manuscript, that the play was entirely Shakespeare's. To retract his attribution after he realized that it was a collaboration would have been seriously damaging to his reputation as a Shakespearean scholar and to his relationship with his patron, so he continued to give lip service to the ascription. Some critics believe that because of this Theobald destroyed his manuscripts, but Freehafer thinks it more likely that Watts acquired them along with the patent. Their disappearance is by no means unique since of "about eighty plays (including *Cardenio*)" originally entered by Moseley, but apparently not published, "only eleven are now known to exist in manuscript. Thus, the loss of Theobald's *Cardenio* manuscript is not remarkable from a statistical standpoint" (p. 512).

Harriet Frazier has written the only book-length account of the relationship between the lost *Cardenio* and *Double Falshood*, and of the authorship of the two plays.[59] She begins with a discussion of the external facts and "a consideration of Theobald's prefaces [in the first and second editions of *Double Falshood*] and matters closely connected with these prefaces" (p. 37). One such matter is the question of whether Theobald knew of Moseley's *Stationers' Register* entry with its implication as to subject matter and authorship. Scholars generally, Frazier says, have assumed Theobald's ignorance of the entry "from the early Nineteenth Century to the present," including Weber, Bradford, Schevill, Oliphant, Graham, Chambers, and Muir. Bradford's comment on the point she considers representative: "That Theobald should have forged such a play . . . with no knowledge of the Shakespeare-Fletcher-*Cardenio* tradition presupposes coincidences which are manifestly impossible" (p. 33). She notes that while Theobald was accused of pedantry and other faults, his contemporaries never branded him ignorant. His plodding qualities would have led him to investigate the *Stationers' Register*. "Though proof of his acquaintance with Moseley's entry is lacking, it seems less than judicious to assume he was necessarily ignorant of it" (p. 35).[60] Another matter is Theobald's change in his statement regarding the date of *Don Quixote* from 1611 in the preface to the first edition to 1605 in the preface to the second. Theobald, Frazier says, "seems to have been well aware of the difficulty of proving Shakespeare's acquaintance with *Don Quixote*," but he knew that the date of 1605 is that of the original Spanish edition—therefore unavailable to Shake-

59. Frazier, *A Babble of Ancestral Voices*, *passim*.

60. Frazier's statement, that Theobald's ignorance of Moseley's entry has been assumed by scholars "to the present" (1974), is in error. Five years earlier, Freehafer had concluded that Theobald knew of the entrance ("*Cardenio*, by Shakespeare and Fletcher," pp. 509–10). He supports his decision and offers an explanation for Theobald's behavior with a reasoned exposition. Frazier seems, inexplicably, to have completely overlooked Freehafer's study, which presents evidence and interpretation tending to alter views of the question previously generally held.

speare who knew no Spanish—and the change "casts some doubt on his integrity" (p. 29). The external evidence does not compel belief that Theobald had an authentic Shakespearean manuscript; but evidence does exist "to support the contention that Theobald not only had the inclination but the ability as well to author a Shakespearian play" (p. 37). Such works of Theobald's as his periodical *The Censor*; his poem, *The Cave of Poverty*; and his adaptation of *Richard II* demonstrate his deep-rooted and early appreciation of Shakespeare. They also make clear "his ability to reweave Shakespeare's phrases in a new fabric . . . [and] to rearrange Shakespeare's lines and couple them with those of his own devising." Certain attributes of his *Richard II* show that he "would not scruple to borrow from a fellow-dramatist," and his *Memoirs of Sir Walter Raleigh* reveals "his willingness to omit relevant facts and imply a non-existent relationship between a Spaniard [Gondomar] and an Englishman [Cecil]" (p. 60). Frazier documents Theobald's remarkable abilities as a Shakespearean editor as exhibited in his edition of the plays and points out that only three of his notes have any bearing on the *Cardenio-Double Falshood* problem, two dealing with *Don Quixote* and only one commenting on a line in *Double Falshood*. She acknowledges a profound respect for Theobald's imagination and for his "knowledge of the Elizabethans. His genius for emendation consistently reveals a brilliantly quirkish mind," but his persistence in suggesting that Shakespeare knew the classics "in the original . . . soars into . . . fancy. Perhaps knowledge, quirk, and fancy combined in mysterious ways the wonders of *The Double Falsehood* to perform" (p. 88).

Frazier comes to grips with the challenge of the authorship question starting with a brief review of the contributions of those students of *Cardenio* and *Double Falshood* who, in the twentieth century, have studied the question in some depth.[61] She finds these studies to be "suggestive rather than definitive" and attributes the reluctance of scholars to make "definite pronouncements" to the lack of a manuscript of *Cardenio*, an unwillingness to consider Theobald "capable of writing a play which anyone might believe Shakespeare's . . . and a failure to examine Theobald's work and times." The pattern of Shakespearean imitation in *Double Falshood* connects the play with Theobald's other work with Shakespeare: "These similarities alone furnish strong proof of Theobald's authorship . . . [and] virtually eliminate the possibility of an author other than Theobald" (pp. 127–28). She cites numerous echoes of *Hamlet* in *Double Falshood*, points out that Theobald had published *Shakespeare Restored*, largely devoted to *Hamlet*,

61. On the authorship question, Frazier cites (pp. 127–30) the work of Bradford, Graham, Muir, and Bertram, one sentence from the introduction to Leech's edition of *The Two Noble Kinsmen* in the Signet Classic series (New York: New American Library, 1966), and Schwartzstein's brief note. She makes no reference to Leech's *John Fletcher Plays*, to Harbage's essay, or to Freehafer's.

just before he produced his adaptation, and says that these echoes point to "Theobald's authorship of the apocryphal play" (p. 140). She supports her contention by finding echoes of other canonical plays, especially those most frequently performed about the time of the premier of *Double Falshood.* She feels confident that still more parallels between the Shakespeare canon and Theobald's adaptation could be discovered, but "the evidence presented here . . . warrants the conclusion that *The Double Falsehood* is neither authored by Shakespeare nor a seventeenth-century imitator of him. . . . The unmitigating presence of *Hamlet* in the revised play points a most accusing finger at Theobald. . . . Equally suggestive . . . is the presence in its text of the language of Shakespeare's plays frequently performed in London in the 1720's." On the basis of this evidence she comes "to the definite conclusion that *The Double Falsehood* is a deliberate forgery of Shakespeare by Theobald" (p. 145).[62]

Brean Hammond believes that only discovery of Theobald's manuscripts or reliable evidence that they existed could clear Theobald's name of forgery. His allusions to manuscripts in his preface to *Double Falshood* and in his letter to the Countess of Oxford are ambiguous because the references could be to Theobald's own *Double Falshood* manuscript. The play was revived on 31 March 1770 and an advertisement in *The Gazeteer* of the same date mentions a printed edition, adding, "The original manuscript of this play is now treasured up in the Museum of Covent-Garden Playhouse." Hammond thinks this refers to a manuscript that pre-dated Theobald, "since Theobald's own holograph would scarcely be worth treasuring up." There were libraries at Covent Garden "which contained, *inter alia*, production copies of plays," all of which were destroyed in the disastrous fire of 19 September 1808 that gutted the theater building and burned all its contents. H. C. Boaden visited Kemble the next day and quotes him as saying, "Yes, it has perished—that magnificent theatre. It is gone with all its treasures of every description. . . . That library, which contained all those immortal productions of our countrymen prepared for the purpose of representation." Hammond concludes, "Perhaps the story of one of Theobald's three playscripts terminates in these ashes."[63]

62. In an essay by Charles Frey, published after Frazier's book, significant structural, thematic, and character development links between *Double Falshood* and Shakespeare's other romances are identified, tending to support his part authorship of *Cardenio* ("'O sacred shadowy, cold and constant queen': Shakespeare's Imperiled and Chastening Daughters of Romance," in *The Woman's Part: Feminist Criticism of Shakespeare*, eds. Carolyn Ruth Swift Lenz, Gayle Greene, and Carol Thomas Neely (Urbana: University of Illinois Press, 1980), pp. 295–313.

63. Brean S. Hammond, "Theobald's *Double Falshood*: an 'Agreeable Cheat'?" *N&Q* 229 (1984): 2–3. Stanley Wells, in the Oxford *Shakespeare* (Oxford: Clarendon Press, 1986), concludes, "It is quite possible that *Double Falsehood* is based (however distantly) on a play of Shakespeare's time; if so, the play is likely to have been the one performed by the King's Men and ascribed by Moseley in 1653 to Fletcher and Shakespeare" (p. 1341).

Moseley's *Stationers' Register* entry, whatever the period following Fletcher's name may signify, provides valuable information about *Cardenio*. It manifestly registers a play because the list of more than fifty titles is described as "the severall Playes following." This is supported by the attributions to authors who are essentially playwrights and by the fact that Moseley is known to have collected play manuscripts. It tells us that the protagonist of the play is named Cardenio, which, taken together with the 1612–1613 date of first performance, points to Shelton's translation of *Don Quixote*. The full title, *The History of Cardenio*, also yields the same indication, since the hero's adventures in the Sierra Morena are referred to under that specific title by Shelton.[64] Leaving aside whatever evidence may be adduced from a study of *Double Falshood*, the existence of the *Stationers' Register* entry, in and of itself, leaves little room for doubt that Moseley had a theater manuscript that, like many others in his possession, had formerly been part of the repertory of the King's Men; and it is nearly as certain that, as the entry says, it was the joint composition of the company's long-term regular poet and their rising new one. Moseley's information on authorship, if not derived from the manuscript itself, may have been supplied to him by surviving members of the company.

The question of the number of Theobald's manuscripts, while of interest, need not be determined for purposes of an attempt to solve the authorship problem. Clearly he claims to have had more than two, and the number is not inherently improbable. Two are separately identifiable. One would have been the Jacobean manuscript, or a copy of it, on the basis of which Moseley registered the play; the other was the Downes manuscript that was heavily cut, particularly in the early part, and probably adapted in anticipation of a Restoration performance of which there is no surviving record. Moseley's uncut original, which may or may not have been in Shakespeare's and Fletcher's autographs, might have been the one that perished in the Covent Garden fire of 1808.

The presence of Theobald's hand in the text of *Double Falshood* is generally acknowledged and is virtually incontrovertible, but it does not establish him as the author of the play. Frazier's numerous examples of Theobaldian admixture prove only that he was what he claimed to be—the adapter and editor. His editorial hand in *Double Falshood* is further attested to by the relative brevity of the script when compared to, for example, *The Two Noble Kinsmen*, but about the same length as Theobald's original plays and his adapted *Richard II*. His presence can also be detected in

64. Freehafer, "*Cardenio*, by Shakespeare and Fletcher," pp. 501–2, tells us that other translations—Edmund Gayton (1654), J[ohn] P[hillips] (1687), John Stevens (1700), Peter Motteux (1700), Edward Ward (1711), and John Ozell (1791)—all differ in this connection, most of them radically so. The closest is that of Stevens, whose work, Freehafer says, "is based on the Shelton translation," which reads, "the Story of *Cardenio*."

abortive actions in the play, such as the matter of the hearse, which is thrice mentioned in *Double Falshood* but yet remains a puzzle. Probably its use was more fully developed in *Cardenio*. There seems to be fairly general scholarly acceptance of the presence of Fletcher in the underlying text, as Bradford argued three quarters of a century ago. A few scholars accept the idea with a measure of reluctance, or merely tacitly; but it seems that some, at least, do so not so much because they have strong doubts about Fletcher's contribution but rather because, as Oliphant pointed out in 1919, once Fletcher's participation is accepted, the critic is immediately faced with the challenge of Shakespeare's possible presence. The evidence for Shakespeare in *Double Falshood* is neither so extensive nor so compelling as that for Fletcher, as such poles-apart critics as Chambers and Frazier, among others, have insisted. Nonetheless, there are passages that are not in the manner of Fletcher and are clearly beyond the poetical powers of Theobald. Scholars have cited several such passages, of which two seem to have a significant Shakespearean ring. In the first of these passages, Julio counsels Leonora to be patient, to which she replies:

> Patient! What else? My Flames are in the Flint.
> Haply, to lose a Husband I may weep;
> Never, to get One: When I cry for Bondage,
> Let Freedom quit me.
>
> (1.2.101–4)

In the second of these passages, Henriques serenades Violante beneath her window, and she bids him to leave:

> Home my Lord,
> What you can say, is most unseasonable; what sing,
> Most absonant and harsh: Nay, your Perfume,
> Which I smell hither, cheers not my Sense
> Like our Field-violet's Breath.
>
> (1.3.57–61)

Such presumptively Shakespearean remains are admittedly neither numerous nor extensive, but it must be remembered that the text of the first part of the play appears to have been more heavily edited and adapted, possibly on two occasions by two different hands, than that of the latter part.

Of all the commentators, Frazier has argued most persistently against the presence of Shakespeare's writing in *Double Falshood*, except as there may have survived some lines from canonical plays filtered through Theobald's mind. She quotes a considerable number and especially cites parallels from *Romeo and Juliet*, *Hamlet*, *Macbeth*, and *Othello*. At least some of these seem to be echoes of thought rather than direct lexical parallels and can be explained as Shakespeare recasting in new language ideas he had earlier expressed, a phenomenon of composition that he exhibits where there is no question of authenticity. Frazier establishes by the evidence she has adduced some grounds for doubt that are sufficient for her, but having established a doubt she then, in a manner that appears almost to be unpremeditated, leaps to certitude that the writing is not Shakespeare—it is Theobald: "Theobald sat down in semi-good faith to write the play which he believed that Shakespeare had already written or which Shakespeare should have written" (pp. 150–51). But her argument is manifestly insufficient to support her conclusion.[65]

The evidence adduced and interpreted by the generality of scholars leads to the conclusion that there was a Shakespeare-Fletcher manuscript of a play entitled *The History of Cardenio*. This manuscript was the one that Moseley entered on the *Stationers' Register*. It found its way, along with an adapted version in Downes's hand, to Theobald. The Downes manuscript is likely to have been entitled *Double Falshood*, the title Theobald consistently employs, and may also have included other Restoration features of the play as it has come down to us. He revised it for the contemporary stage, the result being a drastic alteration of the first half and a less comprehensive editing of the last. In essence, *Double Falshood* is mainly Theobald, or Theobald and an earlier adapter, with a substantial admixture of Fletcher and a modicum of Shakespeare.

Scholars have not found it necessary to give serious consideration to other unlikely authorship suggestions such as Shirley (by Farmer), Massinger (by Malone), and Beaumont (by Oliphant) nor to efforts by Fleay and others to identify the lost *Cardenio* with extant plays, such as Fletcher's *Love's Pilgrimage* or Massinger's *A Very Woman*.[66]

Source

In the case of *Cardenio* we are in the rather unusual position of being reasonably sure that we know its source even though we do not have the play. The name *Cardenio* is rare in English, and it would be a most remarkable coincidence if it should occur in a play title and in a contemporaneous popular novel without a direct connection existing between them. We may

65. Zimansky, in a review of two of Frazier's essays (later incorporated into her book) that form the heart of her argument, says, "Neither of Miss Frazier's papers by itself is at all convincing, though the two together just begin to form a case" (*PQ* 48 [1969]: 401–2). Taylor points out that Frazier's arguments "are not wholly convincing, but even if we accepted them they would not disprove Shakespeare's part-authorship of a lost play, but only Theobald's access to that work" ("The Canon and Chronology of Shakespeare's Plays," *William Shakespeare: A Textual Companion*, by Stanley Wells and Gary Taylor with John Jowett and William Montgomery [Oxford: Clarendon Press, 1987], p. 133).

66. Chambers (*William Shakespeare* 1:542), Gerald Eades Bentley (*Jacobean and Caroline Stage*, 7 vols. [Oxford: Clarendon Press, 1941–1968], 3:370, 4:827, 5:1104–5), and Muir (*Collaborator*, pp. 159–60) dismiss with minimal discussions these and other attributions and identifications.

be fairly certain that the *Stationers' Register* title, *The History of Cardenio,* which is also used in that form in Shelton's translation,[67] is derived from *Don Quixote*; and it is reasonable to carry the idea one step further and conjecture that the plot of the play as well as the name of the hero is taken from the novel.

Cervantes's story of the adventure of Don Quixote in Sierra Morena is also undoubtedly the source of *Double Falshood.* That the basic fabric of this play is adapted from the tale of Cardenio and Luscinda in Shelton's translation is clear despite a complex process of condensation, transposition of incidents, compression of some events and amplification of others, enhancement of a few characters, a round of wholesale name changing, and substantial vocabulary deviation. How much of the process of adaptation was accomplished by Theobald and how much might have been previously incorporated into the Downes manuscript by a Restoration adapter we have no means of telling, but the close affinity between *Double Falshood* and Cervantes's story is manifest. In the editor's preface to the first edition of his play, Theobald, in his effort to wipe out one of the "flying objections," says, concerning the source:

> Another Objection has been started, (which would carry much more Weight with it, were it Fact;) that the Tale of this Play, being built upon a Novel in *Don Quixot,* Chronology is against Us, and *Shakespeare* could not be the Author. But it happens, that *Don Quixot* was publish'd in the Year 1611, and *Shakespeare* did not dye till *April* 1616, a sufficient Interval of Time for All that We want granted.[68]

It is evident that Theobald means that *Don Quixote* is the source of *Cardenio,* but by legitimate extension we may say that it is also, whether directly or indirectly, the source of *Double Falshood.* His assertion was not questioned until Schevill raised the issue of the identity of the direct source of Theobald's adaptation in 1911.[69] Schevill argues that *Double Falshood* is based not directly on Shelton's original translation but on an adapted and rearranged eighteenth-century version of the Cardenio story included by Samuel Croxall in the second edition of his *Select Collection of Novels and Histories* published by Watts, Theobald's printer, under the title "The Adventures on the Black Mountains." The author of "The Adventures" has not been identified. Schevill supports his contention by a three-way comparison of structural elements and parallel passages from Shelton's translation, from Croxall's novel, and from *Double Falshood.* By this means he

67. Fitzmaurice-Kelly, *The History of Don Quixote,* 1:262, for example, where it is spelled *Historie.*

68. The latter portion of this passage is altered in the second edition to read, "But it happens, that the *First* Part of *Don Quixot,* which contains the Novel upon which the Tale of this Play seems to be built, was publish'd in the Year 1605, and our *Shakespeare* did not dye till *April* 1616; an Interval of no less than Eleven Years, and more than sufficient for All that we want granted."

69. Schevill, "Theobald's *Double Falsehood?*"

endeavors to adduce proof that the play could not have been based on Shelton but could have derived from "The Adventures." His study shows that there is a correspondence of the number and kinds of characters in the play that is closer to their counterparts in "The Adventures" than to those in Shelton; that "the plot of the novel . . . present[s] an excellent parallel to the play," whereas *Don Quixote* is diffuse; that incidents in *Double Falshood*, not in "The Adventures," such as Julio's interruption of the wedding of Henriquez and Leonora, the meeting of the fathers, and the reconciliation at the inn, developed from general hints in Croxall's novel; that there is a "similar sequence of events in the novel" and the play; and a "direct imitation by the play of features which do not exist in Shelton and which the author of *Double Falshood* could have taken only from Croxall's version." He concludes that "The Adventures" is based directly on Shelton, and that he has shown that the play's eighteenth-century characteristics are due chiefly to its being based on Croxall's novel. Since the date of the second edition of *Novels and Histories* is 1729, two years or so after the premier of *Double Falshood*, Schevill conjectures that Theobald must have obtained a manuscript copy of the novel from Watts. "At all events, his [Theobald's] name is the only one that can definitely be connected with the authorship of *Double Falshood*" (p. 285).

Graham analyzes Schevill's hypothesis in his 1916 essay, and in the introduction to his edition, and demonstrates that there are some seven key "verbal and phrasal parallels" common to Shelton and the play of which Croxall's novel "has either no parallel passage or one which does not follow Shelton as closely as" does *Double Falshood*. This makes it clear, Graham claims, that "the original author or authors" of the play and the translator of "The Adventures" independently worked from Shelton. This in turn raises a question concerning "the obvious parity of the two in details not found in Shelton." Graham's solution is that the author of Croxall's novel "furbished up Shelton . . . under the conscious or unconscious influence of the play with which he was familiar," and Graham cites changes from the original Cardenio story that "would be made rather for a dramatic purpose than any other." This contention is supported by two references to *Double Falshood* in the volume that includes "The Adventures." He concludes that *Double Falshood* is based not on Croxall's "Adventures" but on Shelton's translation, and that the latter is also the source of *Cardenio*.[70]

Critics who have examined the evidence generally accept (perhaps

70. Graham, "The *Cardenio-Double Falsehood* Problem," pp. 271–74; *Double Falsehood*, pp. 4–8. The two allusions to *Double Falshood* occur in the Preface and on the title page of "The Adventures." The former reads, "The Adventures on the Black Mountains: *This is the Novel, from which the Plan of a Posthumous Play, written originally by* Shakespear, *call'd* Double-Falshood, *was taken*." The latter, after the title, reads, "A TALE, Upon which the Plan of a Posthumous Play, call'd DOUBLE FALSHOOD, was written Originally by W. SHAKESPEARE." Freehafer conjectures that the inclusion by Watts of "Adventures" and these notes in Croxall's collection was intended "to aid in selling remaining copies of *Double Falshood*" ("*Cardenio*, by Shakespeare and Fletcher," p. 513, n. 81).

partly in consideration of Graham's demonstration) Shelton's version of *Don Quixote* as the source of both *Cardenio* and *Double Falshood*,[71] although sometimes with a muted reservation concerning the earlier play, which is understandable since the text is not extant. Some students of *Double Falshood* who have recently written on Theobald's adaptation call attention to possible secondary sources. Muir finds echoes of Shakespeare's previous work, citing specifically *Romeo and Juliet*, *1 Henry IV*, *Hamlet*, and *Troilus and Cressida*, and he conjures up an image of Theobald manufacturing "some scenes . . . with a copy of Shakespeare's works open in front of him." Leech calls attention to similarities between the endings of *Double Falshood* and *All's Well That Ends Well* (the accusation of Henriquez by a disguised Violante of perfidy that Henriquez denies; Violante's leaving the stage to summon a witness; the reading of an incriminating letter; the denouement when Violante reappears as herself) that "seem to constitute a reminiscence of the situation involving Bertram, the King of France, and Bertram's accusers in Shakespeare's play." He also notes that the wanderings of the *Double Falshood* lovers "in mountain-scenery" resemble incidents in *Cymbeline* and *The Winter's Tale*, as well as in *Philaster*. He thinks this is "Fletcher characteristically employing a Shakespearian reminiscence in the play's ending."[72]

Frazier seems to consider Theobald's comment on *Don Quixote* as source in his preface to apply to *Double Falshood*, but not to *Cardenio*, and she therefore addresses herself only to the sources of the later play. Her discussion is consistent with her contention that *Double Falshood* is wholly Theobald's and with her rejection of his claim to possess Jacobean manuscripts: "Though Shelton's *Don Quixote* is the ultimate source of *The Double Falsehood*, it is but one of several sources." Cervantes's story of Cardenio and Luscinda was dramatized several times throughout Europe, especially in France, shortly after the novel was first published and well before the date of Theobald's adaptation. Frazier finds significant influences on *Double Falshood* from one of the several French dramatic versions, Pichou's *Les Folies de Cardenio*, first produced in 1629, printed in 1630, and performed at Paris as late as 4 January 1721. She believes Theobald read *Les Folies* in the published version rather than saw a performance. She also argues that Theobald drew on Aphra Behn's *The Amorous Prince*, produced in 1671 and reprinted as part of her *Works* in 1704, 1711, and 1724; and, to

71. Among them are Chambers, *William Shakespeare*, 1:539; Baldwin Maxwell, *Studies in Beaumont, Fletcher and Massinger*, p. 178; Hazleton Spencer, *The Art and Life of William Shakespeare* (New York: Harcourt, 1940), pp. 412–13, n. 4; Greg, *First Folio*, p. 98; Muir, *Collaborator*, p. 148; and Leech, *Fletcher Plays*, who sums up succinctly, "It is . . . certain that it [*Cardenio*] was a derivative from the story of Cardenio in *Don Quixote*" (p. 140); Freehafer, "*Cardenio*, by Shakespeare and Fletcher," p. 502; and G. R. Proudfoot, "*The Two Noble Kinsmen* and the Apocryphal Plays," in *Shakespeare Select Bibliographical Guides*, ed. Stanley Wells (Oxford: Oxford University Press, 1973), p. 293.

72. Muir, *Collaborator*, pp. 154–59; Leech, *Fletcher Plays*, pp. 152–53. Muir also identifies a parallel in *Double Falshood* to *The Maid's Tragedy* (p. 153).

a lesser extent, on Part 1 of Thomas D'Urfey's *The Comical History of Don Quixote*, first performed in 1694 and frequently revived. She lists ten performances of *The Comical History* between 1720 and 1728. According to this theory, *Double Falshood* adopts elements from Pichou's play, such as Henriquez's soliloquy and the wedding scene; exhibits "several specific similarities in detail" from Behn's *The Amorous Prince* such as "the letter bearing incident . . . similarity in names of the servant Galliard in *The Amorous Prince* and Gerald in *The Double Falsehood*" and two possible verbal echoes; and shares with D'Urfey's *Comical History* the Cardenio story, which was one of two most popular narratives excerpted from *Don Quixote* following the Restoration (the other being the story of the Curious Impertinent). In summary, Frazier finds that Theobald "borrowed least" from D'Urfey's *Comical History*, more extensively from Behn's *Amorous Prince*, "and he relied most heavily for the structure of *The Double Falsehood* on Pichous's *Les Folie de Cardenio*."[73]

There is virtually no room for doubt that Cervantes's tale of Cardenio and Luscinda is the primary source of *Double Falshood*; and, although in the absence of the text of *The History of Cardenio* we cannot be absolutely sure, it seems reasonably certain that *Don Quixote* was also the source of the play that Moseley registered in 1653 [Text 1]. The context of Theobald's comment regarding the source, which is conditioned on the availability of *Don Quixote* while Shakespeare was still writing plays for the King's Men, indicates beyond question that he is saying that Cervantes's novel is the source of *Cardenio*. Even if it were to be assumed that Shakespeare had no hand in the play, Theobald's statement on the source, in the form presented in either the first or second editions of *Double Falshood*, is not adversely affected.

An incident by incident comparison of the events of the play with those of the novel shows that, with a few minor exceptions (none of which amounts to so much as an entire scene), there is an element in the story of Cardenio and Luscinda that the dramatist (or dramatists) carried over to the play almost unaltered, adapted with only minor changes, or expanded and developed from a Cervantes hint. To this general proposition there are a few exceptions, of which two are of some importance. The first centers on a fundamental difference in the wedding ceremony of Fernando and Luscinda. In the novel, they are actually married before Luscinda faints, while Cardenio observes the ceremony, without interfering, from a "hollow roome of a window" concealed by a tapestry. In the play, Julio watches from behind an arras and emerges to interrupt as the wedding service is about to begin. He moves to attack Henriquez but is seized and "drag'd out." At this point Leonora swoons before the crucial point of giving and taking, and she is carried off, unmarried. The second difference is in the reunion of the pairs of lovers with which the play concludes, and which is

73. Frazier, *A Babble of Ancestral Voices*, pp. 115–26.

notably modified from the novel. In *Double Falshood*, Henriquez is confronted by Violante, and, though hesitant to accept her, he eventually does so under pressure from Roderick and, to a lesser extent, from the Duke, his father, and the fathers of Violante and Julio. In *Don Quixote*, Don Fernando is persuaded by Dorotea's pleas and his own conscience to accept her; the three fathers and his brother, unnamed in the novel, are not even present. Other deviations include the changes in the names, transpositions of incidents, and the development of secondary characters who are merely mentioned in the novel. The dramatist may have incorporated one event into his play that, if derived from *Don Quixote*, was inspired by story elements not part of the tale of Cardenio and Luscinda. This is the hearse trick, employed to enable Henriquez, posing as a corpse in the hearse, to gain entry to the convent to which Leonora had fled following the interrupted wedding. His purpose is to abduct her, and in this he is successful. The plan is suggested by Roderick in 4.1, and the action takes place offstage during 4.2. Leonora is in the custody of the brothers by the beginning of the next scene, 5.1. Neither the hearse nor the element of deception are part of the story of Cardenio and Luscinda in *Don Quixote*, nor does the incident take the same form as it does in Theobald's adaptation. In the novel, Don Fernando, aided by three associates, secures the gate to the convent when the porter is absent, then enters and succeeds in "snatching her [Luscinda] away ere she could retire herselfe." Graham says, "The hearse trick . . . probably needs no other sources than the suggestions furnished by two incidents in other parts of *Don Quixote*." One of these incidents is simply a funeral procession, including a body in a hearse, but in its other particulars it is not close to the play. The other possible source consists of two elements that occur in successive chapters, but otherwise are unrelated, concerning a girl confined to a convent and, separately, a procession of clerics and laity formed about a statue of the Virgin Mary shrouded in black going to a mountain hermitage to pray for rain (Text 1, First Booke, Chapter 5; Fourth Booke, Chapters 24–25). It is not a funeral. There are similarities to the play, but the differences are sufficiently significant to invite speculation concerning a different explanation. Perhaps the hearse trick was the invention of one of the writers—Shakespeare, Fletcher, the unidentified Restoration adapter, or Theobald himself; or perhaps it was originally a bit of folklore about separated lovers folded into *Double Falshood* by the author. One comment by Roderick has a touch of realism that may point to an independent existence for such a tale. He says he and Henriquez will never gain entry to the convent except by craving "a Night's Leave to rest the Hearse . . . for to such Charity Strict Zeal and Custom of the House give Way" (4.1 245–47).[74]

74. For Muir's interesting comment concerning the "stratagem of the hearse," in the introduction to the Cornmarket facsimile of *Double Falshood*, see above, n. 50. Graham, *Double Falsehood*, p. 7.

The other sources suggested by students of *Double Falshood* are of lesser significance. Leech's identification of the structural similarity of the ending with that of *All's Well That Ends Well* is certainly valid; but his conjecture that the wanderings of Julio and Violante in the Sierra are somehow related to incidents in *The Winter's Tale* and *Cymbeline*, while possible, is less certain. Lexical and structural parallels to Shakespeare's acknowledged plays, perceived by a number of scholars, are of differing cogency. A few are sound. Violante's appearance at a window is strongly reminiscent of Juliet on the balcony, and Muir's two echoes of passages in *Hamlet* are equally so. The parallels to *Troilus and Cressida* also seem probable, but others are less compelling. Some are reminiscent of Fletcher's practice of recalling Shakespeare; none seem to be Shakespeare restating an idea he had used in earlier plays.

Frazier accepts *Don Quixote* as the primary source, but her speculative designations of the three dramas by other authors on the Cardenio and Luscinda theme as *Double Falshood* sources are not, for the most part, convincing. Possibly Theobald had read Pichou's *Les Folies de Cardenio* in printed form, but the structural elements that she adduces as her primary evidence could have been as easily developed from Cervantes. The publication of Behn's *Complete Works* in 1724 made her *Amorous Prince* available to Theobald before he produced his play, and he could have seen a performance of D'Urfey's *Comical History*, because it was revived on 27 January 1724. Frazier's findings of "unauthorized borrowing on Theobald's part" from *The Amorous Prince* strains her evidence. Of one element, she herself says, "The letter-bearing incident may well be a common dramatic technique." Concerning the relationship between *D'Urfey's Comical History of Don Quixote* and *Double Falshood*, she says in summation, "The influence . . . is to be found neither in structure, in verbal parallels, nor in tone." She explains away the difficulty by saying, "One would scarcely expect Theobald's heavy reliance on a play so frequently performed in the decade immediately preceding the appearance of *The Double Falsehood*." If, as she contends, Theobald engaged in wholesale borrowing from such various sources, the expectations of critics would very probably be quite the opposite.[75]

Stage History

In regard to the stage history of *Cardenio*, students of the play, as with the source problem, are in the unusual position of having records of performances even though they do not have the play; and, if *Double Falshood* is *Cardenio* adapted, we have a documented stage history that compares

75. Frazier, *A Babble of Ancestral Voices*, pp. 121, 122, 125.

favorably to that of some canonical plays. The highlights of the theatrical fortunes of the play are the records of the performances of *Cardenio* at Whitehall and Greenwich; the substantial initial run of *Double Falshood*, longer than most of the early eighteenth-century plays of which we have record; its longevity on the London stage that extends intermittently from 1727 to 1791; and the hilarious one night stand organized by W. C. Day and his anonymous friend in 1847.

There are records of two performances of *Cardenio* at court. The first occurs in the Chamber account for the holiday season of 1612–1613:

> Item paid to John Heminges upon the Cowncells warrant dated att Whitehall xx° die Maij 1613, for presenting before the Princes Highnes the Lady Elizabeth and the Prince Pallatyne Elector fowerteene severall playes. . . . Item paid to the said John Heminges vppon the lyke warrant, dated att Whitehall xx° die Maij 1613, for presentinge sixe severall playes, viz: . . . One other Cardenno.

A later entry in the same account reads:

> Item paid to John Heminges vppon lyke warrant, dated att Whitehall ix° die Julij 1613 for himself and the rest of his fellowes his Majesties servauntes and Players for presentinge a playe before the Duke of Savoyes Embassadour on the viijth daye of June, 1613, called Cardenna, the some of vj^{li}, xxij^{s} iiij^{d}.[76]

These are the only performances of *Cardenio* of which we have record, but it was undoubtedly presented at Blackfriars and possibly at the Globe.

The premiere of *Double Falshood* took place at the Drury Lane theater on 13 December 1727. John Genest lists the principal members of the cast and gives a generally accurate synopsis of the action, including making explicit a bit of stage business of which there is only a hint in the dialogue: "Roderick assists Henriquez in getting Leonora from the nunnery, but takes care not to let her be in his brother's power." He also appends some comments of his own:

> This is a very good play, but certainly not Shakspeare's, as Theobald endeavoured to persuade the world—Dr. Farmer conjectures with much probability that it was Shirley's—Theobald in the preface speaks of having three Manuscript copies of it, one of which was in the hand-writing of Downes, and had been formerly in the possession of Betterton, who intended to have brought out this play, but did not do it—there is a great similarity between the latter part of Julio's character and that of Octavian in the Mountaineers—they are both taken from the story of Cardenio in Don Quixote.

76. Chambers, *William Shakespeare*, 2:343.

Genest notes that on the occasion of the sixth performance (19 December) Barton Booth acted the part of Julio, this "being his 1st appearance since his illness. Booth had rehearsed Julio several times; when the play was ready for acting, he was prevented from appearing in it by illness, and the character was supplied by [Charles] Williams, to whom Booth had given the part to study, as doubting of being able to appear in it himself; but at Theobald's earnest entreaty he good-naturedly disregarded his indisposition and played the part on this evening." Booth, although not fully recovered, continued in the role for the remaining four performances of the initial run. *Double Falshood* was presented again on 9 January 1728 and Genest notes of Booth, "This was his last performance."[77]

Clearly, *Double Falshood* was a stage success. A run of ten consecutive performances was in those times very rare, although not unprecedented. Dramatists hoped that a new play would have a run of three performances because the third was traditionally the playwright's first benefit. The performances of 15, 19, and 22 December 1727 were for the benefit of "the author of Shakespear Restor'd" (Theobald.)[78] The play was next acted at Drury Lane on 18 March 1728 "at the particular Desire of several Ladies of Quality" and for the benefit of Mrs. Booth, no doubt in consideration of the declining health of her husband, who lingered on in pain for five more years. Mrs. Booth was a member of the cast when it was next presented on 1 May 1728 for the benefit of Benjamin Griffin, a well-known actor and a friend of Theobald's who was himself the beneficiary of a performance on 21 April 1729.[79]

Double Falshood was first acted outside of Drury Lane when it moved to Covent Garden during the 1740–1741 season. It was graced with a new prologue for its first Covent Garden presentation of 13 December 1740, which may have contributed somewhat to the substantial receipts of £129 19s. 6d. The second performance two days later realized £35 16s. Receipts were better (at £100) when the play was acted on 15 May 1741 "by Command of their Royal Highnesses the Prince and Princess of Wales, Prince George, and the Lady Augusta. Benefit the last Editor of Shakespear [Theobald]. Written Originally by Shakespear."[80] It was revived, again at Covent Garden, for two more performances, in 1767. The first, on 24 April, was a benefit for William Gibson, an accomplished actor who played

77. John Genest, *Some Account of the English Stage from the Restoration in 1660 to 1830*, 10 vols. (Bath, 1832; rpt. New York: Franklin, 1966), 3:203–5. See also Theophilus Cibber, *The Lives and Characters of the most Eminent Actors and Actresses* (London: 1753), Part 1, pp. 82–83.

78. Emmet Avery, ed., *The London Stage 1660–1800*, 5 parts (Carbondale, Ill.: Southern Illinois University Press, 1960), Part 2, 1700–1729, 2:949–51, 954.

79. Ibid., pp. 965, 973, 1027.

80. Arthur H. Scouten, ed., *The London Stage 1660–1800*, 5 parts (Carbondale, Ill.: Southern Illinois University Press, 1961), Part 3, 1729–1747, 2:873, 917.

Camillo. Total receipts amounted to £104 3s. 6d., yielding to Gibson £37 18s. 6d. plus £30 15s. from tickets. The second presentation, "by Particular Desire," on 6 May had receipts of £93 12s. 6d. yielding Thomas Hull (acting Roderick) £27 5s. 6d. plus £56 6s. from tickets.[81]

Sometime after March 1749, *Double Falshood* was presented, Brean Hammond tells us, as a private entertainment "given by and for the family and friends of the Noel family of Luffenham, county Rutland, probably at their county seat at Luffenham Hall." Parts were acted by Baptist Noel, fourth Earl Gainsborough and Lady Jane Noel. The setting was simplified, only two scenes—"Grove" and "The Street"—being noted in an extant marked copy of the 1728 edition used as a promptbook and now in the Folger Library. Care was taken to provide appropriate music, and Hammond points out that some of the cuts in the text were made in consideration of "what is proper for a Peer to say and what is proper to be said to him."[82]

After an absence of four decades, the play returned to Drury Lane for two performances in 1770. The earlier performance, on March 31, was a benefit for Samuel Reddish, who personated Julio; and the later performance, on May 11, was for Mrs. Bradshaw and Mrs. Dorman, who played two of the *Three Old Women Weatherwise*, the afterpiece. No information on receipts has survived.[83] Its last appearance on London boards for half a century was at Covent Garden on 6 June 1791 when new songs were added and *Fond Echo forbear thy fond sigh*, which was a feature of the original production of 1727 under the title *Fond Echo forbear thy light Strain*, was restored with a new musical setting. The song is said to have been "written by Shakspeare [*recte* Lewis Theobald]." It was a benefit for James Wild, the prompter. Receipts were £188 15s.[84]

Double Falshood was produced by the company of players headquartered at Bath but acting at both the Theatre Royal in Orchard Street, Bath, and in the alternate theater at King Street, Bristol. The celebrated tragedienne Sarah Siddons acted the part of Leonora on 18, 27 (at Bristol), and

81. George Winchester Stone, Jr., ed., *The London Stage 1660–1800*, 5 parts (Carbondale, Ill.: Southern Illinois University Press, 1962), Part 4, 1747–1776, 2:1238, 1243.

82. Brean S. Hammond, "The Performance History of a Pseudo-Shakespearean Play: Theobald's *Double Falshood*," *British Journal for Eighteenth-Century Studies* 7, 1 (1984): 49–60. Hammond reproduces photographically two pages from the Noel promptbook (pl. 4) showing some cuts and notations.

83. Stone, *The London Stage*, Part 4, 3:1466, 1476. A promptbook in the Furness Library at the University of Pennsylvania, brought to light by Hammond, contains information on the Drury Lane performances of 1770, including actors' warnings, notes on entrances, scenery and props, music cues, cuts and one small textual emendation, and a cast list. These are in two hands in a copy of the 1767 edition of *Double Falshood*. Hammond, who identifies the hands as those of Garrick and William Hopkins, his prompter, reproduces two pages from this promptbook ("Performance History," pp. 55–56 and Pl. 3).

84. Charles Beecher Hogan, ed., *The London Stage 1660–1800*, 5 parts (Carbondale, Ill.: Southern Illinois University Press, 1968), Part 5, 1776–1800, 2:1361–62.

28 March 1780, and 19 May 1781, between her 1775 failure in London as Portia to Garrick's Shylock, when she was only twenty, and her very successful return to Drury Lane in 1782, where she established herself as the pre-eminent tragic actress of the English stage.[85]

William C. Day came upon a copy of Theobald's published text of *Double Falshood* in a second-hand bookshop in the autumn of 1847 and decided to mount a performance at the Theatre Royal Olympic in Wych Street, London. It was advertised as *Shakespeare's Last Play*. The cast consisted of Day himself and a friend in the two leading male roles,

> the other parts being filled by seedy professionals out of engagement, with a contingent of subordinates from the amateur stage. Miss Fanny Hamilton, who attained some popularity at the Olympic under George Wild's management, was engaged for the heroine, and Mrs. Graham, long associated with Sadler's Wells, personated the second lady.

There was one performance on 22 November 1847, which was treated as a dubious joke by an audience consisting largely of the "free list." They proved unruly and the play culminated in a cry of "Manager" and "Author." In response to the calls, the partners presented a plaster bust of Shakespeare.[86] Thus, the stage history that began at Whitehall ended—at least for the present—in horse play. However, in an era of many successful annual Shakespeare festivals, when producers range freely throughout the canon and then look to *Sir Thomas More*, *The Two Noble Kinsmen*, and even *Edward III*, there is a possibility that *Double Falshood* may yet be revived in the twentieth century after another hiatus of more than a century.[87]

85. Belville S. Penley, *The Bath Stage* (London: 1892; rpt. New York: Blom, 1971), pp. 56–61; Arnold Hare, ed., *Theatre Royal Bath* (Bath: Kingsmead, 1977), pp. vii–viii, 70, 77, 95, 144, 145.

86. W. C. Day, *Behind the Footlights* (London and New York: Warne, 1885), pp. 60–67.

87. The founder-producer of the Shakespeare Society of America, R. Thad Taylor, who in 1980 completed the Los Angeles Globe Playhouse's presentation of the canonical cycle including *Pericles*, has also produced *The Two Noble Kinsmen* (1979), *Sir Thomas More* (1984), and *Edward III* (1986). Stodder reports that Taylor is planning to mount the North American premier of *Double Falshood*, possibly as part of the 1989 season (Joseph H. Stodder, "Three Apochryphal Plays in Los Angeles," *SQ* 38 [1987]: 243).

1. Source

From *The History of the valorous and wittie Knight-Errant Don-Quixote of the Mancha*, vol. 1*

By Miguel de Cervantes; translated by Thomas Shelton, 1612; edited by James Fitzmaurice-Kelly, 1896

The Third Booke

Chapter 9

Of that which befell the famous Don-Quixote in Siera Morena, which was one of the most rare adventures, which in this or any other so authenticall a History is recounted.

Don-Quixote seeing himselfe in so ill plight, said to his Squire Sancho, I have heard say oft-times, that to doe good to men unthankfull, is to cast water into the Sea. If I had beleeved what thou saidst to me, I might well have prevented all this griefe: but now that is past; patience, and be wiser an other time. You wil take warning as much by this, quoth Sancho, as I am a Turke. But since you say, that if you had beleeved me, you had avoided this griefe, beleeve me now, and you shall eschue a greater: for you must wit, that no Knighthood nor Chivalry is of any authoritie with the Holy brotherhood; for it cares not two farthings for all the Knights Errants in the world, and know, that mee thinkes I heare their arrows buzze about mine eares already. Sancho, thou art a naturall coward, quoth Don-Quixote, but because thou mayest not say, that I am obstinate, and that I never follow thine advice, I will take thy counsell this time, and convey my selfe from that fury which now thou fearest so much: but it shal be on a condition, that thou never tell alive nor dying to any mortall creature, that I retired or withdrew my selfe out of this danger for feare, but onely to satisfie thy requests: For if thou sayest any other thing, thou shalt belie me most falsly: and even from this very time till that, and from thence until now, I give thee the lie herein, and I say thou liest, and shalt lie as oft-times as thou sayest or doest thinke the contrary: and doe not replie to me. For in onely thinking that I withdraw my selfe out of any peril, but principally this, which seemes to carry with it some shadow of feare, I am about to remaine and expect heere alone, not onely for the Holy brotherhood,

*Reproduced from *The History of the valorous and wittie Knight-Errant Don-Quixote of the Mancha* are chapters 9, 10, and 13 (part) of the Third Booke; 1, 2, 3 (part), 5, 9, 10 (part), and 20 (part) of the Fourth Booke. Reproduced as the possible source of the hearse incident are chapters 5 of the Second Booke; 24 and 25 of the Fourth Booke, all in part.

which thou namest and fearest, but also for the brethren of the Twelve Tribes, for the Seven Macchabees, for Castor and Pollux, and for all the other brothers and brotherhoods in the world. Sir, answered Sancho, to retire, is not to flie, nor to expect is wisedome, when the danger exceedeth all hope; and it is the part of a wiseman, to keepe himselfe safe to day for to morrow; and not to adventure himselfe wholly in one day. And know, that although I be but a rude Clowne, yet doe I for all that understand somewhat of that which men call good government: and therefore doe not repent your selfe for following mine advice, but mount on Rozinante if you be able; if not, I wil helpe you, and come after me, for my minde gives me that we shall now have more use of legges then of hands.

Don-Quixote leaped on his horse without replying a word, and Sancho guiding him on his Asse, they both entred into that part of Sierra Morena that was neare unto them; Sancho had a secret designe to crosse over it all, and issue at Viso or Amodovar of Campo, and in the meane time to hide themselves for some daies, among those craggie and intricate rocks, to the end they might not be found by the Holy brotherhood, if it did make after them. And he was the more encouraged to doe this, because he saw their provision which he carried on his Asse, had escapt safely out of the skirmish of the Gally-slaves: a thing which he accounted to be a miracle, considering the diligence that the slaves had used to search and carrie away all things with them. They arrived that night into the very midst and bowels of the mountaine, and there Sancho thought it fittest to spend that night, yea and some other few dayes also, at least as long as their victuals indured, and with this resolution they tooke up their lodging among a number of Corke trees that grew between two Rockes. But fatall chance, which according to the opinion of those that have not the light of faith guideth, directeth, and compoundeth all as it liketh, ordayned that that famous couzener and thiefe Gines de Passamonte, who was before delivered out of chaines by Don-Quixotes force and folly, perswaded through feare he conceived of the Holy brotherhood (whom hee had just cause to feare) resolved to hide himselfe likewise in that mountaine, and his fortune and feares led him just to the place where it had first addrest Don-Quixote and his Squire, just at such time as he might perceive them, and they both at that instant fallen asleepe. And as evillmen are evermore ingratefull, and that necessity forceth a man to attempt that which it urgeth, and likewise that the present redresse prevents the expectation of a future, Gines, who was neither gratefull nor gratious, resolved to steale away Sancho his Asse, making no account of Rozinante, as a thing neither saleable nor pawnable. Sancho slept soundly, and so he stole his beast, and was before morning so farre off from thence, as he feared not to be found.

Aurora sallied forth at last to refresh the earth, and affright Sancho with a most sorrowfull accident, for he presently missed his Asse, and so seeing himselfe deprived of him, he began the most sadde and dolefull lamentation of the world: in such sort as he awaked Don-Quixote with his out-cries, who heard that hee said thus. O childe of my bowels, borne in mine owne house, the sport of my children, the comfort of my wife, and the envie of my neighbours; the ease of my burdens, and finally the sustainer of halfe of my person; for with sixe and twentie Marvediis that I gained daily by thee, I did defray halfe of mine expences. Don-Quixote, who heard the plaint, and knew also the cause, did comfort Sancho with the best words he could devise, and desired him to have patience, promising to give a letter of exchange, to the end that they of his house might deliver him three Asses of five, which he had left at home.

Sancho comforted himselfe againe with this promise, and dried up his teares, moderated his sighes, and gave his Lord thankes for so great a favour. And as they entred in farther among those mountaines, we cannot recount the joy of our Knight, to whom those places seemed most accommodate to atchieve the adventures he searched for. They reduced to his memory the marvellous accidents that had befalne Knights Errant in like solitudes and desarts: and he rode so overwhelmed and transported by these thoughts as he remembred nothing else. Nor Sancho had any other care (after he was out of feare to be taken) but how to fill his belly with some of these relikes which yet remained of the Clericall spoyles; and so hee followed his Lord, taking now and then out of a basket, (which Rozinante carried for want of the Asse) some meat, lining therewithall his paunch; and whilst he went thus imployed, he would not have given a mite to encounter any other adventure how honourable soever.

But whilst he was thus busied, he espyed his Master labouring to take up with the point of his Iaveline, some bulke or other that lay on the ground, and went towards him to see whether he needed his helpe, just at the season that he lifted up a saddle cushion, and a Portmantew fast to it, which were halfe rotten, or rather wholly rotted by the weather; yet they weighed so much, that Sanchoes assistance was requisite to take them up: and straight his Lord commaunded him to see what was in the Wallet. Sancho obeyed with expedition. And although it was shut with a chaine and hanging locke, yet by the parts which were torne he saw what was within, to wit, foure fine holland shirts, and other linnens both curious and cleane: and moreover a handkercher, wherein was a good quantity of gold: which he perceiving, said, Blessed be heaven, which hath once presented to us a beneficiall adventure: and searching for more, he found a Tablet very costly bound. This Don-Quixote tooke of him, commaunding him to keepe the golde with himselfe; for which rich favour Sancho did presently kisse his hands: and after, taking all the linnen, he clapt it up in the bagge of their victuals. Don-Quixote having noted all these things, said, Me thinkes, Sancho (and it cannot be possible any other) that some traveller having left his way, past through this mountaine, and being encountred by thieves, they slew him, and buried him in this secret place. It cannot be so, answered Sancho, for if they were theeves, they would not have left this money behind them. Thou sayest true, quoth Don-Quixote, and therefore I cannot conjecture what it might be: but stay a while, we will see whether there be any thing written in these Tablets, by which wee may vent and finde out that which I desire. Then he opened it, and the first thing that he found written in it, as it were a first draught, but done with a very faire Character, was a Sonnet which he read aloud, that Sancho might also heare it, and was this which ensues:

Or love of understanding quite is voyde:
  Or he abounds in cruelty, or my paine
  Th' occasion equals not; for which I bide
  The torments dyre, he maketh me sustaine.
But if love be a God, I dare maintaine
  He nought ignores: and reason aye decides,
  Gods should not cruell be: then who ordaines
  This paine I worship, which my heart divides?
Filis! I erre, if thou I say it is:
  For so great ill and good cannot consist.
  Nor doth this wracke from heav'n befall, but yet,
That shortly I must die, can no way misse:
  For th'evill, whose cause is hardly well exprest,
  By miracle alone, true cure may get.

Nothing can be learned by that verse, quoth Sancho, if by that Hilo or threed which is said there, you gather not where lies, the rest of the clue. What Hilo is here? quoth Don-Quixote. Me thought, quoth Sancho, that you read Hilo there. I did not, but Fili, said Don-Quixote, which is without doubt the name of the Lady, on whom the Authour of this Sonnet complaines, who in good truth seemes to be a reasonable good Poet, or els I know but little of that Art. Why then, quoth Sancho, belike you doe also understand Poetry? That I doe, and more then thou thinkest, quoth Don-Quixote; as thou shalt see when thou shalt carry a letter from me to my Lady Dulcinea del Toboso, written in verse from the one end to the other: For I would thou shouldest know, Sancho, that all or the greater number of Knights Errant, in times past were great Versifiers and Musitians: for these two qualities, or graces as I may better terme them, are annext to amorous Knights Adventurers. True it is, that the verses of the auncient Knights are not so adorned with words, as they are rich in conceits. I pray you reade more, quoth Sancho, for perhaps you may finde somewhat that may satisfie. Then Don-Quixote turned the leafe, and said, This is prose, and it seemes to be a letter. What Sir, a missive letter? quoth Sancho. No, but rather of love, according to the beginning, quoth Don-Quixote. I pray you therefore, quoth Sancho, reade it loud enough, for I take great delight in these things of love. I am content, quoth Don-Quixote, and reading it loudly as Sancho had requested, it said as ensueth:

Thy false promise and my certaine misfortune, do carry me to such a place, as from thence thou shalt sooner receive newes of my death, then reasons of my just complaints. Thou hast disdained me (O ingrate) for one that hath more, but not for one that is worth more then I am: but if vertue were a treasure of estimation, I would not emulate other mens fortunes, nor weepe thus for mine owne misfortunes. That which thy beauty erected, thy workes have overthrowne: by it I deemed thee to be an Angell, and by these I certainely know thee to be but a woman. Rest in peace (O causer of my warre) and let heaven worke so, that thy spouses deceipts remaine still concealed, to the end thou maist not repent what thou didst, and I bee constrained to take revenge of that I desire not.

Having read the letter, Don-Quixote said, We can collect lesse by this then by the letter, what the Authour is, other then that he is some disdained lover: and so passing over all the booke, he found other Verses and Letters, of which hee could reade some, others not at all. But the summe of them all were, accusations, plaints, and mistrusts, pleasures, griefes, favours, and disdaines, some solemnized, others deplored. And whilest Don-Quixote past over the booke, Sancho past over the mallet, without leaving a corner of it, or the cushion unsearched, or a seame unript, nor a locke of wooll uncarded, to the end nothing might remaine behind for want of diligence, or carelessenesse: the found gold which past a hundred crownes, had stird in him such a greedinesse to have more. And though he got no more then that which he found at the first, yet did he account his flights in the coverlet, his vomiting of the drench, the benedictions of the packestaves, the blowes of the Carrier, the losse of his wallet, the robbing of his Cassocke, and all the hunger, thirst, and wearinesse that he had past in the service of his good Lord and Master, for well imployed; accounting himselfe to be more then well payed, by the gifts received of the money they found. The Knight of the Ilfavoured face was the while possessed with a marvailous desire to know who was the owner of the mallet, conjecturing by the Sonnet, and letter, the gold, and linnen, that the enamoured was some man of worth, whom the disdaine and rigour of his Lady had conducted to some desperate termes. But by reason that no body appeared, through that inhabitable and desart place, by whom he might be informed; hee thought on it no more, but only roade on, without choosing any other way, then that which pleased Rozinante to travaile, who tooke the plainest and easiest to passe through: having still an imagination that there could not want some strange adventure, amidst that Forrest.

And as he rode on with this conceit, he saw a man on the top of a little mountaine that stood just before his face, leape from rocke to rocke, and tuffe to tuffe, with wonderfull dexterity. And as he thought, he was naked, had a blacke and thicke beard, the haires many and confusedly mingled, his feet and legges bare, his thighes were covered with a paire of hose, which seemed to bee of Murry Velvet, but were so torne, that they discovered his flesh in many places: his head was likewise bare, and although he past by with the hast we have recounted, yet did The Knight of the Ilfavoured face note all these particularities, and although he indevoured, yet could not hee follow him, for it was not in Rozinantes power, in that weake state wherein he was, to travaile so swiftly among those rocks, chiefly being naturally very slow and flegmatike. Don-Quixote after espying him, did instantly imagine him to be owner of the cushion and mallet; and therefore resolved to goe on in his search, although he should spend a whole yeare therein among those mountaines: and commanded Sancho to goe about the one side of the mountaine, and he would goe the other, and quoth hee, it may befall that by using this diligence, wee may incounter with that man, which vanished so suddainely out of our sight. I cannot doe so, quoth Sancho, for that in parting one step from you, feare presently so assaults mee, with a thousand visions and affrightments. And let this serve you hereafter for a warning, to the end you may not from henceforth part me the blacke of a naile from your presence. It shall bee so, answereth The Knight of the ill-favoured face. And I am very glad that thou dost thus build upon my valour, the which shall never faile thee, although thou didst want thy very soule: and therefore follow me by little and little, or as thou maist, and make of thine eyes two Lanthornes, for wee give a turne to this little rocke, and perhaps wee may meete with this man whom we saw even now, who doubtlesly can be none other then the owner of our bootie. To which Sancho replyed, It were much better not to finde him: for if we should meet him, and were by chance the owner of this money, it is most evident that I must restore it to him, and therefore it is better without using this unprofitable diligence, to let me possesse it *bona fide*, untill the true Lord shall appeare by some way lesse curious and diligent: which perhaps may fall at such a time as it shall be all spent; and in that case I am freed from all processes by priviledge of the King. Thou deceivest thy selfe, Sancho, therein, quoth Don-Quixote: for seeing wee are falne already into suspition of the owner, wee are bound to search and restore it to him: and when wee would not seeke him out, yet the vehement presumption that we have of it, hath made us possessors *mala fide*, and renders us as culpable, as if he whom we surmise, were verily the true Lord. So that, friend Sancho, be not grieved to seeke him, in respect of the griefe whereof thou shalt free me if he be found. And saying so, spurd Rozinante, and Sancho followed after a foote, animated by the hope of the yong Asses his Master had promised unto him; and having compassed a part of the mountaine, they found a little streame, wherin lay dead, and halfe devoured by dogs and crows, a Mule sadled and bridled, al which confirmed more in them the suspition that hee which fled away, was owner of the Mule and cushion. And as they looked on it, they heard a whistle, much like unto that which Sheepheards use, as they keepe their flocks, and presently appeared at their left hand a great number of Goates, after whom the Goatheard that kept them, who was an aged man, followed on the toppe of the mountaine; and Don-Quixote cried to him, requesting him to come downe to them: who answered them againe as loudly, demanding of them, who had brought them to those desarts, rarely troden by any other then Goats, Wolves, or other savage beastes which frequented those mountaines? Sancho answered him, that if hee would descend where they were, they would give him account thereof. With that the Sheepheard came downe, and arriving to the place where Don-Quixote was, he said, I dare wager that you looke on the hyred Mule which lies dead there in that bottom; well, in good faith he lies in that very place these six moneths. Say, I pray you, have not you met in the way with the master thereof: We have encountred no body but a cushion and a little Mallet, which we found not very farre off from hence. I did likewise finde the same, replyed the Goat-heard, but I would never take it up nor approach to it, fearefull of some misdemeanor, or that I should be hereafter demanded for it as for a stealth. For the Divell is crafty, and now and then something riseth, even from under a mans feete, whereat he stumbles and falles, without knowing how, or how not. That is the very same, I say, quoth Sancho: for I likewise found it, but would not approach it the cast of a stone. There I have left it, and there it remaines as it was; for I would not have a dogge with a bell. Tell me good fellow, quoth Don-Quixote, dost thou know who is the owner of all these things?

That which I can say, answered the Goat-heard, is that about some sixe moneths past, little more or lesse, there arrived at a certaine sheepe-fold some three leagues off, a yong Gentleman of comely personage, and presence, mounted on that very Mule which lies dead there, and with the same Cushion and Mallet which you say you met, but touched not. He demaunded of us which was the most hidden and inaccessable part of the mountaine, and we told him that this wherein we are now: and it is true; for if you did enter but halfe a league farther, perhaps you would not finde the way out againe so readily: and I doe greatly marvell how you could find the way hither it selfe; for there is neither high way nor path that may addresse any to this place. I say then, that the young man, as soone as he heard our answere, hee turned the bridle, and travelled towards the place we shewed to him leaving us all with very great liking of his comelines, and marvell at his demaund and speed wherewith he departed and made towards the mountaine: and after that time, we did not see him a good many of daies, untill by chance one of our sheepheards came by with our provision of victuals, to whom he drew neere, without speaking a word, and spurned and beat him welfavourdly, and after went to the Asse which carried our victuals, and taking away all the bread and cheese that was there, he fled into the mountaine with wonderfull speede. When we heard of this, some of us Goat-heards, wee went to search for him, and spent therein almost two dayes in the most solitary places of this mountaine, and in the end found him lurking in the hollow part of a very tall and great Corke tree; who as soone as he perceived us, came forth to meete us with great stayednes: his apparrell was all torne, his visage disfigured, and tosted with the Sunne in such manner, as we could scarce know him, if it were not that his attire, although rent, by the notice we had of it, did give us to understand, that hee was the man for whom we sought. He saluted us courteously, and in briefe and very good reasons he said, that we ought not to marvell, seeing him goe in that manner: for that it behoved to doe so, that hee might accomplish a certaine penance injoyned to him, for the many sinnes he had committed. We prayed him to tell us what he was: but wee could never perswade him to it. We requested him likewise that whensoever he had any neede of meat (without which he could not live) he should tell us where wee might finde him, and we would bring it to him with great love and diligence; and that if he also did not like of this motion, that he would at leastwise come and aske it, and not take it violently as he had done before from our Sheepheards. Hee thanked us very much for our offer, and intreated pardon of the assaults passed, and promised to aske it from thence forward for Gods sake, without giving annoyance to any one. And touching his dwelling or place of abode, he said that he had none other then that where the night overtooke him, and ended his discourse with so feeling laments, that we might well be accounted stones which heard him, if therein we had not kept him company, considering the state wherein we had seene him first; and that wherein now he was. For as I said, he was a very comely and gracious young man, and shewed by his courteous and orderly speech, that he was well borne, and a courtlike person. For though wee were all Clownes, such as did heare him, his Gentility was such, as could make it selfe knowne, even to rudenesse it selfe: and being in the best of his Discourse, he stopt and grew silent, fixing his eyes on the ground a good while, wherein wee likewise stood still suspended, expecting in what that distraction would end, with no little compassion to behold it; for we easily perceived that some accident of madnes had surprised him, by his staring and beholding the earth so fixedly, without once mooving the eye-lidde, and other times by the shutting of them, the biting of his lips, and bending of his browes. But very speedily after, hee made us certaine thereof himselfe: for rising from the ground (whereon he had throwne himselfe a little before) with great furie, hee set upon him that sate next unto him, with such courage and rage, that if wee had not taken him away, he would have slaine him with blowes and bites, and he did all this, saying, O treacherous Fernando, here, heere thou shalt pay me the injurie that thou didst me: these handes shall rent out the heart, in which do harbour and are heaped all evils together, but principally fraude and deceit: and to these he added other words, all addrest to the dispraise of that Fernando, and to attach him of treason and untruth. We tooke from him at last, not without difficultie, our fellow, and hee without saying a word departed from us, embushing himselfe presently among the bushes and brambles, leaving us wholly disabled to follow him in those rough and unhaunted places. By this we gathered that his madnes comes to him at times, and that some one called Fernando, [had done] some ill work of such waight, as the termes shew, to which it hath brought him. All which hath after beene yet confirmed as often, (which were many times) as he came out to the fields, sometimes to demaund meat of the Sheepheards, and other times to take it of them perforce: for when hee is taken with this fit of madnesse, although the Sheepheards doe offer him meat willingly, yet will not he receive, unlesse he take it with buffets: and when hee is in his right sense, he asks it for Gods sake, with courtesie and humanity, and renders many thanks, and that not without teares. And in very truth, Sirs, I say unto you, quoth the Goatheard, that I and foure others, wherof two are my men, other two my friends, resolved Yesterday to search until we found him; and being found, eyther by force or faire means, we will carry him to the towne of Almodavar, which is but eight leagues from hence; and there will we have him cured, if his disease may be holpen, or at least we shall learne what he is, when he turnes to his wits, and whether he hath any friends to whom notice of his misfortune may be given. This is, Sirs, all that I can say concerning that which you demaunded of mee; and you shall understand that the owner of those things which you saw in the way, is the very same, whom you saw passe by you so naked and nimble. For Don-Quixote had told him by this, that hee had seene that man goe by, leaping among the Rockes.

Don-Quixote rested marvellously admired at the Goatheards tale, and with greater desire to know who that unfortunate mad-man was, purposed with himselfe, as hee had alreadie resolved to search him throughout the mountaines, without leaving a corner or Cave of it unsought, untill he had gotten him. But fortune disposed the matter better then he expected: for he appeared in that very instant in a clift of a Rocke, that answered to the place where they stood speaking, who came towards them, murmuring somewhat to himselfe, which could not be understood neere at hand, and much lesse a farre off. His apparell was such as we have delivered, onely differing in this, as Don-Quixote perceived when he drew neerer, that he wore on him, although torne, a leather Ierkin perfumed with Ambar. By which he thoroughly collected, that the person which wore such attire, was not of the least quality. When the young man came to the place where they discoursed, he saluted them with a hoarce voyce, but with great courtesie: and Don-Quixote returned him his greetings with no lesse complement; and allighting from Rozinante, he advanced to imbrace him with very good carriage and countenance, and held him a good while straightly between his armes, as if he had knowne him of long time. The other, whom we may call the unfortunate Knight of the Rock, as well as Don-Quixote, the Knight of the ill favoured face, after he had permitted himselfe to be imbraced a while, did step a little off from our Knight; and laying his hand on his shoulders, began to behold him earnestly, as one desirous to call to minde whether he had ever seene him before: being perhaps no less admired to see Don-Quixote figure, proportion and armes, then Don-Quixote was to view him. In resolution, the first that spoke after the imbracing, was the ragged Knight, and sayd what we will presently recount.

Chapter 10

Wherein is prosecuted the adventure of Sierra Morena.

The History affirmes, that great was the atention, wherewithall Don-Quixote listened to the unfortunate Knight of the Rock, who began his speech in this manner: Truely, good Sir, whatsoever you be (for I know you not) I doe with all my heart gratifie the signes of affection and courtesie which you have used towards me, and wish heartily that I were in termes to serve with more then my will, the good will you beare towards me, as your courteous intertainment denotes: but my fate is so niggardly, as it affoords me no other meanes to repay good workes done to me, then onely to lend me a good desire sometime to satisfie them. So great is mine affection, replied Don-Quixote, to serve you, as I was fully resolved never to depart out of these mountaines untill I had found you, and known of your selfe whether there might be any kind of remedy found for the griefe that this your so unusuall a kind of life argues, doth possesse your soule. And if it were requisite, to search it out with all possible diligence: and when your disaster were known of those which clap their doors in the face of comfort, I intended in that case to beare a part in your lamentations, and plaine it with the dolefullest note; for it is a consolation in afflictions to have one that condoles in them. And if this my good intention may merit any acceptance, or be gratified by any courtesie, let me intreat you, Sir, by the excesse thereof, which I see accumulated in your bosom; and joyntly I conjure you by that thing which you have, or doe presently most affect, that you will please to disclose unto me who you are, and what the cause hath bin that perswaded you to come, to live and dye in these desarts, like a bruit beast, seeing you live among such, so alienated from your selfe, as both your attire and countenance demonstrate. And I doe vow (quoth

Don-Quixote) by the high order of Chivalrie, which I (although unworthie and a sinner) have received, and by the profession of Knights errant, that if you doe pleasure me herein, to assist you with as good earnest as my profession doth binde me, either by remedying your disaster, if it can be holpen; or els by assisting you to lament it, if it be so desperate.

The Knight of the Rocke, who heard him of the ill favoured face speake in that manner, did nothing else for a great while, but behold him again and again, and re-behold him from top to toe. And after viewing him wel he said; if you have any thing to eate, I pray you give it me for Gods sake, and after I have eaten, I will satisfie your demand thorowly, to gratifie the many courtesies and undeserved proffers you have made unto me. Sancho, and the Goatheard presents the one out of his Wallet, the other out of his Scrip, tooke some meat and gave it to the Knight of the Rocke to allay his hunger, and he did eate so fast, like a distracted man, as he left no intermission between bit and bit, but clapt them up so swiftly, as he rather seemed to swallow then to chew them; and whilst he did eat, neither he or any of the rest spoke a word: and having ended his dinner, he made them signes to follow him, as at last they did, unto a little meadow seated hard by that place, at the folde of a mountaine; where being arrived he stretched himselfe on the grasse, which the rest did likewise in his imitation, without speaking a word, untill that he after setling himselfe in his place, began in this manner: if, Sirs, you please to heare the exceeding greatnesse of my disasters briefly rehearsed, you must promise me, that you will not interrupt the file of my dolefull narration, with eyther demaund or other thing; for in the very instant that you shall do it, there also must remaine that which I say depending. These words of our ragged Knights, called to Don-Quixotes remembrance the tale which his Squire had told unto him when he erred in the account of his Goats, which had passed the river, for which that Historie remained suspended. But returning to our ragged man, he said; this prevention which now I give, is to the end that I may compendiously passe over the discourse of my mishaps: for the revoking of them to remembrance, onely serves me to none other steed then to increase the old by adding of new misfortunes; and by how much the fewer your questions are, by so much the more speedily shal I have finished my pittifull Discourse; and yet I meane not to omit any essential poynt of my woes untoucht, that your desires may be herein sufficiently satisfied. Don-Quixote in his own, and his other companions name, promised to performe his request; whereupon he began his relation in this manner:

My name is Cardenio, the place of my birth, one of the best Cities in Andaluzia, my linage noble, my parents rich, and my misfortunes so great, as I thinke my parents have e're this deplored, and my kinsfolke condoled them; being very little able with their wealth to redresse them; for the goods of fortune are but of smal vertue to remedie the disasters of heaven. There dwelt in the same Citie a heaven, wherein love had placed all the glory that I could desire; so great is the beauty of Luscinda, a damzel as noble and rich as I: but more fortunate and lesse constant then my honourable desires expected. I loved, honoured, and adored this Luscinda, almost from my verie infancy; and she affected me likewise, with all the integritie and good will, which with her so young yeares did accord. Our parents knew our mutuall amity; for which they were nothing agrieved, perceyving very well, that although we continued it, yet could it have none other end but that of Matrimony; a thing which the equality of our blood and substance did of it selfe almost invite us to. Our age and affection increased in such sort, as it seemed fit for Luscinda's father, for certaine good respects, to denie me the entrance of his house any longer; imitating in a manner therein Tisbi, so much solemnized by the poets, her parents; which hinderance served only to adde flame to flame, and desire to desire: for although it set silence to our tongues, yet could they not impose it to our pens, which are wont to expresse to whom it pleased, the most hidden secrecies of our soules, with more libertie then the tong; for the presence of the beloved doth often distract, trouble, and strike dumbe the boldest tongue and firmest resolution. O heavens, how many Letters have I written unto her? What cheerefull and honest answers have I received? How many Ditties and amorous Verses have I composed, wherein my soule declared and published her passions, declined her inflamed desires, intertayned her remembrance, and recreated her will? In effect, perceyving my selfe to be forced, and that my soule consumed with a perpetuall desire to behold her, I resolved to put my desires in execution, and finish in an instant that which I deemed most expedient for the better atchieving of my desired and deserved reward; which was (as I did indeed) to demaund her of her father for my lawfull Spouse. To which he made answere, that he did gratifie the good will which I shewed by honouring him, and desire to honour my selfe with pawnes that were his: but yet seeing my father yet lived, the motion of that matter properly most concerned him. For if it were not done with his good liking and pleasure, Luscinda was not a woman to be taken or given by stealth. I rendred him thankes for his good will, his words seeming unto me very reasonable, as that my father should agree unto them, as soone as I should explane the matter; and therefore departed presently to acquaint him with my desires; who, at the time which I entred into a chamber, wherein he was, stood with a letter open in his hand; and espying me, e're I could breake my mind unto him, gave it me, saying; by that letter, Cardenio, you may gather the desire the Duke Ricardo beares, to doe you any pleasure or favour. This Duke Ricardo, as I thinke you know Sirs already, is a Grande of Spayne, whose Dukedome is seated in the best part of all Andaluzia. I tooke the letter and read it; which appeared so urgent, as I my selfe accounted it would be ill done, if my father did not accomplish the contents thereof, which were endeed, that he should presently addresse me to his court, to the end I might be companion (and not servant) to his eldest sonne; and that he would incharge himselfe with the advancing of me to such preferments as might be answerable unto the value and estimation he made of my person. I past over the whole Letter, and was strucken dumbe at the reading thereof, but chiefly hearing my father to say, Cardenio, thou must depart within two dayes, to accomplish the Dukes desire; and omit not to render Almighty God thankes, which doth thus open the way, by which thou mayest attaine in fine to that which I know thou doest merite; and to these words added certaine others of fatherly counsell and direction. The terme of my departure arrived, and I spoke to my Luscinda on a certaine night, and recounted unto her all that passed, and likewise to her father, intreating him to overslip a few daies, and deferre the bestowing of his daughter else-where, untill I went to understand Duke Ricardo his will: which he promised me, and she confirmed it with a thousand oathes and promises. Finally, I came to Duke Ricardoes Court, and was so friendly received and entertained by him, as even very then envie began to exercise her accustomed function, beeing forthwith emulated by the auncient Servitors; perswading themselves, that the tokens the Duke shewed to doe me favours, could not but turne to their prejudice. But he that rejoyced the most at mine arrivall, was a second sonne of the Dukes, called Fernando, who was young, gallant, very comely, liberall, and amorous; who within a while after my comming, held mee so deerely, as every one wondred thereat: and though the elder loved me well, and did me favour, yet was it in no respect comparable to that wherewithall Don Fernando loved and treated me. It therefore befell, that as there is no secresie amongst friends so great, but they will communicate it the one to the other, and the familiarity which I had with Don Fernando, was now past the limits of favour, and turned into deerest amitie, he revealed unto me all his thoughts, but chiefly one of his love, which did not a little molest him. For he was enamoured on a Farmers daughter that was his fathers vassall, whose parents were marvellous rich, and she her selfe so beautifull, wary, discreete, and honest, as never a one that knew her, could absolutely determine wherein, [or] in which of all her perfections she did most excell or was most accomplished. And those good parts of the beautifull countreymaide, reduced Don Fernando his desires to such an exigent, as he resolved that he might the better gaine her good will, and conquere her integritie, to passe her a promise of marriage; for otherwise he should labour to affect that which was impossible, and but strive against the streame. I, as one bound thereunto by our friendship, did thwart and disswade him from his purpose with the best reasons, and most efficacious words I might: and seeing all could not prevaile, I determined to acquaint the Duke Ricardo his father therewithall. But Don Fernando beeing very crafty and discreete, suspected and feared as much, because hee considered that in the law of a faithfull servant, I was bound not to conceale a thing that would turne so much to the prejudice of the duke my Lord: and therefore both to divert and deceive me at once, that he could finde no meanes so good, to deface the remembrance of that beautie out of his minde, which held his hart in such subjection, then to absent himself for certaine moneths: and he would likewise have that absence to be this, that both of us should depart together, and come to my fathers house, under pretence (as hee would informe the Duke) that he went to see and cheapen certaine great horses that were in the Citie wherein I was borne; a place of breeding the best horses in the world. Scarce had I heard him say this (when borne away by the naturall propension each one hath to his Countrey, and my love joynde) although his designment had not beene so good, yet would I have ratified it, as one of the most expedient that could be imagined, because I saw occasion and oportunity so fairely offred, to returne and see againe my Luscinda. And thereof set on by this thought and desire, I approved his opinion, and did quicken his purpose, perswading him to prosecute it with all possible speede, for absence would in the end work her effect in despite of the most forcible and urgent thoughts; and when he said this to me, hee had already under the title of a husband (as it was afterward knowne) reaped the fruits of his longing desires, from his beautifull countrey maide, and did onely await an opportunity to reaveale it without his owne detriment; fearefull of the Duke his fathers indignation, when he should understand his errour.

It afterward hapned, that as love in young men is not for the most part love but lust, the which (as it ever proposeth to it selfe as his last end and period his delight) so as soone as it obtaineth the same, it likewise decaieth and maketh forcibly to retire that which was termed love; for it cannot transgresse the limits which Nature hath assigned it, which boundings or meares, Nature hath in no wise allotted to true and sincere affection. I would say, that as soone as Don Ferdinando had injoyed his Country lasse, his desires weakened, and his importunities waxed colde; and if at the first he fained an excuse to absent himselfe, that he might with more facility compasse them, he did now in very good earnest procure to depart, to the end he might not put them in execution. The Duke gave him license to depart, and commanded me to accompany him. We came to my Citie, where my father entertayned him according to his calling. I saw Luscinda, and then againe were reviv'd (although indeede they were neither dead nor moritfied) my desires, and acquainted Don Fernando (alas, to my totall ruine) with them, because I thought it was not lawfull by the law of amity to keepe any thing concealed from him. There I dilated to him, on the beauty, wit, and discretion of Luscinda in so ample manner, as my prayses stirred in him a desire to view a Damzell so greatly adorned, and inriched with so rare endowments: and this his desire I through my misfortune satisfied, shewing her unto him by the light of a candle, at a Window where we two were wont to parle together; where he beheld her to be such, as was sufficient to blot out of his memory all the beauties which ever he had viewed before. He stood mute, beside himselfe, and ravished: and moreover rested so greatly enamoured, as you may perceive in the Discourse of this my doleful narration. And to inflame his desires the more, (a thing which I fearefully avoyded, and onely discovered to heaven) fortune so disposed, that he found after me one of her letters, wherein she requested that I would demand her of her father for wife; which was so discreet, honest and amorously penned, as he said after reading it, that in Luscinda alone were included all the graces of beauty and understanding joyntly, which were divided and separate in all the other women of the world. Yet in good sooth I will here confesse the truth, that although I saw cleerely how deservedly Luscinda was thus extold by Don Ferdinando, yet did not her praises please me so much pronounced by him, and therefore began to feare and suspect him, because he let no moment overslip us, without making some mention of Luscinda, and would still himselfe begin the discourse, were the occasion ever so far-fetched: a thing which rowsed in me I cannot tell what jealousie; not that I did feare any traverse in Luscindas loyalty, but yet for all my fates made me the very thing which they most assured mee: and Don Ferdinando procured to read all the papers I sent to Luscinda, or she to me, under pretext that he tooke extraordinary delight to note the witty conceits of us both. It therefore fell out, that Luscinda having demaunded of mee a booke of Chivalry to read, wherein shee tooke marvellous delight, and was that of *Amadis du Gaule*.

Scarce had Don-Quixote well heard him make mention of bookes of Knight-hood, when hee replied to him; if you had, good Sir, but once told me at the beginning of your Historical narration, that your Lady Luscinda was affected to the reading of Knightly adventures, you needed not to have used any amplification to indeere or make plaine unto me the eminencie of her wit; which certainely could not in any wise bee so excellent and perspicuous as you have figured it, if she wanted the propension and feeling you have rehearsed, to the perusing of so pleasing discourses: so that henceforth with me, you need not spend any more words to explaine and manifest the height of her beauty, worthes and understanding; for by this onely notice I have received of her devotion to books of Knighthood, I do confirme her for the most faire and accomplished woman for all perfections in the world: and I would to God, good Sir, that you had also sent her together with *Amadis*, the Histories of the good *Don Rugel of Grecia*; for I am certaine the Lady Luscinda would have taken great delight in Darayda and Garaya, and in the wittie conceits of the Sheepheard Darinel, and in those admirable verses of his Bucolickes, sung and rehearsed by him with such grace, discretion and liberty. but a time may come, wherein this fault may be recompenced, if it shall please you to come with mee to my village; for there I may give you three hundred bookes, which are my soules greatest contentment, and the intertainment of my life; although I do now verily beleeve that none of them are left, thankes be to the malice of evill and envious inchanters. And I beseech you to pardon me this transgression of our agreement (at the first promised) not to interrupt your Discourses: for when I heare any motion made of Chivalry or Knights Errant, it is no more in my power to omit to speake of them, then in the Sunne-beames to leave off warming, or in the Moones to render things humid. And therefore I intreat pardon, and that you will prosecute your History, which is that which most imports us.

Whilest Don-Quixote spoke those words, Cardenio hanged his head on his brest, giving manifest tokens that he was exceeding sad. And although Don-Quixote requested him twice to follow on with his Discourse, yet neither did he lift up his head, or answere a word, till at last, after he had stood a good while musing, hee held up his head and said: it cannot be taken out of my minde, nor is there any one in the world can deprive me of the conceit, or make mee beleeve the contrary: and we were a bottle-head, that would thinke or beleeve otherwise then that the great villaine, Master Elisabat the Barber kept Queene Madasima as his Lemman. That is not so, I vow by such and such, quoth Don-Quixote in great choler (and as he was wont, rapt out three or foure round oathes) and it is great malice, or rather villany to say such a thing. For Queene Madasima was a very noble Lady, and it ought not to be presumed, that so high a Princesse would fall in love with a Quack-salver: and whosoever thinkes the contrary, lies like an arrant villaine; as I will make him understand a horsebacke or a foote, armed or disarmed, by night or by day, or as he best liketh. Cardenio stood beholding him very earnestly as he spoke these words, whom the accident of his madnesse had by this possessed, and was not in plight to prosecute his History: or would Don-Quixote give eare to it, he was so mightily disgusted to heare Queene Madasima detracted. A marvellous accident, for hee tooke her defence as earnestly, as if she were verily his true and naturall Princesse; his wicked bookes had so much distracted him. And Cardenio being by this furiously madde, hearing himselfe answered with the lie, and the denomination of a villaine, with other the like outrages, he tooke the rest in ill part, and lifting up a stone that was neere unto him, gave Don-Quixote such a blow therewithall, as hee overthrew him to the ground on his backe. Sancho Pança seeing his Master so roughly handled, set upon the foole with his fist shut; and the ragged man received his assault in such manner, as he likewise overthrew him at his feete with one fist, and mounting afterward upon him, did worke him with his feete like a piece of dough: and the Goatheard, who thought to succour him, was like to incurre the same danger. And after hee had overthrowne and beaten them all very well, he departed from them and entred into the wood very quietly. Sancho arose, and with rage to see himselfe so belaboured without desert, hee ranne upon the Goatheard to bee revenged on him, saying that he was in the fault, who had not premonished them, how that mans raving fits did take him so at times; for had they beene advertised therof, they might have stood all the while on their guard. The Goatheard answered, that he had already advised them thereof; and if hee had not beene attentive thereunto, yet he was therefore nothing the more culpable. Sancho Pança replied, and the Goatheard made a rejoynder thereunto: but their disputation ended at last, in the catching hold of one anothers beards, and befisting themselves so uncompassionately, as if Don-Quixote had not pacified them, they would have torne one another to pieces. Sancho holding still the Goatheard fast, said unto his Lord, Let mee alone, Sir Knight of the ill favoured face, for on this man who is a Clowne as I am my selfe, and [no] dubbed Knight, I may safely satisfie my selfe of the wrong he hath done me, by fighting with him hand to hand like an honourable man. It is true, quoth Don-Quixote, but I know well that hee is in no wise culpable of that which hath hapned. And saying so, appeased them; and turned againe to demand of the Goatheard, whether it were possible to meet againe with Cardenio; for he remained possessed with an exceeding desire to know the end of his History. The Goat-heard turned again to repeat what he had said at the first, to wit, that he knew not any certaine place of his abode; but if he haunted that Commarke any while, he would some-time meete with him, eyther in his madde or modest humour.

Chapter 13

How the Curate and the Barber put their designe in practise, with many other things, worthy to be recorded in this famous Historie.

Both therefore arresting there quietly under the shadow, there arrived to their hearing the sound of a voyce, which without being accompanied by any instrument, did resound so sweet and melodiously, as they remained greatly admired, because they esteemed not that to be a place wherein any so good a Musitian might make his abode. For although it is usually said, that in the woods and fields are found Shepheards of excellent voyces, yet is this rather a Poeticall indeerement, then an approved truth; and most of all, when they perceived that the verses they heard him singing were not of rusticke composition, but rather of delicate and Courtly invention.

* * *

The Song was concluded with a profound sigh; and both the others lent attentive care to heare if hee would sing any more; but perceyving that the musicke was converted into throbs and dolefull playnts, they resolved to goe and learne who was the wretch, as excellent for his voyce, as dolorous in his sighes: and after they had gone a little at the doubling of the point of a cragge, they perceived one of the very same forme and fashion that Sancho had painted unto them, when he told them the Historie of Cardenio: which man espying them likewise, shewed no semblance of feare, but stood stil with his head hanging on his brest like a male-content, not once lifting up his eyes to behold them from the first time, when they unexpectedly arrived.

The Curate, who was a man very well spoken (as one that had alreadie intelligence of his misfortune, for hee knew him by his signes) drew neerer to him, and prayed and perswaded him with short, but very forcible reasons, to forsake that miserable life, lest he should there eternally lose it, which of all miseries would prove the most miserable. Cardenio at this season was in his right sense, free from the furious accident, that distracted him so often; and therefore viewing them both attyred in so strange and unusuall a fashion from that which was used among those desarts, he rested somewhat admired; but chiefly hearing them speak in his affaire, as in a matter knowne (for so much hee gathered out of the Curates speeches) and therefore answered in this manner: I perceyve well, good Sirs, (whosoever you be) that heaven which hath alwayes care to succour good men, yea even and the wicked many times, hath without any desert addrest unto me by these desarts and places so remote from vulgar haunt, persons, which laying before mine eyes with quicke and pregnant reasons the little I have to lead this kinde of life, doe labour to remove me from this place to a better: and by reason they know not as much as I doe, and that after escaping this harme, I shall fall into a farre greater, they account me perhaps for a man of weake discourse: and what is worse, for one wholly devoid of judgement. And were it so, yet is it no marvell; for it seemes to mee that the force of the imagination of my disasters is so bent and powerfull in my destruction, that I, without being able to make it any resistance, do become like a stone, void of all good feeling and knowledge: and I come to know the certainty of this truth, when some men doe recount and shew unto me tokens of the things I have done, whilst this terrible accident over-rules mee: and after I can doe no more, then be grieved though in vayne, and curse without benefit, my too froward fortune; and render as an excuse of my madnesse, the relation of the cause thereof, to as many as please to heare it: for wisemen perceyving the cause, will not wonder at the effects. And though they give me no remedie, yet at least wil not condemne me, for it will convert the anger they conceive at my misrules, into compassion of my disgraces. And, Sirs, if by chance it be so, that you come with the same intention that others did, I request you, ere you inlarge farther your discreet perswasions, that you will give eare a while to the relation of my mishaps: for perhaps when you have understood it, you may save the labour that you would take, consorting an evil wholly incapable of consolation.

Both of them, which desired nothing so much then to understand from his owne mouth, the occasion of his harmes, did intreat him to relate it, promising to do nothing else in his remedie or comfort, but what himselfe pleased. And with this the sorrowfull Gentleman began his dolefull Historie, with the very same words almost that he had rehearsed it to Don-Quixote and the Goatheard a few dayes past, when by occasion of Master Elisabat and Don-Quixotes curiositie in observing the Decorum of Chivalry, the tale remained imperfect, as our History left it above. But now good fortune so disposed things, that his foolish fit came not upon him, but gave him leisure to continue his storie to the end; and so arriving to the passage that spoke of the Letter Don Ferdinando found in the book of *Amadis du Gaule*, Cardenio said that he had it very well in memorie; and the sense was this:

Luscinda to Cardenio

'I discover daily in thee worthes, that oblige and inforce mee to hold thee deere: and therefore if thou desirest to have me discharge this debt, without serving a writ on my honour, thou mayest easily doe it. I have a father that knowes thee, and loves me likewise well; who without forcing my will, will accomplish that which justly thou oughtest to have: if it be so, that thou esteemest mee as much as thou sayest, and I doe beleeve.'

This Letter moved mee to demand Luscinda of her father for my wife, as I have already recounted; and by it also Luscinda remained in Don Ferdinando's opinion crowned, for one of the most discreet women of her time. And this billet Letter was that which first put him in mind to destroy me, e're I could effect my desires. I tolde to Don Ferdinando wherein consisted all the difficultie of her fathers protracting of the marriage, to wit, in that my father should first demand her; the which I dared not to mention unto him, fearing lest he would not willingly consent thereunto; not for that the qualitie, bountie, vertue, and beautie of Luscinda were to him unknowne, or that she had not parts in her able to ennoblish and adorne any other linage of Spaine whatsoever: but because I understood by him, that he desired not to marrie me, untill he had seene what Duke Ricardo would doe for me. Finally, I tolde him that I dared not reveale it to my father, as well for that inconvenience, as for many others that made mee so affraid, without knowing what they were, as me thought my desires would never take effect. To all this Don Ferdinando made me answer, that he would take upon him to speake to my father, and perswade him to treat of that affaire also with Luscindas. O ambitious Marius. O cruell Cataline. O facinorous Quila. O treacherous Galalon. O trayterous Vellido. O revengefull Iulian. O covetous Iudas. Traytor, cruell, revengefull, and couzening, what indeserts did this wretch commit, who with such plaines discovered to thee the secrets and delights of his heart? What offence committed I against thee? What words did I speake, or counsel did I give, that were not all addrest to the increasing of thine honour and profite? But on what doe I of all wretches the worst complaine, seeing that when the current of the starres doth bring with it mishaps, by reason they come downe precipatately from above, there is no earthly force can with-hold, or humane industry prevent or evacuat them? Who would have imagined that Don Fernando, a noble gentleman, discreet, obliged by my deserts, and powerful to obtaine whatsoever the amorous desire would exact of him, where and whensoever it seazed on his heart, would (as they say) become so corrupt, as to deprive me of one onely sheepe, which yet I did not possesse? But let these considerations be laide apart as unprofitable, that we may knit up againe the broken threede of my unfortunate History. And therefore I say, that Don Ferdinando beleeving, that my presence was a hinderance to put his treacherous and wicked designe in execution, he resolved to send mee to his eldest brother, under pretext to get some money of him, for to buy sixe great horses, that he had of purpose, and onely to the end I might absent my selfe, bought the very same day that he offered to speake himselfe to my father, and would have me goe for the money (because he might bring his treacherous intent the better to passe) could I prevent this treason? Or could I perhaps but once imagine it? No truly; but rather glad for the good merchandize hee had made, did make proffer of my selfe to depart for the money very willingly. I spoke that night to Luscinda, and acquainted her with the agreement past betweene mee and Don Ferdinando, bidding her to hope firmely, that our good just desires would sort a wished and happie end. She answered me againe (as little suspecting Don Ferdinandos treason as my selfe) bidding me to returne with all speed, because she beleeved that the conclusion of our affections should be no longer deferred, then my father deferred to speake unto hers. And what was the cause I know not, but as soone as she had said this unto me, her eyes were filled with teares, and somewhat thwarting her throat, hindred her from saying many other things, which me thought shee strived to speake.

I rested admired at this new accident untill that time never seene in her; for alwaies as many times as my good fortune and diligence graunted it, wee conversed with all sport and delight, without ever intermedling in our discourses, any teares, sighes, complaints, suspitions, or feares. Al my speech was to advance my fortune; for having receyved her from heaven as my Ladie and Mistresse, then would I amplifie her beautie, admire her worth, and prayse her discretion. She on the other side would returne mee the exchange, extolling in mee, what shee as one enamoured accounted worthy of laude and commendation. After this we would recount a hundred thousand toyes and chances befalne our neighbours and acquaintance, and that to which my presumption dared farthest to extend it selfe, was sometimes to take her beautiful and Ivorie hands perforce, and kisse them as well as I might through the rigorous strictnesse of a niggardly yron-grate which devided us. But the precedent night to the day of my sad departure, she wept, sobd, and sighed, and departed, leaving me full of confusion and inward assaults, amazed to behold such new and dolefull tokens of sorrow and feeling in Luscinda. But because I would not murder my hopes, I did attribute all these things to the force of her affection towards me, and to the griefe which absence is wont to stirre in those that love one another deerely. To be briefe, I departed from thence sorrowfull and pensive, my soule being ful of imaginations and suspitions, and yet know not what I suspected or imagined: Cleere tokens, foretelling the sad successe and misfortune which attended me. I arrived to the place where I was sent, and delivered my Letters to Don Ferdinandos brother, and was well intertained, but not well dispatched: for he commanded me to expect (a thing to me most displeasing) eight dayes, and that out of the Duke his fathers presence; because his brother had written unto him to send him certaine moneyes unknowne to his father. And all this was but false Don Ferdinandos invention, for his brother wanted not money wherewithall to have dispatched me presently, had not he written the contrary.

This was so displeasing a commandement and order, as almost it brought me to termes of disobeying it, because it seemed to mee a thing most impossible to sustaine my life so many dayes in the absence of my Luscinda; and specially having left her so sorrowfull as I have recounted; yet notwithstanding I did obey like a good servant, although I knew it would be with the cost of my health. But on the fourth day after I had arrived, there came a man in my search with a letter, which he delivered unto me, and by the indorsement I knew it to be Luscindas; for the hand was like hers. I opened it not without feare and assaylement of my senses, knowing that it must have beene some serious occasion, which could move her to write unto me, being absent, seeing she did it so rarely, even when I was present. I demaunded of the Bearer before I read, who had delivered it to him, and what time he had spent in the way. He answered me, that passing by chance at mid-day thorow a streete of the Citie, a very beautifull Ladie did call him from a certaine window: Her eyes were all beblubbered with teares; and said unto him very hastily, Brother, if thou beest a Christian, as thou appearest to be one, I pray thee for Gods sake, that thou doe forthwith addresse this Letter to the place and person that the superscription assigneth, (for they be well knowen) and therein thou shalt doe our Lord great service. And because thou mayest not want meanes to doe it, take what thou shalt finde wrapped in that Handkerchife: and saying so, she threw out of the Window a handkerchife, wherein were lapped up a hundred Rials, this Ring of Gold which I carie here, and that letter which I delivered unto you; and presently without expecting mine answer shee departed, but first saw me take up the handkerchife and letter; and then I made her signes that I would accomplish herein her command: and after perceyving the paines I might take in bringing you it so well considered, and seeing by the indorsement, that you were the man to whom it was addrest: for, Sir, I know you verie well; and also obliged to doe it by the teares of that beautifull Ladie, I determined not to trust any other with it, but to come and bring it you my selfe in person: and in sixteene houres since it was given unto me, I have travelled the journey you know, which is at least eighteene leagues long. Whilest the thankefull new messenger spake thus unto me, I remained in a manner hanging on his words, and my thighes did tremble in such manner, as I could very hardly sustaine my selfe on foot: yet taking courage, at last I opened the Letter, whereof these were the Contents:

'The word that Don Ferdinando hath past unto you to speake to your father, that he might speake to mine, he hath accomplished more to his owne pleasure then to your profite. For, Sir, you shall understand, that he hath demaunded me for his wife; and my father borne away by the advantage of worthes which he supposes to be in Don Ferdinando more then in you, hath agreed to his demaund in so good earnest, as the espousals shall bee celebrated within these two daies, and that so secretly and alone, as onely the heavens and some folke of the house shall be witnesses. How I remaine, imagine, and whether it be convenient you should returne, you may consider: and the successe of this affaire shall let you to perceive, whether I love you well or no. I beseech Almighty God that this may arrive unto your hands, before mine shall see it selfe in danger to joyne it selfe with his, which keepeth his promised faith so ill.'

These were in summe, the Contents of the Letter, and the motives that perswaded me presently to depart, without attending any other answer, or other monies: for then I conceived clearely, that it was not the buyall of the horses, but that of his delights, which had moved Don Ferdinando to send mee to his brother. The rage which I conceived against him, joyned with the feare to lose the jewell which I had gained by so many yeares service, and desires, did set wings on mee, for I arrived as if I had flien the next day at mine owne Citie, in the houre and moment fit to goe speak to Luscinda. I entred secretly, and left my Mule whereon I rode in the honest mans house, that had brought mee the letter, and my fortune purposing then to be favourable to me, disposed so mine affairs, that I found Luscinda sitting at that yron grate, which was the sole witnesse of our loves. Luscinda knew me straight and I her, but not as we ought to know one another. But who is he in the world which may truly vaunt, that he hath penetrated, and throughly exhausted the confused thoughts, and mutable nature of women? Truly none. I say then, to proceede with my tale, that as soone as Luscinda perceived me, shee said, Cardenio, I am attired with my wedding garments, and in the Hall doe waite for mee, the traitor Don Ferdinando, and my covetous father with other witnesses, which shall rather be such of my death, then of mine espousals; bee not troubled deare friend, but procure to be present at this sacrifice, the which if I cannot hinder by my perswasions and reasons, I carry hidden about me a poynard secretly, which may hinder more resolute forces, by giving end to my life, and a beginning to thee, to know certaine the affection which I have ever borne, and doe beare unto thee. I answered her troubled and hastily, fearing I should not have the leasure to reply unto her, saying, Sweete Ladie, let thy workes verifie thy words for if thou carriest a poynard to defend thy credit, I doe heere likewise beare a sword wherewithall I will defend thee, or kill my selfe, if fortune proove adverse and contrary. I beleave that she could not heare all my words, by reason she was called hastily away as I perceived, for that the bridegroome expected her comming. By this the night of my sorrowes did throughly fall, and the Sunne of my gladnesse was set: and I remained without light in mine eyes, or discourse in my understanding. I could not finde the way into her house, nor could I move my selfe to any part: yet considering at last how important my presence was, for that which might befall in that adventure, I animated my selfe the best I could, and entred into the house; and as one that knew very well all the entries and passages thereof, and specially by reason of the trouble and businesse that was then in hand, I went in unperceived of any. And thus without being seene, I had the oportunitie to place my selfe in the hollow roome of a window of the same Hall, which was covered by the endes of two incountring peeces of tapestry, from whence I could see all that was done in the Hall, remaining my selfe unviewed of any. Who could now describe the assaults and surprisals of my heart whilst I there abode? The thoughts which incountred my mind, the considerations which I had, which were so many and such, as they can neither be said, nor is it reason they should? Let it suffice you to know, that the bridegroome entred into the Hall without any ornament, wearing the ordinary array he was wont, and was accompanied by a cousen Germain of Luscindas, and in all the Hall there was no stranger present, nor any other then the household servants: within a while after, Luscinda came out of the Parlour, accompanied by her mother and two waiting maides of her owne, as richly attired and deckt, as her calling and beautie deserved, and the perfection of courtly pompe and bravery could affoord: my distraction and trouble of minde lent me no time to note particularly the apparell shee wore, and therefore did onely marke the colours, which were carnation, and white; and the splendour which the precious stones and Iewels of her Tires, and all the rest of her garments yeelded: yet did the singular beauty of her faire and golden tresses surpasse them so much, as being in competencie with the precious stones, and flame of foure linkes that lighted in the Hall, yet did the splendour thereof seeme farre more bright and glorious to mine eies. O memory, the mortall enemie of mine ease, to what end serves it now to represent unto me the uncomparable beautie of that my adored enemy? Were it not better, cruel memory, to remember and represent that which shee did then, that being mooved by so manifest a wrong, I may at least endevour to lose my life, since I cannot procure a revenge? Tire not, good sirs, to heare the digressions I make, for my griefe is not of that kinde that may be rehearsed succinctly and speedily, seeing that in mine opinion every passage of it is worthy of a large discourse.

To this the Curate answered, that not onely they were not tyred or wearied, hearing of him, but rather they received marvellous delight to heare him recount each minuitie and circumstance, because they were such, as deserved not to be past over in silence, but rather merited as much attention as the principall parts of the History. You shall then wit (quoth Cardenio) that as they thus stood in the Hall, the Curate of the Parish entred, and taking them both by the hand, to do that which in such an act is required at the saying of, 'Will you Ladie Luscinda take the Lord Don Ferdinando, who is heere present for your lawfull Spouse, according as our holy mother the Church commands?' I thrust out all my head and neck out of the tapistry, and with most attentive eares and a troubled mind, settled my self to heare what Luscinda answered; expecting by it the sentence of my death, or the confirmation of my life. O, if one had dared to sally out at that time, and cried with a loud voice: O Luscinda, Luscinda, see well what thou doest, consider withall what thou owest me! Behold how thou art mine, and that thou canst not be any others; note that thy saying of yea, and the end of my life shall be both in one instant. O traytor Don Ferdinando, robber of my glory, death of my life, what is this thou pretendest? what wilt thou doe? Consider that thou canst not Christianlike atchieve thine intention, seeing Luscinda is my spouse, and I am her husband. O foolish man now that I am absent, and farre from the danger, I say what I should have done, and not what I did. Now after that I have permitted my deare Iewel to be robbed, I exclaime on the theefe, on whom I might have revenged my selfe, had I had as much heart to doe it as I have to complaine. In fine, since I was then a coward and a foole, it is no matter though I now die ashamed, sory, and franticke. The Curate stood expecting Luscindas answer a good while ere she gave it: and in the end, when I hoped that she would take out the Poynard to stab her selfe, or would unloose her tongue to say some truth, or use some reason or perswasion that might redound to my benefit, I heard heere in stead thereof, answer with a dismaied and languishing voice the word, 'I will': and then Don Fernando said the same, and giving her the Ring, they remained tyed with an indissoluble knot. Then the Bridegroome comming to kisse his spouse, she set her hand upon her heart, and fell in a trance betweene her mothers armes.

Now onely remaines untold the case wherein I was, seeing in that, yea, which I had heard my hopes deluded, Luscinda's words and promises falsified; and my selfe wholy disabled to recover in any time the good which I lost in that instant, I rested void of counsell, abandoned (in mine opinion) by heaven, proclaimed an enemy to the earth which upheld me, the ayre denying breath enough for my sighes, and the water, humour sufficient to mine eyes: only the fire increased in such manner, as I burned throughly with rage and jealousie. All the house was in a tumult for this sodaine amazement of Luscinda: and as her mother unclasped her bosome, to give her the ayre, there appeared in it a paper foulded up, which Don Fernando presently seazed on, and went aside to reade it by the light of a torch; and after he had read it, he sate downe in a chayre, laying his hands on his cheeke, with manifest signes of melancholy discontent, without bethinking himselfe of the remedies that were applied to his Spouse, to bring her againe to her selfe. I seeing all the folke of the house thus in an uprore, did adventure my selfe to issue, not waighing much whether I were seene or no; bearing withall a resolution (if I were perceived) to play such a rash part, as all the world should understand the just indignation of my breast, by the revenge I would take on false Don Fernando, and the mutable and dismaied traytresse: But my destinie, which hath reserved me for greater evils, if possibly there may be any greater then mine owne, ordained that instant my wit should abound, whereof ever since I have so great want: and therefore without will to take revenge of my greatest enemies (of whom I might have taken it with all facilitie, by reason they suspected so little my being there) I determined to take it on my selfe, and execute in my selfe the paine which they deserved; and that perhaps with more rigour then I would have used towards them, if I had slaine them at that time, seeing that the sodaine death finisheth presently the paine, but that which doth lingringly torment, kils alwaies without ending the life. To be short, I went out of the house, and came to the other where I had left my Mule, which I caused to be saddled, and without bidding mine hoast adieu, I mounted on her, and rode out of the Citie, without daring like another Lot to turne back and behold it: and then seeing my selfe alone in the fields, and that the darkenesse of the night did cover me, and the silence thereof invite me to complaine, without respect or feare to be heard or knowne, I did let slip my voyce, and untied my tongue with so many curses of Luscinda and Don Ferdinando, as if thereby I might satisfie the wrong they had done me. I gave her the title of cruell, ungratefull, false, and scornefull, but specially of covetous, seeing the riches of mine enemie had shut up the eyes of her affection, to deprive me thereof, and render it to him, with whom fortune had dealt more frankly and liberally: and in the midst of this tune of maledictions and scornes, I did excuse her saying: that it was no marvell that a Mayden kept close in her parents house, made and accustomed alwaies to obey them, should at last condiscend to their will specially, seeing they bestowed upon her for husband, so noble, so rich and proper a Gentleman, as to refuse him, would be reputed in her to proceed either from want of judgement, or from having bestowed her affections else-where, which things must of force greatly prejudice her good opinion and renowne. Presently would I turne againe to say, that though she had told them that I was her spouse, they might easily perceive that in chusing me she had not made so ill an election, that she might not be excused, seeing that before Don Fernando offred himselfe, they themselves could not happen to desire, if their wishes were guided by reason, so fit a match for their daughter as my selfe: and she might easily have said, before she put her selfe in that last and forcible passe of giving her hand, that I had already given her mine, which I would come out to confesse and confirme all that she could any way faine in this case: and concluded in the end, that little love, lesse judgement, much ambition, and desire of greatnesse caused her to forget the wordes, wherewithall she had deceived, intertained, and sustained me in my firme hopes and honest desires.

Using these words, and feeling this unquietnesse in my brest, I travelled all the rest of the night, and strucke about dawning into one of the entries of these mountaines, thorow which I travelled three dayes at random, without following or finding any path or way, untill I arrived at last to certaine meddowes and fieldes, that lie I know not in which part of these mountaines: and finding there certaine heards, I demaunded of them which way lay the most craggy and inaccessible places of these rocks, and they directed me hither; and presently I travelled towards it, with purpose here to end my life: and entring in among those desarts, my Mule, through wearinesse and hunger fell dead under me, or rather as I may better suppose, to disburden him selfe of so vile and unprofitable a burden as he carried in me. I remained a foote, overcome by nature, and pierced thorow and thorow by hunger, without having any helpe, or knowing who might succour me; and remained after that manner, I know not how long prostrate on the ground; and then I arose againe without any hunger, and I found neere unto me certaine Goatheards, who were those doubtlesly that fedde me in my hunger. For they tolde me in what manner they found me, and how I spake so many foolish and madde words, as gave certaine argument that I was devoide of judgement. And I have felt in my selfe since that time, that I enjoy not my wits perfectly, but rather perceive them to be so weakened and impaired, as I commit a hundred follies, tearing mine apparrell, crying loudly thorow these desarts, cursing my fates, and idely repeating the beloved name of mine enemie, without having any other intent or discourse at that time, then to endevour to finish my life ere long: and when I turne to my selfe, I am so broken and tyred, as I am scarce able to stirre me. My most ordinary Mansion-place is in the hollownes of a Corke tree, sufficiently able to cover this wretched carkasse. The Cowheards, and the Goatheards that feede their cattell here in these mountaines, moved by charity, gave me sustenance, leaving meate for me by the wayes, and on the rockes which they suppose I frequent, and where they thinke I may finde it: and so, although I doe then want the use of reason, yet doth naturall necessity induce me to know my meate, and stirreth my appetite to covet, and my will to take it. They tell me when they meete me in my wits; that I doe other times come out to the high-waies, and take it from them violently, even when they themselves doe offer it unto mee willingly. After this manner doe I passe my miserable life, untill heaven shall be pleased to conduct it to the last period, or so change my memorie, as I may no more remember on the beauty and treacherie of Luscinda, or the injurie done by Don Ferdinando; for if it doe me this favour, without depriving my life, then will I convert my thoughts to better discourses: if not, there is no other remedie but to pray God to receive my soule into his mercie; for I neyther finde valour nor strength in my selfe to rid my bodie out of the straites, wherein for my pleasure I did at first willingly intrude it.

This is, Sirs, the bitter relation of my disasters, wherefore judge if it be such as may be celebrated with lesse feeling and compassion then that, which you may by this time have perceived in my selfe: And doe not in vaine labour to perswade or counsel me that which reason should affoord you may bee good for my remedie: for it will worke no other effect in me then a medicine prescribed by a skilfull Physitian, to a Patient that will in no sort receive it. I will have no health without Luscinda; and since she pleaseth to alienate her selfe, being or seeing she ought to be mine: so doe I also take delight to be of the retinue of mishap, although I might be a retainer to good fortune. She hath ordained that her changing shall establish my perdition. And I will labour by procuring mine owne losse, to please and satisfie her wil: and it shall be an example to ensuing ages, that I alone wanted that, wherewithall all other wretches abounded, to whom the impossibility of receiving comfort, proved sometimes a cure, but in me it is an occasion of greater feeling and harme, because I am perswaded that my harmes cannot end even with very death it selfe. Here Cardenio finished his large discourse, and unfortunate and amorous Historie; and just about the time that the Curate was bethinking himselfe of some comfortable reasons to answer and perswade him, he was suspended by a voyce which arrived to his hearing, which with pittifull accents said what shall be recounted in the fourth part of this Narration.

The Fourth Booke

Chapter 1

Wherein is discoursed the new and pleasant adventure that hapned to the Curate and Barber, in Sierra Morena.

Most happy and fortunate were those times, wherein the thrise audacious and bold Knight Don-Quixote of the Mancha was bestowed on the world; by whose most Honorable resolution, to revive and renue in it the already worne out, and welnigh diseased exercise of armes, wee joy in this our so niggard and scant an age of all pastimes, not onely the sweetnesse of his true Historie, but also of the other tales, and digressions contained therein, which are in some respects lesse pleasing, artificiall and true, then the very History it selfe. The which prosecuting the carded, spun, and selfetwined threede of the relation sayes, that as the Curate began to bethinke himselfe upon some answere that might both confort and animate Cardenio, hee was hindered by a voyce which came to his hearing, said very dolefully the words ensuing:

O God! is it possible that I have yet found out the place which may serve for a hidden Sepulchre, to the load of this loathsome body that I unwillingly beare so long? Yes it may be, if the solitarinesse of these rockes doe not illude me, ah unfortunate that I am! How much more gratefull companions will these cragges and thickets prove to my designes, by affoording me leisure to communicate my mishaps to heaven with plaints; then that if any mortall man living, since there is none upon earth from whom may be expected counsell in doubts, ease in complaints, or in harmes remedie. The Curate and his companions heard and understood all the words cleerely, and for as much as they conjectured (as indeed it was) that those plaints were delivered very neere unto them, they did all arise to search out the plaintiffe; and having gone some twenty steppes thence, they beheld a young youth behinde a rocke, sitting under an Ashe tree, and attired like a country Swaine, whom by reason his face was inclined, as hee sate washing of his feete in the cleere streame that glided that way, they could not perfectly discerne; and therefore approched towards him with so great silence, as they were not descryed by him who only attended to the washing of his feet, which were so white, as they properly resembled two pieces of cleere crystall, that grew among the other stones of the streame. The whitenesse and beauty of the feet amazed them, being not made as they well conjectured, to tread cloddes, or measure the steps of lazie Oxen, and holding the Plow, as the youthes apparrell would perswade them; and therefore the Curate, who went before the rest, seeing they were not yet espyed, made signes to the other two that they should divert a little out of the way, or hide themselves behinde some broken cliffes that were neere the place, which they did all of them, noting what the youth did with very great attention. He wore a little browne Capouch, gyrt very neere to his body with a white Towell; also a paire of Breeches and Gamashoes of the same coloured cloth, and on his head a clay-coloured Cap. His Gamashoes were lifted up halfe the legge, which verily seemed to be white Alabaster. Finally, having washed his feet, taking out a linnen Kerchife from under his Cappe, he dried them therewithall, and at the taking out of the Kerchife, he held up his face, and then those which stood gazing on him, had leisure to discerne an unmatchable beautie, so surpassing great, as Cardenio rounding the Curate in the eare, said, This bodie, since it is not Luscinda, can be no humane creature, but a divine. The youth tooke off his Cappe at last, and shaking his head to the one and other part, did disheavell and discover such beautifull haires, as those of Phoebus might justly emulate them: and thereby they knew the supposed Swaine to be a delicate woman, yea and the fairest that ever the first two had seene in their lives, or Cardenio himselfe, the lovely Luscinda excepted; for as he after affirmed, no feature save Luscindas could contend with hers. The long and golden haires did not onely cover her shoulders, but did also hide her round about, in such sort, as (her feet excepted) no other part of her body appeared, they were so neere and long. At this time her hands served her for a Combe, which as her feet seemed pieces of crystall in the water, so did they appeare among her haires like pieces of driven Snow. All which circumstances did possesse the three which stood gazing at her with great admiration, and desire to know what she was; and therefore resolved to shew themselves; and with the noyse which they made when they arose, the beautifull mayden held up her head, and removing her haires from before her eyes with both hands, she espyed those that had made it, and presently arising full of feare and trouble, shee laid hand on a packet that was by her, which seemed to be of apparell, and thought to flie away, without staying to pull on her shooes, or to gather up her haire: But scarce had shee gone sixe paces, when her delicate and tender feete, unable to abide the rough encounter of the stones, made her to fall to the earth. Which the three perceiving, they came out to her, and the Curate arriving first of all, said to her: Lady, whatsoever you be, stay and feare nothing; for we which you beholde here, come only with intention to doe you service, and therefore, you need not pretend so impertinent a flight, which neither your feete can endure nor would we permit. The poore Gyrle remained so amazed and confounded, as shee answered not a word: wherefore the Curate and the rest drawing neerer, he tooke her by the hand, and then hee prosecuted his speech, saying, What your habit concealed from us, Ladie, your haires have bewrayed, being manifest arguments that the causes were of no smal moment, which have thus bemasked your singular beauty, under so unworthy array, and conducted you to this all-abandoned desart; wherein it was a wonderfull chaunce to have met you, if not to remedie your harmes, yet at least to give you some comfort, seeing no evill can afflict and vexe one so much, and plunge him in so deepe extreames, (whilest it deprives not the life) that will wholly abhorre from listening to the advice that is offered, with a good and sincere intention; so that, faire Ladie, or Lord, or what else you shall please to be termed, shake off your affrightment, and rehearse unto us your good or ill fortune, for you shall finde in us joyntly, or in every one apart, companions to helpe you to deplore your disasters.

Whilest the Curate made this speech, the disguised woman stood as one halfe asleepe, now beholding the one, now the other, without once moving her lippe or saying a word; much like unto a rusticke Clowne, when rare and unseene things to him before, are unexpectedly presented to his view. But the Curate insisting and using other perswasive reasons addrest to that effect, won her at last to make a breach on her tedious silence, and with a profound sigh, blow open her curall gates, saying somewhat to this effect: Since the solitarinesse of these rockes hath not beene potent to conceale me, nor the disheaveling of my disordered haires, licensed my tongue to belie my sexe, it were in vaine for me to faine that anew, which, if you beleeved it, would be more for courtesies sake then any other respect. Which presupposed, I say, good Sirs, that I doe gratifie you highly for the liberall offers you have made me; which are such, as have bound me to satisfie your demaund as neere as I may; although I feare the relation which I must make to you of my mishappes, will breede sorrow at once with compassion in you, by reason you shal not be able to find any salve that may cure, comfort, or beguile them: yet notwithstanding, to the end my reputation may not hover longer suspended in your opinions, seeing you know me to be a woman, and view me, young, alone, and thus attyred, being things all of them able either joyned or parted, to overthrow the best credite, I must be enforced to unfold, what I could otherwise most willingly conceale. All this, she that appeared so comely, spoke without stoppe or staggering, with so ready deliverie and so sweete a voice, as her discretion admired them no lesse then her beautie. And renewing againe their complements and intreaties to her, to accomplish speedily her promise, she setting all coynesse apart, drawing on her shooes very modestly, and winding up her haire, sate her downe on a stone, and the other three about her, where she used no little violence to smother certaine rebellious teares that strove to breake forth without her permission: and then with a reposed and cleere voyce she began the Historie of her life in this manner.

In this Province of Andaluzia there is a certaine Towne, from whence a Duke derives his denomination, which makes him one of those in Spain are call'd Grandes: He hath two sonnes, the elder is heire of his States, and likewise, as may be presumed, of his vertues: the younger is heire I know not of what, if it bee not of Vellido his treacheries, or Galalons frauds. My parents are this Noblemans vassals, of humble and low calling; but so rich, as if the goods of nature had equalled those of their fortunes, then should they have had nothing else to desire, nor I feared to see my selfe in the misfortunes, wherein I now am plunged. For perhaps my mishaps proceed from that of theirs, in not being nobly descended. True it is that they are not so base, as they should therefore shame their calling, nor so high as may check my conceit, which perswades me, that my disasters proceede from their lownesse. In conclusion, they are but Farmours, and plaine people, but without any touch or spot of badde bloud, and as we usually say, Olde rustie Christians, yet so rustie and auncient, as it, their riches, and magnificent porte, gaines them by little and little the title of Gentilitie; yea, and of worship also; although the treasure and Nobility, whereof they made most price the account, was to have had me for their daughter: and therefore as well by reason that they had none other heire then my selfe, as also because as affectionate parents, they held mee most deere; I was one of the most made of and cherished daughters that ever father brought up: I was the mirrour wherein they beheld themselves, the staffe of their olde age, and the subject to which they addrest all their desires. From which, because they were most vertuous, mine did not stray an inch: and even in the same manner that I was Ladie of their mindes, so was I also of their goods. By me were servants admitted or dismissed: the notice and account of what was sowed or reaped, past through my hands, of the Oyle-mils, the Wine-presses, the number of great and little cattell, the Bee-hives; in fine, of all that which so rich a Farmour as my Father was, had or could have; I kept the account, and was the Steward thereof and Mistresse, with such care of my side, and pleasure of theirs, as I cannot possibly endeere it enough. The times of leisure that I had in the day, after I had given what was necessary to the head servants, and other labourers, I did entertaine in those exercises, which were both commendable and requisite for maydens, to wit, in sowing, making of bone-lace, and many times handling the Distaffe: and if sometimes I left those exercises to recreate my minde a little, I would then take some godly booke in hand, or play at the Harpe; for experience had taught me, that musicke ordereth disordered mindes, and doth lighten the passions that afflict the spirit. This was the life which I led in my fathers house: the recounting whereof so particularly, hath not beene done for ostentation, nor to give you to understand that I am rich, but to the end you may note how much, without mine owne fault, have I falne from that happy state I have said, unto the unhappie plight into which I am now reduced. The Historie therefore is this, that passing my life in so many occupations, and that with such recollection as might bee compared to a religious life, unseene as I thought by any other person then those of our house: for when I went to Masse, it was commonly so earely, and so accompanied by my mother and other mayd-servants; and I my selfe so coverd and watchfull, as mine eyes did scarce see the earth whereon I treade: and yet notwithstanding those of love, or as I may better terme them, of idlenesse, to which Linces Eyes may not bee compared, did represent me to Don Ferdinandos affection and care; for this is the name of the Dukes younger sonne, of whom I spake before. Scarce had she named Don Ferdinando when Cardenio changed colour, and began to sweate with such alteration of bodie and countenance, as the Curate and Barber which beheld it, feared that the accident of frenzie did assault him which was wont as they had heard to possesse him at times. But Cardenio did nothing else then sweat, and stood still beholding now and then the countrey gyrle imagining straight what she was, who without taking notice of his alteration, followed on her discourse in this manner. And scarce had he seene mee, when (as he himselfe after confest) he abode greatly surprized by my love, as his actions did after give evident demonstration.

But to conclude soone the relation of those misfortunes which have no conclusion, I will overslip in silence the diligences and practises of Don Ferdinando used to declare unto me his affection: he suborned all the folke of the house. He bestowed gifts and favours on my parents: every day was a holy day, and a day of sports in the streets where I dwelled: at night no man could sleepe for musicke; the letters were innumerable that came to my hands, without knowing who brought them; farsed too full of amorous conceits and offers; and contayning more promises and protestations then they had characters. All which, not onely could not mollifie my mind, but rather hardened it as much as if hee were my mortal enemie, and therefore did construe all the indevours he used to gaine my good will, to be practised to a contrary end: which I did not, as accounting Don Ferdinando ungentle, or that I esteemed him too importunat, for I took a kind of delight to see my selfe so highly esteemed and beloved of so noble a Gentleman: nor was I any thing offended to see his papers written in my praise; for if I be not deceived in this point, be we women ever so foule, we love to heare men call us beautifull. But mine honesty was that which opposed it selfe unto all these things, and the continuall admonitions of my parents, which had by this plainely perceived Don Fernandos pretence, as one that cared not all the world should know it. They would often say unto me, that they had deposited their honours and reputation in my vertue alone and discretion, and bad me consider the inequality that was betweene Don Fernando and me, and that I might collect by it how his thoughts (did he ever so much affirme the contrary) were more addrest to compasse his pleasures then my profit: And that if I feared any inconvenience might befall, to the end they might crosse it, and cause him to abandon his so unjust a pursuit, they would match me where I most liked, eyther to the best of that towne, or any other towne adjoyning, saying, they might easily compasse it, both by reason of their great wealth and my good report. I fortified my resolution and integritie with these certaine promises, and the knowne truth which they told me, and therefore would never answer to Don Fernando any word, that might ever so farre of argue the least hope of condiscending to his desires. All which cautions of mine which I thinke he deemed to be disdains, did inflame more his lascivious appetite (for this is the name wherewithall I intitle his affection towards me) which had it beene such as it ought, you had not knowne it now, for then the cause of revealing it had not befalne me. Finally Don Fernando understood how my parents meant to marrie me, to the end they might illude his hope of ever possessing me: or at least set more gards to preserve mine honour, and this newes or surmise was an occasion that he did, what you shall presently heare.

For one night as I sate in my chamber, only attended by a young Mayden that served me, I having shut the doores very safe, for feare lest through any negligence my honestie might incur any danger, without knowing or imagining how it might happen: notwithstanding all my diligences used and preventions, and amidst the solitude of this silence and recollection, he stood before me in my chamber. At his presence I was so troubled, as I lost both sight and speech, and by reason thereof could not crie, nor I thinke he would not, though I had attempted it, permit me. For he presently ranne over to me, and taking me betweene his armes (for as I have said, I was so amazed, as I had no power to defend my selfe) he spake such things to me, as I knew not how it is possible that so many lies should have ability to faine things resembling in shew so much the truth: and the traytor caused teares, to give credit to his words and sighes, to give countenance to his intention. I poore soule being alone amidst my friends, and weakly practised in such affaires, began I know not how to account his leesings for verities, but not in such sort, as his teares or sighes might any wise move me to any compassion that were not commendable. And so the first trouble and amazement of mind being past, I began againe to recover my defective spirits, and then said to him with more courage then I thought I should have had, if as I am, my Lord, betweene your armes, I were betweene the pawes of a fierce Lyon, and that I were made certaine of my liberty on condition to doe or say any thing prejudiciall to mine honour, it would proove as impossible for me to accept it, as for that which once hath beene, to leave off his essence and being. Wherefore even as you have ingyrt my middle with your armes, so likewise have I tied fast my minde with vertuous and forcible desires, that are wholy discrepant from yours, as you shall perceive, if seeking to force me, you presume to passe further with your inordinate designe. I am your vassall, but not your slave, nor hath the nobility of your bloud power, nor ought it to harden, to dishonour, staine or hold in little account the humility of mine; and I doe esteeme my selfe though a countrey wench and farmers daughter, as much as you can your selfe, though a Nobleman and a Lord: With me your violence shall not prevaile, your riches gaine any grace, your words have power to deceive, or your sighes and teares be able to move: yet if I shall finde any of these properties mentioned in him, whom my parents shall please to bestow on mee for my spouse, I will presently subject my will to his, nor shall it ever varie from his minde a jot: So that if I might remaine with honor, although I rested void of delights, yet would I willingly bestow on you, that which you presently labour so much to obtaine: all which I doe say, to divert your straying thought from ever thinking that any one may obtaine of me ought, who is not my lawfull spouse. If the let onely consistes therein, most beautifull Dorotea (for so I am called) answered the disloyall Lord: behold, I give thee here my hand to be thine alone: and let the heavens, from which nothing is concealed; and this Image of our Lady which thou hast heere present, be witnesses of this truth. When Cardenio heard her say that she was called Dorotea, hee fell againe into his former suspicion, and in the end confirmed his first opinion to bee true: but would not interrupt her speech, being desirous to know the successe, which he knew wholy almost before, and therefore said only. Lady, is it possible that you are named Dorotea? I have heard report of another of that name, which perhaps hath runne the like course of your misfortunes: but I request you to continue your relation; for a time may come, wherein I may recount unto you things of the same kinde, which will breed no small admiration. Dorotea noted Cardenios words, and his uncouth and disastrous attire, and then intreated him very instantly, if hee knew any thing of her affaires, he would acquaint her therewithall. For if fortune had left her any good, it was onely the courage which she had to beare patiently any disaster that might befall her, being certaine in her opinion, that no new one could arrive, which might increase a whit those she had alreadie. Ladie, I would not let slip the occasion (quoth Cardenio) to tell you what I thinke, if that which I imagine were true: and yet there is no commoditie left to doe it; nor can it availe you much to know it. Let it be what it list, said Dorotea: but that which after befell of my relation, was this: That Don Fernando took an Image that was in my Chamber for witnesse of our contract, and added withall most forcible words and unusuall oathes, promising unto me to become my husband. Although I warned him before he had ended his speech, to see well what he did, and to weigh the wrath of his father, when he should see him married to one so base, and his vassall, and that therefore he should take heed that my beautie such as it was should not blinde him. Seeing he should not finde therein a sufficient excuse for his errour: and that if he meant to doe me any good, I conjured him by the love that he bore unto me, to license my fortunes to roule in their owne spheare, according as my quality reached: For such unequall matches doe never please long, nor persever with that delight wherewithall they begunne.

All the reasons heere rehearsed, I said unto him, and many moe; which now are falne out of minde, but yet proved of no efficacy to weane him from his obstinate purpose, even like unto one that goeth to buy; with intention never to pay for what he takes: and therefore never considers the price, worthinesse, or faultlesse of the stuffe he takes to credit. I at this season made a briefe discourse, and said thus to my selfe: I may doe this, for I am not the first which by matrimonie hath ascended from a low degree to a high estate: nor shall Don Fernando be the first whom beautie or blind affection (for that is the most certaine) hath induced to make choyce of a consort unequall to his greatnesse. Then since herein I create no new world, nor custome, what error can be committed by embracing the honour wherewithall fortune crownes me? Although it so befell, that his affection to me endured no longer then till he accomplish his will: for before God, I certes shall still remaine his wife. And if I should disdainfully give him the repulse, I see him now in such termes, as perhaps forgetting the dutie of a Noble man, hee may use violence, and then shall I remaine for ever dishonoured, and also without excuse of the imputations of the ignorant which knew not how much without any fault I have falne into this inevitable danger. For, what reasons may be sufficiently forcible to perswade my father and other, that this Noble man did enter into my Chamber without my consent? All these demaunds and answers did I in an instant revolve in mine imagination, and found my selfe chiefly forced (how I cannot tell) to assent to his petition, by the witnesses hee invoked, the teares hee shed, and finally by his sweete disposition and comely feature, which accompanied with so many arguments of unfained affection, were able to conquer and enthrall any other heart, though it were as free and wary as mine owne. Then called I for my waiting maide, that she might on earth accompany the celestiall witnesses. And then Don Fernando turned againe to reiterate and confirme his oathes, and added to his former, other new Saints as witnesses; and wished a thousand succeeding maledictions to light on him, if he did not accomplish his promise to mee. His eyes againe waxed moyst, his sighes increased, and himselfe inwreathed mee more straightly betweene his armes, from which he had never once loosed mee: and with this, and my Maydens departure, I left to be a Mayden, and hee beganne to be a traytor, and disloyall man. The day that succeeded to the night of my mishaps, came not I thinke so soone as Don Fernando desired it: for after a man hath satisfied that which the appetite covets, the greatest delight it can take after is to apart it selfe from the place where the desire was accomplished. I say this, because Don Fernando, did hasten his departure from me, by my Maids industrie, who was the very same that had brought him into my chamber, hee was got in the streete before dawning. And at his departure from mee, he said (although not with so great shew of affection and vehemencie, as hee had used at his comming) that I might bee secure of his faith, and that his oathes were firme most true: and for a more confirmation of his word hee tooke a rich ring off his finger, and put it on mine. In fine he departed and I remained behinde I cannot well say, whether joyfull or sad; but this much I know that I rested confused and pensive, and almost beside my selfe for the late mischance; yet ėyther I had not the heart, or else I forgot to chide my Maide for her treacherie committed by shutting up Don Fernando in my chamber: for as yet I could not determine, whether that which had befalne me, was a good or an evill. I said to Don Fernando at his departure that he might see mee other nights when he pleased by the same meanes hee had come that night seeing I was his owne, and would rest so, until it pleased him to let the world know that I was his wife. But hee never returned againe, but the next night following; [nor] could I see him after, for the space of a moneth eyther in the streete or Church, so as I did but spend time in vaine to expect him: although I understood that hee was still in towne, and rode everie other day a hunting: an exercise to which hee was much addicted.

Those dayes were, I know, unfortunate and accursed to me, and those houres sorrowfull; for in them I began to doubt, nay rather wholly to discredite Don Fernando his faith: and my maide did then heare loudly the checkes I gave unto her for her presumption, ever untill then dissembled. And I was moreover constrained to watch and keepe guard on my teares and countenance, lest I should give occasion to my parents to demaund of mee the cause of my discontents, and thereby ingage me to use ambages or untruthes to cover them. But all this ended in a instant, one moment arriving whereon all these respects stumbled, all honourable discourses ended, patience was lost, and my most hidden secrets issued in publicke: which was, when there was spread a certaine rumour throughout the towne within a few dayes after, that Don Fernando had married in a Citie neere adjoyning, a damzell of surpassing beautie, and of very noble birth, although not so rich, as could deserve by her preferment or dowrie so worthy a husband. It was also said, that she was named Luscinda, with many other things that hapned at their Spousals, worthy of admiration. Cardenio hearing Luscinda named, did nothing else but lift up his shoulders, bite his lippe, bend his browes, and after a little while shedde from his eyes two floods of teares. But yet for all that, Dorotea did not interrupt the file of her Historie, saying, This dolefull newes came to my hearing, and my heart, in steede of freezing thereat, was so inflamed with choler and rage, as I had welnigh runne out to the streets, and with outcries published the deceit and treason that was done to me: but my furie was presently asswaged by the resolution which I made, to doe what I put in execution the very same night, and then I put on this habite which you see, being given unto me by one of those that among us Countrey-folke are called Swaines, who was my fathers servant; to whom I disclosed all my misfortunes, and requested him to accompany me to the Citie, where I understood mine enemie sojourned. He, after he had reprehended my boldnesse, perceiving me to have an inflexible resolution, made offer to attend on mee as hee said, unto the end of the world: and presently after I trussed up in a pillowbeare, a womans attire, some mony and jewels, to prevent necessities that might befall; and in the silence of night, without acquainting my treacherous maide with my purpose, I issued out of my house, accompanied by my servant, and many imaginations: and in that manner set on towards the Citie, and though I went on foote, was yet borne away flying, by my desires, to come, if not time enough to hinder that which was past, yet at least to demaund of Don Fernando that he would tell me with what conscience or soule he had done it. I arrived where I wished within two dayes and a halfe; and at the entry of the Citie I demaunded where Luscinda her father dwelled? and he of whom I first demaunded the question, answered me more then I desired to heare: he shewed me the house, and recounted to me all that befell at the daughters marriage, being a thing so publique and knowne in the Citie, as men made meetings of purpose to discourse thereof. Hee said to me, that the very night wherein Don Fernando was espoused to Luscinda, after that she had given her consent to be his wife, shee was instantly assayled by a terrible accident, that strucke her into a traunce, and her spouse approching to unclaspe her bosome, that she might take the ayre, found a paper foulded in it, written with Luscindas owne hand, wherein she said and declared, that she could not be Don Fernando's wife, because she was already Cardenioes, who was, as the man tolde me, a very principall Gentleman of the same Citie; and that if she had given her consent to Don Fernando, it was onely done, because she would not disobey her parents: in conclusion he tolde mee, that the Billet made also mention, how shee had a resolution to kill her selfe presently after the marriage, and did also lay downe therein the motives she had to doe it. All which, as they say, was confirmed by a poynard that was found hidden about her in her apparrell. Which Don Fernando perceiving, presuming that Luscinda did flout him, and hold him in little account, hee set upon her ere she was come to her selfe, and attempted to kill her with the very same poynard; and had done it, if her father and other friends which were present had not opposed themselves, and hindered his determination. Moreover, they reported that presently after Don Fernando absented himselfe from the Citie, and that Luscinda turned not out of her agony untill the next day, and then recounted to her parents how she was verily Spouse to that Cardenio of whom we spake even now. I learned besides that Cardenio as it is rumour'd, was present at the marriage, and that as soone as he saw her married, being a thing he would never have credited, departed out of the Citie in a desperate moode, but first left behinde him a letter, wherein he shewed at large the wrong Luscinda had done to him, and that hee himselfe meant to goe to some place where people should never after heare of him. All this was notorious, and publiquely bruited throughout the Citie, and every one spoke thereof, but most of all having very soone after understood that Luscinda was missing from her parents house and the Citie; for shee could not be found in neyther of both: for which her parents were almost beside themselves, not knowing what meanes to use to finde her.

These newes reduced my hopes againe to their rancks, and I esteemed it better to find Don Fernando unmarried then married, presuming that yet the gates of my remedy were not wholly shut, I giving my selfe to understand that heaven had peradventure set that impediment on the second marriage, to make him understand what hee ought to the first; and to remember, how he was a Christian, and that he was more obliged to his soule then to humane respects. I revolved all these things in my minde, and comfortlesse did yet comfort my selfe, by faining large yet languishing hopes, to sustaine that life which I now do so much abhor. And whilest I staide thus in the Citie, ignorant what I might doe, seeing I found not Don Fernando, I heard a cryer goe about publikely, promising great rewards to any one that could finde me out, giving signes of the very age and apparrell I wore. And I likewise heard it was bruited abroad, that the youth which came with me had carried me away from my fathers house. A thing that touched my soule very neerely, to view my credit so greatly wrackt, seeing that it was not sufficient to have lost it by my comming away, without the addition him with whom I departed, being a subject so base and unworthy of my loftier thoughts. Having heard this crie, I departed out of the Citie with my servant: who even then began to give tokens that he faultred in the fidelitie he had promised to me: and both of us together entred the very same night into the most hidden parts of this mountaine, fearing lest we might be found. But as it is commonly said, that one evill cals on another, and that the end of one disaster is the beginning of a greater, so proved it with me; for my good servant, untill then faithfull and trustie, rather incited by his owne villany then my beautie, thought to have taken the benefite of the oportunity which these inhabitable places offered; and solicited me of love, with little shame and lesse feare of God, or respect of my selfe: and now seeing that I answered his impudencies with severe and reprehensive words, leaving the intreaties aside, wherewithall hee thought first to have compast his will, he beganne to use his force. But just heaven which seldome or never neglects the just mans assistance, did so favour my proceedings, as with my weake forces, and very little labour; I threw him downe a steepe rocke, and there I left him, I know not whether alive or dead. And presently I entred in among these mountaines, with more swiftnesse then my feare and wearinesse required; having therein no other project or designe, then to hide my selfe in them, and shunne my father and others, which by his intreaty and meanes sought for me everywhere. Some moneths are past since my first comming here, where I found a Heardman, who carried me to a village seated in the midst of these rockes, wherein he dwelled and intertained me, whom I have served as a Shepheard ever since, procuring as much as lay in me to abide still in the fielde, to cover these haires, which have now so unexpectedly betraide me. Yet all my care and industry was not very beneficiall, seeing my Master came at last to the notice that I was no man, but a woman, which was an occasion that the like evill thought sprung in him, as before in my servant. And as fortune gives not alwayes remedie for the difficulties which occurre, I found neither rocke nor downefall to coole and cure my Masters infirmitie, as I had done for my man: and therefore I accounted it a lesse inconvenience to depart thence, and hide my selfe againe among these desarts, then to adventure the triall of my strength or reason with him. Therefore, as I say, I turned to imboske my selfe, and search out some place, where, without any encumbrance I might intreat heaven with my sighes and teares, to have compassion on my mishap; and lend me industry and favour, eyther to issue fortunately out of it, or else to die amidst these solitudes, not leaving any memory of a wretch, who hath ministred matter, although not through her owne default, that men may speake and murmure of her, both in her owne and in other countries.

Chapter 2

Which treates of the discretion of the beautifull Dorotea, and the artificiall manner used to disswade the amorous Knight from continuing his penance: and how hee was gotten away; with many other delightfull and pleasant occurrences.

This is, Sirs, the true relation of my Tragedie: see therefore now and judge, whether the sighes you heard, the words to which you listened, and the teares that gushed out at mine eyes, have not had sufficient occasion to appeare in greater abundance: and having considered the quality of my disgrace; you shall perceive all comfort to bee vaine, seeing the remedie thereof is impossible. Only I will request at your hands one favour which you ought and may easily grant, and is that you will addresse me unto some place, where I may live secure from the feare and suspition I have to be found by those which I know do daily travel in my pursuit: for although I am sure that my parents great affection towards me, doth warrant me to be kindly received and intertained by them: yet the shame is so great that possesseth me, onely to thinke that I shall not returne to their presence in that state which they expect, as I account it farre better to banish my selfe from their sight for ever, then once to beholde their face, with the least suspition that they againe would behold mine divorced from that honestie which whilome my modest behaviour promised. Here she ended, and her face suddenly over-run by a lovely scarlet, perspicuously denoted the feeling and bashfulnesse of her soule.

The audients of her sad storie, felt great motions both of pitie and admiration for her misfortunes: and although the Curate thought to comfort and counsell her forthwith, yet was he prevented by Cardenio, who taking her first by the hand, said at last; Ladie, thou art the beautifull Dorotea, daughter unto rich Cleonardo. Dorotea rested admired when she heard her fathers name, and saw of how little value he seemed, who had named him. For we have already recounted how raggedly Cardenio was clothed; and therefore she said unto him, And who art thou, friend, that knowest so well my fathers name; for untill this houre (if I have not forgotten my selfe) I did not once name him throughout the whole Discourse of my unfortunate tale? I am (answered Cardenio) the unluckie Knight, whom Luscinda (as thou saidst) affirmed to be her husband. I am the disastrous Cardenio, whom the wicked proceeding of him that hath also brought thee to those termes wherein thou art, hath conducted me to the state in which I am, and thou mayest beholde ragged, naked, abandoned by al humane comfort: and what is worse, voyde of sense; seeing I onely enjoy it but at some few short times, and that when heaven pleaseth to lend it me. I am hee, Dorotea, that was present at Don Fernando's unreasonable wedding, and that heard the consent which Luscinda gave him to be his wife. I was hee, that had not the courage to stay and see the end of her traunce, or what became of the paper found in her bosome. For my soule had not power or sufferance, to behold so many disventures at once, and therefore abandoned the place and my patience together, and onely left a Letter with mine Hoste, whom I intreated to deliver it into Luscinda her owne hands, and then came into these desarts, with resolution to end in them my miserable life, which since that houre I have hated as my most mortall enemie. But fortune hath not pleased to deprive me of it, thinking it sufficient to have impaired my wit, perhaps reserving me for the good successe befalne me now in finding of your selfe; for that being true (as I beleeve it is) which you have here discoursed, peradventure it may have reserved yet better hap for us both in our disasters then we doe expect. For presupposing that Luscinda cannot marry with Don Fernando, because she is mine, nor Don Fernando with her because yours: and that she hath declared so manifestly the same: we may well hope that heaven hath meanes to restore to every one that which is his owne, seeing it yet consists in being not made away, or anihilated. And seeing this comfort remaines, not sprung from any very remote hope, nor founded on idle surmises, I request thee faire Ladie to take another resolution in thine honourable thought, seeing I meane to doe it in mine, and let us accommodate our selves to expect better successe. For I doe vow unto thee by the faith of a Gentleman and Christian, not to forsake thee, untill I see thee in Don Fernandoes possession, and when I shall not by reasons be able to induce him to acknowledge how farre he rests indebted to thee, then will I use the liberty graunted to me as a Gentleman, and with just title challenge him to the fielde, in respect of the wrong he hath done unto thee; forgetting wholly mine owne injuries, whose revenge I will leave to heaven, that I may be able to right yours on earth.

Dorotea rested wonderfully admired having knowne and heard Cardenio, and ignoring what competent thankes she might returne him in satisfaction of his large offers, she cast her selfe downe at his feet to have kist them, which Cardenio would not permit: and the Licenciat answered for both, praising greatly Cardenios discourse: and chiefely intreated, prayed, and counselled them, that they would goe with him to his village, where they might fit themselves with such things as they wanted, and also take order how to search out Don Fernando, or carrie Dorotea to her fathers house, or doe else what they deemed most convenient. Cardenio and Dorotea gratified his courtesies, and accepted the favour hee proffered. The Barber also, who had stood all the while silent and suspended, made them a prettie Discourse, with as friendly an offer of himselfe, and his service as Master Curate; and likewise did briefly relate the occasion of their comming thither, with the extravagant kinde of madnesse which Don-Quixote had, and how they expected now his Squires returne, whom they had sent to search for him. Cardenio having heard him named, remembred presently as in a dreame the conflict past betweene them both, and recounted it unto them, but could not in any wise call to minde the occasion thereof.

By this time they heard one call for them, and knew by the voyce, that it was Sancho Panças, who because hee found them not in the place where he had left them, cryed out for them as loudly as he might. They went to meete him, and demaunding for Don-Quixote, he answered, that he found him all naked to his shirt, leane, yellow, almost dead for hunger, and sighing for his Lady Dulcinea: and although he had tolde him, how she commaunded him to repayre presently to Toboso, where she expected him: yet notwithstanding he answered that he was determined never to appeare before her beautie, untill he had done Feats that should make him worthy of her gracious favor. And then the Squire affirmed if that humor passed on any further, hee feared his Lord would be in danger never to become an Emperour as he was bound in honour, no nor a Cardinall, which was the least that could be expected of him. The Licenciat bid him be of good cheere, for they would bring him from thence whether he would or no; and recounted to Cardenio and Dorotea, what they had bethought for Don-Quixotes remedie, or at least for the carrying of him home to his house. To that Dorotea answered, that she would counterfeit the distressed Ladie better then the Barber; and chiefly seeing shee had apparell wherewithall to act it most naturally. And therefore desired them to leave to her charge the representing of all that which should bee needfull for the atchieving of their designe; for she had read many books of Knighthood, and knew well the stile that distressed damzels used, when they requested any favour of Knights adventurous. And then neede we nothing else, quoth the Curate, but onely to put our purpose presently in execution. For questionlesse good successe turnes on our side, seeing it hath so unexpectedly begun alreadie to open the gates of your remedy, and hath also facilitated for us that wherof we had most necessity in this exigent. Dorotea tooke forthwith out of her pillowbeare a whole gowne of very rich stuffe, and a short mantle of another greene stuffe, and a collar and many other rich jewels out of a boxe, wherewithall she adorned her selfe in a trice so gorgeously, as shee seemed a very rich and goodly Ladie. All which and much more she had brought with her as she said from her house, to prevent what might happen, but never had any use of them, untill then. Her grace, gesture and beautie liked them all extremely, and made them account Don Fernando to be a man of little understanding, seeing he contemned such feature. But he which was most of all admired was Sancho Pança, because, as he thought (and it was so indeed) that he had not in all the dayes of his life before seene so faire a creature: and he requested the Curate very seriously to tell him who that beautifull Ladie was? and what she sought among those through-fares? This faire Lady, friend Sancho, answered the Curate, is (as if a man said nothing, she is so great) heire apparent by direct line of the mighty Kingdome of Micomicon, and comes in the search of your Lord, to demaund a boone of him, which is, that he will destroy and undoe a great wrong done unto her by a wicked Giant; and through the great fame which is spread over all Guinea of your Lords prowesse, this Princesse is come to finde him out. A happy searcher, and a fortunate finding, quoth Sancho, and chiefly, if my Master be so happie as to right that injurie, and redresse that wrong by killing that, O! the mighty lubber of a Giant whom you say: yes, he will kill him, I am very certaine, if he can once but meete him, and if he be not a spirit; For my Master hath no kinde of power over spirits. But I must request one favour of you among others most earnestly, good Mr. Licenciat, and tis, that to the end my Lord may not take an humour of becomming a Cardinall (which is the thing I feare most in this world) that you will give him counsell to marry this Princesse presently, and by that meanes he shall remaine incapable of the dignitie of a Cardinall, and will come very easily by his Empyre, and I to the end of my desires: for I have thought well of the matter, and have found that it is in no wise expedient that my Lord should become a Cardinall; for I am wholly unfit for any Ecclesiasticall dignitie, seeing I am a married man: and therefore to trouble my selfe now with seeking of dispensations to injoy Church-livings, having as I have both wife and children, were never to end: so that all my good consists, in that my Lord do marry this Princesse instantly, whose name yet I know not, and therfore I have not said it. She is hight (quoth the Curate) the Princesse Micomicona, for her Kingdome being called Micomicon, it is evident she must be termed so. That is questionlesse, quoth Sancho, for I have knowne many to take their denomination and surname from the place of their birth, calling themselves Peter of Alcala, Iohn of Ubeda, and Iames of Valedolid: and perhaps in Guinea Princes and Queenes use the same custome, and call themselves by the names of their Provinces.

So I thinke, quoth the Curate: and as touching your Masters marriage with her, I will labour therein as much as lies in my power. Wherewithall Sancho remained as well satisfied, as the Curate admired at his simplicitie, and to see how firmely he had fixed in his fantasie the very ravings of his Master, seeing he did beleeve without doubt that his Lord should become an Emperour. Dorotea in this space had gotten upon the Curates Mule, and the Barber had somewhat better fitted the beard which he made of the Oxes tayle on his face, and did after intreat Sancho to guide them to the place where Don-Quixote was, and advertised him withall, that he should in no wise take any notice of the Curate or Barber, or confesse in any sort that he knew them, for therein consisted all the meanes of bringing Don-Quixote to the minde to become an Emperour. Yet Cardenio would not goe with them, fearing lest thereby Don-Quixote might call to minde their contention: and the Curate thinking also that his presence was not expedient, remained with him, letting the others goe before, and these followed a farre off faire and softly on foot, and ere they departed, the Curate instructed Dorotea a new, what she should say, who bid him to feare nothing, for she would discharge her part to his satisfaction, and as bookes of Chivalrie required and laid downe.

They travelled about three quarters of a league, as they espied the Knight, and at last they discovered him among a number of intricate rocks, all apparelled but not armed: and as soone as Dorotea beheld him, she strucke her Palfray, her well bearded Barber following her: and as they approached Don-Quixote, the Barber leaped lightly down from his Mule, and ranne towards Dorotea to take her downe betweene his armes, who allighting, went with a very good grace towards Don-Quixote, and kneeled before him. And although hee strived to make her arise, yet she remaining still on her knees, spake to him in this manner: I will not arise from hence thrice valourous and approoved Knight, untill your bountie and courtesie shall grant unto me one boone, which shall much redound unto your honour and prize of your person, and to the profit of the most disconsolate and wronged Damzell that the Sunne hath ever seene. And if it be so, that the valour of your invincible arme to be correspondent to the bruite of your immortall fame, you are obliged to succour this comfortlesse Wight, that comes from lands so remote, to the sound of your famous name, searching you for to remedie her mishaps. I will not answere you a word, faire Lady, quoth Don-Quixote, nor heare a jot of your affaire, untill you arise from the ground. I will not get up from hence, my Lord, quoth the afflicted Ladie, if first of your wonted bountie you doe not grant to my request. I doe give and grant it, said Don-Quixote, so that it be not a thing that may turne to the dammage or hinederance of my King, my countrey, or of her that keepes the key of my heart and liberty. It shall not turne to the dammage or hinderance of those you have said, good Sir, replied the dolorous Damzell; and as she was saying this, Sancho Pança rounded his Lord in the eare, saying softly to him; Sir, you may very well grant the request she asketh, for it is a matter of nothing, it is onely to kill a monstrous Giant, and shee that demands it is the mightie Princesse Micomicona Queene of the great Kingdome of Micomicon in Ethiopia. Let her be what she will, quoth Don-Quixote, for I will accomplish what I am bound, and my conscience shal informe me conformable to the state I have professed: and then turning to the Damsell, he said, Let your great beautie arise, for I grant to you any boone which you shall please to aske of me. Why then quoth the Damsell that which I demand is, that your magnanimous person come presently away with mee, to the place where I shall carry you, and doe likewise make me a promise, not to undertake any other adventure or demaund untill you revenge me upon a traytour who hath, against all lawes both divine and humane, usurped my kingdome. I say that I grant you all that quoth Don-Quixote, and therefore Ladie you may cast away from this day forward all the melancholy that troubles you, and labour that your languishing and dismaied hopes may recover againe new strength and courage, for by the helpe of God, and that of mine arme you shall see your selfe shortly restored to your kingdome, and enthronized in the chayre of your ancient and great estate, in despite and maugre the traytors that shall dare gainesay it: and therefore Hands to the worke, for they say, that danger alwayes followes delay. The distressed Damsell strove with much ado to kisse his hand: but Don-Quixote, who was a most accomplished Knight for courtesie, would never condescend thereunto, but making her arise, he imbraced her with great kindenesse and respect; and commaunded Sancho to saddle Rozinante, and helpe him to arme himselfe. Sancho tooke downe the armes forthwith, which hung on a tree like trophies, and searching the guirts armed his Lord in a moment, who seeing himselfe armed said, Let us in Gods name depart from hence to assist this great Lady. The barber kneeled all this while, and could with much adoe dissemble his laughter, or keepe on his beard that threatned still to fall off; with whose fall perhaps, they should all have remained without bringing their good purpose to passe: and seeing that the boone was granted, and noted the diligence wherewithall Don-Quixote made himselfe ready to depart and accomplish the same: hee arose and tooke his Ladie by the hand, and both of them together holpe her upon her Mule: and presently after, Don-Quixote leaped on Rozinante, and the Barber got up on his beast, Sancho onely remayning a foote: where hee a fresh renued the memory of the losse of his gray Asse, with the want procured to him thereby. But all this he bore with very great patience, because he supposed that his Lord was now in the way, and next degree to be an Emperour: for he made an infallible account that he would marry that Princesse, and at least be King of Micomicon: but yet it grieved him to thinke how that Kingdome was in the countrey of blacke Moores, and that therefore the Nation which should be given to him for his vassals, should be all blacke: for which difficultie his imagination coyned presently a good remedie: and he discoursed with himselfe in this manner: Why should I care, though my subjects be all blacke Moores, is there any more to be done, then to loade them in a ship, and bring them into Spaine, where I may sell them, and receive the price of them in readie money? And with that money may I buy some title or Office, wherein I may after live at mine ease all the daies of my life? No! but sleepe, and have no wit, nor abilitie to dispose of things, and to sell thirtie or ten thousand vassailes in the space that one would say, give me those strawes. I will dispatch them all, they shall flie the little with the great, or as I can best contrive the matter. And be they ever so blacke, I will transforme them into white or yellow ones: come neere and see whether I cannot sucke well my fingers ends: And thus he travailed so sollicitous and glad, as he quite forgot his paine of travailing a foote. Cardenio and the Curate stood in the meane time beholding all that passed from behind some brambles, where they lay lurking, and where in doubt what meanes to use to issue and joyne in company with them. But the Curate who was an ingenious and prompt plotter, devised instantly what was to bee done, that they might attaine their desire, thus he tooke out of his case a payre of sheares, and cut off Cardenioes beard therewithall in a trice, and then gave unto him to weare a riding Capouch which he himselfe had on, and a blacke cloake; and himselfe walked in a dublet and hose. Cardenio thus attired looked so unlike that he was before, as he would not have knowne himselfe in a looking glasse. This being finished, and the others gone on before whilst they disguised themselves, they sallied out with facility to the high way before Don-Quixote or his company, for the rocks and many other bad passages did not permit those that were a horsebacke, to make so speedie an end of their journey as they: and when they had thorowly past the mountaine, they expected at the foot thereof for the Knight and his companie: and when the Knight appeared, the Curate looked on him very earnestly for a great space, with inkling that he beganne to know him: and after he had a good while beheld him, he ranne towards him with his armes spread abroad, saying, In a good houre be the mirrour of all Knighthood found and my noble country-man Don-Quixote of the Mancha, the flower and the creame of Gentilitie, the shaddow and remedie of the afflicted and the Quintessence of Knights Errant: and saying this he held Don-Quixote his left thigh embraced. Who, admiring at that which he heard that man to say and do, did also review him with attention, and finally knew him, and all amazed to see him, made much ado to alight, but the Curate would not permit him: wherefore Don-Quixote said, good Master Licenciat permit me to alight, for it is in no sort decent that I be a horsebacke, and so reverend a person as you goe on foot. I will never consent thereunto, quoth the Curate, your highnes must needs stay on horsebacke, seeing that thereon you are accustomed to atchieve the greatest feats of Chivalrie and adventures, which were ever seene in our age. For it shall suffice me, who am an unworthy Priest, to get up behinde some one of these other Gentlemen that ride in your company, if they will not take it in bad part, yea, and I will make account that I ride on Pegasus, or the Zebra of the famous Moore Muzaraque, who lies yet inchanted in the steepe rocke Çulema, neere unto Alcala of Henares. Truely I did not thinke upon it good Master Licenciat, answered Don-Quixote, yet I presume that my Lady the Princesse will be well appaide for my sake to commaund her Squire to lend you the use of his saddle, and to get up himselfe on the Croper, if so it be that the beast will beare double. Yes that it will, said the Princesse, for ought I know, and likewise I am sure it will not be necessary to commaund my Squire to alight, for he is of himselfe so courteous and courtly, as he will in no wise condiscend that an Ecclesiasticall man should go a foote, when he may helpe him to a horse. That is most certaine, quoth the Barber; and saying so he alighted, and intreated the Curate to take the saddle; to which courtesie he did easily condescend. But by evill fortune, as the Barber thought to leape up behind him: the Mule which was in effect a hired one (and that is sufficient to say it was unhappy) did lift a little her hinder quarters, and bestowed two or three flings on the ayre, which, had they hit on Master Nicholas his brest or pate, he would have bequeathed the quest of Don-Quixote upon the Divill: but notwithstanding the Barber was so affrighted, as he fell on the ground with so little heed of his beard, as it fell quite off, and lay spread upon the ground: and perceiving himselfe without it, he had no other shift, but to cover his face with both handes, and complaine that all his cheeke-teeth were strucken out. Don-Quixote beholding such a great sheafe of a beard falne away, without jaw or bloud from the face, he said, I vow, this is one of the greatest miracles that ever I saw in my life; it hath taken and pluckt away his beard, as smoothly as if it were done of purpose. The Curate beholding the danger wherein their invention was like to incurre if it were detected, went forthwith, and taking up the beard, came to Master Nicholas that lay still a playing, and with one push bringing his head towards his owne brest, he set it on againe, murmuring the while over him certaine words, which he said were a certaine prayer, appropriated to the setting on of falne beards, as they should soone perceive: And so having set it on handsomly, the Squire remained as well bearded and whole as ever he was in his life: whereat Don-Quixote rested marvellously admired, and requested the Curate to teach him that prayer when they were at leasure. For he supposed that the vertue thereof extended it selfe farther then to the fastning on of beards; since it was manifest that the place whence the beard was torne, must have remained without flesh, wounded and il-dight; and seeing it cured all, it must of force serve for more then the beard. It is true, replyed Master Curate; and then promised to instruct him with the secret, with the first oportunity that was presented.

Then they agreed that the Curate should ride first on the Mule, and after him the other two, each one by turnes untill they arrived to the Inne, which was about some two leagues thence. Three being thus mounted, to wit, Don-Quixote, the Princesse and Curate, and the other three on foote, Cardenio, the Barber, and Sancho Pança. Don-Quixote said to the damzell, Madam, let me intreat your highnesse to leade me the way that most pleaseth you. And before she could answere, the Licenciat said, Towards what Kingdome would you travell? Is it by fortune towards that of Micomicon? I suppose, it should be thitherwards, or else I know but little of Kingdomes. She, who knew very well the Curates meaning, and was her selfe no babe, answered, saying; Yes Sir, my way lies towards that Kingdome. If it be so, quoth the Curate, you must passe thorow the village where I dwell, and from thence direct your course towards Cartagena, where you may luckily embarke your selves. And if you have a prosperous winde, and a quiet and calme Sea, you may come within the space of nine yeares to the sight of the Lake Meona, I meane Meolidas, which stands on this side of your Highnesse Kingdome some hundred dayes journey or more. I take you to be deceived good Sir, quoth shee; for it is not yet fully two yeares since I departed from thence; and truely I never almost had any faire weather, and yet notwithstanding I have arrived, and come to see that which I so much longed for, to wit, the presence of the worthy Don-Quixote of the Mancha, whose renowne came to my notice as soone as I touched the earth of Spaine with my foote, and moved me to search for him, to commend my selfe to his courtesie, and commit the justice of my cause to the valour of his invincible arme. No more, quoth Don-Quixote, I cannot abide to heare my selfe praysed. For I am a sworne enemy of all adulation. And although this be not such, yet notwithstanding the like discourses do offend my chaste eares. What I can say to you, faire Princesse is, that whether I have valour or not; that which I have or have not, shalbe imploied in your service, even to the very losse of my life. And so omitting that til his time, let me intreat good Master Licenciat, to tell me the occasion which hath brought him heere to these quarters so alone, without attendants, and so slightly attired, as it strikes me in no little admiration? To this I will answere with brevity, quoth the Curate: You shall understand that Master Nicolas the Barber, our very good friend, and my selfe, travelled towards Sivill, to recover certaine summes of money, which a kinseman of mine, who dwels this many yeeres in the Indias hath sent unto me. The summe is not a little one, for it surmounted seventy thousand Rials of eight, all of good waight: see if it was not a rich gift. And passing yesterday through this way, we were set upon by foure robbers, which dispoiled us of all, even to our very beardes, and that in such sort, as the Barber was forced to set on a counterfeit one: and this yong man that goeth here with us (meaning Cardenio) was transformed by them anew. And the best of it is, that it is publikely bruited about all this Commarke, that those which surprized us, were Galley-slaves, who were set at liberty, as it is reported, much about this same place, by so valiant a Knight, as in despite of the Commissarie and the guard he freed them all. And questionlesse hee either was wood, or else as great a knave as themselves, or some one that wanted both soule and conscience, seeing he let slip the Wolves amidst the Sheepe, the Foxe among the Hennes, and Flies hard by Honie, and did frustrate justice, rebell against his naturall Lord and King, for he did so by oppugning his just commandements, and hath deprived the Gallies of their feete, and set all the Holy brotherhood in an uprore, which hath reposed these many yeares past. And finally, would doe an act, by which he should lose his soule, and yet not gaine his bodie. Sancho had rehearsed to the Curate and Barber the adventure of the slaves, which his Lord had accomplished with such glorie; and therefore the Curate did use this vehemencie as he repeated it, to see what Don-Quixote would say or doe, whose colour changed at every word, and durst not confesse that he was himselfe, and the deliverer of that good people: and these, quoth the Curate, were they that have robbed us: and God of his infinite mercy pardon him who hindered their going to receive the punishment they had so well deserved.

Chapter 3

Of many pleasant discourses passed betweene Don-Quixote, and those of his companie, after he had abandoned the rigorous place of his penance.

Scarce had the Curate finished his speech throughly, when Sancho said: By my faith, Master Licenciat, he that did that feate, was my Lord, and that not for want of warning, for I told him before hand, and advised him, that he should see well what he did, and that it was a sinne to deliver them, because they were all sent to the Gallies for very great villanies they had played. You bottlehead, replyed Don-Quixote, hearing him speake, it concerneth not Knights Errant to examine whether the afflicted, inchained, and oppressed, which they encounter by the way, be carried in that fashion, or are plunged in that distresse, through their owne default or disgrace; but onely are obliged to assist them as needie and oppressed, setting their eyes upon their paines, and not on their crimes. I met with a Rosarie or beades of inserted people, sorrowfull and unfortunate, and I did for them that which my religion exacts, as for the rest, let them verifie it elsewhere: and to whosoever the holy dignitie and honourable person of Master Licenciat excepted, it shall seeme evill: I say hee knowes but slightly what belongs to Chivalrie; and hee lies like a whoreson and a villaine borne: and this will I make him know with the broad side of my sword. These words he said, settling himselfe in his stirrups, and addressing his Morion (for the Barbers bason, which he accounted to be Mambrino his Helmet, he carried hanging at the pomell of his saddle, untill he might have it repaired of the crazings the Galley-slave had wrought in it.) Dorotea who was very discreete and pleasant, and that was by this well acquainted with Don-Quixotes faultie humour, and saw all the rest make a jest of him, Sancho Pança excepted, would also shew her conceit to bee as good as some others, and therefore said unto him, Sir Knight, remember your selfe of the boone you have promised unto mee, whereunto conforming your selfe, you cannot intermeddle in any other adventure, be it ever so urgent. Therefore asswage your stomacke, for if Master Licenciat had known that the gallislaves were delivered by your invincible arme, he would rather have given unto himselfe three blowes on the mouth, and also bit his tongue thrice then have spoken any word whence might result your indignation. That I dare sweare, quoth the Curate, yea and besides torne away one of my Mustachioes. Madame said Don-Quixote, I will hold my peace, and suppresse the just choler already inkindled in my breast, and will ride quietly and peaceably, until I have accomplished the thing I have promised: and I request you in recompence of this my good desire, if it be not displeasing to you, to tell mee your grievance, and how many, which, and what the persons be, of whom I must take due, sufficient, and entyre revenge? I will promptly performe your will herein answered Dorotea, if it will not bee irkesome to you to listen to disasters. In no sort good Madam, said Don-Quixote: to which Dorotea, answered thus, be then attentive to my relation. Scarce had she said so, when Cardenio and the Barber came by her side, desirous to heare how the discreete Dorotea would faine her tale: and the same did Sancho, which was as much deceived in her person as his Lord Don-Quixote and she, after dressing her selfe well in the saddle, bethought and provided her selfe whilst she coughed and used other gestures, and then began to speake in this manner.

First of all good Sirs I would have you note that I am called: and heere she stood suspended a while, by reason she had forgotten the name that the Curate had given unto her; but he presently occurd to her succour, understanding the cause, and said. It is no wonder great Ladie that you be troubled and stagger, whilest you recount your misfortunes, seeing it is their ordinarie custome of disasters to deprive those whom they torment and distract their memorie in such sort, as they cannot remember themselves, even of their owne very names; as now it proves done in your Highnesse, which forgets it selfe, that you are called the Princesse Micomicona lawfull inheritrix of the great Kingdome of Micomicon: and with this note, you may easily reduce into your dolefull memory, all that which you shall please to rehearse. It is very true (quoth the Damsell) and from henceforth I thinke it will not be needfull to prompt me any more; for I will arrive into a safe port, with the narration of my authenticke Historie: which is, that my father, who was called The wise Tinacrio, was very expert in that which is called Art Magick, and he knew by his science, that my Mother, who was called Queene Xaramilla should die before he deceased, and that he should also passe from this life within a while after, and leave me an Orphane, but he was woont to say, how that did not afflict his mind so much, as that he was very certaine that a huge Giant, Lord of a great Iland neere unto my Kingdome, called Pandafilando, of the duskie sight: because, although his eyes stand in their right places, yet doe they still looke a squint, which he doth to terrifie the beholders. I say that my father knew, that this Giant when he should heare of his death, would passe with a maine power into my land, and deprive me therof, not leaving me the lest village, wherein I might hide my head. Yet might all this be excused, if I would marry with him, but as he found out by his science, he knew I would never condiscend thereunto, or incline mine affection to so unequall a marriage: and herein he said nothing but truth, for it never past once my thought, to espouse that Giant, nor with any other, were he ever so unreasonable, great and mightie: my father likewise added then, that after his death, I should see Landafilando usurpe my Kingdome, and that I should in no wise stand to my defence, for that would prove my destruction; but leaving to him the kingdome freely without troubles, if I meant to excuse mine owne death, and the totall ruine of my good and loyall subjects, for it would be impossible to defend my selfe from the divellish force of the giant; I should presently direct my course towards Spayne, where I should find a redresse of my harmes, by incountring with a Knight Errant, whose fame should extend it selfe much about that time throughout that kingdome, and his name should be if I forget not my selfe, Don Açote or Don Gigote. Ladie, you would say Don-Quixote quoth Sancho Pança, or as hee is called by another name, the Knight of the ilfavoured face. You have reason replied Dorotea: he said moreover, that he should bee high of stature, have a withered face, and that on the right side, a little under the left shoulder, or thereabouts, he should have a tawny spot with certaine haires like to bristles. Don-Quixote hearing this said to his Squire, hold my horse heere, sonne Sancho; and helpe me to take off mine apparrell, for I will see whether I be the Knight, of whom the wise king hath prophesied. Why would you now put off your cloaths? quoth Dorotea. To see whether I have that spot which your father mentioned, answered Don-Quixote: You need not undoe your apparrell for that purpose said Sancho, for I know alreadie that you have a spot with the tokens she named on the very ridges of your backe, and argues you to bee a very strong man. That is sufficient quoth Dorotea: for wee must not looke too neere, or be over curious in our friends affaires, and whether it be on the shoulder, or ridge of the backe it imports but little: for the substance consists onely in having such a marke, and that wheresoever it shall be; seeing all is one, and the selfesame flesh: and doubtlesly my good father did ayme well at all, and I likewise in commending my selfe to Don-Quixote: for surely he is the man of whom my father spoke, seeing the signes of his face agree with those of the great renowne that is spread abroad of this Knight, not onely in Spayne, but also in Aethiopia: for I had no sooner landed in Osuna, when I heard so many of his prowesses recounted, as my minde gave me presently, that hee was the man in whose search I travailed. But how did you land in Osuna good Madam quoth Don-Quixote, seeing it is no Seatowne? Marrie sir quoth the Curate, anticipating Dorotea's answere, the Princesse would say that after she had landed in Malaga, the first place wherein she heard tidings of you, was at Osuna. So I would have said quoth Dorotea. And it may be very wel quoth the Curate, and I desire your Majestie to continue your discourse: there needs no farther continuation quoth Dorotea, but that finally my Fortune hath beene so favourable in finding of Don-Quixote, as I doe alreadie hold and account my selfe for Queene and Ladie of all mine estate, seeing that hee of his wonted bountie and magnificence hath promised mee the boone to accompany me wheresoever I shall guide him, which shall be to none other place then to set him before Pandafilando of the duskie sight, to the end you may sley him, and restore mee to that which hee hath so wrongfully usurped: for all will succeed in the twinkling of an eye, as the wise Tinacrio my good father hath already foretold: who said moreover, and also left it written in Chaldaicall or Greeke characters, (for I cannot read them,) that if the Knight of the Prophecie, after having beheaded the Giant, would take me to wife, that I should in no sort refuse him, but instantly admitting him for my Spouse, make him at once possessor of my selfe and my Kingdome.

What thinkest thou of this friend Sancho? quoth Don-Quixote then, when he heard her say so: how likest this point? did not I tell thee thus much before? see now, whether we have not a kingdome to commaund, and a Queene whom wee may marry? I sweare as much quoth Sancho, a poxe on the knave that will not marry as soone as Master Pandahilado his windepipes are cut. Mount then and see whether the Queene bee il or no: I would to God all the fleas of my bed were turned to be such. And saying so, he gave two or three friskles in the ayre, with very great signes of contentment, and presently went to Dorotea, and taking her Mule by the bridle he withheld it, and laying himselfe downe on his knees before her requested her very submissively to give him her hands to kisse them, in signe that hee received her for his Queene and Ladie. Which of the beholders could abstaine from laughter, perceiving the masters madnesse, and the servants simplicity? To be briefe, Dorotea must needes give them unto him, and promised to make him a great Lord in her Kingdome, when heaven became so propitious to her, as to let her once recover and posesse it peaceablie. And Sancho returned her thankes, with such words as made them all laugh a new.

This is my Historie noble Sirs, quoth Dorotea, whereof onely restes untold, that none of all the traine which I brought out of my Kingdome to attend on me, is now extant, but this well bearded Squire; for all of them were drowned in a great storme that overtooke us in the very sight of the Harborough, whence hee and I escaped, and came to land by the helpe of two plankes, on which we laid hold, almost by miracle; as also the whole discourse and mysterie of my life seemes none other then a miracle, as you might have noted: And if in any part of the relation I have exceeded, or not observed a due decorum, you must impute it to that which Master Lecenciat said to the first of my History, that continuall paines and afflictions of mind deprives them that suffer the like of their memory. That shall not hinder mee (O high and valorous Ladie) quoth Don-Quixote, from enduring as many as I shall suffer in your service be they ever so great or difficult. And therefore I doe anew ratifie and confirme the promise I have made, and doe sweare to goe with you to the end of the world untill I find out your fierce enemy, whose proud head I meane to slice off by the helpe of God, and my valorous arme, with the edge of this (I will not say a good) sword: thankes be to Gines of Passamonte, which tooke away mine owne: this he said murmuring to himselfe, and then prosecuted saying: and after I have cut it off, and left you peaceably in the possession of your state, it shal rest in your owne will to dispose of your person as you like best. For as long as I shall have my memory possessed, and my will captived, and my understanding yeelded to her, I will say no more, it is not possible that ever I may induce my selfe to marry any other, although shee were a Phoenix.

That which Don-Quixote had said last of all, of not marrying, disliked Sancho so much, as lifting his voyce with great anger, he said, I vow and sweare by my selfe, that you are not in your right wits, Sir Don-

Quixote: for how is it possible, that you can call the matter of contracting so high a Princesse as this is in doubt? do you think that Fortune will offer you at every corners end the like happe of this which is now proffered? Is my Ladie Dulcinea perhaps more beautiful? No certainely, nor halfe so faire, nay I am rather about to say, that she comes not to her shoo that is here present. In an ill howre shall I arrive to possesse that unfortunate Earldome which I expect if you goe thus seeking for Mushrubs in the bottome of the Sea: Marry, marry your selfe presently; the divell take you for me, and take that Kingdome comes into your hands, and being a King make me presently a Marquesse, or Admirall, and instantly after let the divell take all if he pleaseth. Don-Quixote, who heard such blasphemies spoken against his Ladie Dulcinea, could not beare them any longer: and therefore lifting up his Iaveline without speaking any word to Sancho, gave him therewithall too such blowes as hee overthrew him to the earth: and had not Dorotea cried to him, to hold his hand, he had doubtesly slaine him in the place. Thinkest thou (quoth he after a while) base peasant, that I shall have alwaies leasure and disposition to thrust my hand into my pouch, and that there be nothing else but thou still erring, and I pardoning; and doest not thou think of it (excommunicated rascall) for certainely thou art excommunicated, seeing thou hast talked so broadly of the peerelesse Dulcinea, and doest not thou know, base slave, Vagabond, that if it were not for the valour shee infuseth into mine arme, that I should not have sufficient forces to kill a flea, Say, scoffer with the vipers tongue, who dost thou thinke hath gained this kingdome, and cut the head of this Giant, and made thee a Marquesse? (For I give all this for done alreadie, and for a matter ended and judged) but the worthes and valour of Dulcinea: using mine arme as the instrument of her act. She fights under my person, and overcomes in mee: And I live and breathe in her, and from her I hold my life and being. O whoreson villaine, how ungratefull art thou, that seest thy selfe exalted out from the dust of the earth to be a Nobleman, and yet dost repay so great a benefit, with detracting the person that bestowed it on thee.

Sancho was not so sore hurt, but that he could heare all his Masters reasons very well: wherefore arising somewhat hastily, hee ranne behinde Dorotea her Palfray, and from thence said to his Lord: Tell me Sir if you bee not determined to marry with this Princesse, it is most cleere that the kingdome shall not be yours: and if it bee not, what favours can you bee able to doe to me? It is of this that I complaine me, marrie your selfe one for one with this Princesse, now that we have her here, as it were rained to us downe from heaven, and you may after turne to my Ladie Dulcinea, for I thinke there bee Kings in the world, that keepe Lemmons. As for beauty, I will not intermeddle; for if I must say the truth, each of both is very faire, although I have never seene the Ladie Dulcinea. How, hast not thou seene her, blasphemous traytor? quoth Don-Quixote, if thou didst but even now bring mee a message from her? I say, quoth Sancho, I have not seene her so leasurely, as I might particularly note her beautie and good partes one by one, but yet in a clap as I saw them, they liked me very well. I doe excuse thee now, said Don-Quixote, and pardon me the displeasure which I have given unto thee, for the first motions are not in our handes. I see that well, quoth Sancho, and that is the reason why talke is in me of one of those first motions. And I cannot omit to speake once at least, that which comes to my tongue. For all that Sancho, replied Don-Quixote, see well what thou speakest, for the earthen pitcher goes so oft to the water, I will say no more.

Well then answered Sancho, God is in heaven, who seeth all these guiles, and shall be one day judge of him that sinnes most, of mee in not speaking well, or of you by not doing well. Let there be no more, quoth Dorotea; but run, Sancho, and kisse your Lords hand, and aske him forgivenesse, and from henceforth take more heede how you praise or dispraise any body, and speake no ill of that Ladie Toboso, whom I doe not know otherwise then to doe her service: and have confidence in God, for thou shalt not want a Lordship wherein thou mayest live like a King. Sancho went with his head hanging downward, and demaunded his Lords hand, which he gave unto him with a grave countenance, and after hee had kissed it, he gave him his blessing, and said to him, that hee had somewhat to say unto him, and therefore bade him to come somewhat forward that he might speake unto him. Sancho obeyed, and both of them going a little a side, Don-Quixote said unto him, I have not had leisure after thy comming to demaund of thee in particular concerning the Embassage that thou carriedst, and the answere that thou broughtest backe; and therefore now Fortune lends us some oportunitie and leisure, doe not denie mee the happinesse which thou mayest give me by thy good newes. Demaund what you please, quoth Sancho, and I will answere you, and I request you good my Lord, that you bee not from henceforth so wrathfull. Why doest thou say so, Sancho? quoth Don-Quixote. I say it, replied Sancho, because that these blowes which thou bestowed now, were rather given in revenge of the dissention which the Divell stirred betweene us two the other night, then for any thing I said against my Lady Dulcinea, whom I doe honour and reverence as a relike, although she be none, onely because she is yours. I pray thee good Sancho, said Don-Quixote, fal not again into those discourses, for they offend me. I did pardon thee then, and thou knowest that a new offence must have a new penance.

Chapter 5

Treating of that which befell all Don-Quixote his traine in the Inne.

The dinner being ended, they saddled and went to horse presently, and travelled all that day, and the next without incountring any adventure of price, untill they arrived at the only bugge and scar-crow of Sancho Pança: and though hee would full faine have excused his entry into it, yet could he in no wise avoide it: the Inkeeper, the Hostesse her daughter, and Maritornes seeing Don-Quixote and Sancho returne, went out to receive them with tokens of great love and joy, and he intertained them with grave countenance and applause, and bade them to make him ready a better bedde then the other which they had given unto him the time before. Sir, quoth the Hostesse, if you would pay us better then the last time, we would give you one for a Prince. Don-Quixote answered that he would; they prepared a reasonable good bedde for him in the same wide roome where he lay before: and he went presently to bedde, by reason that he arrived much tyred, and voide of wit. And scarce was he gotten into his chamber, when the Hostesse leaping suddenly on the Barber, and taking him by the beard, said, Now by my selfe blissed, thou shalt use my taile no more for a beard, and thou shalt turne me my taile; for my husbands combe goes throwne up and down the floore, that it is a shame to see it: I meane the combe that I was wont to hang up in my good taile. The Barber would not give it unto her for all her drawing, until the Licenciate bad him to restore it, that they had now no more use thereof, but that he might now very well discover himselfe, and appeare in his owne shape, and said to Don-Quixote, that after the Galley-slaves had robd him, he fledde to that Inne; and if Don-Quixote demaunded by chaunce for the Princesse her Squire, that they should tell him, how she had sent him before to her kingdome, to give intelligence to her subjects, that she returned, bringing with her him that should free and give them all libertie. With this the Barber surrendred the taile willingly to the Hostesse, and likewise all the other borrowed wares which she had lent for Don-Quixotes deliverie. All those of the Inne rested wonderfull amazed at Doroteas beautie, and also at the comelinesse of the Shepheard Cardenio. Then the Curate gave order to make readie for them such meat as the Inne could affoord: and the Inkeeper, in hope of better payment, did dresse very speedily for them a reasonable good dinner. Don-Quixote slept all this while, and they were of opinion to let him take his rest, seeing sleepe was more requisite for his disease then meate. At the Table they discoursed (the Inkeeper, his wife, daughter and Maritornes, and all the other travellers being present) of Don-Quixotes strange frensie, and of the maner wherein they found him. The Hostesse eftsoones recounted what had hapned there betweene him and the Carrier; and looking to see whether Sancho were present, perceiving that hee was away, she tolde likewise all the story of his canvasing, whereat they conceived no little content and pastime. And as the Curate said, that the originall cause of Don-Quixotes madnesse proceeded from the reading of bookes of Knighthood; the In-keeper answered.

I cannot conceive how that may be, for (as I beleeve) there is no reading so delightfull in this world: and I my selfe have two or three bookes of that kinde with other papers, which doe verily keepe me alive, and not onely me, but many other. For in the reaping times, many of the reapers repaire to this place in the heates of mid-day, and there is evermore some one or other among them that can reade, who takes one of these bookes in hand, and then some thirtie or more of us doe compasse him about, and doe listen to him with such pleasure, as it hinders a thousand hoary haires: for I dare say at least of my selfe, that when I heare tell of those furious and terrible blowes that Knights Errant give, it inflames me with a desire to become such a one my selfe, and could finde in my heart to be hearing of them day and night. I am just of the same minde no more, nor no lesse, said the Hostesse, for I never have any quiet houre in my house, but when thou art hearing those bookes whereon thou art so besotted, as then thou doest onely forget to chide, which is thy ordinarie exercise at other times. That is very true, said Maritornes. And I in good sooth doe take great delight to heare those things, for they are very fine, and especially when they tell how such a Ladie lies embraced by her Knight under an Orange tree, and that a certaine Damsell keepeth watch all the while, readie to burst for envie that she hath not likewise her sweet heart: And very much afraid. I say that all those things are as sweete as honey to mee. And you, quoth the Curate to the Inkeepers daughter, what do you thinke? I know not in good sooth Sir quoth she, but I do likewise give eare, and in truth although I understand it not, yet doe I take some pleasure to heare them, but I mislike greatly those blowes, which please my father so much; and onely delight in the lamentations that Knightes make, being absent from their Ladies: which in sooth doe now and then make mee weepe through the compassion I take of them. Well then, quoth Dorotea, belike, faire Maiden, you would remedie them, if such plaints were breathed for your owne sake? I know not what I would doe, answered the Gyrle, onely this I know, that there are some of those Ladies so cruell, as their Knights call them Tigres and Lyons, and a thousand other wild beasts. And good Iesus, I knew not what unsouled folke they bee, and so without conscience, that because they will not once behold an honorable man, they suffer him either to die or run mad. And I know not to what end serves all that coynesse. For if they doe it for honesties sake, let them marry with them, for the Knights desire nothing more: Peace, childe, quoth the Hostesse, for it seemes that thou knowest too much of those matters, and it is not decent that maidens should know or speake so much: I speake, quoth she, by reason that this good Sir made me the demaund. And I could not in courtesie omit to answere him: Well, said the Curate, let me intreat you good mine Host, to bring us here those bookes, for I would faine see them.

I am pleased, said the Inkeeper: and then entring into his chamber, he brought forth a little old Mallet shut up with a chaine, and opening thereof, he tooke out three great bookes and certaine papers written with a very faire letter. The first booke he opened, was that of *Don Cirongilio of Thracie*. The other *Felixmarte of Hircania*: And the third, *The Historie of the great Captaine, Gonçalo Hernandez of Cordova*, with the life of *Diego Garcia of Paredes*, adjoyned. As soone as the Curate had read the titles of the two bookes, he said to the Barber, We have now great want of our friends, the old woman and Neece. Not so much as you thinke, quoth the Barber, for I know also the way to the yard, or the chimney, and in good sooth, there is a fire in it good enough for that purpose. Would you then, quoth the Host burne my bookes? No more of them, quoth the Curate, but these first two of *Don Cirongilio* and *Felixmarte*. Are my bookes perhaps, quoth the Inkeeper, hereticall or flegmaticall, that you would thus roughtly handle them? Schismaticall thou wouldest have said, quoth the Barber, and not flegmaticall. It is so, said the Inkeeper, but if you will needs burne any, I pray you rather let it be that of the *Great Captaine*, and of that *Diego Garcia*, for I would rather suffer one of my sonnes to be burned, then any one of those other two. Good friend, these two bookes are lying and full of follies and vanities, but that of the *Great Captaine* is true, and containeth the artes of Gonçalo Hernandez of Cordova: who for his sundrie and noble acts, merited to be termed by all the world, The great Captaine, a name famous, illustrious, and onely deserved by himselfe, and this other Diego Garcia of Paredes was a noble Gentleman, borne in the Citie of Truxillo in Estremadura, and was a most valorous souldier, and of so surpassing force, as hee would detaine a mill wheele with one hand from turning in the midst of the speediest motion: and standing once at the end of a bridge with a two handed sword, defended the passage against a mightie armie that attempted to passe over it: and did so many other things, that if another, who were a stranger and unpassionate, had written them, as he did himselfe who was the relater and historiographer of his owne acts, and therefore recounted them with the modestie of a Gentleman, and proper Chronicler; they would have drowned all the Hectors, Achillises and Rolands in oblivion.

There is a jest, quoth the Inkeeper, deale with my father, I pray you, see at what you wonder. A wise tale, at the withholding of the wheele of a mill. I sweare you ought to read that which is read in *Felixmarte of Hircania*, who with one thwart blow cut five mightie Giants in halfes, as if they were of beanes, like to the little Friers that children make of bean-cods. And set another time upon a great and most powerful army of more then a million and sixe hundred thousand souldiers, and overthrew and scattered them all like a flocke of sheepe. What then can you say to me of the good Don Cirongilio of Thracia, who was so animous and valiant as may be seene in his booke: wherein is laid downe, that as he sayled along a River, there issued out of the middest of the water a serpent, of fire, and he, as soone as he perceived it, leaped upon her, and hanging by her squamie shoulders he wroong her throat so straitly betweene both his armes, that the Serpent perceiving her selfe to bee well-nigh strangled, had no other way to save her selfe, but by diving down into the deeps, carrying the knight away with her, who would never let goe his gripe, and when they came to the bottome, he found himselfe by a Pallace in such faire and pleasant gardens, as it was a wonder: and presently the Serpent turned into an old man, which said to him such things as there is no more to be desired. Two figs for the Great Captaine, and that Diego Garcia, of whom you speake.

Dorotea hearing him speake thus, said to Cardenio, mee thinks our host wants but litle to make up a second part of Don-Quixote? So it seemes to me likewise replied Cardenio, for as we may conjecture by his words, he certainly beleeves that every thing written in those bookes passed just as it is laid down, and barefooted friers would be scarce able to perswade him the contrary. Know, friend (quoth the Curate to the Inkeeper) that there was never any such man as Felixmarte of Hircania, or Don Cirongilio of Thracie, nor other such Knights, as books of Chivalry recount. For all is but a device and fiction of idle wits that composed them, to the end that thou sayest, to passe over the time, as your readers do in reading of them. For I sincerely sweare unto thee, that there were never such knights in the world, nor such adventures and ravings hapned in it. Cast that bone to another dog, quoth the Inkeeper, as though I knew not how many numbers are five, and where the shoo wrests me now. I pray you, Sir, goe not about to give me pappe, for by the Lord I am not so white. Is it not a good sport that you labour to perswade mee that al that which these good books say, are but ravings and fables, they being printed by grace and priviledge of the Lords of the privie Counsel; as if they were folke that would permit so many lies to be printed at once: and so many battels and inchantments, as are able to make a man runne out of his wits. I have told thee already, friend (said the Curate) that this is done for the recreation of our idle thoughts: and so even as in welgovernd commonwealths, the plaies of Chesse, Tennis, and Trucks are tollerated for the pastime of some men, which have none other occupation, and either ought not, or cannot work: even so such books are permitted to be printed: presuming (as in truth they ought) that no man would be found so simple and ignorant, as to hold any of these bookes for a true history. And if my leasure permitted, and that it were a thing requisite for this auditory, I could say many things concerning the subject of books of knighthood, to the end that they should be well contrived, and also be pleasant and profitable to the readers: but I hope sometime to have the commoditie to communicate my conceit with those that may redresse it. And in the meane while you may beleeve good mine host what I have said, and take to you your bookes, and agree with their truthes or leasings as you please, and much good may it do you. And I pray God that you hault not in time on the foot that your guest Don-Quixote halteth. Not so, quoth the Inkeeper, for I will never be so wood as to become a Knight errant, for I see well, that what was used in the times of these famous Knights, is now in no use nor request.

Sancho came in about the midst of this discourse, and rested much confounded and pensative of that which he heard them say, that Knights Errant were now in no request, and that the bookes of Chivalry, onely contained follies and lies: and purposed with himselfe to see the end of that voyage of his Lords, and that if it sorted not the wished successe which he expected, he resolved to leave him and returne home to his wife and children, and accustomed labour. The Inkeeper thought to take away his bookes and budget, but the Curate withheld him, saying, stay a while, for I would see what papers are those which are written in so faire a character. The host took them out and gave them to him to read, being in number some eight sheets with a title written in text letters, which said, *The History of the curious impertinent*: The Curate read two or three lines softly to himselfe, and said after, truly, the title of this History doth not mislike mee, and therefore I am about to reade it through. The Inkeeper hearing him, said, your reverence may very well do it, for I assure you, that some guests which have read it here as they travelled, did commend it exceedingly, and have begd it of me as earnestly, but I would never bestow it, hoping some day to restore it to the owner of this Mallet, who forgot it heere behind him with these bookes and papers, for it may be that he will sometime returne, and although I know that I shall have great want of the bookes, yet will I make to him restitution, for although I am an Inkeeper, yet God be thanked I am a Christian therewithall. You have great reason my friend, quoth the Curate, but yet notwithstanding if the tast like me, thou must give me leave to take a copie thereof; with all my heart, replied the host.

Chapter 9

Which treates of many rare successes, befalne in the Inne.

Whilst they discoursed, thus, the Inkeeper, who stood all the while at the dore, said, heere comes a faire troupe of guests; and if they will here alight, wee may sing *Gaudeamus*. What folke is it? quoth Cardenio. Foure men a horsebacke, quoth the Host, and ride gennetwise, with launces and targets, and maskes on their faces, and with them comes likewise a woman, apparelled in white, in a side saddle, and her face also masked, and two Lackeys, that run with them a foote. Are they neere? quoth the Curate. So neare, replyed the Inkeeper, as they do now arrive. Dorotea hearing him say so, covered her face, and Cardenio entred into Don-Quixotes Chamber, and scarce had they leisure to doe it, when the others, of whom the Host spake, entred into the Inne: and the foure Horsemen alighting, which were all of very comely and gallant disposition, they went to helpe downe the Lady that rode in the side saddle; and one of them taking her downe in his armes, did seat her in a chaire that stood at the chamber dore, into which Cardenio had entred and all this while neither shee, nor they, tooke off their maskes, or spake a word, onely the Gentlewoman, at her sitting downe in the Chaire, breathed forth a very deepe sigh, and let fall her armes, like a sicke and dismayed person. The Lackeyes carried away their Horses to the Stable. Master Curate seeing and noting all this, and curious to know what they were that came to the Inne in so unwonted an attyre, and kept such profound silence therein, went to the Lackeies, and demaunded of one of them that which he desired to know. Who answered him In good faith Sir I cannot tell you what folke this is, only this I know, that they seeme to be very Noble, but chiefly hee that went and tooke downe the Ladie in his armes that you see there: and this I say, because all the others doe respect him very much, and nothing is done, but what hee ordaines and commaunds. And the Ladie, what is shee? quoth the Curate. I can as hardly informe you, quoth the Lackey, for I have not once seene her face in all this journey, yet I have heard her often grone, and breathe out so profound sighes, as it seemes shee would give up the Ghost at every one of them: and it is no marvaile, that we should know no more then wee have said, for my companion and my selfe have beene in their companie but two dayes: for they incountred us on the way, and prayed and perswaded us to goe with them unto Andaluzia, promising that they would recompence our paines largely. And hast thou heard them name one another? said the Curate. No truly, answered the Lackey; for they all travaile with such silence, as it is a wonder: for you shall not heare a word among them, but the sighs and throbs of the poore Ladie, which doe move in us very great compassion, and we doe questionlesse perswade our selves, that she is forced wheresoever shee goes: and as it may bee collected by her attyre shee is a Nunne, or as is most probable goes to be one; and perhaps shee goeth so sorrowfull as it seemes, because shee hath no desire to become religious. It may very well be so, quoth the Curate; and so leaving them hee returned to the place where he had left Dorotea, who hearing the disguised Ladie to sigh so often, mooved by the native compassion of that sexe, drew neare her and said, what ailes you good Madam? I pray you thinke if it be any of those inconveniences to which women bee subject, and whereof they may have use and experience to cure them: I doe offer unto you my service, assistance, and good will, to helpe you as much as lies in my power. To all those complements the dolefull Ladie answered nothing, and although Dorotea made her againe larger offers of her service, yet stood shee ever silent untill the bemasked Gentleman (whom the

Lackey said, the rest did obay) came over and said to Dorotea: Ladie doe not trouble your selfe, to offer any thing to that woman, for shee is of a most ingratefull nature, and is never wont to gratifie any curtesie, nor doe you seeke her to answer unto your demaunds, if you would not heare some lie from her mouth. I never said any (quoth the silent Ladie) but rather because I am so true and sincere without guiles, I am now drowned here in those misfortunes, and of this I would have thy selfe beare witnesse, seeing my pure truth makes thee to be so false and disloyal.

Cardenio overheard these words very cleere and distinctly, as one that stood so neere unto her that said them, as onely Don-Quixotes chamber doore stood between them, and instantly when he heard them, he said with a very loud voyce, good God, what is this that I heare? what voyce is this that hath touched mine eare? The Ladie moved with a sodaine passion, turned her head at those outcries, and seeing shee could not perceive him that gave them, she got up, and would have entred into the roome, which the Gentleman espying, withheld her, and would not let her stirre out of the place: and with the alteration and sodaine motion the maske fell off her face, and she discovered an incomparable beautie, and an angelicall countenance, although it was somewhat wanne and pale, and turned heere and there with her eyes to every place so earnestly as she seemed to be distracted: which motions without knowing the reason why they were made, strucke Dorotea and the rest that beheld her into very great compassion. The Gentleman held her very strongly fast by the shoulders, and was so busied as hee could not hold up the maske, that hee wore on his own face that was falling, as it did in the end wholy: Dorotea, who had likewise embraced the Ladie, lifting up her eyes by chance, saw that he, which did also embrace the Ladie was her spouse Don Fernando: and scarce had she known him, when breathing out a long and most pittifull 'Alas' from the bottome of her heart, she fell backward in a trance. And if the Barber had not bin by good hap at hand, she would have falne on the ground with all the waight of her bodie: the Curate presently repaired to take off the vaile of her face, and cast water thereon: and as soone as he did discover it, Don Fernando, who was he indeed that held fast the other, knew her, and looked, like a dead man as soone as he viewed her, but did not all this [while] let go Luscinda, who was the other whom he held so fast, and that laboured so much to escape out of his hands. Cardenio likewise heard the 'Alas' that Dorotea said, when she fell into a trance, and beleeving that it was his Luscinda, issued out of the chamber greatly altered, and the first he espied was Don Fernando, which held Luscinda fast; who forthwith knew him: and all the three, Luscinda, Cardenio, and Dorotea, stood dumbe and amazed, as folke that knew not what had befalne unto them. All of them held their peace, and beheld one another. Dorotea looked on Don Fernando, Don Fernando on Cardenio, Cardenio on Luscinda, and

Luscinda againe on Cardenio: but Luscinda was the first that broke silence, speaking to Don Fernando in this manner. Leave me off, Lord Fernando, I conjure thee, by that thou shouldest bee, for that which thou art; if thou wilt not doe it for any other respect: let me cleave to the wall, whose Ivie I am, to the supporter from whom neither thy importunities nor threats, promises or gifts could once deflect me. Note how heaven, by unusuall, unfrequented, and from us concealed waies, hath set my true spouse before mine eyes: and thou doest know well by a thousand costly experiences, that onely death is potent to blot forth his remembrance out of my memory: let then so manifest truthes be of power (if thou must doe none other) to convert thine affliction into rage, and thy good will into despight, and therewithall end my life: for if I may render up the ghost in the presence of my deere spouse, I shall account it fortunately lost. Perhaps by my death he will remaine satisfied of the faith, which I ever kept sincere towards him, untill the last period of my life. By this time Dorotea was come to her selfe, and listned to most of Luscindas reasons, and by them came to the knowledge of her selfe: but seeing that Don Fernando did not yet let her depart from betweene his armes, nor answer any thing to her words, encouraging her selfe the best that she might, she arose, and kneeling at his feete, and shedding a number of Cristall and penetrating teares, she spoke to him thus.

If it be not so my Lord, that the beames of that Sunne which thou holdest eclipsed betweene thine armes, doe darken and deprive those of thine eyes, thou mightest have by this perceived how she that is prostrated at thy feet is the unfortunate (untill thou shalt please) and the disastrous Dorotea. I am that poore humble countriwoman, whom thou eyther through thy bountie, or for thy pleasure didst deigne to raise to that height that she might call thee her owne. I am she which sometime immured within the limits of honestie did lead a most contented life, untill it opened the gates of her recollection and wearinesse, to thine importunitie, and seeming just, and amorous requests, and rendred up to thee the keyes of her libertie, a greefe by thee so ill recompensed, as the finding my selfe in so remote a place as this: wherein you have met with mee, and I seene you, may cleerely testifie, but yet for all this, I would not have you to imagine that I come heere, guided by dishonourable steps being onely hither conducted by the tracts of dolour, and feeling to see my selfe thus forgotten by thee. It was thy will, that I should be thine owne, and thou didst desire it in such a manner, as although now thou wouldst not have it so, yet canst not thou possibly leave off to be mine. Know my deare Lord that the matchlesse affections that I do beare towards thee, may recompense and be equivalent to her beautie and nobilitie, for whom thou doest abandon mee. Thou canst not be the beautifull Luscindas, because thou art mine: nor she thine, for as much as shee belongs to Cardenio, and it will be more easie, if you will note it well, to reduce thy will to love her that adores thee, then to addresse hers that hates thee, to beare thee affection: Thou diddest sollicite my wretchlesnesse; thou prayedst to mine integritie, and wast not ignorant of my qualitie: thou knowest also very well upon what termes I subjected my selfe to thy will, so as there remaines no place, nor colour to terme it a fraud or deceit. And all this being so, as in veritie it is, and that thou beest as Christian as thou art noble, why doest thou with these so many untoward wreathings dilate the making of mine end happy, whose commencement thou diddest illustrate so much? and if thou wilt not have mee for what I am, who am thy true and lawfull spouse; yet at least take and admit me for thy slave, for so that I may be in thy possession, I will account my selfe happy and fortunate. Doe not permit that by leaving and abandoning me, meetings may be made to discourse of my dishonour. Doe not vexe thus the declining yeeres of my parents, seeing that the loyall services which they ever have done as vassailes to thine, deserve not so honest a recompence. And if thou esteemest that thy bloud by medling with mine shall be stayned or embased: consider how few Noble howses, or rather none at all are there in the world, which have not runne the same way: and that the womans side is not essentially requisite for the illustrating of noble descents, how much more, seeing that true nobilitie consists in vertue, which if it shall want in thee, by refusing that which thou owest mee so justly, I shall remaine with many more degrees of nobilitie then thou shalt. And in conclusion, that which I will lastly say, is, that whether thou wilt or no, I am thy wife, the witnesses are thine owne words, which neither should nor ought to lie, if thou doest prize thy selfe of that for whose want thou despisest mee. Witnesse shall also be thine owne hand writing. Witnesse heaven, which thou didst invoke to beare witnesse of that which thou didst promise unto mee: and when all this shal faile, thy very conscience shall never fayle from using clamours, being silent in thy mirth and turning, for this truth which I have said to thee now, shall trouble thy greatest pleasure and delight.

These and many other like reasons did the sweetly grieved Dorotea use with such feeling and abundance of teares, as all those that were present, as well such as accompanied Don Fernando, as all the others that did accompany her. Don Fernando listned to her without replying a word, untill she had ended her speech, and given beginning to so many sighes and sobs, as the heart that could indure to behold them without moving, were harder then brasse. Luscinda did also regard her, no lesse compassionate of her sorrow, then admired at her discretion and beautie: and although she would have approched to her, and used some consolatorie words, yet was she hindred by Don Fernandoes armes, which held her still embraced; who full of confusion and marvell, after he had stood very attentively beholding Dorotea a good while, opening his armes, and leaving

Luscinda free, said, Thou hast vanquished: O beautifull Dorotea, thou hast vanquished me. For it is not possible to resist or deny so many united truthes. Luscinda through her former trance and weakenesse, as Don Fernando left her, was like to fall, if Cardenio, who stoode behind Don Fernando all the while, lest he should be knowne, shaking off all feare and indangering his person, had not started forward to stay her from falling: and clasping her sweetly between his armes, he said, if pittifull heaven be pleased, and would have thee now at last take some ease, my loyall, constant and beautifull ladie, I presume that thou canst not possesse it more sêcurely, then betweene these armes which do now receive thee, as whilome they did when fortune was pleased, that I might call thee mine owne: and then Luscinda first severing her eyelids, beheld Cardenio, and having first taken notice of him by his voyce, and confirmed it againe by her sight, like one quite distracted, without farther regarding modest respects, she cast both her armes about his necke, and joyning her face to his, said; yea, thou indeed art my Lord: thou, the true owner of this poore captive, howsoever adverse fortune shall thwart it, or this life, which is only sustained and lives by thine, be ever so much thretned. This was a marvellous spectacle to Don Fernando, and all the rest of the beholders, which did universally admire at this so unexpected an event: and Dorotea perceiving Don Fernando to change color, as one resolving to take revenge on Cardenio, for he had set hand to his sword; which she conjecturing, did with marvellous expedition kneele, and catching hold on his legges, kissing them, she strained them with so loving embracements, as he could not stirre out of the place, and then with her eyes overflowen with teares, said unto him: what meanest thou to doe my onely refuge in this unexpected traunce? Thou hast heere thine owne spouse at thy feete, and her whom thou wouldest faine possesse, is betweene her owne husbands armes: judge then whether it become thee, or is a thing possible to dissolve that which heaven hath knit, or whether it be any wise laudable to indevour to raise and equall to thy selfe her, who contemning all dangers and inconveniences, and confirmed in faith and constancy, doth in thy presence bathe her eyes with amorous liquor of her true loves face and bosome. I desire thee for Gods sake, and by thine owne worths, I request thee that this so notorious a verity may not onely asswage thy choler, but also diminish it in such sort, as thou mayest quietly and peaceably permit those two lovers to enjoy their desires without any encumbrance, all the time that heaven shall grant it to them: and herein thou shalt shew the generositie of thy magnanimous and noble breast, and give the world to understand how reason prevaileth in thee, and dominereth over passion. All the time Dorotea spoke thus to Don Fernando, although Cardenio held Luscinda betweene his armes, yet did he never take his eye of Don Fernando, with resolution, that if he did see him once stir in his prejudice, he would labour both to defend himself, and offend his adversary, and all those that shuld joine with him to do him any harme as much as he could although it were with the rest of his life: but Don Fernandos friends, the Curate and Barber who were present, and saw all that was past repayred in the meane season, without omitting the good Sancho Pança, and all of them together compassed Don Fernando, intreating him to have regard of the beautifull Doroteas teares, and it being true (as they beleeved it was) which she had said he should not permit her to remain defrauded of her so just and lawful hopes. And that he should ponder how it was not by chance, but rather by the particular providence and disposition of the heavens, that they had al met together so unexpectedly. And that he should remember, as Master Curate said very wel, that only death could sever Luscinda from her Cardenio. And that although the edge of a sword might devide and part them asunder, yet in that case they would account their death most happy, and that in irremedilesse events, it was highest prudence, by straining and overcomming himselfe to shew a generous minde, permitting that he might conquer his owne will they two should joy that good, which heaven had alreadie granted to them, and that he should convert his eyes to behold the beautie of Dorotea, and he should see that few or none could for feature paragon with her; and much lesse excell her, and that he should confer her humilitie and extreme love which she bore to him, with her other indowments; and principally, that if he gloried in the titles of Nobility or Christianitie, hee could not doe any other then accomplish the promise that he had past to her: and that by fulfilling it, hee should please God, and satisfie discreet persons, which know very well, how it is a speciall prerogative of beautie, though it be in an humble and meane subject, if it bee consorted with modestie and vertue, to exalt and equall it selfe to any dignitie, without disparagement of him which doth helpe to raise, or unite it to himselfe. And when the strong lawes of delight are accomplished (so that there intercurre no sinne in the acting thereof) he is not to bee condemned which doth follow them. Finally, they added to these reasons, others so many and forcible, that the valerous breast of Don Fernando (as commonly all those that are warmed and nourished by Noble bloud are wont) was mollified, and permitted it selfe to bee vanquished by that truth which he could not denie though hee would: and the token that hee gave of his being overcome, was to stoupe downe and imbrace Dorotea, saying unto her, arise ladie, for it is not just that shee be prostrated at my feete, whose Image I have erected in my minde, and if I have not hitherto given demonstrations of what I now averre, it hath perhaps befallen through the disposition of heaven, to the end that I might by noting the constancie and faith wherewithall thou dost affect me, know after how to valewe and esteeme thee according unto thy merits: and that which in recompence thereof I doe intreat of thee is, that thou wilt excuse in me mine ill maner of proceeding, and exceeding carelesnesse in repaying thy good will. For the very occasion and violent passions that made mee to accept thee as mine, the very same did also impell me againe not to be thine: and for the more verifying of mine assertion, doe but once behold the eyes of the now contented Luscinda, and thou mayest read in them a thousand excuses for mine errour: and seeing shee hath found and obtained her hearts desire; and I have in thee also gotten what is most convenient: for I wish she may live securely and joyfully, many and happy yeeres with her Cardenio, for I will pray the same, that it will license mee to enjoy my beloved Dorotea: and saying so, he embraced her againe, and joyned his face to hers with so lovely motion, as it constrayned him to hold watch over his teares, lest violently bursting forth, they should give doubtlesse arguments of his fervent love, and remorse.

Cardenio, Luscinda, and almost all the rest could not doe so, for the greater number of them shed so many teares, some for their private contentment, and others for their friends, as it seemed, that some grievous and heavy misfortune had betided them all: even very Sancho Pança wept, although hee excused it afterward, saying, that he wept only because that he saw that Dorotea was not the Queene Micomicona, as he had imagined, of whom he hoped to have received so great gifts and favours. The admiration and teares joyned, indured in them all for a pretty space, and presently after Cardenio and Luscinda went and kneeled to Don Fernando, yeelding him thankes for the favour that he had done to them, with so courteous complements, as he knew not what to answere; and therefore lifted them up, and embraced them with very great affection and kindenesse; and presently after he demaunded of Dorotea how she came to that place so farre from her owne dwelling? And she recounted unto him all that she had told to Cardenio: whereat Don Fernando and those which came with him tooke so great delight, as they could have wished that her story had continued a longer time in the telling then it did, so great was Doroteas grace in setting out of her misfortunes. And as soone as she had ended, Don Fernando told all that had befalne him in the Citie, after that he had found the scroule in Luscinda's bosome, wherein shee declared Cardenio to be her husband; and that he therefore could not marry her, and also how he attempted to kill her, and would have done it, were it not that her parents hindred him, and that hee therefore departed out of the house full of shame and despite, with resolution to revenge himselfe more commodiously; and how he understood the next day following, how Luscinda was secretly departed from her fathers house, and gone no body knew where; but that he finally learned within a few moneths after that she had entred into a certaine Monastery, with intention to remaine there all the daies of her life, if she could not passe them with Cardenio: and that as soone as he had learned that, choosing those three Gentlemen for his associates, hee came to the place where she was, but would not speake to her, fearing lest that as soone as they knew of his being there, they would increase the guardes of the Monastery, and therefore expected untill he found on a day the gates of the Monastery open; and leaving two of his fellowes to keepe the doore, he with the other entred into the Abbey in Luscindas search, whom they found talking with a Nunne in the Cloyster, and snatching her away ere she could retire her selfe, they brought her to a certaine village, where they disguised themselves in that sort they were; for so it was requisite for to bring her away. All which they did with the more facility, that the Monastery was seated abroad in the fields, a good way from any village. He likewise told that as soone as Luscinda saw her selfe in his power, she fell into a sound and that after she had returned to her selfe, she never did any other thing but weepe and sigh, without speaking a word; and that in that manner, accompanied with silence and teares, they had arrived to that Inne, which was to him as gratefull as an arrivall to heaven, wherein all earthly mishaps are concluded and finished.

Chapter 10

Wherein is prosecuted the Historie of the famous Princess Micomicona, with other delightfull adventures.

Sancho gave eare to all this with no small griefe of minde, seeing that all the hopes of his Lordship vanished away like smoake, and that the faire Princesse Micomicona was turned into Dorotea, and the Giant into Don Fernando, and that his Master slept so soundly and carelesse of all that had hapned. Dorotea could not yet assure her selfe whether the happinesse that she possest was a dreame, or no. Cardenio was in the very same taking, and also Luscindas thought run the same race. Don Fernando yeelded many thanks unto heaven for having dealt with him so propitiously, and unwinded him out of the intricate Labyrinth, wherein straying, hee was at the point to have lost at once his soule and credite, and finally, as many as were in the Inne, were very glad and joyfull of the successe of so thwart, intricate, and desperate affaires. The Curate compounded and ordered all things through his discretion, and congratulated every one of the good he obtayned: but she that kept greatest Iubilee and joy, was the Hostesse for the promise that Cardenio and the Curate had made to pay her the damages and harmes committed by Don-Quixote; onely Sancho, as we have said, was afflicted, unfortunate, and sorrowfull. And thus he entred with melancholy semblance to his Lord, who did but then awake, and said to him.

Well and securely may you sleepe, Sir Knight of the heavie countenance, as long as it shall please your selfe, without troubling your selfe with any care of killing any Giant, or of restoring the Queene to her Kingdome, for all is concluded and done already. I beleeve thee very easily, replyed Don-Quixote, for I have had the monstrousest and most terrible battell with that Giant, that ever I thinke to have all the dayes of my life with any; and yet with one thwart blow thawacke, I overthrew his head to the ground: and there issued so much bloud, as the streames thereof ranne along the earth, as if they were of water. As if they were of red wine, you might better have said, replied Sancho Pança: for I would let you to understand, if you know it not already, that the dead Giant is a bored wine bagge: and the bloud, sixe and thirty gallons of redde Wine, which it contayned in his belly: the head that was flasht off so neately, is the whoore my mother and let the Divell take all away for mee. And what is this thou sayest madde man (quoth Don-Quixote)? Art thou in thy right wits? Get up, Sir (quoth Sancho) and you your selfe shall see the faire stuffe you have made, and what we have to pay, and you shall behold the Queene transformed into a particular Ladie called Dorotea, with other successes, which if you may once conceive them aright, will strike you into admiration. I would marvell at nothing, quoth Don-Quixote, for if thou beest well remembred, I tolde thee the other time that we were here, how all that succeeded in this place, was done by inchantment, and what wonder then if now the like should eftsoones befall? I could easily be induced to beleeve all, replied Sancho, if my canvassing in the Coverlet were of that nature. But indeed it was not, but most reall and certaine. And I saw well how the Inkeeper that is here yet this very day alive, held one end of the Coverlet, and did tosse me up towards heaven with very good grace and strength, no lesse merrily then lightly: and where the notice of parties intercurs, I doe beleeve, although I am a simple man, and a sinner, that there is no kind of inchantment, but rather much trouble, brusing and misfortune. Well, God will remedie all, said Don-Quixote, and give me mine apparrell, for I will get up and goe forth, and see those successes and transformations which thou speakest of. Sancho gave him his cloathes, and whilst he was making of him readie, the Curate recounted to Don Fernando and to the rest, Don-Quixotes mad pranks, and the guile hee had used to bring him away out of the poore Rocke, wherein he imagined that hee lived exiled through the disdaine of his Lady. Hee told them moreover all the other adventures, which Sancho had discovered, whereat they did not laugh a little and wonder withall, because it seemed to them all to be one of the extravagantest kinds of madnesse, that ever befell a distracted braine. The Curate also added, that seeing the good successe of the Lady Dorotea did impeach the farther prosecuting of their designe, that it was requisite to invent and finde some other way, how to carry him home to his owne village. Cardenio offred himselfe to prosecute the adventure, and Luscinda should represent Doroteas person. No, quoth Don-Fernando, it shal not be so, for I will have Dorotea to prosecute her owne invention. For so that the Village of this good Gentleman be not very far off from hence, I will be very glad to procure his remedy. It is no more then two daies journey from hence, said the Curate. Wel though it were more replied Don Fernando, I wold be pleased to travel them, in exchange of doing so good a worke. Don-Quixote sallied out at this time completely armed with Mambrinos Helmet, (although with a great hole in it) on his head, his target on his arme, and leaned on his Trunke or Iaveline: his strange countenance and gate amazed Don Fernando and his companions very much, seeing his ilfavoured visage so withered and yealow, the inequalitie and insutability of his armes, and his grave manner of proceeding; and stood all silent to see what he would: who casting his eyes on the beautiful Dorotea, with very great gravitie and stayednesse said.

I am informed (beautifull Ladie) by this my Squire, that your greatnesse is annihilated, and your being destroyed; for of a Queene and mightie Princesse which you were wont to bee, you are now become a particular Damzell: which if it hath bene done by particular order of the magicall king your Father, dreading that I would not bee able to give you the necessarie and requisite helpe for your restitution; I say, that he neither knew nor doth know the one halfe of the enterprise, and that he was very little acquainted with Histories of chivalry, for if he had read them, or passed them over with so great attention and leisure, as I have done and read them, he should have found at every other step how other knights of a great deale lesse fame then my selfe, have ended more desperate adventures, seeing it is not so great a matter to kill a Giant, be he ever so arrogant: for it is not many howres since I my selfe fought with one, and what insued I will not say, least they should tell me that I doe lie, but time the detector of all things will disclose it, when wee doe least thinke thereof. Thou foughtest with two wine bagges, and not with a Giant, quoth the Host at this season, but Don Fernando commaunded him to be silent, and not interrupt Don-Quixote in any wise, who prosecuted his speech saying. In fine I say high and disinherited Ladie, that if your father hath made this metamorphoses in your person for the causes related, give him no credit: for there is no perill so great on earth, but my sword shall open a way through it, wherewithall I overthrowing your enemies head to the ground, will set your Crowne on your owne head within a few dayes. Heere Don-Quixote held his peace, and awaited the Princesse her answere, who knowing Don Fernando's determination and will, that she should continue the commenced guile untill Don-Quixote were carried home againe, answered with a very good grace and countenance in this manner. Whosoever informed you valorous Knight of the ill favored face, that I have altered and changed my being, hath not told you the truth: for I am the very same to day, that I was yesterday: true it is, that some unexpected yet fortunate successes have wrought some alteration in mee by bestowing on me better hap, then I hoped for, or could wish my selfe: but yet for all that, I have not left off to be that which before, or to have the very same thoughts, which I ever had, to helpe my selfe by the valour of your most valorous and invincible arme. And therefore I request you good my Lord of your accustomed bounty, to returne my father his honour againe, and account of him as of a very discreete and prudent man; seeing that he found by this skill, so easie and so infallible a way to redresse my disgraces. For I doe certainly beleeve, that if it had not beene by your meanes, I should never have hapned to attaine to the good fortune, which now I possesse, as all those Noblemen present may witnesse: what therefore rests, is, that to morrow morning we doe set forward, for to day is now alreadie so overgone, as we should not be able to travaile very farre from hence: as for the conclusion of the good successe that I doe hourely expect, I referre that to God, and the valour of your invincible arme.

Thus much the discreet Dorotea said, and Don-Quixote having heard her, hee turned him to Sancho with very manifest tokens of indignation, and said. Now I say unto thee little Sancho, that thou art the veryest rascall that is in all Spaine: tell me theefe and vagabond, didst not thou but even very now say unto mee, that this Princesse was turned into a Damsell, and that called Dorotea? and that the heade which I thought I had slashed from a giants shoulders, was the whore which bore thee? with a thousand other follies, which did plunge mee into the greatest confusion that ever I was in, in my life? I vow (and then he looked upon heaven, and did crash his teeth together) that I am about to make such a swacke on thee, as shall beate wit into the pates of all the lying Squires that shall ever hereafter serve Knights Errant in this world. I pray you have patience, good my Lord, answered Sancho, for it may very well befall me, to bee deceived in that which toucheth the transmutation of the Ladie and Princesse Micomicona: but in that which concerneth the Giants head, or at least the boaring of the wine bagges, and that the bloud was but red wine, I am not deceived I sweare. For the bagges lie yet wounded there within at your owne beds head: and the red wine hath made a lake in the Chamber: and if it bee not so, it shall be perceived at the frying of the egges, I meane, that you shall see it, when Master Inkeepers worship, who is heere present, shall demand the losse and dammage: I say thee, Sancho, quoth Don-Quixote, that thou art a mad-cap: pardon me, and so it is enough. It is enough indeed quoth Don Fernando: and therefore let me intreate you to say no more of this: and seeing my Ladie the Princesse saies she will goe away to morrow, seeing it is now to late to depart to day, let it be so agreed on, and we will spend this night in pleasant discourses, untill the approach of the insuing day, wherein wee will all accompany and attend on the worthy Knight Sir Don-Quixote, because we would be eye-witnesses of the valorous and unmatchable feates of armes, which he shall doe in the pursuit of this weightie enterprize, which hee hath taken upon him: I am hee that will serve and accompany you good my Lord, replyed Don-Quixote, and I doe highly gratifie the honour that is done me, and the good opinion that is held of me, the which I will indevour to verifie and approove, or it shall cost mee my life, or more, if more it might cost mee.

Chapter 20

Wherein is prosecuted the manner of Don-Quixotes inchauntment, with other famous occurrences.

Whilest the Ladies of the Castle were thus intertained by Don-Quixote, the Curate and Barber tooke leave of Don Fernando and his companions, of the Captaine and his brother, and of all the contented Ladies, specially of Dorotea and Luscinda; all of them embraced and promised to acquaint one another with their succeeding fortunes: Don Fernando intreating the Curate to write unto him what became of Don-Quixote, assuring him that no affaire he could informe him of should please him better then that, and that he would in lieu thereof acquaint him with all occurrences which he thought would delight him.

2. Possible Source

The Second Booke

Chapter 5

Wherein is finished the History of the Pastora Marcela, with other accidents.

And as they travelled in these discourses, they beheld discending betwixt the clift of two loftie mountaines, to the number of twenty Sheepheards, all apparelled in skinnes of blacke wooll, and crowned with garlands; which as they perceived afterward, were all of Ewe and Cipresse; sixe of them carried a Beare, covered with many sorts of flowers and boughes. Which one of the Goatheards espying, hee said, those that come there, are they which bring Grisostoms body, and the foot of that mountaine is the place where he hath commaunded them to burie him. These words were occasion to make them haste to arrive in time; which they did just about the instant that the others had laid downe the corpes on the ground: and foure of them with sharpe pickaxes, did digge the grave at the side of a hard rocke. The one and the others saluted themselves very courteously: and then Don-Quixote, and such as came with him, beganne to behold the Beare, wherein they saw laid a dead body all covered with flowers, and apparrelled like a Sheepheard, of some thirtie years old; and his dead countenance shewed that he was very beautifull, and an able-bodied man. He had placed round about him in the Beare certaine bookes, and many papers, some open and some shut, and all together, as well those that beheld this, as they which made the grave, and all the others that were present kept a marvellous silence, untill one of them which had carried the dead man, said to another, See well, Ambrosio, whether this bee the place that Grisostome said, seeing that thou wouldest have all so punctually observed, which hee commanded in his Testament? This is it, answered Ambrosio: for many times my unfortunate friend recounted to me in it the History of his mishaps: even there he told me that he had seene that cruell enemy of mankinde first; and there it was, wher he first broke his affection too, as honest as they were amorous: and there was the last time, wherein Marcela did end to resolve, and began to disdaine him, in such sort as she set end to the Tragedie of his miserable life. And here in memory of so many misfortunes, he commaunded himselfe to be committed to the bowels of eternall oblivion: and converting himselfe to Don-Quixote, and to the other travellers he said: This body, Sirs, which you do now behold with pitifull eyes, was the treasury of a soule, wherein heaven had hourded up an infinite part of his treasures. This is the body of Grisostome, who was peerelesse in wit, without fellow for courtesie, rare for comelinesse, a Phaenix for friendship, magnificent without measure, grave without presumption, pleasant without offence; and finally the first in all that which is good, and second to none in all unfortunate mischances. He loved well, and was hated; he adored and was disdained; hee prayed to one no lesse savage then a beast; he importuned a heart as hard as Marble; he pursued the winde, he cried to desarts, he served ingratitude, and hee obtayned for reward the spoyles of death in the midst of the Cariere of his life: to which a Sheepheardesse hath given end, whom he laboured to eternize, to the end shee might ever live in the memories of men: as those papers which you see there might very well prove, had he not commanded mee to sacrifice them to the fire, as soone as his body was rendred to the earth.

If you did so, quoth Vivaldo, you would use greater rigour and crueltie towards them then their very Lord, nor is it discreete or justly done, that his will bee accomplished, who commands any thing repugnant to reason. Nor should Augustus Caesar himselfe have gained the reputation of wisedome, if he had permitted that to bee put in execution, which the divine Mantuan had by his will ordeined. So that, Seignior Ambrosio, now that you commit your friends body to the earth, do not therefore commit his labour to oblivion: for though hee ordeined it as one injured, yet are not you to accomplish it, as one void of discretion: but rather cause, by giving life to these Papers, that the crueltie of Marcela may live eternally, that it may serve as a document to those that shall breathe in insuing ages, how they may avoid and shunne the like downefals: for both my selfe and all those that come here in my companie, doe already know the Historie of your enamoured and despairing friend, the occasion of his death, and what he commaunded eare hee deceased. Out of which lamentable relation may be collected, how great hath beene the crueltie of Marcela, the love of Grisostome, the faith of your affection, and the conclusion which those make, which doe rashly runne through that way, which indiscreete love doeth present to their view. Wee understood yesternight of Grisostomes death, and that he should be entred in this place, and therefore wee omitted our intended journyes, both for curiositie and pitie, and resolved to come and behold with our eyes that, the relation whereof did so much grieve us in the hearing; and therefore we desire thee (discreete Ambrosio) both in reward of this our compassion, and also of the desire which springs in our brests, to remedie this disaster if it were possible; but chiefly I for my part request thee, that omitting to burne these Papers, thou wilt licence mee to take away some of them. And saying so, without expecting the Shepheards answere, hee stretched out his hand, and tooke some of them that were next to him. Which Ambrosio perceiving, said, I will consent, Sir, for courtesies sake, that you remaine Lord of those which you have ceased upon, but to imagine that I would omit to burne these that rest, were a very vaine thought.

The Fourth Booke

Chapter 24

Relating that which the Goat-heard told to those that carried away Don-Quixote.

This souldier therefore, whom I have deciphered, this Vincente of the Rose, this braggard, this Musician, this Poet, eyed and beheld many times by Leandra from a certaine window of her house that looked into the Market place; and the golden shew of his attire enamoured her: and his Ditties inchanted her; for hee would give twentie Copies of every one he composed: The report of his worthy acts, beautified by himselfe, came also unto her eares, and finally (for so it is likely the Divell had ordered the matter) she became in Love with him, before he presumed to think once of soliciting her. And as in Love adventures no one is accomplished with more facilitie, then that which is favoured by the womans desire; Leandra and Vincente made a short and easie agreement: and ere any one of her suiters could once suspect her desires, shee had fully satisfied them, abandoned her deere and loving Fathers house, (for her mother lives not) and running away from the Village with the Souldier, who departed with more triumph from that enterprise, then from all the others which he had arrogated to himselfe. The accident amazed all the Towne, yea and all those to whome the rumour thereof arrived, were astonished, Anselmo amazed, her father sorrowfull, her kinsfolke ashamed. The ministers of Iustice carefull, and the Troupers readie to make pursuit; all the wayes were laide, and the woods, and every other place meerely searched; and at the end of three dayes, they found the lustfull Leandra hidden in a Cave within a wood, naked in her smocke, and dispoyled of a great summe of money, and many precious Iewels, which shee had brought away with her: they returned her to her dolefull fathers presence, where asking how shee became so dispoyled, shee presently confessed, that Vincent of the Rose had decevied her: for having passed his word to make her his wife, he perswaded her to leave her fathers house, and made her beleeve that hee would carrie her to the richest, and most delightfull Citie of the world, which was Naples. And that shee through indiscretion, and his fraude, had given credit to his words, and robbing her father, stole away with him the very same night that shee was missed; and that he caried her to a very rough Thicket, and shut her up in that Cave wherein they found her: She also recounted how the Souldier, without touching her honour, had robd her of all that shee carried, and leaving her in that Cave, was fled away; which successe stroke us into greater admiration then all the rest: for wee could hardly be induced to beleeve the yong gallants continencie, but shee did so earnestly protest it, as it did not a little comfort her comfortlesse father, who made no reckoning of the riches hee had lost, seeing his daughter had yet reserved that Iewell, which being once gone, could never againe be recovered. The same day that Leandra appeared, shee also vanished out of our sights, being conveied away by her Father, and shut up in a Nunnerie at a certaine Towne not farre off; hoping that time would illiterate some part of the bad opinion already conceived of his daughters facilitie. Leandra her youth served to excuse her errour, at least with those which gained nothing by her being good or ill; but such as knew her discretion, and great wit, did not attribute her sinne to ignorance, but rather to her too much lightnesse, and the naturall infirmitie of that sexe, which for the most part is inconsiderate, and slipperie.

Chapter 25

Of the falling out of Don-Quixote and the Goateheard: with the adventure of the disciplinants, to which the Knight gave end to his cost.

The Goateheard beheld him, and seeing the Knight so ill arrayed, and of so evill-favoured a countenance, hee wondred, and questioned the Barber, who sate neare to him, thus: I pray you Sir, who is this man, of so strange a figure, and that speakes so odly? who else should he be, answered the Barber, but the famous Don-Quixote of the Mancha, the righter of wrongs, the redresser of injuries, the protector of Damzels, the affrighter of Giants, and the overcommer of battails? that which you say of this man, answered the Goateheard, is very like that which in bookes of Chivalrie is written of Knights Errant; who did all those things which you apply to this man? and yet I beleeve that either you jest, or else that this Gentlemans head is voide of braines. Thou art a great villaine, said Don-Quixote, and thou art hee whose pate wants braines; for mine is fuller then the very, very whoores that bore thee; and saying so, and snatching up a loafe of bread that stoode by him, he raught the Goateheard so furious a blow withall, as it beate his nose flat to his face: but the other, who was not acquainted with such jests, and saw how ill he was handled, without having respect to the Carpet, Napkins, or those that were eating, he leaped upon Don-Quixote, and taking hold of his collar with both the hands, would certainely have strangled him if Sancho Pança had not arrived at that very instant, and taking him fast behinde, had not throwen him backe on the Table, crushing dishes, breaking glasses, and shedding, and overthrowing all that did lie upon it. Don-Quixote seeing himselfe free, returned to get upon the Goateheard, who all besmeered with bloud, and trampled to pieces under Sancho's feete, groped here and there groveling as hee was for some knife or other to take a bloudy revenge withall, but the Canon and Curate prevented his purpose; and yet, by the Barbers assistance, he got under him Don-Quixote, on whome hee rained such a shower of buffets, as hee powred as much bloud from the poore Knights face, as had done from his owne: The Canon and Curate were ready to burst for laughter: The Troupers danced for sport; every one hissed, as men use to do when Dogges fall out, and quarrell together: onely Sancho Pança was wood, because he could not get from one of the Canons Servingmen, who withheld him from going to helpe his Master. In conclusion, all being verie merry, save the two buffetants, that tugged one another extremely, they heard the sound of a trumpet so dolefull, as it made them turne their faces towards that part from whence it seemed to come: but hee that was most troubled at the noyse thereof, was Don-Quixote; who although he was under the Goatheard, full sore against his will, and by him exceedingly bruised and battered, yet said unto him: brother divell (for it is impossible that thou canst be any other, seeing that thou hast had valour and strength to subject my forces) I pray thee let us make truce for one onely houre; for the dolorous sound of that trumpet which toucheth our eares, doth mee thinks, invite me to some new adventure. The Goatheard, who was weary of buffeting, and being beaten, left him off incontinently, and Don-Quixote stood up, and turned himselfe towards the place from whence he imagined the noyse to proceede, and presently he espyed descending from a certaine height many men apparelled in white like disciplinants. The matter indeed was, that the clowdes had that yeere denyed to bestow their due on the earth, and therefore they did institute Rogations, Processions, and Disciplines, throughout all that Countrey, to desire almighty God to open the hands of his mercy, and to bestow some raine upon them: and to this effect, the people of a Village, neere unto that place, came in Procession to a devout Eremitage builded upon one of the hilles that invironed that Vally.

Don-Quixote noting the strange attyre of the Disciplinants, without any calling to memorie how hee had often seen the like before, did forthwith imagine that it was some new adventure, and that the triall thereof only appertained to him, as to a Knight errant: and this his presumption was fortified the more, by beleeving that an Image which they carried all covered over with blacke, was some principall Lady whom those miscreants and discourteous Knights did beare away perforce. And as soone as this fell into his brain, he leaped lightly towards Rozinante, that went feeding up and downe the Plaines, and dismounting from his pomell the bridle, and his target that hanged thereat, he bridled him in a trice; and taking his sword from Sancho, got instantly upon his horse, and then imbracing his target, said in a loud voyce to all those that were present: you shall now see, O valorous company, how important a thing it is to have in the world such Knights as professe the order of Chivalrie errant: now I say, you shall discerne by the freeing of that good Ladie, who is there carryed captive away, whether Knights adventurous are to be held in price; and saying so, he strucke Rozinante with his heeles (for spurres he had none) and making him to gallop (for it is not read in any part of this true Historie, that Rozinante did ever passe one formall or full career) he posted to incounter the disciplinants, although the Curate, Canon, and Barber, did what they might to withhold him, but all was not possible; and much lesse could he be detained by these outcries of Sancho, saying, whether do you goe, Sir Don-Quixote? what Divels doe you beare in your brest that incite you to runne thus against the Catholike faith? see Sir, unfortunate that I am, how that is a Procession of disciplinants, and that the Lady whom they beare, is the blessed Image of the immaculate Virgin, looke Sir, what you doe, for at this time it may well be said, that you are not you know what. But Sancho laboured in vaine, for his Lord rode with so greedie a desire to encounter the white men, and deliver the morning Ladie, as he heard not a word, and although he had, yet would he not then have returned back at the Kings commandement. Being come at last, neere to the Procession, and stopping Rozinante (who had already a great desire to rest himselfe a while) he said with a troubled and hoarse voice: O you that cover your faces, perhaps because you are not good men, give eare and listen to what I shall say: the first that stood at this alarme, were those which carried the Image; and one of the foure Priests which sung the Litanies, beholding the strange shape of Don-Quixote, the leannesse of Rozinante, and other circumstances worthy of laughter, which he noted in our Knight, returned him quickly this answere Good Sir, if you would say any thing to us, say it instantly; for these honest men, as you see, are toiled extremely; and therefore wee cannot, nor is it reason wee should stand lingring to heare any thing, if it be not so brief, as it may be delivered in two words; I will say it in one, said Don-Quixote, and it is this, that you doe forthwith give libertie to that beautifull Lady, whose teares and pittifull semblance cleerely denote, that you carrie her away against her will, and have done her some notable injurie; and I, who was borne to right such wrongs, will not permit her to passe one step forward, untill shee be wholly possessed of the freedome shee doth so much desire and deserve. All those that over-heard Don-Quixote, gathered by his words that he was some distracted man; and therefore beganne to laugh very hartily, which laughing seemed to adde gun-powder to his choler; for laying his hand on his sword without any more words, he presently assaulted the Image-carriers; one whereof leaving the charge of the burden to his fellowes, came out to encounter the Knight with a wooden forke (whereon he supported the beere whensoever they made a stand) and receyving upon it a great blow which Don-Quixote discharged at him, it parted the forke in two; and yet hee with the peece that remained in his hand, returned the Knight such a thwacke upon the shoulder, on the sword side, as his target not being able to make resistance against that rusticall force, poore Don-Quixote was overthrowen to the ground, and extremely bruised.

THE TWO NOBLE KINSMEN

THE

TWO NOBLE KINSMEN:

Presented at the Blackfriers by the Kings Maiesties servants, with great applause:

Written by the memorable Worthies of their time;

{Mr. *John Fletcher*, and} Gent.
{Mr. *William Shakspeare*.}

Printed at *London* by *Tho. Cotes*, for *Iohn Waterson*: and are to be sold at the signe of the *Crowne* in *Pauls* Church-yard. 1634.

INTRODUCTION

Publication

The Two Noble Kinsmen was entered on the *Stationers' Register* on "8° Aprilis [1634]." Following that date the entrance reads: M[r]. Io: Waterson Entred for his Copy vnder the hands of S[r]. Hen: Herbert & m[r] Aspley warden a TragiComedy called the two noble kinsmen by Io: ffletcher & W[m]. Shakespeare vjd.[1] Waterson published the play promptly with the title page reproduced in figure 5. Forty-five copies of Waterson's quarto are known.[2] A materially altered adaptation of *The Two Noble Kinsmen* entitled *The Rivals* was published anonymously in 1668. It was attributed, probably correctly, to Sir William Davenant by the prompter of his stage company, John Downes, and by the printer, William Cademan.[3] *The Two Noble Kinsmen* was included in the second Beaumont and Fletcher Folio of 1679 and regularly reprinted as part of the Beaumont and Fletcher canon during the eighteenth century and the first half of the nineteenth century.[4] Not until two centuries after the original quarto was it published with Shakespeare's plays, when Charles Knight included it in the volume of disputed plays as part of his *Pictorial Shakspere* of 1841. Alexander Dyce printed it in an edition of Beaumont and Fletcher (1846), excluded it from

1. W. W. Greg, ed., *A Bibliography of the English Printed Drama to the Restoration*, 4 vols. (London: The Bibliographical Society, 1939–1959), 1: 43; S. Schoenbaum, *William Shakespeare Records and Images* (New York: Oxford University Press, 1981), prints a photographic facsimile of the entrance (Pl. 148, p. 226).

2. Stanley Wells and Gary Taylor with John Jowett and William Montgomery, *William Shakespeare: A Textual Companion* (Oxford: Clarendon Press, 1987), p. 625.

3. Arthur Freeman, ed., *Roscius Anglicanus or an Historical Review of the Stage by John Downes*, a photographic facsimile of Folger copy PN2592 D6 of the original 1708 edition (New York: Garland, 1972), p. 23; Gerard Langbaine, *An Account of the English Dramatick Poets* (Oxford: 1691; rpt. New York: Franklin, n.d.), p. 547. For a discussion of D'Avenant's adaptation, see Arthur H. Nethercot, *Sir William D'Avenant Poet Laureate and Playwright—Manager* (Chicago: University of Chicago Press, 1938), pp. 388–91.

4. Editions of Beaumont and Fletcher of that era which included *The Two Noble Kinsmen* are the one printed by Tonson (London, 1711) and those edited by Theobald, Seward, and Sympson (London, 1750), George Colman the elder (London, 1778), and Henry Weber (Edinburgh, 1812). Weber's text was reprinted with an introduction by George Darley (London, 1839). The play was also included in *The Dramatic Works of Ben Jonson, and Beaumont & Fletcher* published by John Stockdale (London, 1811), and in *The Modern British Drama* printed for William Miller (London, 1811). The texts of most of these early editions derive from the Beaumont and Fletcher second folio of 1679, sometimes through intermediaries, except for Colman's and Weber's, which are based on Q. See E. K. Chambers, *The Elizabethan Stage*, 4 vols. (Oxford: Clarendon Press, 1923), 3:203–4; and Paul Bertram, *Shakespeare and the Two Noble Kinsmen* (New Brunswick: Rutgers University Press, 1965), Appendix B, pp. 297–99.

his first edition of Shakespeare's *Works* (1857), but then reversed himself and included it in his second (1864–1867) and third (1875–1876) editions of Shakespeare. Knight, in the second edition of his *Pictorial Shakspere* (1867), significantly revised his text and notes in the light of Dyce's edition of 1864–1867. An edition by Sir Walter Scott was issued in the Modern British Drama series (1811). The play was printed by William Gilmore Simms in *A Supplement to the Plays of William Shakspeare* (1848), comprising seven questionably Shakespearean plays, and by Henry Tyrrell in his *Doubtful Plays of Shakspere* (1851). W. W. Skeat published a bowdlerized school text in 1875.

The most comprehensive edition of the play is by Harold Littledale, which was issued in three parts (numbers 7, 8, and 15) in the plays series of the New Shakspere Society *Publications*. Number 7 is a type facsimile, "reprinted literally" in Littledale's words (p. v), of the 1634 quarto, preceded by a "Bibliography," not quite complete, of prior scholarly editions. Number 8, designated part 1 of the critical edition, comprises an edited text and Littledale's textual and commentary notes. Number 15, part 2 of the critical edition, prints the general introduction and a "list of words," a concordance. Although Littledale's edition has been superseded in part, most of it is so sound and comprehensive that it remains the standard a full century after it was completed.[5]

Following Littledale's edition, *The Two Noble Kinsmen* was included in a number of editions of Shakespeare's *Works* such as those of Delius (1877), Collier (1878), Hudson (1881), Rolfe (1883), Wright (*The New Century*, 1901), Raleigh (1904), and Farjeon (*Nonesuch*, 1933). A. F. Hopkinson printed it as one of *Shakespeare's Doubtful Plays* (1894), and C. H. Herford published an edition in *The Temple Dramatists* series (1897). Arnold Glover and A. R. Waller reprinted the 1679 Folio text in volume 5 of their variorum edition of *The Works of Beaumont and Fletcher* (Cambridge: Cambridge University Press, 1905–1912). Notable among the editions of plays doubtfully assigned to Shakespeare in which *The Two Noble Kinsmen* appears is that of C. F. Tucker Brooke, whose *Shakespeare Apocrypha* was first issued by the Oxford University Press in 1908 and was reprinted several times.[6] Kittredge admitted the play to his influential edition of Shakespeare (Boston: Ginn, 1936; revised edition by Irving Ribner, 1971). Sylvan Barnet included the play in the Signet Classic series (edited by Clifford Leech, 1963), and this was reprinted in *The Complete Signet Classic Shakespeare* (New York: Harcourt, 1972). G. Blakemore Evans published an edition by Hallett Smith in *The Riverside Shakespeare* (Boston: Houghton-

5. Harold Littledale, *The Two Noble Kinsmen. Reprint of the Quarto, 1634* (London: for The New Shakspere Society). Nos. 7 and 8 were issued in 1876; No. 15 in 1885. Rpt. Vaduz: Kraus, 1965. A modern spelling version of Littledale's text was included in the 1877 Leopold *Shakespeare* (Littledale, ed. cit., p. 20*).

6. Because *TNK* is readily available in modern scholarly texts, it will not be included in G. R. Proudfoot's projected new edition of the *Shakespeare Apocrypha*.

Mifflin, 1973); and Stanley Wells and Gary Taylor admitted the play to their Oxford *Shakespeare* (Oxford: Clarendon Press, 1986). Alfred Harbage and David Bevington omitted it from their editions of Shakespeare's *Collected Works* (1969 and 1980, respectively). Fredson Bowers has included an edition in volume 7 (forthcoming) of his *Beaumont and Fletcher Canon*. In addition to Leech's Signet Classic *Two Noble Kinsmen*, other single volume editions have been issued in *The Kittredge Shakespeares*, edited by Irving Ribner (1969); in the *Regents Renaissance Drama* series, edited by G. R. Proudfoot (1970); and in the *Penguin Shakespeare* series, by N. W. Bawcutt (1977). Others are scheduled to be published in the single volume Oxford *Shakespeare* and the updated *New Cambridge* and *New Arden Shakespeare* series. Two photographic facsimiles of the 1634 quarto have been issued: John S. Farmer's Tudor Facsimile Texts (1910) and the more recent (1981) Huntington Library copy in *Shakespeare's Plays in Quarto*.[7]

The King's Men's promptbook was very probably the copy for the quarto. There is substantial evidence for this, including the mention of names of two players in stage directions (Thomas Tuck[field] and Curtis [Greville]) and several anticipatory warnings of the need for stage properties (for example, "3 Hearses ready"). The provenance of the promptbook is subject to question. The actors named are known to have been associated together with the King's Men only circa 1625–1626, which may mean that the promptbook dates from that year and therefore that the surviving text may have been subject to revision in preparation for a revival. The prologue and especially the epilogue are thought by some scholars to be of that era. However, it is also possible that the promptbook may have been the one prepared for the original production circa 1613, the actors' names being inserted about 1625. In spite of textual anomalies that present some difficulties, it seems that the promptbook was the annotated foul papers of the two playwrights. Frederick Waller, who has examined the question in depth, offers an alternative hypothesis that the basis for the promptbook was a composite of Shakespeare's foul papers and a scribal transcript of Fletcher's, which goes far to explain most of the textual irregularities, but he also says, "It seems clear enough that foul papers are the ultimate basis for the quarto *Kinsmen*."[8]

7. John S. Farmer, ed., *The Two Noble Kinsmen*, Tudor Facsimile Texts No. 141 (Edinburgh and London: by the editor, 1910). The copy reproduced is British Library C.34, g.23. Michael J. B. Allen and Kenneth Muir, eds., *Shakespeare's Plays in Quarto: A Facsimile Edition of Copies Primarily from the Henry E. Huntington Library* (Berkeley: University of California Press, 1981), pp. 836–81. The *Two Noble Kinsmen* Q copied is Huntington 59780.

8. The warning about the hearses occurs in the margin twenty-four lines before they are needed on stage. See the Farmer *Two Noble Kinsmen* facsimile, sig. C4v and, for the actor's names, sigs. I4v and L4v. In the Allen and Muir facsimile, see pp. 845, 869, and 877. Frederick O. Waller, "Printer's Copy for *The Two Noble Kinsmen*," *SB* 11 (1958): 61–84. The sentence quoted is on p. 75. Bertram, *Shakespeare and the Two Noble Kinsmen*, pp. 58–121, advances a hypothesis that the promptbook was Shakespeare's original manuscript annotated by the bookkeeper. For a full discussion by William Montgomery of the nature of the manuscript underlying Q, see *William Shakespeare: A Textual Companion*.

Date

The Two Noble Kinsmen was almost certainly written during the summer of 1613. The earliest possible time is shortly after 20 February 1613 and the latest date is 31 October 1614, but other evidence points to a first date of performance at Blackfriars in the autumn of 1613.

Francis Beaumont composed a masque danced at Whitehall on 20 February 1613 by the gentlemen of the Inner Temple and Gray's Inn as part of the festivities on the occasion of the wedding on St. Valentine's day of Princess Elizabeth and Count Frederick, Elector Palatine.[9] The masque was a success, and the second antimasque adapted for the play was particularly well received.[10] The earliest date of composition would therefore be shortly after the masque was danced at court, that is, March or April 1613. The terminus ad quem is provided by three allusions in Jonson's *Bartholomew Fair*, the induction of which is precisely dated "the one and thirtieth day of October, 1614."[11] Quarlous and Winwife are contending for the hand of Grace Wellborn, who persuades them to settle the matter by a kind of lottery, a feature of which is that each selects a name.

> Quarlous. Well, my word is out of the *Arcadia*
> then: "Argalus."
> Winwife. And mine out of the play, "Palamon."

Subsequently, Grace reveals that Palamon is the winner and Quarlous exclaims:

> Palamon? Fare you well, fare you well.

Later he congratulates Winwife:

> Master Winwife, give you joy, you are Palamon; you are possessed of the gentlewoman.[12]

9. Philip Edwards, ed., *The Masque of the Inner Temple and Gray's Inn, in A Book of Masques in Honour of Allerdyce Nicoll*, eds. T. J. B. Spencer and Stanley Wells (Cambridge: Cambridge University Press, 1967; rpt. 1970, 1980), pp. 125–48. It is also printed with a textual introduction by Fredson Bowers, *The Dramatic Works in the Beaumont and Fletcher Canon* (Cambridge: Cambridge University Press, 1966), 1:113–44. The original Q is undated, but it was entered on the *SR* on 27 February 1613 and is dated in that year by Greg (*Bibliography*, 1:28 and 450, no. 309). Littledale, ed. cit., pp. 55* and 69*, was the first to note the significance of the date of Beaumont's *Masque* to the dating of *The Two Noble Kinsmen*. He was supported by Ashley H. Thorndike, "Influence of the Court-Masques on the Drama, 1608–15," *PMLA* 15 (1900): 114–20.

10. See below in the Sources section for a discussion of Beaumont's *Masque* and its relationship to *The Two Noble Kinsmen*.

11. *Ben Jonson*, eds. C. H. Herford and Percy and Evelyn Simpson, 11 vols. (Oxford: Oxford University Press, 1925–1952), 6:15.

12. Herford and Simpson, *Ben Jonson*, 4.3.68–70; 5.2.27; 5.6.83–84. Eugene M. Waith notes that both "Argalus and Palamon are typical romance lovers" (*Ben Jonson's Bartholomew Fair* [New Haven: Yale University Press, 1963], p. 132, n. 65).

A character named Palaemon also occurs in a play by Samuel Daniel entitled *The Queen's Arcadia*, first performed at Christ Church, Oxford, in 1605 before Queen Anne and published in 1606. Some have thought that Daniel's is the play to which Winwife alludes, perhaps under the influence of Quarlous's choice of Argalus from the *Arcadia*, which is, of course, Sidney's poem.[13] Counterbalancing that possibility is Quarlous's line in act 5 of *Bartholomew Fair*, which, in saying to Winwife, "You are possessed of the gentlewoman," seems to reflect the concluding scene of *The Two Noble Kinsmen*. Furthermore, most commentators have decided against Daniel's play and in favor of *The Two Noble Kinsmen*, since *The Queen's Arcadia* was a university play and was acted, apparently only once, nine years before *Batholomew Fair*. There is no record of a London performance. Jonson is far more likely to have mentioned in October 1614 a play "presented," as the 1634 quarto title page says, "at the Blackfriers by the Kings Maiesties servants, with great applause" during the immediately preceding season.[14]

A possible echo of a passage from *The Two Noble Kinsmen* that reads, "Extremity that sharpens sundry wits / Makes me a Foole" (1.1 118–19), occurs in *The Honest Man's Fortune*:

Cunning Calamity,
That others' gross wits uses to refine,
When I most need it, dulls the edge of mine.

On the fly leaf of the surviving manuscript of *The Honest Man's Fortune*, it is said to have been "plaide in the yeare 1613,"[15] providing some further support that *The Two Noble Kinsmen* may have been written in the same year. The absence of criticism of the single combat between Palamon and Arcite points to a date before 1615. King James had taken action against duelling beginning in October 1613 that culminated in a royal edict against private combats issued late in the following year. In his plays composed in 1615 and after, Fletcher includes arguments against duelling.[16] A comment in the prologue may allude to another event of 1613, or possibly to events that took place near the revival of circa 1625. The passage reads:

13. Frederick Gard Fleay, *A Biographical Chronicle of the English Drama 1559–1642*, 2 vols. (London: 1891; rpt. New York: Franklin, 1969), 1:377–78; E. K. Chambers, *William Shakespeare: A Study of Facts and Problems*, 2 vols. (Oxford: Clarendon Press, 1930), 1:530.

14. Chambers, *The Elizabethan Stage*, 3:276 and 373; Clifford Leech, ed., *The Two Noble Kinsmen*, Signet *Shakespeare* (New York: New American Library, 1966; rpt. *Complete Signet Classic Shakespeare*, New York: Harcourt, 1972), p. 1616; Irving Ribner, ed., *The Two Noble Kinsmen*, in The *Kittredge Shakespeares* (Waltham, Mass.: Blaisdell, 1969), p. xi.

15. Littledale, ed. cit., pp. 117 and 69*. For a discussion of the date of composition and the first date of performance, see Johan Gerritsen, ed., *The Honest Man's Fortune* (Groningen: Wolters, 1952), pp. xl–xli. The year 1613 is accepted as the date of the first performance by Gerald Eades Bentley, *The Jacobean and Caroline Stage*, 7 vols. (Oxford: Clarendon Press, 1941–1968), 2:544, 612. References to *TNK* are to the Hallett Smith edition in the *Riverside Shakespeare*.

16. Baldwin Maxwell, *Studies in Beaumont, Fletcher and Massinger* (Chapel Hill: University of North Carolina Press, 1939; rpt. New York: Octagon, 1974), pp. 84–106.

If this play doe not keepe,
A little dull time from us, we perceave
Our losses fall so thicke, we must needs leave.
(Prologue, 30–32)

To many students of the play, the losses mentioned can only be the disastrous burning to the ground of the Globe on 29 June 1613. If this premise is accepted, then the comments in the prologue to "new plays" (l. 1) and "the first sound this child hear" (l. 16) indicate that *The Two Noble Kinsmen* was first produced shortly after the Globe fire. An alternative explanation, emphasizing the plural—"losses" (l. 32)—is that the prologue was written for the revival of circa 1625 and that the allusion is to the deaths in that year of James I and Fletcher and to the closing of the playhouses because of the plague. Although all the evidence—and its interpretation—unfortunately does not point in the same direction, on balance it appears that the composition of *The Two Noble Kinsmen* was begun after Beaumont's masque was presented at court and completed after 29 June 1613 in time for presentation at the Blackfriars in the autumn of that year, when income was badly needed to help meet the expenses of rebuilding the Globe.

Authorship

Scholars are not agreed on the authorship of *The Two Noble Kinsmen.* Some hold the opinion, in spite of the external evidence for collaboration, that it is the work of a single hand, usually, though not always, thought to be either Shakespeare or Fletcher. Of those who accept the idea that the play is, in fact, of divided authorship, most believe it was written by Shakespeare and Fletcher, but others admit the presence of a third dramatist. Some believe that it is the fruit of a cooperative effort of Fletcher and another playwright, not Shakespeare. In connection with the various combinations, with or without Shakespeare or Fletcher, the names of Marlowe, Beaumont, Chapman, Jonson, Massinger, Tourneur, Middleton, and Rowley have been mentioned. A large majority of scholars who have studied the authorship question have determined that the play is a collaboration between Shakespeare and Fletcher. The grounds for this conclusion are the external evidence of the *Stationers' Register* entry and the title page of the 1634 quarto, including its attribution to Shakespeare and Fletcher and its identification as a King's Men's play; the presence in the play of two palpably different dramatic styles; the equally manifest differences in dramatic technique, verse, and characterization; structure and use of the source.

Some of the external evidence argues against collaboration. Most notable is its absence from the Shakespeare First Folio. Also, when Waterson transferred his rights in "*The Noble kinsman*" along with those in *The Elder Brother* and *Monsieur Thomas*, to Humphrey Moseley in 1646, all three plays were bracketed in the *Stationers' Register* entrance with the note "by M^{r} ffesher." Subsequently, *The Two Noble Kinsmen* was included in the Second Beaumont and Fletcher Folio of 1679 but was not printed with the seven apocryphal plays (including *Pericles*) in either the second issue (1664) of the Shakespeare Third Folio or the Fourth Folio (1685). All of these bits of evidence point toward authorship by Fletcher. Three publishers' catalogues issued during the Commonwealth that listed printed plays available for sale included *The Two Noble Kinsmen*. In the catalogue by Richard Rogers and William Ley (1656), the play is unattributed. In Edward Archer's list (also 1656), the play is given to Shakespeare; Francis Kirkman's catalogue (1661, expanded and reissued 1671) assigns it to Fletcher.[17]

Early critical comment on authorship generally does not offer any detailed discussion of the question. Langbaine tells us only that "this play was written by Mr. *Fletcher* and Mr. *Shakespear*," which, as Littledale points out, at least indicates that Langbaine knew of no reason to doubt the quarto title-page attribution.[18] Pope notes what may have been theatrical gossip regarding Shakespeare's possible sole authorship. In the course of a comment on Shakespeare's use of Chaucer as a source in the preface to his first edition of Shakespeare, he says in regard to *The Two Noble Kinsmen*, "If that Play be his, as there goes a tradition it was, (and indeed it has little resemblance of *Fletcher* and more of our Author than some of those which have been received as genuine)."[19] However, Pope excluded the play from his edition. Theobald in a letter to Warburton refers to "Fletcher's Two Noble Kinsmen . . . in the writing which Play Shakespeare assisted; and indeed his workmanship is very discoverable in a number of places."[20] Warburton is himself similarly casual, remarking that "the whole first Act of *Fletcher's Two Noble Kinsmen* was wrote by *Shakespear*, but in his worst manner."[21] A comment by Richard Farmer is tangential. In discussing a

17. Greg, *Bibliography*, 1:57 and 3:1319–62. Although some critics attach significance to the evidence from such bookseller's lists as having some bearing on authenticity questions, it is by others considered merely confirmatory or dismissed altogether. Oliphant similarly expresses the opinion that the inclusion of *The Two Noble Kinsmen* in the Beaumont and Fletcher second folio "need not be held to add very materially to Fletcher's claim, nor even to greatly detract from Shakespeare's," and Chambers concurs (E. H. C. Oliphant, *The Plays of Beaumont and Fletcher* [New Haven: Yale University Press, 1927; rpt. New York: Phaeton, 1970], p. 327; Chambers, *William Shakespeare*, 1:531).

18. Langbaine, *An Account of the English Dramatick Poets*, p. 215. Littledale, ed. cit., no. 7, p. vii.

19. Alexander Pope, ed., *Works*, 6 vols. (London: 1723–1725), Preface, 1:xi. Preface reprinted by D. Nicoll Smith, ed., *Eighteenth Century Essays on Shakespeare* (Edinburgh: MacLehose, 1903; rpt. New York: Russell, 1962), p. 54. Chambers (*William Shakespeare*, 1:531) suggests that the tradition "mentioned by Pope may only rest on the title-page."

20. John Nichols, *Illustrations of the Literary History of the Eighteenth Century*, 8 vols. (London: 1817–1858), 2:623.

21. William Warburton, ed., *Works of Shakespear*, 8 vols. (Dublin, 1747), 1:sig. d7^{v}.

crux in *Cymbeline* he cites in support of an emendation, the "rose" dialogue (2.2.135–43) between Emilia and her woman, "those beautiful lines in the *Two Noble Kinsmen* which I have no doubt were written by *Shakepeare*."[22] Colman recognizes the stylistic disparities in the different parts of *The Two Noble Kinsmen* and decides that it is a work of collaboration. He emphasizes the play's absence from the Shakespeare Folios, which argues against his being "one of the joint authors," and its presence in the Beaumont and Fletcher Second Folio, which indicates that it was the work of those two playwrights, saying, "We cannot find one plausible argument for ascribing to Shakespeare any part of the Two Noble Kinsmen."[23]

Steevens offers what he calls "a few words" in regard to Shakespeare's imputed share in *The Two Noble Kinsmen* in the course of a long note on the authorship of *Pericles*. He attaches significance to the absence of *The Two Noble Kinsmen* from the later Shakespeare Folios, finds Shakespeare's "intimacy with [Fletcher] . . . unaccountable," and thinks it unlikely that Fletcher, a gentleman of family and fortune, would have "united with Shakespeare [whom he classifies with "needy poets and mercenary players"] in the same composition." He lists almost two score parallels between *The Two Noble Kinsmen* and canonical Shakespearean plays, which to Steevens, by means of a strange process of reasoning, demonstrates the play "to have been written by Fletcher in silent *imitation* of our author's [Shakespeare's] manner." Furthermore, parallels to *Midsummer Night's Dream, Love's Labor's Lost, Hamlet*, and *Macbeth* show "that the general current of the style was even throughout the whole, and bore no marks of a divided hand." At the time of composition ("after 1611"), Shakespeare was in Warwickshire while Fletcher was in London, "and without frequent interviews between confederate writers, a consistent tragedy can hardly be produced." The infrequent use of hemistiches "is some indication of a writer more studious of neatness in composition than the pretended associate of Fletcher." He concludes that this evidence points to a single playwright, not Shakespeare, but one writing under his influence, and that the dramatist must have been Fletcher.[24] Lamb, in a note in which he drew an oft-quoted comparison between characteristic stylistic qualities of Shakespeare and Fletcher, also briefly discusses the question of authorship:

> This scene [2.2.1–110] bears indubitable marks of Fletcher: the two which precede it give strong countenance to the tradition that Shakspeare

22. Farmer in Shakespeare, *Works*, First Variorum, 1773, ed. Samuel Johnson and George Steevens, vol. 10, sig. Qq3v.

23. Colman, ed. cit., 10:123–24.

24. Edmond Malone, ed., *The Plays and Poems of William Shakespeare*, 21 vols., Third Variorum, Prepared for the press by James Boswell (London: 1821), 21:233–41. For a discussion of Steevens's note (first printed in Malone's *Supplement to the Edition of Shakespeare Published in 1778* [London: 1780], 2:168–75), see Bertram, *Shakespeare and the Two Noble Kinsmen*, pp. 202–8.

> had a hand in this play. The same judgment may be formed of the death of Arcite, and some other passages, not here given. They have a luxuriance in them which strongly resembles Shakspeare's manner in those parts of his plays where the progress of the interest being subordinate, the poet was at leisure for description. I might fetch instances from Troilus and Timon. That Fletcher should have copied Shakspeare's manner through so many entire scenes (which is the theory of Mr. Steevens) is not very probable, that he could have done it with such facility is to me not certain. . . . If Fletcher wrote some scenes in imitation, why did he stop?[25]

Henry Weber, in a fourteen volume edition of Beaumont and Fletcher's plays, the first substantial critical edition, appended to the text of the play a section entitled "Observations on the Participation of Shakspeare in the Two Noble Kinsmen." He surveys at some length prior opinion on Shakespeare's part authorship and puts forth his own views in the form of a refutation of Steevens's. In the course of a comparison of style in acts 1 and 2, Weber draws attention to differences in "language, metaphor and versification," the first act exhibiting the characteristics of Shakespeare and the manifestly different second act those of Fletcher. Unlike Steevens, he sees no reason why Fletcher, who collaborated with Daborne, Massinger, and Field, would not have collaborated with Shakespeare, and he does not attach major significance to the play's absence from the Shakespeare Folios. He reexamines Steevens's parallel passages and concludes that two-thirds of them support Shakespeare's presence in *The Two Noble Kinsmen.* He then systematically assigns, for the first time scene-by-scene, the segments of the play composed by the two dramatists. That Shakespeare wrote the first act

> is supported strongly by internal evidence. . . . The second act bears all the marks of Fletcher's style . . . of the third, I should be inclined to ascribe the first scene to Shakspeare, and in the fourth, the third scene, which is written in prose; while the other scenes, in which the madness of the Jailor's Daughter is delineated, are in verse, according to the usual practice of Fletcher. The entire last act, perhaps with the exception of the fourth scene, strongly indicates that it was the composition of Fletcher's illustrious associate.[26]

William Spalding published in epistolary form (1833) the first comprehensive discussion of the authorship of *The Two Noble Kinsmen.*[27] He

25. Charles Lamb, ed., *Specimens of English Dramatic Poets Who Lived about the Time of Shakespeare* (London: 1808; 2d ed. 1813), p. 419.

26. Weber, ed. cit., 13:151–69. Weber's own opinion is set forth on pp. 166–69.

27. W[illiam] S[palding], *A Letter on Shakspeare's Authorship of The Two Noble Kinsmen: A Drama Commonly Ascribed to John Fletcher* (Edinburgh: 1833; rpt. *NSST* 8, 1 [1867]: 1–109). In his Forewords to the *NSST* rpt. of Spalding's *Letter,* Furnivall cites a later review

says at the beginning of his monograph (p. 3) that "it has not been doubted, and may be assumed, that Fletcher had a share in the work; the only question is,—Whether Shakspeare wrote any part of it, and what parts, if any?" In spite of the thrust of his question, he endeavors, as a consequence of his attempt to identify the parts contributed by the two playwrights, to establish the features of Fletcher's dramatic composition as well as those of Shakespeare. He turns first to external evidence of authorship: the title page of the 1634 quarto and the Shakespeare First Folio. He sees no intrinsic reason to doubt the quarto title-page ascription, which is supported further by the identification of the theater and the acting company with which both collaborators were associated. The publisher could have had no motive for falsely printing Shakespeare's name because by 1634 he was less popular than Fletcher (pp. 4–5). The absence of *The Two Noble Kinsmen* from the Shakespeare First Folio is not conclusive. *Pericles,* which was also omitted, is now accepted into the canon. The exclusion of both plays may have been due to the unavailability of an acceptable text. The First Folio provides no evidence of authorship one way or the other (pp. 6–9).

Spalding then turns to internal evidence. He identifies the now well-known characteristics of late Shakespearean verse and the qualities of Fletcher's verse (smooth, lines complete, double endings); their contrasting diction (Fletcher is sweet and flowing; Shakespeare is stately, solemn, vehement); and their differing imagery (Fletcher is diffuse, deliberate, delicate, pleasing, frequently romantic; Shakespeare is concise, brief, conveyed by hints, energetic, often unexpected, poetic). Spalding does not accept the view of other critics that the presence of classical allusions per se points to Fletcher because Shakespeare knew some Latin and there were many translations of the classics available to him. The most important element distinguishing the one playwright from the other is in the range and depth of thought. Shakespeare exhibits a prevailing tendency to reflection, serious when the theme is lofty, shrewd when the subject is familiar; and the originality, reach, and comprehension of his mind is as remarkable as its activity. "Fletcher is a poet of much and sterling merit; but his fund of thought is small indeed when placed beside Shakespeare's" (pp. 15–27).

Employing these individual characteristics as touchstones, Spalding assigns the acts and scenes of *The Two Noble Kinsmen* to the collaborators. "The whole of the First Act may be safely pronounced to be Shakspeare's," including the opening bridal song, which "has several marks of distinction,

by Spalding of Dyce's edition in which he says, "The question of Shakespeare's share in this play is really insoluble," which Furnivall takes as meaning that Spalding is "less decided" than formerly about Shakespeare's participation. Spalding's subsequent discussion in the review does not support Furnivall's interpretation (pp. vii–ix). Citations in the text refer to Spalding's original *Letter*.

and is very unlike the more formal and polished rhymes of Fletcher" (p. 28), and the well-known couplet with which the act closes. "In the Second Act," he says, "no part seems to have been taken by Shakspeare," but his discussion here and there conveys a muted note of uncertainty, particularly in regard to the first scene. He points out that the first portion of this scene is written in prose and therefore might be thought to be Shakespeare's, but the dullness of the subplot (of which the nineteenth-century critics had a low opinion) absolves "Shakspeare from the charge of having written it" (p. 36). The dialogue of the verse continuation of the scene (or scene 2 as marked in the quarto[28]) Spalding thinks is "in many respects admirable." It exhibits some Shakespearean qualities and some Fletcherian. "On the whole, however, this scene, if it be Fletcher's, (of which I have no doubt,) is among the very finest he ever wrote; and there are many passages . . . [which reflect the] flame and inspiration" of Shakespeare (p. 37). Spalding finds "nothing in the Third Act [that] can with confidence be attributed to Shakspeare, except the first scene," which exhibits imagery and liveliness of dialogue in the Shakespearean manner. Scenes 2 and 4, being part of the underplot and written in verse, are assigned to Fletcher, as is scene 5 (the morris dance), which Spalding thinks of as being associated with the Jailer's Daughter sequence. Scenes 3 and 6, between Palamon and Arcite, were also written by Fletcher. Of the former, he comments, "In most respects the scene is not very characteristic of either writer, but leans towards Fletcher"; and of the latter, he says, "The scene is good, but in the flowing style of Fletcher, not the more manly one of Shakspeare" (p. 41–45). Concerning "the Fourth Act," Spalding says that it "may safely be pronounced wholly Fletcher's. . . . All of it, except one scene, is taken up by the episodical adventures of the jailor's daughter," the one exception being the second scene (that of Emilia and the pictures of Palamon and Arcite), the effects of which "resemble the extravagant stage effects of the King and No King" (pp. 45–46). "In the Fifth Act we again feel the presence of the Master. . . . The whole act, a very long one, may be boldly attributed to him, with the exception of one episodical scene" (5.2), which again concerns the Jailer's Daughter, and which Spalding tells us "is disgusting and imbecile in the extreme." He also notes a passage concerning the Jailer's Daughter in the final scene (5.4.23–38) and believes it may be a Fletcherian interpolation into a Shakespearean scene (pp. 46–57). Spalding concludes his discussion of authorship by reiterating his conviction that there are clearly two hands in the play and that one of them is Fletcher's; that Shakespeare's hand can be traced frequently and unequivocally; and that the suggestions that the second hand was Marlowe's, Jonson's, Massinger's, or Middleton's can safely be set aside (pp. 57–58).

28. Hallett Smith, in his *Riverside Shakespeare* edition, follows Q in designating the verse sequence scene 2.

At the end of his discussion, Spalding takes up the question of whether it is possible to attribute to Shakespeare "the design of the work." He is confident the play "owes to Shakspeare much more than the composition of a few scenes,—that he was the poet who chose the story" (pp. 61–62). He examines the subplot, which in some particulars resembles elements of acknowledged Shakespearean plays. He links the Jailer's Daughter to Ophelia and Lear; the Physician and some of his remarks are close to the same elements in *Macbeth*; the schoolmaster is a repetition of the pedagogue in *Love's Labor's Lost*; and the "exhibition of the clowns which he directs" resembles parts of *Love's Labor's Lost* and *A Midsummer Night's Dream*. Likenesses of style that he has cited in regard to authorship show a trend of development from earlier plays, but these facets of the underplot are mere imitations that show little change, and such change that occurs is in the direction of deterioration. The inferiority of execution is palpable, and Shakespeare could not have, for example, decided on an imitation of Ophelia executed in a far lower tone. If Shakespeare had made the attempt, he "could not have failed so utterly." These elements of *The Two Noble Kinsmen* constitute a "designed imitation of Shakspeare" by Fletcher. He concludes that Shakespeare had nothing to do with the underplot (pp. 62–64). In regard to the main plot, Spalding notes that Shakespeare frequently chose stories that were already familiar in their essentials to his audience, that may have been the subject of earlier plays, and that dealt with chivalric, romantic, and classical subjects, sometimes in combination. Younger dramatists, including Fletcher, "avoid such known subjects, and attempt to create an adventitious interest . . . by appealing to the passion of curiosity, and feeding it with novelty of incident." The story of Palamon and Arcite has many of the qualities in which Shakespeare had previously demonstrated an interest, as in *A Midsummer Night's Dream, Troilus and Cressida*, and *Pericles*. It incorporates elements of chivalry, romance, and the classics and was the subject of at least two earlier plays. These characteristics were not those that would recommend themselves to Fletcher. "The person who chose this subject was not Fletcher . . . the choice was made by Shakspeare" (pp. 64–75). Spalding also finds that in the "Arrangement of the Plot," the characteristics point toward Shakespeare and away from Fletcher. It is Shakespearean in its simplicity as contrasted to Fletcher's fondness for "hurry, surprise, and rapid and romantic revolution of incident . . . rather than tragic strength or even stage effect. . . . Fletcher either would not have chosen so bare a story, or he would have treated it in another guise." The economy and concentration of individual scenes is also much like Shakespeare and not like the more diffuse structure exhibited by Fletcher (pp. 75–80). The conception of the motivating passions—love and jealousy—is Shakespeare's in its "loftiness and magnanimity" and in the "singleness and coherence of design." Fletcher "is unable to preserve any one form of passion or of character skilfully in the foreground." If he tries to do so, "he either degenerates into the exhibition of a few over-wrought dramatic contrasts, or loses his way altogether amidst the complicated adventures with which he encumbers his stories. This inability to keep sight of an uniform design is in truth one striking argument of inferiority." The single informing conception—friendship—and the multifarious and subtle ways in which it shapes the action, "this singular harmony of parts, was an idea perfectly beyond Fletcher's reach" (pp. 80–83). Following a philosophical discussion of the value of poetry, Spalding sums up. The external evidence of authorship cannot be ignored, but it should not be overemphasized. The story is "ill-suited" to Fletcher, "belongs to a class of subjects at variance with his style of thought, and not elsewhere chosen by him. . . . It is not unlikely that Shakspeare may have suggested it." The structure and "execution . . . of the drama . . . presents circumstances of likeness to him so numerous that they cannot possibly have been accidental, and so strikingly characteristic that we cannot conceive them to be the product of imitation." The play is inferior to his best, but "imperfect as it is, however, it would, if it were admitted among Shakspeare's acknowledged works, outshine many, and do discredit to none" (pp. 109–11).

In an "Introductory Notice" to his edition of *The Two Noble Kinsmen*, Knight gives his reason for printing it in his volume of Doubtful Plays: "Without prejudging the question as to Shakspere's participation in the authorship of The Two Noble Kinsmen, we have thought it the most satisfactory course to print the play entire. The reader will be better prepared for entering upon the examination of the authorship after its perusal."[29] In his "Notice on the Authorship of The Two Noble Kinsmen," on the basis of the singular form of the word "wrighter" in the prologue, Knight dismisses the evidence of the dual attribution on the quarto title page as to Shakespeare and then feels compelled, for consistency's sake, to dismiss it as to Fletcher. He is therefore, as he says, "thrown upon the examination of the internal evidence" (p. 170). He notes the complete absence from *The Knight's Tale* of the play's subplot and observes, "It is perfectly evident that this underplot was of a nature not to be conceived of by him [Shakespeare] and further not to be tolerated in any work with which he was concerned," because of what Knight believes to be salacious passages (p. 178). He acknowledges that the play in parts "bears a most remarkable resemblance to Shakspere in the qualities of detached thought, of expression, of versification . . . [as exhibited in] the peculiarities of his later period. But we hold,

29. Although Knight says he prints "the play entire," he omits the prologue and epilogue (Charles Knight, ed., *The Pictorial Edition of the Works of Shakspere*, 8 vols., 2d ed. rev. [London: 1876], 7:123, 169–87). Knight prints the "Notice on Authorship," substantially unchanged, in his *Studies of Shakspere* (London: 1849), pp. 428–47.

at the same time, that the management of the subject is equally *unlike* Shakspere" (p. 179). The style, however, is readily distinguishable from Fletcher's, and he feels bound "to produce a theory which may attempt, however imperfectly, to reconcile these difficulties . . . [his theory is] a mere conjecture, not hurriedly adopted, but certainly propounded without any great confidence in its validity." Fletcher had a coadjutor who was not Shakespeare nor, as Coleridge suggested, Jonson, but George Chapman (pp. 182–84). He supports this proposal by finding that the non-Fletcher parts are descriptive and didactic in tone and classical in content, therefore appropriate to Chapman's talents. The resemblances to Shakespeare in the scenes that Chapman contributed are present because "in a limited range, he approached Shakspere" in earnestness, language, style, and "a tendency to reflect and philosophize," and he cites some parallels. Although certain passages have "with great probability been attributed to Shakspere, it is clear to us that" the two hands in the play are Fletcher and Chapman (pp. 185–87).

In an essay prefaced by Dyce to his edition of *Beaumont & Fletcher* entitled "Some Account of the Lives and Writings of Beaumont and Fletcher," he sets forth his view of the authorship of *The Two Noble Kinsmen*. In general, Dyce accepts Spalding's determination, though he believes that some of the scenes given to Shakespeare "have suffered by alterations and interpolations from the pen of Fletcher." The stylistic contrasts in the play he compares to an imagined "picture painted partly by Michael Angelo and partly by Coreggio." Dyce rejects Knight's contention for Chapman because his style lacks the "compression of thought" seen in *The Two Noble Kinsmen* and is "composed on another system of versification." The play as we have it is a Shakespearean revision of the anonymous *Palamon and Arsett* of 1594, later altered by Fletcher.[30]

Samuel Hickson surveyed the authorship findings set forth in Spalding's Letter (1833), in Knight's *Pictorial Shakspere* (1841), and in Dyce's edition of the Beaumont and Fletcher plays (1846). Hickson's judicious review article combines a critical examination of the opinions of his three predecessors with a persuasive presentation of his own determinations. The result, a conflation of the fruits of Spalding's investigations adjusted by Hickson's own perceptions especially as regards the subplot, with a hint or two from Knight and Dyce, establishes the assignment of the contributions of the collaborators. Despite an occasional critical cavil, the broad outline he defines has endured and has been reconfirmed by mainstream scholarly examination from time to time during the past half century. Hickson commences his review with the statement that there is one point on which "all are agreed:—That two writers, of dissimilar and unequal powers, were

30. Alexander Dyce, ed., *Works of Beaumont & Fletcher*, 11 vols. (London: 1843–1846; rpt. Freeport, NY: Books for Libraries, 1970), 1:lxxx–lxxxvii.

engaged in this play there appears to be quite sufficient internal evidence." This evidence he identifies as the character of the verse, structural qualities, imagery, vocabulary, metrical features, and stylistic preferences. He finds, on the basis of such evidence, that scenes 1, 3, 4, and 5 of act 1 are Shakespeare's. The early part of scene 1.2 seems to be a conflation of the two styles, but from the entrance of Valerius it is entirely Shakespeare's. Scene 2.1 introduces the subplot of the Jailer's Daughter. It is written in prose, which Fletcher only very rarely uses, exhibits other Shakespearean characteristics, and is reminiscent of the opening scene of *The Winter's Tale*. The remaining scenes of act 2 (2 through 6) are not as effective as act 1, and the verse is unlike Shakespeare. They are assigned to Fletcher. The stronger voice of Shakespeare is again heard in 3.1, and the depth of insight into the character of the Jailer's Daughter in the next scene indicates that it is also Shakespeare's. Scene 3.3, the second encounter between Palamon and Arcite in the woods, is clearly inferior to 3.1 and is therefore of Fletcher's authorship, as are 3.4 through 6 and 4.1. Three of these latter scenes are concerned with the underplot, including the morris dance, but one is the duel between the noble kinsmen that Theseus interrupts. Hickson thinks 4.2, in which Emilia soliloquizes over the pictures of her contending suitors, is "Fletcher's masterpiece" in this play, successful both as drama and as poetry. He believes this is so because Fletcher had a superior model in the somewhat similar scene in *Hamlet*. Scene 4.3, which shows the progressive deterioration of the Jailer's Daughter's mental state, again exhibits a penetrating understanding of a disordered mind that is beyond Fletcher. It parallels but does not imitate analogous scenes in *King Lear* and *Macbeth*. For these reasons and because it is prose, he gives it to Shakespeare. Of the four scenes of act 5, three were composed by Shakespeare and one by Fletcher. Scenes 5.1 (the prayers of Arcite, Palamon, and Emilia to Mars, Venus, and Diana, respectively), 5.3 (the tournament), and 5.4 (in which Palamon wins Emilia as a consequence of Arcite's fatal accident) comprise a masterful sequence that is clearly the best conceived and written of the play and worthy of Shakespeare. Hickson compares these scenes to a "stately march or the procession of a triumph." Fletcher wrote scene 5.2, the "tone and moral effect" of which is so degraded that Shakespeare could not have participated in it. As to the style of the scene, it is Fletcher's at a low ebb. Hickson points out in his conclusion that his alterations in the assignment of the scenes to the two collaborators as proposed by Spalding, which he bases on manifest differences in dramaturgy and style, means that each of the significant actions of *The Two Noble Kinsmen* is initiated by Shakespeare, that with the partial exception of

> Arcite, every character, even to the doctor who makes his first appearance at the end of the Fourth Act, was introduced by Shakespere. We have here, then, not only the framework of the play, but the groundwork of

> every character; in each case we find that Shakspere goes first, and Fletcher follows; and even then we find that the latter is most successful in the parts where he had Chaucer for a guide.

In the course of his review of the subplot, he rejects "the idea of anything like *equal* cooperation in the work . . . there was a superior and directing, and an inferior and subordinate mind engaged upon it." He reiterates his opinion that "the framework of the play is Shakspere's," which he bases in part on the fact that "the first scene in which Fletcher appears is the second of the Second Act." *The Two Noble Kinsmen* is a play "to which Shakspere possesses a better title than can be *proved* for him to *Pericles* . . . to him belong its entire plan and general arrangement." Thus Hickson implicitly rejects Dyce's more complex hypothesis of authorship. As to Knight's theory of a Fletcher-Chapman collaboration, he says that he doubts "whether he has made a single convert to his theory." In these judgments, he has been generally followed with only sporadic divergences.[31]

Littledale's closely reasoned discussion of the composition of *The Two Noble Kinsmen*[32] leads him to the conclusion that the play is a collaboration. In this he is in agreement with those of his predecessors who discuss the question in some depth (Weber, Spalding, Dyce, Hickson).[33] In the few instances in which their opinions on scene assignments differ, Littledale's analysis sometimes places him with one or another combination of the four. He assigns only one scene (1.5) in contradiction to all of the earlier scholars. It must be borne in mind in evaluating Littledale's comments that he had accepted the idea that Shakespeare began and wrote some scenes of *The Two Noble Kinsmen* and outlined others, then "left the imperfect draft for Fletcher to complete" (p. 12*). This hypothesis, or a variant of it, had been mentioned earlier (for example, by Spalding and Hickson)[34] but merely as one possible non-controlling theory of origin. His assumption conditions Littledale's reasoning throughout. This may be seen in his discussion of characterization, where he notes, "We have only two acts to base our judgment on, two fifths of a complete play" (p. 25*); and in his scene-by-scene analysis that he precedes with the note, "It must never by forgot-

31. S. Hickson, "The Shares of Shakspere and Fletcher in *The Two Noble Kinsmen*," *Westminster and Foreign Quarterly Review* 92 (1847): 59–88. Rpt. *NSST* 1, 1 (1874): Appendix, pp. 25*–61*. Hickson, in the essay, is the first to assign parts of the subplot to Shakespeare. Following the *NSST* reprint are notes by Fleay and Furnivall confirming, by means of verse tests, Hickson's results (pp. 61*–65*).

32. Littledale, ed. cit., pp. 12*–68*, and notes to critical text pp. 107–70 *passim*.

33. Littledale prints a useful chart (p. 14*) of the scene assignments made by his forerunners, including those by Dowden, Nicholson, Hargrove, Furnivall, Skeat, Swinburne, Lamb, Coleridge, and De Quincey in addition to his own and those of the four scholars mentioned above. Elsewhere in his discussion of authorship, he takes note of the contributions of other commentators.

34. Spalding, *Letter*, p. 111; Hickson, "The Shares of Shakspere and Fletcher," *NSST* rpt., pp. 60*–61*.

ten too that only a first rough, fragmentary sketch is being compared with finished and carefully-elaborated productions" (p. 29*).

Littledale takes the quarto title page to be presumptive evidence that *The Two Noble Kinsmen* is a collaboration between Shakespeare and Fletcher, rejecting the attacks by earlier critics. The internal evidence of authorship he adduces "is three-fold:—metrical similarities, artistic handling . . . and style of thought and imagery" (p. 18*). Four metrical tests are employed: rhyme, light and weak ending, stopped line, and double-ending. These tests were devised by others (Fleay, Ingram, Furnivall), and he considers them useful in discriminating between playwrights. On the basis of this evidence, he finds that Shakespeare wrote the first four scenes of act 1, refusing to accept Hickson's contention that scene 1.2 either was composed by the two dramatists in conjunction or is Fletcher revised and partially re-written by Shakespeare.[35] Concerning the opening hymeneal song and the first seventeen lines, he has reservations but inclines toward Shakespeare. Scene 1.5 he thinks is Fletcher's because it is generally imitative of Shakespeare and because the funeral song is "very poor stuff and contains several Fletcherian phrases" (p. 45*). Littledale has serious problems with the underplot, in no single scene of which "can we feel absolutely certain of his [Shakespeare's] hand throughout" (p. 46*). However, because its characterization is Shakespearean and because it is written in prose and is reminiscent of Plutarch, Littledale feels confident that scene 2.1 is Shakespeare's (pp. 46*–48*). In scene 2.2 he finds parallels to Fletcher's other plays and concludes that it is "Fletcher's, beyond a doubt" (p. 49*), as are the ensuing four scenes of this act, which Littledale assigns on the basis of Fletcherian lexical preferences and parallels. Scene 3.2 and the first seventy-six lines of 3.1 "are certainly" Shakespeare's, but the crudeness of the rest makes him think that it was expanded from rough notes by Shakespeare "into its present form by Fletcher" (p. 50*). The remainder of act 3—scenes 3, 4, 5 (the morris dance), and 6—and 4.1 and 2 are all Fletcher's. The next scene, 4.3 (part of the subplot of the Jailer's Daughter), Littledale discusses at some length. Originally accepting Hickson's determination that the scene is Shakespeare's, he continues to believe it was originally written by Shakespeare but that Fletcher "interpolated some passages" (p. 57*). He points to inconsistencies in characterization and thinks that lines 51–56 are "certainly more in Fletcher's style than Shakspere's" (p. 61*). He also notes, however, the difficulty in finding the style to be Fletcher's, since it is written in prose and the Doctor exhibits qualities in the manner of Shakespeare. Littledale's conclusion is that Shakespeare wrote "much of the scene . . . but that Fletcher has touched up and modified" it (pp. 61*–62*). The exordium of 5.1 is Fletcher's because it has thirteen double endings in seventeen lines. Beyond that, the entire scene is

35. Hickson, "The Shares of Shakspere and Fletcher," p. 36*.

Shakespeare's because it exhibits lexical affinities with his acknowledged plays. The next scene (5.2), the "basest" of the Jailer's Daughter's scenes, "has given rise to the undue depreciation of any potentialities of merit which may be in the subplot" (p. 65*). Scene 5.3 (the tournament) "is partly by Shakespere but has been touched by Fletcher, and perhaps by Beaumont also. . . . The word play in l. 46 . . . is very Shaksperian, and the dramatic construction of the scene is especially worthy of his genius." Fletcher had a hand in the scene—"ll. 105–14 and 136–46 . . . are decidedly in his manner"—but Littledale says this "may be heresy" (pp. 65*–66*). He does not tell us which lines he thinks are Beaumont's. Littledale emphasizes parallels and vocabulary preferences in awarding the bulk of 5.4 to Shakespeare, but "ll. 84–98 are unmistakeably from Fletcher's pen" (p. 67*). The prologue and epilogue were composed by Fletcher (pp. 12* and 68*).

Oliphant twice studied the authorship of *The Two Noble Kinsmen*, slightly revising the assignments to Shakespeare and Fletcher in the second version from his initial determination.[36] Differing in a few places from Littledale, Oliphant assigns to Shakespeare all of act 1; the first part of 2.1 to the Daughter's exit; 3.1 and 2; 5.1, from Theseus's exit to the end; and 5.3 and 4. He denies any part to Massinger and, although he does "not feel absolutely certain," he believes that the hand of Beaumont can be detected. This is a belief, however, to which he has come "somewhat reluctantly." The parts he assigns to Beaumont are "the burlesque nonsense in the latter part of III.v; [the] May dance [which] is clearly a repetition of the anti-masque in Beaumont's masque of 1612–13; [and] the latter part of IV.iii (from the Daughter's exit)," which he says, "Speaks most clearly of Beaumont." His grounds are mainly style and imagery and one phrase that he thinks "decidedly points to Beaumont" (p. 345).[37] Herford, finding Spalding's argument has made his case "appear even more plausible" than it is and emphasizing Spalding's later hesitation, raises doubts concerning Shakespeare's participation. The "subject, plot and characterisation" have features that may have attracted Shakespeare's interest, but while they are not incompatible with Shakespeare's authorship they do not proclaim it and some repudiate it. "Not a single character is definitely Shaksperean. . . . It remains open to much doubt whether the considerable poet . . . was really Shakspere. . . . In default of Shakspere, no dramatist has so good a claim as Massinger." A. W. Ward discusses earlier ascriptions of the non-

36. E. H. C. Oliphant, "The Works of Beaumont and Fletcher," *Englische Studien* 15 (1891): 322–27, and *Plays of Beaumont and Fletcher*, pp. 325–48. Quotations are from the latter. Oliphant designates each of the prayers in 5.1 as a separate scene, as do also Wells and Taylor in the *Oxford Shakespeare* (1986).

37. The parallel to the line from Beaumont's poem *The Remedie of Love* is in *The Two Noble Kinsmen* at 4.3.87–88, "carve her, drink to her." Shakespeare, according to Littledale, uses the *carve* locution twice (Littledale, ed. cit., note pp. 156–57), and there are other possibilities, so its evidence for Beaumont's participation, while possible, is not compelling.

Fletcherian portions of *The Two Noble Kinsmen* by Knight (to Chapman), Boyle (to Massinger), and Fleay (to Beaumont), and also notes the hesitations of other "oracles" (Dowden, Furnivall, and ten Brinck). He adheres to the "twofold conviction" and accepts Fletcher but not the "supposition of Shakspere's authorship," which he finds "both improbable and unproved—unless by the negative argument that the claims of no other contemporary dramatist call for comparative consideration."[38]

Thorndike accepts the joint authorship of *The Two Noble Kinsmen* on the basis of the external evidence, rejecting specifically the claims for Beaumont and Massinger. He believes that Shakespeare developed the plan, that both playwrights had a clear understanding of the "outline of the play," and, on the model of other dramatic collaborations, that each wrote a series of scenes in both the main and the subplot. Either Shakespeare or the two poets jointly assigned the scenes. Fletcher's work is entirely his. Shakespeare scenes, on the other hand, show signs of interpolation, probably by Fletcher, "only at the beginnings or ends." He points out that in a play written in 1613 and still popular in 1634 there is a "manifest possibility that the text was subject to some alteration and revision." There is no hard evidence that Shakespeare had left London by 1613, and Thorndike concludes that the two authors worked together as equal partners. He analyzes the scenes of the principal plot and subplot separately and demonstrates that in each the contributions of the collaborators are linked in spite of some minor disparities. "The method of composition seems to have been collaboration pure and simple" by the two dramatists. He rejects a number of conjectures by predecessor critics. Some earlier students of the play had put forward the idea that Shakespeare would not have tolerated the "trash" of the underplot, especially in scenes 4.1 and 3, and 5.2, presumed to be from the pen of Fletcher, but Thorndike notes that there is equivalent "trash" in *Pericles* "which he managed to endure." It has been argued that the degraded imitations of Ophelia and Holofernes would have offended Shakespeare, but Thorndike thinks Shakespeare planned them and left the writing for Fletcher to do, the result being inferior. These earlier hypotheses imply that Shakespeare could not have taken part in a play including such offensive elements. Thorndike negates the inference. He argues effectively against another earlier theory—that Shakespeare left an unfinished play at his death which was completed by Fletcher—by pointing out that none of the scenes is incomplete. He also reexamines Littledale's identification of the morris dance scene (3.5) with Beaumont's antimasque, finds "the connection . . . unmistakeable," and endorses Littledale's dating of the play.[39]

38. Herford and Simpson, *Ben Jonson*, pp. v–xii; Adolphus William Ward, *A History of English Dramatic Literature to the Death of Queen Anne*, 3 vols., rev. ed. (London: Macmillan, 1899), 2:237–43, 743–47.

39. Ashley H. Thorndike, *The Influence of Beaumont and Fletcher on Shakspere* (Worcester, Mass.: Wood, 1901; rpt. New York: AMS, 1966), pp. 44–55.

Tucker Brooke finds modern critics unanimous on two points: *The Two Noble Kinsmen* was written by two poets "very different in style, genius and character" and the weaker part is "mainly or exclusively the work of Fletcher." He notes that metrical tests demonstrate that the non-Fletcherian portion exhibits stylistic features like those observed in *The Winter's Tale* and *The Tempest*. In solving the authorship puzzle, the characteristics of the style must be balanced against the un-Shakespearean characterization. The elements ascribed to Shakespeare are strongly reminiscent of his style, but they fall short of authenticity. The parts of the play that are obviously not Fletcher's contain some brilliant poetry but are deficient in the psychological insight and philosophy of life characteristic of Shakespeare. On these counts, Emilia cannot compare to Imogen or Miranda. The best scenes in the play are the first of acts 1 and 5, but Brooke denies them to Shakespeare because they lack dramatic unity and propriety. Shakespeare's authorship is "quite undemonstrable." He considers Massinger a more likely claimant for Fletcher's partner.[40] Willard Farnham introduced a stylistic test based on the frequency of colloquial contractions used by Beaumont, Fletcher, Massinger, and Shakespeare but employed by each of the playwrights at different rates. In his study of *The Two Noble Kinsmen*, he identifies 37 such contractions occurring 141 times in the play. Studies of acknowledged plays in the case of each dramatist—for Shakespeare the plays are *The Merchant of Venice, Romeo and Juliet, Othello*, and *The Winter's Tale*—provide the basis for comparison. The use of the contractions ranges from a low for Massinger, followed by Beaumont, then Fletcher, to a high for Shakespeare. The frequencies in *The Two Noble Kinsmen* eliminate Massinger and Beaumont, identify Fletcher, and show a usage characteristic of Shakespeare in the scenes not traditionally assigned to Fletcher. "Consequently," Farnham concludes, "the evidence points to Shakespeare more than to any other as the author of the non-Fletcherian scenes of *The Two Noble Kinsmen*."[41]

H. Dugdale Sykes marshals numerous parallels between *The Two Noble Kinsmen* and several of Massinger's plays in support of his candidacy as Fletcher's collaborator, almost all of which can be explained on grounds other than the assumption of Massinger's presence in the play. Some are

40. C. F. Tucker Brooke, ed., *The Shakespeare Apocrypha* (Oxford: Clarendon Press, 1908), pp. xl–xlv. Brooke puts forth Massinger, based on the opinions of Robert Boyle and Fleay. The latter (in his *Biographical Chronicle* 1:189–92) subsequently rejected Massinger and settled on Beaumont as Fletcher's collaborator. For Boyle's view, see "On Massinger and *The Two Noble Kinsmen*," *NSST* 1, 9 (1881): 371–99, and "Beaumont, Fletcher and Massinger," *Englische Studien* 5 (1882): 74–96. A. H. Cruickshank (*Philip Massinger* [Oxford: Blackwell, 1920], pp. 92–104) rejects Boyle's arguments and denies that Massinger wrote any part of *The Two Noble Kinsmen*. He reiterates his opinion in his lecture *Massinger and "The Two Noble Kinsmen"* (Oxford: Blackwell, 1922). Brooke, forty years later, seems to have accepted a Shakespeare-Fletcher collaboration (*A Literary History of England*, ed. Albert C. Baugh [New York: Appleton, 1948], pp. 540 and 576).

41. Willard Edward Farnham, "Colloquial Contractions in Beaumont, Fletcher, Massinger and Shakespeare as a Test of Authorship," *PMLA* 31 (1916): 326–58.

commonplaces, a few are not convincing, most may be the result of Massinger's well-known proclivity for echoing Shakespeare, which Sykes acknowledges. "It must be admitted that the language of the play occasionally rises to a poetic height rarely achieved by Massinger elsewhere, and that it sometimes exhibits a peculiarly 'Shakespearean' directness and brevity of expression." Yet the evidence he has presented, he says, "cannot be rebutted by arguments in favour of Shakespeare's authorship based upon mere aesthetic impression," which, as it happens, are the kinds of arguments he offers for Massinger's authorship. Sykes mentions, but does not attempt to refute, the external evidence.[42] Henry David Gray takes up the question of "Beaumont and *The Two Noble Kinsmen*." He examines the play in the light of a dozen of "Beaumont's characteristics as given by Professor Gayley." These are almost exclusively stylistic preferences.[43] Gray finds all of them except one in *The Two Noble Kinsmen* and says that they occur in scenes "written in a manner which is like Shakespeare's . . . but the trouble is they are only *like* Shakespeare," as contrasted to others that are "splendidly Shakespearean," such as Emilia's prayer to Diana. He concludes that there are then "two dramatists (aside from Fletcher), of whom one was Shakespeare and the other" possibly Beaumont. The non-Fletcher scenes "were planned and partly written by Beaumont, and finished, somewhat hastily, by Shakespeare." Gray posits the following sequence: Fletcher started the play, then enlisted the services of Beaumont, who incorporated his own antimasque and wrote other scenes of the Jailer's Daughter and "a series of scenes dealing with the main plot," but then he married and went to live in Kent. Fletcher at this point turned to Shakespeare for assistance, and he completed the play.[44]

A. C. Bradley compiles statistics of part-line scene endings in Shakespeare and seven other dramatists. His figures show that Shakespeare employs this mannerism more frequently in late plays than he does in earlier ones, and at a significantly higher rate than the other dramatists, with one aberration: collaborative Beaumont and Fletcher plays exhibit a frequency approaching Shakespeare's, but Fletcher writing alone shows a much lower rate. The twelve scenes of *The Two Noble Kinsmen* usually assigned to Shakespeare have a rate characteristic of him, while the other twelve are closer to Fletcher's frequency. Massinger, whose plays include very few such part-line scene endings, is by this test eliminated as a possible author of the non-Fletcherian scenes.[45]

42. H. Dugdale Sykes, "The Two Noble Kinsmen," in *Sidelights on Shakespeare* (Stratford-upon-Avon: Shakespeare Head Press, 1919), pp. 1–17.

43. Charles Mills Gayley, *Beaumont the Dramatist* (New York: Century, 1914), pp. 281–99.

44. Henry David Gray, "Beaumont and *The Two Noble Kinsmen*," *PQ* 2 (1923): 112–31.

45. Andrew C. Bradley, "Scene-Endings in Shakespeare and in *The Two Noble Kinsmen*," in *A Miscellany* (London: Macmillan, 1929; rpt. Freeport, NY: Books for Libraries, n.d.), pp. 218–24.

Sir Edmund Chambers sees "clearly . . . at least two hands in the play. . . . Fletcher's is unmistakeable . . . metrically, the non-Fletcherian verse agrees with that of Shakespeare, in its latest stage." The converging evidence of *The Two Noble Kinsmen* and *Henry VIII* with the slighter indication of *Cardenio*, "all pointing to 1613, is strong for some collaboration between Shakespeare and Fletcher in that year . . . stylistic features, other than metrical, are confirmatory." The invocations in act 5 are beyond the capability of "Tourneur, Rowley, or Chapman who have been loosely talked of . . . [and] are quite outside the imaginative range of Massinger." It is thought that Beaumont might have helped Fletcher in 3.5, "and of course it is his mask that is drawn upon." Possibly the prose of 2.1 and 4.3 "might be his, rather than Shakespeare's. Either is more likely than Fletcher, who did not make much use of prose."[46] Alfred Hart studies the vocabulary of the two parts of *The Two Noble Kinsmen*, as traditionally divided, in an effort to determine if differences exhibited in the text are sufficient to support the presumed divided authorship. As controls he uses *Antony and Cleopatra, Coriolanus, Cymbeline, The Winter's Tale*, and *The Tempest.* He investigates such vocabulary phenomena as rare words, those previously unused in the late plays, new words, and original word forms such as those beginning with *un* and *dis* and those ending with *like, ance, ment, ful*, and *less*. The incidence of such words and word forms in the two parts of the play demonstrates a significant difference, those that occur in the presumed Shakespearean portion of *The Two Noble Kinsmen* occurring at a rate consistent with the rates in the control plays while those seen in the Fletcher part vary from a rate of occurrence of fifty percent of the Shakespearean segments to zero. Hart concludes that the diction of the scenes customarily assigned to Shakespeare "bears the stamp of the essential qualities of his vocabulary" and that the evidence adduced "strongly supports the claim made by many critics that *The Two Noble Kinsmen* should be included in the Shakespeare canon."[47]

On the basis of the external evidence of the title page, Kittredge, with characteristic directness, says, "The ascription to Fletcher and Shakespeare in the title page is undoubtedly correct," and he conjectures that "probably they worked in active collaboration." As to Beaumont's possible participation, he finds that "nothing indicates that Beaumont had any share in the text of the drama" but says that perhaps his hand may be detected "in the Schoolmaster's long speech as Presenter of the dance" borrowed from his masque. Peter Alexander and Mark van Doren briefly discuss *The Two Noble Kinsmen* and both deny Shakespeare's authorship, the former because it was not admitted to the Shakespeare First Folio; the latter because the

46. Chambers, *William Shakespeare*, 1:531–32.

47. Alfred Hart, "Shakespeare and the Vocabulary of *The Two Noble Kinsmen*," *RES* 10 (1934): 274–87. Reprinted substantially unchanged in *Shakespeare and the Homilies* (Melbourne: Melbourne University Press, 1934; rpt. New York: Octagon, 1970), pp. 242–56.

style and characterization are un-Shakespearean.[48] Theodore Spencer, in two of the few perceptively appreciative essays on *The Two Noble Kinsmen*, determines with minimal discussion that it is the result of a collaboration between Shakespeare and Fletcher.[49] Hazleton Spencer says (not quite accurately) that the only external evidence is the title page, the truth of which has not been demonstrated. He notes that "some evidence against it" is the play's omission from the Shakespeare First Folio and its inclusion in the Beaumont and Fletcher Second Folio. Internal evidence, "always risky," supports Shakespeare's presence. "It is reasonably certain that two playwrights wrote this dramatic romance . . . [in] close collaboration." One is Fletcher; it "seems probable [that] the other coauthor is Shakespeare. . . . Nothing excludes the possibility that the collaborators revised each other's work."[50] Sir Walter Greg does not systematically examine the question of Shakespeare's participation in the authorship but says, in the course of a discussion of the authenticity of *Pericles*, that based on the testimony of the title page, *The Two Noble Kinsmen* is "the product of collaboration on Shakespeare's part." Later he reiterates, "*Henry VIII* and *The Two Noble Kinsmen* are generally held to be the outcome of collaboration between Shakespeare and John Fletcher."[51]

Edward Armstrong first identified, defined, and described characteristic Shakespearean "image clusters," linked images not logically connected that seem to have arisen from the poet's memory of past personal experiences. Some of the image clusters occur in more than one play, some in several written over a period of years, and thus may be employed as an aid in determining Shakespearean authorship questions, especially since they seem to occur only rarely in other dramatists. In the second revised edition of his study, Armstrong investigates "Shakespearean Imagery in *The Two Noble Kinsmen*." He searches for previously identified image clusters, of which he finds several, and analyzes the parts of the play customarily thought to be Shakespearean, identifying three clusters that are also found in other plays, especially *Coriolanus* and the earlier romantic comedies. One new cluster is of unusual interest because it conflates two that occur separately in *The Tempest*. Armstrong notes that while "cluster

48. Kittredge, ed., *Works*, p. 1409; Peter Alexander, *Shakespeare's Life and Art* (London: Nisbet, 1939; rpt. New York: New York University Press, 1967), pp. 220–21 n.; Mark van Doren, *Shakespeare* (New York: Holt, 1939), pp. 335–36.

49. Theodore Spencer, "*The Two Noble Kinsmen*," *MP* 36 (1939): 255–76, and "Appearance and Reality in Shakespeare's Last Plays," *MP* 39 (1942): 265–74. Both are reprinted in *Theodore Spencer: Selected Essays*, edited by Alan C. Purves (New Brunswick: Rutgers University Press, 1966), nos. 14 and 16. See also "Shakespeare's Last Plays," *Shakespeare and the Nature of Man* (New York: Macmillan, 1942; 2d ed., 1949), pp. 177–202.

50. Hazelton Spencer, *The Art and Life of William Shakespeare* (New York: Harcourt, 1943), pp. 378–82.

51. W. W. Greg, *The Editorial Problem in Shakespeare* (Oxford: Clarendon Press, 1942; 3d ed., 1954), pp. 19–20, and *The Shakespeare First Folio* (Oxford: Clarendon Press, 1955), p. 98.

analysis has supplied definitive proof that Shakespeare wrote [most of] the scenes" usually assigned to him, the clusters are dispersed over longer passages than in earlier plays. He attributes this to the fact that the poet's "creative imagination had passed its prime." This explains "peculiarities in the imagery such as the loosening of linkages and dispersal of the clusters. . . . The spontaneous fluidity of association seems to be impeded." Armstrong thinks that his analysis reveals that Shakespeare was aware of "approaching infirmity" when he wrote *The Two Noble Kinsmen*, that "he had done the work he set out to do" and took part in the collaboration "urged on, it may be by others."[52] Gerald Eades Bentley, like Greg, does not present a methodical examination of the authorship of the play, but it is apparent that he accepts Shakespeare's participation by linking it with *Cymbeline, The Winter's Tale*, and *The Tempest* as a Shakespearean romance and by raising the question of why it was not included in the First Folio.[53]

In an essay on authorship, Marco Mincoff judges the external evidence of the *Stationers' Register* entry and the quarto title page as being "extraordinarily strong, so strong that it cannot be dismissed without very cogent counterarguments." The vague contention that the style is similar to Shakespeare's but that the genius is lacking is not compelling. He points out that while some contemporary attributions of authorship are in error, most are substantially correct; and, further, if the publisher, Waterson, "who bears a good name for honesty," was in any doubt he could have attached Beaumont's name at a time when the well-known pair's popularity was at its height. "This attribution is in itself of considerable weight." He acknowledges the negative evidentiary value of *The Two Noble Kinsmen* being omitted from the Shakespeare First Folio but points out that the manuscript may have been mislaid or that Heminges and Condell might have felt justified in excluding it because Shakespeare contributed only "about a quarter of the whole." The omission he considers, however, to be "scarcely damning." He examines many of the arguments against Shakespeare's participation on the basis of internal evidence and shows that the so-called un-Shakespearean elements of characterization, style, and imagery can be paralleled from canonical plays, particularly the other romances. In fact, the internal evidence points to Shakespeare's last period

52. Edward A. Armstrong, *Shakespeare's Imagination* (London: Drummond, 1946; 2d ed., rev. Lincoln: University of Nebraska Press 1963), Appendix B, "Shakespearean Imagery in *The Two Noble Kinsmen*," pp. 203–17. See also C. H. Hobday, "Why the Sweets Melted: A Study in Shakespeare's Imagery," *SQ* 16 (1965): 3–17. Of course, the stylistic phenomena may be accounted for in ways other than a failure of dramatic powers. Theodore Spencer, for example, attributed such qualities to intractable source materials (*Selected Essays*, pp. 221–22).

53. Gerald Eades Bentley, "Shakespeare and the Blackfriars Theatre," *ShS* 1 (1948): 38–50, and *Shakespeare: A Biographical Handbook* (New Haven: Yale University Press, 1961), pp. 130, 192.

and thus supports the external evidence. He adduces a significant and persuasive body of metrical, stylistic, and imagistic evidence in support of his claim for Shakespeare's presence in the play.[54]

Many students of *The Two Noble Kinsmen* have drawn attention to the palpable divergences in style and verse in different parts of the play. One of the arguments for Fletcher that has been generally accepted is the frequency of feminine endings, although a few scholars—notably Alexander—have challenged its use as a discriminant between Fletcher and Shakespeare because the latter, especially late in his career, increasingly employed the feminine ending.[55] In an effort to resolve this aspect of the authorship dispute, Ants Oras devised a verse test to distinguish between the two playwrights, assuming there are two, in both *The Two Noble Kinsmen* and *Henry VIII*. He studied the incidence of extra monosyllables—those forming the last unstressed part of feminine endings—as compared to the total number of feminine endings in the blank verse of the two plays. He excluded incomplete lines—those of fewer than five "metrical beats"—and of course rhymed verses; and three scenes of *The Two Noble Kinsmen* concerning the authorship of which critics are not agreed. The rate of occurrence of unstressed final monosyllables in the scenes traditionally given to Fletcher is 36%; the rate in Shakespearean scenes is 19.4%. Applied as a control to *Cymbeline, The Winter's Tale*, and *The Tempest*, the same test yields 18.1%, 20.2%, and 23.2%, respectively. For *Valentinian, Bonduca*, and *Monsieur Thomas*—all accepted as completely Fletcher's—the incidence is 32.4%, 30.4%, and 42.4%, respectively. Oras tentatively concludes that these quantitative results show measurable differences between the Shakespeare and the Fletcher parts, but he then looks for potential qualitative distinctions. He finds that in the Shakespeare control plays "care appears to have been taken not to impede the flow of the verse . . . it looks indeed as if Shakespeare had been careful to keep his monosyllables from obstructing the free progress of his blank verse. Much the same impression is created by his endings in" the two plays under study. The fluent ease noted contrasts with the Fletcherian sections, in which many of the extra monosyllables are heavily weighted, and in which there occur series of the same final monosyllables in close succession. Fletcher seems to choose parallelism, Shakespeare prefers variety. "Shakespeare's extra monosyllables are varied, usually light, and, when heavier . . . fit naturally and smoothly into their metrical context. . . . Fletcher's monosyllables . . . appear artificially weighted . . . the writer seems to be lingering on them." His qualitative evidence, Oras concludes, supports his statistics and adds another link to

54. M. Mincoff, "The Authorship of *The Two Noble Kinsmen*," *Englische Studien* 33 (1952): 97–115.

55. Peter Alexander, "Conjectural History, or Shakespeare's *Henry VIII*," *E&S* 16 (1930): 85–120.

the chain of argument supporting the tradition of a Shakespeare-Fletcher collaboration.[56]

Kenneth Muir reexamines the metrical tests employed by Littledale and Chambers and finds them valid in establishing the presence of two playwrights in *The Two Noble Kinsmen* and in identifying the hand in the non-Fletcherian parts of the play as Shakespeare's. He also analyzes Hart's vocabulary tests and concludes that they strengthen the case for Shakespeare's part-authorship. Mincoff's study of the imagery, especially of that drawn from nature, exhibits characteristic marks of Shakespeare. He looks at the style as poetry in contrast to mere rhetoric from the points of view of Ellis-Feror, who concludes that it is brilliant but only rhetoric, and De Quincey, who thinks the poet meant his lines to be rhetorical although the furnace of composition transmuted their substance. Armstrong's image clusters establish the passages in which they occur as the work of a conscious imitator of Shakespeare or Shakespeare himself. Some of them are so cogent that it can hardly be denied that Shakespeare is the author. Muir analyzes the play scene by scene and concludes that the qualities of style and structure support the traditional division of the play between the two playwrights. He considers it significant that *The Two Noble Kinsmen* conforms to the pattern of the other late Shakespearean plays in containing theophanies, but in other respects it differs. It does not deal with forgiveness, reconciliation of fathers through the love of children, the restoration of a lost wife or child, the recovery of a lost kingdom, or evil jealousy or ambition. It is possible that the play was written in a hurry. Perhaps while Shakespeare was on a visit to London he sketched out a play and wrote part of it. Fletcher wrote the remaining scenes and made necessary alterations in Shakespeare's parts.[57]

In reading *Henry VIII* along with contemporary plays of Fletcher and Shakespeare, Robert Adger Law became aware of the use by Fletcher of a "trick of style . . . ending a feminine line with a verb followed by an unstressed pronoun." Shakespeare also employs such line endings. Law tabulates the occurrences of this phenomenon in both *Henry VIII* and *The Two Noble Kinsmen*, and, as controls, in *Cymbeline, The Winter's Tale*, and *The Tempest*, and in three unaided Fletcher plays: *Bonduca, Valentinian*, and *The Wild Goose Chase*. In *The Two Noble Kinsmen*, Law finds this line ending

56. Ants Oras, "'Extra Monosyllables' in *Henry VIII* and the Problem of Authorship," *JEGP* 52 (1953): 198–213.

57. Kenneth Muir, "Shakespeare's Hand in *The Two Noble Kinsmen*," *ShS* 11 (1958): 50–59. Reprinted in revised form in *Shakespeare as Collaborator* (London: Methuen, 1960), pp. 98–147. See also "The Kite Cluster in *The Two Noble Kinsmen*," *N&Q* 199 (1954): 52–53; "A Trick of Style and Some Implications," *ShakS* 6 (1973): 305–10; "Theophanies in the Last Plays," in *Shakespeare's Last Plays: Essays in Honor of Charles Crow*, edited by Richard T. Tobias and Paul G. Zalbrod (Athens, Ohio: Ohio University Press 1974), pp. 32–43; and *Shakespeare's Comic Sequence* (Liverpool: Liverpool University Press, 1979), pp. 192–202.

appearing in 9.4% of the blank verse lines of the scenes usually considered Fletcher's and at a rate of 2.5% in Shakespearean scenes. The control plays have 9%, 10%, and 11.2%, respectively, for Fletcher, and 3.1%, 3.1%, and 3.6%, respectively, for Shakespeare. Law concludes that the test shows a clear distinction in style between the two parts of the drama.[58] Una Ellis-Fermor studies the quality and characteristics of the non-Fletcherian parts of the play—the aesthetic evidence. The vocabulary, the syntax, the imagery, and the verbal music are chiefly responsible for the "undeniable Shakespearean tone," but she believes that these qualities, and the characterization, do not demonstrate the presence of Shakespeare. They are "a dazzling imitation of Shakespeare's hand rather than Shakespeare's hand itself." The imitation achieves surprising "and, be it admitted, imaginative feats of reproduction" that are like Shakespeare but are seen to be unlike him "when they are dissected." The planning of the play is different from Shakespeare's known designs, and there is a theatrical over-heightening at all levels that raises the question of what kind of collaboration is involved. She puts forth the suggestion that the scenes assigned to Shakespeare were composed by the team of Beaumont and Fletcher. The disharmony between the elements of style and the total effect of the play is without parallel in any of Shakespeare's mature work.[59]

In the course of a comprehensive linguistic investigation into Fletcherian dramatic collaboration, Cyrus Hoy examines the possible collaborative efforts by Fletcher and Shakespeare in *The Two Noble Kinsmen.* Concerning Fletcher's share in the play, he finds "no real difficulty. The linguistic evidence is sufficient to point with reasonable clarity to the specific scenes of his authorship." As to Shakespeare's presence, "all that can be said is that the linguistic pattern displayed in the non-Fletcherian scenes . . . is not inconsistent with the pattern of [Shakespeare's] linguistic preferences." The case for Shakespeare, "based solely on stylistic grounds, is a strong one, and I think it abundantly supports the claim of the quarto title page that Shakespeare is a partial author of the play." The language practices that distinguish the two authors are the *ye-you, em-them, has-hath, does-doth* preferences and the uses of contractions. Comparisons of these usages in canonical Shakespearean late plays and plays that are Fletcher's unaided work distinguish the two playwrights, generally along the lines of the traditional division of *The Two Noble Kinsmen.* The assignments are supported by statistical tables that "complete the linguistic evidence for

58. Robert Adger Law, "The Double Authorship of *Henry VIII,*" *SP* 56 (1959): 471–88.

59. Una Ellis-Fermor, "*The Two Noble Kinsmen,*" in *Shakespeare the Dramatist,* edited by Kenneth Muir (London: Methuen; and New York: Barnes & Noble, 1961), pp. 177–86. Originally read as the British Academy Shakespeare lecture of 1948. Muir appends a note that Ellis-Fermor, "although continuing to deny Shakespeare's part-authorship of the play, was not in 1957 as positive as she had been."

differentiating their shares in a play of their joint authorship."[60] Philip Edwards, in one of the more insightful essays on the play, finds a complex design in the progress of the chief characters from the innocence of spontaneous friendship to the mixed joys of sexual awakening that can only be Shakespearean. The doubts about his authorship arise because of a conviction that the play is inane, but there is purposeful thought in *The Two Noble Kinsmen*, especially in the first and last acts, in its insistence that mature love means abandoning something more worthwhile. Since Edwards addresses the Shakespearean quality of the play's design, he says little about Fletcher's participation, which he assumes, except to note that "Shakespeare's grand design sags when Fletcher takes over."[61]

A. C. Partridge conjectures that the play was excluded from the First Folio because Heminges and Condell knew that "their colleague wrote little of it, if anything at all." The subject of the play was Shakespeare's choice, but the planning is unlike his practice. He set about revising the old play, *Palamon and Arsett*, about 1611 but did not get very far. Beaumont and Fletcher rewrote it with Fletcher doing most of the work for the production of 1613. An unknown writer retouched it for the revival of 1626.[62] In the introduction to his edition of *The Two Noble Kinsmen*, Clifford Leech examines the external evidence and notes that "there is an inordinately strong case for accepting the title page's statement of authorship." If Waterson had been trying to enhance custom, it would have been at least as effective to attribute the play to Beaumont and Fletcher. The internal evidence, chiefly that from style, supports the external. "If we accept the commonly held view of the two writers' shares (and there is little reason to be skeptical about it), it was Shakespeare who wrote the beginning and the ending and introduced all the major characters and strands of action." He may have been less regularly at the playhouse than formerly, so Fletcher did the final putting together of the manuscript. It seems likely that the main planning of the play was Shakespeare's because of resemblances to his earlier romances in which the gods are freely involved and play a direct part in the action. The play shares structural features with *Pericles* and *The Tempest* and themes with *The Winter's Tale*. Because it seems likely that Fletcher had the task of integrating his and Shakespeare's work, the dominant, though not exclusive, tone is Fletcher's.[63]

60. Cyrus Hoy, "The Shares of Fletcher and his Collaborators in the Beaumont and Fletcher Canon (VII)," *SB* 15 (1962): 71–90.

61. Philip Edwards, "On the Design of *The Two Noble Kinsmen*," *RES* 5 (1964): 89–105. See also *Shakespeare and the Confines of Art* (London: Methuen, 1968), pp. 153–59.

62. A. C. Partridge, *Orthography in Shakespeare and the Elizabethan Drama* (London: Arnold; and Lincoln: Nebraska University Press, 1964), pp. 162, 180–81.

63. Leech, *The Two Noble Kinsmen*, pp. 1615–21. See also *The John Fletcher Plays* (Cambridge: Harvard University Press, 1962), pp. 144–68, and "Masking and Unmasking in the Last Plays," in *Shakespeare's Romances Reconsidered*, edited by Carol McGinnis Kay and Henry E. Jacobs (Lincoln: University of Nebraska Press, 1978), pp. 40–59.

In the course of his reading of the prior scholarship on the authorship question, Bertram takes note of the tendency of many students of the play to cite the assumed dual authorship of *Henry VIII* and *Cardenio* as establishing a practice that encompasses the three plays, thus supporting an opinion that *The Two Noble Kinsmen* is a collaboration. For this reason he addresses himself to the authorship of the other two plays. He cites the only external evidence regarding the authorship of *Henry VIII*—its inclusion in the Shakespeare First Folio—and points out that the question concerning divided authorship was raised very late by James Spedding (in 1850) and following Spalding's and Hickson's determination of the shared authorship of *The Two Noble Kinsmen*. He attacks Spedding's rationale, which he considers weak, and Hickson's even thinner subsequent support, and cites both Alexander's strong defense of Shakespeare as sole author of *Henry VIII* and the tide of recent critical opinion tending in the same direction, culminating in R. A. Foakes's persuasive assessment in his New Arden edition. He concludes with Foakes that the play is wholly Shakespeare's. When he comes to the lost *Cardenio*, Bertram quotes Greg's evaluation of the external evidence (Moseley's *Stationers' Register* entrance of 9 September 1653) and the relationship of Moseley's manuscript of the play to Theobald's *Double Falshood* but impugns the authenticity of the ascription to Shakespeare and Fletcher by citing other doubtful and erroneous Moseley attributions. He accepts Theobald's story that his adaptation was based on *Cardenio* but repudiates Theobald's assertion that the source play was Shakespeare's: "The most reasonable position with respect to the authorship of *Cardenio* is that, whoever wrote the play, Shakespeare had nothing to do with it" (p. 196). By this means he aims at negating any evidence adduced by analogy from *Henry VIII* and *Cardenio* to put forth an hypothesis of collaborative authorship of *The Two Noble Kinsmen*.[64] He then turns to his main purpose, which is, he says, "to demonstrate the integrity of the play and . . . to prove the case for Shakespeare" (p. 244). He argues that the adaptation of some of the elements from *The Knight's Tale*, which includes the transposition of incidents from Chaucer to different positions in the sequence of events in the play, is handled with such

64. J[ames] S[pedding], "Who Wrote Shakspere's Henry VIII?" *Gentlemen's Magazine* 178 (1850): 115–24, 381–82; S. Hickson, "Who Wrote Shakspeare's Henry VIII?" *N&Q* 43 (24 April 1850): 198. See also Anon., "Further Notes on the Authorship of Shakspeare's Henry VIII," *N&Q* 50 (12 October 1850): 306–7; Hickson, "Authorship of 'Henry VIII,'" *N&Q* 55 (16 November 1850): 401–3; and Hickson, "Authorship of Henry VIII," *N&Q* 64 (18 January 1851): 33–34. Alexander, "Conjectural History, or Shakespeare's *Henry VIII*," *E&S* 16 (1930): 85–120; R. A. Foakes, ed., *Henry VIII*, New Arden *Shakespeare* (London: Methuen, 1957). In his revised edition (1964), Foakes seems more receptive to Fletcher's participation. Scholarly opinion is divided, with respected voices speaking for a Shakespeare-Fletcher collaboration. See Law, "The Double Authorship of *Henry VIII*," pp. 471–72, n. 3, who lists the proponents of both theories; Hoy, "The Shares of Fletcher and his Collaborators in the Beaumont and Fletcher Canon (VII)," pp. 71 and 76–90; Bertram, *Shakespeare and the Two Noble Kinsmen*, pp. 124–96.

care that the main plot is virtually seamless and therefore could only have been the work of one hand. The method of adaptation and the resultant structure is typically Shakespearean. In support of this thesis, he points to consistency in characterization, noting specifically the compatibility in different places in the play of the parts of Theseus and Emilia. He also points to some elements of design such as the marriage symbolism that occurs, as could have been anticipated, in the opening scene and as part of Emilia's prayer to Diana, but also, less expectedly, in the subplot. He takes up the frequently stated opinion that Palamon and Arcite are not sufficiently distinguished and discerns subtle yet significant differences between them, although they are equally noble, which "shows how Shakespeare uses breadth of social reference, to enhance, indeed to create, individual human dignity" (p. 282). He concludes by crediting Shakespeare with the development of the plot.[65]

John Cutts analyzes elements of masque, song, and music, and elements of the symbolism of flowers and colors that occur throughout the main plot of *The Two Noble Kinsmen* and compares them to similar features in canonical Shakespeare and Fletcher plays, especially, in the case of Shakespeare, his romances. He finds that in all these aspects of the play there is a close affinity with the handling of such elements in the acknowledged plays of Shakespeare and very little or none at all with those of Fletcher. *The Two Noble Kinsmen*, he decides, "in its main plot is thoroughly in tune with the techniques and philosophy of Shakespeare's late romances."[66] Unlike Kittredge, his mentor, Ribner has reservations about the authorship of the play. He acknowledges the external facts but says there is "no other evidence for Shakespeare's authorship . . . [and] the work is so different in its general tone and effect from anything we know him to have written, that it is difficult to believe that he could have had more than a slight hand in a few scenes." It was omitted from the 1623 Shakespeare Folio and from subsequent editions of Shakespeare, although generally included in editions of Beaumont and Fletcher, until Knight printed it with his "Doubtful Plays," which indicates the uncertainty of the early editors. He notes, without endorsement, that it is believed Shakespeare was responsible for the beginning and ending and that "Fletcher filled in the play which Shakespeare initially had devised."[67]

"Fletcher's claim to the greater part of *The Two Noble Kinsmen* has rarely been questioned," according to Proudfoot in his edition of the play, but the identity of Fletcher's collaborator or collaborators "has been the subject of much controversy." Beaumont may have participated by writing elements of the subplot, but Massinger's candidacy, except possibly for

65. Bertram, *Shakespeare and the Two Noble Kinsmen*, pp. 197–282.

66. John P. Cutts, "Shakespeare's Song and Masque Hand in *The Two Noble Kinsmen*," *EM* 18 (1967): 55–85.

67. Ribner, *Two Noble Kinsmen*, pp. ix–xi.

author of the prologue and epilogue, "has been generally rejected." Shakespeare's authorship of the non-Fletcher scenes "is now as well established as it is ever likely to be." Residual hesitation arises "from the feeling that it is not a good enough play to have his name attached to it." The external evidence consists of the 1634 registration, the quarto title page, and its absence from the Shakespeare First Folio and from the second issue of the Third Folio. His suggested explanation for the decision of Heminges and Condell to exclude it from the First Folio is that "they knew it to be a collaborative play in which his [Shakespeare's] was a minor share." The title-page attribution "has high authority. . . . He [Waterson] evidently obtained the manuscript from the King's Men and they were better placed than anyone else to know who wrote the play." Internal evidence of style, meter, verbal parallels, imagery and image clusters, preferences for colloquial and contracted verbal forms, and the characterization demonstrates the presence of two distinctly different hands and broadly establishes the shares written by the two dramatists: the play "begins and ends with a splendor of language that is not sustained in the middle acts."[68] Frank Kermode points out, "As Shakespeare grew older he necessarily associated with the younger playwrights who were to succeed him . . . [and he finds] nothing improbable about the view that he collaborated with Fletcher in *The Two Noble Kinsmen.*" He accepts Fletcher as one of the dramatists and defines the problem as identifying his associate. Massinger and Beaumont, as well as Shakespeare, are candidates. The first scene is attributed to Shakespeare, but Kermode doubts that he planned it; the "*ordonnance*" of the work suggests Fletcher. There is an "un-Shakespearian over-extension of the possibilities . . . the description of Emilia [in 2.2] is grossly over-developed and mechanical." These and other qualities "support the view that although he probably wrote a great deal of the play Shakespeare had nothing to do with its plot." *The Two Noble Kinsmen* "is best thought of as a play by Fletcher to which Shakespeare contributed."[69] Hallett Smith cites the external evidence for a Shakespeare-Fletcher collaboration and notes that Waterson, the stationer who was the source of the ascription, had printed other King's Men's plays, that the copy for his quarto was "a theatre manuscript that must have been made available by them, and from them he would have had reliable information about the authorship of the play." Its exclusion, on the other hand, from the Shakespeare First Folio

68. G. R. Proudfoot, ed., *Two Noble Kinsmen*, in the *Regents Renaissance Drama* series (1970), pp. xiii–xix. See also "Shakespeare and the New Dramatists of the King's Men, 1606–1613," in *Later Shakespeare*, Stratford-upon-Avon Studies 8, edited by John Russell Brown and Bernard Harris (London: Arnold, 1966), pp. 235–61; "*The Two Noble Kinsmen* and the Apocryphal Plays," in *Shakespeare: Select Bibliographical Guides*, edited by Stanley Wells (London: Oxford University Press, 1973), pp. 389–97.

69. Frank Kermode, *Shakespeare, Spencer, Donne: Renaissance Essays* (London: Routledge, 1971), pp. 256–58. See also *William Shakespeare: The Final Plays*, Writers and their Work, No. 155 (London: Longmans, 1963), p. 52.

may be "somehow related to the facts of authorship." Perhaps Heminges and Condell knew that Fletcher had the controlling hand in the play. But the case for Shakespeare as part author has strong adherents and Smith decides that the play is a collaborative work. M. C. Bradbrook accepts the statement of the 1634 title page that the play is a collaboration and finds "the case for Shakespeare's part-authorship . . . strong." She speculates that it "was perhaps only commissioned to provide a setting for the anti-masque" borrowed from Beaumont's masque, at which the courtly "audience were deeply stirred and diverted," prompting the King's Men to mount "a repeat performance before a select audience at Blackfriars . . . [which] would be highly profitable."[70]

Concentrating his attention chiefly on the poetic, dramatic, and theatrical qualities of *The Two Noble Kinsmen* in the introduction to his edition,[71] Bawcutt identifies two different hands. He notes, for example, that in the characterization of the two kinsmen, who are distinguishable, there is some confusion and clumsiness. Throughout the latter part of the play, Palamon is presented as the lover and Arcite as the soldier, "as in Chaucer" (p. 23). In 1.2, however, Palamon is the stronger, more military of the two. Act 1 as a whole exhibits "an impressive poise and assurance . . . [and] a rich background of themes and associations, many of which are taken up again in Act V" (p. 27). The intervening portion of the play, except for 3.1, lacks the largeness and resonance of Act 1. One writer presents ceremony and ritual, the other drama and excitement, "the stress falls on human psychology and mental conflict rather than morality or the supernatural order . . . a gain in variety and liveliness . . . is paid for by a loss in significance." The style of the better poet develops spontaneously with unexpected changes of direction and unusual and arresting images that create "a rich context of feeling, a living texture of thought" (p. 28). The verse of the lesser poet is more orderly and rhetorical. The characters he depicts seem more concerned with making effects and scoring points than with exploring their inner feelings. His metaphors tend toward the commonplace, are sometimes blurred, and have an air of elaborate, self-conscious set-pieces. There is a frequently noted difference in the characterization of the two principals. One playwright shows them behaving with stoic dignity and an absence of self-pity. The other presents them as more openly emotional, indulging in a kind of self-regarding pathos. The

70. Smith, *Two Noble Kinsmen*, in the *Riverside Shakespeare*, pp. 1639–41. See also "Shakespeare's Last Plays: Facts and Problems," *Shakespearean Research Opportunities* 3 (1967): 9–16, and *Shakespeare's Romances: A Study of Some Ways of the Imagination* (San Marino: Huntington Library, 1972), pp. 33–35. M. C. Bradbrook, *The Living Monument Shakespeare and the Theatre of his Time* (Cambridge: Cambridge University Press, 1976), pp. 235–41. She reiterates her view in *Shakespeare the Poet in his World* (New York: Columbia University Press, 1978), pp. 234–36.

71. N. W. Bawcutt, ed., *Two Noble Kinsmen*, in the *Penguin Shakespeare* (1977), pp. 7–46.

distribution, based on his analysis, of the parts between Shakespeare and Fletcher follows the accepted lines that Bawcutt has no wish to challenge. He believes the two playwrights collaborated closely and that they worked together in planning the play.

In a book on Shakespeare's use of Chaucer as a source, Ann Thompson says that she arrived at the conclusion that *The Two Noble Kinsmen* is a collaboration between Shakespeare and Fletcher because her "detailed study of the use of the source in different parts of the play confirmed it so strongly." She accepts "the orthodox position on the division" between the playwrights and rejects Bertram's contention that the play exhibits a high degree of internal consistency (and must therefore be of single authorship) because of the discrepant "treatment of *The Knight's Tale*" in different scenes. Addressing only the question of Shakespeare's participation, Taylor considers that "the attribution is supported by the fact that it occurs in the Stationers' Register as well as the first edition, and by the hypothesis that the text was printed from a manuscript annotated by the book-keeper of Shakespeare's company. . . . The independent external evidence for *Cardenio* and internal evidence for *All is True* . . . establishes that Shakespeare was probably collaborating with Fletcher at the time when *Kinsmen* was composed. . . . The external evidence for Shakespeare's part-authorship of *Kinsmen* therefore appears to be reliable." The internal evidence from vocabulary, imagery, linguistics, parallels, pause patterns, sources, and meter marshalled by a variety of scholars "all corroborate the external evidence, discriminating two stylistic patterns in the play, one remarkably congruent with late Shakespeare, the other equally congruent with middle Fletcher." Wells cites the quarto title page and says, "There is no reason to disbelieve this ascription. . . . Studies of style suggest that Shakespeare was primarily responsible for the rhetorically and ritualistically impressive Act 1; for Act 2, Scene 1; Act 3, Scenes 1 and 2; and for most of Act 5 (Scene 4 excepted), which includes emblematically spectacular episodes related to his other late plays."[72]

As can be seen from the foregoing survey of the debate concerning the authorship of *The Two Noble Kinsmen*, there has been little inclination since 1930 to give serious consideration to the claims on behalf of Chapman and Massinger, let alone the even more wayward sponsorship of such unlikely candidates as Jonson and Tourneur. The alternative answers to the question that have, in recent years, merited the attention of scholars are a) Shakespeare is the sole author; b) Fletcher is the sole author; or c) the play is the result of a collaboration between Shakespeare and Fletcher. There is

72. Ann Thompson, *Shakespeare's Chaucer: A Study in Literary Origins*, Liverpool English Texts and Studies, ed. Philip Edwards (Liverpool: Liverpool University Press; and New York: Harper and Row, 1978), pp. 126–27, 186–87. Gary Taylor, "The Canon and Chronology of Shakespeare's Plays," in *William Shakespeare: A Textual Companion*, p. 134. Wells, *Oxford Shakespeare*, p. 1379.

added a coda holding that the morris dance, and perhaps other parts of the subplot, may have been the work of a third dramatist, possibly Beaumont. To those, notably Bertram, who champion Shakespeare's sole authorship, there is the problem of explaining the passages that are palpably infra-Shakespearean. Their unsatisfactory quality is explained as the result of aging, fatigue, disaffection, or illness, although in regard to the last, there is, in fact, no evidence of physical debility in 1613, three years before his death. The challenge for the Fletcher advocates is to account for the passages that are knotty in style, complex in syntax, pregnant in meaning, and of a measurably higher poetical order than the writing in his unaided plays. The explanation offered is that these parts of the play were written by Fletcher under the influence of Shakespeare. Alternatively, these phenomena may be accounted for by viewing the passages that are fundamentally different from Fletcher's writing as being Shakespearean in origin; and those that are unlike Shakespeare come from the pen of Fletcher. It may be that the play is in fact a collaboration of the two poets, as the external evidence of the *Stationers' Register* and the title page tells us. To this determination the authorship of *Henry VIII* and *Cardenio* is largely irrelevant. Whether or not *All is True* is a collaboration or, as much scholarly opinion now runs, entirely Shakespeare's does not shed determinative light on the authorship of *The Two Noble Kinsmen*. If *Henry VIII* is in reality Shakespeare's unaided work, that does not preclude the possibility that *The Two Noble Kinsmen* is a collaborative play. Nor, if new evidence should be adduced proving that *Henry VIII* is of dual Shakespeare-Fletcher authorship, would that significantly bolster the contention that *The Two Noble Kinsmen* is a cooperation of the two playwrights, because that possibility is already established by the objective evidence. Similarly, whether *Double Falshood* is an original work of Theobald or is an adaptation of a play composed by Shakespeare and Fletcher can, at most, only indicate a potential solution for *The Two Noble Kinsmen* authorship puzzle. It cannot solve the problem. In the instance of each of the three plays, the determination of authorship must be based on evidence that can be independently adduced concerning each one of them without regard to the evidence concerning the other two.

The hypothesis of Fletcher's sole authorship of *The Two Noble Kinsmen* is the weakest of the three possibilities. As Lamb asked, if Fletcher could have in this play written nearly as well as Shakespeare at his best, why did he not continue to do so? Yet he never did. Whatever may be the estimate of Fletcher's capability as a dramatist, no one can doubt that, as a critic, he surely recognized Shakespeare's work as of an order to which he should aspire and, if he could, equal in his own way. That he tried seems clear; that he did not succeed is demonstrated by the body of his unaided work. The only rational explanation is that the better poetry and the better dramaturgy in *The Two Noble Kinsmen* is beyond the capability of Fletcher as well as every other contemporary playwright except Shakespeare. The unevenness in Shakespeare's part of the play may be traceable to his not having been throughout at his best, as Sir Edmund Chambers tellingly pointed out concerning his work in general in the 1924 British Academy lecture on "The Disintegration of Shakespeare." This would be especially understandable if he were writing under the pressure of the urgent need for a new play with which the King's Men could open the autumn season at Blackfriars and thus gather funds for the rebuilding of the Globe. The lower level of effectiveness of parts of the play's poetic and dramatic content is not merely attenuated Shakespeare, it is a lesser accomplishment of a different kind, as William Spalding argued so effectively in 1833. Not even Bertram's incisive and persuasive analysis can quite overcome either the magnitude or the character of the disparity between the two segments of the play nor surmount the obstacle, as Hoy says in his review of Bertram's book, of the accumulated metrical, linguistic, and bibliographical evidence for Fletcher's hand in the play.[73]

We are left then, by a process of elimination, with the third alternative, that *The Two Noble Kinsmen* is a collaboration between Shakespeare and Fletcher in which Shakespeare planned the play, possibly in association with Fletcher, started all the major themes of the main plot and the Jailer's Daughter part of the subplot, advanced the play to its climax, and wrote the catastrophe. Fletcher composed the whole middle stretch of the play, except for 3.1 and the two prose scenes (2.1 and 4.3), perhaps in consultation with Shakespeare and assuredly working at least from a scenario upon which the two poets had agreed. Under the influence of Shakespeare, the younger playwright wrote some of his best dramatic poetry, incorporating, perhaps not consciously, Shakespearean themes and conceptions and elements of his style. He may also have written some brief links to integrate the two contributions and perhaps inserted a few lines of dialogue in other places, such as the passage concerning the Jailer's Daughter in the aborted execution scene to complete her story. Solutions to the question of just

73. Cyrus Hoy, rev. art. of Bertram's book, *MP* 67 (1969): 83–88. See also Leech, *Two Noble Kinsmen*, p. 1621; Ribner, *Two Noble Kinsmen*, p. x; and Bawcutt, ed. cit., pp. 48, 49, none of whom accept Bertram's thesis. Smith, *Riverside Shakespeare*, p. 1639, calls Bertram's "the minority view." Critics who favor single authorship of *TNK* sometimes cite in support of their contention the singular "wrighter" that occurs at line 19 of the prologue. However, there are ten plural pronouns and pronominal adjectives (*we, us, our*) in the prologue, and while some of these may refer to the players, others (especially *we* in lines 15, 21, and 24) are more readily understood as linked to authorship. Furthermore, the phrase reads (Chaucer speaking): "O fan From me the witles chaffe of such a wrighter," which does not clearly imply a single dramatist, merely a single example. The number has been thought by some to be the result of the exigencies of the rhyme. Leech, *Two Noble Kinsmen*, p. 1626, n. 19, sums up, "The singular is notable, but by no means decisive on the question of authorship."

how the collaboration was conducted are largely conjectural, including the one just outlined, but there may be a bit of support in the stage directions. Many of them are comprehensively descriptive and literary in tone, some setting forth specifically how certain stage business is to be conducted and even various details of costume. They are especially elaborate in act 1 and the first scene of act 5, which are generally agreed to be Shakespeare's. This could be attributable to their having been written while he was absent from London and feeling the need to provide detailed instructions to both Fletcher and the King's Men's managers so that they would understand his conception of the scenes he was contributing.[74] The absence of *The Two Noble Kinsmen* from the First Folio has not been satisfactorily explained. Some scholars, thinking in terms of mere quantity of verses contributed, believe the play was excluded because it is mostly Fletcher's, but if Shakespeare selected the story and started all the themes, it is essentially as much his as Fletcher's.

There remains the conjectural presence of Beaumont in the play, possibly only in two scenes: in 3.5, the morris dance and, less surely, in 2.4, in which four countrymen discuss, in sprightly fashion, plans for maying and the entertainment for Duke Theseus. Some, however, think he may have been responsible for the entire subplot. Advocacy for Beaumont may be said to have commenced with the inclusion of *The Two Noble Kinsmen* in the Second Beaumont and Fletcher Folio (1679), and more specifically by Colman's attribution to the two dramatists in 1778. Littledale and Oliphant detect touches of Beaumont's hand, and Gray conjectures a deeper involvement. Chambers thinks that the dance based on Beaumont's antimasque and the two prose scenes in the subplot could be his writing, while Kittredge focuses on Gerrold's speech as presenter of the morris. Of the recent students of the play, Proudfoot has set forth the most persuasive case for Beaumont's participation in *The Two Noble Kinsmen*. In his essay in *Later Shakespeare*, he notes the potential separability of the subplot (the Jailer's Daughter sequence and the morris) and conjectures on the basis of

74. Dover Wilson, seconded by Chambers, thinks that the similarly detailed stage directions in *Tmp.* point to Shakespeare's absence from London while that play was being written. Wilson, ed., *The Tempest*, New Cambridge *Shakespeare* (Cambridge: Cambridge University Press, 1921), p. 80. E. K. Chambers, *Shakespearean Gleanings* (Oxford: Oxford University Press, 1944), p. 80. For a dissent see John Jowett, "New Created Creatures: Ralph Crane and the Stage Directions in *The Tempest*," *ShS* 36 (1983): 107–20, especially 107–8. Glynne Wickham posits a unique rationale for the collaboration. He points out that the King's Men and their ordinary poet took care to have one play a year ready to present at court from the time they entered the royal service in 1603. The only exception, up to Shakespeare's retirement, was the 1606–1607 season when the company presented *Philaster*, which "would also mark the company's decision to train Fletcher to follow Shakespeare in this role and account for their subsequent collaborative plays." "*The Two Noble Kinsmen* or *A Midsummer Night's Dream, Part II?*" *The Elizabethan Theatre VII*, ed. G. R. Hibbard (Ontario: Meany; and Hamden, Conn.: Archon, 1980), pp. 174–75 and n. 11.

the stage directions in 2.1 and 2.2 that the underplot scenes were composed after 2.2, "or at least independently of the main plot and perhaps by a third collaborator who was neither Shakespeare nor Fletcher," whose collaboration in the main plot "may have been supplemented by the work of a third author who provided the subplot of the Jailer's Daughter and may have had something to do with the morris dance scenes." In this essay, Proudfoot does not identify "the third dramatist," but in his edition of the play he says that "Beaumont may have had a hand in the writing of the subplot, especially the scenes involving the morris dance" (2.4, 3.5). In the absence of external evidence comparable to that for Shakespeare and Fletcher, the case for a contribution by Beaumont to *The Two Noble Kinsmen* remains speculative, yet persuasive argument on the bases of style and content has been put forth by a number of scholars, particularly by Proudfoot, so that a collaboration of the three playwrights is at least a strong possibility.[75]

Sources

It [Our Play] has a noble Breeder, and a pure,
A learned, and a Poet never went
More famous yet twixt Po and silver Trent.
Chaucer (of all admir'd) the story gives,
There constant to Eternity it lives;
If we let fall the Noblenesse of this,
And the first sound this child heare, be a hisse,
How will it shake the bones of that good man,
And make him cry from under ground, O fan
From me the witles chaffe of such a wrighter
That blastes my Bayes, and my fam'd workes makes lighter
Then Robin Hood? This is the feare we bring;
For to say Truth, it were an endlesse thing,

75. Proudfoot, "Shakespeare and the New Dramatists," pp. 251, 260; *Two Noble Kinsmen*, p. xiv. In the course of a computer-assisted analysis of the writing habits exhibited in *TNK* employing the method of statistical stylometry developed by A. Q. Morton and his colleagues at the University of Edinburgh, which generally corroborates the traditional division of the play between Shakespeare and Fletcher, Morton detected an anomaly in the subplot in scene 3.5, the morris dance. The habits of composition evident in that scene he found to be unlike Shakespeare and equally unlike Fletcher. This points to a possible contribution of a third collaborator. Although there are not at present any stylometric studies of Beaumont's habits of composition employing the Edinburgh technique that would confirm the identification of him as the third dramatist, it is clear that Morton's as yet unpublished stylometric study tends to support the arguments of scholars who have detected his presence. For the Edinburgh system of stylometry and its application to Shakespearean authorship studies, see A. Q. Morton, *Literary Detection* (Epping: Bowker; and New York: Scribner's, 1978); and Metz, "Disputed Shakespearean Texts and Stylometric Analysis," *TEXT* 2 (1985): 149–71.

And too ambitious to aspire to him;
Weake as we are, and almost breathelesse swim
In this deepe water. Do but you hold out
Your helping hands, and we shall take about,
And something do to save us: You shall heare
Sceanes though below his Art, may yet appeare
Worth two houres travell. To his bones sweet sleepe:
(Prol. 10–29)

These lines (in the original spelling) from the prologue to *The Two Noble Kinsmen* constitute the most specific source acknowledgment of any play associated with Shakespeare. The "story" mentioned is *The Knight's Tale* (Text 1), the first of the *Canterbury Tales* and one of the most popular of Chaucer's poems, yielding place only to *Troilus and Criseyde.*[76] A comparative reading of the play and the tale unequivocally supports the statement in the lines cited above. Almost all the incidents in the main plot of *The Two Noble Kinsmen* are present in *The Knight's Tale*. At the beginning of the poem, as in the play, mourning widows of slain opponents of Creon accost Theseus and his wedding party—after the nuptials as the Knight tells it—with their pleas for help to enable them to bury their dead husbands. Theseus yields to their petitions and sets off for Thebes, sending Ypolita and Emelye on to Athens. In battle he destroys the Theban forces "and to the ladyes he restored agayn The bones of hir freends that were slayn To doon obsequies" (991–93).[77] His pillagers find two young princes, Arcite and Palamon, "Nat fully quyke, ne fully dede" (1015) and present them to Theseus, who sends them "To Atthenes to dwellen in prisoun" (1023). Emelye walks in the garden adjacent to the tower in which the kinsmen are imprisoned and Palamon, seeing her, cries out, "As though he stongen were unto the herte" (1079). Arcite counsels patience in adversity, but Palamon explains that he has fallen in love. Arcite then sees the lady and says he must "have hir mercy and hir grace" (1120). Palamon reminds Arcite of their oath, "neither of us in love to hyndre oother" (1135), and since Palamon "loved hire first" (1146), Arcite is bound to help him, "Or else artow fals" (1151). Arcite points out that Palamon looks on Emelye as a goddess while he—Arcite—views her as a woman, therefore "Thyn is affeccioun of hoolynesse, And myn is love, as to a creature" (1158–59). It is "Ech man for hymself . . . for I love and ay shal" (1182–83). Consequently, "Greet was the strif and long betwix hem tweye" (1187). Perotheus, who had known Arcite at Thebes before The-

76. Caroline F. E. Spurgeon, *Five Hundred Years of Chaucer Criticism and Allusion 1357–1900* (Cambridge: Cambridge University Press, 1925; rpt. New York: Russell, 1960), pp. lxxvi–lxxix.

77. Line references are to *KnT* in *The Riverside Chaucer*, gen. ed. Larry D. Benson, based on *The Works of Geoffrey Chaucer*, ed. F. N. Robinson (Boston: Houghton Mifflin, 1987), pp. 37–66. "Freends" in the passage quoted is glossed "husbands."

seus's attack, petitions for his release from prison, which Theseus grants, but banishes him from Athens. Arcite is happy to be free but envies Palamon's good fortune in being able to see Emelye, who, in his turn, is jealous of Arcite's freedom and thinks his cousin, being free, will devise a way to win the lady. In banishment in Thebes, Arcite is visited by Mercury in a dream and counseled to return to Athens in disguise. He dresses as a laborer and performs menial duties for Emelye's chamberlain so efficiently that Theseus takes note of him and makes him his squire. Palamon, love desperate, "By helpying of a freend, brak his prisoun" (1468) with the object either to "lese his lif, Or wynnen Emelye unto his wyf" (1485–86). He conceals himself in a wood. Arcite rises early "for to doon his observaunce to May" (1500) and roams the wood bewailing his fate. Palamon, overhearing him, "stirte him up out of the buskes thikke" (1579), accuses Arcite of being a wicked false traitor to presume to love Palamon's lady, and challenges him to a fight to settle the issue. Arcite says he will return with weapons and "mete and drynke. . . . Ynough for thee" (1615–16), which he does the next day. "Everich of him heelp for to armen oother As freendly as he were his owene brother" (1651–52) and they fight like a "wood leon And . . . a crueel tigre" (1656–57) until they are "Up to the ancle . . . in hir blood" (1660). Theseus, in pursuit of a hart, comes upon the noble kinsmen fighting and commands them to stop. Palamon explains the cause of the fight and Theseus condemns them to death, but Ypolita and Emelye plead for their lives. He pardons the kinsmen but notes that they cannot both have Emelye and proposes a tournament between the two, "this day fifty wykes" (1850), each supported by a hundred knights, a proposal which both Palamon and Arcite gladly accept. They return in a year, each with his retinue. Palamon's principal supporter is Lygurge, king of Trace, and Arcite's is Emetreus, king of Inde. On the day of the tourney, Palamon prays to Venus, petitioning not for victory but to "have fully possession of Emelye . . . the statue of Venus shook, And made a signe, whereby that he took That his preyere accepted was that day" (2242–43; 2265–67). Emelye, in her plea to Diana, expresses her "Desire to ben a mayden al my lyfe, Ne nevere wol I be no love ne wyf" (2305–6); but the goddess appears "With bowe in honde" (2347) and counsels Emelye to "stynt thyn hevynesse" (2348) because the gods have affirmed that "Thou shalt ben wedded unto oon of tho That han for thee so muchel care and wo" (2351–52). With a clatter of the arrows, the goddess disappears, leaving Emelye puzzled as to the meaning of her words. Arcite petitions Mars to "Yif me victorie; I aske thee namoore" (2420). In response to his prayer, the doors clatter, the hauberk on the statue of the god rings and a murmur "lowe and dym . . . seyde thus, 'Victorie!'" (2433), which leaves Arcite "with joye and hope wel to fare" (2435). Immediately there is strife in heaven between Venus and Mars over the contradictory promises to Palamon and Arcite, but Saturn, old and experienced, promises to find a way that "Palamon . . . shal have his lady. . . . Though Mars shal helpe his knyght" (2471–73).

Before the tournament begins, Theseus announces through a herald that the only weapons to be permitted are the spear, the long sword, and the mace so that none of the contestants may be slain but instead brought by force to stakes on either side. If either chieftain is taken, "No lenger shal the turneiynge laste" (2557). With Palamon and Arcite on either side of him, Theseus proceeds to the lists accompanied by Ypolita, Emelye, and other ladies. The tournament begins and, after much fighting, Palamon is brought to the stake. Theseus calls a halt and declares that "Arcite of Thebes shal have Emelie, That by his fortune hath hire faire ywonne" (2658–59). Venus weeps at Palamon's misfortune but Saturn promises her comfort. Arcite rides up and down the lists in triumph and looks up at Emelye, who casts him a friendly eye, but an infernal fury sent by Pluto "out of the ground" (2684) at the request of Saturn causes the horse to founder in fear and to fall on Arcite, who "lay as he were dead" (2690). He lingers for some days, but as death approaches he calls for Emelye and Palamon, bequeaths the service of his ghost to Emelye, tells her if ever she "shul ben a wyf, foryet nat Palamon, the gentil man" (2796–97), and expires. Theseus erects a funeral pyre in the grove where the noble kinsmen had fought, and "Arcite is brent to asshen colde" (2957). Emelye and Palamon mourn "by lengthe of certyn yeres" (2967) and then Theseus brings them together, persuades them to marry, "And thus with alle blisse and melodye Hath Palamon ywedded Emelye" (3097–98).

As can be seen from this brief outline of the action of *The Knight's Tale*, which omits a few incidents and a great deal of description that have no part in *The Two Noble Kinsmen*, the central core of the play's main plot and most of its subsidiary events have their origin in Chaucer's poem. While the story is significantly modified by the playwrights in a number of ways, a few elements have been altered without fundamental change. In the passage in which Chaucer tells of the mourners who accost the wedding party, no number is mentioned. The queens and duchesses are described as "A compaignye of ladyes, tweye and tweye, Ech after oother" (898–99). Apparently, their number is considerable,[78] but only one, "whilom wyf to king Cappaneus" (932), addresses Theseus. In *The Two Noble Kinsmen*, the number is reduced. There are only three queens, but each speaks in appeal to Theseus, Hippolyta, and Emilia. Another example, which consists only in rearranging a sequence of actions, is the change in the order of the prayers to the deities of the kinsmen and Emelye. In *The Knight's Tale*, the sequence is determined by the hours of the day custom-

78. Leech, *Two Noble Kinsmen*, p. 1622, says there is "a crowd of queens and duchesses."

arily dedicated to the three gods (2216–17, 2271–74, 2367),[79] with Palamon offering the first prayer followed by Emelye and Arcite. In the play the order is Arcite, Palamon, and Emilia. In this connection a noteworthy deviation from the source is seen in the responses of the gods in *The Two Noble Kinsmen*. To Arcite the theophany is represented by a clanging of armor and a short thunder as the burst of a battle; to Palamon there is music, and doves are seen to flutter; to Emilia there is a sudden twang of instruments and a rose falls from a tree that is on Diana's altar. Another alteration comparable to the change in the order of the prayers is the transfer of the cousins' principal supporting knights in the tourney. Though neither is named in the play and the descriptions are somewhat intermingled, it is clear that Lygurge of Thrace has become Arcite's second and Emetreus of India has become Palamon's, which is the reverse of the tale. These changes, and others like them, are clearly intended to improve the dramatic effectiveness of the story, and in that they are successful.

Even some passages that are original in the play may have been developed from a hint in Chaucer. One of these is the substance of Palamon's prayer to Venus. Chaucer's Palamon speaks only of his own difficulties in love, which are those of a young man, but in the play Palamon expatiates on the problems of aged lovers, successively men of seventy, eighty, and ninety winters, with debilities, such as hoarseness, cramps, and gout, associated with the elderly. Phrases in Chaucer that might have inspired the alteration in the prayer are Palamon's mention of his "bittre teeris smerte" (2225) and "the tormentz of myn helle" (2228); and an earlier comment by Theseus on the extravagance of lovers, "a man moot ben a fool, or yong or oold" (1812). These may have suggested to the middle-aged Shakespeare the kind of supplication he composed.

There are additional traces of Chaucer's poem in the play that editors, in particular, have noted. Two are in the fourth scene of the first act. Theseus inquires as to the identity of the wounded Palamon and Arcite and is told they are "Men of great quality. . . . Sisters' children, nephews to the King" (1.4.14–16). This echoes *The Knight's Tale*:

> they that were of the blood roial
> Of Thebes, and of sustren two yborn.
> (1018–19)

Theseus then asks, "They are not dead?" and the Herald responds, "Nor in a state of life" (1.4.24–25). Chaucer describes them as "Nat fully quyke, ne fully dede" (1015). The final couplet of the first act reads

> This world's a city full of straying streets,
> And death's the market-place, where each one meets.
> (1.5.15–16)

79. Benson, *The Riverside Chaucer*, p. 837, n. 2217, explains the astrological system of the hours.

while Chaucer has

> This world nys but a thurghfare ful of wo,
> And we been pilgrymes, passynge to and fro.
> Deeth is an endé of every worldly soore.[80]
> (2847–49)

There are several other verbal echoes.[81]

All the names of the principals in the main plot of the play appear in *The Knight's Tale*: Theseus, Hippolyta, Emilia, Pirithous, and, of course, Palamon and Arcite. Theseus and Hippolyta appear in *A Midsummer Night's Dream*, but the other four are not mentioned. The names of minor characters in *The Two Noble Kinsmen*—Artesius, Valerius, Gerrold—do not occur in *The Knight's Tale*; but those of Capaneus and Creon, who are alluded to in the play, appear in the tale. However, the collaborators could have known at least these last two names without having read them in Chaucer.[82]

Leech notes a slightly different phenomenon, which he designates "some quite incidental echoes of Chaucer." One of the countrymen is named Arcas, which is the name of the son of Callisto, referred to as "Calistopee" in the poem. The story of Meleager and Atalanta and the Calydonian boar is mentioned by Gerrold, the schoolmaster, and also in *The Knight's Tale*. In *The Two Noble Kinsmen*, the tournament is held where the kinsmen fight over Emilia. In Chaucer it is the place of Arcite's funeral pyre. Palamon's speech at the block to his knightly companions, Leech says, "bears an obvious relation to the arguments that Theseus uses . . . to persuade Palamon and Emilia to give up their mourning for Arcite and

80. Littledale, ed. cit., pp. 131–32, and 45*–46*, cites evidence tending to show that the aphorism is proverbial, although it is not clear that his examples date from before the date of composition of *TNK*. Morris P. Tilley lists the two elements of the expression in *A Dictionary of the Proverbs in England in the Sixteenth and Seventeenth Centuries* (Ann Arbor: University of Michigan Press, 1950), D140 and W176. In the latter, he quotes the *TNK* formulation not duplicated in his other citations. Perhaps Shakespeare was reminded of the saying by Chaucer's lines.

81. Cf. 2.2.162–65 and 1156–59; 2.5.50–51 and 1500; 3.6.98–100 and 2809–10; 3.6.132–35 and 1710–13; 3.6.172–79 and 1719–26; 4.2.81–82 and 2131–33 (Bawcutt points out [ed. cit., p. 219] that the descriptions of the knights supporting Palamon and Arcite are "indebted to *The Knight's Tale* lines 2128–78 but with a number of modifications"); 5.1.54 ("armipotent") and 1982 and 2441 (Shakespeare used the term earlier, twice in *LLL* and once in *AWW*); 5.1.53–56 and 2463–64; 5.4.62 ("Cold . . . Saturn") and 2443; 5.4.112 and 3099–3100.

82. The names Theseus, Hippolyta, and Pirithous occur also in the "Life of Theseus." Several of the deities are common to the play and the tale, but one—Bellona, the goddess of war, who is thrice mentioned in the play (1.1.75, 1.3.13, and 4.2.106)—does not appear in *KnT*. Thompson (*Shakespeare's Chaucer: A Study in Literary Origins*, p. 70) thinks that the source of her name "was very probably" Chaucer's *Anelida and Arcite* (Benson, *Riverside Chaucer*, p. 376, l. 6). Shakespeare, as she notes, had known the name because Macbeth is called "Bellona's bridegroom" (1.2.54) in that play of some six or seven years earlier. The goddess is also alluded to as "the fire-ey'd maid of smoky war" in *1H4* (4.1.114) of 1598. Neither is connected to Chaucer.

enter into marriage." The "obvious relation" is that of parallels of thought. "Such points of casual resemblance between play and poem, with the dramatists freely manipulating the words and images they found in Chaucer, show the intimacy of their acquaintance with the source."[83]

Just as Chaucer freely adapted the *Teseida* to his purposes, compressing and deleting elements of Boccaccio's epic of Theseus and developing and expanding portions that fit into his plan,[84] so the collaborators of *The Two Noble Kinsmen* with equal freedom altered their source in Chaucer. The playwrights' adaptation seems clearly designed to meet the constraints and to take advantage of the opportunities offered by the stage. Most of Chaucer's descriptive passages are either entirely absent from the play or survive in truncated form. The tournament, for example, the events of which Chaucer relates in detail, is condensed and merely reported by the playwrights. There are also elements of the main plot in the play of which there are no hints in *The Knight's Tale*. These include the dialogue between Palamon and Arcite on the corruption in Thebes (1.2), Emilia's recital of her girlish friendship with Flavina (1.3), and Emilia's monologue on the portraits of her two suitors (4.2). Each of these serves a manifest theatrical purpose, and they are therefore likely to be original with the playwrights.

In her study of *The Knight's Tale* as source, Thompson detects a distinct difference in the handling of the events of the tale in different parts of the play. She allows room for the possibility that some aspects of the difference may be traceable to unlike interpretations of the source but believes that the fundamental nature of the divergence arises from varying objectives. Shakespeare adapts Chaucer's tale to the stage, exploring certain themes such as "the destructive effects of amorous passions on other relationships and the extent to which men can control their own destinies." To Fletcher, the source poem "simply becomes the quarry from which . . . [he] extracts the situations which he proceeds to elaborate with maximum sensational effect." He produces a result in keeping with his conception of tragicomedy, while Shakespeare is generating something of a different order—a dramatic romance. Thompson supports her determination with examples and perceptive analysis. Shakespeare and Fletcher clearly saw different things in *The Knight's Tale* and dramatized it in independent ways.[85]

In "A Note on the Source" in his edition, Leech says that "in the

83. Leech, *Two Noble Kinsmen*, p. 1622. Arcas: 2.3.37; 3.5.46 and 2056. Meleager: 3.5.18 and 2070–71. Tourney: 3.6.292 and 2853–65. Palamon's speech: 5.4.1–13 and 3041–56.

84. Robinson (*Works of Chaucer*, 2d ed., pp. 4–5) says, "Only about a third of the English poem is actually translated from the Italian . . . yet his debt to Boccaccio . . . can hardly be overstated." Other scholars emphasize the importance of Chaucer's deviations from and additions to the *Teseida*. See Robert A. Pratt, "Chaucer's Use of the *Teseida*," *PMLA* 62 (1947): 598–621; and V. A. Kolve, *Chaucer and the Imagery of Narrative* (Stanford: Stanford University Press, 1984), pp. 85–157, especially pp. 134–36.

85. Thompson, *Shakespeare's Chaucer: A Study in Literary Origins*, pp. 208–15.

dramatization a considerable number of changes were made" to Chaucer's story. He cites the compression of time in several places, such as in the interval after Arcite's accident before he dies—he lingers in the tale but expires quickly in the play—which "gives an effect of tighter structure to what is in Chaucer a diffuse narrative." Changes for dramatic effectiveness include having the queens interrupt the progress of the wedding procession *before* Theseus and Hippolyta are married; providing Emilia with a confidant to talk with in the garden; and reducing the kinsmen's attendant knights to three from one hundred each. A sense of disturbance is introduced by use of powerfully harsh terms in Palamon's petition to Venus; the falling of the rose in response to Emilia's prayer to Diana; and the decree of Theseus that the defeated knights shall die. Chaucer describes the quarrel of the gods, which emphasizes their division, but the play makes us feel that "a single power speaks through . . . [them], that the matter is predetermined."[86]

The characterization of some of the principals is significantly altered from *The Knight's Tale*. Theseus is changed least, but Hippolyta and Emilia are both developed to a greater extent in *The Two Noble Kinsmen* than they are in Chaucer. They take an active part in helping Theseus to decide to aid the petitioning queens in the play, of which there is no trace in Chaucer. They both exhibit a depth of thoughtfulness in their discussion of the different values of love and friendship (1.3.26–97) and in other ways are better rounded characters and more active participants in the action in the play than they are in the tale. Emilia assumes a more central position in the play than Chaucer assigns to her. In the events of *The Knight's Tale*, she is a passive participant awaiting the outcome of the contest for her hand with equanimity. A heroine of chivalric romance, her most significant action is to cast an approving glance at the victor of the tournament (2680). Chaucer observes of her that like most women she follows "the favour of Fortune" (2682), but in the play she is a much more complex personality who is unable to make a choice between the two equally noble cousins and would prefer to remain a maiden votary of Diana than to become a wife. She is also sensitive to her role as the prize of the tournament and to the fact that, unwillingly, she will be the cause of the death of one of the two young men. When Theseus informs Emilia that Arcite is the winner, she exclaims, thinking only of Palamon's impending execution:

> Is this winning?
> Oh all you heavenly powers where is you[r] mercy?
> (5.3.138–39)

And in the final scene, when the dying Arcite yields to Palamon his claim to Emilia, she thinks only of his tragic end:

86. Leech, *Two Noble Kinsmen*, pp. 1621–22. Waith studies shifts of emphasis in *TNK* from *KnT* in "Shakespeare and Fletcher on Love and Friendship," *ShakS* 18 (1986): 235–50.

blessed souls be with thee!
. . . and while I live,
This day I give to tears.
(5.3.96–98)

The action of the drama requires that Palamon and Arcite be the same in worth, chivalry, and honor. Emilia reflects their uniform value when, with the help of Hippolyta and Pirithous having succeeded in persuading Theseus to rescind his sentence of death on the noble cousins, she refuses his bidding to choose one as her husband, saying, "I cannot Sir, they are both too excellent" (3.6.286). She reiterates this sentiment when she studies their portraits and finds much to admire in each but is again unable to choose:

What a meere child is fancy,
That having two faire gauds of equal sweetness,
Cannot distinguish, but must cry for both.
(4.2.52–54)

The dramatists, as can be seen from these examples, strove to portray the kinsmen as exactly equal in the admirable qualities of character. Some commentators see this as a defect in characterization, even while acknowledging the theatrical necessity for it, and complain that the two are not sufficiently differentiated. Muir, for example, says, "The twin heroes are as indistinguishable as Tweedledum and Tweedledee."[87] Other critics believe that, within their equality of merit, they exhibit traits that are different. By and large, and without uniform consistency, Palamon is the lover and Arcite is the warrior. These distinctions are most evident in the prayers in the opening scene of act 5, in their choice of deities to whom they address their petitions, and in the terms in which they pray. Both seek victory, but Arcite asks for "military skill" while Palamon says victory would be "true love's merit" (5.1.58 and 128). Earlier in the play, these roles are not so manifest. When the kinsmen first appear (in 1.2), it is Palamon who seems the more martial of the two, but when they quarrel over Emilia upon first seeing her (in 2.2), Palamon is more clearly the lover. However, in the interchange between the two leading up to their duel for Emilia (3.1, 3, and 6), Palamon reverts to a more aggressive stance. Bawcutt, while rejecting the view that the two are indistinguishable, acknowledges that there is "some degree of confusion or clumsiness . . . in the efforts of both Shakespeare and Fletcher to characterize the two men [but] from Act III onwards Palamon is clearly presented as the lover, the follower of Venus, and Arcite as the soldier, the follower of Mars."[88]

In sum, while the basic conception of the main plot and most of the essential themes, characters, and events are drawn from *The Knight's Tale*,

87. Muir, *Collaborator*, p. 127.
88. Bawcutt, ed. cit., p. 23.

Chaucer's poem is altered freely by the playwrights for dramatic and theatrical purposes, and there are some elements of independent origin.

Until recently it had been assumed by most scholars that the version of the *Canterbury Tales* employed by the playwrights was Thomas Speght's first edition of Chaucer's *Works* published in 1598. Robert K. Turner has shown, however, that it was Speght's second edition of 1602. In the 1598 edition, Emetreus, King of Inde, is described as having "crispe heer like rynges was yronne" (2165). By error this became in the 1602 edition "His crispe haire like rings was of yron," which explains a puzzling expression in the play:

His head's yellow,
Hard-hair'd, and curl'd
(4.2.103–4)

and demonstrates that it was Speght's 1602 edition that was used.[89]

E. C. Pettet traces the roots and the tone of the story of Palamon and Arcite back beyond *The Canterbury Tales* and notes that the playwrights, unlike Chaucer, whose viewpoint in *The Knight's Tale* is ironic, adopt a serious stance toward the events they dramatize. "What really marks *The Two Noble Kinsmen* off from the rest of the [Shakespearean] romances is that its substance and spirit derive . . . from the oldest layer of the romantic tradition. [It] is unique among the plays in which Shakespeare had a hand for its dependence upon and fidelity to the chivalric code." Theseus acts "like a true knight" in taking up the cause of the queens, and Palamon and Arcite stress the chivalric theme of honor in contemplating flight from corrupt Thebes. They are constrained, also by honor, from doing so when Creon is about to be attacked. Like feudal knights, they owe a duty to Thebes. Their sentiments of friendship expressed in prison are "entirely of a chivalric kind," and they behave "like true romantic lovers" when they catch sight of Emilia in the garden. Their "single-hearted, fanatical dedication . . . to their mistress, their courtesy to one another, as when each helps to arm the other . . . Arcite's refusal to take advantage of Palamon when he is unarmed, weak from hunger and in shackles . . . their refusal to accept the ignominious offer of life with banishment from Emilia and their eager acquiescence in Theseus' plan of a tourney . . . all the spirit and motion of the play are obviously generated from the old chivalric code." The setting is also typical of narrative romance—"the castle, the rose garden, the woods, the May morning and the field of tournament."[90]

89. Robert K. Turner, Jr., "*The Two Noble Kinsmen* and Speght's Chaucer," *N&Q* 225 (1980): 175–76.

90. E. C. Pettet, *Shakespeare and the Romance Tradition* (London: Staples, 1949), pp. 170–74. A number of other critics have noted the chivalric underpinnings of the main plot. See, for example, Spalding, *Letter*, pp. 67–70; Ribner, *Two Noble Kinsmen*, pp. xi–xii; E. Talbot Donaldson, *The Swan at the Well: Shakespeare Reading Chaucer* (New Haven: Yale University Press, 1985), pp. 50–73. Dorothy Bethurum Loomis, however, while recogniz-

There are records of two earlier plays based on Chaucer's *Knight's Tale*, one or both of which might have been sources of *The Two Noble Kinsmen*. The earlier *Palaemon and Arcyte*, which was written by Richard Edwards, an Oxford scholar, a dramatist, and Master of the Chapel Children, was presented as an entertainment to Queen Elizabeth in Christ Church common during her visit to the university in 1566. Although the play is lost, several detailed descriptions of it are extant.[91] The later *Palamon and Arsett* was performed four times on 17 September, 16 and 27 October, and 9 November by the Admiral's Men at Newington during the short season of 1594, according to entries in Henslowe's *Diary*. We do not have the text and nothing else is known of the play.[92] It is, however, conceivable that Shakespeare saw this version of the story since his *Titus Andronicus* was performed at Newington as late as the preceding 12 June. It is much less likely that he would have had access to the accounts of the Oxford production of Edwards's play. Most scholars are of the opinion that *The Two Noble Kinsmen* is not indebted to either of the predecessor plays primarily because its links to *The Knight's Tale* are so manifest and pervasive that there is scarcely any possibility of an intermediary. A few critics, however, do not rule out entirely the possibility of a secondary influence from the earlier plays. In his Shakespeare Society edition of Henslowe's *Diary*, J. Payne Collier notes that the 1594 play is "obviously [based] on Chaucer's Palamon and Arcite. This might be an alteration of Edwards's play acted before Queen Elizabeth in 1566. . . . The Two Noble Kinsmen, in which

ing the chivalric qualities of Palamon and Arcite, sees them in their relationship to each other as "sophisticated Jacobean courtiers" ("Chaucer and Shakespeare," in *Chaucer's Mind and Art*, ed. A. C. Cawley [Edinburgh: Oliver & Boyd, 1969], p. 182). Proudfoot (*Two Noble Kinsmen*, p. xx) observes, "Some classical texts relating to Thebes, such as the *Thebais* of Statius, were probably known to Shakespeare or Fletcher." He notes specifically "Palamon's allusion to Juno's jealousy of Thebes, at I.ii.20–22, [which] implies a fuller knowledge of the story of Thebes than Chaucer could supply."

91. Three of the descriptions, two translated from the Latin, are printed by W. Y. Durand ("*Palaemon and Arcyte, Progne, Marcus Geminus*, and the Theatre in which they were acted, as described by John Bereblock [1566]," *PMLA* 20 [1905]: 503–28). He discusses the performances in that essay and in "Palaemon and Arcyte not a Source of *The Two Noble Kinsmen*," *JEGP* 4 (1902): 365–69. Anthony a Wood also wrote a lively and circumstantial account that Littledale prints in full, ed. cit., pp. 9*–11*. See also Frederick S. Boas, *University Drama in the Tudor Age* (Oxford: Oxford University Press, 1914; rpt. New York: Blom, 1966), pp. 98–106. One character, Trecatio, and two incidents, a fox hunt and the burning of Arcite's body, among other details mentioned in these accounts that are not in *TNK*, make it unlikely that Edwards's play is a source. Weber in his edition of Beaumont and Fletcher says (13:3) *Palaemon and Arcyte* "was . . . printed in 1585"; and Charles Plummer notes that "the play has been several times printed" (*Elizabethan Oxford* [Oxford: Clarendon Press, 1887], p. xxi). If so, no copy seems to have survived. Weber may have had in mind another Edwards play, *Damon and Pithias*, printed in 1571 (STC 7514), or his *Paradise of Dainty Devices*, which survives in a 1585 print (STC 7520).

92. R. A. Foakes and R. T. Rickert, eds., *Henslowe's Diary* (Cambridge: Cambridge University Press, 1961), pp. 24–25. Malone (1821 Variorum 3:303) makes this comment on the entry in the *Diary*: "On this old play The Two Noble Kinsmen was probably founded."

Shakespeare is stated to have had some concern, is founded on the same incidents. It is very possible that he did something for it when it was acted on the 17th Sept. 1594, by the Lord Chamberlain's Players, (performing with the Lord Admiral's men) and that the alterations and additions he made were employed by Fletcher in the play as it was printed in 1634."[93] Dyce rejects Collier's notion that the two early plays are connected and that the Shakespearean portions of *The Two Noble Kinsmen* "were composed as early as 1594,—stamped as they every where are with the manner of Shakespeare's later years," but he thinks he might have subsequently (perhaps in 1609–1610) revised the 1594 play that was then remodeled by Fletcher, who retained "those additions which had been made to it by Shakespeare, but tamper[ed] with them here and there" to give us the text that we have.[94]

The subplot of *The Two Noble Kinsmen* consists of two separate elements. One element is the sequence of the Jailer's Daughter that comprises nine complete scenes plus part of the morris dance scene in which she sings, speaks briefly, and dances. Altogether, these total almost six hundred lines, or just under one-fifth of the play. The other underplot element might be designated the maying sequence consisting of the concluding sixty lines of 2.3 (in which the countrymen talk of may games and tell Arcite about them) and the whole of the morris dance scene, 3.5. Both of these elements are loosely connected to the main plot primarily through the Jailer's Daughter. Her love for Palamon and her success in releasing him from prison give rise to references to her when Palamon secures her and her father's pardon (4.1); and when he speaks to the Jailer about her at the block (5.4); and also through her presence in the country pastime presented before Theseus and his train. The source of the dance is clearly the second antimasque from Beaumont's *Masque of the Inner Temple and Grayes Inne*, the text of which, including a commentary on the performance, was published in a quarto of 1613.[95] The direction for the second antimasque and the brief but illuminating account of its reception comprise Text 2.[96]

93. J. Payne Collier, ed., *The Diary of Philip Henslowe* (London: For the Shakespeare Society, 1845), p. 41. Collier is in error about the acting troupe. The two companies separated on 15 June 1594 (W. W. Greg, *Henslowe's Diary*, 2 vols. [London: Bullen, 1904–1908], 2:84–85). *Palamon and Arsett* was performed by the Admiral's Men.

94. Dyce, *Beaumont & Fletcher*, 1:lxxxv–lxxxvi. Possibly the choice of title for *TNK* was a purposeful attempt by the playwrights to distinguish it from the earlier plays.

95. Greg, *Bibliography*, 1:450, no. 309. The title page of Q survives in two states, one including Beaumont's name, spelled "Beamont," which was canceled, and one without it (STC 1663, 1664).

96. A shorter version of the Q text of the masque representing a variant tradition was printed in the Beaumont and Fletcher Folios of 1647 and 1679. The descriptions are omitted and the directions are brief, but Beaumont's name is included, spelled, as in the earlier state of Q, "Beamont" (Edwards, *Masque of the Inner Temple*, pp. 143–45; Bowers, *Dramatic Works in the Beaumont and Fletcher Canon*, pp. 113–20). Colman and Darley reprinted the Q text, but neither mentions any connection between the second antimasque and the morris in the play. Weber also prints the masque with an introduction and says in a note: "The Pedant evidently appears in the same character as Gerrold in The Two Noble Kinsmen" (14:337, n.

Gerrold, the Schoolmaster in the play who corresponds to the Pedant in Beaumont's antimasque, addresses an elaborate introduction to Theseus and his train. He says:

> I first appear, though rude, and raw, and muddy,
> To speak before thy noble grace, this tenner:
> At whose great feet I offer up my penner.
> The next the Lord of May, and Lady bright,
> The Chambermaid, and Servingman by night
> That seeke out silent hanging. Then mine Host
> And his fat Spouse, that welcomes to their cost
> The galled traveller, and with a beckining
> Informs the tapster to inflame the reckining:
> Then the beast-eating Clown, and next the Fool,
> The Bavian with long tail, and eke long tool,
> *Cum multis aliis* that make a dance,
> Say "Ay," and all shall presently advance.
> (3.5.123–34)

In view of the close correspondences of the dancers, there can be little doubt that the one entertainment influenced the other. In *The Two Noble Kinsmen*, the morris dance is clearly detachable. Theseus and his party had been pursuing a stag when they were accosted by Gerrold and his village dancers. After the morris, he says, "Now to our sports again," and they depart with minimal ceremony to the winding of horns. In Beaumont's masque, by contrast, the second antimasque is an integral element of the whole connected through Iris—one of the two presenters—and especially connected by her dialogue with Mercury to both the main masque and the first antimasque. Furthermore, it is not likely that Beaumont would have borrowed an element from a King's Men's play acted in a public theater to piece out a composition to be presented before the royal family at an important wedding celebration. On the other hand, Shakespeare's company, some of whom were probably the "actors" who danced the second antimasque, would have, by incorporating it into their play, benefited from the attendance of Londoners who had heard about the court masque but had not been privileged to attend. A respected critic has even speculated that *The Two Noble Kinsmen* may have been commissioned specifically "to provide a setting for the anti-masque" and thus to take advantage of the favorable royal reception.[97] A few scholars have raised doubts about the source of the morris dance scene because it seems to them that the pairs of dancers

5); but he does not connect the dancers in Beaumont's antimasque to those in the play. Littledale was the first to note the similarities between the antimasque and *TNK* (pp. 145, 53*–54*) and to interpret correctly their significance. He thinks that Fletcher wrote both the masque (which indicates that he ignored the ascription to Beaumont in Q and in the two B&F Folios) and scene 3.5 (p. 54*).

97. Bradbrook, *The Living Monument*, p. 236.

in the play do not exactly match the pairs in the antimasque. The grounds for these doubts are twofold: Gerrold mentions only nine dancers in his presentation; and the opening stage direction for the scene in the quarto lists only four countrymen, a Baum (baboon), two or three wenches, and a Taborer. However, in the dialogue, six girls are named—Friz, Mauldine, Luce, Barbary, Nell, and Cecily. The last named is absent, and Gerrold says, "Here is a woman wanting." Her place is subsequently taken by the Jailer's Daughter. In Gerrold's address to Theseus, he names by title all six of Beaumont's male roles but only three female roles. However, he concludes with "*Cum multis aliis* that make a dance," so it is clear that, while only three female parts are mentioned, there are others who complete the six pairs of dancers.[98] The identification of the source is conclusive because the roles designated by Beaumont are substantially duplicated in *The Two Noble Kinsmen*, and further because this particular antimasque constituted an innovation consisting, as it says in the argument, "not of any suited (i.e., identically costumed) persons, but of a confusion or commixture of all such persons as are natural and proper for country sports."[99] Therefore, it is most improbable that it was an element of an earlier masque or play.

In regard to the Jailer's Daughter's sequence, scholars have either considered it an invention of the dramatists based upon a minimal hint in Chaucer that "a freend" helped Palamon "brak his prisoun" (1467–74); or they have contented themselves with the simple statement that its source has not been identified. But Thompson may have discovered its origin in the story of Mopsa in *The Countess of Pembroke's Arcadia* [Text 3]. "There are obvious resemblances [between the romance and the play] in the presentation of an apparently mad daughter who is obsessed with thoughts of her own marriage to the point that she can callously discuss the possibility that her father will be hanged tomorrow as a mere trifle." She calls attention to other similarities to elements in the play such as the girl's unrequited love for a social superior and the fact that her father is a jailer from whose custody an important prisoner (Pamela) has escaped. Thompson calls her discovery a parallel and refrains from designating the *Arcadia* as the source of the subplot, although she says, "There is no other obvious source." She points out that there is evidence in other Fletcher plays that he knew Sid-

98. 3.5.25–44 and 133. Some scholars (for example, Proudfoot, *Two Noble Kinsmen*, p. xx) count only eight dancers in Gerrold's list (there are actually nine), apparently considering the second elements in one or other of two locutions—"Then the beast-eating Clown, and next the Fool" or "and next the Fool, The Bavian" (3.5.131–32)—to be in apposition to the first, but the syntax does not support such an interpretation, and if Gerrold had the six girls he mentions as dancers, his list of male dancers would have to be read as six, not five.

99. Edwards, *Masque of the Inner Temple*, p. 134. The antimasque was a relatively recent introduction into the court masque. Jonson says that Queen Anne suggested to him incorporating into *The Masque of Queenes* (1609) "some *Daunce*, or shew" that would be "a foyle, or False-*Masque*" (Herford and Simpson, *Ben Jonson*, 7:282).

ney's romance well and thinks it "highly likely" that he would have recalled it when he was "working on the somewhat similar subject-matter of *The Two Noble Kinsmen.*"[100]

During the course of the play, the Jailer's Daughter sings all or part of eight songs, and she or another character mentions six others. All are associated with the portrayal of her deteriorating mental condition. When we first encounter her (2.1), she is normally rational. The next time she appears, she speaks of her love for Palamon and hints at her emotional vulnerability because she is his social inferior (2.4). She expands on this in her third scene, in which she tells of having freed Palamon, says she is desperate, and complains of his failure to thank her or to kiss her (2.6). The first significant evidence of decline is in her next scene (3.2), in which, having lost track of Palamon in the wood, she laments his apparent decision to go on his way without thought of her and speaks of her own death, perhaps even by suicide. In her next soliloquy (3.4), she is hallucinating and for the first time she sings part of a ballad. Other snatches are sung in the succeeding scenes as she continues to deteriorate (3.5, 4.1, 4.3), but when her condition seems to be stabilizing in her final scene (5.2), she does not sing. Some of the songs—both those she sings on stage and those that are merely mentioned—have been identified, but some have not. Most are well-known ballads such as *Child Waters, Nut Brown Maid, George Aloo, Broom,* and *Bonny Robin.*[101] Others are exceptional. One that begins in *The Two Noble Kinsmen* quarto, "There was three fooles, fell out about an howlet," is probably a child's rhyme.[102] Another, referred to by the Jailer's Daughter as "*Quipassa,*" has been identified as an Italian dance tune, "Chi passa per questa strada" (Who passes along this street).[103] A third, described in the text as "O faire, oh sweete, &c." is thought to be a setting of the seventh of Sidney's *Certain Sonnets.*[104] Four songs that are mentioned but that the Jailer's Daughter does not sing occur in canonical plays. "Willow, willow, willow" is a sad song alluded to by Desdemona. Ophelia bids Laertes to sing "A-down-a" and she herself sings one line of "Bonny Robin." A tune

100. Ann Thompson, "Jailers' Daughters in *The Arcadia* and *The Two Noble Kinsmen,*" *N&Q* 224 (1979): 140–41. Shakespeare also, of course, knew Sidney's romance and drew upon it, most notably for the story of the king of Paphlagonia in *Lr* (Geoffrey Bullough, *Narrative and Dramatic Sources of Shakespeare*, 8 vols. [London: Routledge; New York: Columbia University Press, 1957–1975], 7:284–85). But Bullough also traces the *Arcadia* in *TGV* (1:207), *Tim.* (6:235), *Per.* (6:355–56), *Ham.* (7:47–8), and *WT* (8:125–26). He lists the *Arcadia* with other important sources and says Shakespeare enjoyed reading it (8:347).

101. Kittredge, ed., *Works*, p. 1410. Skeat, *Two Noble Kinsmen* (1875), p. 128, n. 19. Bawcutt, *Two Noble Kinsmen*, pp. 205–6, nn. 19–20; p. 208, n. 60; p. 216, nn. 107, 108. Leech, *Two Noble Kinsmen*, p. 1652, nn. 107, 108.

102. 3.5.67. Iona and Peter Opie, eds., *The Oxford Dictionary of Nursery Rhymes* (Oxford: Clarendon Press, 1951), pp. 421–23, no. 525.

103. 3.5.86. See Bawcutt, *Two Noble Kinsmen*, p. 209, n. 87.

104. 4.1.113. See Leech, *Two Noble Kinsmen*, p. 1652, n. 114; and Bawcutt, *Two Noble Kinsmen*, p. 216, n. 114.

called "Light a'love" is mentioned once in *The Two Gentlemen of Verona* and twice in *Much Ado About Nothing.*[105] Singing by the Jailer's Daughter appears to be, in the main, limited to fragments of song. The most extensive song text incorporated into the play consists of eight lines from *George Aloo*, a ballad that in one version runs to fifty-two lines.[106] However, in four instances the first line of a song is followed by "&c." These are "May you never more enjoy the light;" "O faire, oh sweete;" "When Cinthia with her borrowed light;" and "I will be true, my stars, my fate."[107] The appended "&c." may mean that in each case the complete song—or most of it—is to be sung, but of this we cannot be certain. Perhaps only two or three lines are rendered.[108]

It has been established that Shakespeare consulted Plutarch's "Life of Theseus" as well as *The Knight's Tale* in preparation for writing *A Midsummer Night's Dream*. It is not clear whether he read it again before composing *The Two Noble Kinsmen*, but there seems to be no doubt that he was influenced by Plutarch, at least in some specific aspects of the story, such as the friendship between Theseus and Pirithous [Text 4]. Theseus in *The Two Noble Kinsmen* is less the romantic bridegroom, as he is in *A Midsummer Night's Dream*, and more the judge, the arbiter, and the experienced warrior. Of the tourney's "subdude"—Palamon and his knights—he says, "Give them our present Iustice, since I know Their lives but pinch 'em" (5.3.131–33), which reflects qualities in Plutarch's portrait of Theseus not emphasized in *A Midsummer Night's Dream*. He is not stern, however, as some critics have thought, for he twice yields to the pleading of Hippolyta and Emilia and changes his decisions. One unattractive feature of Theseus's character described by Plutarch—his ravishing of Perigouna, Ariadne, Antiope, and Helen—is not reflected in *The Two Noble Kinsmen*, although Shakespeare knew of it and alluded to his aggression and lack of faith in *The Two Gentlemen of Verona* (4.4.167–68) and in *A Midsummer Night's Dream* (2.1.77–80). It appears that the collaborators suppressed elements from this source so as to present Theseus in a favorable light.

Numerous reminiscences of canonical Shakespearean plays are woven into the fabric of *The Two Noble Kinsmen*, as nearly everyone who has studied the play points out. The most thoroughgoing examination of this

105. "Willow," *TNK* 4.1.80; *Oth.* 4.3.28. "Robin," *TNK* 4.1.108; *Ham.* 4.5.187. "A-down-a," *TNK* 4.3.12; *Ham.* 4.5.171–72. "Light a'love," *TNK* 5.2.54; *TGV* 1.2.80; *Ado* 3.4.44 and 47.

106. Francis James Child, ed., *The English and Scottish Popular Ballads*, 5 vols. (Boston: 1882–1898; rpt. New York: Cooper Square, 1962), 5:133–35, no. 285.

107. "May you," 4.1.104. "O faire," 4.1.113. "When Cinthia," 4.1.152. "I will be true," 4.3.57.

108. William R. Bowden, in *The English Dramatic Lyric, 1603–42* (New Haven: Yale University Press, 1951; rpt. Hamden, Conn.: Archon, 1969), on the basis of a study of "mad singing" in the Stuart drama, concludes that it "is more likely" that the songs were sung "in snatches by the Gaoler's Daughter in her madness" (pp. 38 and nn. 7 and 8; and 147).

phenomenon is the scene-by-scene analysis by Littledale in the introduction to his edition. Littledale recognizes that these resemblances occur in the parts of the play generally thought to be Fletcher's as well as in those ascribed to Shakespeare, but he distinguishes between borrowings and "self-reproduction." The latter arises "naturally, incidentally; some familiar word associates an old train of ideas, or some fresh idea finds its easiest embodiment in some old familiar phrase" (p. 29*). Although Littledale diligently adduces many verbal and grammatical parallels, he does not limit his evidence to such echoes. Resemblances of thought, character, situation, and staging are also noted. The "self-resemblances" (as distinguished from Fletcherian "imitations") are of varying cogency. Most of Littledale's parallels have been found by later commentators to be persuasive,[109] although some have been considered tenuous. All in all, Littledale finds common elements between *The Two Noble Kinsmen* and twenty-eight canonical Shakespearean plays,[110] as well as a few similarities to the poems. While some early plays are included, such as *2 Henry VI* and *The Comedy of Errors*, a majority of those associated with *The Two Noble Kinsmen* are late. As might have been expected, the romances are heavily represented. Earlier plays are thematically connected. *The Two Gentlemen of Verona* has a similar love-friendship plot element, as, in a different way, does *Love's Labor's Lost*; and *A Midsummer Night's Dream* shares the Theseus-Hippolyta story. The Jailer's Daughter's madness scenes echo related elements regarding derangement in *Hamlet* and *King Lear*, and even in *Timon of Athens*. As Sir Edmund Chambers broadly sums up, the majority of the connections are "to his late plays, [but] there are also several to *Midsummer Night's Dream*, associations with which the resumed handling of Theseus may well have evoked."[111]

Some students of the sources have discerned a connection between Gerrold and the pedagogues Holofernes in *Love's Labor's Lost* and Rombus in Sidney's untitled entertainment usually designated *The Lady of May* [Text 5]. The undoubted immediate origin of Gerrold is the Pedant who ushers in the dancers in Beaumont's *Masque* but speaks no lines. There are a number of characteristics that are common to Rombus, Holofernes, and Gerrold. They speak pedantically, all making more or less frequent use of inkhorn terms and Latin phrases, refer to deities, employ alliteration and catalogues of synonyms, and speak slightingly of their less educated associ-

109. For example, Brooke, *Shakespeare Apocrypha*, pp. xli, xliv; Chambers, *William Shakespeare*, 1:531; Leech, *Two Noble Kinsmen*, pp. 1616–18; Ribner, *Two Noble Kinsmen*, p. xii; Proudfoot, *Two Noble Kinsmen*, p. xx; Smith, *Riverside Shakespeare*, p. 1640; Bawcutt, *Two Noble Kinsmen*, pp. 177, 195, 221.

110. Littledale, ed. cit., pp. 30*–68*. The canonical plays are *Ant.*, *AYL*, *Cor.*, *Cym.*, *Err.*, *Ham.*, *1* and *2H4*, *H5*, *2H6*, *H8*, *JC*, *Jn.*, *LLL*, *Lr.*, *Mac.*, *MM*, *MND*, *Per.*, *R2*, *Rom.*, *Tim.*, *Tmp.*, *TN*, *Tro.*, *TGV*, *Wiv.*, and *WT*. Thompson, *Shakespeare's Chaucer*, p. 205, n. 7, adds an echo from *MV*.

111. *William Shakespeare*, 1:531.

ates. They participate in oratorical presentations to royalty or nobility: in the case of Rombus it is a petition; in the case of the others it is an entertainment. The manner of each, though varied, is essentially the same. Each acknowledges that he is a schoolmaster. In addition to the similarities, there are differences. While their speech is dotted with Latin, no Latin tag uttered by one character is identical to that spoken by another. There is no other material lexical affinity, not even of the names of the gods, although both Rombus and Gerrold mention Jove. Perhaps the most significant difference is that while Rombus and Holofernes are, in their presentations, discomfited, Gerrold is applauded, praised, and rewarded in his. He concludes the morris dance scene happily by commending his dancers: "*Dii deaeque omnes* [gods and goddesses all], ye have danc'd rarely, wenches." Bullough ends a short discussion of possible antecedents of Holofernes with the observation that "the relationship is generic rather than particular," and the same comment may apply to the relationship of Gerrold to Rombus and Holofernes.[112]

A possible source of a passage in Arcite's prayer to Mars is Barnabe Barnes's *Foure Bookes of Offices* (p. 161), but this is not established. Barnes's treatise is dated 1606, several years before *The Two Noble Kinsmen*; and, other than one or two commonplace words such as "corrector," the only shared term is "pluresie," which Arcite connects with "people" whereas Barnes's uses the word in the phrase "plurasies of peace." Furthermore, Shakespeare uses the word in *Hamlet* (4.7.117), which antedates the *Foure Bookes*.[113]

Stage History

The title page of the 1634 quarto tells us that *The Two Noble Kinsmen* was presented at the Blackfriars to great applause, but no records survive concerning the specific dates of performances. The premier is likely to have taken place within a few months of the date of Beaumont's masque, which was danced at Whitehall on 20 February 1613. Probably it was the first play scheduled in the autumn of that year at the King's Men's private playhouse. The allusions to the play in Ben Jonson's *Bartholomew Fair* dated 31 October 1614 shows that it was probably still in the repertory at that time. Scraps of paper from the office of the revels found inserted into Sir George Buc's

112. Bullough, *Sources*, 1:426–27. Dover Wilson points out that Shakespeare's schoolmasters are unsympathetically portrayed ("figures of fun"). Gerrould certainly is not. Though he is designated a schoolmaster, he is more of a dancemaster. The differences lend some support to the idea that the morris is the work of a third playwright ("The Schoolmaster in Shakespeare's Plays," *Transactions of the Royal Society of Literature*, n.s. 9 [1930]: 9–34).

113. Paul A. Jorgensen, *Shakespeare's Military World* (Berkeley: University of California Press, 1956), pp. 176–78, 188.

manuscript *History of Richard III* contain lists of plays including "*The 2 Noble Kinesman.*" Chambers thinks they represent plays that were under consideration for performance at court. He dates the lists about 1619–1620, which indicates that the King's Men were acting it at the time.[114] The two players whose names appear in stage directions in the quarto—Thomas Tuckfield and Curtis Greville—are known to have acted together with the King's Men for a short time circa 1624–1626. Since their names would only have been noted in the promptbook (from which the quarto derived) to facilitate performance, it is very likely that the play was being acted about that time. The publication of Waterson's quarto of 1634 is evidence of a continuing interest in *The Two Noble Kinsmen* probably based on current performances, although we have no records of them. We also lack contemporary accounts of the early staging, but the printed stage directions, particularly those in 1.1 and 1.5 and those describing the staging of the supplications to the gods in 5.1, show that the production was colorful and elaborate and the costuming rich.

There is no evidence of any production of *The Two Noble Kinsmen* employing the original text for nearly three centuries after the Jacobean performances until the Old Vic presented it in 1928. Davenant's adaptation of the play entitled *The Rivals* was first produced at Lincoln's Inn Fields in 1664. Downes records that its initial run continued for nine successive performances "with a full Audience,"[115] which was unusual for its day, and it was revived on a number of occasions thereafter.[116] Pepys attended a performance of *The Rivals* on 10 September 1664 and again on 2 December. The casts were different. On neither occasion was he pleased with the play, although he praised the acting. On the first occasion, Winifred Gosnell, who took the part corresponding to the Jailer's Daughter, after a good start singing and dancing later wandered off key. In December he noted: "The play not good nor anything but the good actings of Betterton and his wife and Harris." Possibly he saw it performed again on 31 May 1668, but we cannot be sure because he does not mention the play's title.[117] A Lord Chamberlain's warrant shows that Charles II attended a performance by the Duke of York's Company on 19 November 1667.[118] Davenant's version is radically altered from the original and provided with a happy ending. The play begins with the defeat of Creon, the rest of act 1 being cut as well as the whole of act 5. The victory of Theseus is largely due to the Provost, who, although of a higher rank, corresponds to the Jailer in

114. Chambers, review of Frank Marcham, "The King's Office of the Revels 1610–1622," *RES* 1 (1925): 479–84; *William Shakespeare*, 2:346.

115. Freeman, ed., *Roscius Anglicanus*, pp. 23–24.

116. Nethercot, *Sir William D'Avenant Poet Laureate and Playwright—Manager*, p. 389.

117. Helen McAfee, ed., *Pepys on the Restoration Stage* (New Haven: Yale University Press, 1916; rpt. New York: Blom, n.d. [1966]), pp. 142–43, 242 n. 4.

118. A. C. Sprague, *Beaumont and Fletcher on the Restoration Stage* (Cambridge: Harvard University Press, 1926), p. 29.

The Two Noble Kinsmen. His daughter (Celania) is close to Emilia (Heraclia), who has her choice of the noble cousins renamed Philander and Theocles. Celania releases Philander from prison, and much of the middle action of the original is preserved though freely adapted. The morris, for example, is presented without Gerrold. In the final scene, Heraclea, knowing Celania is in love with Philander, chooses Theocles for herself, and Philander, at first with little enthusiasm, accepts Celania.[119]

William Charles Macready in January 1828 acted the part of Ribemont in *Edward the Black Prince,* a pastiche assembled by Frederick Reynolds from elements of *The Two Noble Kinsmen, Philaster,* and *Bonduca.* It was played twice in what one observer called "a beautiful performance."[120]

The Old Vic production of the original play, which ran for six performances in 1928, was greeted with mixed reviews. The theater critics expressed reservations about the possibility of Shakespeare's authorship participation and about the stageworthiness of the text, particularly in the more serious passages. Similarly, they were unfavorably impressed by the noble characters even though they commended the actors who played those parts, especially Ernest Milton, who acted Palamon with comic overtones. The presentation of the subplot characters was better received, and Jean Forbes-Robertson as the Jailer's Daughter was generally praised. A. G. Macdonell called her performance outstanding, noting "her dainty freshness at the beginning of the play and her terribly intense acting as the mad girl." James Agate complimented the Old Vic for having "mounted [the play] in good Chaucerian vein."[121]

Following the 1928 production, there was a pause in stage activity until the mid-1950s, when *The Two Noble Kinsmen* was produced twice in the United States, the first a student production at Harvard University and the second the premier American professional production by the Antioch Area Theatre under the direction of Arthur Lithgow. At Harvard in 1954, the play was presented alternately with *The Comedy of Errors* in a classical arena setting.[122] The Antioch production the following year was greeted warmly by one reviewer who found "the costuming spectacular . . . [and] the production . . . interesting, entertaining and well acted. . . . Jacqueline Brooks as the Jailer's Daughter couldn't have been better." The reviewer

119. Ibid., pp. 129–37, provides a detailed analysis of the adaptation. The citation, in a variant text, of the closing couplet of act 1 in a 1674 miscellany seems unlikely to indicate performance. *The Shakspere Allusion Book . . . from 1591 to 1700,* comp. C. M. Ingleby, L. Toulmin Smith, and F. J. Furnivall (London, 1874, 1879, 1886), rev. ed., John Munro (London, 1909), rpt. with a preface by Sir Edmund Chambers, 2 vols. (London: Oxford University Press, 1932), 2:204.

120. Alan S. Downer, *The Eminent Tragedian William Charles Macready* (Cambridge: Harvard University Press, 1966), p. 111.

121. A. G. Macdonell, "Chronicles: The Drama," *The London Mercury* 17, 102 (1928): 696–97; James Agate, *Brief Chronicles* (London: Cape, 1943), pp. 153–56. See also Gordon Crosse, *Shakespearean Playgoing 1890–1952* (London: Mowbray, 1953), p. 66.

122. Mary C. Hyde, comp., "Current Theatre Notes," *SQ* 6 (1955): 88.

also praised the singing and the "light-hearted characters" of the subplot, and wondered why a play that "is well worth doing" is rarely performed.[123] It was acted eight times.

The venue shifted back to Britain for the next twenty years, where the play was produced on five occasions. The Reading University Dramatic Society acted the play six times in the open air at Stratford-upon-Avon in 1959. The Department of Drama of the University of Bristol presented it at Dartington Hall, Devon, and in the Gardens of the Royal Fort, Bristol, for a total of nine performances in July 1964.[124] A brief run consisting of only two performances in modern dress was presented in an arena theater in the British Council's residence hall in February 1970. The *Financial Times* theater critic found it a full Elizabethan treatment of Chaucer's tale of sibling amorous rivalry—"duels, drunkenness, mad scenes, country dances, eccentric schoolmaster, vows on the altars of the gods, plus a rather tedious subplot"—but concluded that the interpretation of the play fell short "in many respects of the brilliant revival it surely deserves."[125] In an unpublished review, Ann Thompson praised the "remarkably cheerful" production as a "valiant attempt" and noted especially that director Michael Friend had taken pains to preserve almost all of Shakespeare's lines. Palamon was played in an ironic vein, "Hippolyta was one of the most successful parts," and the "schoolmaster and his rustics . . . were surprisingly funny . . . the jailer's daughter was . . . excellent throughout." But she had many reservations about the value of the production and especially of the textual alterations.

One of the more original stagings was mounted by the York Theatre Royal in 1973. The production was admired by reviewers for its acting as well as its "striking setting." The stage was a white platform, draped at the back in stark white, with giant white balloons floating in the central space. The text was cut—the morris dance, for example, was dropped—and altered, but the Shakespearean flavor of the poetry was preserved. The *Guardian* theater critic found this *Two Noble Kinsmen* "gay, sweeping and exuberantly romantic" and said it "crowned the York Festival."[126]

Mervyn Willis, who had produced the York Theatre Royal presentation, mounted a second production by the New Shakespeare Company in Regent's Park the next year. There were nine performances. J. C. Trewin reported that it was "exciting audiences," and he commended the acting of much of the cast, although "the Jailer's Daughter goes madder than Ophe-

123. Dayton (Ohio) *Daily News*, 11 August 1955.

124. Alice Griffin, comp., "Current Theatre Notes," *SQ* 11 (1960): 106; Glynne Wickham, *Shakespeare's Dramatic Heritage* (New York: Barnes & Noble, 1969), p. 30; M. G. Jones, "*The Two Noble Kinsmen*," *New Theatre Magazine* 5:2 (1964): 18–19.

125. *Financial Times* (London), 4 February 1970.

126. "*Two Noble Kinsmen* at York Theatre Royal," *The Manchester Guardian*, 5 July 1973; "1634 Play," *York Evening Press*, 5 July 1973; "Impressive *Noble Kinsmen*," *Stage and Television Today*, 12 July 1973; Bawcutt, ed. cit., p. 16.

lia." He also regretted the omission of the opening hymeneal song but noted that most of the Shakespearean "beauties" were retained.[127]

The following year saw the first of two entirely different productions of *The Two Noble Kinsmen* mounted by Richard H. Abrams in America, the first at the University of Texas-Austin, presented by the English and Classics departments in 1975; and the second at Richmond, acted in 1979 by an independent theater group. Professor Abrams thus matched in the United States the accomplishment of Mervyn Willis in Britain. The Austin production was presented "virtually bare-stage" while that at Richmond was elaborately costumed. Each production ran for seven performances.[128]

The Cherub Company produced a "heavily cut but still lucid . . . production" with an all-male cast at the New Chaplaincy Center in the 1979 Edinburgh International Festival, which Gerald Berkowitz thought "frequently exciting." The noble youths were effectively differentiated, and Charles Grant as Emilia conveyed "her turmoil and unhappiness at being a pawn in a game." The abbreviated text successfully "illuminate[d] structural patterns in the play." The production was continued at the Young Vic Studio in London, at which Tony Howard experienced a mixed reaction. He found the Jailer's Daughter shrill and "in her madness embarrassing"; and the emphasis on sexuality "a sly anti-feminine joke . . . the audience was evidently gripped by Fletcher's compelling narrative line in Acts II and III, [and] the tender ferocity of the arming scene was most striking," but the "striving for effect marred the close." To G. M. Pearce, "the production was well balanced [exhibiting] delight in disguise, much sexual innuendo and a strong element of comedy." Anthony Best as the Jailer's Daughter managed her "difficult mad scene with its echoes of Ophelia with great sensitivity and conveyed the sexual longings of the young girl naturally and without ridicule." There were a total of twenty-eight performances at the two locations.[129] Professor Hugh Richmond presented the play with a student cast in 1978 at the University of California-Berkeley.[130]

R. Thad Taylor, the executive producer of the Los Angeles Globe Playhouse, mounted a *Two Noble Kinsmen* in 1979 as part of a thirty-eight-

127. J. C. Trewin, *Illustrated London News*, October 1974, p. 107. For further discussion of this production by Barbara Hodgdon, see Samuel L. Leiter, ed., *Shakespeare Around the Globe* (Westport, Conn.: Greenwood, 1986), pp. 808–9. A San Francisco acting group called Birnam Wood in 1974–1975 presented an "underrehearsed half-thought abridgment" of *The Two Noble Kinsmen* that according to Stephen Booth was a failure (*SQ* 27 [1976]: 103–4).

128. Production details provided by Professor Abrams, who also directed a performance of 2.2 as part of a *KnT* colloquium at the University of Southern Maine in 1981.

129. Gerald M. Berkowitz, "Shakespeare in Edinburgh," *SQ* 31, 2 (1980): 165–66; Tony Howard, comp., "Census of Renaissance Drama Productions," *RORD* 22 (1979): 75; G. M. Pearce, "*The Two Noble Kinsmen*," *Cahiers Elisabéthains* 17 (1980): 100–101.

130. *Fest Folio*, Berkeley Shakespeare Festival study guide, 1985, No. 4, p. 2.

play Shakespearean cycle within three and a half years. Reviewers, both scholarly and periodical, were complimentary about the production for its general excellence and specifically for the part of the Jailer's Daughter as conceived by director Walter Scholz and played by Suzanna Peters. Joseph Stodder and Lillian Wilds noted especially Scholz's projection of "plot and character largely through use of dance and ritual . . . the fight choreography and the dance choreography were superbly wrought; each contributed much to the successful development of the ritualistic center of this production." The production and Peters's acting won Los Angeles Drama Critics Awards. It was acted seventeen times.[131]

"The ambitiously literary Jean Cocteau Repertory Company"—so designated by Maurice Charney and Arthur Ganz—presented the play in New York City in the winter of 1981. The critics did not find it "satisfyingly poetic," attributable, perhaps, to the chivalric elements adapted from *The Knight's Tale*, but they did commend the portrayal of the Jailer's Daughter, "very winningly played by Phyllis Deitschel." There were sixteen performances.[132] Director Julian Lopez-Morillas conceived of his 1985 Berkeley Shakespeare Festival *Two Noble Kinsmen* as a criticism of the rigidities of the code of chivalry, a plea by the playwrights for leaving human relationships to the benevolent vagaries of affection and chance. Phyllis Brooks was in general favorably impressed by the production. Noting that "so much of [the play] is intractable to staging," she cites as problems "long soliloquies, debates with foregone conclusions, set speeches and detailed narratives." The director's solutions, which she found successful, were "to cut, . . . to introduce figures in order to increase the on-stage energy, to complicate the dynamics, perhaps to divert. Thus, the jailer's daughter fiddled with a rag doll as she soliloquized." Some episodes not normally thought amusing, such as the theophanies and Arcite's death, "got particularly big laughs. . . . The comic scenes . . . suffered in comparison, offering . . . a less sophisticated kind of humor." In sum she points out that the director "neither insisted on the play's silliness nor tried to prevent us from deciding that the play is often quite silly. Instead he let us discover the play for ourselves." It was acted twenty-one times.[133]

The Royal Shakespeare Company's first production of *The Two Noble Kinsmen* was presented in 1986 in its new Swan Theatre at Stratford-upon-

131. Joseph H. Stodder and Lillian Wilds, "Shakespeare in Southern California and Visalia," *SQ* 31, 2 (1980): 258–59.

132. Maurice Charney and Arthur Ganz, "Shakespeare in New York City," *SQ* 33, 2 (1982): 218–22.

133. Phyllis Brooks, "Berkeley Shakespeare Festival: Summer 1985" *SQ* 37, 3 (1986): 396–97. The press reviewers praised Nancy Carlin's acting as the Jailer's Daughter and, surprisingly, Louis Latorto and Chiron Alston in the parts of Palamon and Arcite, which are seldom singled out for approval. They were thought believable and vibrant (*San Francisco Chronicle*, 30 July 1985; *Express*, 2 August 1985).

Avon, which was constructed in the shell of the old Memorial Theatre destroyed in a 1926 fire. Keith Brown considered the play-text "a formidable challenge." Shakespeare's style is "clogged" and "elliptical," and Fletcher's contribution "discrepant in tone and episodic . . . the irrelevant Morris-dance episode . . . seems an obvious device . . . for enlivening a dullish story." In spite of these difficulties, director Barry Kyle "achieves a distinct triumph" by clarifying the theme and formalizing the action with Japanese costumes. "Palamon and Arcite are crisply distinguished . . . the former . . . does often seem mad . . . Arcite is a cooler intelligence . . . Imogen Stubbs's moving and delightful . . . Gaoler's Daughter . . . provides the highlight of the evening." He criticized the "needless volume of shouting and hysteria that mars the later stages." Other reviews were also mixed. Irving Wardle liked Stubbs's "mischievous, spectacularly athletic playing" of the Jailer's Daughter and the director's decision to "abandon the traditional moral equality of the two lovers and follow the text," but he thinks the choice of *The Two Noble Kinsmen* as a "baptismal production . . . eccentric." Michael Billington finds that the play only "comes dramatically alive in the contrasted attitudes of the wanly indecisive Emilia" and the passionate and stark-mad Jailer's Daughter. Kyle may not have uncovered a masterpiece, but "he has taken the cobwebs off a theatrically workable piece." To Roger Warren, "the production matched the full range of the play, from the stylized chivalric gestures of the samurai to the world of pawky Northern English humor inhabited by the Gaoler's daughter." The kinsmen were "ideally contrasted," the Emilia of Amanda Harris and Stubbs's Jailer's Daughter were effectively and "increasingly counterpointed," Richard Moore doubled a quietly pedantic schoolmaster with a quietly humane doctor, and the temple scene, in which "the three principals were sharply differentiated [was] the powerful climax of the play." At the close the themes of male friendship and great loss were presented in bitter ironic comparison to "a final image of the destructiveness of love." His judgment is that Kyle's *Kinsmen* was "stimulating." Tony Howard notes that Kyle made numerous changes and cuts in the text, eliminating some 350 lines, including the reference to the close bond between Theseus and Pirithous, reducing Emilia's account of her friendship with Flavina, making the queens in 1.5 "a kind of stylized morbid chorus," removing references to "the force and rightness of the heavens," and subverting the text's acceptance of the justice of the "heavenly charmers" in the final scene. "In short, Barry Kyle attempted to edit the play into a tragedy," in which he was not entirely successful. Imogen Stubbs "gave a fine performance" as the Jailer's Daughter. However, Theseus and Pirithous were "brittle and thuggish" and Palamon was spiteful; Arcite was frank and generous. Howard reports that Gerard Murphy (Palamon) spoke of difficulties with the character's dense language; and that Kyle during rehearsals became sure that the play is "to a large extent Shakespearean and that all its scenes connect organically."[134]

In the spring of 1987, the production was transferred from Stratford to the RSC's third London house, the refurbished Mermaid Theatre. It opened to mixed reviews. The only press critic who reported on both versions (Michael Billington) noted that the production at the Mermaid "hangs fire a bit in the first half" and that it was "missing something of its initial spring, [but] comes most alive" in the second half in the acting of Amanda Harris as Emilia and Imogen Stubbs as the Jailer's Daughter. Charles Osborne found the play "long winded . . . hallowed only by time and its possible association with Shakespeare . . . a creaky old vehicle. . . . The verse speaking in this production . . . is sometimes poor [and Emilia is] colourless and indecisive." However, the "two noble kinsmen are splendidly acted. . . . The play is worth seeing for these two engaging performances." Jeremy Kingston thought the staging "stylish" and mentioned favorably the "simplified Japanese" costumes and the duelling sequence, especially the "tender grace" of the Kinsmen's arming. He particularly admired the Jailer's Daughter "bewitchingly played by Imogen Stubbs," who conveyed her emotions "with gesture, turns of the head, hesitations and delicate variety of voice. . . . [She] catches with rare skill and beauty the shimmering nebulous time between childhood and the maid. . . . For its visual delight and every appearance of the Gaoler's Daughter, the production is a marvel." Gerald Berkowitz observed some of the same deficiencies in the Mermaid performace that reviewers found at the Swan, but he also noted that "the play's central conflict of love and loyalty was effectively explored . . . [and that] in the subplot Imogen Stubbs perfectly caught the combination of nymphet sexuality and vulnerability in the Jailer's Daughter." There were seventy-four performances at the Swan and twenty-six at the Mermaid for an even one hundred, by far the play's longest run on record.[135]

The New Jersey Shakespeare Festival also produced the play in 1986. The first act was, except for a few lines from 1.4, entirely cut, and the action telescoped into the beginning of 2.2. In compensation, Arcite's wrestling match was shown on-stage rather than briefly reported as in the original. Palamon and Arcite were presented as twins of honor without sufficient effort made to distinguish one from the other. The best performances were those of Margaret Emory, who played the Jailer's Daughter

134. Keith Brown, "Deftly disinterred," *TLS*, 23 May 1986, p. 563; *The Times*, 10 May 1986; *The Guardian*, 10 May 1986; Roger Warren, "Shakespeare at Stratford-upon-Avon, 1986," *SQ* 38, 1 (1987): 83–84; Tony Howard, "Census of Renaissance Drama Productions (1986)," *RORD* 29 (1986–87): 50–52.

135. *Guardian*, 28 May 1987; *Daily Telegraph*, 28 May 1987; *The Times*, 27 May 1987. Gerald M. Berkowitz, "Shakespeare in London, January-July 1987," *SQ* 38, 4 (1987): 498–99.

in a fey, mildly comic manner that was pathetic without being unduly disturbing; and of Don Perkins, who effectively conveyed a happy Gerrold and an understanding Doctor, and who spoke the prologue and epilogue, all with professional distinction and without a change of costume. The morris was danced with jolly gusto and was the highlight of the production. A serious limitation was the commonplace flatness with which most of the cast delivered the lines. David Gould described the production as a "lively, clever, well-acted production—one with an emphasis on evoking laughter . . . the roles of Theseus, Pirithous, and Hippolyta . . . were greatly reduced. . . . Robin Leary . . . was a most attractive Emilia, one who could very well cause two lifelong friends to fight for her. Brian Hugh O'Neill was an endearingly funny and gallant Arcite . . . [but] Rick Parks did not fare quite as well as Palamon, due largely to the one-note nature of the character. . . . Don Perkins . . . was at his best as Gerrold, the Mountebank/schoolmaster. Delivering the Prologue with a devilish grin . . . he set the tone for the entire play. . . . As the Jailer's Daughter, Margaret Emory was the best of a very good cast. She handled the fluctuating moods of this complex character masterfully. . . . Her movement into madness was quite believable . . . she evoked both laughter . . . and sympathy." Gould concluded by posing a question: "Playing *The Two Noble Kinsmen* for laughs does present a problem—the ending. After an evening of laughter, wrestling, and dancing, what is to be made of the death of Arcite, the qualified pairing of Palamon and Emilia, and the matching of the Jailer's Daughter with a man she believes is someone else?" Nevertheless, he found the presentation truly entertaining, "worthy of sharing a summer with *Julius Caesar* and *Antony and Cleopatra.*" The Festival acted the play twenty-six times.[136]

It is apparent from this performance history that the part of the Jailer's Daughter is by a wide margin the most effective on stage, beginning with Jean Forbes-Robertsons' portrayal of 1928. Although there are occasional criticisms that the role is overplayed or that it compares poorly with that of Ophelia, even those reviewers who are not completely pleased attest to its significance to the performance. There is considerable diversity observable in the idea of the role, varying from palpable madness to mere discontinuity of the character's perception of the real world. The task of differentiating the two noble cousins is a more difficult challenge that some directors have successfully met but others have not. There is no doubt that they must be equal in chivalric honor, which tends to have a leveling effect on the stage. This arises from the text and is not easily overcome, but a few productions have managed it. The part of Emilia has met with equally mixed success and this again is implicit in the dramatic situation. Consid-

136. David Gould, *The Two Noble Kinsmen, BNYSS* 5 (1987): 21–22.

erable directorial ingenuity is called for to make the character seem something other than indecisive. In several productions it has turned out that the morris dance scene, taking into account only purely theatrical considerations, is the peak of the play, lending "a spirit of country jollity" (as the note to Beaumont's masque says) that is apparently welcome to audiences.

1. Source

From *The Canterbury Tales: The Knyghtes Tale*

By Geoffrey Chaucer; in *The Riverside Chaucer*, general editor Larry D. Benson, 1987

Heere bigynneth the Knyghtes Tale.

Iamque domos patrias, Scithice post aspera gentis Prelia, laurigero, &c.

Whilom, as olde stories tellen us,
Ther was a duc that highte Theseus;
Of Atthenes he was lord and governour,
And in his tyme swich a conquerour
That gretter was ther noon under the sonne.
Ful many riche contree hadde he wonne;
What with his wysdom and his chivalrie,
He conquered al the regne of Femenye,
That whilom was ycleped Scithia,
And weddede the queene Ypolita,
And broghte hire hoom with hym in his contree
With muchel glorie and greet solempnytee,
And eek hir yonge suster Emelye.
And thus with victorie and with melodye
Lete I this noble duc to Atthenes ryde,
And al his hoost in armes hym bisyde.
And certes, if it nere to long to heere,
I wolde have toold yow fully the manere
How wonnen was the regne of Femenye
By Theseus and by his chivalrye;
And of the grete bataille for the nones
Bitwixen Atthenes and Amazones;
And how asseged was Ypolita,
The faire, hardy queene of Scithia;
And of the feste that was at hir weddynge,
And of the tempest at hir hoom-comynge;
But al that thyng I moot as now forbere.
I have, God woot, a large feeld to ere,
And wayke been the oxen in my plough.
The remenant of the tale is long ynough.
I wol nat letten eek noon of this route;
Lat every felawe telle his tale aboute,
And lat se now who shal the soper wynne;
And ther I lefte, I wol ayeyn bigynne.

This duc, of whom I make mencioun,
Whan he was come almoost unto the toun,
In al his wele and in his mooste pride,
He was war, as he caste his eye aside,
Where that ther kneled in the heighe weye
A compaignye of ladyes, tweye and tweye,
Ech after oother clad in clothes blake;
But swich a cry and swich a wo they make
That in this world nys creature lyvynge
That herde swich another waymentynge;
And of this cry they nolde nevere stenten
Til they the reynes of his brydel henten.
"What folk been ye, that at myn homcomynge
Perturben so my feste with criynge?"
Quod Theseus. "Have ye so greet envye
Of myn honour, that thus compleyne and crye?
Or who hath yow mysboden or offended?
And telleth me if it may been amended,
And why that ye been clothed thus in blak."
The eldeste lady of hem alle spak,
Whan she hadde swowned with a deedly cheere,
That it was routhe for to seen and heere;
She seyde, "Lord, to whom Fortune hath yiven
Victorie, and as a conqueror to lyven,
Nat greveth us youre glorie and youre honour,
But we biseken mercy and socour.
Have mercy on oure wo and oure distresse!
Som drope of pitee, thurgh thy gentillesse,
Upon us wrecched wommen lat thou falle,
For, certes, lord, ther is noon of us alle
That she ne hath been a duchesse or a queene.
Now be we caytyves, as it is wel seene,
Thanked be Fortune and hire false wheel,
That noon estaat assureth to be weel.
And certes, lord, to abyden youre presence,
Heere in this temple of the goddesse Clemence
We han ben waitynge al this fourtenyght.
Now help us, lord, sith it is in thy myght.
"I, wrecche, which that wepe and wayle thus,
Was whilom wyf to kyng Cappaneus,
That starf at Thebes—cursed be that day!—
And alle we that been in this array
And maken al this lamentacioun,
We losten alle oure housbondes at that toun,

Whil that the seege theraboute lay.
And yet now the olde Creon—weylaway!—
That lord is now of Thebes the citee,
Fulfild of ire and of iniquitee,
He, for despit and for his tirannye,
To do the dede bodyes vileynye
Of alle oure lordes whiche that been yslawe,
Hath alle the bodyes on a heep ydrawe,
And wol nat suffren hem, by noon assent,
Neither to been yburyed nor ybrent,
But maketh houndes ete hem in despit."
 And with that word, withouten moore respit,
They fillen gruf and criden pitously,
"Have on us wrecched wommen som mercy,
And lat oure sorwe synken in thyn herte."
 This gentil duc doun from his courser sterte
With herte pitous, whan he herde hem speke.
Hym thoughte that his herte wolde breke,
Whan he saugh hem so pitous and so maat,
That whilom weren of so greet estaat;
And in his armes he hem alle up hente,
And hem conforteth in ful good entente,
And swoor his ooth, as he was trewe knyght,
He wolde doon so ferforthly his myght
Upon the tiraunt Creon hem to wreke
That al the peple of Grece sholde speke
How Creon was of Theseus yserved
As he that hadde his deeth ful wel deserved.
And right anoon, withouten moore abood,
His baner he desplayeth, and forth rood
To Thebes-ward, and al his hoost biside.
No neer Atthenes wolde he go ne ride,
Ne take his ese fully half a day,
But onward on his wey that nyght he lay,
And sente anon Ypolita the queene,
And Emelye, hir yonge suster sheene,
Unto the toun of Atthenes to dwelle,
And forth he rit; ther is namoore to telle.
 The rede statue of Mars, with spere and targe,
So shyneth in his white baner large
That alle the feeldes glyteren up and doun;
And by his baner born is his penoun
Of gold ful riche, in which ther was ybete
The Mynotaur, which that he wan in Crete.
Thus rit this duc, thus rit this conquerour,

And in his hoost of chivalrie the flour,
Til that he cam to Thebes and alighte
Faire in a feeld, ther as he thoughte to fighte.
But shortly for to speken of this thyng,
With Creon, which that was of Thebes kyng,
He faught, and slough hym manly as a knyght
In pleyn bataille, and putte the folk to flyght;
And by assaut he wan the citee after,
And rente adoun bothe wall and sparre and rafter;
And to the ladyes he restored agayn
The bones of hir freendes that were slayn,
To doon obsequies, as was tho the gyse.
But it were al to longe for to devyse
The grete clamour and the waymentynge
That the ladyes made at the brennynge
Of the bodies, and the grete honour
That Theseus, the noble conquerour,
Dooth to the ladyes, whan they from hym wente;
But shortly for to telle is myn entente.
Whan that this worthy duc, this Theseus,
Hath Creon slayn and wonne Thebes thus,
Stille in that feeld he took al nyght his reste,
And dide with al the contree as hym leste.
To ransake in the taas of bodyes dede,
Hem for to strepe of harneys and of wede,
The pilours diden bisynesse and cure
After the bataille and disconfiture.
And so bifel that in the taas they founde,
Thurgh-girt with many a grevous blody wounde,
Two yonge knyghtes liggynge by and by,
Bothe in oon armes, wroght ful richely,
Of whiche two Arcita highte that oon,
And that oother knyght highte Palamon.
Nat fully quyke, ne fully dede they were,
But by hir cote-armures and by hir gere
The heraudes knewe hem best in special
As they that weren of the blood roial
Of Thebes, and of sustren two yborn.
Out of the taas the pilours han hem torn,
And han hem caried softe unto the tente
Of Theseus; and he ful soone hem sente
To Atthenes, to dwellen in prisoun
Perpetuelly—he nolde no raunsoun.
And whan this worthy duc hath thus ydon,
He took his hoost, and hoom he rit anon

With laurer crowned as a conquerour;
And ther he lyveth in joye and in honour
Terme of his lyf; what nedeth wordes mo?
And in a tour, in angwissh and in wo,
This Palamon and his felawe Arcite
For everemoore; ther may no gold hem quite.
This passeth yeer by yeer and day by day,
Till it fil ones, in a morwe of May,
That Emelye, that fairer was to sene
Than is the lylie upon his stalke grene,
And fressher than the May with floures newe—
For with the rose colour stroof hire hewe,
I noot which was the fyner of hem two—
Er it were day, as was hir wone to do,
She was arisen and al redy dight,
For May wole have no slogardie anyght.
The sesoun priketh every gentil herte,
And maketh it out of his slep to sterte,
And seith "Arys, and do thyn observaunce."
This maked Emelye have remembraunce
To doon honour to May, and for to ryse.
Yclothed was she fressh, for to devyse:
Hir yelow heer was broyded in a tresse
Bihynde hir bak, a yerde long, I gesse.
And in the gardyn, at the sonne upriste,
She walketh up and doun, and as hire liste
She gadereth floures, party white and rede,
To make a subtil gerland for hire hede;
And as an aungel hevenysshly she soong.
The grete tour, that was so thikke and stroong,
Which of the castel was the chief dongeoun
(Ther as the knyghtes weren in prisoun
Of which I tolde yow and tellen shal),
Was evene joynant to the gardyn wal
Ther as this Emelye hadde hir pleyynge.
Bright was the sonne and cleer that morwenynge,
And Palamoun, this woful prisoner,
As was his wone, by leve of his gayler,
Was risen and romed in a chambre an heigh,
In which he al the noble citee seigh,
And eek the gardyn, ful of braunches grene,
Ther as this fresshe Emelye the shene
Was in hire walk, and romed up and doun.
This sorweful prisoner, this Palamoun,
Goth in the chambre romynge to and fro

And to hymself compleynynge of his wo.
That he was born, ful ofte he seyde, "allas!"
And so bifel, by adventure or cas,
That thurgh a wyndow, thikke of many a barre
Of iren greet and square as any sparre,
He cast his eye upon Emelya,
And therwithal he bleynte and cride, "A!"
As though he stongen were unto the herte.
And with that cry Arcite anon up sterte
And seyde, "Cosyn myn, what eyleth thee,
That art so pale and deedly on to see?
Why cridestow? Who hath thee doon offence?
For Goddes love, taak al in pacience
Oure prisoun, for it may noon oother be.
Fortune hath yeven us this adversitee.
Som wikke aspect or disposicioun
Of Saturne, by som constellacioun,
Hath yeven us this, although we hadde it sworn;
So stood the hevene whan that we were born.
We moste endure it; this is the short and playn."
This Palamon answerde and seyde agayn,
"Cosyn, for sothe, of this opinioun
Thow hast a veyn ymaginacioun.
This prison caused me nat for to crye,
But I was hurt right now thurghout myn ye
Into myn herte, that wol my bane be.
The fairnesse of that lady that I see
Yond in the gardyn romen to and fro
Is cause of al my criyng and my wo.
I noot wher she be womman or goddesse,
But Venus is it soothly, as I gesse."
And therwithal on knees doun he fil,
And seyde, "Venus, if it be thy wil
Yow in this gardyn thus to transfigure
Bifore me, sorweful, wrecched creature,
Out of this prisoun help that we may scapen.
And if so be my destynee be shapen
By eterne word to dyen in prisoun,
Of oure lynage have som compassioun,
That is so lowe ybroght by tirannye."
And with that word Arcite gan espye
Wher as this lady romed to and fro,
And with that sighte hir beautee hurte hym so,
That, if that Palamon was wounded sore,
Arcite is hurt as muche as he, or moore.

And with a sigh he seyde pitously,
"The fresshe beautee sleeth me sodeynly
Of hire that rometh in the yonder place;
And but I have hir mercy and hir grace,
That I may seen hire atte leeste weye,
I nam but deed; ther nis namoore to seye."
This Palamon, whan he tho wordes herde,
Dispitously he looked and answerde,
"Wheither seistow this in ernest or in pley?"
"Nay," quod Arcite, "in ernest, by my fey!
God helpe me so, me list ful yvele pleye."
This Palamon gan knytte his browes tweye.
"It nere," quod he, "to thee no greet honour
For to be fals, ne for to be traitour
To me, that am thy cosyn and thy brother
Ysworn ful depe, and ech of us til oother,
That nevere, for to dyen in the peyne,
Til that the deeth departe shal us tweyne,
Neither of us in love to hyndre oother,
Ne in noon oother cas, my leeve brother,
But that thou sholdest trewely forthren me
In every cas, as I shal forthren thee—This was thyn ooth, and
myn also, certeyn;
I woot right wel, thou darst it nat withseyn.
Thus artow of my conseil, out of doute,
And now thow woldest falsly been aboute
To love my lady, whom I love and serve,
And evere shal til that myn herte sterve.
Nay, certes, false Arcite, thow shalt nat so.
I loved hire first, and tolde thee my wo
As to my conseil and my brother sworn
To forthre me, as I have toold biforn.
For which thou art ybounden as a knyght
To helpen me, if it lay in thy myght,
Or elles artow fals, I dar wel seyn."
This Arcite ful proudly spak ageyn:
"Thow shalt," quod he, "be rather fals than I;
And thou art fals, I telle thee outrely,
For paramour I loved hire first er thow.
What wiltow seyen? Thou woost nat yet now
Wheither she be a womman or goddesse!
Thyn is affeccioun of hoolynesse,
And myn is love as to a creature;
For which I tolde thee myn aventure
As to my cosyn and my brother sworn.

I pose that thow lovedest hire biforn;
Wostow nat wel the olde clerkes sawe,
That 'who shal yeve a lovere any lawe?'
Love is a gretter lawe, by my pan,
Than may be yeve to any erthely man;
And therfore positif lawe and swich decree
Is broken al day for love in ech degree.
A man moot nedes love, maugree his heed;
He may nat fleen it, thogh he sholde be deed,
Al be she mayde, or wydwe, or elles wyf.
And eek it is nat likly al thy lyf
To stonden in hir grace; namoore shal I;
For wel thou woost thyselven, verraily,
That thou and I be dampned to prisoun
Perpetuelly; us gayneth no raunsoun.
We stryve as dide the houndes for the boon;
They foughte al day, and yet hir part was noon.
Ther cam a kyte, whil that they were so wrothe,
And baar awey the boon bitwixe hem bothe.
And therfore, at the kynges court, my brother,
Ech man for hymself, ther is noon oother.
Love, if thee list, for I love and ay shal;
And soothly, leeve brother, this is al.
Heere in this prisoun moote we endure,
And everich of us take his aventure."

Greet was the strif and long bitwix hem tweye,
If that I hadde leyser for to seye;
But to th'effect. It happed on a day,
To telle it yow as shortly as I may,
A worthy duc that highte Perotheus,
That felawe was unto duc Theseus
Syn thilke day that they were children lite,
Was come to Atthenes his felawe to visite,
And for to pleye as he was wont to do;
For in this world he loved no man so,
And he loved hym als tendrely agayn.
So wel they lovede, as olde bookes sayn,
That whan that oon was deed, soothly to telle,
His felawe wente and soughte hym doun in helle—
But of that storie list me nat to write.
Duc Perotheus loved wel Arcite,
And hadde hym knowe at Thebes yeer by yere,
And finally at requeste and preyere
Of Perotheus, withouten any raunsoun,
Duc Theseus hym leet out of prisoun

Frely to goon wher that hym liste over al,
In swich a gyse as I you tellen shal.
    This was the forward, pleynly for t'endite,
Bitwixen Theseus and hym Arcite:
That if so were that Arcite were yfounde
Evere in his lif, by day or nyght, oo stounde
In any contree of this Theseus,
And he were caught, it was acorded thus,
That with a swerd he sholde lese his heed.
Ther nas noon oother remedie ne reed;
But taketh his leve, and homward he him spedde.
Lat hym be war! His nekke lith to wedde.
    How greet a sorwe suffreth now Arcite!
The deeth he feeleth thurgh his herte smyte;
He wepeth, wayleth, crieth pitously;
To sleen hymself he waiteth prively.
He seyde, "Allas that day that I was born!
Now is my prisoun worse than biforn;
Now is me shape eternally to dwelle
Noght in purgatorie, but in helle.
Allas, that evere knew I Perotheus!
For elles hadde I dwelled with Theseus,
Yfetered in his prisoun everemo.
Thanne hadde I been in blisse and nat in wo.
Oonly the sighte of hire whom that I serve,
Though that I nevere hir grace may deserve,
Wolde han suffised right ynough for me.
O deere cosyn Palamon," quod he,
"Thyn is the victorie of this aventure.
Ful blisfully in prison maistow dure—
In prison? Certes nay, but in paradys!
Wel hath Fortune yturned thee the dys,
That hast the sighte of hire, and I th'absence.
For possible is, syn thou hast hire presence,
And art a knyght, a worthy and an able,
That by som cas, syn Fortune is chaungeable,
Thow maist to thy desir somtyme atteyne.
But I, that am exiled and bareyne
Of alle grace, and in so greet dispeir
That ther nys erthe, water, fir, ne eir,
Ne creature that of hem maked is,
That may me helpe or doon confort in this,
Wel oughte I sterve in wanhope and distresse.
Farwel my lif, my lust, and my gladnesse!
    "Allas, why pleynen folk so in commune

On purveiaunce of God, or of Fortune,
That yeveth hem ful ofte in many a gyse
Wel bettre than they kan hemself devyse?
Som man desireth for to han richesse,
That cause is of his mordre or greet siknesse;
And som man wolde out of his prisoun fayn,
That in his hous is of his meynee slayn.
Infinite harmes been in this mateere.
We witen nat what thing we preyen heere;
We faren as he that dronke is as a mous.
A dronke man woot wel he hath an hous,
But he noot which the righte wey is thider,
And to a dronke man the wey is slider.
And certes, in this world so faren we;
We seken faste after felicitee,
But we goon wrong ful often, trewely.
Thus may we seyen alle, and namely I,
That wende and hadde a greet opinioun
That if I myghte escapen from prisoun,
Thanne hadde I been in joye and parfit heele,
Ther now I am exiled fro my wele.
Syn that I may nat seen you, Emelye,
I nam but deed; ther nys no remedye."
Upon that oother syde Palamon,
Whan that he wiste Arcite was agon,
Swich sorwe he maketh that the grete tour
Resouneth of his youlyng and clamour.
The pure fettres on his shynes grete
Weren of his bittre, salte teeres wete.
"Allas," quod he, "Arcita, cosyn myn,
Of al oure strif, God woot, the fruyt is thyn.
Thow walkest now in Thebes at thy large,
And of my wo thow yevest litel charge.
Thou mayst, syn thou hast wisdom and manhede,
Assemblen all the folk of oure kynrede,
And make a werre so sharp on this citee
That by som aventure or some tretee
Thow mayst have hire to lady and to wyf
For whom that I moste nedes lese my lyf.
For, as by wey of possibilitee,
Sith thou art at thy large, of prisoun free,
And art a lord, greet is thyn avauntage
Moore than is myn, that sterve here in a cage.
For I moot wepe and wayle, whil I lyve,
With al the wo that prison may me yive,

And eek with peyne that love me yeveth also,
That doubleth al my torment and my wo."
Therwith the fyr of jalousie up sterte
Withinne his brest, and hente him by the herte
So woodly that he lyk was to biholde
The boxtree or the asshen dede and colde.
    Thanne seyde he, "O crueel goddes that governe
This world with byndyng of youre word eterne,
And writen in the table of atthamaunt
Youre parlement and youre eterne graunt,
What is mankynde moore unto you holde
Than is the sheep that rouketh in the folde?
For slayn is man right as another beest,
And dwelleth eek in prison and arreest,
And hath siknesse and greet adversitee,
And ofte tymes giltelees, pardee.
    "What governance is in this prescience,
That giltelees tormenteth innocence?
And yet encresseth this al my penaunce,
That man is bounded to his observaunce,
For Goddes sake, to letten of his wille,
Ther as a beest may al his lust fulfille.
And whan a beest is deed he hath no peyne;
But man after his deeth moot wepe and pleyne,
Though in this world he have care and wo.
Withouten doute it may stonden so.
The answere of this lete I to dyvynys,
But wel I woot that in this world greet pyne ys.
Allas, I se a serpent or a theef,
That many a trewe man hath doon mescheef,
Goon at his large, and where hym list may turne.
But I moot been in prisoun thurgh Saturne,
And eek thurgh Juno, jalous and eek wood,
That hath destroyed wel ny al the blood
Of Thebes with his waste walles wyde;
And Venus sleeth me on that oother syde
For jalousie and fere of hym Arcite."
    Now wol I stynte of Palamon a lite,
And lete hym in his prisoun stille dwelle,
And of Arcita forth I wol yow telle.
    The somer passeth, and the nyghtes longe
Encressen double wise the peynes stronge
Bothe of the lovere and the prisoner.
I noot which hath the wofuller mester.
For, shortly for to seyn, this Palamoun

Perpetuelly is dampned to prisoun,
In cheynes and in fettres to been deed;
And Arcite is exiled upon his heed
For everemo, as out of that contree,
Ne nevere mo ne shal his lady see.
Yow loveres axe I now this questioun:
Who hath the worse, Arcite or Palamoun?
That oon may seen his lady day by day,
But in prison he moot dwelle alway;
That oother wher hym list may ride or go,
But seen his lady shal he nevere mo.
Now demeth as yow liste, ye that kan,
For I wol telle forth as I bigan.

Explicit prima pars

Sequitur pars secunda

Whan that Arcite to Thebes comen was,
Ful ofte a day he swelte and seyde "Allas!"
For seen his lady shal he nevere mo.
And shortly to concluden al his wo,
So muche sorwe hadde nevere creature
That is, or shal, whil that the world may dure.
His slep, his mete, his drynke, is hym biraft,
That lene he wex and drye as is a shaft;
His eyen holwe and grisly to biholde,
His hewe falow and pale as asshen colde,
And solitarie he was and evere allone,
And waillynge al the nyght, makynge his mone;
And if he herde song or instrument,
Thanne wolde he wepe, he myghte nat be stent.
So feble eek were his spiritz, and so lowe,
And chaunged so, that no man koude knowe
His speche nor his voys, though men it herde.
And in his geere for al the world he ferde
Nat oonly lik the loveris maladye
Of Hereos, but rather lyk manye,
Engendred of humour malencolik
Biforen, in his celle fantastik.
And shortly, turned was al up so doun
Bothe habit and eek disposicioun
Of hym, this woful lovere daun Arcite.
What sholde I al day of his wo endite?
Whan he endured hadde a yeer or two
This crueel torment and this peyne and wo,

At Thebes, in his contree, as I seyde,
Upon a nyght in sleep as he hym leyde,
Hym thoughte how that the wynged god Mercurie
Biforn hym stood and bad hym to be murie.
His slepy yerde in hond he bar uprighte;
And hat he werede upon his heris brighte.
Arrayed was this god, as he took keep,
As he was whan that Argus took his sleep;
And seyde hym thus: "To Atthenes shaltou wende,
Ther is thee shapen of thy wo an ende."
And with that word Arcite wook and sterte.
"Now trewely, hou soore that me smerte,"
Quod he, "to Atthenes right now wol I fare,
Ne for the drede of deeth shal I nat spare
To se my lady, that I love and serve.
In hire presence I recche nat to sterve."
    And with that word he caughte a greet mirour,
And saugh that chaunged was al his colour,
And saugh his visage al in another kynde.
And right anon it ran hym in his mynde,
That, sith his face was so disfigured
Of maladye the which he hadde endured,
He myghte wel, if that he bar hym lowe,
Lyve in Atthenes everemoore unknowe,
And seen his lady wel ny day by day.
And right anon he chaunged his array,
And cladde hym as a povre laborer,
And al allone, save oonly a squier
That knew his privetee and al his cas,
Which was disgised povrely as he was,
To Atthenes is he goon the nexte way.
And to the court he wente upon a day,
And at the gate he profreth his servyse
To drugge and drawe, what so men wol devyse.
And shortly of this matere for to seyn,
He fil in office with a chamberleyn
The which that dwellynge was with Emelye,
For he was wys and koude soone espye,
Of every servaunt, which that serveth here.
Wel koude he hewen wode, and water bere,
For he was yong and myghty for the nones,
And therto he was long and big of bones
To doon that any wight kan hym devyse.
A yeer or two he was in this servyse,
Page of the chambre of Emelye the brighte,

And Philostrate he seyde that he highte.
But half so wel biloved a man as he
Ne was ther nevere in court of his degree;
He was so gentil of condicioun
That thurghout al the court was his renoun.
They seyden that it were a charitee
That Theseus wolde enhauncen his degree,
And putten hym in worshipful servyse,
Ther as he myghte his vertu excercise.
And thus withinne a while his name is spronge,
Bothe of his dedes and his goode tonge,
That Theseus hath taken hym so neer
That of his chambre he made hym a squier,
And gaf hym gold to mayntene his degree.
And eek men broghte hym out of his contree,
From yeer to yeer, ful pryvely his rente;
But honestly and slyly he it spente,
That no man wondred how that he it hadde.
And thre yeer in this wise his lif he ladde,
And bar hym so, in pees and eek in werre,
Ther was no man that Theseus hath derre.
And in this blisse lete I now Arcite,
And speke I wole of Palamon a lite.
In derknesse and horrible and strong prisoun
Thise seven yeer hath seten Palamoun
Forpyned, what for wo and for distresse.
Who feeleth double soor and hevynesse
But Palamon, that love destreyneth so
That wood out of his wit he goth for wo?
And eek therto he is a prisoner
Perpetuelly, noght oonly for a yer.
Who koude ryme in Englyssh proprely
His martirdom? For sothe it am nat I;
Therfore I passe as lightly as I may.
It fel that in the seventhe yer, of May
The thridde nyght (as olde bookds seyn,
That al this storie tellen moore pleyn),
Were it by aventure or destynee—
As, whan a thyng is shapen, it shal be—
That soone after the mydnyght Palamoun,
By helpyng of a freend, brak his prisoun
And fleeth the citee faste as he may go.
For he hadde yeve his gayler drynke so
Of a clarree maad of a certeyn wyn,
With nercotikes and opie of Thebes fyn,

That al that nyght, thogh that men wolde him shake,
The gayler sleep; he myghte nat awake.
And thus he fleeth as faste as evere he may.
The nyght was short and faste by the day
That nedes cost he moot hymselven hyde,
And til a grove faste ther bisyde
With dredeful foot thanne stalketh Palamon.
For, shortly, this was his opinion:
That in that grove he wolde hym hyde al day,
And in the nyght thanne wolde he take his way
To Thebes-ward, his freendes for to preye
On Theseus to helpe him to werreye;
And shortly, outher he wolde lese his lif
Or wynnen Emelye unto his wyf.
This is th'effect and his entente pleyn.
  Now wol I turne to Arcite ageyn,
That litel wiste how ny that was his care,
Til that Fortune had broght him in the snare.
  The bisy larke, messager of day,
Salueth in hir song the morwe gray,
And firy Phebus riseth up so bright
That al the orient laugheth of the light,
And with his stremes dryeth in the greves
The silver dropes hangynge on the leves.
And Arcita, that in the court roial
With Theseus is squier principal,
Is risen and looketh on the myrie day.
And for to doon his observaunce to May,
Remembrynge on the poynt of his desir,
He on a courser, startlynge as the fir,
Is riden into the feeldes hym to pleye,
Out of the court, were it a myle or tweye.
And to the grove of which that I yow tolde
By aventure his wey he gan to holde
To maken hym a gerland of the greves,
Were it of wodebynde or hawethorn leves,
And loude he song ayeyn the sonne shene:
"May, with alle thy floures and thy grene,
Welcome be thou, faire, fresshe May,
In hope that I som grene gete may."
And from his courser, with a lusty herte,
Into the grove ful hastily he sterte,
And in a path he rometh up and doun,
Ther as by aventure this Palamoun
Was in a bussh, that no man myghte hym se,

For soore afered of his deeth was he.
No thyng ne knew he that it was Arcite;
God woot he wolde have trowed it ful lite.
But sooth is seyd, go sithen many yeres,
That "feeld hath eyen and the wode hath eres."
It is ful fair a man to bere hym evene,
For al day meeteth men at unset stevene.
Ful litel woot Arcite of his felawe,
That was so ny to herknen al his sawe,
For in the bussh he sitteth now ful stille.
Whan that Arcite hadde romed al his fille,
And songen al the roundel lustily,
Into a studie he fil sodeynly,
As doon thise loveres in hir queynte geres,
Now in the crope, now doun in the breres,
Now up, now doun, as boket in a welle.
Right as the Friday, soothly for to telle,
Now it shyneth, now it reyneth faste,
Right so kan geery Venus overcaste
The hertes of hir folk; right as hir day
Is gereful, right so chaungeth she array.
Selde is the Friday al the wowke ylike.
Whan that Arcite had songe, he gan to sike
And sette hym doun withouten any moore.
"Allas," quod he, "that day that I was bore!
How longe, Juno, thurgh thy crueltee,
Woltow werreyen Thebes the citee?
Allas, ybroght is to confusioun
The blood roial of Cadme and Amphioun—
Of Cadmus, which that was the firste man
That Thebes bulte, or first the toun bigan,
And of the citee first was crouned kyng.
Of his lynage am I and his ofspryng
By verray ligne, as of the stok roial,
And now I am so caytyf and so thral,
That he that is my mortal enemy,
I serve hym as his squier povrely.
And yet dooth Juno me wel moore shame,
For I dar noght biknowe myn owene name;
But ther as I was wont to highte Arcite,
Now highte I Philostrate, noght worth a myte.
Allas, thou felle Mars! Allas, Juno!
Thus hath youre ire oure lynage al fordo,
Save oonly me and wrecched Palamoun,
That Theseus martireth in prisoun.

And over al this, to sleen me outrely
Love hath his firy dart so brennyngly
Ystiked thurgh my trewe, careful herte
That shapen was my deeth erst than my sherte.
Ye sleen me with youre eyen, Emelye!
Ye been the cause wherfore that I dye.
Of al the remenant of myn oother care
Ne sette I nat the montance of a tare,
So that I koude doon aught to youre plesaunce."
And with that word he fil doun in a traunce
A longe tyme, and after he up sterte.
    This Palamoun, that thoughte that thurgh his herte
He felte a coold swerd sodeynliche glyde,
For ire he quook; no lenger wolde he byde.
And whan that he had herd Arcites tale,
As he were wood, with face deed and pale,
He stirte hym up out of the bushkes thikke
And seide: "Arcite, false traytour wikke,
Now artow hent, that lovest my lady so,
For whom that I have al this peyne and wo,
And art my blood, and to my conseil sworn,
As I ful ofte have told thee heerbiforn,
And hast byjaped heere duc Theseus,
And falsly chaunged hast thy name thus!
I wol be deed, or elles thou shalt dye.
Thou shalt nat love my lady Emelye,
But I wol love hire oonly and namo;
For I am Palamon, thy mortal foo.
And though that I no wepene have in this place,
But out of prison am astert by grace,
I drede noght that outher thow shalt dye,
Or thow ne shalt nat loven Emelye.
Chees which thou wolt, or thou shalt nat asterte!"
    This Arcite, with ful despitous herte,
Whan he hym knew, and hadde his tale herd,
As fiers as leon pulled out his swerd,
And seyde thus: "By God that sit above,
Nere it that thou art sik and wood for love,
And eek that thow no wepne hast in this place,
Thou sholdest nevere out of this grove pace,
That thou ne sholdest dyen of myn hond.
For I defye the seurete and the bond
Which that thou seist that I have maad to thee.
What! Verray fool, thynk wel that love is free,
And I wol love hire maugree al thy myght!

But for as muche thou art a worthy knyght
And wilnest to darreyne hire by bataille,
Have heer my trouthe; tomorwe I wol nat faille,
Withoute wityng of any oother wight,
That heere I wol be founden as a knyght,
And bryngen harneys right ynough for thee;
And ches the beste, and leef the worste for me.
And mete and drynke this nyght wol I brynge
Ynough for thee, and clothes for thy beddynge.
And if so be that thou my lady wynne,
And sle me in this wode ther I am inne,
Thow mayst wel have thy lady as for me."
    This Palamon answerde, "I grounte it thee."
And thus they been departed til amorwe,
Whan ech of hem had leyd his feith to borwe.
    O Cupide, out of alle charitee!
O regne, that wolt no felawe have with thee!
Ful sooth is seyd that love ne lordshipe
Wol noght, his thankes, have no felawshipe.
Wel fynden that Arcite and Palamoun.
Arcite is riden anon unto the toun,
And on the morwe, er it were dayes light,
Ful prively two harneys hath he dight,
Bothe suffisaunt and mete to darreyne
The bataille in the feeld bitwix hem tweyne;
And on his hors, allone as he was born,
He carieth al the harneys hym biforn.
And in the grove, at tyme and place yset,
This Arcite and this Palamon ben met.
To chaungen gan the colour in hir face;
Right as the hunters in the regne of Trace,
That stondeth at the gappe with a spere,
Whan hunted is the leon or the bere,
And hereth hym come russhyng in the greves,
And breketh bothe bowes and the leves,
And thynketh, "Heere cometh my mortal enemy!
Withoute faille, he moot be deed, or I,
For outher I moot sleen hym at the gappe,
Or he moot sleen me, if that me myshappe."
So ferden they in chaungyng of hir hewe,
As fer as everich of hem oother knewe.
    Ther nas no good day, ne no saluyng,
But streight, withouten word or rehersyng,
Everich of hem heelp for to armen oother
As freendly as he were his owene brother;

And after that, with sharpe speres stronge
They foynen ech at oother wonder longe.
Thou myghtest wene that this Palamon
In his fightyng were a wood leon,
And as a crueel tigre was Arcite;
As wilde bores gonne they to smyte,
That frothen whit as foom for ire wood.
Up to the ancle foghte they in hir blood.
And in this wise I lete hem fightyng dwelle,
And forth I wole of Theseus yow telle.
    The destinee, ministre general,
That executeth in the world over al
The purveiaunce that God hath seyn biforn,
So strong it is that, though the world had sworn
The contrarie of a thyng by ye or nay,
Yet somtyme it shal fallen on a day
That falleth nat eft withinne a thousand yeer.
For certeinly, oure appetites heer,
Be it of werre, or pees, or hate, or love,
Al is this reuled by the sighte above.
    This mene I now by myghty Theseus,
That for to hunten is so desirus,
And namely at the grete hert in May,
That in his bed ther daweth hym no day
That he nys clad, and redy for to ryde
With hunte and horn and houndes hym bisyde.
For in his huntyng hath he swich delit
That it is al his joye and appetit
To been hymself the grete hertes bane,
For after Mars he serveth now Dyane.
    Cleer was the day, as I have toold er this,
And Theseus with alle joye and blis,
With his Ypolita, the faire queene,
And Emelye, clothed al in grene,
On huntyng be they riden roially.
And to the grove that stood ful faste by,
In which ther was an hert, as men hym tolde,
Duc Theseus the streighte wey hath holde.
And to the launde he rideth hym ful right,
For thider was the hert wont have his flight,
And over a brook, and so forth on his weye.
This duc wol han a cours at hym or tweye
With houndes swiche as that hym list comaunde.
    And whan this duc was come unto the launde,
Under the sonne he looketh, and anon

He was war of Arcite and Palamon,
That foughten breme as it were bores two.
The brighte swerdes wenten to and fro
So hidously that with the leeste strook
It semed as it wolde felle an ook.
But what they were, no thyng he ne woot.
This duc his courser with his spores smoot,
And at a stert he was bitwix hem two,
And pulled out a swerd and cride, "Hoo!
Namoore, up peyne of lesynge of youre heed!
By myghty Mars, he shal anon be deed
That smyteth any strook that I may seen.
But telleth me what myster men ye been,
That been so hardy for to fighten heere
Withouten juge or oother officere,
As it were in a lystes roially."
    This Palamon answerde hastily
And seyde, "Sire, what nedeth wordes mo?
We have the deeth disserved bothe two.
Two woful wrecches been we, two caytyves,
That been encombred of oure owene lyves;
And as thou art a rightful lord and juge,
Ne yif us neither mercy ne refuge,
But sle me first, for seinte charitee!
But sle my felawe eek as wel as me;
Or sle hym first, for though thow knowest it lite,
This is thy mortal foo, this is Arcite,
That from thy lond is banysshed on his heed,
For which he hath deserved to be deed.
For this is he that cam unto thy gate
And seyde that he highte Philostrate.
Thus hath he japed thee ful many a yer,
And thou hast maked hym thy chief squier;
And this is he that loveth Emelye.
For sith the day is come that I shal dye,
I make pleynly my confessioun
That I am thilke woful Palamoun
That hath thy prisoun broken wikkedly.
I am thy mortal foo, and it am I
That loveth so hoote Emelye the brighte
That I wol dye present in hir sighte.
Wherfore I axe deeth and my juwise;
But sle my felawe in the same wise,
For bothe han we deserved to be slayn."
    This worthy duc answerde anon agayn,

And seyde, "This is a short conclusioun.
Youre owene mouth, by youre confessioun,
Hath dampned yow, and I wol it recorde;
It nedeth noght to pyne yow with the corde.
Ye shal be deed, by myghty Mars the rede!"
    The queene anon, for verray wommanhede,
Gan for to wepe, and so dide Emelye,
And alle the ladyes in the compaignye.
Greet pitee was it, as it thoughte hem alle,
That evere swich a chaunce sholde falle,
For gentil men they were of greet estaat,
And no thyng but for love was this debaat;
And saugh hir blody woundes wyde and soore,
And alle crieden, bothe lasse and moore,
"Have mercy, Lord, upon us wommen alle!"
And on hir bare knees adoun they falle
And wolde have kist his feet ther as he stood;
Til at the laste aslaked was his mood,
For pitee renneth soone in gentil herte.
And though he first for ire quook and sterte,
He hath considered shortly, in a clause,
The trespas of hem bothe, and eek the cause,
And although that his ire hir gilt accused,
Yet in his resoun he hem bothe excused,
As thus: he thoghte wel that every man
Wol helpe hymself in love, if that he kan,
And eek delivere hymself out of prisoun.
And eek his herte hadde compassioun
Of wommen, for they wepen evere in oon,
And in his gentil herte he thoughte anon,
And softe unto hymself he seyde, "Fy
Upon a lord that wol have no mercy,
But been a leon, bothe in word and dede,
To hem that been in repentaunce and drede,
As wel as to a proud despitous man
That wol mayntene that he first bigan.
That lord hath litel of discrecioun,
That in swich cas kan no divisioun
But weyeth pride and humblesse after oon."
And shortly, whan his ire is thus agoon,
He gan to looken up with eyen lighte
And spak thise same wordes al on highte:
    "The god of love, a benedicite!
How myghty and how greet a lord is he!

Ayeyns his myght ther gayneth none obstacles.
He may be cleped a god for his myracles,
For he kan maken, at his owene gyse,
Of everich herte as that hym list divyse.
Lo heere this Arcite and this Palamoun,
That quitly weren out of my prisoun,
And myghte han lyved in Thebes roially,
And witen I am hir mortal enemy,
And that hir deth lith in my myght also,
And yet hath love, maugree hir eyen two,
Broght hem hyder bothe for to dye.
Now looketh, is nat that an heigh folye?
Who may been a fool but if he love?
Bihoold, for Goddes sake that sit above,
Se how they blede! Be they noght wel arrayed?
Thus hath hir lord, the god of love, ypayed
Hir wages and hir fees for hir servyse!
And yet they wenen for to been ful wyse
That serven love, for aught that may bifalle.
But this is yet the beste game of alle,
That she for whom they han this jolitee
Kan hem therfore as muche thank as me.
She woot namoore of al this hoote fare,
By God, than woot a cokkow or an hare!
But all moot ben assayed, hoot and coold;
A man moot ben a fool, or yong or oold—
I woot it by myself ful yore agon,
For in my tyme a servant was I oon.
And therfore, syn I knowe of loves peyne
And woot hou soore it kan a man distreyne,
As he that hath ben caught ofte in his laas,
I yow foryeve al hoolly this trespaas,
At requeste of the queene, that kneleth heere,
And eek of Emelye, my suster deere.
And ye shul bothe anon unto me swere
That nevere mo ye shal my contree dere,
Ne make werre upon me nyght ne day,
But been my freendes in all that ye may.
I yow foryeve this trespas every deel."
And they hym sworen his axyng faire and weel,
And hym of lordshipe and of mercy preyde,
And he hem graunteth grace, and thus he seyde:
"To speke of roial lynage and richesse,
Though that she were a queene or a princesse,

Ech of you bothe is worthy, doutelees,
To wedden whan tyme is; but nathelees—
I speke as for my suster Emelye,
For whom ye have this strif and jalousye—
Ye woot yourself she may nat wedden two
Atones, though ye fighten everemo,
That oon of you, al be hym looth or lief,
He moot go pipen in an yvy leef;
This is to seyn, she may nat now han bothe,
Al be ye never so jalouse ne so wrothe.
And forthy I yow putte in this degree,
That ech of yow shal have his destynee
As hym is shape, and herkneth in what wyse;
Lo, heere youre ende of that I shal devyse.
    My wyl is this, for plat conclusioun,
Withouten any repplicacioun—
If that you liketh, take it for the beste:
That everich of you shal goon where hym leste
Frely, withouten raunson or daunger,
And this day fifty wykes, fer ne ner,
Everich of you shal brynge an hundred knyghtes
Armed for lystes up at alle rightes,
Al redy to darreyne hire by bataille.
And this bihote I yow withouten faille,
Upon my trouthe, and as I am a knyghte,
That wheither of yow bothe that hath myght—
This is to seyn, that wheither he or thow
May with his hundred, as I spak of now,
Sleen his contrarie, or out of lystes dryve,
Thanne shal I yeve Emelya to wyve
To whom that Fortune yeveth so fair a grace.
The lystes shal I maken in this place,
And God so wisly on my soule rewe
As I shal evene juge been and trewe.
Ye shul noon oother ende with me maken,
That oon of yow ne shal be deed or taken.
And if yow thynketh this is weel ysayd.
Seyeth youre avys, and holdeth you apayd.
This is youre ende and youre conclusioun."
    Who looketh lightly now but Palamoun?
Who spryngeth up for joye but Arcite?
Who kouthe telle, or who kouthe it endite,
The joye that is maked in the place
Whan Theseus hath doon so fair a grace?
But doun on knees wente every maner wight,

And thonked hym with al hir herte and myght,
And namely the Thebans often sithe.
And thus with good hope and with herte blithe
They taken hir leve, and homward gonne they ride
To Thebes with his olde walles wyde.

Explicit secunda pars

Sequitur pars tercia

I trowe men wolde deme it necligence
If I foryete to tellen the dispence
Of Theseus, that gooth so bisily
To maken up the lystes roially,
That swich a noble theatre as it was
I dar wel seyen in this world ther nas.
The circuit a myle was aboute,
Walled of stoon, and dyched al withoute.
Round was the shap, in manere of compas,
Ful of degrees, the heighte of sixty pas,
That whan a man was set on o degree,
He letted nat his felawe for to see.
Estward ther stood a gate of marbul whit,
Westward right swich another in the opposit.
And shortly to concluden, swich a place
Was noon in erthe, as in so litel space;
For in the lond ther was no crafty man
That geometrie or ars-metrike kan,
Ne portreyour, ne kervere of ymages,
That Theseus ne yaf him mete and wages
The theatre for to maken and devyse.
And for to doon his ryte and sacrifise,
He estward hath, upon the gate above,
In worshipe of Venus, goddesse of love,
Doon make an auter and an oratorie;
And on the gate westward, in memorie
Of Mars, he maked hath right swich another,
That coste largely of gold a fother.
And northward, in a touret on the wal,
Of alabastre whit and reed coral,
An oratorie, riche for to see,
In worshipe of Dyane of chastitee,
Hath Theseus doon wroght in noble wyse.
But yet hadde I foryeten to devyse
The noble kervyng and the portreitures,
The shap, the contenaunce, and the figures

That weren in this oratories thre.
    First in the temple of Venus maystow se
Wroght on the wal, ful pitous to biholde,
The broken slepes, and the sikes colde,
The sacred teeris, and the waymentynge,
The firy strokes of the desirynge
That loves servantz in this lyf enduren;
The othes that hir covenantz assuren;
Plesaunce and Hope, Desir, Foolhardynesse,
Beautee and Youthe, Bauderie, Richesse,
Charmes and Force, Lesynges, Flaterye,
Despense, Bisynesse, and Jalousye,
That wered of yelewe gooldes a gerland,
And a cokkow sittnyge on hir hand;
Festes, instrumentz, caroles, daunces,
Lust and array, and alle the circumstaunces
Of love, which that I rekned and rekne shal,
By ordre weren peynted on the wal,
And mo than I kan make of mencioun.
For soothly al the mount of Citheroun,
Ther Venus hath hir principal dwellynge,
Was shewed on the wal in portreyynge,
With al the gardyn and the lustynesse.
Nat was foryeten the porter, Ydelnesse,
Ne Narcisus the faire of yore agon,
Ne yet the folye of kyng Salomon,
Ne yet the grete strenghte of Ercules—
Th'enchauntementz of Medea and Circes—
Ne of Turnus, with the hardy fiers corage,
The riche Cresus, kaytyf in servage.
Thus may ye seen that wysdom ne richesse,
Beautee ne sleighte, strengthe ne hardynesse,
Ne may with Venus holde champartie,
For as hir list the world than may she gye.
Lo, alle thise folk so caught were in hir las,
Til they for wo ful ofte seyde "allas!"
Suffiseth heere ensamples oon or two,
And though I koude rekene a thousand mo.
    The statue of Venus, glorious for to se,
Was naked, fletynge in the large see,
And fro the navele doun al covered was
With wawes grene, and brighte as any glas.
A citole in hir right hand hadde she,
And on hir heed, ful semely for to se,
A rose gerland, fressh and wel smellynge;

Above hir heed hir dowves flikeryngе.
Biforn hire stood hir sone Cupido;
Upon his shuldres wynges hadde he two,
And blynd he was, as it is often seene;
A bowe he bar and arwes brighte and kene.
Why sholde I noght as wel eek telle yow al
The portreiture that was upon the wal
Withinne the temple of myghty Mars the rede?
Al peynted was the wal, in lengthe and brede,
Lyk to the estres of the grisly place
That highte the grete temple of Mars in Trace,
In thilke colde, frosty regioun
Ther as Mars hath his sovereyn mansioun.
First on the wal was peynted a forest,
In which ther dwelleth neither man ne best,
With knotty, knarry, bareyne trees olde,
Of stubbes sharpe and hidouse to biholde,
In which ther ran a rumbel in a swough,
As though a storm sholde bresten every bough.
And dounward from an hille, under a bente,
Ther stood the temple of Mars armypotente,
Wroght al of burned steel, of which the entree
Was long and streit, and gastly for to see.
And therout came a rage and swich a veze
That it made al the gate for to rese.
The northren lyght in at the dores shoon,
For wyndowe on the wal ne was ther noon,
Thurgh which men myghten any light discerne.
The dore was al of adamant eterne,
Yclenched overthwart and endelong
With iren tough; and for to make it strong,
Every pyler, the temple to sustene,
Was tonne-greet, of iren bright and shene.
Ther saugh I first the derke ymaginyng
Of Felonye, and al the compassyng;
The crueel Ire, reed as any gleede;
The pykepurs, and eek the pale Drede;
The smylere with the knyf under the cloke;
The shepne brennynge with the blake smoke;
The tresoun of the mordrynge in the bedde;
The open werre, with woundes al bibledde;
Contek, with blody knyf and sharp manace.
Al ful of chirkyng was that sory place.
The sleere of hymself yet saugh I ther—
His herte-blood hath bathed al his heer—

The nayl ydryven in the shode anyght;
The colde deeth, with mouth gapyng upright.
Amyddes of the temple sat Meschaunce,
With disconfort and sory contenaunce.
Yet saugh I Woodnesse, laughynge in his rage,
Armed Compleint, Outhees, and fiers Outrage;
The careyne in the busk, with throte ycorve;
A thousand slayn, and nat of qualm ystorve;
The tiraunt, with the pray by force yraft;
The toun destroyed, ther was no thyng laft.
Yet saugh I brent the shippes hoppesteres;
The hunte strangled with the wilde beres;
The sowe freten the child right in the cradel;
The cook yscalded, for al his longe ladel.
Noght was foryeten by the infortune of Marte.
The cartere overryden with his carte—
Under the wheel ful lowe he lay adoun.
Ther were also, of Martes divisioun,
The barbour, and the bocher, and the smyth,
That forgeth sharpe swerdes on his styth.
And al above, depeynted in a tour,
Saugh I Conquest, sittynge in greet honour,
With the sharpe swerd over his heed
Hangynge by a soutil twynes threed.
Depeynted was the slaughtre of Julius,
Of grete Nero, and of Antonius;
Al be that thilke tyme they were unborn,
Yet was hir deth depeynted ther-biforn
By manasynge of Mars, right by figure;
So was it shewed in that portreiture,
As is depeynted in the sterres above
Who shal be slayn or elles deed for love.
Suffiseth oon ensample in stories olde;
I may nat rekene hem alle though I wolde.
The statue of Mars upon a carte stood
Armed, and looked grym as he were wood;
And over his heed ther shynen two figures
Of sterres, that been cleped in scriptures,
That oon Puella, that oother Rubeus—
This god of armes was arrayed thus.
A wolf ther stood biforn hym at his feet
With eyen rede, and of a man he eet;
With soutil pencel was depeynted this storie
In redoutynge of Mars and of his glorie.
Now to the temple of Dyane the chaste,

As shortly as I kan, I wol me haste,
To telle yow al the descripsioun.
Depeynted been the walles up and doun
Of huntyng and of shamefast chastitee.
Ther saugh I how woful Calistopee,
What that Diane agreved was with here,
Was turned from a womman til a bere,
And after was she maad the loode-sterre.
Thus was it peynted; I kan sey yow no ferre.
Hir sone is eek a sterre, as men may see.
Ther saugh I Dane, yturned til a tree—
I mene nat the goddesse Diane,
But Penneus doghter, which that highte Dane.
Ther saugh I Attheon an hert ymaked,
For vengeaunce that he saugh Diane al naked;
I saugh how that his houndes have hym caught
And freeten hym, for that they knewe hym naught.
Yet peynted was a litel forther moor
How Atthalante hunted the wilde boor,
And Meleagre, and many another mo,
For which Dyane wroghte hym care and wo.
Ther saugh I many another wonder storie,
The which me list nat drawen to memorie.
    This goddesse on an hert ful hye seet,
With smale houndes al aboute hir feet,
And undernethe hir feet she hadde a moone—
Wexynge it was and sholde wanye soone.
In gaude grene hir statue clothed was,
With bowe in honde and arwes in a cas.
Hir eyen caste she ful lowe adoun
Ther Pluto hath his derke regioun.
A womman travaillynge was hire biforn;
But for hir child so longe was unborn,
Ful pitously Lucyna gan she calle
And seyde, "Help, for thou mayst best of alle!"
Wel koude he peynten lifly that it wroghte;
With many a floryn he the hewes boghte.
    Now been thise lystes maad, and Theseus,
That at his grete cost arrayed thus
The temples and the theatre every deel,
Whan it was doon, hym lyked wonder weel.
But stynte I wole of Theseus a lite,
And speke of Palamon and of Arcite.
    The day approcheth of hir retournynge,
That everich sholde an hundred knyghtes brynge

The bataille to darreyne, as I yow tolde.
And til Atthenes, hir covenant for to holde,
Hath everich of hem broght an hundred knyghtes,
Wel armed for the werre at alle rightes.
And sikerly ther trowed many a man
That nevere, sithen that the world bigan,
As for to speke of knyghthod of hir hond,
As fer as God hath maked see or lond,
Nas of so fewe so noble a compaignye.
For every wight that lovede chivalrye
And wolde, his thankes, han a passant name,
Hath preyed that he myghte been of that game;
And wel was hym that therto chosen was,
For if ther fille tomorwe swich a cas,
Ye knowen wel that every lusty knyght
That loveth paramours and hath his myght,
Were it in Engelond or elleswhere,
They wolde, hir thankes, wilnen to be there—
To fighte for a lady, benedicitee!
It were a lusty sighte for to see.

And right so ferden they with Palamon.
With hym ther wenten knyghtes many on;
Som wol ben armed in an haubergeoun,
And in a brestplate and a light gypoun;
And som wol have a paire plates large;
And som wol have a Pruce sheeld or a targe;
Som wol ben armed on his legges weel,
And have an ax, and som a mace of steel—
Ther is no newe gyse that it nas old.
Armed were they, as I have yow told,
Everych after his opinioun.

Ther maistow seen, comynge with Palamoun,
Lygurge hymself, the grete kyng of Trace.
Blak was his berd, and manly was his face;
The cercles of his eyen in his heed,
They gloweden bitwixen yelow and reed,
And lik a grifphon looked he aboute,
With kempe heeris on his browes stoute;
His lymes grete, his brawnes harde and stronge,
His shuldres brode, his armes rounde and longe;
And as the gyse was in his contree,
Ful hye upon a chaar of gold stood he,
With foure white boles in the trays.
In stede of cote-armure over his harnays,
With nayles yelewe and brighte as any gold,

He hadde a beres skyn, col-blak for old.
His longe heer was kembd bihynde his bak;
As any ravenes fethere it shoon for blak;
A wrethe of gold, arm-greet, of huge wighte,
Upon his heed, set ful of stones brighte,
Of fyne rubyes and of dyamauntz.
Aboute his chaar ther wenten white alauntz,
Twenty and mo, as grete as any steer,
To hunten at the leoun or the deer,
And folwed hym with mosel faste ybounde,
Colered of gold, and tourettes fyled rounde.
An hundred lordes hadde he in his route,
Armed ful wel, with hertes stierne and stoute.
 With Arcita, in stories as men fynde,
The grete Emetreus, the kyng of Inde,
Upon a steede bay trapped in steel,
Covered in clooth of gold, dyapred weel,
Cam ridynge lyk the god of armes, Mars.
His cote-armure was of clooth of Tars
Couched with perles white and rounde and grete;
His sadel was of brend gold newe ybete;
A mantelet upon his shulder hangynge,
Bret-ful of rubyes rede as fyr sparklynge;
His crispe heer lyk rynges was yronne,
And that was yelow, and glytered as the sonne.
His nose was heigh, his eyen bright citryn,
His lippes rounde, his colour was sangwyn;
A fewe frakenes in his face yspreynd,
Bitwixen yelow and somdel blak ymeynd;
And as a leon he his lookyng caste.
Of fyve and twenty yeer his age I caste.
His berd was wel bigonne for to sprynge;
His voys was as a trompe thonderynge.
Upon his heed he wered of laurer grene
A gerland, fressh and lusty for to sene.
Upon his hand he bar for his deduyt
An egle tame, as any lilye whyt.
An hundred lordes hadde he with hym there,
Al armed, save hir heddes, in al hir gere,
Ful richely in alle maner thynges.
For trusteth wel that dukes, erles, kynges
Were gadered in this noble compaignye,
For love and for encrees of chivalrye.
Aboute this kyng ther ran on every part
Ful many a tame leon and leopart.

And in this wise thise lordes, alle and some,
Been on the Sonday to the citee come
Aboute pryme, and in the toun alight.
This Theseus, this duc, this worthy knyght,
Whan he had broght hem into his citee,
And inned hem, everich at his degree,
He festeth hem, and dooth so greet labour
To esen hem and doon hem al honour
That yet men wenen that no mannes wit
Of noon estaat ne koude amenden it.
The mynstralcye, the service at the feeste,
The grete yiftes to the meeste and leeste,
The riche array of Theseus paleys,
Ne who sat first ne last upon the deys,
What ladyes fairest been or best daunsynge,
Or which of hem kan dauncen best and synge,
Ne who moost felyngly speketh of love;
What haukes sitten on the perche above,
What houndes liggen on the floor adoun—
Of al this make I now no mencioun,
But al th'effect; that thynketh me the beste,
Now cometh the point, and herkneth if yow leste.
The Sonday nyght, er day bigan to sprynge,
Whan Palamon the larke herde synge
(Although it nere nat day by houres two,
Yet song the larke) and Palamon right tho
With hooly herte and with an heigh corage,
He roos to wenden on his pilgrymage
Unto the blisful Citherea benigne—
I mene Venus, honurable and digne.
And in hir houre he walketh forth a pas
Unto the lystes ther hire temple was,
And doun he kneleth, and with humble cheere
And herte soor he seyde as ye shal heere:
"Faireste of faire, O lady myn, Venus,
Doughter to Jove and spouse of Vulcanus,
Thow gladere of the mount of Citheron,
For thilke love thow haddest to Adoon,
Have pitee of my bittre teeris smerte,
And taak myn humble preyere at thyn herte.
Allas! I ne have no langage to telle
Th'effectes ne the tormentz of myn helle;
Myn herte may myne harmes nat biwreye;
I am so confus that I kan noght seys
But 'Mercy, lady bright, that knowest weele

My thought and seest what harmes that I feele!'
Considere al this and rewe upon my soore,
As wisly as I shal for everemoore,
Emforth my myght, thy trewe servant be,
And holden werre alwey with chastitee.
That make I myn avow, so ye me helpe!
I kepe noght of armes for to yelpe,
Ne I ne axe nat tomorowe to have victorie,
Ne renoun in this cas, ne veyne glorie
Of pris of armes blowen up and doun;
But I wolde have fully possessioun
Of Emelye, and dye in thy servyse.
Fynd thow the manere hou and in what wyse:
I recche nat but it may bettre be
To have victorie of hem, or they of me,
So that I have my lady in myne armes.
For though so be that Mars is god of armes,
Youre vertu is so greet in hevene above
That if yow list, I shal wel have my love.
Thy temple wol I worshipe everemo,
And on thyn auter, where I ride or go,
I wol doon sacrifice and fires beete.
And if ye wol nat so, my lady sweete,
Thanne preye I thee, tomorwe with a spere
That Arcita me thurgh the herte bere.
Thanne rekke I noght, whan I have lost my lyf,
Though that Arcita wynne hire to his wyf.
This is th'effect and ende of my preyere:
Yif me my love, thow blisful lady deere."
  When the orison was doon of Palamon,
His sacrifice he dide, and that anon,
Ful pitously, with alle circumstaunces,
Al telle I noght as now his observaunces;
But atte laste the statue of Venus shook,
And made a signe, wherby that he took
That his preyere accepted was that day.
For thogh the signe shewed a delay,
Yet wiste he wel that graunted was his boone,
And with glad herte he wente hym hoom ful soone.
  The thridde houre inequal that Palamon
Bigan to Venus temple for to gon,
Up roos the sonne, and up roos Emelye
And to the temple of Dyane gan hye.
Hir maydens, that she thider with hire ladde,
Ful redily with hem the fyr they hadde,

Th'encens, the clothes, and the remenant al
That to the sacrifice longen shal;
The hornes fulle of meeth, as was the gyse—
Ther lakked noght to doon hir sacrifise.
Smokynge the temple, ful of clothes faire,
This Emelye, with herte debonaire,
Hir body wessh with water of a welle.
But hou she dide hir ryte I dar nat telle,
But it be any thing in general;
And yet it were a game to heeren al.
To hym that meneth wel it were no charge;
But it is good a man been at his large.
Hir brighte heer was kembd, untressed al;
A coroune of a grene ook cerial
Upon hir heed was set ful fair and meete.
Two fyres on the auter gan she beete,
And dide hir thynges, as men may biholde
In Stace of Thebes and thise bookes olde.
Whan kyndled was the fyr, with pitous cheere
Unto Dyane she spak as ye may heere:
"O chaste goddesse of the wodes grene,
To whom bothe hevene and erthe and see is sene,
Queene of the regne of Pluto derk and lowe,
Goddesse of maydens, that myn herte hast knowe
Ful many a yeer, and woost what I desire,
As keepe me fro thy vengeaunce and thyn ire,
That Attheon aboughte cruelly.
Chaste goddesse, wel wostow that I
Desire to ben a mayden al my lyf,
Ne nevere wol I be no love ne wyf.
I am, thow woost, yet of thy compaignye,
A mayde, and love huntynge and venerye,
And for to walken in the wodes wilde,
And noght to ben a wyf and be with childe.
Noght wol I knowe compaignye of man.
Now help me, lady, sith ye may and kan,
For tho thre formes that thou hast in thee.
And Palamon, that hath swich love to me,
And eek Arcite, that loveth me so soore,
This grace I preye thee withoute moore,
As sende love and pees bitwixe hem two,
And fro me turne awey hir hertes so
That al hire hoote love and hir desir,
And al hir bisy torment, and hir fir
Be queynt, or turned in another place.
And if so be thou wolt nat do me grace,

Or if my destynee be shapen so
That I shal nedes have oon of hem two,
As sende me hym that moost desireth me.
Bihoold, goddesse of clene chastitee,
The bittre teeris that on my chekes falle.
Syn thou art mayde and kepere of us alle,
My maydenhede thou kepe and wel conserve,
And whil I lyve, a mayde I wol thee serve."
    The fires brenne upon the auter cleere,
Whil Emelye was thus in hir preyere.
But sodeynly she saugh a sighte queynte,
For right anon oon of the fyres queynte
And quyked agayn, and after that anon
That oother fyr was queynt and al agon;
And as it queynte it made a whistelynge,
As doon thise wete brondes in hir brennynge,
And at the brondes ende out ran anon
As it were blody dropes many oon;
For which so soore agast was Emelye
That she was wel ny mad and gan to crye,
For she ne wiste what it signyfied,
But oonly for the feere thus hath she cried,
And weep that it was pitee for to heere.
And therwithal Dyane gan appeere,
With bowe in honde, right as an hunteresse,
And seyde, "Doghter, stynt thyn hevynesse.
Among the goddes hye it is affermed,
And by eterne word writen and confermed,
Thou shalt ben wedded unto oon of tho
That han for thee so muchel care and wo,
But unto which of hem I may nat telle.
Farwel, for I ne may no lenger dwelle.
The fires which that on myn auter breene
Shulle thee declaren, er that thou go henne,
Thyn aventure of love, as in this cas."
And with that word, the arwes in the caas
Of the goddesse clateren faste and rynge,
And forth she wente and made a vanysshynge;
For which this Emelye astoned was,
And seyde, "What amounteth this, allas?
I putte me in thy proteccioun,
Dyane, and in thy disposicioun."
And hoom she goth anon the nexte weye.
This is th'effect; ther is namoore to seye.
    The nexte houre of Mars folwynge this,
Arcite unto the temple walked is

Of fierse Mars to doon his sacrifise,
With alle the rytes of his payen wyse.
With pitous herte and heigh devocioun,
Right thus to Mars he seyde his orisoun:
"O stronge god, that in the regnes colde
Of Trace honoured art and lord yholde,
And hast in every regne and every lond
Of armes al the brydel in thyn hond,
And hem fortunest as thee lyst devyse,
Accepte of me my pitous sacrifise.
If so be that my youthe may deserve,
And that my myght be worthy for to serve
Thy godhede, that I may been oon of thyne,
Thanne preye I thee to rewe upon my pyne.
For thilke peyne and thilke hoote fir
In which thow whilom brendest for desir,
Whan that thow usedest the beautee
Of faire, yonge, fresshe Venus free,
And haddest hire in armes at thy wille—
Although thee ones on a tyme mysfille,
Whan Vulcanus hadde caught thee in his las
And foond thee liggynge by his wyf, allas!—
For thilke sorwe that was in thyn herte,
Have routhe as wel upon my peynes smerte.
I am yong and unkonnynge, as thow woost,
And, as I trowe, with love offended moost
That evere was any lyves creature,
For she that dooth me al this wo endure
Ne reccheth nevere wher I synke or fleete.
And wel I woot, er she me mercy heete,
I moot with strengthe wynne hire in the place,
And wel I woot, withouten help or grace
Of thee ne may my strengthe noght availle.
Thanne help me, lord, tomorwe in my bataille,
For thilke fyr that whilom brente thee,
As wel as thilke fyr now brenneth me,
And do that I tomorwe have victorie.
Myn be the travaille, and thyn be the glorie!
Thy sovereyn temple wol I moost honouren
Of any place, and alwey moost labouren
In thy plesaunce and in thy craftes stronge,
And in thy temple I wol my baner honge
And alle the armes of my compaignye,
And everemo, unto that day I dye,
Eterne fir I wol bifore thee fynde.

And eek to this avow I wol me bynde:
My beerd, myn heer, that hongeth long adoun,
That nevere yet ne felte offensioun
Of rasour nor of shere, I wol thee yive,
And ben thy trewe servant whil I lyve.
Now, lord, have routhe upon my sorwes soore;
Yif me [victorie]; I aske thee namoore."
    The preyere stynt of Arcita the stronge,
The rynges on the temple dore that honge,
And eek the dores, clatereden ful faste,
Of which Arcita somwhat hym agaste.
The fyres brenden upon the auter brighte
That it gan al the temple for to lighte;
A sweete smel the ground anon up yaf,
And Arcita anon his hand up haf,
And moore encens into the fyr he caste,
With othere rytes mo; and atte laste
The statue of Mars bigan his hauberk rynge,
And with that soun he herde a murmurynge
Ful lowe and dym, and seyde thus, "Victorie!"
For which he yaf to Mars honour and glorie.
And thus with joye and hope wel to fare
Arcite anon unto his in is fare,
As fayn as fowel is of the brighte sonne.
    And right anon swich strif ther is bigonne,
For thilke grauntyng, in the hevene above,
Bitwixe Venus, the goddesse of love,
And Mars, the stierne god armypotente,
That Juppiter was bisy it to stente,
Til that the pale Saturnus the colde,
That knew so manye of aventures olde,
Foond in his olde experience an art
That he ful soone hath plesed every part.
As sooth is seyd, elde hath greet avantage;
In elde is bothe wysdom and usage;
Men may the olde atrenne and noght atrede.
Saturne anon, to stynten strif and drede,
Al be it that it is agayn his kynde,
Of al this strif he gan remedie fynde.
    "My deere doghter Venus," quod Saturne,
"My cours, that hath so wyde for to turne,
Hath moore power than woot any man.
Myn is the drenchyng in the see so wan;
Myn is the prison in the derke cote;
Myn is the stranglyng and hangyng by the throte,

The murmure and the cherles rebellyng,
The groynynge, and the pryvee empoysonyng;
I do vengeance and pleyn correccioun,
Whil I dwelle in the signe of the leoun.
Myn is the ruyne of the hye halles,
The fallynge of the toures and of the walles
Upon the mynour or the carpenter.
I slow Sampsoun, shakynge the piler;
And myne be the maladyes colde,
The derke tresons, and the castes olde;
My lookyng is the fader of pestilence.
Now weep namoore; I shal doon diligence
That Palamon, that is thyn owene knyght,
Shal have his lady, as thou hast him hight.
Though Mars shal helpe his knyght, yet nathelees
Bitwixe yow ther moot be som tyme pees,
Al be ye noght of o compleccioun,
That causeth al day swich divisioun.
I am thyn aiel, redy at thy wille;
Weep now namoore; I wol thy lust fulfille."
    Now wol I stynten of the goddes above,
Of Mars, and of Venus, goddesse of love,
And telle yow as pleynly as I kan
The grete effect, for which that I bygan.

Explicit tercia pars

Sequitur pars quarta

    Greet was the feeste in Atthenes that day,
And eek the lusty seson of that May
Made every wight to been in swich plesaunce
That al that Monday justen they and daunce,
And spenden it in Venus heigh servyse.
But by the cause that they sholde ryse
Eerly, for to seen the grete fight,
Unto hir reste wenten they at nyght.
And on the morwe, whan that day gan sprynge,
Of hors and harneys noyse and claterynge
Ther was in hostelryes al aboute,
And to the paleys rood ther many a route
Of lordes upon steedes and palfreys.
Ther maystow seen devisynge of harneys
So unkouth and so riche, and wroght so weel
Of goldsmythrye, of browdynge, and of steel;
The sheeldes brighte, testeres, and trappures,

Gold-hewen helmes, hauberkes, cote-armures;
Lordes in parementz on hir courseres,
Knyghtes of retenue, and eek squieres
Nailynge the speres, and helmes bokelynge;
Giggynge of sheeldes, with layneres lacynge—
There as nede is they weren no thyng ydel;
The fomy steedes on the golden brydel
Gnawynge, and faste the armurers also
With fyle and hamer prikynge to and fro;
Yemen on foote, and communes many oon
With shorte staves, thikke as they may goon;
Pypes, trompes, nakers, clariounes,
That in the bataille blowen blody sounes;
The paleys ful of peple up and doun,
Heere thre, ther ten, holdynge hir questioun,
Dyvynynge of this Thebane knyghtes two.
Somme seyden thus, somme seyde "it shal be so";
Somme helden with hym with the blake berd,
Somme with the balled, somme with the thikke herd;
Somme seyde he looked grymme, and he wolde fighte:
"He hath a sparth of twenty pound of wighte."
Thus was the halle ful of divynynge,
Longe after that the sonne gan to sprynge.
The grete Theseus, that of his sleep awaked
With mynstralcie and noyse that was maked,
Heeld yet the chambre of his paleys riche
Til that the Thebane knyghtes, bothe yliche
Honured, were into the paleys fet.
Duc Theseus was at a wyndow set,
Arrayed right as he were a god in trone.
The peple preesseth thiderward ful soone
Hym for to seen, and doon heigh reverence,
And eek to herkne his heste and his sentence.
An heraud on a scaffold made an "Oo!"
Til al the noyse of peple was ydo,
And whan he saugh the peple of noyse al stille,
Tho shewed he the myghty dukes wille:
"The lord hath of his heigh discrecioun
Considered that it were destruccioun
To gentil blood to fighten in the gyse
Of mortal bataille now in this emprise.
Wherfore, to shapen that they shal nat dye,
He wol his firste purpos modifye.
No man therfore, up peyne of los of lyf,
No maner shot, ne polax, ne short knyf

Into the lystes sende or thider brynge;
Ne short swerd, for to stoke with poynt bitynge,
No man ne drawe, ne bere it by his syde.
Ne no man shal unto his felawe ryde
But o cours with a sharpe ygrounde spere;
Foyne, if hym list, on foote, hymself to were.
And he that is at meschief shal be take
And noght slayn, but be broght unto the stake
That shal ben ordeyned on either syde;
But thider he shal by force, and there abyde.
And if so falle the chieftayn be take
On outher syde, or elles sleen his make,
No lenger shal the turneiynge laste.
God spede you! Gooth forth and ley on faste!
With long swerd and with mace fighteth youre fille.
Gooth now youre wey; this is the lordes wille."
    The voys of peple touchede the hevene,
So loude cride they with murie stevene,
"God save swich a lord, that is so good
He wilneth no destruccion of blood!"
Up goon the trompes and the melodye,
And to the lystes rit the compaignye,
By ordinance, thurghout the citee large,
Hanged with clooth of gold, and nat with sarge.
    Ful lik a lord this noble duc gan ryde,
Thise two Thebans upon either syde,
And after rood the queene and Emelye,
And after that another compaignye
Of oon and oother, after hir degree.
And thus they passen thurghout the citee,
And to the lystes come they by tyme.
It nas nat of the day yet fully pryme
Whan set was Theseus ful riche and hye,
Ypolita the queene, and Emelye,
And othere ladys in degrees aboute.
Unto the seetes preesseth al the route.
And westward, thurgh the gates under Marte,
Arcite, and eek the hondred of his parte,
With baner reed is entred right anon;
And in that selve moment Palamon
Is under Venus, estward in the place,
With baner whyt and hardy chiere and face.
In al the world, to seken up and doun,
So evene, withouten variacioun,
Ther nere swiche compaignyes tweye,
For ther was noon so wys that koude seye

That any hadde of oother avauntage
Of worthynesse, ne of estaat, ne age,
So evene were they chosen, for to gesse.
And in two renges faire they hem dresse.
Whan that hir names rad were everichon,
That in hir nombre gyle were ther noon,
Tho were the gates shet, and cried was loude:
"Do now youre devoir, yonge knyghtes proude!"
    The heraudes lefte hir prikyng up and doun;
Now ryngen trompes loude and clarioun.
Ther is namoore to seyn, but west and est
In goon the speres ful sadly in arrest;
In gooth the sharpe spore into the syde.
Ther seen men who kan juste and who kan ryde;
Ther shyveren shaftes upon sheeldes thikke;
He feeleth thurgh the herte-spoon the prikke.
Up spryngen speres twenty foot on highte;
Out goon the swerdes as the silver brighte;
The helmes they tohewen and toshrede;
Out brest the blood with stierne stremes rede;
With myghty maces the bones they tobreste.
He thurgh the thikkeste of the throng gan threste;
Ther stomblen steedes stronge, and doun gooth al,
He rolleth under foot as dooth a bal;
He foyneth on his feet with his tronchoun,
And he hym hurtleth with his hors adoun;
He thurgh the body is hurt and sithen take,
Maugree his heed, and broght unto the stake;
As forward was, right there he moste abyde.
Another lad is on that oother syde.
And some tyme dooth hem Theseus to reste,
Hem to refresshe and drynken, if hem leste.
Ful ofte a day han thise Thebanes two
Togydre ymet, and wroght his felawe wo;
Unhorsed hath ech oother of hem tweye.
Ther was no tygre in the vale of Galgopheye,
Whan that hir whelp is stole whan it is lite,
So crueel on the hunte as is Arcite
For jelous herte upon this Palamon.
Ne in Belmarye ther nys so fel leon,
That hunted is, or for his hunger wood,
Ne of his praye desireth so the blood,
As Palamon to sleen his foo Arcite.
The jelous strokes on hir helmes byte;
Out renneth blood on bothe hir sydes rede.
    Som tyme an ende ther is of every dede.

For er the sonne unto the reste wente,
The stronge kyng Emetreus gan hente
This Palamon, as he faught with Arcite,
And made his swerd depe in his flessh to byte,
And by the force of twenty is he take
Unyolden, and ydrawen to the stake.
And in the rescus of this Palamoun
The stronge kyng Lygurge is born adoun,
And kyng Emetreus, for al his strengthe,
Is born out of his sadel a swerdes lengthe,
So hitte him Palamoun er he were take.
But al for noght; he was broght to the stake.
His hardy herte myghte hym helpe naught:
He moste abyde, whan that he was caught,
By force and eek by composicioun.
 Who sorweth now but woful Palamoun,
That moot namoore goon agayn to fighte?
And whan that Theseus hadde seyn this sighte,
Unto the folk that foghten thus echon
He cryde, "Hoo! namoore, for it is doon!
I wol be trewe juge, and no partie.
Arcite of Thebes shal have Emelie,
That by his fortune hath hire faire ywonne."
Anon ther is a noyse of peple bigonne
For joye of this, so loude and heighe withalle
It semed that the lystes sholde falle.
 What kan now faire Venus doon above?
What seith she now? What dooth this queene of love,
But wepeth so, for wantynge of hir wille,
Til that hir teeres in the lystes fille?
She seyde, "I am ashamed, doutelees."
 Saturnus seyde, "Doghter, hoold thy pees!
Mars hath his wille, his knyght hath al his boone,
And, by myn heed, thow shalt been esed soone."
 The trompours, with the loude mynstralcie,
The heraudes, that ful loude yelle and crie,
Been in hire wele for joye of daun Arcite.
But herkneth me, and stynteth noyse a lite,
Which a myracle ther bifel anon.
 This fierse Arcite hath of his helm ydon,
And on a courser, for to shewe his face,
He priketh endelong the large place
Lokynge upward upon this Emelye;
And she agayn hym caste a freendlich ye
(For wommen, as to speken in comune,

Thei folwen alle the favour of Fortune)
And was al his chiere, as in his herte.
    Out of the ground a furie infernal sterte,
From Pluto sent at requeste of Saturne,
For which his hors for fere gan to turne,
And leep aside, and foundred as he leep;
And er that Arcite may taken keep,
He pighte hym on the pomel of his heed,
That in the place he lay as he were deed,
His brest tobrosten with his sadel-bowe.
As blak he lay as any cole or crowe,
So was the blood yronnen in his face.
Anon he was yborn out of the place,
With herte soor, to Theseus paleys.
Tho was he korven out of his harneys
And in a bed ybrought ful faire and blyve,
For he was yet in memorie and alyve,
And alwey criynge after Emelye.
    Duc Theseus, with al his compaignye,
Is comen hoom to Atthenes his citee,
With alle blisse and greet solempnitee.
Al be it that this aventure was falle,
He nolde noght disconforten hem alle.
Men seyde eek that Arcite shal nat dye;
He shal been heeled of his maladye.
And of another thyng they weren as fayn,
That of hem alle was ther noon yslayn,
Al were they soore yhurt, and namely oon,
That with a spere was thirled his brest boon.
To othere woundes and to broken armes
Somme hadden salves, and somme hadden charmes;
Fermacies of herbes, and eek save
They dronken, for they wolde hir lymes have.
For which this noble duc, as he wel kan,
Conforteth and honoureth every man,
And made revel al the longe nyght
Unto the straunge lordes, as was right.
Ne ther was holden no disconfitynge
But as a justes or a tourneiynge;
For soothly ther was no disconfiture.
For fallyng nys nat but an aventure,
Ne to be lad by force unto the stake
Unyolden, and with twenty knyghtes take,
O persone allone, withouten mo,
And haryed forth by arme, foot, and too,

And eke his steede dryven forth with staves
With footmen, bothe yemen and eek knaves—
It nas arretted hym no vileynye;
Ther may no man clepen it cowardye.
For which anon duc Theseus leet crye,
To stynten alle rancour and envye,
The gree as wel of o syde as of oother,
And eyther syde ylik as ootheres brother;
And yaf hem yiftes after hir degree,
And fully heeld a feeste dayes three,
And conveyed the kynges worthily
Out of his toun a journee largely.
And hoom wente every man the righte way.
Ther was namoore but "Fare wel, have good day!"
Of this bataille I wol namoore endite,
But speke of Palamon and of Arcite.
    Swelleth the brest of Arcite, and the soore
Encreesseth at his herte moore and moore.
The clothered blood, for any lechcraft,
Corrupteth, and is in his bouk ylaft,
That neither veyne-blood, ne ventusynge,
Ne drynke of herbes may ben his helpynge.
The vertu expulsif, or animal,
Fro thilke vertu cleped natural
Ne may the venym voyden ne expelle.
The pipes of his longes gonne to swelle,
And every lacerte in his brest adoun
Is shent with venym and corrupcioun.
Hym gayneth neither, for to gete his lif,
Vomyt upward, ne dounward laxatif.
Al is tobrosten thilke regioun;
Nature hath now no dominacioun.
And certeinly, ther Nature wol nat wirche,
Fare wel phisik! Go ber the man to chirche!
This al and som, that Arcita moot dye;
For which he sendeth after Emelye,
And Palamon, that was his cosyn deere.
Thanne seyde he thus, as ye shal after heere:
"Naught may the woful spirit in myn herte
Declare o point of alle my sorwes smerte
To yow, my lady, that I love moost,
But I bequethe the servyce of my goost
To yow aboven every creature,
Syn that my lyf may no lenger dure.
Allas, the wo! Allas, the peynes stronge,
That I for yow have suffred, and so longe!

Allas, the deeth! Allas, myn Emelye!
Allas, departynge of oure compaignye!
Allas, myn hertes queene! Allas, my wyf,
Myn hertes lady, endere of my lyf!
What is this world? What asketh men to have?
Now with his love, now in his colde grave
Allone, withouten any compaignye.
Fare wel, my sweete foo, myn Emelye!
And softe taak me in youre armes tweye,
For love of God, and herkneth what I seye.

"I have heer with my cosyn Palamon
Had strif and rancour many a day agon
For love of yow, and for my jalousye.
And Juppiter so wys my soule gye,
To speken of a servaunt proprely,
With alle circumstances trewely—
That is to seyen, trouthe, honour, knyghthede,
Wysdom, humblesse, estaat, and heigh kynrede,
Fredom, and al that longeth to that art—
So Juppiter have of my soule part,
As in this world right now ne knowe I non
So worthy to ben loved as Palamon,
That serveth yow, and wol doon al his lyf.
And if that evere ye shul ben a wyf,
Foryet nat Palamon, the gentil man."
And with that word his speche faille gan,
For from his feet up to his brest was come
The coold of deeth, that hadde hym overcome,
And yet mooreover, for in his armes two
The vital strengthe is lost and al ago.
Oonly the intellect, withouten moore,
That dwelled in his herte syk and soore,
Gan faillen whan the herte felte deeth.
Dusked his eyen two, and failled breeth,
But on his lady yet caste he his ye;
His laste word was, "Mercy, Emelye!"
His spirit chaunged hous and wente ther,
As I cam nevere, I kan nat tellen wher.
Therfore I stynte; I nam no divinistre;
Of soules fynde I nat in this registre,
Ne me ne list thilke opinions to telle
Of hem, though that they writen wher they dwelle.
Arcite is coold, ther Mars his soule gye!
Now wol I speken forth of Emelye.

Shrighte Emelye, and howleth Palamon,
And Theseus his suster took anon

Swownynge, and baar hire fro the corps away.
What helpeth it to tarien forth the day
To tellen how she weep bothe eve and morwe?
For in swich cas wommen have swich sorwe,
Whan that hir housbondes ben from hem ago,
That for the moore part they sorwen so,
Or ellis fallen in swich maladye
That at the laste certeinly they dye.
Infinite been the sorwes and the teeres
Of olde folk and folk of tendre yeeres
In al the toun for deeth of this Theban.
For hym ther wepeth bothe child and man;
So greet wepyng was ther noon, certayn,
Whan Ector was ybroght, al fressh yslayn,
To Troye, Allas, the pitee that was ther,
Cracchynge of chekes, rentynge eek of heer.
"Why woldestow be deed," thise wommen crye,
"And haddest gold ynough, and Emelye?"
No man myghte gladen Theseus,
Savynge his olde fader Egeus,
That knew this worldes transmutacioun,
As he hadde seyn it chaunge bothe up and doun,
Joye after wo, and wo after gladnesse,
And shewed hem ensamples and liknesse.
"Right as ther dyed nevere man," quod he,
"That he ne lyvede in erthe in some degree,
Right so ther lyvede never man," he seyde,
"In al this world, that som tyme he ne deyde.
This world nys but a thurghfare ful of wo,
And we been pilgrymes, passynge to and fro.
Deeth is an ende of every worldly soore."
And over al this yet seyde he muchel moore
To this effect, ful wisely to enhorte
The peple that they sholde hem reconforte.
Duc Theseus, with al his bisy cure,
Caste now wher that the sepulture
Of goode Arcite may best ymaked be,
And eek moost honurable in his degree.
And at the laste he took conclusioun
That ther as first Arcite and Palamoun
Hadden for love the bataille hem bitwene,
That in that selve grove, swoote and grene,
Ther as he hadde his amorouse desires,
His compleynte, and for love his hoote fires,
He wolde make a fyr in which the office

Funeral he myghte al accomplice.
And leet comande anon to hakke and hewe
The okes olde, and leye hem on a rewe
In colpons wel arrayed for to brenne.
His officers with swifte feet they renne
And ryde anon at his comandement.
And after this, Theseus hath ysent
After a beere, and it al overspradde
With clooth of gold, the richeste that he hadde.
And of the same suyte he cladde Arcite;
Upon his hondes hadde he gloves white,
Eek on his heed a coroune of laurer grene,
And in his hond a swerd ful bright and kene.
He leyde hym, bare the visage, on the beere;
Therwith he weep that pitee was to heere.
And for the peple sholde seen hym alle,
Whan it was day, he broghte hym to the halle,
That roreth of the criyng and the soun.
Tho cam this woful Theban Palamoun,
With flotery berd and ruggy, asshy heeres,
In clothes blake, ydropped al with teeres;
And, passynge othere of wepynge, Emelye,
The rewefulleste of al the compaignye.
In as muche as the servyce sholde be
The moore noble and riche in his degree,
Duc Theseus leet forth thre steedes brynge,
That trapped were in steel al gliterynge,
And covered with the armes of daun Arcite.
Upon thise steedes, that weren grete and white,
Ther seten folk, of whiche oon baar his sheeld,
Another his spere up on his hondes heeld,
The thridde baar with hym his bowe Turkeys
(Of brend gold was the caas and eek the harneys);
And riden forth a paas with sorweful cheere
Toward the grove, as ye shul after heere.
The nobleste of the Grekes that ther were
Upon hir shuldres caryeden the beere,
With slakke paas and eyen rede and wete,
Thurghout the citee by the maister strete,
That sprad was al with blak, and wonder hye
Right of the same is the strete ywrye.
Upon the right hond wente olde Egeus,
And on that oother syde duc Theseus,
With vessels in hir hand of gold ful fyn,
Al ful of hony, milk, and blood, and wyn;

Eek Palamon, with ful greet compaignye;
And after that cam woful Emelye,
With fyr in honde, as was that tyme the gyse,
To do the office of funeral servyse.
Heigh labour and ful greet apparaillynge
Was at the service and the fyr-makynge,
That with his grene top the hevene raughte;
And twenty fadme of brede the armes straughte—
This is to seyn, the bowes weren so brode.
Of stree first ther was leyd ful many a lode.
But how the fyr was maked upon highte,
Ne eek the names that the trees highte,
As ook, firre, birch, aspe, alder, holm, popler,
Wylugh, elm, plane, assh, box, chasteyn, lynde, laurer,
Mapul, thorn, bech, hasel, ew, whippeltree—
How they weren feld shal nat be toold for me;
Ne hou the goddes ronnen up and doun,
Disherited of hire habitacioun,
In which they woneden in reste and pees
Nymphes, fawnes and amadrides;
Ne hou the beestes and the briddes alle
Fledden for fere, whan the wode was falle;
Ne how the ground agast was of the light,
That was nat wont to seen the sonne bright;
Ne how the fyr was couched first with stree,
And thanne with drye stikkes cloven a thre,
And thanne with grene wode and spicerye,
And thanne with clooth of gold and with perrye,
And gerlandes, hangynge with ful many a flour;
The mirre, th'encens, with al so greet adour;
Ne how Arcite lay among al this,
Ne what richesse aboute his body is;
Ne how that Emelye, as was the gyse,
Putte in the fyr of funeral servyse;
Ne how she swowned whan men made the fyr,
Ne what she spak, ne what was hir desir;
Ne what jeweles men in the fyre caste,
Whan that the fyr was greet and brente faste;
Ne how somme caste hir sheeld, and somme hir spere,
And of hire vestimentz, whiche that they were,
And coppes fulle of wyn, and milk, and blood,
Into the fyr, that brente as it were wood;
Ne how the Grekes, with an huge route,
Thries riden al the fyr aboute
Upon the left hand, with a loud shoutynge,

And thries with hir speres claterynge;
And thries how the ladyes gonne crye;
And how that lad was homward Emelye;
Ne how Arcite is brent to asshen colde;
Ne how that lyche-wake was yholde
Al thilke nyght; ne how the Grekes pleye
The wake-pleyes; ne kepe I nat to seye
Who wrastleth best naked with oille enoynt,
Ne who that baar hym best, in no disjoynt.
I wol nat tellen eek how that they goon
Hoom til Atthenes, whan the pley is doon;
But shortly to the point thanne wol I wende
And maken of my longe tale an ende.
 By processe and by lengthe of certeyn yeres,
Al stynted is the moornynge and the teres
Of Grekes, by oon general assent.
Thanne semed me ther was a parlement
At Atthenes, upon certein pointz and caas;
Among the whiche pointz yspoken was,
To have with certein contrees alliaunce,
And have fully of Thebans obeisaunce.
For which this noble Theseus anon
Leet senden after gentil Palamon,
Unwist of hym what was the cause and why,
But in his blake clothes sorwefully
He cam at his comandement in hye.
Tho sente Theseus for Emelye.
Whan they were set, and hust was al the place,
And Theseus abiden hadde a space
Er any word cam fram his wise brest,
His eyen sette he ther as was his lest.
And with a sad visage he siked stille,
And after that right thus he seyde his wille:
 "The Firste Moevere of the cause above,
Whan he first made the faire cheyne of love,
Greet was th'effect, and heigh was his entente.
Wel wiste he why, and what thereof he mente,
For with that faire cheyne of love he bond
The fyr, the eyr, the water, and the lond
In certeyn boundes, that they may nat flee.
That same Prince and that Moevere," quod he,
"Hath stablissed in this wrecched world adoun
Certeyne dayes and duracioun
To al that is engendred in this place,
Over the whiche day they may nat pace,

Al mowe they yet tho dayes wel abregge.
Ther nedeth noght noon auctoritee t'allegge,
For it is preeved by experience,
But that me list declaren my sentence.
Thanne may men by this ordre wel discerne
That thilke Moevere stable is and eterne.
Wel may men knowe, but it be a fool,
That every part dirryveth from his hool,
For nature hath nat taken his bigynnyng
Of no partie or cantel of a thyng,
But of a thyng that parfit is and stable,
Descendynge so til it be corrumpable.
And therfore, of his wise purveiaunce,
He hath so wel biset his ordinaunce
That speces of thynges and progressiouns
Shullen enduren by successiouns,
And nat eterne, withouten any lye.
This maystow understonde and seen at ye.
"Loo the ook, that hath so long a norisshynge
From tyme that it first bigynneth to sprynge,
And hath so long a lif, as we may see,
Yet at the laste wasted is the tree.
"Considereth eek how that the harde stoon
Under oure feet, on which we trede and goon,
Yet wasteth it as it lyth by the weye.
The brode ryver somtyme wexeth dreye;
The grete tounes se we wane and wende.
Thanne may ye se that al this thyng hath ende.
"Of man and womman seen we wel also
That nedes, in oon of thise termes two—
This is to seyn, in youthe or elles age—
He moot be deed, the kyng as shal a page;
Som in his bed, som in the depe see,
Som in the large feeld, as men may see;
Ther helpeth noght; al goth that ilke weye.
Thanne may I seyn that al this thyng moot deye.
"What maketh this but Juppiter, the kyng,
That is prince and cause of alle thyng,
Convertynge al unto his propre welle
From which it is dirryved, sooth to telle?
And heer-agayns no creature on lyve,
Of no degree, availleth for to stryve.
"Thanne is it wysdom, as it thynketh me,
To maken vertu of necessitee,
And take it weel that we may nat eschue,

And namely that to us alle is due.
And whoso gruccheth ought, he dooth folye,
And rebel is to hym that al may gye.
And certeinly a man hath moost honour
To dyen in his excellence and flour,
Whan he is siker of his goode name;
Thanne hath he doon his freend, ne hym, no shame.
And gladder oghte his freend been of his deeth,
Whan with honour up yolden is his breeth,
Than whan his name apalled is for age,
For al forgeten is his vassellage.
Thanne is it best, as for a worthy fame,
To dyen whan that he is best of name.
"The contrarie of al this is wilfulnesse.
Why grucchen we, why have we hevynesse,
That goode Arcite, of chivalrie flour,
Departed is with duetee and honour
Out of this foule prisoun of this lyf?
Why grucchen heere his cosyn and his wyf
Of his welfare, that loved hem so weel?
Kan he hem thank? Nay, God woot, never a deel,
That both his soule and eek hemself offende,
And het they mowe hir lustes nat amende.
"What may I conclude of this longe serye,
But after wo I rede us to be merye
And thanken Juppiter of al his grace?
And er that we departen from this place
I rede that we make of sorwes two
O parfit joye, lastynge everemo.
And looketh now, wher moost sorwe is herinne,
Ther wol we first amenden and bigynne.
"Suster," quod he, "this is my fulle assent,
With al th'avys heere of my parlement,
That gentil Palamon, youre owene knyght,
That serveth yow with wille, herte, and myght,
And ever hath doon syn ye first hym knewe,
That ye shul of youre grace upon hym rewe,
And taken hym for housbonde and for lord.
Lene me youre hond, for this is oure accord.
Lat se now of youre wommanly pitee.
He is a kynges brother sone, pardee;
And though he were a povre bacheler,
Syn he hath served yow so many a yeer,
And had for yow so greet adversitee,
It moste been considered, leeveth me,

For gentil mercy oghte to passen right."
Thanne seyde he thus to Palamon the knight:
"I trowe ther nedeth litel sermonyng
To make yow assente to this thyng.
Com neer, and taak youre lady by the hond."
Bitwixen hem was maad anon the bond
That highte matrimoigne or mariage,
By al the conseil and the baronage.
And thus with alle blisse and melodye
Hath Palamon ywedded Emelye.
And God, that al this wyde world hath wroght,
Sende hym his love that hath it deere aboght;
For now is Palamon in alle wele,
Lyvynge in blisse, in richesse, and in heele,
And Emelye hym loveth so tendrely,
And he hire serveth so gentilly,
That nevere was ther no word hem bitwene
Of jalousie or any oother teene.
Thus endeth Palamon and Emelye;
And God save al this faire compaignye! Amen.

Heere is ended the Knyghtes Tale.

2. Source

From *The Masque of the Inner Temple and Grayes Inne* (1613)

By Francis Beaumont

Iris,

Iust match this shew; or my Inuention failes,
Had it beene worthier, I would haue inuok'd
The blazing Comets, Clouds and falling Starres,
And all my kindred Meteors of the Ayre
To haue excell'd it, but I now must striue
To imitate Confusion, therefore thou
Delightfull *Flora*, if thou euer felt'st
Encrease of sweetnesse in those blooming plants,
On which the hornes of my faire bow decline;
Send hither all the Rurall company,
Which decke the May-games with their Countrey sports;
Iuno will haue it so.

The second Anti-masque rush in, daunce their Measure, and as rudely depart, consisting of a Pedant.

May Lord,	May Lady.
Seruingman,	Chambermaide.
A Countrey Clowne, or Shepheard,	Countrey Wench.
An Host,	Hostesse.
A Hee Baboone,	Shee Baboone.
A Hee Foole,	Shee Foole vshe-ring them in.

All these persons apparelled to the life, the Men issuing out of one side of the Boscage, and the Woemen from the other: the Musicke was extremely well fitted, hauing such a spirit of Countrey iolitie, as can hardly be imagined, but the perpetuall laughter and applause was aboue the Musicke.

The dance likewise was of the same strain, and the Dancers, or rather Actors expressed euery one their part so naturally, and aptly, as when a Mans eye was caught with the one, and then past on to the other, hee could not satisfie himselfe which did best. It pleased his Maiestie to call for it againe at the end, as he did likewise for the first Anti-masque, but one of the *Statuaes* by that time was vndressed.

3. Possible Source

From *The Countess of Pembroke's Arcadia* (1590)

By Sir Philip Sidney; edited by Albert Feuillerat, 1912

The Fourthe Booke or Acte

So then home ageane went *Dametas* punished in Conceipt, as in Conceipt hee had erred, till hee had founde hym self there from a fancyed Losse falne into an essentiall misery: For entering into his howse three howers w[th]in nighte, (in steade of the Lightsome Countenance of *Pamela* w[ch] gave suche an Inward decking to that lodge, as proudest pallaces mighte have cause to envy yt, and of the gratefull Conversation of *Dorus*, whose witty behavyour made that Lonelynes seeme full of good Company) in steade of the lowde scoulding of *Miso* and the buysy tumbling up and downe of *Mopsa* (whiche thoughe they were so shorte as quyte Contrary to the others prayse worthynes, yet were they farr before them in filling of a howse) hee founde no thinge but a solitary Darckenes (whiche as naturally yt breedes a kynde of yrcksome gastfullnes, so yt was to him a moste present terror) remembring the Charge hee had lefte behynde, whiche hee well knewe imported no less then his Lyfe unto hym. Therefore Lighting a Candle there was no place a Mouse coulde have dwelled in, but, that hee with quaking diligence soughte into, but when hee sawe, (hee coulde see no thing of that hee moste Cared for) then became hee the Right Paterne of a wretche dejected, with feare, for Crying and howling, knocking his heade to y[e] walles hee began to make pittyfull Complayntes where no body coulde heare hym: And with too muche Dread hee shoulde not recover her leave all Consideracyons howe to recover her. But at lengthe looking lyke a Shee gote, when shee castes her Kydd for very sorowe hee tooke in his owne behalf, oute of the Lodge hee went ronning as fast as hee coulde having now Receyved the very forme of hanging into his Consideracyon: Thus ronning as a man that woulde have ronne from hym self, yt was his foolish fortune, to espy by the glimmering Lighte the Moone did then yeelde hym, one standing alofte amonge the Bowghes of a fayre Ashe. Hee that woulde at that tyme have asked Counsell of a Dogg, Cast up his face, as yf his toothe had beene Drawyng oute, and wth muche bending his sighte, hee perceyved yt was Mistris *Mopsa*, fittly seated there for her witt and dignity: There, (I will not say wth Joy, for howe coulde hee taste of Joy, whose Imaginacyon was fallen from a Pallace to a gallowes) but yet with some Refresshing of Comforte in hope hee shoulde learne better tydinges over, hee began to Crye oute, O *Mopsa* my beloved Chickyn here am I thyne owne Father *Dametas*, never in suche a towardnes to hanging, yf thow can not help mee. But never a worde coulde his Eloquence procure of *Mopsa*, who in deede was there attending for greate matters: This was yet a newe Burden to *Dametas* who thought all the worlde was conspired ageanst hym, and therefore with a silly Choller hee began an other Tune. Thow vyle *Mopsa* saide hee now the vengeance of my Fatherly Curse light overthwart thee yf thow doo not streighte answer mee: But neyther blessing nor Cursing coulde prevayle with *Mopsa*, who was nowe greate with Chylde wth thexpectation of her May game hopes, and did longe to bee delivered, with the thirde tyme beeyng named, w[ch] by and by followed. For *Dametas* rubbing his ellbowe, stampping, and whyning, seeying neither of these take place began to throwe stones at her, and with all to Conjure her by the Name of Hellish *Mopsa*: But, when hee had named her the thirde tyme, No Chyme can more sodenly follow the stryking of a Clock, then shee (verily thincking yt was the God that used her Fathers voyce, throwyng her armes abrode, and not Considering shee was muffled uppon so hye a Tree) came fluttering downe like a hooded Hawke, like enough to have broken her neck, but that the Tree full of Bowghes, tost her from one Boughe to an other, and lastly well bruysed brought her to receyve an unffrendly salutatyon of the Earthe. *Dametas*, assoone, as shee was Downe came Ronning unto her, and fynding her so Close wrapt pulde of the scarlett Cloake in good tyme for her, for with the sorenes of the Falle, yf shee had not had breathe given her, shee had delivered a Foolish sowle to *Pluto*; But then *Dametas* began a fressh to desyer his Daughter, not to forgett the paynes hee had taken for her in her Chyldehoode (w[ch] hee was sure shee coulde not remember) and to tell hym where *Pamela* was. O good *Appollo* sayde *Mopsa*, yf ever thow didst beare Love to *Phaetons* Mother, Lett mee have a kinge to my husband? Alas, what speakest thow of *Phaeton* sayde *Dametas*, yf by thy Circumspect meanes I fynde not oute *Pamela*, thy Father will bee hanged to morowe: It ys no matter thoughe hee bee hanged sayde *Mopsa*, doo but thow make *Dorus* a Kinge and lett hym bee my husband, good *Appollo*, for my Corage dothe muche prick mee towardes hym. Ah *Mopsa* cryed oute *Dametas* where ys thy witt doest thow not knowe thy Father? haste thow forgotten thy self? I do not aske witt of thee myne owne good *Appollo* sayde shee, but I see thow wouldest have mee Remember my Father, and in deede forgett my self; No, no, a good husband. Thow shalte have thy fill of Husbandes saide *Dametas*, and do but answer mee my questyon. O I thancke thee sayde *Mopsa* with all my hart hartely, but lett them bee all Kinges. *Dametas* seeyng no other way prevayle, fell downe on his knees, *Mopsa, Mopsa* sayde hee doo not thus cruelly torment mee? I am allredy wretched ynoughe, alas eyther help mee, or tell mee thow canst not: Shee that woulde [not] bee behynde *Appollo* in Curtisy, kneeled downe on the other syde, I will never leave tormenting thee (sayde *Mopsa*) untill thow haste satisfyed my Longing, but I will proclayme thee a promyse breaker: that even *Jupiter* shall heare yt. Nowe, by the Fostering thow haste receyved in this place, save my Lyfe saide *Dametas*: Nowe by this fayre Ashe (answered *Mopsa*) where thow didest receyve so greate a good turne, graunte poste haste to my burning fancy? O where ys *Pamela*, sayde *Dametas*? O a Lusty husband sayde *Mopsa: Dametas* that now verely assured hym self his Daughter was madd, began utterly to dispayre of his Lyfe, and therefore amazed, catching her in his Armes, to see whether hee coulde bringe her to her self, Hee mighte feele the weighte of a great Cudgell light uppon his shoulders: And for his first greeting hee knewe his wyfe *Misos* voyce, by the Calling hym Ribalde, villayne, and asking hym whether shee coulde not serve his turne aswell as *Charita*.

4. Source

From *The Lives of the Noble Grecians and Romans: The Life of Theseus*

By Plutarch; "Dryden Translation," 1683; edited by Edmund Fuller, 1959

The Amazons, he says, being naturally lovers of men, were so far from avoiding Theseus when he touched upon their coasts, that they sent him presents to his ship; but he, having invited Antiope, who brought them, to come aboard, immediately set sail and carried her away.

This was the origin and cause of the Amazonian invasion of Attica, which would seem to have been no slight or womanish enterprise. For it is impossible that they should have placed their camp in the very city, and joined battle close by the Pnyx and the hill called Museum, unless, having first conquered the country around about, they had thus with impunity advanced to the city. That they made so long a journey by land, and passed the Cimmerian Bosphorus, when frozen, as Hellanicus writes, is difficult to be believed. That they encamped all but in the city is certain, and may be sufficiently confirmed by the names that the places hereabout yet retain, and the graves and monuments of those that fell in the battle. Both armies being in sight, there was a long pause and doubt on each side which should give the first onset; at last Theseus, having sacrificed to Fear, in obedience to the command of an oracle he had received, gave them battle; and this happened in the month of Boedromion, in which to this very day the Athenians celebrate the Feast Boedromia. Clidemus, desirous to be very circumstantial, writes that the left wing of the Amazons moved towards the place which is yet called Amazonium and the right towards the Pnyx, near Chrysa, that with this wing the Athenians, issuing from behind the Museum, engaged, and that the graves of those that were slain are to be seen in the street that leads to the gate called the Piraic, by the chapel of the hero Chalcodon; and that here the Athenians were routed, and gave way before the women, as far as to the temple of the Furies, but, fresh supplies coming in from the Palladium, Ardettus, and the Lyceum, they charged their right wing, and beat them back into their tents, in which action a great number of the Amazons were slain. At length, after four months, a peace was concluded between them by the mediation of Hippolyta (for so this historian calls the Amazon whom Theseus married, and not Antiope), though others write that she was slain with a dart by Molpadia, while fighting by Theseus's side, and that the pillar which stands by the temple of Olympian Earth was erected to her honour. Nor is it to be wondered at, that in events of such antiquity, history should be in disorder. For indeed we are also told that those of the Amazons that were wounded were privately sent away by Antiope to Chalcis, where many by her care recovered, but some that died were buried there in the place that is to this time called Amazonium. That this war, however, was ended by a treaty is evident, both from the name of the place adjoining to the temple of Theseus, called, from the solemn oath there taken, Horcomosium; and also from the ancient sacrifice which used to be celebrated to the Amazons the day before the Feast of Theseus.

This is as much as is worth telling concerning the Amazons. For the account which the author of the poem called the Theseid gives of this rising of the Amazons, how Antiope, to revenge herself upon Theseus for refusing her and marrying Phaedra, came down upon the city with her train of Amazons, whom Hercules slew, is manifestly nothing else but fable and invention. It is true, indeed, that Theseus married Phaedra, but that was after the death of Antiope, by whom he had a son called Hippolytus, or, as Pindar writes, Demophon. The calamities which befell Phaedra and this son, since none of the historians have contradicted the tragic poets that have written of them, we must suppose happened as represented uniformly by them.

There are also other traditions of the marriages of Theseus, neither honourable in their occasions nor fortunate in their events, which yet were never represented in the Greek plays. For he is said to have carried off Anaxo, a Troezenian, and having slain Sinnis and Cercyon, to have ravished their daughters; to have married Periboea, the mother of Ajax, and then Phereboea, and then Iope, the daughter of Iphicles. And further, he is accused of deserting Ariadne (as is before related), being in love with Aegle, the daughter of Panopeus, neither justly nor honourably; and lastly, of the rape of Helen, which filled all Attica with war and blood, and was in the end the occasion of his banishment and death, as will presently be related.

Herodorus is of opinion, that though there were many famous expeditions undertaken by the bravest men of his time, yet Theseus never joined in any of them, once only excepted, with the Lapithae, in their war against the Centaurs; but others say that he accompanied Jason to Colchis and Meleager to the slaying of the Calydonian boar, and that hence it came to be a proverb, *Not without Theseus*; that he himself, however, without aid of any one, performed many glorious exploits, and that from him began the saying, *He is a second Hercules*. He also joined Adrastus in recovering the bodies of those that were slain before Thebes, but not as Euripides in his tragedy says, by force of arms, but by persuasion and mutual agreement and composition, for so the greater part of the historians write; Philochorus adds further that this was the first treaty that ever was made for the recovering the bodies of the dead, but in the history of Hercules, it is shown that it was he who first gave leave to his enemies to carry off their slain. The burying-places of the most part are yet to be seen in the village called Eleutherae: those of the commanders, at Eleusis, where Theseus allotted them a place, to oblige Adrastus. The story of Euripides in his suppliants is disproved by Aeschylus in his Eleusinians, where Theseus himself relates the facts as here told.

The celebrated friendship between Theseus and Pirithoüs is said to have thus begun; the fame of the strength and valor of Theseus being spread through Greece, Pirithoüs was desirous to make a trial and proof of it himself, and to this end seized a herd of oxen which belonged to Theseus, and was driving them away from Marathon, and, when the news was brought that Theseus pursued him in arms, he did not fly, but turned back and went to meet him. But as soon as they had viewed one another, each so admired the gracefulness and beauty, and was seized with such respect for the courage of the other, that they forgot all thoughts of fighting; and Pirithoüs, first stretching out his hand to Theseus, bade him be judge in this case himself, and promised to submit willingly to any penalty he should impose. But Theseus not only forgave him all, but entreated him to be his friend and brother in arms; and they ratified their friendship by oaths. After this Pirithoüs married Deidamia, and invited Theseus to the wedding, entreating him to come and see his country, and make acquaintance with the Lapithae; he had at the same time invited the Centaurs to the feast, who growing hot with wine and beginning to be insolent and wild, and offering violence to the women, the Lapithae took immediate revenge upon them, slaying many of them upon the place, and afterwards, having overcome them in battle, drove the whole race of them out of their country, Theseus all along taking their part and fighting on their side. But Herodorus gives a different relation of these things; that Theseus came not to the assistance of the Lapithae till the war was already begun; and that it was in this journey that he had his first sight of Hercules, having made it his business to find him out at Trachis, where he had chosen to rest himself after all his wanderings and his labours; and that this interview was honourably performed on each part, with extreme respect, and good-will, and admiration of each other. Yet it is more credible, as others write, that there were, before, frequent interviews between them, and that it was by the means of Theseus that Hercules was initiated at Eleusis, and purified before initiation, upon account of several rash actions of his former life.

Theseus was now fifty years old, as Hellanicus states, when he carried off Helen, who was yet too young to be married. Some writers, to take away this accusation of one of the greatest crimes laid to his charge, say, that he did not steal away Helen himself, but that Idas and Lynceus were the ravishers, who brought her to him, and committed her to his charge, and that, therefore, he refused to restore her at the demand of Castor and Pollux; or, indeed, they say her own father, Tyndarus, had sent her to be kept by him, for fear of Enarophorus, the son of Hippocoön, who would have carried her away by force when she was yet a child. But the most probable account, and that which has most witnesses on its side, is this: Theseus and Pirithoüs went both together to Sparta, and, having seized the young lady as she was dancing in the temple Diana Orthia, fled away with her. There were presently men sent in arms to pursue, but they followed no further than to Tegea; and Theseus and Pirithoüs, being now out of danger, having passed through Peloponnesus, made an agreement between themselves, that he to whom the lot should fall should have Helen to his wife, but should be obliged to assist in procuring another for his friend. The lot fell upon Theseus, who conveyed her to Aphidnae, not being yet marriageable, and delivered her to one of his allies, called Aphidnus, and, having sent his mother, Aethra, after to take care of her, desired him to keep them so secretly, that none might know where they were; which done, to return the same service to his friend Pirithoüs, he accompanied him in his journey to Epirus, in order to steal away the king of the Molossians' daughter. The king, his own name being Aidoneus, or Pluto, called his wife Proserpina, and his daughter Cora, and a great dog, which he kept, Cerberus, with whom he ordered all that came as suitors to his daughter to fight, and promised her to him that should overcome the beast. But having been informed that the design of Pirithoüs and his companion was not to court his daughter, but to force her away, he caused them both to be seized, and threw Pirithoüs to be torn in pieces by his dog, and put Theseus into prison, and kept him.

About this time, Menestheus, the son of Peteus, grandson of Orneus, and great-grandson of Erechtheus, the first man that is recorded to have affected popularity and ingratiated himself with the multitude, stirred up and exasperated the most eminent men of the city, who had long borne a secret grudge to Theseus, conceiving that he had robbed them of their several little kingdoms and lordships, and having pent them all up in one city, was using them as his subjects and slaves. He put also the meaner people into commotion, telling them, that, deluded with a mere dream of liberty, though indeed they were deprived of both that and of their proper homes and religious usages, instead of many good and gracious kings of their own, they had given themselves up to be lorded over by a newcomer and a stranger. Whilst he was thus busied in infecting the minds of the citizens, the war that Castor and Pollux brought against Athens came very opportunely to further the sedition he had been promoting, and some say that by his persuasions was wholly the cause of their invading the city. At their first approach, they committed no acts of hostility, but peaceably demanded their sister Helen; but the Athenians returning answer that they neither had her there nor knew where she was disposed of, they prepared to assault the city, when Academus, having, by whatever means, found it out, disclosed to them that she was secretly kept at Aphidnae. For which reason he was both highly honoured during his life by Castor and Pollux, and the Lacedaemonians, when often in aftertimes they made incursions into Attica, and destroyed all the country round about, spared the Academy for the sake of Academus.

5. Possible Source

From *The Lady of May* (1590)

By Sir Philip Sidney; edited by Albert Feuillerat, 1912

Herewith the woman-suiter being gone, there was heard in the woods a confused noyse, and forthwith there came out six sheapheards with as many fosters haling and pulling, to whether side they should draw the Lady of May, who seemed to encline neither to the one nor other side. Among them was Maister *Rombus* a schoole-maister of a village thereby, who being fully perswaded of his owne learned wisedome, came thither, with his authority to part their fray; where for aunswer he received many unlearned blowes. But the Queene comming to the place where she was seene of them, though they knew not her estate, yet something there was which made them startle aside and gaze upon her: till old father *Lalus* stepped forth (one of the substantiallest shepheards) and making a legge or two, said these few words.

May it please your benignity to give a little superfluous intelligence to that, which with the opening of my mouth, my tongue and teeth shall deliver unto you. So it is right worshipfull audience, that a certaine she creature, which we shepheards call a woman, of a minsicall countenance, but by my white Lambe not three quarters so beautious as yore selfe, hath disanulled the braine pan of two of our featioust yong men. And wil you wot how? by my mother *Kits* soule, with a certaine fransicall maladie they cal Love, when I was a yong man they called it flat follie. But here is a substantiall schoole-maister can better disnounce the whole foundation of the matter, although in sooth for all his loquence our young men were nothing dutious to his clarkeship; Come on, Come on Maister schoole-maister, be not so bashlesse, we say, that the fairest are ever the gentlest: tell the whole case, for you can much better vent the points of it then I.

Then came forward Maister Rombus, and with many speciall graces made this learned oration.

Now the thunderthumping *Jove* transfund his dotes into your excellent formositie, which have with your resplendent beames thus segregated the emnitie of these rurall animals: I am *Potentissima Domina*, a schoolemaister, that is to say, a Pedagogue, one not a litle versed in the disciplinating of the juventall frie, wherein (to my laud I say it) I use such geometricall proportion, as neither wanted mansuetude nor correction, for so it is described.

Parcare Subjectos & debellire superbos.

Yet hath not the pulchritude of my vertues protected me from the contaminating hands of these plebeians; for comming, *solummodo* to have parted their sanguinolent fray, they yeelded me no more reverence, then if I had bin some *Pecorius Asinus*. I, even I, that am, who am I? *Dixi verbus sapiento satum est.* But what sayd that Troian *Aeneas*, when he sojorned in the surging sulkes of the sandiferous seas, *Haec olim memonasse juvebit.* Well well, *ad propositos revertebo*, the puritie of the veritie is, that a certaine *Pulchra puella profectò* elected and constituted by the integrated determination of all this topographicall region, as the soveraigne Lady of this Dame Maias month, hath bene *quodammodo* hunted, as you would say, pursued by two, a brace, a couple, a cast of yong men, to whom the crafty coward *Cupid* had *inquam* delivered his dire-dolorous dart.

But here the May Lady interrupted his speech, saying to him:

Away away you tedious foole, your eyes are not worthy to looke to yonder Princelie sight, much lesse your foolish tongue to trouble her wise eares.

At which Maister Rombus in a great chafe cried out:

O Tempori, ô Moribus! in profession a childe, in dignitie a woman, in yeares a Lady, *in caeteris* a maid, should thus turpifie the reputation of my doctrine, with the superscription of a foole, *ô Tempori, ô Moribus!*

But here againe the May Ladie saying to him,

Leave off good Latine foole, and let me satisfie the long desire I have had to feede mine eyes with the only sight this age hath graunted to the world.

The poore scholemaister went his way backe.

* * *

Rombus the schoole-maister.

Heu, Ehem, hei, Insipidum, Inscitium vulgorum & populorum. Why you brute Nebulons have you had my *Corpusculum* so long among you, and cannot yet tell how to edifie an argument? Attend and throw your eares to me, for I am gravidated with child, till I have endoctrinated your plumbeous cerebrosities. First you must divisionate your point, *quasi* you should cut a cheese into two particles, for thus must I uniforme my speech to your obtuse conceptions; for *Prius dividendum oratio antequam definiendum exemplum gratia*, either *Therion* must conquer this Dame *Maias* Nimphe, or *Espilus* must overthrow her, and that *secundum* their dignity, which must also be subdivisionated into three equall *species*, either according to the penetrancie of their singing, or the meliority of their functions, or lastly the superancy of their merits *De* singing *satis*. *Nunc* are you to argumentate of the qualifying of their estate first, and then whether hath more infernally, I meane deepely deserved.

* * *

Rombus the schoole-maister.

O tace, tace, or all the fat wil be ignified, first let me dilucidate the very intrinsicall maribone of the matter. He doth use a certaine rhetoricall invasion into the point, as if in deed he had conference with his Lams, but the troth is he doth equitate you in the meane time maister *Rixus*, for thus he sayth, that sheepe are good, *ergo* the shepheard is good, An *Enthimeme à loco contingentibus*, as my finger and my thumbe are *Contingentes*: againe he sayth, who liveth well is likewise good, but shepheards live well, *Ergo* they are good; a *Sillogisme* in *Darius* king of *Persia* a *Conjugatis*; as you would say, a man coupled to his wife, two bodies but one soule: but do you but acquiescate to my exhortation, and you shall extinguish him. Tell him his major is a knave, his minor is a foole, and his conclusion both, *Et ecce homo blancatus quasi liliũ.*

Rixus. I was saying the shepheards life had some goodnesse in it, because it borrowed of the countrey quietnesse something like ours, but that is not all, for ours besides that quiet part, doth both strengthen the body, and raise up the mind with this gallant sort of activity.

* * *

Rombus. Bene bene, nunc de questione prepositus, that is as much to say, as well well, [n]ow of the proposed question, that was, whether the many great services and many great faults of *Therion*, or the few small services and no faults of *Espilus*, be to be preferred, incepted or accepted the former.

The May Lady.

No no, your ordinarie traines shall not deale in that matter, I have already submitted it to one, whose sweete spirit hath passed thorough greater difficulties, neither will I that your blockheads lie in her way.

INDEX TO THE INTRODUCTIONS